Oct: 1968.

Ann beh beh cont + Ad law 4

Public Law 303, 315, 316, 320

CONSTITUTIONAL LAW

CONSTITUTIONAL LAW

By

J. D. B. MITCHELL,

LL.D., PH.D., DR.(H.C.) UNIV. LILLE

*Salvesen Professor of European Institutions
in the University of Edinburgh*

*" Non enim propter gloriam, divitias
aut honores pugnamus, sed propter
libertatem solummodo, quam nemo
bonus nisi simul cum vita amittit."*

SECOND EDITION

Published under the auspices of
THE SCOTTISH UNIVERSITIES LAW INSTITUTE

EDINBURGH
W. GREEN & SON LTD.
1968

First Published 1964
Second Edition 1968

SBN 414 00504 X

Printed in Great Britain
by
The Eastern Press, Ltd.,
of London and Reading

For my wife and family

PREFACE

THERE is, as was remarked in the first edition of this book, no right time at which to produce a book on constitutional law, and the second edition of this one has had to be prepared in difficult circumstances. There have been many changes (some of detail) in the world in which constitutional law works. A renewed burst of creating or reorganising nationalised industries is evident. Winds of change are supposedly sweeping through government, though some of the changes (particularly in parliamentary procedure) have not long endured, and others are not working smoothly. Reform of the House of Lords has been proposed, and events may quicken that process. There is much talk of devolution which would have substantial constitutional effects, as would British adhesion to the Treaty of Rome. Two Royal Commissions on Local Government are, reputedly, about to report, as is the Fulton Committee on the Civil Service. Overall there is uncertainty and no clear pattern has emerged.

In such circumstances, when so much was fluid, it has been thought best to leave the main structure of the book unchanged and modify the text as was necessary. The main purposes of the book remain those set out in the Preface to the first edition and the policy has again been followed of giving in the footnotes references to a wide range of material, legal and non-legal, which is essential to any real understanding of constitutional law as a subject having an intimate connection with government and politics. The material should be read, but the incorporation of much of it would have made the book too long. The introductory matter in Part One has been considerably revised. The Parliamentary Commissioner for Administration will be found discussed in the chapter devoted to " Public Authorities in the Courts," for it is in that context that the deficiencies of the office and of the concept become abundantly clear. Account has been taken of the tentative moves to create new " Specialised Committees " of the House of Commons, and there has been printed as an Appendix an extract from the European Convention for the Protection of Human Rights as a reminder that lawyers must now take this Convention seriously, though it is too early to judge its internal effects.

These uncertainties do not render unnecessary a new edition at this time. If they did not exist others would. Indeed they can, paradoxically, justify a new edition. All of this uncertainty is a sign of a widespread feeling that the traditional machinery and ideas are not working satisfactorily in practice, yet the changes are piecemeal and have a random air—often one is inconsistent in principle with another. There is a need for more consistent re-thinking—hence the emphasis that has been placed on revising some of the introductory material. In particular one question underlies the whole work, and much of the uncertainty, namely, the place of courts and of law in a modern state. When it is said " I am sure that most Members feel that a written constitution would be in grave danger of infringing the principle of parliamentary sovereignty " (762 H.C.Deb. 1070) all sorts of assumptions are made. It is assumed that that principle exists or can be proved to exist (which is at best doubtful), and that that principle is necessarily always beneficent in operation (which is even more doubtful), and that it is somehow wrong in a civilised country to have standards against which political conduct may be measured. Indeed the statement is essentially inconsistent with the acceptance of the European Convention on Human Rights. On the other hand it is true that in the field of public law the traditional machinery of the law has shown its inadequacy to deal with the problems of a modern state. The emergence of that state (which, in itself, is to be welcomed) poses many problems, but above all (in this field) those of the balance of political and legal controls, of the efficacy of each, and of the impact of each form of control on the efficiency of the administration. It must be remembered that individual citizens have an interest not only in those controls, but also in that efficiency. The two aspects cannot be separated. It is these problems and their sequels which underlie a great deal of the book, since it is my conviction that, if the rule of law is to have any real meaning and not become merely an empty catch-phrase, much re-thinking is needed. The book is intended as a contribution to the debate on such topics, which cannot, however, be discussed in isolation from the general background.

The difficulties of preparing this edition were enhanced by the complications involved in a move within the University. It is to be hoped that these difficulties have not left too many marks. Once again my thanks are due to many, to the publishers, to Mr. H. McN. Henderson for help in revising the chapter on Local Government, but above all to my wife for tolerance which made the difficulties supportable and then for sharing with Miss Margaret Ainslie the burden of proof-reading.

J. D. B. M.

May 28, 1968.
Centre of European Governmental Studies,
The University of Edinburgh.

PREFACE TO THE FIRST EDITION

THERE are both universal and local aspects of constitutional law. The rules may be local, but the problems are universal. The Declaration of Arbroath (from which the quotation on the title page is taken) emphasises both these aspects. The fact that (as Lord Cooper pointed out) it was not entirely original, and the fact of its local significance, demonstrate how the universal and the local may blend. Similarly there are both ephemeral and eternal aspects. Since constitutional law is about power and the exercise of power there is some tendency to concentrate upon contemporary issues, which may be of short-lived interest. The enduring object of the rules—liberty—so forcefully emphasised by the Declaration of Arbroath should not, however, be lost to sight. Too great a concentration upon what is local and may be ephemeral can be harmful unless other elements are borne in mind.

Nevertheless, there is perhaps no good time at which to write a book on constitutional law. Continuous change is a greater force than it is often believed to be, and any writer becomes increasingly conscious of circumstances equivalent to those which (reputedly) tempted Professor Thomas Reed Powell to change the title of his course from Constitutional Law to Current Affairs. When this book was in its final stages, the Peerage Act 1963 was enacted, the reform of local government in Scotland was projected, and litigation such as the *Burmah Oil* case, capable of casting light on fundamentals, was in train. At the proof stage the problem of selecting a Prime Minister once again became prominent. Of some of these and similar matters it has been possible to take some note, but no proper exploration was practicable. Had the book been held back to make a fuller treatment possible, other like events would doubtless have happened meanwhile.

In one sense timing does not perhaps matter. The purpose of the book is to treat central institutions, central ideas, and their relationships. In the interest of clarity much detail has therefore been omitted, and an attempt has been made (as the Commissioners of 1707 would have put it) not to stir into any matter which was not essential to the primary purpose. Within these limits the book is, for the most part, concerned with Great Britain. The proper consideration of the position in Northern Ireland, the Channel Isles or the Isle of Man would have involved too many strands of argument. Within Great Britain the emphasis is upon Scottish institutions and rules. Where possible comparison is made where there

ix

is significance in differences. This pattern was chosen not merely because of the provenance of the book, but also in the interests of brevity and clarity; an account of both the Scottish and English systems of local government could well be confusing to the student. Nevertheless, since the emphasis is upon central institutions and ideas, it is hoped that the book will have a general utility. For similar reasons, despite what has been said earlier, comparison with other systems beyond the United Kingdom has been limited, though it is to be hoped that opportunity will arise for the proper development of such comparative aspects. No general account has been given of the development of the Commonwealth or of the relationship of the United Kingdom to the Commonwealth since it is conceived that these matters are appropriate to specialist studies. If excuse or justification must be offered for this concentration it might be said that our constitutional institutions and ideas are not thought to have such perfection that an examination of them alone, without further distraction, or complication, is out of place.

In relation to matters falling within the scope thus designated descriptive material has been cut down, particularly where there already exists adequate literature. References to such literature have been made, and the references should be pursued. There is little point in summarising familiar printed sources or other men's work (or indeed the fuller statements of the author's views which have appeared elsewhere). It is better that students should resort to originals. Further, since an attempt has been made to concentrate upon matters of principle, it will be found that on occasion the position is somewhat baldly stated. Again it is hoped that the material given in the footnotes is adequate for the reader to be able to check and to challenge the propositions which are made. The student reader should be urged to resort to original sources, other readers will no doubt prefer so to do. This method of treatment means, however, that, on occasion, the footnotes are of more significance than is sometimes the case in somewhat similar works.

The book appears in connection with the Law Institute for Scotland, endowed by the Carnegie Trust for the Universities of Scotland. Thanks are due to both those institutions. Mr. W. I. R. Fraser, Q.C. (as he then was), read the whole of the manuscript while he was still at the Bar, and although he has no responsibility for errors in the text, the author's thanks are due to him in particular. Thanks are also due to others who read the manuscript, but who, for professional reasons, wish to remain anonymous. It is hoped that they will accept this Preface as an expression of thanks which, otherwise, would be more explicit.

Within the University, my thanks are due to Mr. H. McN. Henderson and Dr. V. S. MacKinnon, my colleagues in the Department of Constitutional Law, who have read the whole or part of the text, and to many of my other colleagues in the Faculty of Law in the University of Edinburgh for their comments and their tolerance of my questions. Particular thanks are due to my students who have accepted my lectures with graceful forbearance, prompted me by questions, and presented a continuous if courteous challenge. The publishers have also been called upon to exercise the virtue of forbearance, and for so doing and for their other virtues they have earned thanks. I am grateful to several secretaries and, in particular, to Miss A. J. Allan, who has borne the brunt of dealing with a script which I would not readily accept from students. Above all I am grateful to my family, even more for its tolerance during the long period of gestation than for its help in proof-reading. While credit must rightly be shared among so many, blame must lie upon the author alone.

In principle, the law is intended to be stated as at early summer 1963.

J. D. B. MITCHELL.

January 1964.

CONTENTS

Part Three

THE INTERLOCKING OF INSTITUTIONS AND CONSTITUTIONAL BALANCE

Appendix

TABLE OF CASES

xv

TABLE OF STATUTES

Part One

THE BACKGROUND

CHAPTER 1

THE SCOPE AND NATURE OF CONSTITUTIONAL LAW

Introduction. The primary concern of constitutional law is with the creation and regulation of power within the state. That concern must have a double aspect. The recognition of the rights, liberties and obligations of individuals as against the state is clearly the counterpart of the recognition of those of the state and its organs. To describe the primary concern of constitutional law in terms of state power is not to imply a primacy for the state and its organs, or to deny or minimise the importance, in this field, of individual liberties. State power and individual liberty cannot be separated. Each reacts upon the other. Neither can be regarded in isolation, and the rights and obligations of the state on the one hand and of the individual on the other should not be regarded as essentially opposed to each other. Indeed, the rights of the state are in a sense nothing but the communal rights of the individuals who make up the state. Any conflict that there is is between two groups of rights both of which are connected with individuals.

The limits of the one group of rights and obligations as against the other are not unchangeably determined, but are constantly being adjusted in the interest of a desired end. Thus, the relationship between the two groups will clearly differ in war and in peace.[1] The chief concern of the constitutional lawyer, at least when he is an expositor, is with the description of the balance, or limits between the two, and of the means by which that balance is preserved, or those limits are maintained. He is not concerned with passing judgment upon the desired ends which cause that balance to change. As a critic, however, he may well be concerned to point out that the attainment of a particular end involves an unaccustomed predominance of one group of powers, or a serious sacrifice of another group of liberties, or else that the end could better be achieved by different means which would not disturb the established balance. The choice of ends, however, normally remains a political and not a legal choice, although, as will appear, there are circumstances in which this distinction cannot be clearly made.

Concern with the balance of the rights and powers of the state and of the individual leads to a concern with the organisation or machinery

[1] Compare, however, the statement of Lord Atkin in *Liversidge* v. *Anderson* [1942] A.C. 206 at 244 with cases such as *Smith* v. *Jeffrey*, Jan. 24, 1817, F.C. (particularly the opinion of Lord Robertson) or *The Case of Saltpetre* (1607) 12 Co.Rep. 12. The point is implicit in the opinions in *Burmah Oil Co.* (*Burma Trading*) *Ltd.* v. *Lord Advocate*, 1964 S.C.(H.L.) 117, *e.g.*, *per* Lord Reid at p. 122, and is explicitly made by Windeyer J. in *Parker* v. *The Commonwealth* (1965) 112 C.L.R. 295 at 301. The balance may not change uniformly in respect of all liberties.

of the state, and the relationship of the various organs of government to each other. Although much of the law governing the organisation of the state will be primarily of internal concern to the administration, and will thus be of no direct concern to the individual, most of it will, even if only indirectly, affect the individual, since it will affect both the means by which he can protect and enforce his rights and the security, or stability, of the balance which has been established. Indeed, it can be asserted that all this body of law is of concern to the individual, since he has an interest in the regularity of administration, and in the efficiency of the machinery of government as a means to attaining desired ends. Although this general interest of the individual may be unprotected by law in the ordinary courts, being regarded as insufficiently personal to afford the foundation of a title to sue,[2] the whole of this body of law must be treated as falling within constitutional law if a true picture of the instruments of state power is to be given.

In regard to the United Kingdom the branch of constitutional law which concerns the organisation of the state assumes greater importance than is sometimes recognised to be the case. Within that Kingdom there are not merely problems of the relationship of central to local government, but also problems which spring from the fact that its constitution is neither federal nor strictly unitary. Further, that Kingdom is itself part of a larger whole, the Commonwealth of Nations. The relationship of the parts of this whole, and the position of the United Kingdom therein, fall properly within the scope of constitutional law, for the reasons already given. These latter matters have, however, been largely neglected in the present volume, not because they lack importance, but because they have been frequently and adequately dealt with elsewhere. Present concern is rather with the more narrowly domestic issues of constitutional law, and in particular with some which have not, at least in relation to Scotland, been fully discussed. Within these limits some selection has to be made. While it is impossible, with us, to divide administrative law from constitutional law by a satisfactory definition, some division is necessary for the purposes of exposition. The only satisfactory division is to include within constitutional law major rules and broad principles, and to leave the detailed application and discussion of these rules to administrative law. The selection of what are to be regarded as major rules is a personal one, and cannot always be justified or governed by reasons which would command universal acceptance. For present purposes this process of selection must also be governed by different considerations. Constitutional law is a practical subject. Hence in selection the emphasis must be placed upon those parts of the constitution which appear to the expositor to be of current importance.

---

2 Thus in Scotland the scope of the *actio popularis* is limited and in England the Attorney-General must often be joined before an action against a public authority for the enforcement of a public duty can be raised; see, *e.g., L.C.C.* v. *Att.-Gen.* [1902] A.C. 165 and *L.P.T.B.* v. *Moscrop* [1942] A.C. 332.

Again the criteria of selection are personal, and objection may well be made to the results in particular cases.[3]

Constitutional law should not, however, be regarded as solely concerned with the organisation of the state, and of the relationship of the state to the individual. It may also be concerned with the relationship of one individual to another. Encroachments upon the liberty of an individual may be attributable to state action but this is not necessarily so, particularly in the field of individual liberties. Personal freedom must be protected against the unreasonable actions of guardians as well as those of the state. Freedom of speech is limited not merely by the law of sedition but also by the law of defamation. Similarly private concentrations of power may need regulation by law in the public interest. Attempts at such regulation of monopolies, for example, are of long standing, and the growth of such concentrations of power may raise new problems of constitutional law, or accentuate old ones.[4] Thus constitutional law may overlap or embrace branches of what might be regarded as private law. Here, however, our concern can only be with the general principles and not with the details.

The nature of constitutional law. Because of its subject-matter constitutional law has several peculiarities when compared with other branches of law. In this branch law reaches its farthest extreme. This is true in the sense that constitutional law is concerned with the establishment of mechanisms which are themselves sources of other branches of law (as well as of detailed rules of constitutional law itself), such as Parliament or the courts. It is also true in the sense that here rules of law tend to merge with principles of a different order. It becomes difficult to distinguish constitutional principles from political theories, or philosophical concepts of the state and of the proper position of man in society. Thus, theories of kingship may merge into the constitutional rules governing the position of the monarch. It is often difficult to determine what is political theory and what is constitutional law, since in many respects the legal position is undefined. With us, the absence of a comprehensive written constitution means that the law concerning even central institutions may not always be clear.[5] The gaps may be filled by deductions as to what are alleged to be rules of law, yet those

---

[3] As an extreme example, Cobden's gibe that the British constitution was a great jaggle " of monopolies and churchcraft and sinecures, armorial hocus pocus, primogeniture and pageantry " can, of course, be justified if there is an undue concentration upon certain rules and aspects which could rightly be called constitutional.

[4] See the issues discussed by Lord MacDermott in the later chapters of *Protection from Power under English Law.*

[5] Thus the succession to the Throne where the sovereign died leaving only daughters was not clearly determined until 1937, and then only by declarations of the Law Officers, which are not in themselves binding. See generally, C. d'O. Farran, " The Law of the Accession " (1953) 16 M.L.R. 140. For a further example, see Heuston, *Lives of the Lord Chancellors 1885–1940* at p. 327. We are, of course, not alone in this. In the U.S.A. important issues relating to the disability of the President are left unresolved by law.

deductions may, despite what has been said above, be no more than expressions of political theory. Moreover, in cases of doubt, the choice of the appropriate legal rule may be made in the light of political theory. The decisions upon prerogative in the seventeenth century both in England and in Scotland depended not so much upon legal precedents as upon conceptions which in truth belong to the field of political theory in the broad sense and not to law.[6] In the same way questions of the limits of the power of Parliament tend to be determined by general conceptions of the place and nature of Parliament which are formulated as a result of beliefs as to what is a good or desirable constitution.[7] To the lawyer these concepts may be fundamental constitutional principles, and as such to be treated as law; to the political philosopher they may have other names and be differently regarded. It is thus much more common for principles of constitutional law to be determined by reference to extra-legal considerations than is the case with the principles of other branches of law.[8]

This becomes obvious when an extreme case is taken. It is difficult to speak with any degree of clarity and certainty of legality except of legality *within* a constitutional system. It is hard to speak with certainty of the legality or otherwise of that system itself, simply because its lawfulness must be judged by principles which do not conform to the type of those which underlie, say, the law of reparation. The revolution of 1688 could be regarded by its supporters not as a revolution, but as the re-establishment of a pre-existing legal order which had been wrongfully disrupted. The opponents of that revolution could in their turn, and perhaps with as much justification, regard it, as a revolution properly so called, as a usurpation of power. Both sides could rely upon principles which they believed, or professed to believe, to be legal, but which belonged as much to the world of politics as of law. The Claim of Right asserts that James VII " did invade the fundamental constitution and altered it from a legal limited monarchy to an arbitrary despotic power." The soundness of this judgment depends *inter alia* upon the relative weight to be given to theories sometimes expressed, or to practices which often conflicted with theory. There was a similar diversity of theory. George Buchanan could, in *De Jure Regni apud Scotos*, support his views of a limited, or popular, monarchy by suitably selected precedents.[9] Sir George Mackenzie could support, in *Jus*

---

[6] See the introductory essay to the part on *Prerogative* in Keir and Lawson, *Cases in Constitutional Law*.

[7] Thus the modern development of the legal theory of the sovereignty of Parliament has been greatly influenced by the political developments since 1832.

[8] This process operates throughout the whole field of constitutional law; see, *e.g.*, the process of reasoning based upon the supposed position of nationalised industries in *British Oxygen Co. Ltd.* v. *South West Scotland Electricity Board*, 1956 S.L.T. 278 and 1956 S.C.(H.L.) 112, and see *British Oxygen Co. Ltd.* v. *South of Scotland Electricity Board*, 1959 S.L.T. 181; 1959 S.C.(H.L.) 17.

[9] See the discussion in the article by W. S. McKechnie in the *Glasgow Quatercentenary Studies on George Buchanan*.

Regium, the opposite views by a different selection. Both authors could invoke long-standing precedents, for the banning of *De Jure Regni* in August 1688 [10] cannot be regarded simply as a mark of a sudden temporary " invasion " by James VII. The book had first been banned in 1584, and it was again banned in 1664. The choice between the two views involves a choice between two constitutional theories, each of which had from time to time been dominant in the law of the land,[11] and that choice cannot, therefore, be determined by reference to law alone. Indeed, it is, at this time, clearly pointless, in any practical sense, to argue the legality of 1688. Factual developments are on the side of George Buchanan. While the dealings of the Cromwellian Commonwealth may be dismissed as illegal, 1688 must simply be accepted. Yet the difference may well be merely that the revolutionary settlement endured and the Commonwealth did not.

It is not only what would normally be called revolutions that provoke such arguments. They can arise, for example, over the consequences of the Union of 1707, and are inevitable simply because constitutional law deals with the fundamentals of the state. At that level of thought there are strict limits to the scope of arguments based upon purely legal principles. The stage is reached when justification must be found simply in facts, or in the broad acceptance of certain generally formulated principles. This circumstance causes many of our basic constitutional principles to be subsequent explanations of factual situations. Hence our constitutional law is formed for us as a result of the activities of men and institutions working towards ends which are often broadly conceived and only partially defined, or, indeed, understood by the actors. The explanations of the results of their activities may be called constitutional principles, yet they may differ from the ideas which influenced those activities. In part this difference may be due to the fact that the formative event, and its explanation, may not become

---

[10] See Wodrow, *History of the Sufferings of the Church*, App. CXLI (Vol. IV, p. 443, 1880 ed.), and W. Croft Dickinson's Introduction (p. xlii) to Knox, *History of the Reformation in Scotland*. This issue of law and fact runs through the judgments in *Madzimbamuto* v. *Lardner-Burke and Ors.*, 1966 (4) S.A. 462, recognising as unlawful the Rhodesian régime, but accepting some of its measures as a " factual government." See the comment in (1967) 83 L.Q.R. at p. 64 *et seq.* The situation in that case was, of course, complicated by the problem of the relationship of Rhodesia to the United Kingdom superimposed on the domestic problem. The Scottish problem was a single-layered one.

[11] A choice must be made, for example, between the attitudes which governed the Act anent the election of officers, etc., 1641 (A.P.S. V, 354), the Act of 1563 upon taxation, war and peace (A.P.S. II, 543), or the Act Anent Peace and War, 1703 (A.P.S. XI, 107), on the one hand, and such Acts as that of 1606 Anent the Kingis majesteis prerogative (A.P.S. IV, 281) or the somewhat similar Acts of 1661 (A.P.S. VII, 10, 13) on the other. Any of these Acts could be explained away by reference to particular political circumstances of the time, but all were for the time the effective constitutional law, and the mere addition of precedents upon one side or the other can neither justify nor condemn the events of 1688. See, too, Cosmo Innes' judgment on appearance and realities, *Scotch Legal Antiquities*, p. 144.

known at the same time.[12] In part the difference may also be attributed to subsequent events. Thus, immediately after the Statute of Westminster there was considerable tendency to regard that statute and the events leading up to it as indicating the " separateness " of the Dominions. Subsequent events, notably the troubled state of international affairs which provoked a much greater interest in unity, tended, at least for a time, to impose a new interpretation with a corresponding shift of emphasis.[13] Thus subsequent events may provoke a fresh interpretation of past events, with an emphasis on different principles. While, as will be seen, constitutional practice may, by itself, have something of the effect of precedent elsewhere in the common law, these *ex post facto* explanations may also have their own independent effect on the development of major rules of constitutional law. This is particularly so when they amount to new principles intended to reconcile new constitutional phenomena with the existing framework. The explanation which is chosen will be influenced by the general ideas of the sort already discussed and will itself influence those ideas. In such circumstances the methods of constitutional law may be more deductive than are those of the common law, at least in England.

The importance of these general ideas is then seen, not only in determining the existence of the principles of constitutional law, but also in determining their interpretation. It is frequently true that, because of their fundamental nature, principles are laid down in general terms. Their interpretation in particular instances thus becomes a matter of considerable importance, and often of greater practical importance than the formulation of the principles themselves. Even when constitutional principles are embodied in formal documents, or statutes, their interpretation cannot be governed exclusively by normal canons, but will be guided and informed by general ideas of the same order as those that determined the existence of the principles themselves. Thus constitutional interpretation tends to enjoy peculiar characteristics, and, at times, to lack the consistency of other types of legal interpretation. To a great extent the absence of a complete written constitution obscures this distinction. It is possible to assert that, with us, there is no fundamental law, and that constitutional law is " part of the ordinary law of the land." [14] Formally this is no doubt true. It is also true in the sense that, with few possible exceptions, none of our constitutional laws are entrenched or specially protected. A constitutional statute is made by the same methods and bears the same appearance as any other.

---

[12] Thus the real reasons for the selection of Mr. Baldwin instead of Lord Curzon as Prime Minister in 1923 were not publicly known until the publication of Sir Harold Nicolson's *King George V*, and are still debatable—see the later *Unknown Prime Minister*, by Robert Blake, Chap. 32.

[13] See S. A. de Smith, " The Royal Style and Titles " (1958) 2 I.C.L.Q. at p. 272. The whole of the post-war evolution of the Commonwealth provides an admirable example of factual situations moulding theory.

[14] Dicey, *Law of the Constitution*, 11th ed., p. 203.

The Statute of Westminster 1931, the Electricity Act 1947 and the Protection of Birds Act 1954 all bear the same form, yet the first, in its entirety, and the second, in parts, affect the constitution. Nevertheless in substance distinctions may be made. It is evident that of these three the Statute of Westminster affects the constitution profoundly. In fact it appears that the attitude of the courts to such statutes does differ from that adopted to others. The provisions of the Bill of Rights and Claim of Right against taxation without parliamentary sanction are treated as having such authority that an implied derogation from them is not possible.[15] In the same way certain cases are regarded as having a particular authority,[16] though here possible instances are fewer since many of what could be regarded as fundamental principles are incorporated into statutes. In Scotland in particular, fundamental liberties can more easily be traced to statutory provisions rather than to notable cases.[17] Nevertheless it would take very clear words to derogate from the broad principles of cases such as *Knight* v. *Wedderburn*.[18]

The statutes and decisions which are treated with this special reverence are, however, few. Not everything which has a constitutional bearing is to be thus regarded. Within the constitutional field the provisions of the Statute of Westminster are of a different order to those of the Electricity Act. This special regard is limited to the relatively few statutes and cases which establish the framework of the state and the broad principles which govern it. Moreover, this special regard should not be thought to render principles immutable in their practical application. There are few basic constitutional principles which can be reduced to clear and certain formulae. No one principle can be regarded as dominant in all circumstances. Principles of liberty must on occasion give way before the needs of state defence. Principles of the separation of powers, even if acceptable, can only be regarded as general rules which may be departed from in particular circumstances. In the same way, although the forms in which basic constitutional principles are expressed may endure, their substantive application will vary according to the conditions of the time, and the practical interpretation of one generation will vary greatly from that of another. The conception of individual liberty may be expanded to include new fields, but may also be restricted because of a changed emphasis upon other principles, such as that of equality. The concept of " property " as it is protected by law obviously changes as the regulation of land-use in the interest of society becomes more common and more acceptable.

15　*Att.-Gen.* v. *Wilts United Dairies* (1921) 37 T.L.R. 884 at 886, *per* Atkin L.J. (affirmed (1922) 38 T.L.R. 781); though see *Att.-Gen. for Canada* v. *Hallet and Carey Ltd.* [1952] A.C. 427, 450 and the cases there referred to.

16　Notably those concerned with individual liberties.

17　The seventeenth-century litigation in England concerning the royal prerogative had no real counterpart in Scotland. Hence the Claim of Right which incorporated many of the principles which emerged from that litigation is all the more important.

18　(1778) Mor. 14545.

In this way constitutional law may have a greater durability but at the same time a greater pliability than other branches of law. This pliability is all the greater in those parts of constitutional law which are mainly derived from sources which differ from those of the ordinary law. Doctrines, such as those which govern the Cabinet, are formed by practice and are rarely crystallised either by statutory regulation or judicial decision. Since no formal step is then required to alter the rule, shifts may be frequent and rapid, and indeed unobserved for some time after their occurrence. This pliability tends to accentuate still more the uncertainty which is caused by the subject-matter of constitutional law.

Written and unwritten constitutions. These characteristics of constitutional law are universal and to a great extent they reduce the importance of the fact that a constitution happens to be written or unwritten, or that constitutional liberties are specifically guaranteed or protected in some way. Our own constitution may be said to be unwritten only in the sense that there is no one document or series of documents which may be pointed to as " The Constitution." It can in another sense be regarded as written—in the sense that a great number, and perhaps the majority, of our constitutional rules are to be found in statutes.[19] But in the narrower sense the contrast between constitutional law under written and unwritten constitutions is also not as great as might be thought. The same circumstances, which make it difficult for us to define our constitutional principles except in very general terms, also make it difficult, and probably undesirable, to draft a constitution except with a similar generality. To compress the constitution of a country into seven articles and twenty-five amendments (as with the U.S.A.) is an impossible task unless broad principles only are to be laid down, and in that case their real significance can only be appreciated in the light of judicial interpretation and of subsequent practical developments.[20] Moreover, the generality of expression also makes it possible for interpretation to vary greatly from generation to generation.[21] While formal amendments may be relatively rare, and thus the constitution has the appearance of rigidity, amendment by judicial interpretation is a continuing and effective process and may in the course of time amount to a complete reversal of former doctrines.

[19] By the use of scissors and paste it would be possible to produce out of the Statute Book a " constitution " which would be very nearly complete.

[20] The definition of the monarchy as a " constitutional monarchy " in Art. 2 of the Danish Constitution of 1953 is, in itself, almost meaningless.

[21] The well-known sentence of Chief Justice Warren in *Brown* v. *Board of Education*, 347 U.S. 483 (1954)—one of the " Segregation Cases " is a sufficient illustration—" In approaching this problem we cannot turn the clock back to 1866 when the Amendment [*scil*. the Fourteenth] was adopted, or even to 1896 when *Plessy* v. *Ferguson* was written. We must consider the public education in the light of its full development and its present place in American life. . . ."

The existence of a written constitution may certainly be of importance in providing a framework which facilitates judicial intervention, though the importance of that framework may be overemphasised. Thus, in *Liyanage* v. *R*.[22] Lord Pearce, giving the opinion of the Judicial Committee of the Privy Council, placed considerable stress upon the differences between written constitutions and others, and as a result held invalid, as being *ultra vires*, certain legislation. It is arguable that too great a stress was placed upon the written nature of the constitution. In effect the court, being faced with a written constitution, imported limitations (which were not themselves written into the constitution) upon the powers of the legislature. These were imported because of the weight attributed to certain general propositions. Logically there is no reason why identical limitations could not be contemplated even in the absence of a written constitution, since the limitation depended upon a conception of " correct " definition of the powers of government. The fundamental importance of a principle does not (save on a very simple view) depend upon its being written down. At best the process, in modern times, of importing limitations upon legislatures, is eased by having a written document as a convenient starting-point for argument. Even if the existence of such a document facilitates intervention of courts it does not, however, compel that intervention at least in relation to legislation. While Chief Justice Marshall took such a document as implying the necessity for judicial review,[23] it has always been held in France that even the existence of a written constitution with limitations upon the legislature did not entitle the courts to pass upon the validity of what was properly primary legislation.[24]

Thus the important distinction is not between written and unwritten constitutions, but between the condition under unwritten constitutions and conditions where the constitution is written and there exists a power of judicial review. In the latter case the principal consequence of the existence of a written constitution may be the increase in the importance of the courts as a means of constitutional adjustment. Whatever the form of constitution, whether written or unwritten, the pressures in society which necessitate constitutional change exist and, if the constitution is not to become unsuited to contemporary conditions, those pressures will, where the difficulties of formal amendment are great, be met by judicial reinterpretation of the original constitutional provisions. Where the means of formal amendment are easier and quicker to operate it is possible for the courts to take a less active role.[25] Clearly, however, the degree to which the courts will serve as a means of constitutional adjustment depends not only on the conception which

---

[22] [1967] A.C. 259. Compare the comment of Gèny on attitudes to written law, *Méthode d'Interpretation et sources en droit privé positif*, Vol. I, pp. 255–256.
[23] *Marbury* v. *Madison* (1803) 1 Cransh. 103.
[24] See Favoreu, *Du Déni de Justice en Droit Public Français*, Chap. I.
[25] See generally *Federalism and Constitutional Change* by W. S. Livingston.

individual judges have of their functions (and is therefore not constant), but also upon the emergence of justiciable issues. While therefore the role of the courts may be considerable in determining the limits, from time to time, of governmental powers, the adjustment of constitutional machinery to changing needs must often be carried out by other means, notably by the development of administrative practices. Hence convention may play as great a part under written as under unwritten constitutions.

The existence of a written constitution does mean that the constitutional law is more easily distinguished. Not only are its limits more obviously fixed but also the peculiarity of some of its methods of development is emphasised. Constitutional interpretation is more widely recognised as being governed by principles not generally applicable to ordinary statutes, and the treatment of judicial decisions (where doctrines of precedent are important) tends, for similar reasons, to differ in this branch of law from the treatment in other branches. In both these ways the influence of the broad general principles which have been already discussed is made more apparent. While the existence of a written constitution may facilitate the discussion of constitutional law and may also emphasise its special characteristics and problems, the substantial effect of such a written constitution as importing certainty and rigidity can be overemphasised.

It is even more important to note that the protection given to the so-called fundamental liberties by a written constitution can be overemphasised. In the first place any civilised system of law may well reach broadly similar results irrespective of constitutional forms.[26] In the second place, if obedience is required to special rules for any constitutional amendment, or is required for those affecting fundamental rights, direct abolition of such rights is obviously difficult. Yet, direct repeal is not usually the greatest danger; the attempt at such repeal will provoke a sufficient opposition. Much more serious is the erosion of liberties, by the gradual extension of legitimate powers, so that while in form liberties may still be protected, in substance they largely cease to exist. The maintenance of this substance depends ultimately upon general public opinion, but more immediately upon the activities of legislatures and especially of courts. In one case arising under a written constitution it was said: " The case confronts us again with the duty our system places on the courts to say where the individual's freedom ends and the State's power begins. Choice on that border, now as always delicate, is perhaps more so where the usual presumption supporting legislation is balanced by the preferred place given in our scheme to the great, the indispensable democratic freedoms secured by the

---

[26] Compare *R.* v. *Howes* [1964] 2 Q.B. 459 and *Gibbs* v. *Burke, Warden,* 337 U.S. 773 (1949). In Scotland the Faculty of Advocates had long accepted a right to counsel.

First Amendment." [27] In other words, the ordinary citizen, whether he lives under a written or unwritten constitution, must normally rely for his protection on the consciences of those who work that constitution. The form of constitution may merely alter the weight of the burden which falls on one particular group. In one case the main burden may lie upon Parliament, in another upon the courts.

The mere fact of there being a written constitution does not by itself necessarily mean that the courts play any greater role in protecting individual rights or policing the constitution. Where there is such a constitution but the courts do not possess the power to declare legislation unconstitutional, the only means by which the courts can protect the basic principles of that constitution from encroachment or erosion is by the restrictive interpretation of legislation. In such circumstances the position of the courts and the protection for fundamental constitutional principles do not differ materially from those which exist when there is no written constitution. The only difference in such circumstances is that by setting out principles the constitution may emphasise their existence. It is, of course, arguable whether or not a principle receives more emphasis from being incorporated in a formal constitutional document than from its enunciation in a leading case.

As has been pointed out, the real contrast with our own system is afforded by a system under which there is not only a written constitution but also a recognised power in the courts to declare legislation invalid as being unconstitutional. Under such a system it might appear that the basic principles of the constitution are much more surely protected. [28] Yet even in such circumstances the decision that the legislature has encroached upon forbidden territory is one which depends upon the limits which the courts will set for that territory and upon the meaning which the courts will give to the challenged legislation and upon the deference which the courts have for the judgment of the legislature. All these are once again matters of interpretation and approach. Hence, at times, the difference between this process, and the process, with us, of giving a restricted interpretation to apparently unambiguous words in a statute, [29] is not great. Although the existence of a power of quashing a statute clearly facilitates judicial intervention, the process of determining validity does not in such cases differ essentially from the judicial treatment of a statute where there is neither a written constitution nor the power of judicial review of legislation. In any of these situations the courts openly or covertly found their opinions upon principles which are not in themselves rules of law. While it is true

[27] Mr. Justice Rutledge in *Thomas* v. *Collins*, 323 U.S. 516 at 529–530 (1945). Whether or not the First Amendment freedoms are thus preferred is a matter of dispute; that question is not involved here.
[28] See the opinion of Chief Justice Centlivres in *Minister of Interior* v. *Harris*, 1952 (4) S.A. 769 (A.D.) and consider *Liyanage* v. *R.* [1967] A.C. 259.
[29] See *Nairn* v. *University of St. Andrews*, 1909 S.C.(H.L.) 10; [1909] A.C. 147 or *Viscountess Rhondda's Claim* [1922] 2 A.C. 339.

that the power of judicial review may in some circumstances be of major importance, it is nevertheless also true that in large areas of constitutional law the existence of the latter power affects only the means of protection, and not the extent of protection.[30]

It is clear that the existence of the power of judicial review increases the importance of the courts in the state. This increase in importance when added to that which, as has already been noticed, can come from the rigidity of a written constitution means that, although the security of the rights of the individual citizen may not be materially affected by the form of his constitution, that form will alter the relative importance of the different parts of the state machinery established by the constitution, and may itself influence general constitutional ideas. Thus, under one system there may be a greater readiness to accept a diversity of controlling mechanisms, while under another there may be a tendency to concentrate almost entirely on one. So, under our system the importance of Parliament as a guardian of the constitution is reflected in ideas of ministerial responsibility and perhaps in our conception of the sovereignty or supremacy of Parliament, whereas the much greater part which the Supreme Court has to play under the constitution of the U.S.A. has been a contributory cause in determining the role of, and the general attitude to, Congress. It might almost be said that to a British lawyer the legislator is regarded as the typical source of law, to the American lawyer that source is the judge. In these more oblique ways the form of a constitution may be more important than it is in its direct effect upon rights and obligations.

The place of the courts. One further general characteristic of constitutional law may here be mentioned, since it bears upon the role of the courts. In this branch of law in particular it is necessary to remember that there are limits to the judicial enforcement of rules of law, and that in constitutional law the existence of rules without apparent sanction, or without sanctions of the usual types, is fairly common. The exclusion of the courts may be due to a variety of reasons. One reason may be a respect for the status of some other constitutional body. Thus the courts have precluded themselves from inquiry into the internal working of Parliament,[31] and a similar limitation has been imposed by the Parliament Act 1911.[32] Another may be the reluctance or inability of the courts to intervene in disputes which involve too great an element of policy: our courts will not control the exercise of the prerogative (in the sense of controlling the reasonableness of the exercise of a

---

[30] See Holmes, *Collected Papers*, p. 295.
[31] *Bradlaugh* v. *Gossett* (1884) 12 Q.B.D. 271; *Bribery Commissioner* v. *Ranasinge* [1965] A.C. 172 at 195; and see the subsequent discussion of, among other things, parliamentary privilege.
[32] s. 3.

prerogative power), but will merely establish its limits or existence.[33] Again, the courts may deny judicial remedies where administrative ones are available.[34] In the same way as they will treat the internal affairs of Parliament as a matter for Parliament alone, so also, though not so broadly, they will regard the internal affairs of the administrative branch of government as being outside their scope.[35] The administrative control of the Crown could exclude even interested parties from bringing suits which concerned the administration of the common good of a burgh.[36] Questions of the fulfilment of statutory obligations to provide educational facilities may (at any rate as to matters of substance) be regarded as being suited only to administrative determination.[37] The regulation and discipline of members of the administrative staffs may be left to rules which are not themselves susceptible of enforcement in the ordinary courts, but are enforced by administrative action.[38] In these cases the jurisdiction of the courts may be excluded by their own decisions, but in others the limitation on the powers of the courts may be the result of statutes. The exclusion of the courts does not, however, mean that the administration has an exclusive jurisdiction over its own affairs. In many cases the proper forum for the enforcement of obligations is Parliament itself, and the doctrine of ministerial responsibility may itself be one of the reasons why the courts will deny jurisdiction.[39]

Many of these rules can be justified historically, but it is at any rate arguable whether today the limits of the activities of courts have, under our present constitution, been drawn at places which are appropriate to modern conditions, and a variety of situations must be considered. Undoubtedly it is socially desirable if, as is attempted by the Race Relations Act 1965, some matters can be left to the processes

[33] Modern cases such as *Liversidge* v. *Anderson* [1942] A.C. 206; *R.* v. *Bottrill, ex p. Kuechenmeister* [1947] K.B. 41 (particularly at p. 52) are really illustrations of this principle. See, too, *Pollok School Co. Ltd.* v. *Glasgow Town Clerk*, 1946 S.C. 373 at 384, *per* Lord President Normand, and Chap. 17, *post*.

[34] See as to burgh funds Ersk. I, 41, 23; *Conn* v. *Magistrates of Renfrew* (1906) 8 F. 905. The alternative remedy may be a strictly administrative one or may be by complaint in another form—*Fife C.C.* v. *Railway Executive*, 1951 S.C. 499. See also Griffith and Street, *Principles of Administrative Law* at p. 236, and Chaps. 12 and 17, *post*.

[35] See the remarks of Lord Sorn in *Griffin* v. *Lord Advocate*, 1950 S.C. 448 at 451. On the other hand, it appears that the real control over *ultra vires* expenditure may be exercised through the Treasury and the Public Accounts Committee. Thus in one case referred to in the report of the latter Committee on *ultra vires* expenditure by the Foreign Office, it is difficult to see who could have had a title to raise the matter in the courts (see H.C. 1956–57 75 (1)).

[36] See the discussion of these cases by Lord Dunedin in *D. & J. Nicol* v. *Dundee Harbour Trustees*, 1915 S.C.(H.L.) 7.

[37] *Watt* v. *Kesteven C.C.* [1955] 1 Q.B. 408 at 425, *per* Denning L.J.; in cases such as *M'Leman* v. *Moray & Nairn Joint C.C.*, 1955 S.L.T.(Sh.Ct.) 14 there was a statutory right of appeal to the courts.

[38] See such cases as *Rodwell* v. *Thomas* [1944] 1 K.B. 596 and the discussion of the internal remedies by L. Blair, " The Civil Servant—Political Reality and Legal Myth " [1958] *Public Law* 32.

[39] See the cases referred to in notes 33 and 35, *supra*. *The Epitome of Reports from Committees of Public Accounts* provides a digest of the sort of control which would elsewhere appear in the record of the Cour des Comptes.

of conciliation, education and good sense. While courts can act as a stimulus to the public conscience, too much activity on their part may have the effect of impeding the development of that conscience. In such fields the desired ends may be better obtained by such means. On the other hand, when the activities of government are in issue there are two obvious dangers. Courts are not the appropriate arenas in which policy (in the largest sense) should be determined, at any rate in a democratic society. On the other hand the power of government needs to be matched by the power of the law if the individual is to be secure.[40] Sometimes the individual must look for relief in one way, sometimes in another. The appropriateness and the effectiveness of the various ways are matters which pervade any discussion of constitutional law.

At the outset therefore the student of constitutional law must be warned to be critical, and to be prepared to find rules of law which differ substantially from rules of private law in the manner of their enforcement. Here again he is faced by rules which exist at the extremes of law. At times the rules will be said to be mere conventions, or to be administrative practices, lacking the full force of law. These rules may, however, often be rightly regarded as law, but as " *internal* " law, that is to say, law governing the domestic affairs of branches of government other than the courts, having, at most, only an oblique effect on the rights of the citizen and falling outside the province of the ordinary courts.[41] The recognition of the possibility of the existence of these rules of internal law, differing as they do in their sanctions and the forum for their enforcement, may often help to resolve difficulties of classification which otherwise arise, particularly in regard to conventions and parliamentary privilege.

It is, however, one of the functions of the courts, in the absence of any statutory provision, to determine whether a rule can be judicially enforced. The discharge of this function involves not merely a consideration of the appropriate forum, but also of the appropriate parties, for the duties of public law have often different subjects from those

40 See as a general introduction Mitchell, " Administrative Law and Parliamentary Control " (1967) 38 *Political Quarterly* 360. The issue is one with many facets; see, *e.g.*, Friedmann, " The Limits of Judicial Law-Making and Prospective Overruling " (1966) 29 M.L.R. 593; Stevens, " The Role of a Final Appeal Court in a Democracy: The House of Lords Today " (1965) 28 M.L.R. 509; Sawer, " Political Questions " (1963) 15 University of Toronto L.J. 49; or Wechsler, " The Courts and the Constitution " (1965) 65 Columbia L.R. 1001.

41 The difference of view between the two Houses of Parliament as to the " laying " of instruments under the Statutory Instruments Act 1946 makes this point. The details of the Act are discussed subsequently; here it is enough to note that while the House of Commons originally thought that the whole matter was one of its own concern, and could thus be regulated by Standing Order, the House of Lords conceived that in view of possible repercussions on private rights the matter should be regulated by or under general law, which was subsequently made possible by the Laying of Documents before Parliament (Interpretation) Act 1948. See also Transport Act 1962, s. 3 (4); and compare Goodhart, " An Apology for Jurisprudence," in *Interpretation of Modern Legal Philosophies* with Hood Phillips, " Constitutional Conventions: A Conventional Reply " (1964) 8 J.S.P.T.L. 60.

of private law. It is for that reason that problems of the title to sue may be of more general importance in constitutional and administrative law than in pure private law. In constitutional and administrative law there is not only the question of whether duties are to be judicially enforced, but since the duties are often imposed in favour of the public at large, there is also the question of whether any one individual is entitled to seek their enforcement. To some extent this problem is of greater importance in Scotland than in England. In England it is recognised that the Attorney-General is a necessary party in any action seeking to enforce duties owed to the public at large, where particular injury cannot be shown. The Lord Advocate does not enjoy the same position.[42] Nevertheless there are limits to the right of the individual to challenge public acts. It has been suggested that something akin to a proprietary right is necessary to the pursuer in an *actio popularis*, that is to say, that the title of the individual to sue must be founded upon a particular injury.[43] In the same way the definition of a " person aggrieved " who is entitled to challenge an administrative act will generally exclude those who are merely disappointed by, or who merely disapprove of, a particular decision. These restrictions do, of course, protect the courts from becoming too much involved in questions of policy but they also mean, much more frequently than in private law, that in the field of constitutional and administrative law duties are, apparently, of imperfect obligation, or at least cannot be readily enforced by the courts. These difficulties which may face an individual again emphasise that judicial remedies, while they are important, must in this branch of law be regarded as only one means of enforcing law. Both in its substance and in its methods public law, in the sense of constitutional and administrative law, has material differences from private law which have generally been too little observed hitherto.[44]

[42] *Griffin* v. *Lord Advocate*, 1950 S.C. 448.
[43] *D. & J. Nicol* v. *Dundee Harbour Trustees*, 1915 S.C.(H.L.) 7 at 17.
[44] The fact that Widgery J. in *Phillips* v. *Berkshire C.C.* [1967] 2 All E.R. 675 at 678 described the law as to who was " a person aggrieved " as a bewildering mass of authority is only one small mark of this.

CHAPTER 2

THE SOURCES OF CONSTITUTIONAL LAW

Introduction: the civil law. To a great extent, the sources of constitutional law are the same as those of other branches of the law. The relative importance of particular sources does, however, differ. Custom or convention is, for example, a source of much greater importance in constitutional law than it is in other branches of law. On the one hand, the civil law, which in Scotland influenced private law greatly and continues to have some influence, had much less effect upon public law. In that field of law it is probably true to say that at one stage the civil law was of considerable importance, but that importance has diminished greatly. It will often be found that there is a civil law foundation for rules which are now expressed in the terminology of the common law.[1] The appeal to Roman law was emphasised by Erskine,[2] and the influence can be seen in his treatment of highways.[3] The early immunities of a Commissioner to the Parliament of Scotland were founded upon the doctrine that he was *absens reipublicae causa*,[4] a doctrine which endured for a short while after the Union.[5] Thereafter circumstances caused a substantial decrease in reliance upon civil law. Gaps were filled in by reference rather to English cases,[6] and it is now only in cases involving the proprietary rights of public authorities that the civil law origins are much apparent. In any event, the reliance upon the civil law in this branch of law tends to be less than in others. Sir John Nisbet remarked: " But as to Questions of State and Government, the Civil Law is of no use with us, in respect the Laws of all Nations, concerning their State and Government are only Municipal." [7] With the development of modern forms of state it is clear that, in the rules which govern political institutions in

---

[1] See cases such as *Phin* v. *Magistrates of Auchtermuchty* (1827) 5 S. 690 founding upon the doctrine of *res extra commercium*, later overtaken by the doctrine of trust. For a modern instance see particularly *Burmah Oil Co. (Burma Trading) Ltd.* v. *Lord Advocate*, 1963 S.C. 410; 1964 S.C.(H.L.) 117; and for a comment on the methods of handling civilian writers see Prosser [1963] *Public Law* 12 *et seq.*

[2] Inst. I, 1, 4. See earlier Craig, *Jus Feudale*, particularly Book I, Tits. 15 and 16. Craig used the civil law as the justification of many rules of public law—see, *e.g.,* I, 10, 11, but contrast I, 16, 48. Erskine appealed to it for authority even for rules which are everywhere accepted, such as the limitation of judicial review to superior courts.

[3] Inst. II, 1, 5 and II, 6, 17.

[4] See *Molison* v. *Clark* (1707) Mor. 10398 and *Morton* v. *Fleming* (1569) Mor. 7325.

[5] See the cases collected in Morison, *Dict., s.v.* " Member of Parliament," Tit. I.

[6] See Erskine's treatment of parliamentary privilege or Bankton's treatment of the rules governing governmental institutions in Book IV of his *Institutes.*

[7] *Dirleton's Doubts, s.v.* " Prerogative "; and see *University of Glasgow* v. *Faculty of Physicians and Surgeons* (1837) 15 S. 736.

free societies, native characteristics will tend to predominate. Not all rules connected with such institutions (for example, those which also affect the rights of individuals) necessarily have this peculiar character. Even in relation to rules affecting the rights of individuals, there is after the Union much less reliance upon the civil law. Despite this the civil law background may still have to be borne in mind when the extension of an old rule to new circumstances is in question. Our present concern is, however, with major modern sources. These are statutes, judicial decisions, customs and convention and books of authority.

STATUTES

It will already have become apparent that many of the statutes which are important in constitutional law are not necessarily easily distinguishable as such by their title. They may be chiefly concerned with other matters and their constitutional importance may be incidental. The Criminal Procedure (Scotland) Act 1887 is general by its title, and many of its provisions relate to details of the criminal law, but parts of it are of major constitutional importance. Section 43, concerning the prevention of delay in trials, fulfils some of the purposes of the Habeas Corpus Acts.[8] On the other hand, some statutes are clearly and almost exclusively constitutional; the Acts of Union 1707, the Parliament Acts 1911 and 1949, the Act of Settlement 1700, or the Act of 1532 establishing the College of Justice,[9] are obvious examples of these.

These examples emphasise two problems concerning statutes as a source of constitutional law. The first is whether there are or can be any purely constitutional statutes of a different kind from those regulating private law. Is it true that, in Dicey's phrase,[10] "neither the Act of Union with Scotland nor the Dentists Act 1878 has more claim than the other to be considered as supreme law"? This problem involves discussion of the sovereignty of Parliament and may be left until later. The second problem arises from the existence of the Union. As the examples show, the constitutional lawyer is concerned not only with the statutes of the United Kingdom Parliament (and with them questions arise on the extent of their application) but also with those of the former Parliaments of the constituent parts of the Kingdom. The Acts of Union 1707 did not repeal any existing legislation except that which was inconsistent with the Acts of Union themselves, nor did they

---

[8] The writ of habeas corpus was general, applying to all persons in detention. The Act of 1679 was concerned with detention in criminal matters, the Act of 1816 extended it to other forms of imprisonment. The Scots Act is limited to criminal matters, other than treason, and re-enacts with amendments provisions of the Act for preventing wrongous Imprisonment 1701 (A.P.S. X, 272). See generally Chap. 18, *post*.

[9] A.P.S. II, 335.

[10] *Law of the Constitution*, 10th ed., p. 145.

generally extend to the other part of the United Kingdom legislation which had hitherto applied only to one part.[11] The constitutional lawyer is therefore still concerned with pre-Union legislation. A complete account of the constitutional law of the Kingdom would involve, for instance, a discussion of both the Claim of Right and the Bill of Rights. Such an account is beyond the scope of the present book and for a full discussion of those statutes which are primarily English, both in origin and present significance, the student is referred to standard English textbooks.

Nowadays little question arises about the extent of operation of post-Union statutes. Normally the terms of the statute itself make it clear whether it is a United Kingdom statute or not, and in the absence of any application clause there is some presumption that the statute applies to all parts of the Kingdom.[12] The modern relative certainty did not always exist,[13] but the position of most of the older statutes has been clarified either by judicial decision or by subsequent legislation,[14] though questions may still arise over interpretation. In older statutes terminology was often inapt for one jurisdiction. The difficulty could be surmounted by disregarding the inappropriate words[15] or by giving an approximate meaning.[16] Again, changes in draftsmanship and in legislative techniques have caused this difficulty to arise less often in modern times.

One problem, however, remains. So long as there exist two separate jurisdictions within the one Kingdom it is inevitable that the same words

---

[11] See Arts. XXV and XVIII of the Treaty. The succession to the Throne was regulated according to English statutes by Art. II, and other incidental alterations were made to existing laws by Arts. XVI, XVII and XVIII, some of which were of enduring importance, as to which see Chaps. 5 and 9, *post*.

[12] " The Application of Statutes to Scotland " by A. E. Anton, 1956 S.L.T.(News) 112. See, too, *Ryan* v. *Ross* [1963] 1 All E.R. 853.

[13] See, *e.g.*, *Duke of Douglas* v. *Lockhart* (1755) 6 Pat.App. 706, in which case the Court of Session was itself of two minds, Kames, Sel.Dec. 42; or *H.M. Advocate* v. *Hughes*, June 24, 1816, F.C.; 19 F.C.App. 5; or, later, *Conn* v. *Magistrates of Renfrew* (1906) 8 F. 905; or as to the continued effectiveness of the Act of 1690, c. 33 (A.P.S. IX, 225), regarding forfeiture, despite the Act of 1708 (7 Anne, c. 21) unifying the law of treason, see *Further Report of Commissioners of Inquiry*, 1716, and *Gordon* v. *King's Advocate* (1750) Mor. 4728.

[14] Thus the question of the disqualifications for membership of the new United Kingdom Parliament was dealt with by the Succession to the Crown Act 1707, ss. 24, 25 and 29. Uniformity as to the manner of conducting parliamentary elections was introduced by the Reform Act 1832; see, too, the Parliamentary Privilege Act 1770.

[15] *e.g.*, *Guthrie* v. *Cowan*, Dec. 10, 1807, F.C. More recently differences in background caused much the same effect in *Bissett* v. *Anderson*, 1949 J.C. 106.

[16] *Gordon* v. *King's Advocate* (1750) Mor. 4728; *Murray* v. *Comptroller-General of Patents*, 1932 S.C. 726; *H.M. Advocate* v. *Burns*, 1967 S.L.T. 170. The opinions in *Bridges* v. *Fordyce* (1844) 6 D. 968 (affd. (1847) 6 Bell App. 1) illustrate the difficulties well. These difficulties could easily arise under a system indicated by Lord Jeffrey in the last case. He had been Lord Advocate at the time and stated: " having given directions that notice of all proposed measures affecting Scotland should be given to me, if I had been asked at the time if such an Act had been passed, I should have said ' No '—no notice having been given to the officer whose duty and right it was to be advised of any change proposed to be made in the law of this country." For the present position see *Royal Commission on Scottish Affairs*—Minutes of Evidence Day 1, Q. 10 and 11 (evidence of Sir David Milne).

in a statute may have different meanings or effects in each jurisdiction.[17] Under the Crown Proceedings Act 1947, proviso (1) to section 47 (applicable to Scotland) is identical in form to the proviso to section 28 (applicable to England), yet the effect of the two provisos differs.[18] It has been said that the decision, even in an English appeal, of the House of Lords on a United Kingdom statute is binding on the Scottish courts,[19] but in view of these considerations the proposition appears to be doubtful as laying down a universal rule.[20] On the other hand, although a statute or part of a statute may, in terms, only apply to one jurisdiction, yet those provisions and the interpretation placed upon them by the courts of that jurisdiction may have considerable weight when different provisions with a similar general purpose fall to be interpreted in the other jurisdiction. This is particularly true when parallel statutes are enacted [21]; in other cases the weight to be given to the interpretation in one jurisdiction must depend upon the importance to be attached to differences in the circumambient rules of law.

Moreover, difficulties can arise as to pre-Union statutes. The attitude of the courts to the old Scots Acts is not the same as their attitude to modern statutes. In particular the method of interpretation has been more liberal (and would remain so where the interpretation has not become fixed),[22] and the doctrine of desuetude applies.[23] It was at

---

[17] As to the interpretation of United Kingdom statutes generally see *Earl of Breadalbane* v. *Lord Advocate* (1870) 8 M. 835 and *I.R.C.* v. *City of Glasgow Police Athletic Association*, 1953 S.C.(H.L.) 13, or earlier, *Lord Advocate* v. *Earl of Saltoun* (1860) 3 Macq. 659 at 671.

[18] As a result of *Glasgow Corporation* v. *Central Land Board*, 1956 S.C.(H.L.) 1, s. 11 of the same Act, although universal, might have a different effect in each jurisdiction. See for the ebb and flow in England *Conway* v. *Rimmer* [1967] 2 All E.R. 1260; and consider *Magistrates of Ayr* v. *S. of S. for Scotland*, 1966 S.L.T. 16 at 18 (*per* Lord Fraser) on the question of interim relief against the Crown.

[19] By implication in *Orr Ewing's Trs.* v. *Orr Ewing* (1885) 13 R.(H.L.) 1, and accepted J. C. Gardner, *Judicial Precedent in Scots Law*, p. 47, and T. B. Smith, *Judicial Precedent in Scots Law*, pp. 55, 59 and 62.

[20] The proposition is doubtless true so far as revenue statutes are concerned as a result of Art. XVII of the Treaty of Union and the Exchequer Court (Scotland) Act 1707, s. 13; see, *e.g.*, *I.R.C.* v. *City of Glasgow Police Athletic Association*, 1953 S.C.(H.L.) 13; its general application is doubtless subject to the considerations discussed in Chap. 14.

[21] In a similar situation English practice relating to Crown proceedings had great influence in Scotland where the practice differed—*Argyll C.C.* v. *L.A.*, 1950 S.C. 304. For a counterpart in England, see *De Demko* v. *Home Secretary* [1959] A.C. 654; and *Regional Properties Ltd.* v. *Frankenschwerth* [1951] 1 K.B. 631 at 637; *Daly* v. *Hargreaves* [1961] 1 All E.R. 552.

[22] *Graham* v. *Irving* (1899) 2 F. 29 at 36, *per* Lord M'Laren.

[23] For a general account of the doctrine, see Ersk. I, 1, 45; " Desuetude " by W. C. Smith (1895) 7 J.R. 173, and " Some Reflections on Desuetude " by Sir Randall Philip (1931) 43 J.R. 260. For the distinction between ancient and modern statutes, see *Governors of George Heriot's Trust* v. *Paton's Trustees*, 1912 S.C. 1123 at 1134–1135, *per* Lord President Dunedin, and *Johnstone* v. *Stotts* (1802) 4 Pat.App. 274 at 285. The application of the doctrine is no doubt affected by such statutes as the Statute Law Revision (Scotland) Acts 1906 and 1964. It seems doubtful, however, if the omission in the Act of 1906 to repeal the whole of a statute even where part is dealt with can be taken as excluding the operation of the doctrine of desuetude as to the remaining parts; consider the Act of 1593 for the Puneisement of thame that trublis the Parliament, etc. (A.P.S. IV, 22). The Act of 1585 Aganis leaguis and

one time held that this doctrine did not apply to statutes concerning the public good of the Kingdom,[24] but thereafter the views changed, and it came to be accepted that the doctrine applied to such statutes also.[25] Nevertheless some distinction between the two types of statute appears to remain. The burden of proof that a general statute for the public good had fallen into desuetude would be heavy. Isolated or local instances of non-observance would not suffice; what would be required would be such a change of circumstances that the Act could no longer be rationally applied.[26]

Apart from the application of this doctrine, pre-Union statutes may, as has been said, have ceased to have effect because of inconsistency with the terms of the Articles of Union. The main provisions in Articles 18 and 25 of the Treaty of Union are general, and in the absence of detailed provisions for repeal this inconsistency must be spelled out as a matter of construction. Many of the difficulties which could have arisen have been removed by subsequent legislation, and examples of pre-Union statutes which have not been specifically repealed but which are in direct conflict are difficult to find.[27] The conflict may not be apparent on the face of the statute, but may depend upon the method of interpretation of either the terms of the Act of Union or of the statute in question. In the latter case there may be some resemblance to the doctrine of desuetude in the line of argument. Such cases may still arise.[28]

bandis (A.P.S. III, 376) is one which, although not referred to in the Act of 1906, was likely to be treated as being in desuetude. Both are so treated in the Statute Law Revision (Scotland) Act 1964.

24 *Jack* v. *Town of Stirling* (1681) Mor. 1838 and Bankt. I, 1, 60.

25 The altered view appears to have been accepted in *Anderson* v. *Magistrates of Wick* (1749) Mor. 1842; although this view was not always regarded as certain, see *Gilchrist* v. *Provost, etc., of Kinghorn* (1771) Mor. 7366, it was affirmed in *Dunbar* v. *Macleod* (1757) Mor. 1855 and in *Bute* v. *More* (1870) 9 M. 180, and acted on in *M'Ara* v. *Magistrates of Edinburgh*, 1913 S.C. 1059. See, too, Ersk. I, 1, 45, where Erskine adopts the reasoning and words of the argument for the pursuers in *Anderson*. The Act 1661 (A.P.S. VII, 12) Anent his Majesties prerogative in making of Leagues and the convention of the subjects might be treated in the same way as the legislation there involved.

26 *Bute* v. *More* (1870) 9 M. 180 at 190, *per* Lord Deas. The Act of 1606 regulating meetings, which was discussed in *M'Ara's Case*, 1913 S.C. 1059, illustrates such a change. At pp. 1075–1076 Lord President Dunedin emphasises the altered circumstances of political debate since 1832.

27 Thus much of the pre-Union legislation relating to Parliament would have been inconsistent, but the Statute Law Revision (Scotland) Act 1906 has now repealed the legislation concerned, and the process has been continued by the Statute Law Revision (Scotland) Act 1964.

28 For one example, see *Macao* v. *Officers of State* (1822) 1 Shaw App. 138, in which the majority of the Scottish judges and of the House of Lords was prepared to hold that an Act of 1695, making naturalised Scotsmen of all persons who should take shares in the Bank of Scotland, was inconsistent with the Act of Union and therefore no longer effective. The effect of the Act of Union upon the English pre-Union statute under which Prince Ernest of Hanover successfully claimed British nationality was not argued—see *Att.-Gen.* v. *Prince Ernest of Hanover* [1957] A.C. 436. A majority of the House of Lords reserved their opinion on that point. See 1956 S.L.T.(News) 89 and (1957) 30 M.L.R. 270 and T. B. Smith, *Studies Critical and Comparative*.

Today a substantial number of the detailed rules will be found, not in statutes themselves, but in orders made under statutory authority, and it is becoming increasingly dangerous for the student to neglect this material. For the most part these instruments are now published in the statutory instrument series. The problems of interpretation and the like which arise in connection with such instruments are largely similar to those connected with statutes and more detailed problems can be left until later.[29]

CASE-LAW

It has been said that "the general principles of the constitution (as, for example, the right to public liberty, or the right of public meeting), are with us the result of judicial decisions."[30] That statement may be debatable,[31] but it is nevertheless true that judicial precedent is of considerable importance, either as an original source of principle[32] or as a secondary source, when the courts are interpreting a statute.[33] Here again problems arise from the fact that the Union of 1707 was in some senses incomplete. Separate systems of courts were then preserved, and thus English decisions (outside revenue matters) are not binding upon Scottish courts,[34] and it is possible for conflicting decisions to be arrived at in the different jurisdictions.[35] These conflicts are not necessarily resolved by the existence of the House of Lords as a common ultimate court of appeal in civil matters. The capacity in which the House sits is not entirely clear—it may sit as a United Kingdom court or as an English or, as the case may be, a Scottish court.[36] Moreover, since it is possible for the constitutional rules to differ in the two jurisdictions, the decisions of the House cannot be taken as being

[29] See Chap. 15, *post*. Apart from individual instruments, volumes of S.I. are published in the same way as, before 1947, roughly equivalent instruments were published as statutory rules and orders. In 1948 S.R. & O. and S.I. Revised (Third Edition) was published, giving the then extant instruments.

[30] Dicey, *Law of the Constitution*, 10th ed., p. 195.

[31] See Chap. 1 as to the influence of statutory law, and as to the significance of this remark, even if true.

[32] As in *Knight* v. *Wedderburn* (1778) Mor. 14545; *Somersett's Case* (1772) 20 St.Tr. 1, or *Smellie* v. *Struthers*, May 12, 1803, F.C., in which the underlying assumption is a fundamental right of property.

[33] As in *Att.-Gen.* v. *Wilts United Dairies* (1921) 37 T.L.R. 884.

[34] See Art. XIX of the Act of Union and the Court of Exchequer (Scotland) Act 1707, s. 6.

[35] Compare *Nottingham No. 1 Area Hospital Management Committee* v. *Owen* [1958] 1 Q.B. 50, holding the hospital premises to be occupied in the public service of the Crown (the argument also implying that in litigation the Committee was to be treated as a Crown servant), with *Adams and Ors.* v. *Sec. of State for Scotland and South-Eastern Regional Hospital Board*, 1958 S.L.T. 258, in which an interdict was granted against the hospital board, which was incompetent were the board a Crown servant.

[36] In *Johnstone* v. *Stotts* (1802) 4 Pat.App. 274 at 282 Lord Eldon roundly declared: "I need not remind your Lordships that . . . we sit here as a Scotch court—a Court of Session," and this view appears to be the correct one, yet it has not always been accepted or acted on; see, *e.g.*, the cases referred to in T. B. Smith, *Judicial Precedent in Scots Law*, pp. 49–50.

necessarily universally binding.[37]   Allowance must also be made for
the fact that the treatment of judicial precedent differs in Scots and
English law.   Under the former system the doctrine is less rigid than
under the latter, and there is machinery for convening a Full Court
which can be used to overrule older decisions, even of the Inner House.
The declaration of the House of Lords in 1966 on the binding effect of
decisions of the House goes some way to create uniformity.[38]

Nevertheless, the fact remains that there is a United Kingdom, and
none of the component jurisdictions can be looked at in isolation.
Developments in one have a reaction in the others.   There are, too,
strong pressures towards uniformity, notably the pressure of administrative convenience.[39]   In the absence of authority upon a particular
point in one jurisdiction weight must be given to relevant decisions
in the other, the exact weight being dependent upon the field of law
concerned—whether or not it is one in which the differences between
the systems are strongly marked.   Unless this is done there may be
certain constitutional topics upon which it is difficult to say that there
is any law at all or, at least, any modern law.   Thus, it is difficult to
find any modern cases upon parliamentary privilege in Scotland except
for a few immediately after the Union.   These cases do little more than
demonstrate the then existing uncertainty about the state of the law,
though they do show that the law was changing not merely in its
application but in its basis.[40]   In these circumstances a Scottish
constitutional lawyer cannot neglect the major English cases on
parliamentary privilege, particularly those of the eighteenth and nineteenth centuries.   Indeed, his reliance on English cases must be
continuous.   The chances of litigation mean, for example, that most
of the cases on this topic must arise in England,[41] and, as in other

---

[37] *Glasgow Corporation* v. *Central Land Board*, 1956 S.C.(H.L.) 1.   For a general
discussion, see T. B. Smith, *op. cit.* pp. 54–66 and 103–104.   The situation can be
still further complicated.   There was discussion in the House of Lords in the
Burmah Oil Case, 1964 S.C.(H.L.) 117 as to why the case had, in the courts below,
been dealt with on the basis of Scots law.   Lord Radcliffe affirmed (at p. 132) that
the proper law was English—the legal foundation for this conclusion being found in
the speech of Lord Pearce (at p. 159).   In fact what was really being debated was a
generalised United Kingdom principle, since in fact the decision would, despite its
origin, determine law for the whole Kingdom.

[38] See, for the declaration [1966] 3 All E.R. 77.   A full discussion of these issues
would be out of place here, and the reader is referred to T. B. Smith, *op. cit.*, and
to Gardner, *Judicial Precedent in Scots Law*.   In the older reports it is, moreover,
often difficult to determine a *ratio*, only the decision being given, a habit which
originated with the older Practicks, and died hard.

[39] *Lord Advocate* v. *Argyllshire C.C.*, 1950 S.C. 304 at 307 and *Moffat Hydropathic
Co. Ltd.* v. *Lord Advocate*, 1919, 1 S.L.T. 82 at 86, and see note 21, *supra*.

[40] *Grant* v. *Earl of Sutherland* (1708) Mor. 8562; *Lady Greenock* v. *Sir John Shaw*
(1709) Mor. 8563.   Some cases, such as *Mill* v. *Reid* (1723) Rob.App. 452 (Mor.App.
15), were decided on grounds which could not now be tenable.   This uncertainty is
reflected in the Lord Advocate's evidence to the Select Committee on Privilege,
H.C. (1955–56) 35, or in the authorities cited on the subject in works such as Hill
Burton's *Manual* or Bankton, *Institutes* IV, 1, 63.

[41] Thus *R.* v. *Graham-Campbell, ex p. Herbert* [1935] 1 K.B. 594 could only have
arisen in London.

branches of the law, differences in the bulk of litigation also cause doctrines to be more fully developed in England than in Scotland. While these influences towards uniformity exist, the problem of assessment nevertheless remains. The relevant case-law must be weighed in its particular context, and it may be that in the past there has been in some branches of the subject too great a readiness to accept into one jurisdiction decisions from the other without adequate consideration.[42]

BOOKS OF AUTHORITY

Books of varying types may be either sources of constitutional law, or sources of our knowledge of facts and events upon which the law is founded or from which it is deduced. In the first group are the books on law, such as Blackstone's *Commentaries*, Chitty, *On the Royal Prerogative* and the like. Many more of such books are to be found in England than in Scotland, where the great constitutional writers tended not to discuss public law so fully as private law. Again, there is the familiar problem of assessment. While Blackstone has been cited in argument and relied on in judgment in Scotland, because of differences in general law not all that is contained in English authoritative works can be regarded as necessarily having equal authority in Scotland.[43] The *Institutions* of Stair contain few titles which refer specifically to constitutional law,[44] those of Erskine (who wrote in more settled times) rather more. In both works constitutional law has often to be sought in the interstices of private law, and some of their introductory generalities which bear upon the subject do not carry the same weight as do their more precise pronouncements in the field of private law. Bankton on the other hand purported to treat fully of public law, but lacks the weight of the former writers and, moreover, probably underestimated the differences in public law between England and Scotland. In other cases, too, statements on constitutional law by writers whose work is of high standing in relation to other branches of law do not, for a variety of reasons, command the same respect. Sir George Mackenzie cannot be relied upon as an impartial observer as far as matters affecting the Crown are concerned [45] and, at a later date, Baron Hume's views on

---

[42] See, *e.g.*, Mitchell, "The Royal Prerogative in Modern Scots Law" [1957] *Public Law* 304.

[43] *Cf.* the remarks of Lord Cooper in *MacCormick* v. *Lord Advocate*, 1953 S.C. 396 at 411.

[44] Though in his *Apology*, which outlines some of his constitutional views, he states that he has written on the prerogative, the book (if it was ever completed) does not now exist.

[45] Thus his remarks upon prerogative in his *Vindication* or in the *Jus Regium* (*Works*, Vol. II) must be treated with caution. The fault often lay as much in the times as in the man. Other writers avoided dangerous issues—Sir John Nisbet was content to dismiss the extent of prerogative as "a point of State and Policy of the highest nature and importance and not to be defined by the opinions of Lawyers"—*Doubts* 138 *s.v.* Prerogative. In quieter times Stuart in his *Answers* could only add: "But to define its Extent is too delicate a point to be farther insisted on." In England,

public law were criticised both from the Bench and elsewhere.[46] On the older law, material is to be found dispersed through Craig's *Jus Feudale* or works such as Balfour's *Practicks* or Hope's *Major Practicks*, which stand halfway between a collection of precedents and an Institute. At a later stage Lord Kames' writings contain valuable material on certain constitutional matters; and other works, which are often, like Stuart's *Observations Concerning Public Law*, mainly historical, are also valuable sources. On the whole, it may be said that Scotland has not had the specialised treatises on the subject which exist elsewhere, and more reference must be made to the general books on law.[47]

In modern times a different type of book cannot be neglected by the constitutional lawyer. In certain branches of the subject, notably in connection with the Cabinet and the central government, the law emerges as a result of practice. These practices often only become generally known as a result of the publication of biographies, volumes of letters and the like, and of accounts of official activities.[48] Care must, however, be taken in the use of such material, since memory is fallible and knowledge may be incomplete.[49]

CONVENTION

The two types of rule. There remains one further source—custom or convention—which assumes particular importance in constitutional law. As a source of law custom is not confined to constitutional law, but in that branch of law it plays a more prominent part and is governed by somewhat different rules from those which prevail elsewhere.[50] The conventions of the constitution have received much emphasis from all modern writers on British constitutional law, and from Dicey in particular. Speaking of our constitutional rules, Dicey said that there were some rules which were laws in the strictest sense, but that there was another set of rules and this " other set of rules consist of con- ventions, understandings, habits, or practices which, though they may regulate the conduct of the several members of the sovereign power, of the Ministry, or of other officials, are not in reality laws at all since

Coke, too, was content to let some of his more contentious writing wait for publica- tion, and his views upon the Crown were not uniform throughout his career. Others both in Scotland and England, while discerning unconstitutional acts, would yet connive in them.
[46] See *H.M. Advocate* v. *Grant* (1848) Shaw (J.) 17 at 92; and see Campbell Paton's biography of Baron Hume—*Hume's Lectures*, Vol. VI, p. 354 *et seq.* (Stair Society ed.).
[47] As to these, see generally *Sources and Literature of Scots Law*—(Stair Society, Vol. I) and in particular the valuable article on constitutional law by Sir Randall Philip.
[48] Such as the *Whitehall* and *New Whitehall Series*. For an indication of the use of the other material referred to see, *e.g.*, the notes to Jennings, *Cabinet Government*; Mackintosh, *The British Cabinet*.
[49] See, *e.g.*, Bassett, *1931 Political Crisis*.
[50] Compare the general discussion of custom as a source of law in Sir Carleton Allen's *Law in the Making*.

they are not enforced by the courts. This portion of constitutional law may, for the sake of distinction, be termed the 'conventions of the constitution,' or constitutional morality." [51] Dicey added that the lawyer, as such, had no direct concern with these conventions.[52] Nevertheless in Part III of *The Law of the Constitution* he did much to underline the importance and clarify the nature of these conventions. Their common quality or property was, he asserted, that " they are all, or at any rate most of them, rules for determining the mode in which the discretionary powers of the Crown (or of the Ministers as servants of the Crown) ought to be exercised." [53]

While the views of Dicey have tended to dominate the discussion of conventions, he was not the first to observe the gap between the practical working constitution and the constitution which is contained exclusively in rules of law.[54] But because of their dominance it will be convenient to take Dicey's views as the starting-point for the present discussion. First, however, it must be emphasised that, just as custom or convention may be important in other branches of law, so also it is important in other constitutional systems. In France under the Third and Fourth Republics the role of the President was determined as much by conventional as by legal rules. In the United States of America the working of the Electoral Colleges in a Presidential election is governed by convention which has also produced rules such as that of Senatorial courtesy.[55] These examples could be multiplied, and the most that can be said is that with us (and with constitutions derived from our own) constitutional conventions are perhaps more important and more widespread than elsewhere.

This importance is due to a number of simple factual considerations. In particular we had our overt revolutions early, and at a time when it was not the habit to crown a revolution with a new constitution, if that could be avoided. Obviously the Cromwellian Commonwealth had to have an Instrument of Government—there had been a breach with established order. Equally obviously after 1688, when it was asserted that all that was really happening was a return to the true traditional legal and constitutional system, there was little incentive to produce a " constitution " in a formal sense. Thereafter, the historical accident of not having a written constitution came to be regarded as a virtue. The evolution of the machinery of government continued and in general

---

[51] *Law of the Constitution*, 10th ed., p. 24.
[52] *Op. cit.* p. 30.   [53] *Op. cit.* pp. 422–423.
[54] Dicey himself refers to Freeman's *Growth of the English Constitution*; earlier, Alphaeus Todd had commented in the general introduction to his *Parliamentary Government in England* on the wide discrepancies between legal rules and modern constitutional usage. Similar observations are to be found in most books on the subject. Gilbert Stuart, writing in 1779 in his *Public Law of Scotland*, comments (at p. 61): " Habits lead to establish a rule; and custom is often as effectual as law." The history of the word and idea is explored in " Constitutional Conventions: Dicey's Predecessors " (1966) 29 M.L.R. 137 by O. Hood Phillips.
[55] For an account see Horwill, *The Usages of the American Constitution*.

there was no desire to reduce the constitution to writing. On the contrary, it was felt that to do so would be wrong. Typically no attempt was made by any formal process of law-making to formulate relations between the House of Lords and House of Commons until the determination of some to disregard the understood rules made such a formulation inevitable, with the result that the Parliament Act 1911 was passed. Such episodes were rare. In general the "rules" for the conduct of government emerged in practice even in vitally important areas (such as those governing the powers of the Sovereign); often even their emergence was not fully noted by the writers of books for some time. Thus, when they were noticed there was felt to be no need to formalise them—they had worked perfectly well in the past as they were, and indeed there were good reasons why the process of "formalising" the rules should not be embarked upon in relation to some matters. Conventions were the primary means for evolving a constitution, and until it was certain that a right or enduring shape had been found it could have been wrong to crystallise the rules. But it is important to note that whether formalised or not they existed, were known to exist and were expected to be observed. Mr. Gladstone, for example, would clearly have expected Queen Victoria to observe certain rules and if necessary would have taken appropriate steps to ensure that result, just as George V was courteously but sharply reminded that the internal proceedings of the House of Commons were no affair of his.[56] Thus rules which would normally appear in a written constitution emerged (and in a form closely akin to the way in which a "convention" would be formulated by a commentator [57]) and were left in an unwritten customary form until a deliberate attempt was made to breach them, or some other circumstance required their formal enunciation. The Parliament Act 1911, already mentioned, is one example [58]; so too is the Statute of Westminster 1931 (and the words "established constitutional position" in the preamble to that Act should be noted).[59] To what extent this formal change is more significant than, for example, the codification or clarification of pre-existing law by the Sale of Goods Act 1893, or by the Bills of Exchange Act 1882, must be discussed shortly. What is important at this stage is to observe that conventions are rules, and are accepted as such.

It is, however, possible for different rules within any legal system to have different juridical values. There may be a hierarchy of rules.

56 Nicolson, *George V*, pp. 428–429.
57 *Cf.* s. 33 (10) of the constitution of Western Nigeria referred to in *Adegbenro* v. *Akintola* [1963] A.C. 614.
58 See p. 149, *post*. The Twenty-Second Amendment to the American Constitution could be regarded as illustrating the same process.
59 It is also relevant to note in the period from 1923–31 which rules governing the Commonwealth were reduced to legislative form, and which were clarified as conventions. The treatment of different rules illustrates the above thesis. But see Marshall & Moodie, *Some Problems of the Constitution*, Chap. 2.

Thus, the pre-eminence of statutory rules over other rules of law was one of the inventions of the seventeenth century, and the common law may thus be regarded as being lower in the hierarchy than statute. Hence, statutes like the Sale of Goods Act do have an effect of confining judicial inventiveness within limits defined by the statute, and the common law cannot fly in the face of statute. Clearly conventions share many of these characteristics. While convention could modify the way in which the Colonial Laws Validity Act was applied, it could not get rid of that Act. For that reason alone the Statute of Westminster was needed. All that conventions can do is to modify or control the way in which a legal institution works, provided that that modification is not in direct contradiction to any other rule of law. As the parallel of the common law indicates, this " inferiority " of convention within the hierarchy of norms does not, of itself, mean that conventions are not law, any more than the fact that the existence of the Sale of Goods Act limits the formative role of mercantile custom prevents valid mercantile custom from being recognised as law. It does not mean, therefore, that conventions are necessarily to be regarded as different in kind from other rules of law, unless undue weight is given to certain purely formal considerations, and the important historical background of the way in which our constitution emerged is disregarded.

Moreover, what has earlier been said of the nature of constitutional law, and of the problems of enforcement of law (and the range of mechanisms for enforcement of law) at this extreme, must also be borne in mind in any discussion of the nature of conventions and of their relationship to law. It suffices for the moment to insist that the possibility that conventions are a form of law is, in the light of the considerations that have been discussed, a real one. Neither history nor nomenclature has excluded that possibility, but before turning to that issue something more should be said of the rules that are normally classed as " conventions."

Types of convention. In a domestic sense the major conventions still operate in the fields indicated by Dicey. It is these conventions which have, as he pointed out, been the principal means of transferring effective power from a sovereign to ministers responsible to Parliament, and of regulating the relationship of Government to Parliament and of the Houses of Parliament to each other. Conventions govern the Sovereign's choice of Prime Minister, the position of the Prime Minister in relation to his colleagues, or the resignation of a government as a result of an adverse vote in the House of Commons. While the Parliament Acts of 1911 and 1949 regulate the relationship of Lords and Commons in some cases of conflict, that relationship is more continuously regulated by rules of privilege which can be regarded as conventional. Examples of such rules are the Commons' claims in respect of Money Bills and the Lords' countervailing claim to a right to object to the " tacking " of

other matters on to Money Bills. It is impossible here to give a full
list of such conventions: to do so would be to compress major parts of
the book into one chapter. Enough has been said to emphasise the
importance of conventional rules in this part of our constitution. They
are those which, as Sir Ivor Jennings has said, make the legal constitution
work by keeping it in touch with the growth of ideas.[60]

Conventions are, however, operative in branches of constitutional
law not covered by Dicey's formulation. Most important of these
other groups of convention is, no doubt, the group of those which govern
the relationship *inter se* of members of the Commonwealth, and which
had not emerged with any clarity at the time when Dicey wrote. Some
of these are the result of practices, others of resolutions of Imperial
Conferences and the like, still others result from a combination of the
two. This group of conventions may be illustrated by those recited in
the preamble to the Statute of Westminster 1931, or by the principles
formulated by the Imperial Conference 1926.[61] While these conventions
perform the function described by Sir Ivor Jennings, they do so in a
different sphere, since they regulate the relationships between separate
and equal governments and not between the different parts of the
machinery of one government. Moreover, these conventions are, far
more than others, the source of the " real " constitution; in this area
rules of strict law are built upon conventional foundations (rather than
the other way round) to a far greater extent than elsewhere. Thus in
this area of constitutional law the role of convention has been
particularly important. Dominion or member status is the child of
convention, and the Statute of Westminster 1931 is, in important
respects, nothing but an enactment of conventions [62] and assumes the
background of a very wide range of conventions beyond the legislative
matters with which it was primarily concerned. This process of
conventional development still continues. The initial recognition of a
republican form of government as being consistent with membership
of the Commonwealth, even though it substantially altered the previously
accepted views of the nature of the Commonwealth and of the place of
the Crown therein, was not granted by any recognised method for the
formulation of rules of law.[63]

---

60 *The Law and the Constitution*, 5th ed., p. 82. Though, correspondingly, unless the
   reasons for the existence of particular conventions are observed, the sheer dead
   weight of accustomed ways may have the opposite effect.
61 *Imperial Conference 1926: Summary of Proceedings* (Cmd. 2768); some of these
   resolutions simply expressed existing practice; others, although having some foundation in practice, were new formulations of principles to be applied in the future.
   See also Keith, *Speeches and Documents on the British Dominions 1918–1931*.
62 *Copyright Owners Reproduction Soc. Ltd.* v. *E.M.I. (Australia) Pty. Ltd.* (1958) 100
   C.L.R. 597.
63 This recognition was granted in the Final Communiqué of the Commonwealth Prime
   Ministers' Meeting 1949—for the text, see Mansergh, *Speeches and Documents on
   British Commonwealth Affairs*, 1931–59, Vol. II, p. 846. The India (Consequential
   Provisions) Act 1949, which made necessary adjustments in British law, assumes the
   background of a changed situation in the position of India in the Commonwealth.

Even within the United Kingdom there are some conventions which are not clearly comprised within Dicey's definition. The relationship of Government to Opposition is regulated by convention, as is the position of Leader of the Opposition.[64] Thus, for example, the use of Supply Days to debate matters selected by the Opposition [65] is purely conventional. Indeed many of the rules falling under the heading " Law and custom of Parliament " and regulating the internal working of Parliament outside the narrow relationship of Government and Opposition may be regarded as conventional. Such, for example, are the rules which lay down the commonly understood, though imprecisely defined, limits to Private Bill legislation [66] or which, varying the ordinary rules, recognise the Second Reading of a Private Bill promoted by a nationalised industy as affording an opportunity for a general debate on that industry.[67] Some of this group of rules have become part of the Standing Orders of one or other House, others remain as practices or understandings.[68] In both cases the full import of the rule is only apparent after a study of precedents and Speaker's rulings.[69]

Similarly, within the administrative branch of government much is regulated by convention. The position of one of the Joint Permanent Secretaries of the Treasury as head of the civil service is the creation of convention,[70] and the rules governing the methods of selection for the most senior appointments in each department have a similar origin.[71] The particular position of the Secretary of State as " Scotland's Minister " (which gives him influence beyond his sphere of legal responsibility) rests upon convention.[72] The civil service itself is governed by a mass

[64] Though the existence of the position was recognised by the Ministers of the Crown Act 1937, s. 3. The Ministerial Salaries and Members' Pensions Act 1965, s. 2, carries the process further by recognising in the same way, and providing for payments to, the Chief Opposition Whips in both Houses as well as the Leader of the Opposition in the House of Lords.

[65] See Morrison, *Government and Parliament from Within* (3rd ed.), p. 120.

[66] See *Report of Joint Committee on Private Bill Procedure* (1955–56) H.C. 137–1, Q. 343 *et seq.* and the proceedings on the Kent County Council Bill 1958 (H.L. 209, 473–540).

[67] See *Report of Joint Committee on Private Bill Procedure* (1955–56) H.C. 137, § 15.

[68] An example of the former type is the convention that Standing Committees should, as far as possible, reflect the composition of the House of Commons (S.O. 58). See, too, S.O. 78 (recommendations from the Crown for applications relating to public money). The examples given in the text are conventions which have not been incorporated into Standing Orders.

[69] See, *e.g.*, the precedents collected in Erskine May, 16th ed., p. 369 *et seq.*, in relation to adjournments under S.O. 9 or in relation to the scope of Finance Bills and tacking, *op. cit.* pp. 800 and 812.

[70] The present arrangement was announced by Mr. Macmillan on July 30, 1962, whereby in addition to the two Joint Permanent Secretaries to the Treasury (one of whom is head of the home civil service) a separate post of Secretary to the Cabinet was created. For the superseded situation, see 557 H.C.Deb. 639–642. The position of head of the civil service was of gradual growth; see 125 H.L.Deb. 275 *et seq.*; and see Bridges, *The Treasury*, pp. 164–165 (2nd ed.).

[71] Morrison, *op. cit.* 337 (3rd ed.); Bridges, *The Treasury*, p. 177 (2nd ed.).

[72] *Report of Royal Commission on Scottish Affairs* 1952–54 (Cmd. 9212), §§ 177–179. Some of the conventional devolution referred to in Chap. VII of that report has since been made " legal " by Orders made under the Ministers of the Crown (Transfer of Functions) Act 1946.

of regulations, some of them statutory, some contained in Royal Warrants or in Treasury Minutes and Instructions. These regulations may, in some cases, be regarded as law; in other cases they cannot be so regarded within Dicey's scheme, since often these regulations take effect within the service only and are not enforceable in ordinary courts of law.[73] They are, however, the effective rules, and must be recognised as conventions or as the internal law of the civil service.[74]

Conventions are important not only where they regulate the relationship of different parts of government or operate within one part. In formulating legislation any government will consult with outside bodies and, indeed, it has been said that any other course would be unthinkable. The limits of consultation appropriate to different types of legislation are also defined by conventional understandings. It is possible, too, that the regulations and attitudes of political parties must, on occasion, be regarded as conventional parts of constitutional law. If the rule is that the Sovereign must send for the leader of the majority party in the House of Commons, then the rules by which the leader is chosen cease to be of purely domestic concern to the party. The regulation of the relationship of Back-Benchers' Committees to the Government or to the Opposition Shadow Cabinet, or the place of the party organisation in the selection of Cabinet Ministers, may also be said to be conventional. There is no doubt that in an Australian context the caucus system would be thus regarded,[75] and so must be the different rules which obtain here. Moreover, conventions are recognised which have a " party " origin. In the general conduct of government the practices of one government tend to be followed by succeeding governments even of a different colour. The unilateral declarations of one party may in the course of time come to be generally accepted. Thus the " Ponsonby Rules," while in origin nothing more than the declaration of intention of one party,[76] have come to be accepted, subject to dispute as to their scope, by all governments.[77]

---

73 See *Rodwell* v. *Thomas* [1944] 1 K.B. 596.
74 The rules may differ from ordinary law. Thus the standard of probity expected from the civil service under its own code is higher than that imposed by ordinary law. (See, *e.g.*, the *Memorandum on the Acceptance of Business Appointments by Officers of the Crown Service* (1937) Cmd. 5517.) It is, however, the higher standard which would be enforced, by sanction if necessary, within the service.
75 See Sawer, " Councils, Ministers and Cabinets in Australia " [1956] *Public Law* at pp. 118–120. There is nothing surprising about this. In the U.S.A. the party customary devices of primary elections, even where they are not formally embodied in the electoral laws, are, nevertheless, recognised by law—see *Terry* v. *Adams*, 345 U.S. 461 (1953).
76 The " rules " were contained in a declaration of policy of the first Labour Government in 1924. See 171 H.C.Deb. 2001–2005.
77 See 577 H.C.Deb. 491, where the " rules " were accepted by the then Conservative Foreign Secretary, though there was no agreement on their exact scope. See, however, the rejection of the " rules ": 179 H.C.Deb. 565. The declaration by Lord Carrington of the circumstances in which the House of Lords should use to the full its legislative powers (280 H.L.Deb. 420 and 285 H.L.Deb. 1459–1460) could have the same effect unless other events change the House radically.

The origins of convention. It is clear that, partly because of the widely different areas in which conventions operate, the origins of conventional rules are even more varied than those of ordinary rules of law. While it is true that the great majority of conventions have their origin in practice and are founded upon precedents, others are founded upon declarations which, although they may have some roots in past practice, express broader rules than would be justified by past precedents alone. Such, for example, were the rules declared in 1926 governing relationships within the Commonwealth. It must not, however, be thought that one precedent necessarily makes a rule (though it may), since the weight to be given to any precedent depends upon the whole surrounding circumstances.[78] It is thus often difficult to state with certainty the moment at which any convention was accepted as such. One common element is, however, that of acceptance, which, backed by precedent or declaration, makes a convention; but it should be noted that this acceptance need not be general, it may be limited to those primarily concerned with the working of a rule. Thus, a convention may be accepted and operated within Parliament before it has been recognised outside. Acceptance should not, however, be confused with agreement. It is, as has been shown, possible for a declaration of principle of conduct by one political party to grow into a convention. The so-called "Ponsonby Rules," to which reference has been made, are an illustration of this.[79]

Another common element, which gives to conventions particular advantages and disadvantages, is that these rules are formulated by those who are concerned with operating the machinery of government. In this, conventions may be compared with some rules of mercantile or international law. As a result conventions are essentially pragmatic in character and, while general theory has influenced the practices upon which they are based, the rules themselves look much more to the practice than to the theory. There are obvious advantages in this practical origin (it may, for example, mean that the rules are more sensible than they would otherwise be), but it means that to a large extent conventional rules escape the various safeguards which are involved in the formation of other sorts of constitutional rules. In

---

[78] See Jennings, *Cabinet Government*, 3rd ed., pp. 6–8. It was possible to construe, in the normal way in which lawyers treat their precedents, the choice of Mr. Baldwin in preference to Lord Curzon.

[79] Similarly, it seems that some regard must be had to the unilateral declaration of the Parliamentary Labour Party on the procedure for the selection of a new Prime Minister during the life of a Parliament. See [1957] *Public Law* 4. Again, while parliamentary parties persist in recognising a Deputy Prime Minister, the office is not recognised by the Sovereign (see Morrison, *Government and Parliament from Within* (3rd ed.), pp. 90–91, and Wheeler Bennett, *George VI*, p. 797). It is thought likely that adherence to its original views by one group of persons " affected " may, in time, force acceptance by another group. Compare, in connection with the relationship between the choice of Prime Minister and the election of a party leader, Robert Blake, *The Unknown Prime Minister* at p. 460.

particular it must be remembered that Government and Opposition in many of the areas in which conventions operate cannot be regarded as opposed forces, like gamekeepers and poachers. They share common interests—those of politicians—and rules made by politicians for politicians are not necessarily the rules which would be chosen by the generality of those interested in constitutions.

While this practical origin must be emphasised, it must also be said that not all governmental or parliamentary practices are to be classed as conventions. Conventions are those rules which, despite their practical origin, seek to attain some constitutional end, as distinct from an end of pure convenience. The allocation of certain days for parliamentary questions directed at certain ministers has an obvious basis of administrative convenience or necessity, but there is no constitutional principle underlying that practice, as there is, for example, underlying the practices or rules which limit questions on the exercise of the prerogative of mercy. The latter may be regarded as conventions, the former cannot be so regarded.[80]

The nature of conventions. From the examples already given it is clear that conventions cannot be regarded as less important than rules of law. Often the legal rule is the less important. In relation to subject-matter the two types of rule overlap: in form they are often not clearly distinguishable. The preamble to the Statute of Westminster is as precisely phrased as is section 4, and may well have at least as much binding force[81]; indeed very many conventions are capable of being expressed with the precision of a rule of law, or of being incorporated into law.[82] Precedent is as operative in the formation of convention as it is in that of law.[83] It cannot be said that a rule of law is necessarily more certain than is a convention.[84] It may, therefore, be asked whether it is right to distinguish law from convention, particularly if the considerations relating to the formation of our constitution which have earlier been discussed are borne in mind. The distinction drawn by Dicey was that, whereas law could be directly enforced in the courts,

---

80 Again, this distinction is not a clear one. Practical and constitutional reasons often coalesce, or are both operative at the same time, or may change their character. This interplay of principle and practical convenience is admirably brought out by M. René Massigli, *Sur Quelques Maladies de l'Etat.*

81 This depends upon arguments as to the effect of s. 4. As to which, see Chap. 4, *post.*

82 This was done, for example, by s. 4 (2) of the Ceylon (Constitution) Order in Council 1946 or in the constitution of West Nigeria—see p. 28, *ante.*

83 The form of precedent may differ, there are Speaker's rulings, decisions by a sovereign, etc., but these differences are accounted for by the circumstances in which the principles must be formulated.

84 This is, of course, particularly true when the rule of law depends upon judicial decision, but it can also be true where the law is statutory; see, *e.g.,* the uncertainty felt about what is a " general direction " under the Coal Industry Nationalisation Act 1946. See *Report of the Select Committee on Nationalised Industries (Reports and Accounts)* [1957–58] H.C. 187–191, Q. 65.

conventions could not.[85] The sanction for convention was, he asserted, to be found in the fact that a breach of convention would ultimately lead to a breach of the law.[86] This thesis is open to attack in two ways. In the first place not all law, particularly in the realm of constitutional law, is capable of enforcement in the courts. Thus, section 3 of the Parliament Act 1911 makes the Speaker's certificate as to what is a Money Bill for the purposes of that Act conclusive and unchallengeable in any court. Effectively the limiting legal definition of a Money Bill contained in the Act is thus made incapable of enforcement in a court of law in Dicey's sense.[87] Indeed, in the post-war constitutions of the Commonwealth it was a commonplace to exclude the jurisdiction of the courts in relation to matters which were most highly political. On the other hand it is not clear that no conventions are enforced in a court of law. The authorities are conflicting,[88] and much depends upon what is meant by "enforcement." It is certainly true that on occasion courts of law will recognise the existence of conventions and derive legal consequences from them.[89] When Lord Radcliffe in *Ibralebbe* v. *The Queen* [90] says: "Their Lordships take it to be clear therefore that the Order in Council which gives effect to a Judicial Committee report is a judicial order " he is asserting that the result of the application of a series of conventions is the emergence of a distinctive legal phenomenon, from which he draws further legal consequences. In effect he is thus " enforcing " the conventional rules and not the legal forms. In the context of constitutional law this is often as far as " enforcement " could go, and it must be remembered that conventions operate in those parts of constitutional law in which litigation is most difficult and often impossible to initiate.

One sort of difficulty is well illustrated by *Adegbenro* v. *Akintola*,[91] in which a declaration was sought that the Governor had acted contrary to the constitution in dismissing the Prime Minister. The Judicial

[85] See the quotation given on pp. 26–27, *ante*. The view is restated and re-argued by Prof. Hood Phillips in 8 J.S.P.T.L.(N.S.) 60, "Constitutional Conventions: Conventional Reply "; and see the discussion in Marshall and Moodie, *Some Problems of the Constitution*, Chap. 2.

[86] *Law of the Constitution*, 10th ed., p. 446.

[87] There are many other examples: see, *e.g.*, s. 3 (2) of the Iron and Steel Act 1949, Transport Act 1962, s. 3 (4). Both as to common law rules and as to statutory rules the same position may be reached, because of limitations upon the title to sue; see as a modern case *Griffin* v. *L.A.*, 1950 S.C. 448. For an older one see *Stewart* v. *Bothwell*, Feb. 26, 1742, F.C., though compare *Craigie* v. *Hepburn*, Dec. 22, 1809, F.C.

[88] See *Re Minimum Wages Act* [1936] S.C.R. 461 and the other cases discussed by Sir Ivor Jennings in his article " The Statute of Westminster and Appeals " in 52 L.Q.R. 173 and in *Constitutional Law of the Commonwealth* and *The Law and the Constitution*. To these may be added *R.* v. *Davenport* (1877) 3 App.Cas. 115; *Smith* v. *The Crown* (1913) 17 C.L.R. 356.

[89] *Adair* v. *Hill*, 1943 J.C. 9; and *Re Bristol S.E. Parliamentary Election* [1961] 3 All E.R. 354 at 370. Other illustrations could be added, most recently and importantly the *Copyright Owners Case* (1958) 100 C.L.R. 597, where (at pp. 612–613) conventions are described as rules which courts would be expected to obey.

[90] [1964] A.C. 900 at 921.

[91] [1963] A.C. 614.

Committee upheld the validity of the Governor's action, and the immediate results were the passing of a constitutional amendment nullifying the decision of the Judicial Committee and a fresh constitutional crisis.[92] Throughout the opinion Lord Radcliffe indicates the difficulty of the situation both for the Governor and the courts, and he approaches the heart of the problem when he says: " But the practical application of these principles to a given situation if it arose in the United Kingdom would depend less on any simple statement of principle than on the actual facts of that situation and the good sense and political sensitivity of the main actors." That is to say that the problem of enforcement of conventions of this order arises in what are virtually revolutionary situations (when admittedly that good sense and political sensitivity, so attractive to lawyers, will *ex hypothesi*, be lacking or else the situation would not have arisen). Thus at this point "enforcement" becomes a pure matter of fact. At a lower level of convention, again the terminology may mislead or obscure. There is recognised an area, commonly called " political questions," in which the courts hold back from exercising a jurisdiction which they could claim.[93] Terminology has concealed the kinship between conventions and the rules of admitted law which exist in this area. Thus, quite apart from any question of the concept of enforcement being fundamental to the idea of law [94] Dicey's attempted differentiation of law and convention on the grounds of enforcement or non-enforcement in courts breaks down on either leg. It does so because insufficient regard is had to the particular nature of constitutional law, as being law at the farthest extreme, and the group of rules here in question are among those in which this characteristic is most marked.

Nor can Dicey's theory of the ultimate sanction of convention be accepted. It is a theory which can work in relation to the conventions with which he was primarily concerned (*i.e.*, those regulating the relationships of Government and Parliament), but which will not work generally.[95] Breaches of convention in the field of Commonwealth relationships, while they might lead to a disruption of the Commonwealth, would not lead to breaches of law, and even in the field of internal affairs Dicey's theory is not always true.[96] Rejecting Dicey's view, and asserting that there is no fundamental distinction between

---

[92] See S. A. de Smith, *The New Commonwealth and its Constitutions*, p. 89; and see (1967) 16 I.C.L.Q. 452, Keith, " Courts and Conventions of the Constitution," and (1964) 13 I.C.L.Q. 280–284.

[93] See Sawer, " Political Questions," in (1963) 15 Univ. Toronto L.J. 49; Scharpf, " Judicial Review and the Political Question—A Functional Analysis," in (1966) 75 Yale L.J. 517; and consider in this context *Harper* v. *Home Secretary* [1955] Ch. 238.

[94] See Goodhart, " An Apology for Jurisprudence," in *Interpretations of Modern Legal Philosophies*.

[95] In Dicey's narrow field, the theory is supported by cases such as *New South Wales* v. *The Commonwealth* (1931) 46 C.L.R. 155 and (1932) 46 C.L.R. 246.

[96] See Jennings, *Law and the Constitution*, 5th ed., p. 129 *et seq.*

law and convention, Sir Ivor Jennings has suggested that Dicey's problem, of why conventions are obeyed, is solved by recognising that all rules, whether legal or conventional, are normally obeyed because of habits of conformity and acceptance. Both law and convention are thus founded upon acceptance.[97]

Even if the substantial truth of this solution be accepted, it may be argued that although it explains why conventions are obeyed, it does not solve the problem of why they *should* be obeyed. From what has been said it is clear that between the two sets of rules there can be found no fundamental distinction in origin, scope, or nature, which is universally valid. It is also apparent that Dicey's formulation of his distinction was greatly influenced by Austinian theories which linked law with a sanction, and thus with courts. As has already been emphasised, in the field of constitutional law both the sanctions (where they exist) of rules and the forum wherein the rules are to be enforced differ greatly from those of private law. If this is accepted, then to a large extent the difficulty is removed. If the place of the ordinary courts in the definition of law is not given the emphasis which Dicey gave it, then there remains no real difficulty in regarding " law " and " convention " as names for groups of rules which are essentially similar. To a great extent conventions operate in the field of what has earlier been called " internal law," [98] or in the field where courts may be less appropriate institutions for enforcement than other more political institutions. To say that, however, does not mean either that the choice of the forum for enforcement is now always correctly made, or that courts have no role even when political sensitivity is lacking. All that is meant is that rules commonly called conventions, if properly so classed, share the same nature as rules of law.

Thus the effort to distinguish the two by any general definition of either, or to distinguish them on the grounds of their substance, or of the consequences of the breach of the different sets of rules, is bound to fail. To say this does not mean that there is no point in preserving the two names. There are good reasons of convenience for so doing. The function of convention in all the different circumstances which have been discussed remains constant. It is to ensure the smooth working of the constitution in changing conditions. In effect, with us, convention has been a major instrument of constitutional adjustment and reform. Through convention, rules have been devised by those who are concerned with the practical working of government and

[97] *Op. cit.* p. 330 *et seq.* In *Cabinet Government*, 3rd ed. at p. 3, Sir Ivor remarks that " The distinction between laws and conventions is not really of fundamental importance." See, however, Chap. 1, note 41, *ante*, for an instance where regulation in the ordinary course of law rather than regulation by the conventional means of Standing Orders was thought necessary.

[98] That is to say, they operate in areas in which courts are in any event most disinclined to operate, and might well decline jurisdiction even in relation to rules of law.

experiment has been possible in an effort to find the most satisfactory rules. This pliability even owes something to the difference in names; changes may be made the more readily because of the absence of that formality which marks a change in law. The positive step of declaring a new rule provokes doubt and hesitation which are absent from a mere change of custom. The abandonment of a conventional rule which has ceased to serve a sound purpose is facilitated, since the stigma attached to unconventionality is less than that attached to illegality. Most important, since there are limits to human imagination and draftsmanship, but not to possible combinations of circumstances, convention remains necessary to allow the necessary flexibility to meet exceptional circumstances. Without any illegality Mr. MacDonald could in 1924 break the accepted rules of collective responsibility to Parliament, and, in effect, declare his own rules which his government would observe.[99] While this departure from rule was required by the special circumstances of the formation of his government, the circumstances (and the rules to meet them) could not have been satisfactorily defined in advance by law.

This pliability which is at the same time the mark and result of convention accounts both for the continuance of conventional rules and for their periodic enactment as rules of law. Where an institution is still developing it will remain governed, to a large extent, by convention,[1] but when experience has shown that rules can and ought to be formulated with clarity and certainty convention may well be superseded by law.[2] In this sense law may be regarded as convention which has crystallised. Such crystallising may be a consequence of a variety of causes. A political crisis may prompt clarification, or it may be felt that a particular stage in development has been reached which should be marked in some signal way.[3] In both cases the fact that, while convention may modify the operation of law, it cannot directly contradict law may be important.[4] The result may be the repeal of a

---

[99] 169 H.C.Deb. 749–750. Similarly with the narrowest of majorities in 1964 Mr. Wilson could adopt broadly similar rules.

[1] Thus there is only a bare minimum of legislation relating to the Cabinet. While salaries are provided for by law, composition is not, subject to some limiting rules which are accepted as necessary: House of Commons Disqualification Act 1957, Sched. II; Ministers of the Crown Act 1937.

[2] The Imperial Conference of 1926, the Conference on the Operation of Dominion Legislation and the resulting Statute of Westminster 1931 provide a clear example of this process.

[3] The rules determined in 1926 relating to the position of a Governor General were the result of the earlier dispute between Lord Byng and Mr. Mackenzie King. The clarification was achieved while leaving the rules conventional. On the other hand, the Statute of Westminster 1931 served not only to repeal (as far as the then Dominions desired) the Colonial Laws Validity Act 1865 but also as a landmark. Thus a convenient way of marking the emergence of a new Dominion in the years immediately following 1945 was simply to bring it within the scope of the Statute of Westminster. Thereafter techniques changed.

[4] This is particularly true of statute law. It is, however, arguable that the declaration of 1949 (see note 63, *supra*) did affect the legal foundation of the Commonwealth.

law which is no longer desired. Although what has just been said may appear to recognise a greater certainty and durability in law than there is in convention, this is not necessarily so, and the choice of the form for the declaration of the rules is governed by other general considerations.

In order, however, that conventions may be regarded in this way, as being of the same nature as law, it is necessary that conventions should be distinguished from mere practices. In any organisation a pattern of activity develops and is continued out of habit or simply for the sake of convenience. Such patterns exist in constitutional matters. There are, for example, limits to parliamentary debate dictated by nothing more than the limits of physical endurance. On the other hand there are patterns which persist because a constitutional principle extending beyond mere practical convenience underlies them. It is these latter patterns which may be regarded as " conventional." Thus the rejection of Lord Curzon as Prime Minister in 1924 may be taken as marking or establishing a convention because the decision was governed by the considerations dependent upon the constitutional relationship of the two Houses of Parliament. While the distinction between practices and conventions cannot always be clearly and conclusively drawn it is nevertheless sufficiently precise to have value and to be of considerable importance when the nature of conventions is analysed.[5] Finally both this element of principle which is inherent in conventions and their real nature as part of the law of the constitution should be emphasised for another reason. It is only thus that the fundamental importance of conventions will be fully realised, and the danger of sliding into the view " If it works, it is constitutional " can be avoided.[6]

---

[5] See, too, Marshall and Moodie, *Some Problems of the Constitution*, Chap. 2.
[6] *Cf.* Professor Griffith in [1963] *Public Law* 401–402, where he elegantly condemns as pointless those pages in books on constitutional law devoted to this topic.

CHAPTER 3

GENERAL DOCTRINES OF THE CONSTITUTION

IN any discussion of constitutional law certain general doctrines are prominent. The doctrines of separation of powers and of the rule of law are among these, and to them must be added in the discussion of the British Constitution the doctrine of the sovereignty of Parliament. It is these doctrines which form the subject-matter of this and the following chapters.

THE SEPARATION OF POWERS

At the outset it should be said that the doctrine of separation of powers has exercised a peculiar fascination for British lawyers perhaps because of its very simplicity in the English version, and because of the dominance of Blackstone and thus of his interpretation in specifically British terms of Montesquieu's theory. The doctrine also appeals to lawyers because of its application in respect of courts. In any event, for whatever reason, the doctrine has for them almost assumed the air of one of the eternal verities. This view of the doctrine is, however, a blinkered one. The doctrine has to be seen as one of a number of successive theories about constitutional structures, all of which were aimed at the prevention of despotism, absolutism or arbitrary government.[1] Theories of " balanced " or of mixed government are among these, and each had at certain points of time considerable influence upon constitutional thought and structure, for example, in relation to the House of Lords. Moreover, there is no single doctrine of the separation of powers. There are many variants of it which depend for their origin upon particular patterns of national thought, or national history; and at the outset it must be emphasised that the doctrine is inconsistent with other theories upon which politicians, political scientists and administrators build our constitutional machinery, whether the lawyers like it or not. That said, since the doctrine has had this importance, and in some respects continues to have it,[2] it must be briefly discussed.

---

[1] No other advice can be given to the student but that he should read Vile, *Constitutionalism and the Separation of Powers*, which is a masterly survey of the origin and development of the doctrine and of the problems of theory which face anyone who wants to think about the structure of a modern state rather than simply to accept the legacies of the past, whether or not they be appropriate. With this prefatory injunction the present treatment can remain brief. In particular, the young lawyer must read Chap. VIII of Vile.

[2] *Bribery Commissioner* v. *Ranasinghe* [1965] A.C. 172 at 190, and especially its sequel, *Liyanage* v. *The Queen* [1967] A.C. 259, which also brings out the continuing importance of Blackstone's interpretation.

This doctrine is commonly associated with Montesquieu's *L'Esprit des Lois*, in which, in Book XI, Chap. VI, the author distinguished three sorts of power—the legislative power, the power exercising matters falling within the law of nations (which he called the executive power), and the power exercising matters falling within the civil law (which he called the judicial power). If, said Montesquieu, any two, or more, of these powers were combined in the same person or body of persons, there could be no liberty. After considering the nature of the person or body in which each power should be vested, Montesquieu might be taken (and was taken) to conclude that the then existing law of England conformed to this ideal pattern and provided the necessary framework for liberty. In truth, at the end of Chapter VI Montesquieu was describing an idealised and not an actual country. At first sight Montesquieu's division does not correspond to what is now generally understood by the phrase " separation of powers," namely, the separation of legislative, executive and judicial powers. Montesquieu's second power is essentially and almost exclusively connected with foreign affairs, his third power extends beyond what is generally accepted as being the scope of the judicial power. It should be noted that, on the one hand, in the eighteenth century, the administrative functions of the central government were almost limited to foreign affairs and related matters, and, on the other, in Montesquieu's development of his theme, his executive branch becomes somewhat broader, being also concerned with the execution of the law within the kingdom. There is some confusion in his use of terms, but, nevertheless, there is thus some foundation here for the modern doctrine of the separation of powers.

It must be emphasised that there is a considerable background to this chapter by Montesquieu. Somewhat similar ideas are to be found in Aristotle's *Politics*,[3] and, closer to Montesquieu's time, and perhaps to his work, in Locke. The latter, having distinguished [4] the legislative and judicial powers, further discussed an executive power (concerned with the execution of the municipal laws) and a federative power (concerned with foreign affairs); these last two powers, being intimately connected, were, he said, almost always united. The three powers which thus resulted from his analysis should, he argued, be separated both for practical and theoretical reasons. Somewhat earlier than Locke, in the same stream of thought, George Buchanan had, in his *De Jure Regni apud Scotos*, distinguished the three elements of government, and had emphasised the necessity for some separation.[5] In later years

---

[3] Book IV, § 14. On all this see Vile, *op. cit.* Chap. II.
[4] *Second Treatise on Civil Government*, Chap. XII.
[5] Thus Buchanan asserts: " When you allow the King to interpret the laws you afford him an opening to make the law say what its author intended, not what is just and good for the community but what is to the interest of the interpreter ": *De Jure Regni* (trans. R. Macfarlan), p. 252. A passage which finds an echo in Montesquieu's assertion that if the executive and judicial powers are joined " the judge would have the strength of an oppressor." Similarly Buchanan separates the legislative function,

the doctrine has had a varied career. It has been incorporated, explicitly or impliedly, in a variety of constitutions,[6] but it has also undergone something of a modification by way of explanation. Thus Madison asserted [7] that it was only when the whole of one power was exercised by a body which also exercised another power that there was danger to liberty. Hence, in one form, the doctrine became one "of mutual restraints or checks and balances." [8] Others have asserted that what merit there is in the theory is to be found simply in the resultant dispersal of power among many hands.[9]

It is possible to raise objections to all of these theories or variants. In relation to our own constitution it is obvious that in earlier times it would be difficult to maintain any theory of separation. The story of the development of institutions is one of increasing specialisation of function, and thus of the separation of bodies which at one stage were united in a single body with multifarious functions. " In the administration of civil justice during the fifteenth century the most marked feature is the gradual differentiation within the *curia regis*, creating a distinction between the executive and the judicial functions of the Council, and in the sixteenth century gradually delimiting the spheres without completely separating the personnel of Privy Council and Council and Session," wrote Professor Hannay.[10] On the other side the Lords Auditors appointed by Parliament also form part of the background of the Court of Session. The process of specialisation or separation was, however, never complete throughout the history of Scotland as an independent state. Any of the volumes of the Acts of the Parliament of Scotland will show that body acting in judicial, administrative or legislative capacities.[11] In modern times it is equally easy to point to departures

entrusting it in the first place to a council. The executive functions are to remain with the King advised by counsellors. This dispersal of power being, according to his argument, a necessary protection against tyranny.

6 It was regarded as fundamental to the existence of a constitution in the Declaration of the Rights of Man 1789 (Art. 16), and was explicitly incorporated, for example, in the original constitution of the Commonwealth of Massachusetts, by implication, at least at first glance, in such constitutions as that of the U.S.A. or of Australia. Vile, *op. cit.*, discusses in detail the evolution of the doctrine in France and the United States. In Australia it can, on occasion, still be an effective force; see, *e.g.*, *Att.-Gen. for Australia* v. *The Queen and the Boilermakers Society of Australia* [1957] A.C. 288.

7 *The Federalist* No. 47.

8 See Sir Carleton Allen, *Law and Orders*. For an account of the development of the idea upon the Continent see Esmein, *Eléments de Droit Constitutionnel*, Chap. 3.

9 Griffith and Street, *Principles of Administrative Law*, Chap. I.

10 *Judicial Administration in Session and Justiciary*, Stair Soc., Vol. I, p. 398; see too his *College of Justice* (particularly Chaps. III and V) and A. A. M. Duncan's *The Central Courts before 1532* in Stair Soc., Vol. XX. A like process of specialisation was of course operative in England; see, *e.g.*, Plucknett, *Concise History of the Common Law*, Chap. 3, and Richardson and Sayles, *Parliaments and Great Councils in Medieval England*, and Adam Smith, *Wealth of Nations*, Book V, Chap. I, Pt. II.

11 In its latter years as part of the struggle against the Crown or as part of the legislative skirmishing which preceded the Union of 1707 that Parliament was claiming to control specific administrative acts, see Act anent Peace and War 1703 (A.P.S. XI, 107), and earlier see Act anent the election of officers 1641 (A.P.S. V, 354), repealed 1661 (A.P.S. VII, 10); and on the judicial side see, *e.g.*, " Judicial Proceedings in the Parliaments of Scotland 1660–1688 " (1924) 36 J.R. 135.

from the doctrine. At one extreme our doctrine of cabinet government is founded upon the intermingling of Parliament and executive, which in itself was the result of applying a different theory (that of " balance ") rather than of specifically not applying the theory of the separation of powers. At the other extreme the sheriff has a mass of administrative functions; and work which at times is entrusted to a court, for example, that of the Dean of Guild, is at other times entrusted to an administrative body—a local authority committee in the landward areas of a county.[12] At one time the Court of Session acted in ways which can be regarded as administrative or legislative. Acts of Sederunt might regulate branches of law, being in time replaced by statutes,[13] and the court might be called upon to draft or consider legislation.[14] Similarly by Act of Sederunt the Lords were prepared to regulate the price of wine or direct brewers to continue their trade,[15] and in the form of judicial decisions were equally prepared to undertake administrative acts,[16] to amplify statutes,[17] or indeed to accept or create new heads of jurisdiction without statutory authority.[18] While Sir George Mackenzie and Sir Ilay Campbell might protest that such activities of courts were due merely to the difficulty of the times, it remains possible to find modern examples not entirely dissimilar.[19] If one looks at other branches of government a

---

[12] See *Report of the Committee on Building Legislation in Scotland* (1957) Cmnd. 269.

[13] The Act of Sederunt of 1620 against unlawful dispositions made by bankrupts, replaced by the Act of 1621 (A.P.S. IV, 615), is perhaps the best known example. Others are to be found in the Report by the Lords of Session to the House of Lords on Feb. 27, 1810, upon Acts of Sederunt (Ilay Campbell, *Acts of Sederunt*, II, 52). See, too, Sir George Mackenzie's comments on the legislative powers of the Court of Session in his *Observations* on the Act of 1621 (Works, Vol. II) and those of Sir Ilay Campbell in his preface to his collection of *Acts of Sederunt*.

[14] See, *e.g.*, Act of Sederunt, Jan. 24, 1754, approving a draft of the Act for preventing clandestine marriages and forwarding it to the Lord Chancellor (Ilay Campbell, *Acts of Sederunt*, II, 476).

[15] July 6, 1692 (Ilay Campbell, I, 201), and July 31, 1725 (Ilay Campbell, I, 283). At other times the court was directly charged by statute with specifically administrative functions, *e.g.*, under the Act of 1686 for cleaning the streets of Edinburgh (A.P.S. VIII, 595).

[16] See, *e.g.*, *Moderator of the Presbytery of Caithness* v. *Heritors of Reay* (1773) Mor. 7449, or *Paterson* v. *Magistrates of Linlithgow*, Feb. 28, 1783, F.C. Indeed in his preface to the *Acts of Sederunt* Sir Ilay Campbell considers the *nobile officium* to be an encroachment upon the executive power of government, and often its exercise is essentially administrative; see, *e.g.*, *Lord Advocate, Petitioner* (1885) 12 R. 925; or *Glasgow Magdalene Institution, Petitioner*, 1964 S.L.T. 184.

[17] *Duke of Gordon* v. *Sir James Grant* (1776) Mor.App.Juris. 3; and see the remarks of Lord Chancellor Eldon in *Johnstone* v. *Stotts* (1802) 4 Pat.App. 274 at 283.

[18] Kames, *Historical Law Tracts*, p. 228; and see the comments of Lord Cockburn upon *Pryde* v. *Heritors and the Kirk Session of Ceres* (1843) 5 D. 552 in his *Journal*, Vol. II, pp. 1 and 257.

[19] The power to make such Acts of Sederunt may be granted by statute—see, *e.g.*, Act of Sederunt (Adoption of Children) 1959 (S.I. 763 (33)), but it is not always so. Thus, in England, the Probate Registrar's Direction of April 23, 1953, in relation to the place of signature of a will has a quasi-legislative effect. Similarly, the Act of Sederunt, Dec. 4, 1850 (Alexander's *Abridgement*, 2nd Supp. 68), constituting one body of solicitors before the court and regulating their qualification and admission can only be regarded as a legislative act. See also *Ward* v. *James* [1966] 1 Q.B. 273 as a clear example of judicial legislation.

similar admixture of functions can be found, both in individuals and institutions.[20]

For this admixture of functions in any one body there are a variety of reasons. There is in the first place no consistent theory which dominates our constitutional structures. Sometimes there is no theory at all, but even where there is a theory the chances are that it will only be applied within one area of the constitution. Here there is one of the observable effects of not having a written constitution. Given the need to produce such a document, there is a compulsion to hammer out a theory which will as far as possible make the document coherent. In the absence of such a need (or in the absence of feeling such a need) pressures for the evolution of particular parts of the constitution will be felt at different times. Thus, solutions which are found in respect of certain parts or areas of the constitution (Parliament and Cabinet, for example) will be found under the influence of theories which may be dominant at the time, but which are inconsistent (or only partially consistent) with theories which dominated at different times in relation to other parts of the constitution. Moreover, particular theories may be especially attractive in relation to certain institutions. The doctrine of the separation of powers is attractive in relation to courts as an aid to judicial neutrality. It is not attractive as far as the relationship of Cabinet to Parliament is concerned. There is a second fundamental reason. It appears to be impossible to formulate any satisfactory definition of legislative, executive or administrative acts which will in all cases clearly distinguish one from the other. It is possible to distinguish such acts by definitions which depend upon the form of the act rather than its nature, but such definitions are clearly unsatisfactory for present purposes.[21] Thus, even if a continuous attempt to carry

---

[20] To overcome difficulties arising from this fact there have been occasions when Lords of Appeal in Ordinary have expressed the view that they should not enter into debates on legislation lest they should in another capacity have to interpret it; see Bromhead, *The House of Lords in Contemporary Politics*, Chap. IV. This principle is certainly not universally observed or accepted. See *Bonnybridge Roman Catholic School* v. *Stirlingshire Education Authority*, 1928 S.C. 855 at 875, where Lord Alness's phrase " Whatever source of information may be open to one; that policy [*scil*. of the Act] must be ascertained from the provisions of the Act, and from those alone " covers a somewhat similar situation. Lord Alness, who as Secretary for Scotland had been responsible for piloting the Education (Scotland) Act 1918 through Parliament, was in a minority in the Second Division on a question of interpreting the Act, though his views were ultimately accepted in the House of Lords. See, too, *Gardner* v. *Beresford's Trustees* (1875) 5 R.(H.L.) 105 at 118, *per* Lord Gordon.

[21] Definitions such as that of Lord Atkin in *R.* v. *Electricity Commissioners* [1924] 1 K.B. 171 of what is judicial are circular. The distinctions drawn in the *Report of the Committee on Ministers' Powers* (1932) Cmd. 4060 are unsatisfactory, since on closer examination the characteristics which are there isolated and seen in a judicial decision exist to a greater or lesser degree in an administrative one. It is noticeable that more recently the *Report of the Committee on Tribunals and Inquiries* (1957) Cmnd. 218 (commonly called the Franks Committee and Franks Report) did not venture upon definitions, urging an empirical approach (§ 30). See the discussion of the distinction between judicial and administrative acts in de Smith, *Judicial*

out the separation of powers were made, this gradual merging of one form of act into another form means that it will never be possible to say with certainty that a true separation has been achieved or that that is desirable. Thirdly, the fact that constitutional machinery has been evolved rather than been made increases the likelihood of this admixture of functions. Once a function has been entrusted to a body it may remain with that body even though, on grounds of pure principle, it would not (or should not) be there placed. In Scotland, the Lord Advocate, in addition to those functions which would naturally fall to him as a Law Officer, still retains others of a somewhat different type which to a large extent adhere to the office because of what it once was. In England the fact that local government was once predominantly the affair of the justices in quarter session still has its consequences.[22] Nor is the machinery of government created with a tidiness which would permit a neat separation. The Lord Chancellor is intended to be in part an administrative officer, but, because for many purposes the Lord President of the Court of Session is to be regarded as his equivalent in Scotland, administrative functions fall to the Lord President, even though that office was not in intention an administrative one.[23] To these considerations must be added another major one. The whole process of government must be one of collaborative effort towards a desired end. Any rigid separation of the departments of government would frustrate this collaboration. For the same reason any rigid adoption of a system of checks and balances, or of the dispersal of power, could be dangerous, leading to inertia in government when movement and vitality is required, or, equally dangerously, leading to the blurring of lines of responsibility with, as a consequence, the failure of systems of accountability.

In any of its forms an extreme application of the doctrine is likely to be undesirable. Nevertheless the doctrine is a significant one. Often, in law, phrases which are incapable of precise definition are useful, hence the consequences which might be thought to flow from difficulties of so defining words such as " legislative " can be overemphasised.[24]

Review of Administrative Action, Chap. II; Paton, *Jurisprudence*, § 73; and Robson, *Justice and Administrative Law*, Chap. 1. The War Damage Act 1965 is an example. Despite its apparent generality it was in truth highly specific.

[22] In Scotland the *Report of the Committee on Building Legislation* (1957) Cmnd. 269 makes this point.

[23] This equivalence is not always drawn; see, *e.g.*, the *Royal Commission on Scottish Affairs* (1954) Cmd. 9212, § 144. Generally it must be borne in mind that in the course of time offices may change their character substantially without losing all their old characteristics; compare, *e.g.*, the development of the offices of Master of the Rolls and of Lord Justice-Clerk—Lord Evershed, *The Office of Master of the Rolls*; Hannay's " The Office of the Justice-Clerk " (1935) 47 J.R. 311; and Malcolm, " The Lord Justice Clerk of Scotland " (1915) 27 J.R. 342 at 375.

[24] Even if the words are incapable of precise definition a minimum content of meaning may be accepted and be used effectively by the courts: *Tuker* v. *Ministry of Agriculture, Fisheries and Food* [1960] 2 All E.R. 834; in which the Court of Appeal founded upon such a minimum content of the word " legislation."

Moreover, there are few, if any, absolute principles in constitutional law; all are matters of degree, and certainly the difficulties with this doctrine arise mainly if an attempt is made to regard it as absolute.[25] Certainly the doctrine continues to shape constitutional arrangements,[26] and influences decisions,[27] and in some limited form is necessary both for efficiency and liberty.   Sometimes, as with the separation of the investigating and prosecuting functions in the criminal law, it is the conception of the dispersal of power which is important.[28]   At other times it is the classical doctrine which matters.   The Ordinance of James V in 1526 communicating to the Lords in Council that " his heines promittis that he sall gif na lettres to stop justice "[29] was founded on sound doctrine of which Montesquieu would have approved.   The frequent repetition in one form or another of the substance of this promise, and its prominence in the settlement of 1688,[30] is an indication

[25] Compare, on the difficulties of striking a balance between checking administrative action in the interest of liberty and allowing activity in the same interest, the majority and minority views in *Liversidge* v. *Anderson* [1942] A.C. 206, or in *Youngstown Steel & Tube Co.* v. *Sawyer*, 343 U.S. 574 (1952). The warnings of, for example, Mr. Justice Holmes against the Supreme Court carrying its function of " checking " too far were numerous.   In this country many of the difficulties which have resulted from the *Report of the Committee on Ministers' Powers* (Cmd. 4060) were rooted in the attempt of the Committee to separate, in ways that were far too rigid, the functions of adjudication and administration.

[26] See, *e.g.*, the Franks Report (1957) Cmnd. 218 and the resultant Tribunals and Inquiries Act 1958.   On a larger scale the doctrine has played a part in determining the powers of the courts and of Parliament in relation to the privileges of the latter.

[27] On the one hand there are the rules of the House of Commons that a matter which is *sub judice* should not be there debated; see *Report of Select Committee on Procedure* (1962–63) H.C. 156.   On the other hand, decisions such as *Duncan* v. *Crighton* (1892) 19 R. 594 or, more recently, *Land Realisation Co.* v. *Postmaster General* [1950] Ch. 435 are clearly affected by the doctrine, as (in relation to the separation between judicial and legislative activities) were such decisions as that in *The Sheriff-Clerks, Petitioners* (1783) Mor. 7393.   Indeed the modern increased insistence on principles of natural justice has often an element of substantial reliance upon the doctrine; compare the readiness with which formerly the Court of Session dealt with the immunity of the College of Justice from taxation (Fount. I, 440) (and the whole history of this matter in Ross, *Privileges of the College of Justice*) with the doubts and difficulties expressed in some of the opinions in *Carron Co.* v. *Hislop*, 1930 S.C. 1050 as to the review of the validity of an Act of Sederunt.   Such cases emphasise equally the difficulty of applying the doctrine absolutely and the sort of difficulty which can arise from an admixture of functions. Recent instances of the effect of the doctrine are *Liyanage* v. *The Queen* [1967] A.C. 259 or *Att.-Gen. for Australia* v. *The Queen and the Boilermakers' Society of Australia* [1957] A.C. 288.

[28] As it is also in relation to warrants, arrest or to search, though again the principle is departed from when other interests become dominant.   See Chap. 18, *post*.   This principle has wide applications.   The existence of what may be called institutional checks is important.   These may be administrative, *e.g.*, the size of the Cabinet Secretariat and the place of the Treasury in the general scheme of government, or they may be difficult to classify, such as the Select Committee on Statutory Instruments, but, nevertheless, bodies whose existence and potential activities are significant.

[29] A.D.C. III, 256.   Compare the insistence on an independent court by Chief Justice Centlivres in *Harris* v. *Donges*, 1952 (2) S.A. 428 (A.D.) and *Liyanage* v. *The Queen* [1967] A.C. 259.

[30] " That the Sending letters to the courts of Justice, Ordaining the Judges to stop or desist from determining causes, or ordaining how to proceed in cases depending before them, and the changing of the nature of the Judges gifts *ad vitam aut culpam* into Commissions *durante bene placito* are contrary to law ": the Claim of Right 1689.   It is to be noticed that there was also the habit of nominating the King's

of its importance. Indeed, it is perhaps true that the greatest importance of the doctrine is to be found in this sphere as securing the independence of the judiciary, and this is a partial explanation of the favour with which lawyers (in particular) continue to regard it. In other branches of government weight must be given to other considerations. Thus, in relation to legislation, it is necessary in a modern society that some legislative functions should be conferred upon the administration. Equally it may be said that in a modern complex society much that must be formally classed as legislation is a mode or facet of administration. It may well be that limits should be set to this admixture of power. These limits may be found through an application of the traditional doctrine of the separation of powers in the interest of preventing a possible abuse of power, and also of promoting the efficient discharge of one function.[31] They may also, especially in regard to the more political parts of constitutional machinery, have to be found through the application of other theories, such as that of balance.

It is also true that some apparent departures from the doctrine may be necessary if the aims desired by those who advance the doctrine are to be attained. In relation to the administration it may be said that the principle of ministerial responsibility, while on the face of it denying the traditional doctrine of the separation of powers, does much, in its operation, to preserve the essence of that doctrine. The separation between the politically responsible minister and the politically neutral administrator is preserved by that system, and is assisted by other devices.[32] The maintenance of that separation, which assists the attainment of Montesquieu's aim while at the same time being made possible by a contradiction of his principle, has become of even greater importance in altered circumstances.[33] This particular separation of functions is

Advocate as a member of the Court of Session (Sir John Nisbet (1664) being the last so appointed), and the Advocate had to be specially served in any matter affecting the King's interest.

[31] Thus on the one side in *Yakus* v. *U.S.*, 321 U.S. 414 (1944) there is an insistence on Congress determining standards, because that is the essential part of the legislative process, and thus cannot be entrusted to an administrative body. On the other side there are assertions such as that of Lord Thring in his *Practical Legislation* that Parliament should only concern itself with principle, delegating the power to legislate in detail, since only thus can Parliament discharge its legislative function effectively. There is a reflection of this attitude also in the *Yakus* case, but the twofold purposes which the doctrine of the separation of powers can serve are well shown by the two viewpoints. See, too, note 24, *supra*, and Chap. 15, *post*.

[32] Thus, the limitations in the terms of reference of Committees of the House of Commons (such as the Select Committees on Statutory Instruments, or on Estimates) which are likely to take evidence from individual civil servants are to be noted. In general they exclude matters of policy which are the proper responsibility of the Minister; see, too, *Special Report of the Select Committee on the House of Commons Disqualification Bill* (1955–56) H.C. 349, Q. 147–Q. 153, for an illustration of the sort of difficulties which may arise. Most recently difficulties have arisen in relation to the " Specialised Committees " of the House. Above all that on agriculture; see *Report from the Select Committee on Agriculture* (1966–67) H.C. 378. The answer of the Lord President of the Council (753 H.C.Deb., col. 1254) makes clear the clash of contradictory theories.

[33] See Massigli, *Sur Quelques Maladies de l'Etat*, Chap. IV.

desirable on the purely practical grounds that it tends to produce more acceptable decisions,[34] as well as on the more general grounds of constitutional theory.

The doctrine has therefore both a functional and a theoretical basis, and both remain important. The benefits to be derived from a process of specialisation can be as great in government as they are in industry. The ends intended to be achieved by the adoption of the doctrine—the prevention of the abuse of power and the preservation of liberty—are as important today as they were at any time in its development, and the doctrine still points to a satisfactory method of achieving those ends. Both the functional and theoretical approach have been important in the evolution of institutions. Perhaps the history of the development and gradual separation of institutions is, with us, to be attributed even more to practical considerations than to any striving after an ideal state of affairs in the interest of liberty. Nevertheless while the classical doctrine of the separation of powers may be important, it must not be regarded as a principle to be applied universally. Just as other theories about what structure is appropriate for a part of the governmental machine if certain desired ends are to be achieved may, in particular circumstances, assume greater importance than the theory of the separation of powers, so also other practical considerations influence any decision of whether the classical theory of separation or one of its variants or some altogether different doctrine is to be given effect in designing that structure.

Economic or industrial analogies on the benefits of specialisation can be pressed too hard. The concept of efficiency in government does not necessarily mean that decisions should be taken or put into effect as rapidly as may be. Though such matters are important, efficiency must also be judged by the extent to which the willing collaboration of those affected can be secured.[35] This problem is of increasing importance in a modern society and its solution must often involve an attempt to ensure that decisions are taken by a body appropriate to the decision in question irrespective of whether the solution can be reconciled with any doctrine of the separation of powers. At extremes, it is obvious that broad questions of policy should be decided by a different sort of body from that which should decide a disputed interpretation of a will or ownership of a particular piece of land. If weight is given to such considerations, then the doctrine of the separation of powers (in any of its forms) tends to be submerged, or be affected by

---

[34] See Lord Strang, *Home and Abroad*, Chap. XII. This, too, is illustrated by the House of Commons Disqualification Act 1957. Some of the disqualifications contained therein are partly explicable on the basis of the traditional doctrine of separation, others on more functional grounds.

[35] *Report of the Committee on Administrative Tribunals and Enquiries* (1957) Cmnd. 218, § 21; similarly many of the conventional rules are intended, in their own spheres, to achieve this end.

doctrines more properly grouped under the title of the distribution of power.

This last doctrine is not well developed with us, because of the form of our state, and yet it is significant and does affect the application of any doctrine of the separation of powers. The desire that a decision should be taken locally may conflict with, and overcome, a desire to observe the doctrine of the separation of powers.[36] More generally the conception of the distribution of power may control the shape of government machinery [37] and with the growing complexity of that machinery this matter may be of increasing importance, even though at this stage it is difficult to define the governing conceptions with precision. The distribution of power cannot today be conceived of simply as a distribution between central and local government (though there are many serious problems in that field). It must also be considered in relation to public corporations of all types and the regulatory devices that surround them. In that field much remains to be discovered about the arrangements of power which are most conducive to the general well-being. All that is certain is that neither in relation to the distribution nor the separation of powers can any one version or interpretation of the doctrine be accepted as being universally or necessarily applicable. Past events and the influence of other ideas must in any context determine the weight to be given to the doctrine. While either may provide a yardstick for measuring the merits of an institution or rule, neither can ever be the sole yardstick and, in particular cases, neither may be the most important.

What must be sought is a clear idea of the benefits to be gained from the application of a range of principles, and then a reconciliation of these principles within the whole institutional framework must be attempted so that as many of these benefits may be received as is possible. This in itself requires a clearer functional analysis of the processes of government and of the different parts of the machinery of the state than is always undertaken. The simplified view of a state which could be tolerable at the time of Montesquieu is no longer adequate, and may be positively unhelpful to thought, except as a starting-point. If this closer analysis is carried through there is a greater chance both that the safeguards against abuse of power will be more effective and that there will be sufficient room for the dynamism which is necessary within government to operate, since controls or safeguards will be applied in appropriate ways. Some of these matters may become clearer when the issue of the rule of law is considered.

---

[36] See *post*, Chap. 16, for the discussion of administrative tribunals.
[37] See *Royal Commission on Scottish Affairs* (1954) Cmd. 9212, § 12 *et seq.* (*cf. The Council for Wales and Monmouthshire* (*Fourth Memorandum and the Reply of the Prime Minister*) (1959) Cmnd. 631); or the White Papers on Local Government and Local Government Finance (1955) Cmd. 9831 and (1956) Cmnd. 208 and 209.

THE RULE OF LAW

" Dispositions maid to the King for just fear ar null et datur restitutio, and the king's successor (being minor) must answer notwithstanding his minoritie." [38] Such propositions emphasise the obvious and elementary meaning of the phrase " The Rule of Law "—that affairs should be regulated by law and not by brute force. In this simple form the principle of the rule of law is common to all civilised societies,[39] applies to rulers and subjects alike, and, despite its elementary nature, still continues to have importance.[40] In relation to the operation of the principle between subjects little difficulty arises here. Questions about the proper limits of self-help are best dealt with in other branches of the law, and, while the principle has obviously shaped doctrines such as those relating to mobbing and rioting,[41] the real importance of the principle in constitutional law is to be found in its application to the regulation of activities of the state.

In that context there are both theoretical and practical difficulties springing from the fact that the state through various organs both makes and enforces the law.[42] If the state makes law, how, it may be asked, can it also be subject to law? This question clearly becomes one of much greater practical importance once the Government (within the limits of political expediency) is effectively in control of the legislature. Apart from the jurisprudential issues (which are not of present concern), the arguments about this question relate both to detailed rules,[43] and to general principles of law. The general principles underlay the seventeenth-century constitutional litigation in England, and also, to

---

[38] Hope, *Major Practicks*, VI, 38, § 26, a proposition founded upon *Gray* v. *Earl of Lauderdale* (1685) Mor. 16497. The actions of the Earl of Lauderdale are, perhaps, a good illustration of the necessity for this principle of the rule of law. As George Buchanan put it, " many causes might induce a king (or indeed anyone in authority) to deviate from rectitude, where the powers of making and interpreting the law are united ": *De Jure Regni* (trans. Macfarlan) at p. 247. Sir George Mackenzie's views were very different; see his *Vindication*.

[39] Various manifestations of the rule in differing national and legal contexts are shown in *Government under Law* (ed. Arthur E. Sutherland), and for a comparison see " The Rule of Law as Understood in France " by M. Letourneur and R. Drago, *American Journal of Comparative Law* (1958), Vol. 7, p. 148.

[40] See such cases as *H.M. Advocate* v. *Gollan* (1882) 5 Coup. 317, *per* Lord Justice-Clerk Moncrieff, or *Clark* v. *Syme*, 1957 J.C. 1 at 5, *per* Lord President Clyde.

[41] See Lord Cowan's charge to the jury in *H.M. Advocate* v. *Wild* (1854) 1 Irv. 552 at 558.

[42] There are glossed over here many problems about the nature of the state or of organs of the state. As an introduction to these, see Paton, *Jurisprudence*, Chap. XIV, § 75, or Friedman, *Legal Theory*, Part VII, Chap. 28, or G. Sawer's essay " Government as a Personalised Legal Entity " in *Legal Personality and Political Pluralism* (ed. Leicester C. Webb); Kelsen, *General Theory of Law and the State*, Part II, Chap. 1; *The Law and the State*, particularly at pp. 182 and 197 *et seq.*

[43] Thus there is the difficulty in relation to a narrow field posed by Hamilton in *The Federalist* saying, " it is in theory impossible to reconcile the idea of a promise which obliges with a power to make a law which can vary the effect of it." (See, too, Mr. Justice Holmes in *Kawananakoa* v. *Polyblank*, 205 U.S. 349 at 353 (1907), posing the issue more generally.) In the broader field the arguments turn upon such matters as the nature and control of the prerogative or the relationship of courts to other branches of government.

some degree, in Scotland; that litigation, itself, was not conclusive. The actual decision in the *Case of Ship Money*, for example, had to be reversed by statute,[44] and, while the litigation may have had constitutional importance in leading to the final assertion of the rule of law, constitutional motives were not the only ones which inspired it.[45] Nevertheless theories which could be broadly summed up in contrasting maxims, the one, derived from Bodin, *Princeps Legibus Solutus*, and the other (that of Knox, Buchanan, Coke and Bracton, among others) *Rex non debet esse sub homine sed sub Deo et lege*,[46] were debated both in the courts and in battle, and the eventual victory of the second maxim is indicated by the declaration in the Claim of Right that James VII had altered the fundamental constitution of the kingdom " from a legal limited monarchy, to an arbitrary Despotick Power " and the reassertion of the former basis. Such declarations [47] can be regarded as subjecting governments to the rule of law.

That subjection, in so far as it was achieved in 1688, was not complete, permanent, nor necessarily advantageous to Fountainhall's populace and mobile. It was not complete in the sense that the whole of government activity cannot be regulated by law and by law alone. A government must have substantial discretionary powers, the degree of discretion varying according to the nature of the power; it may, for example, be much greater in the field of foreign, than of home, affairs. Law can govern the existence of such powers. It cannot, save within narrow limits, control the exercise of many of them. Thus the control of law must be supplemented by other controls (which with us have been found in responsible government) if the aim of preventing the abuse of

---

[44] 16 Car. 1, c. 14.

[45] Fountainhall's comment upon *Gray* v. *Lauderdale* (Fount. I, 388) is revealing: " The preparative of their processes may be very useful for the common people to be some check to deter great men from oppressing them grossly; but the processes are only created and fomented by interest, malice and passion, to ruine some fallen courtier, or to incapacitate him from ever rising to avenge himself again; so that I dare say that thir processes against concussion are never designed mainly to repair the injured parties; tho' it be some pleasure to the populace and mobile to see their oppressors repaid in their own coin, albeit no material advantage redound to them from thence." Lauderdale's actions in themselves point sufficiently to the need.

[46] Thus, John Knox reports one of his interviews with Mary Queen of Scots: " *Queen Mary*: Think ye that subjects having power may resist their princes. *John Knox*: if their princes exceed their bounds, Madam, no doubt they should be resisted even by power "; this argument in a slightly different shape he carried into the more general field of politics in his debate with Lethington:
" *Lethington*: Then ye will make subjects control their princes and rulers. *Knox*: And what harm should the commonwealth receive, if the corrupt affections of ignorant rulers were moderated and so bridled by the wisdom and discretion of godly subjects that they should do no wrong nor violence to no man ": *History of the Reformation* (ed. Dickinson), Vol. II, pp. 16–17, and Vol. II, p. 120. It must be remembered that a " prince " does not necessarily become respectable by being elected. All " princes " tend to behave in the same way, whether they are called President or Prime Minister.

[47] And the provisions in the Bill of Rights, such as those curtailing the suspending and dispensing powers.

power is to be attained.[48]   In this sense the Revolutionary Settlement of 1688 was as much the beginning as the end of a story.   If it were to be successful in achieving the aims of its makers legal controls of government had to be supplemented by political controls still to be evolved, a statement which in itself indicates that any rigid formulation of the separation of powers is unworkable.   Leaving that argument on one side, the subjection of government to law was not permanent in the sense that thereafter no question could arise.   If the price of liberty is eternal vigilance, the courts have had to continue to pay part of that price, even in what may be regarded as the traditional areas of operation of the rule.[49]   Whether they have in vital areas of activity of a modern state is a question that must hereafter be discussed.

Further, even if the rule may be taken as established at the Revolution, it nevertheless requires to be maintained in changing circumstances.   In relation to both individuals or private organisations and to governments, altered conditions raise new problems of the application of legal controls.[50]   Such statements assume that the establishment of the rule of law is advantageous.   That belief underlies most assertions on the subject.   When George Buchanan wrote that " They [the people] were taught by many experiences that it was better to trust their liberty to laws than to Kings " [51] or when, in modern times, it is said that " The Rule of Law stands for the view that decisions should be made by the application of known principles or laws," [52] it is clear that the authors of such phrases have in mind laws which are designed to achieve certain desired ends, individual liberty and the like, or laws which are consonant with certain moral or political ideals.[53]   If the law is such that all who act upon His Majesty's commission are protected against " all pursutes or complaints that can be raised against them," or that " the King is

---

[48] Compare *Boyesen* v. *Nixon*, Jan. 16, 1813, F.C., with *Smith* v. *Jeffrey and Ors.*, Jan. 24, 1817, F.C., and consider the weight given to government policy in the context of recognition of foreign states and contrast the attitude in relation to domestic affairs.   *Monkland* v. *Jack Barclay Ltd*. [1951] 2 K.B. 252 at 265.   See, too, *Chandler* v. *D.P.P.* [1964] A.C. 763 and Chap. 9, *post*.

[49] See *Kuechenmeister* v. *Home Office* [1958] 1 Q.B. 496 and Report of the Committee of Privy Councillors to inquire into the interception of communications (1957) Cmnd. 283.

[50] See such cases as *Russell* v. *Duke of Norfolk* [1949] 1 All E.R. 109; *Bonsor* v. *Musicians' Union* [1956] A.C. 104; *Nagle* v. *Feilden* [1966] 2 Q.B. 633; or the Restrictive Trade Practices Act 1956 as to the first group, and *Blackpool Corporation* v. *Locker* [1948] 1 K.B. 349, or *British Oxygen Co. Ltd*. v. *S. of Scotland Electricity Board*, 1959 S.C.(H.L.) 17, or the Franks Report (1957) Cmnd. 218 as to governmental bodies, and the Privy Councillors' Report (Cmnd. 283) referred to above, as to the second group.

[51] *De Jure Regni* (trans. Macfarlan), p. 247.

[52] Franks Report (1957) Cmnd. 218, § 29.   There is, of course, once again a concealed over-simplification.   There must be discretionary powers in government allowed by the law.   All that can be hoped for is that the discretion be appropriately limited and that mechanisms be devised to ensure that it is used in an even-handed way; see Chap. 17, *post*.

[53] Thus some of the grievances recited in the Claim of Right as contrary to the fundamental laws of the Kingdom and thus inconsistent with the rule of law were nevertheless consistent, at the time, with particular statutes; see, *e.g.*, the Act obliging Husbands to be lyable for their wyves fynes 1685 (A.P.S. VIII, 461).

sovereign monarch, absolute prince, judge and governor over all persons, estates and causes both spiritual and temporal " [54] so that, as Sir George Mackenzie put it, " He is only a tyrant who has no right to reign," [55] there is clearly no advantage in living under a rule of law, for that rule will do nothing to protect from oppression. The legality of tyranny is a conception fundamentally opposed to the general ideas underlying the normal use of the phrase " rule of law."

A moral or political content to the rule of law was clearly assumed by Dicey, whose formulation of the rule in his *Law of the Constitution* [56] has tended to govern modern discussions of the subject in this country. For Dicey the rule of law had three particular meanings: (1) " The absolute supremacy or predominance of regular law as opposed to the influence of arbitrary power . . . Englishmen are ruled by the law, and by the law alone "; (2) " the equal subjection of all classes to the ordinary law of the land administered by the ordinary law courts; the ' rule of law ' in this sense excludes the idea of any exemption of officials or others from the duty of obedience to the law which governs other citizens or from the jurisdiction of the ordinary tribunals "; (3) " that with us the law of the constitution, the rules which in foreign countries naturally form part of a constitutional code, are not the source but the consequence of the rights of individuals, as defined and enforced by the courts; . . . the constitution is the result of the ordinary law of the land."

Dicey's formulation may be criticised on many grounds. That there is no antithesis between the rule of law and arbitrary power, unless assumptions are made about the substance of law, has already been demonstrated. Dicey's third point also has its difficulties. If it is to be accepted, then documents such as the Bill of Rights or the Claim of Right must be regarded as " not so much ' declaration of rights ' in the foreign sense of the term, as judicial condemnations of claims or practices on the part of the Crown which are thereby pronounced illegal." [57] That

---

[54] See the Act for Security of Officers of State 1685 (A.P.S. VIII, 484), the Acknowledgment of H.M. Prerogative 1661 (A.P.S. VII, 45) and the Act anent restitution of bishops 1606 (A.P.S. IV, 282), wherein these and similar provisions are commonplace.

[55] *Jus Regium* (*Works*, Vol. II, p. 451). Sir George Mackenzie also there argued that it was necessary for the King to be above the law, " for strict and rigid law is a greater tyrant than absolute Monarchy ": *ibid.* p. 450.

[56] See particularly Chap. IV. Dicey's views as there expressed are more fully grasped against the background of his *Law and Opinion.* They must be read together with Sir Ivor Jennings' comment and criticism in his *Law and the Constitution*; and see Lawson, " Dicey Revisited " (1959) 7 *Political Studies*, pp. 109, 207, and Arndt, " The Origin of Dicey's Concept of the Rule of Law " (1957) 31 A.L.J. 117. So far as Dicey wrote of general institutions the adjective " English " is inapt. So far as he wrote upon particular rules, the general principles of which he wrote may be applicable throughout the Kingdom, but some of the rules are accurately described as English, having counterparts, but not copies, in Scotland.

[57] Though, later, Dicey, writing of the development of particular liberties, expresses views which are not entirely consistent with this; see, *e.g.*, Chap. VI, on the Right to Freedom of Discussion. It must also be remembered that the essential document which allowed the Supreme Court of the U.S.A. to maintain its role as the stimulus to the latent conscience of the people in such cases as *Brown* v. *The Board of*

view can only with difficulty be reconciled either with the contemporary
views of such documents or with their subsequent treatment in the
courts.[58]   The dependence of constitutional law upon the hazards of
ordinary litigation has many disadvantages which may outweigh gains,[59]
particularly where, as with us, the courts will accept (as is appropriate
perhaps in private law) the passive role as arbiter; in public law the
issues may be too important to be confined to those which, in pleading,
the parties find convenient.   On the other hand, within the confines of
the United Kingdom, the role of the courts in establishing many of the
fundamental rules in modern constitutional law can be greatly
exaggerated, as can the strength of the maxim *ubi jus ibi remedium* upon
which Dicey relies.   In the field of public law in England, particularly
in relation to judicial review, the converse, *ubi remedium ibi jus*, is far
more true.   Modern experience elsewhere also suggests that the value
of general declarations may be underrated by Dicey; what matters is
an attitude of mind, particularly among members of governments, courts
and legislatures, and that attitude may be better strengthened, according
to circumstances by tradition or by general declarations.   Further,
developments in society, which were only starting in Dicey's day, have
reached such proportions that today any strict application of his
principles is in many respects quite impracticable.[60]   These detailed
criticisms can be so important that Sir Ivor Jennings was inclined
to dismiss the rule of law as an unruly horse, either being merely
synonymous with law and order, or else " apt to express the political
views of the theorists and not to be an analysis of the practice of
government " or to be merely a phrase distinguishing democratic or
constitutional government from dictatorship.[61]

Education, 347 U.S. 438 (1954) was precisely one of those " declarations of rights."
It provided the ground upon which a good man could stand.   It takes a greater
effort for a court, such as the Conseil d'Etat, to achieve a similar result without this
ground, as in *Canal*, C.E., Oct. 19, 1962, 1962 D(J) 687.

[58] It is impossible, for example, to consider measures such as the Act for Security of
the Church of Scotland as being accurately thus described, and, even in the particular
context of which Dicey wrote, consider the treatment of the Bill of Rights in such
cases as *Att.-Gen.* v. *Wilts United Dairies Ltd.* (1921) 37 T.L.R. 884 and *Re the
Parliamentary Privilege Act 1770* [1958] A.C. 331 at 350.

[59] On the one hand, major constitutional issues, while relevant, may not, for a variety
of reasons, be dealt with; see, *e.g.*, *Att.-Gen.* v. *Ernest Augustus (Prince) of Hanover*
[1957] A.C. 436; on the other, pronouncements upon constitutional issues may be
made in cases where they are not strictly necessary for the decision or have not been
properly argued, *e.g.*, *Ellen Street Estates Ltd.* v. *Minister of Health* [1934] 1 K.B.
590.   Equally, the argument upon basic principles, such as that of *égalité devant les
charges publiques*, may have been so weak that legislative correction becomes
inevitable; see *Burmah Oil Co. (Burma Trading) Ltd.* v. *Lord Advocate*, 1964
S.C.(H.L.) 117 and the resultant War Damage Act 1965, which perhaps overcorrected.

[60] Especially the development of administrative tribunals, which is both a sign and a
consequence of other developments of which Dicey elsewhere took account; see
" The Development of Administrative Law in England " (1915) 21 L.Q.R. 148.
More particularly, see Mitchell, " The Causes and Consequences of the Absence
of a System of Public Law in the United Kingdom " [1965] *Public Law* 95.

[61] *Law and the Constitution*, 5th ed., p. 60.

Nevertheless, even at risk of merely demonstrating the truth of the first of Sir Ivor Jennings' possibilities, further discussion of the rule of law as it is commonly understood since Dicey's day appears necessary. His whole exposition is marked by an insistence upon the ordinary law (and of equality before it), upon the role of the ordinary courts, and upon the need to limit discretions. As makers of law the courts have declined in importance. In part this is the obvious result of the development of Parliament, in part it is the result of changes in ideas about the functions of a state. The development of the " Welfare State " (or, as Dicey would have called it, the " Collectivist State ") has meant that rights with which individuals are increasingly concerned, protections or hedges against poverty, ill health, and the like, cannot be the creation of judge-made law as could be the rights of free speech, etc., with which Dicey was concerned. These newer rights can only be the result of complex legislation. Moreover, the same development has involved a movement from a law of obligation to a law of standards. The eternal questions of the type What do I owe? or What am I owed? persist, but steadily other questions, What is consistent with good husbandry, good architecture, good town planning? affect individuals more and more. Questions of land-use have become more important than questions of land-ownership. For a variety of reasons such questions are not suitable to the ordinary courts, in the first instance at any rate. Nor are many of the modern questions of obligation. The procedure of the ordinary courts is not well fitted to the determination of questions of entitlement to pensions, etc. Thus, of necessity, there has grown up another system of courts—administrative tribunals—apart from the ordinary or traditional courts with which Dicey was concerned and increasingly it is these newer courts which must concern ordinary individuals.[62] Nevertheless the virtues which were associated with the ordinary courts remain important, and one of the problems of modern constitutional law is to ensure the maintenance of those virtues (such as regularity and impartiality) and at the same time to meet the requirements of these new forms of adjudication. The importance of the ordinary courts may today be as supervisors and as the ultimate guardians of essentials, and not as creators or as places of first resort.[63]

The limitation of discretion, with which Dicey was concerned, clearly remains important. There is a need for known rules, as against arbitrariness, and the rules must be applied in an even-handed way. This proviso is of importance, since it is clear that, human foresight being limited, the rules must allow for discretionary powers, and their abuse may be checked either by limitations upon their extent or upon

[62] See Chap. 16, *post*, and as an instance of this development, " Some Constitutional Features of the Scottish Land Court," 1956 S.L.T.(News) 65.

[63] *Kennedy* v. *Johnstone*, 1956 S.L.T. 73 at 82, and earlier the insistence in such cases as *Jeffray* v. *Angus*, 1909 S.C. 400 upon the powers of supreme courts to correct injustices.

the mode of their exercise.[64]   As has been seen, the latter may be one function of the doctrine of the separation of powers or of the distribution of power.[65]   The limitation of discretionary power has a long history in which both courts and Parliament have played a part, and, within limits, was rightly insisted upon by Dicey.   The principle is, however, somewhat broader than Dicey suggested.   He was concerned with the limitation of the power of the executive.[66]   While it is necessary to limit or control such power, wide discretions conferred on other bodies may well be equally injurious to the interests of individuals.   Regularity has its place in the courts also,[67] and there the limitations have been largely self-imposed.[68]   The great exception which apparently exists is the unlimited discretion of the legislature.   In fact that exception may not be as great as it appears.   As has been suggested, it is a mistake in considering constitutional mechanisms designed to control or limit to concentrate exclusively on the courts.   Particularly in relation to legislation judicial controls are often either ineffective or inappropriate [69] and other devices either legal or conventional must be considered.   Conventions, understandings, or mere habits of thought, which are the products of parliamentary life, impose limits upon the legislative activities of the

---

[64] See, e.g., Emergency Powers (Defence) Act 1939, s. 11; Supplies and Services (Transitional Powers) Act 1945; and the Supplies and Services (Extended Purposes) Act 1947; and for the attitude to this legislation, see Wheeler Bennett, King George VI, and Morrison, Government and Parliament, 2nd ed., p. 194 et seq.

[65] p. 46, ante; and see A. v. B. (1538) Mor. 7854 or Balfour v. Balfour (1569) Mor. 7855.   Both are early cases of the subjection of the King to the rule of law, and both show how the objectives of the law may, at times, be attained by the separation or dispersal of power; see, e.g., Act remitting the interpretation of the Act of Oblivion to the Lords of Session 1587 (A.P.S. III, 448).   Indeed formality, if not carried to excess, was early found to be a check upon the abuse of power, and may still be so: L.C.C. v. Farren [1956] 1 W.L.R. 1297; Becker v. Crosby Corporation [1952] 1 All E.R. 1350; Commissioners of Customs and Excise v. Cure & Deeley Ltd. [1962] 1 Q.B. 340.

[66] Law of the Constitution, 10th ed., in particular Chap. XII and p. 188.   The attitude persists, " State power is the great antagonist against which the rule of law must for ever be addressed ": Jones, " The Rule of Law and the Welfare State," 58 Col.L.R. at p. 144.   This statement implies an antagonism between state and individual which need not and may not exist.

[67] " It has been said over and over again that the greatest restraint and discretion should be used by the court in dealing with contempt of court, lest a process, the purpose of which is to prevent interference with the administration of justice, should degenerate into an oppressive or vindictive abuse of the courts' powers ": Milburn, 1946 S.C. 301 at 315, per Lord President Normand.   Similar warnings have been issued about parliamentary powers to commit for contempt.

[68] Compare the attitude of the court in relation to the nobile officium in Duke of Gordon v. Grant (1776) Mor.App.Juris. 3, and commented upon by Lord Eldon in Johnstone v. Stotts (1802) 4 Pat.App. 274 at 282–283, with that of the court in Crichton-Stewart's Tutrix, 1921 S.C. 840.   See, too, on the evolution of rules fettering discretionary powers, Milne v. M'Nicol, 1944 J.C. 151; W. A. Elliott, " Nulla Poena Sine Lege," 1956 J.R. 22; and Gordon, Criminal Law, p. 21 et seq.; and Blackstone's comments upon the " Liberty of considering all cases in an equitable light "—Commentaries, I, 62.   Cf. as to the scope of the declaratory order in England the remarks of Denning L.J. in Barnard v. National Dock Labour Board [1953] 2 Q.B. 18 at 41; and see Pyx Granite Co. Ltd. v. Min. of Housing and Local Government [1960] A.C. 260.   In administrative law the equivalent of the length of the Chancellor's foot may still exist as a criterion of jurisdiction.

[69] Consider the dissent of Mr. Justice Holmes in Lochner v. New York, 198 U.S. 45 (1905) and the subsequent history of the majority opinions.

central government [70]; the broad discretionary power to legislate for good rule and government conferred upon local authorities is limited in law by the requirement of confirmation [71] and, in practice, by administrative pressures, and in both cases such checks as are provided by the electoral process are also present. Unless allowance is made for such matters a false impression is gained. If allowance is made for them it will be seen that these apparently wide discretionary legislative powers are not as wide as they appear at first sight.

Thus there remains importance in a principle which is opposed to the existence of wide or uncontrolled discretionary powers, though the principle must be wider in its application than appears from Dicey's formulation, and the principle may, in some respects, be nothing more than an alternative expression of the results of the application of other principles, such as that of the separation of powers. Nevertheless, while broader in application than Dicey's formulation suggests, it is true that the most serious problems exist in the control of administrative discretion. It was possible, until the control by the executive over Parliament had grown to present proportions, and while the area of administrative discretionary powers was limited, for Parliament with some aid from the courts to exercise the necessary control. Parliament could then operate since the points of immediate contact (and thus of potential legal friction) between the state and the individual were limited. These conditions no longer exist, and it is here that the question of the " ordinary law " and the " ordinary courts " emerges in a more profound form than has yet been mentioned. It is impossible to escape the truth of the maxim of Portalis, " *Juger l'administration, c'est aussi administrer* ": yet with us the courts have so severed themselves from the administrative process in thought that their methods have become inappropriate in a variety of ways. The instruments of control which are at their disposal are often too blunt to be used, their techniques are such that control is often no more than a control over form and not of substance.[72] To a large extent this situation results from an unreasonable acceptance of one aspect of Dicey's formulation of the " Rule of Law." His insistence upon the subjection of all, whether officials or otherwise, to the ordinary law of the land may not be sound or useful, and unfortunately it is this aspect to which much attention has been given. A confusion of thought underlies the principle.

---

[70] Apart from limitations in the field of general legislation consider such proceedings as those on the Wedgwood Benn (Renunciation) Bill 1955, and the precedents cited there ((1955) H.L. 23), as shedding light upon the attitude taken to the exercise of admitted powers. That a power exists does not necessarily mean that its exercise will be regarded as proper.

[71] See Local Government (Scotland) Act 1947, s. 300; Local Government Act 1933, s. 249. These other checks are recognised by the courts as affecting their powers: *Glasgow Insurance Committee* v. *Scottish Insurance Commissioners*, 1915 S.C. 504; *Aldred* v. *Miller*, 1925 J.C. 21.

[72] See Mitchell, " The State of Public Law in the United Kingdom " (1966) 15 I.C.L.Q. 133.

While the subjection of officials to law is desirable, it does not follow that this should in all cases, or generally, be a subjection to the law which is applicable to the ordinary citizen. Dicey's proposition has become more true in some ways than it was when he wrote. Thus, in his time, in England, the Crown could not be sued in tort and the only remedy available in contract was the somewhat unsatisfactory one by way of a Petition of Right. In Scotland the law was somewhat more benevolent to the subject.[73] In both jurisdictions the Crown Proceedings Act 1947, in general, increased the remedies available to the subject, and brought litigation by an individual against the Crown more into line with litigation between individuals.[74] This could be read as an indication of the acceptance and general desirability of Dicey's views. Yet it is to be noticed that some provisions of the same Act carefully preserved privileges of the Crown,[75] and the question remains whether these provisions or the more general ones are to be taken as indicating the nature of the underlying principle.

The difficulty is that it is clear that the powers of government cannot be those of an ordinary citizen. At common law extraordinary powers to act for the common good have long been recognised,[76] and with the development of society, the need of governmental bodies for special powers grows. Revenue authorities must be able to require information, public authorities must be able to acquire land and other rights compulsorily. The list of such abnormal but necessary powers is lengthy, and it is clear that as far as rights are concerned public bodies and public officials cannot be governed by the ordinary law.[77] On the side of obligation or duties, Dicey claimed that " with us every official . . . is under the same responsibility for every act done without legal justification as any other citizen." [78] This proposition cannot be supported as historically true, nor, it is thought, can it be urged as theoretically desirable, as a general proposition. Officials and public authorities have long been protected, in the absence of malice, from the consequences of

[73] An action lay in contract, and while the maxim that " The King can do no wrong " had been applied in delict, *Macgregor* v. *Lord Advocate*, 1921 S.C. 847, this application of the maxim was a late development. See Sir Randall Philip, " The Crown as Litigant in Scotland " (1928) 40 J.R. 238, and Mitchell, " The Royal Prerogative in Modern Scots Law " [1957] *Public Law* 304.

[74] See *post*, Chap. 17. S. 2 (2) of the Act enacts in a particular context Dicey's principle in so many words. Similarly, the Public Authorities Protection Act 1893 has been repealed.

[75] Crown Proceedings Act 1947, ss. 28 and 47.

[76] See, *e.g.*, Hume's *Lectures* (The Stair Society), Vol. III, pp. 205–206, and *The Case of Saltpetre* (1607) 12 Co.Rep. 12 ; the lawfulness of the act was not in question in *Burmah Oil Co. (Burma Trading) Ltd*. v. *Lord Advocate*, 1964 S.C.(H.L.) 117. What was in dispute was the liability to compensate for an admittedly lawful act.

[77] The extent of the special rights may depend upon the degree of public interest or urgency. Consider the regulation of police rights to search or arrest without warrant, or on a lower plane the provisions of the Rights of Entry (Gas and Electricity Boards) Act 1954.

[78] *Law of the Constitution*, 10th ed., p. 193.

acts where a private individual would not be,[79] particular rules have long been applied to public officers,[80] and to public property,[81] and important variations have long been made to general law because of the circumstances of public bodies.[82] Those circumstances may operate either to relieve of liability which would otherwise attach, as in many of the cases already mentioned, or to impose additional liability. Powers conferred for public ends can be abused and put to private purposes. Thus special rules have long been aimed at public officers who abuse or neglect their offices [83] (albeit that at some of the times when they were most needed these rules were least enforced) and the imposition of additional liabilities as a guard against abuse of powers continues.[84] This general issue does not arise only in relation to obligations or liabilities in the narrow sense of contractual or delictual ones. As has already been pointed out, the relationship of public authorities *inter se*, even in such matters as agency, may not be governed by ordinary rules, the duties of public authorities may be enforceable by means other than those appropriate to the normal enforcement of duties. Other liabilities such as fiscal ones may differ because of the character of the body which is liable or of the service which it provides.[85] This differentiation is

[79] *Beaton* v. *Ivory* (1887) 14 R. 1057; *Macaulay* v. *N. Uist School Board* (1887) 15 R. 99; *Wallace* v. *Mooney* (1885) 12 R. 710; *Everett* v. *Griffiths* [1921] 1 A.C. 631 at 635. The justification of this rule in *Henderson* v. *Scott* (1793) Mor. 17072 remains sound. The special protections afforded to persons acting in a public capacity were re-emphasised in *Robertson* v. *Keith*, 1936 S.C. 29 (argued before a court of seven judges), in which *Shields* v. *Shearer*, 1914 S.C.(H.L.) 33, which might have been taken to affect the older law, was explained. See also *Parker* v. *The Commonwealth* (1965) 38 A.L.J.R. p. 444, *per* Windeyer J., for a particular application, and Ganz, " The Limits of Judicial Control over the Exercise of Discretion " [1964] *Public Law* 367 at 372–373.

[80] Thus in *Magistrates of Montrose* v. *Strachan* (1710) Mor. 13118 limitations were imposed upon the ability of the magistrates to dismiss a schoolmaster because of the public character of his employment. Generally the public character of an office has imposed limitations upon tenure. See, too, Hume's reasons for limiting or excluding the liability of a public officer for the acts of his subordinates: *Lectures*, III, 193. Similarly, special rules are applied because of the office held. See as to the Attorney-General, *Att.-Gen.* v. *Harris* [1960] 1 Q.B. 74; *Hester* v. *Macdonald and Ors.*, 1961 S.L.T. 414; it is to be questioned whether this last case does not go too far.

[81] Craig, *Jus Feudale*, I, 15, 16 and 17. Many of the rules governing rights falling *inter regalia* and the common good of burghs, while too often disregarded in practice, nevertheless, in legal theory, point in the same direction. For more modern cases, see, *e.g.*, *Paterson* v. *Magistrates of St. Andrews* (1879) 7 R. 712.

[82] Stair, II, 4, 2, and II, 12, 27; and as more modern examples, see *Hall* v. *Beckenham Corporation* [1949] 1 K.B. 716 or *Plank* v. *Magistrates of Stirling*, 1956 S.C. 92; *cf. McPhail* v. *Lanark C.C.*, 1951 S.C. 301. Though subsequent legislation has affected the detailed rules involved in these cases, they remain apt illustrations in this context.

[83] See Hume's definition of oppression, *Criminal Law*, Vol. I, Chap. IX, and his remarks on the neglect of duty in public officers, *op. cit.* Vol. I, Chap. XV, and on the prosecution of Sir John Carnegie and John Arbuthnot (1709), *op. cit.* Vol. II, Chap. I, and *H.M. Advocate* v. *Jeffrey* (1840) 2 Swin. 479.

[84] See Clean Air Act 1956, s. 26. Civil and criminal liability need not be determined by the same rules: *Gaynor* v. *Allen* [1959] 2 Q.B. 403.

[85] See, *e.g.*, *Glasgow Corporation* v. *I.R.C.*, 1959 S.C. 203, and the cases there referred to, where for tax purposes a distinction is drawn between non-profit-making activities of a local authority and similar activities of other bodies.

not, however, uniform, but it is arguable that in some cases where it is not made the results would be more satisfactory if it were.[86]

The subjection of public authorities and officials to the ordinary law has not always been attempted, nor, despite the modern legislation to which reference has been made, is it now complete. The desirability of that subjection as a general rule appears to be doubtful because of the different powers and purposes of public authorities. Indeed that subjection when it is achieved may, as a necessary concession to the requirements of government, be followed by a limitation of remedies, and thus the purposes of justice which it was intended to serve by that subjection are in the end frustrated. Yet, once again the doctrine cannot be entirely rejected. Its historical background includes the Star Chamber, a " special " court remembered for the evils of its latter days rather than for any good it earlier did. It could include the Privy Council (and its offshoots) in Scotland which also exercised a supervisory jurisdiction over the administration.[87] Courts other than the ordinary courts did in the past, with us, give good grounds for distrust, and even in more modern times have had to be watched.[88] There is, however, no inherent reason why a specialised court should not protect individuals more effectively than ordinary courts. Similarly claims to procedural advantages,[89] or to the benefits of substantive privileges,[90] need to be scrutinised, and at times rejected lest they be advanced farther than is necessary. Constantly there is a conflict between the desires and

---

[86] Consider *Glasgow Corporation* v. *I.R.C.*, 1959 S.C. 203, where it was held that no action would lie for repetition of money paid under a misinterpretation of a statute in settlement of tax claimed. In the converse case, where the Revenue authorities have underclaimed on a taxpayer for a like reason, they may later claim the additional sums: *Lord Advocate* v. *Duke of Hamilton* (1891) 29 S.L.R. 213; *Lord Advocate* v. *Mirrielees' Trs.*, 1943 S.C. 587 at 594, *per* Lord Keith (the subsequent proceedings in this case are not here relevant). In the former situation a very good case can be made for saying that, while as between individuals money paid under a mistake of law should not be recoverable, a public authority should be expected to act according to higher standards and forgo such unintended benefits. In the fields of ordinary law, consider the result in *McPhail* v. *Lanark C.C.*, 1951 S.C. 301. The rule referred to by Lord Keith has a long history, running back to the Act of 1600, c. 14 (A.P.S. IV, 231), on which see " Some Aspects of the Royal Prerogative " (1923) 25 J.R. 49.

[87] Though formerly the jurisdiction of the Council extended to " matters of state, and preserving of the public peace, and determining and punishing all riots and encroachments upon lawful possession " (Stair, IV, 1, 58), it was, at times, widely and oppressively extended.

[88] See *William Reid, Suppliant* (1765) Mor. 7361, where the only purpose in seeking to maintain the jurisdiction of the Court of Exchequer could have been the hope of more benevolent treatment of official misconduct. Compare *Ramsay* v. *Adderton* (1747) Mor. 7590, where the jurisdiction of the Exchequer was upheld, no irregularity being alleged against the revenue officer concerned.

[89] *Ramsay* v. *M'Laren*, 1936 S.L.T. 35.

[90] *Robert Baird Ltd.* v. *Glasgow Corporation*, 1934 S.C. 359 at 361, *per* the Lord President (Clyde); and see such cases as *Hayward* v. *Edinburgh Board of Management*, 1954 S.C. 453; *M'Ginty* v. *Board of Management Glasgow Victoria Hospitals*, 1951 S.C. 200; and compare as to the liability of a board for its own acts *Davis* v. *Glasgow Victoria Hospitals Board*, 1950 S.C. 382 and *Bullard* v. *Croydon Hospital Group Management Committee* [1953] 1 Q.B. 511. Much of the former complexity in interpreting the Public Authorities Protection Act 1893 was due to a desire to restrict the operation of that Act within narrow bounds.

needs of the individual and the desires and needs of governmental bodies.[91] Sometimes it is the interests of one group which must prevail, sometimes those of the other. A proper balance in the law is unlikely to be achieved if a starting-point is taken which overlooks the peculiar position and purposes of governmental bodies. If it be accepted that the state is something which is the representative of the collective interests of individuals and not something which is somehow beyond and opposed to individuals, it becomes apparent that the terms of legal debate have frequently been changed when the state is a party to the dispute. A dispute between two private individuals (whether one party is one of the small folk of Canterbury and the other is a great commercial corporation, or whether both are of the same order of size) is different from most disputes between an individual (whether human or corporate) and the state. In the first, interests of the same legal order, private interests, are in issue. In the second, interests of different orders are in conflict: private interests conflict with public or collective interests. The rules of " ordinary " law, following the tradition of Locke, are designed to work justice in the first form of conflict. In the second form, the change in the interests in issue dictates a change in the rules both substantive and procedural if justice is to be done. It is unreasonable that the state (with the power and moral obligation to act) should be allowed to act like the Gaullish warrior, casting its sword upon the scales, crying *Vae victis* [92]; but if the state is to be allowed to act appropriately to protect the collective interest, and those individuals who suffer exceptionally as a result of such actions are also to be protected, the rules of law must be designed to deal with this special situation. The " ordinary law " which is designed for situations in which neither party has this sort of moral or political obligation will not work. Thus, in dealings with the state the virtue of the " ordinary law " is now in question. Equally, since specialisation of thought and of procedure are important, this same argument brings into question the " ordinary courts," not in the sense that administrative tribunals (as we know them) may be needed but in the sense that a real administrative jurisdiction which can consistently and specifically attune its thought to doing justice to individual and state alike in these changed terms of debate may be vital to any real rule of law.[93] It is, indeed, difficult to formulate any general principle beyond asserting that the law must have regard to that position and those purposes, a regard which is inconsistent with Dicey's formulation as it is generally interpreted. Such a general formulation is all that can be expected since on

[91] Compare *Glasgow Corporation* v. *Central Land Board*, 1956 S.C.(H.L.) 1 and *Duncan* v. *Cammell Laird & Co. Ltd.* [1942] A.C. 624.

[92] The simile is that of M. Latournerie in *Cie des Scieries Africaines*, C.E., Mar. 9, 1928, R.D.P. 323.

[93] See the arguments and proposals in (1967) 38 *Political Quarterly* 360 *et seq.* and Chap. 17, *post.*

the one hand (as has been suggested) that regard will not always mean that there must be any departure from the general rules of law as applied between individuals; and on the other hand the peculiar attributes of governmental bodies do not mark all their activities. While contracts for the production of defence equipment may require special regulation,[94] contracts for the supply of stationery may not be similarly marked by any special considerations.[95] Further, just as activities of public bodies may be stamped to a greater or lesser degree, so also may the character of bodies themselves. Public corporations form a spectrum from those which are indistinguishable from other government agencies as instruments for carrying out government policy to those which are to all intents and purposes indistinguishable from private organisations.[96]

In such circumstances any general rule purporting to govern all relationships of governmental bodies is likely to be either misleading or to be so hedged with qualifications that its usefulness is restricted. As a principle of general validity this branch of Dicey's formulation of the rule of law must be rejected. It must also be rejected as an expression of an approach which is generally likely to produce the most desirable results. It can only be accepted as an indication that governmental bodies should be subject to law. Often that subjection may be facilitated by a recognition of their special characteristics, where those are significant. Without that recognition there is a tendency to withdraw important matters from regulation by law to regulation according to administrative convenience.[97] A solution to this whole problem can probably only be found through the creation of a specific court charged with the task of evolving rules which are appropriate to the peculiarities of the legal situation which exists. Only in that way can the " Rule of Law " be made a reality. No solution can be found, at this stage, by the formulation of a general code of rules purporting to govern all relationships of governmental bodies. Such a code would be impossible to draw. What is required is a mechanism which can duplicate the evolutionary process of the common law in the field of public law.

94 See, *inter alia*, the Defence Contracts Act 1958.
95 The separation of these activities is not an easy process. See Mitchell, *The Contracts of Public Authorities*, Chap. V, and the references there given. See also note 79, *supra*, and *Racecourse Betting Control Board* v. *Young* [1959] 3 All E.R. 215.
96 Compare the operations of the Bank of England, which in effect shares certain essentially governmental responsibilities in relation to the national economy with the Treasury (see the Radcliffe Report (1959) Cmnd. 827), with the Crown Estates Commissioners under the Crown Estate Act 1956, which, although a public corporation, is intended to act as much as possible like any ordinary private land-owner (see Report of Committee on Crown Lands (1955) Cmd. 9483).
97 The result in *Duncan* v. *Cammell Laird & Co. Ltd.* [1942] A.C. 624 and subsequent developments such as the statement of the Lord Chancellor in the House of Lords (197 H.L.Deb. 741–748 (1569)) exemplify that tendency. See, too, *Nottingham No. 1 Area Hospital Management Committee* v. *Owen* [1958] 1 Q.B. 50 and Clean Air Act 1956, s. 22.

CHAPTER 4

THE SOVEREIGNTY OR SUPREMACY OF PARLIAMENT

Introduction. Constitutions and constitutional doctrines are the result of history. As has already been emphasised, our overt revolutions occurred relatively early in the history of the modern state, and at times when the writing of a full constitution to crown the revolution had not become customary. These factors affect as strongly the doctrines relating to Parliament as they do doctrines such as those related to conventions. While the position and powers of Parliament have, in some respects, been hedged about with protections, there are few specific attributions of power to it.[1] In this, Parliament is no different from many of our other institutions, but this circumstance is, perhaps, particularly important in relation to Parliament, since it is an institution peculiarly liable to growth and change as a result of a changing climate of opinion. This background must be borne in mind when considering the doctrine of the sovereignty of Parliament, for some of the precedents, some of the authoritative writings, must be considered (to an extent at least) in the light of the Parliament which existed contemporaneously with them, and which may be materially different from that which now exists, either in itself or in general acceptance.[2]

This varying background is also important since, on the whole, no theory about the sovereignty of Parliament can be proved, in the way that other legal concepts can be, by a chain of elucidatory decisions. This peculiarity of proof is partly due to the fact that cases must be rare in which the issue could be raised both properly and inescapably.[3] Such precedents as do exist may also be inappropriate today, since, inevitably, they reflect the then current political facts. This difficulty of proof is concerned with one of the fundamentals of the constitution. To such matters a different attitude must be adopted to that which is

---

[1] Some of the provisions of the Claim of Right or Bill of Rights serve both purposes.
[2] The sequence of events starting in 1832 has substantially affected modern ideas of Parliament, and to take two authors at random, Coke wrote at the close of the Middle Ages, Kames at a period when natural law theories were at their height. Both circumstances were important in relation to the authors; neither now exists. See generally for such influences Gough, *Fundamental Law in English Constitutional History*, and Sir Owen Dixon, " The Common Law as an Ultimate Constitutional Foundation " (1957) 31 A.L.J. 240.
[3] Thus in *MacCormick* v. *Lord Advocate*, 1953 S.C. 396, which in recent times came nearest to this issue, the decision rested upon questions of relevance and title to sue. What was said upon the fundamental question by, *e.g.*, Lord President Cooper (at p. 411 *et seq.*) is strictly *obiter*. Other cases, such as *Vauxhall Estates Ltd.* v. *Liverpool Corporation* [1932] 1 K.B. 733, were often susceptible of decision upon very narrow grounds, and were so decided; see p. 77, *post*. This attitude of the courts is common; *cf.* Dowling and Edwards, *American Constitutional Law*, p. 88 *et seq.*

appropriate when dealing with subsidiary or derivative rules of law. The one set of rules creates or is the legal foundation of the state, the other is built upon that foundation. Because of these differences, too, uncertainty about the doctrine as it exists at any one moment of time is increased.

The meaning of the doctrine. By the sovereignty of Parliament is generally meant the absence of any legal restraint upon the legislative power of the United Kingdom Parliament.[4] This absence of legal restraint has two aspects. The positive one would mean that Parliament is competent to legislate upon any subject-matter, and the negative aspect implies that once Parliament has legislated no court or other body can pass upon the validity of the legislation. These two aspects are obviously related, but must, for some purposes, be distinguished. Even if it were said that the legislative competence of Parliament is limited it does not follow that any court has power to review the validity of legislation.[5] Both aspects were most unequivocally asserted by Dicey,[6] but events and argument since Dicey's time have made necessary further discussion before his views can be accepted or rejected.

The doctrine has an initial attraction. Parliament has had such an outstanding part in the development of the modern constitution, and today remains apparently outstanding in the legislative field. The Revolution of 1688 was, in both jurisdictions, a parliamentary revolution, the Union of 1707 was likewise a parliamentary Union, the title to the Crown is a parliamentary one.[7] This pre-eminence of Parliament is emphasised both by its position as virtually the sole source, either directly or indirectly, of legislation, and by its freedom from the restraints of any other system of law. Prerogative powers of legislation, in an internal sense, have disappeared,[8] and within the United Kingdom subordinate

---

4 It can be argued whether " sovereignty," " supremacy," or some other words such as " legislative omnipotence," are apt—see Jennings, *Law and the Constitution*, 5th ed., p. 152 *et seq*. It is true that the use of the word " sovereignty " can lead to such difficulties as Dicey's separation of legal and political sovereignty, and that the word " sovereignty " lacks any one universally accepted meaning. Nevertheless it is the word most often used in this context and will be here used in the general sense indicated.

5 Waline asserts (*Droit Administratif*, 8th ed., p. 427) that no court in France will accept this jurisdiction. For an explanation of the curious and limited jurisdiction of the Conseil Constitutionnel see Prélot, *Institutions Politiques*, p. 789. Earlier the conclusions of Chief Justice Marshall did not follow of necessity from his premisses. For a short general survey see Cappelletti & Adams, " Judicial Review of Legislation; European Antecedents and Adaptations " (1966) 79 Harvard L.R. 1207.

6 *Law of the Constitution*, Chap. I. Others who had earlier made somewhat similar assertions had also put forward elsewhere views difficult to reconcile with the general proposition; see Jennings, *op. cit.* App. III, *Was Lord Coke also a Heretic?*

7 Consider the terms of the English and Scottish Acts, 1705, authorising the appointment of Commissioners to treat for the Union (A.P.S. XI, 292). By British theory His Majesty's Declaration of Abdication Act 1936 was necessary to enable Edward VIII's declaration of abdication to be effective in law.

8 *Grieve* v. *Edinburgh and District Water Trustees*, 1918 S.C. 700 at 713, *per* the Lord Justice-Clerk (Scott Dickson); *The Case of Proclamations* (1611) 12 Co.Rep. 74 and Mackenzie, Inst. I, 1, incorporating the effect of this decision. Matters formerly falling within the prerogative such as the regulation of the entry of aliens have also

legislative bodies derive their significant legislative powers from Parliament.[9] It is clear that legislation cannot be confined by international law,[10] or by morality or natural law,[11] and, indeed, may abolish any legal significance of physical differences between distinct things, and to that extent be freed from physical laws. It is also clear that legislation is not limited in time,[12] nor space,[13] nor in relation to persons.[14]

The apparent absence of limitations. Because of these factors there has thus grown up a belief in the legal ability of Parliament to pass any legislation at all. It is generally admitted that this apparent omnicompetence may be limited by factual considerations, such as the ability to enforce obedience, by rules of interpretation which may operate, in the absence of very clear wording, to restrict the operation of a statute,

been taken over by statute. Much earlier Balfour laid down in his *Practicks*: " na jugeis within the realme has power to mak any lawes or statutes save the Parliament allanerlie "—Tit. *of Law*. To a limited extent prerogative powers of legislation may continue to exist in relation to some colonies: *Sammut* v. *Strickland* [1938] A.C. 678.

[9] While common law corporations, such as Royal Burghs, might have extensive internal legislative powers (see *University of Glasgow* v. *Faculty of Physicians and Surgeons of Glasgow* (1837) 15 S. 736, and the instances there cited) the important powers today are those conferred by statute, and conferment of powers by statute may have a restricting effect on common law powers; *Graham* v. *Glasgow Corporation*, 1936 S.C. 108; *Att.-Gen.* v. *Leicester Corporation* [1943] Ch. 86.

[10] *Mortensen* v. *Peters* (1906) 8 F.(J.) 93 at 100, *per* Lord Dunedin, though the rules of international law may where that is possible by the terms of the Act influence interpretation; *Co-operative Committee on Japanese Canadians* v. *Att.-Gen. for Canada* [1947] A.C. 87 at 104, *per* Lord Wright; and *I.R.C.* v. *Collco Dealings Ltd.* [1960] Ch. 592 (affirmed [1962] A.C. 1).

[11] Many earlier assertions to the contrary can be found; see in England *Day* v. *Savage* (1615) Hob. 85, *per* Hobart C.J.; *Dr. Bonham's Case* (1610) 8 Co.Rep. 113b at 118a, *per* Coke C.J.; and, in Scotland, Ersk. Inst. I, 1, 20: " What the law of nature hath commanded cannot be forbidden or even dispensed with by positive law "; Kames, *Equity*, Book II, Chap. 3, writing that the " trust " upon which Parliament holds its power will not include the power to do injustice or to oppress. Stair (Inst. I, 1, 15) goes no further than saying that nations are happiest when the laws come nearest to natural equity. The stronger assertions could no longer be supported; compare Lord Wright in *Liversidge* v. *Anderson* [1942] A.C. 206 at 261: " Parliament is supreme. It can enact extraordinary powers of interfering with personal liberty." These survivals of natural law theories have now been translated into presumptions in statutory interpretation (see below) and for a general account of them see Gough, *Fundamental Law in English Constitutional History*, and the authorities there referred to. There are many assertions particularly in Coke on the equation of natural, or moral, law with the common law, and in this respect Stair may be noticed. He comments (I, 1, 16) on the superiority of the common law as against statute law on the ground that desuetude does not affect the former, and then demonstrates that certain statutes were held inoperative because of the superior moral principles of the common law with which they conflicted.

[12] Again formerly different views found expression: Ersk. Inst. I, 1, 23 (against retrospective legislation); and compare Mackenzie, Inst. I, 1, on the difference between declaratory and other laws in this context.

[13] For a strong case see *Boissevain* v. *Weil* [1950] A.C. 327, in which it is possible that neither party to the transaction in question was aware of the legislation; and consider the Criminal Justice Act 1948, s. 31, in conjunction with the Criminal Justice (Scotland) Act 1949, s. 29. See too *R.* v. *Martin* [1956] 2 Q.B. 272; *R.* v. *Naylor* [1962] 2 Q.B. 527.

[14] Again Erskine (I, 1, 22) excluded laws affecting individuals from " proper law " on the principle that legislation must be general; today one must accept that such Acts as the Niall Macpherson Indemnity Act 1954 as law. It remains true that private Acts may be somewhat differently regarded: *Scottish Drainage and Improvement Co.* v. *Campbell* (1889) 16 R.(H.L.) 16.

See *Poll v Ld. Adv* 180 *infra* where Gen. sought *injunch* to restrain *cate of feance*

and by conventional rules governing the preparation of legislation. For the most part what were formerly asserted to be limitations upon the legislative capacity of Parliament have become presumptions of interpretation. So, a statute is presumed, in the absence of clear words to the contrary, not to take away property without compensation, not to exclude the jurisdiction of the courts, not to be retrospective, not to impose taxation.[15] These presumptions may be more or less strong in particular circumstances, and while they do not impose any restriction upon Parliament they indicate the broad acceptance in normal times of general and fundamental constitutional ideas, which were once translated in theory, but not in practice, into restrictions upon Parliament in the name of natural law, or other names.

Through these presumptions some protection can be given to what would be regarded as fundamental rights, and that is advantageous, but in other contexts these presumptions may cause difficulty. In effect the recognition of the superiority of statute over common law was itself the work of the common law and of common lawyers. Yet, while generally this superiority is accepted there may from time to time become apparent a reluctance to allow that acceptance to be whole-hearted, and at such times these presumptions become particularly important. Through them the reluctance becomes effective. What is involved in such cases is often not so much a conflict of rules within a hierarchy, but a conflict of basic ideas. Especially in the field of public law, statute may represent modern theories of the role of the state, whereas a different theory underlies the common law. Such a conflict is apparent in *Allen* v. *Thorn Electrical Industries*,[16] in which there underlay the legislation in question a theory of the role appropriate to the state in regulating the economy, while the economic theory underlying the much older common law rules that were in question was radically different. In such cases the application of these presumptions may cause difficulties, which could be avoided were the debate conducted in different terms, which brought out more clearly the constitutional issues.

Conventional limitations are generally of more current importance. These may take the form of procedural rules or may relate to substance. Those that may be called procedural have some constitutional importance in helping to preserve the responsiveness and responsibility of government. Thus it is accepted that convention (as well as practical considerations) requires that a government consult interests likely to be affected by general legislation. For obvious reasons much financial legislation falls outside this rule, and it must be emphasised that at most it is consultation and not agreement which is required. Recently some

---

15 *Att.-Gen.* v. *Wilts United Dairies Ltd.* (1922) 91 L.J.K.B. 897. As to taking without compensation, see *Hartnell* v. *Minister of Housing and Local Government* [1965] A.C. 1134 at 1157; and for a more general statement of the principle, see *Allen* v. *Thorn Electrical Industries* [1967] 2 All E.R. 1137 at 1143.

16 [1967] 2 All E.R. 1137.

attempt has been made to formalise the process, as in the " Green Paper " of 1967 on the then proposed regional employment premiums, but it appears doubtful if much progress can be made along these lines. Similarly, conventional rules govern the preparation of measures of electoral reform and probably of measures affecting major changes in constitutional machinery.[17] The precise limits of such rules are by no means clear, and it is evident that in the last resort they impose no effective or enforceable limitation upon Parliament.

The substantive limitation of this type which is often urged is the doctrine of mandate. That doctrine can have several meanings. It may mean that a government should not introduce major changes by legislation unless they have been an issue in a general election, and that, correspondingly, a waning government which has lost general support in the country should not force major legislation through Parliament shortly before an election, even though that legislation may have been in its electoral programme. It may also, at times, be given the meaning that a government has an obligation to carry onto the Statute Book the main heads of its electoral programme. At first sight this doctrine in any of its forms fits easily into theories of representative government, and, while it is true that instances can be given in which it has been disregarded, there are notable instances, such as the events leading up to the Parliament Act 1911, which tend to support it. There are certainly many more instances where the doctrine has been invoked on behalf of or against proposed actions. This support may be more apparent than real. Recent evidence suggests that what may be thought to be a determining factor in an election (and thus the necessary foundation for a mandate) may in fact play a much less significant part in determining the result of the election than was once thought to be the case.[18] Again, it is clear that if the doctrine is not restricted to constitutional changes, but is extended, as is often the case, to major legislation generally, its force is greatly weakened by the fact that any government must determine policy (including legislative policy) in the light of current facts which may be materially different from those which were known to party leaders, or which existed at the time of an election. Further, on a proper examination, there are implications in the doctrine of theories of direct government which may be inconsistent with other constitutional doctrines.[19] It may also assume a level of factual knowledge, political wisdom and rational assessment higher than that which

---

[17] Generally see, *e.g.*, (1944) Cmd. 6502. As to measures of electoral reform and the use of Speakers' Conferences, etc., see 595 H.C.Deb. 1030; and as to measures of constitutional change, see 753 H.C.Deb. 19 and 28–30.

[18] H. G. Nicholas, *The British General Election 1950*; *The General Election in Glasgow, February 1950*, ed. S. B. Chrimes; Budge and Urwin, *Scottish Political Behaviour*, Chap. 7.

[19] Matters such as the relationship of a Member of Parliament to his constituency, or whether that whole theory of government (whether that of Bagehot or Barker) of a pyramidal structure ending with the Cabinet as a committee of Parliament is to be accepted or not, are, for example, involved.

always exists in the electorate at large. The doctrine then is not one
which is clear cut or which has a clear foundation, and, even if difficulties
of the classification of conventions are neglected, it cannot therefore be
said to amount to any substantial limitation upon Parliament beyond
those which already result from the general democratic theory as
practised in this country.

The apparent impossibility of challenging a statute. There is thus
the appearance of unlimited legislative competence, which is little
touched by the conventional limitations. The most significant of the
latter—the doctrine of mandate—is of doubtful validity. Other conventional limitations, which are of greater validity, operate " behind the
curtain " and thus do not detract from the appearance. Thus a predisposition to accept the " positive " aspect of the sovereignty of
Parliament is built up, and that view is all the more readily accepted
since it could be regarded as a logical extension of the idea of the
superiority of statute law. A like predisposition to accept the " negative " aspect arises since any possibility of challenging the validity of
legislation is, at best, so extremely rare that there has grown up a belief
that any such challenge is impossible, and, indeed, even were some of the
so-called conventional limitations more precisely formulated and accepted
as limitations, the possibilities would probably not be increased.[20] The
view that any such challenge is impossible is strengthened by citation
from writers of authority,[21] so that Lord Shaw could dismiss the whole
doctrine as being the " merest platitude." [22] Such views have also been
partly dependent on, partly productive of, the view that there are in law
no limitations upon Parliament, and that Parliament is incapable of
imposing any such limitations upon itself. It will be convenient to
examine these latter views before returning to the question of the
possibility of challenge, for, as has already been said, the two questions
are severable, even though interlocking. Before entering upon the discussion, however, it may be as well to emphasise that recent litigation
has given much cause to re-examine and reassess traditional views.

The apparent freedom from statutory limitations. Again there is
strong support among writers of authority for the proposition that
Parliament cannot bind itself,[23] and instances abound where one

---

[20] Compare *Thorneloe & Clarkson Ltd.* v. *Board of Trade* [1950] 2 All E.R. 245. In
Bribery Commissioner v. *Ranasinghe* [1965] A.C. 172 at 195 Lord Pearce emphasises
how a predisposition to accept extreme limitations on judicial review results from
the shape of the British Constitution.
[21] Coke, 4 Inst. 36; Blackstone, 1 Comm. 91. See too *Officers of State* v. *Cowtie &
Ors.* (1611) Mor. 7327.
[22] *Legislature and Judiciary.*
[23] " Whatever a Parliament can do at one time, in making of law, or determining of
causes may be at their pleasure abrogate or derogate ": Stair, Ins. IV, 1, 61. See
too Erskine, Ins. I, 1, 19; Blackstone, 1 Comm. 160; Coke, 4 Inst. 25.

Parliament has overthrown the work of another.[24]   Equally there can be found judicial support for the same principle.[25]   To it there has been admitted from time to time the possible exception that Parliament could abdicate its power to another,[26] and this exception seems now to have received judicial acceptance.[27]   More recently, some reconsideration of the principle was prompted by litigation in South Africa, and subsequently doubts found expression here in *MacCormick* v. *Lord Advocate*,[28] particularly in the opinion of Lord President Cooper.   In discussing the general proposition it seems necessary to distinguish, though this has not always been done, different types of limitation. There is first the limitation which may exist in a constituent document, there is secondly the limitation which Parliament, once created, may subsequently impose upon itself.   The second form of limitation could again take various forms, the abdication or denial of legislative power, or the imposition of restrictions as to time, form or content of legislation, or any combination of these last limitations.   Different principles may apply in each case.

WAS PARLIAMENT BORN UNFREE?

The Acts of Union. Taking first the point of a constituent document, if it be accepted (as it seems it must be, because of their terms and origin) that the Acts of Union of 1707 were intended to be, and were,

---

[24] To the instance of the statute of Henry VIII (28 Hen. 8, c. 17; repealed during the minority of Edward VI, 1 Edw. 6, c. 11) commonly cited can be added references to the statutes restoring episcopacy in Scotland which others had abolished in all time coming; and those dealing with the Crown in Scotland. What in 1681 (A.P.S. VIII, 238) Parliament declared to be beyond legislative competence was achieved by Parliament in 1689 and accepted. Sir George Mackenzie asserted that Parliament was bound by certain fundamentals, influenced, no doubt, by the fear of just such happenings as later occurred in 1707 (see his *Observations on the Acts*, 17th Parliament of James VI). Consider also the development since 1592 (briefly recited in the Act Ratifying the Confession of Faith 1690, A.P.S. IX, 133) in the light of the phraseology of the Act for abolisheing of the actis contrair to the trew religion 1592 (A.P.S. III, 541); and see *Duke of Douglas and Ors.* v. *The King's Advocate* (1748) Mor. 7695, wherein grants ratified in Parliament were upheld, even though the procedure which Parliament itself had imposed had not been followed. It is, though, arguable whether such cases do not rather reflect a situation of power more than they reflect any constitutional theory. It will be noted that these precedents relate to both pre-Union and post-Union times, which may affect the weight of some. For the moment it will be convenient to leave on one side the changes in the Acts of Union with Scotland and with Ireland.

[25] *British Coal Corporation* v. *The King* [1935] A.C. 500 at 520, *per* Lord Sankey L.C.; *Vauxhall Estates Co. Ltd.* v. *Liverpool Corporation* [1932] 1 K.B. 733; *Ellen Street Estates Co. Ltd.* v. *Minister of Health* [1934] 1 K.B. 590; *Godden* v. *Hales* (1686) 11 St.Tr. 1166 at 1697.

[26] Anson, " Government of Ireland Bill and the Sovereignty of Parliament " (1886) 2 L.Q.R. 427 at 437–438; Dicey, *Law of the Constitution*, 10th ed., p. 69n., though this may be inconsistent with one reading of the views, referred to above, of Lord Sankey in the *British Coal Corporation* case.

[27] *Ibralebbe* v. *The Queen* [1964] A.C. 900 at 924. See too Lord Gardiner in 282 H.L.Deb. 1202–1203.

[28] 1953 S.C. 396. See also the reaction in Northey, " The New Zealand Constitution," in *The A. G. Davis Essays in Law*, pp. 164–179.

constituent Acts, then 1707 forms a fresh starting-point. Logical difficulties about the transfer of legislative power from a sovereign to a
non-sovereign body need not be too heavily stressed.[29] Moreover, it is
not clear that in 1707 either that the English Parliament was accepted
as " sovereign " in the sense in which the word is now used[30] or that,
alternatively, the Scottish Parliament could not, in legal theory, be said
to be as " sovereign " then as was the English one.[31] It is more probable
that, in the modern acceptance of that term, the doctrine, if it exists, is
a post-Union development closely linked with the ideas underlying the
reforms of 1832.[32] It is certainly possible that as constituent documents
the Acts of Union could have imposed limitations, and it is equally
clear that some of those responsible for them hoped so to do.[33] This
possibility is enhanced by the terminology of the Acts. Too much
cannot be built upon such phrases as " in all time coming " or " for
ever," which were of common occurrence in the Acts of the Parliament
of Scotland; nevertheless, the insistence upon the protection of the
church, of the courts, and of equality, marks out such provisions, and
they have equally been emphasised in decisions which isolate them as
of particular importance.[34]

29 Though this supposed difficulty is emphasised by Lord Cooper: 1953 S.C. at p. 411.
30 Consider the doubts expressed about the validity of the Septennial Act 1715.
31 The very rapid growth of the Parliament of Scotland between 1688 and 1707 is often
    overlooked; and see note 24, *supra*. The argument based upon the existence of the
    doctrine of desuetude is weak, and the operation of that doctrine was itself at the
    mercy of Parliament.
32 Apart from the uncertainties which were expressed in the early part of the 18th
    century, *e.g.*, as to the validity of the Septennial Act 1715, or the possibility of the
    repeal of the Acts of Union in 1713 (see *Hist. and Proceedings of the House of Lords*
    (1742), ii, pp. 394–397). The doctrine is dependent upon the development of the
    political power of Parliament. So long as it can be maintained that it is dangerous
    for a Parliament to continue after the death of a King " for then a Parliament
    called by a King might continue without the consent of the King that succeeds and
    make Acts prejudicial to him " (Fount. I, 339), it is clearly difficult to maintain, as
    accepted theory, the principle of the sovereignty of Parliament. Parliament is on that
    basis to be subservient. Legal theory feeds upon political fact, and the growth of
    the theory of the sovereignty of Parliament depends on the growth of Parliament.
    Such remarks as that of Lord Hardwicke in the debate upon the Bill for the abolition
    of the Heritable Jurisdictions that " In all countries the legislative power must to a
    general extent be absolute " (Campbell, *Lives of the Chancellors*, Vol. X, p. 122)
    assume a different position of Parliament in the state (though it may be noted in
    passing that Lord Hardwicke asserts that the United Kingdom Parliament inherited
    the sovereign position of the Parliament of Scotland (*loc. cit.*)). That assumption is
    equally apparent elsewhere: see, *e.g.*, Brodie's annotations to Stair, I, 1, 16; see
    Ersk. I, 1, 45 for the ideas underlying his doctrine that the posterior statute may
    always derogate from the anterior one.
33 Lang Mathieson in his *Scotland and the Union* at p. 213 recognises the intention to
    create fundamental provisions, though denying the possibility in law of so doing.
    Taylor Innes, in his *Law of Creeds in Scotland*, puts it that " the royal sanction on
    the 6th March, 1707, consummated the Union on the basis of fundamental conditions
    not to be altered or derogated from in any sort for ever " (p. 58). The understanding
    of the church is shown by the Memorial of 1712 against the restoration of lay
    patronage, and continued in protests until the Claim of Right of the Church of
    Scotland Assembly 1842, which argued that the Act for Securing the Protestant
    Religion had removed from the " cognisance and power of the federal legislature
    created by " the Union all matters dealt with in that Act.
34 See particularly *Minister of Prestonkirk* v. *The Heritors*, Feb. 3, 1808, F.C. (the
    opinions are fully set out from the Session Papers in *Connell on Tithes*, Vol. III).
    " Our Ancestors, at the Union, provided that the regulations applicable to our

The scope of entrenchment. The degree and consequences of entrenchment are not so clear. In the first place, if it be conceded that the Acts of Union are to be regarded as constituent, then it follows that they should be interpreted in the flexible manner normally used in constitutional interpretation. Thus, the meaning of the phrases " public right " or " private right " cannot be taken to have been fixed in 1707.[35] In the next place allowance must be made for other changes in ideas. Ideas of the nature and purposes of education change, and these changes are reflected in the way in which certain provisions in the Act for Securing the Protestant Religion are to be regarded.[36] On a wider scale ideas about the relationship of church and state fluctuate. The conception of Parliament as the temporal head of the church which could be advanced in 1843 [37] is rejected by Parliament itself in the Church of

national church, should be absolutely irrevocable, and that the Parliament of Great Britain should have no power to alter or repeal those provisions ": *per* the Lord Justice-Clerk (Hope) at p. 321. " The people of Scotland, at the period of the Union, were most careful to preserve unalterably all the rights of their Presbyterian Church as by law established ": *per* the Lord President (Blair) at p. 376. See, too, *Duke of Queensberry* v. *Officers of State*, Dec. 15, 1807, F.C. (Mor.Jurisdict.App.No. 19). Contrast *The Strathbogie Case* (1840) 2 D. 585 at 594, where Lord Gillies accepts Blackstone's proposition that Parliament can alter the established religion. In contrast there are to be found in both the majority and minority decisions in the " Disruption Cases " assertions of the fundamental nature of the Act for Security, though these declarations are more frequent in the minority opinions. Thus Lord Moncrieff in the *Auchterarder Case* (Robertson's Report, Vol. ii, p. 333) asserted that the Act for Security had rendered the law " definite and unalterable," and (at p. 329) treated the Act as " fundamental and essential " to the state. See too in the *Auchterarder Case* (Robertson's Report, Vol. ii) at p. 381, *per* Lord Jeffrey, and at p. 148, *per* Lord Medwyn (Lord Medwyn's " compact theory " necessarily involved this idea). In *Cruickshank* v. *Gordon* (1843) 5 D. 909 at 1000 Lord President Boyle would, it seems, regard the Act as binding upon both church and state. See too *per* Lord Fullerton in the *Culsalmond Case* (1842) 4 D. 957. The Act for Securing the Protestant Religion is also recognised by the Regency Act 1937, s. 4 (2), as having a special position, though that particular section is ambiguous; while recognising that special position it impliedly contemplates the possibility of repeal in circumstances outside the scope of the Regency Act.

35 It is difficult to imagine that today a customs duty granted to a town could be regarded as a private, as distinct from public, right as it was in *Reid & Kerr* v. *Magistrates of Edinburgh* (1712) II Fount. 696.

36 The provisions imposing the test upon those who taught in universities and schools might well have been regarded as fundamental by the draftsman, and they continued to be so regarded by some at a much later period (see *The Protest, Declaration and Testimony*, 1849, of the Church of Scotland, which regarded the control by the church of schools as being as important as the establishment of Presbyterianism itself). Nevertheless changed attitudes to education, and the Disruption itself, meant that this view was no longer generally held. The Universities (Scotland) Act 1853, limiting the test, was, in effect, put forward by the church itself, and few would have considered the Education Act 1872 (creating school boards) as being in conflict with the Union legislation. Moreover, the history of the church's attitude to tests, and the whole of the legislative history in this matter, tend to the conclusion that what was intended to be entrenched was general. See particularly " Doctrinal Subscription in the Church of Scotland " by Lord Sands (1905) 17 J.R. 221. See also (1900) 12 J.R. 194. For the modern formula for the admission of a minister see Cox, *Practice and Procedure of the Church of Scotland*.

37 The *Auchterarder Case* (Robertson's Report, Vol. ii, p. 10). At p. 13, the Lord President refers to the Act of 1690 as " an admission on the part of the Church, of its dependence on the Legislature, and of the necessity of the authority of Parliament to render even its doctrines and creed valid in law." See too Lord Gillies in the *Strathbogie Case* (1840) 2 D. 585 at 594.

Scotland Act 1921.[38] This shift of opinion on the relationship of church and state cannot be without effect upon the interpretation of and attitude to the Union legislation, as, indeed, the contrasts between the majority and minority opinions in the Disruption litigation show clearly. Thus the thing which is " entrenched " is not, for a variety of reasons, anything which is absolutely constant.

Even if these external matters are disregarded, and the Act for Securing the Protestant Religion is looked at in isolation, parts of it must be read as ancillary to the primary purpose of securing a Presbyterian Church. It is true that the Act itself declares that its terms shall be fundamental and essential conditions of the Union, without any alteration or derogation, and thus, all its terms are, on the surface, of absolute and equal authority. Yet some Acts, notably that of 1690, are picked out " more especially," other provisions are added " for greater security," above all the Confession of Faith, ratified in 1690 and incorporated by reference in the Act of 1707, contains both machinery for alteration and an admission that it may incorporate error. Chapter XXXI states that " it belongeth to Synods and Councills . . . to set down rules for the better ordering the publick worship of God and government of his Church " and also that " All Synods or Councills since the Apostles time whether generall or particular may err and many have erred, therefore they are not to be made the rule of faith or practise but to be used as a help in both." Thus too rigid an interpretation of this Act might conflict with the expressed intentions of those for whose benefit entrenchment was contemplated. A looser interpretation, that is to say, that the Act intended to protect a protestant presbyterian church in general rather than in detail, accords with opinions later expressed.[39] It equally is the interpretation which reconciles the Church of Scotland Act 1921 and the Act for Securing the Protestant Religion, to which the 1921 Act makes express reference.[40]

The same type of construction is, it seems, applicable to Article XIX of the Act of Union, relating to the Court of Session. That provision is on the face of it less rigid than the provisions relating to the church since it contemplates regulation " for the better administration of justice." Nevertheless, it seems that the essential point of a distinct court

[38] See particularly Art. V of the Schedule thereto. For an account of the shifting views see Sjölinder, *Presbyterian Re-union in Scotland, 1907–1921.*
[39] See *Report as to the Subscription of Tests* of the Scottish Universities Commission, 1892 (C. 6790). Apart from the doubts expressed by some Professors of Divinity on the Confession of Faith as a doctrinal test, the Church of Scotland itself proposed arrangements which, while consistent with the interpretation suggested above, were inconsistent with a more rigid interpretation (see particularly *Report*, pp. xvii and xix). See too Lord Sands' article referred to in note 36 above. Moreover, it is only by such an interpretation that the law can match church doctrine. There are considerable difficulties otherwise in reconciling what the lawyers did with what the church wanted; see, *e.g.,* Burleigh, " The Presbyter in Presbyterianism " (1949) 2 *Scottish Journal of Theology* 293 at 309, where he describes the Claim of Right as neither theologically nor ecclesiastically accurate.
[40] Consider particularly s. 2 and Arts. II and V of the Schedule to the Act of 1921. The treatment of Art. I is in accord with the interpretation here suggested.

may be regarded as fundamental. In *MacCormick* v. *Lord Advocate*[41] Lord Russell expressly reserved his opinion on this matter, and in 1807 the Memorial to the House of Lords from the Senators of the College of Justice clearly envisaged limits to the power of regulation such as would be imposed by such an interpretation.[42]

Suggested effects of the Acts of Union. Thus it seems that hypothetically the Acts of Union could have imposed limitations upon the Union Parliament, being antecedent to it, and that those limitations could be valid. It also appears that such was the intention of the framers and that this intention has been recognised, indirectly at least, in some of the decisions. The limitations are, however, few and imposed in such a way that any infringement of them is improbable. Direct proof of such propositions is difficult. It depends upon the attempted breach of an entrenched provision and a challenge to that breach. It is doubtful if there has as yet been any breach, and in the case coming nearest to a breach (the sequence of legislation starting with the Universities (Scotland) Act 1853) that " breach," if it be one, was in effect carried out at the request and with the consent of the body most able to express national opinion upon the topic.[43] Should the breach involve parliamentary legislation, proof would also depend upon the acceptance by the courts of jurisdiction to listen to a challenge to the validity of the later Act, a matter which is treated hereafter.

The Irish Union. The somewhat similar position which existed in relation to Ireland should be noticed. The Union between Ireland and Great Britain brought about by the Union with Ireland Act 1800 was stated to be " for ever after " January 1, 1801, and the Churches of England and Ireland were, at the same time, united, the continuance of the United Church being said to be an essential and fundamental part of the Union of the Kingdoms. Yet, in 1869, by the Irish Church Act, the Union of the Churches was broken and the Irish Church disestablished and in 1922 the Union of the Kingdom was broken. The situations appear to be parallel, yet perhaps they are not. As has already been said, too much cannot be built upon the words " for ever "; strong and enduring nationalist movements cannot ultimately be confined by words upon the Statute Book, and law must eventually come

---

[41] 1953 S.C. 396 at 417.

[42] " We are of opinion that on fair bona fide construction, as between two independent nations, it cannot be held to have been in the contemplation of either, that any law should, in future times, be considered as merely a regulation for the better administration of justice which goes to subvert the supreme jurisdiction of the Court of Session, and to render it subordinate to a new court, unknown to our ancestors." This protest and others like it had its effect upon the shape of the reforms then made.

[43] See particularly the speech of the Duke of Argyll introducing the Bill for the 1853 Act into Parliament. It is noticeable that in the patronage cases the direct issue of the validity of the Patronage Act 1711 was evaded, perhaps necessarily so in view of the very uncertain position of the law on that matter in the years preceding the Union. As to the Union generally, see Chap. 5, *post.*

into step with reality, as it did to some extent in 1922, the process being carried further by the Ireland Act 1949. As to the churches, the Church of Ireland was not in 1800 or in 1869 a national church in the same way as the Church of Scotland was in 1707 and remains. By 1869 it had become clear that the Union and the supposed fundamental provision would not both endure, though it was not yet clear that neither could. Historically the Irish Church Act 1869 must be regarded as part of the process of dissolution of the Union. Looked at in that light, the Irish precedent, even in so far as it can be relevant, does not therefore necessarily conflict with what has been said.

The attitude to constituent documents. Nevertheless, the dependence of law on political fact which it re-emphasises remains important. Words like " ever " or " never " in such contexts must be read in a relative sense, and it is impossible, in any absolute sense, to confine the evolution of societies by the Statute Book. That certainly is not done by a written constitution, and when the process of formal constitutional amendment is too slow, or is for other reasons inappropriate or ineffective, other means are found of keeping constitutional words in touch with life. It may be that those words are " illumined " in different ways from time to time, as Lord Wright put it,[44] or the process of changing interpretation may be more open.[45] A constitution which attempted to protect too much, and which contained no method of adjustment, would prove unworkable. Just as on a smaller scale it has been found necessary to restrict the ability of testators and settlors to plan for future generations, so on a larger scale succeeding generations must have or will find opportunities of development according to their ideals. Granted then the shape of the Union legislation, which contains no machinery for constitutional amendment, the looser interpretation of the " entrenching " provisions suggested above is the one which in practice is most likely to fulfil the needs of the societies for which it was intended. Nevertheless, it must be emphasised that although the suggested interpretation can have practical advantages, it does not rely on them for justification. It can, it is thought, be justified by ordinary methods of interpreting the documents and other materials alone.

CAN PARLIAMENT BIND ITSELF?

The background. The second question relating to the sovereignty of Parliament is whether a Parliament can fetter its successors. There is a substantial body of authority which denies that this can be done, and for good reason. When Stair asserts that " Parliament can never exclude the full liberty of themselves, or their successors, no more than persons can by one resolution secure that they cannot resolve the

44 *James* v. *The Commonwealth* [1936] A.C. 578.
45 *Brown* v. *Board of Education*, 347 U.S. 483 (1954).

contrary, and, therefore, the same Session of Parliament may judge that to be unjust, that it judged to be just, and contrarywise, as oft as they will; and much more may different Parliaments: for, whatever a Parliament can do at one time, in making laws, or determining of causes, may be at their pleasure abrogate or derogate," [46] he may have been thinking mainly of Parliament as a court, but he specifically includes Parliament as a legislature. The considerations which underlie, in the judicial field, arguments in favour of a loose doctrine of precedent, or of devices, such as that of convening a Full Court,[47] to remove obsolete or inconvenient decisions, are just as important in the legislative field. At lowest this is but a necessary concession to the fallibility of human reasoning, understanding and foresight, and to the freedom of successive generations to mould the law to their liking or to the requirements of their age, a freedom which in any event they will take even if they are not given it.[48]

The precedents. Before the Union the Parliament of Scotland demonstrated, as has been shown, a willingness to repeal or amend statutes which earlier Parliaments had attempted, at least by the appearance of the statute, to make binding upon their successors, and to disobey formal limitations.[49] In post-Union times there has equally been acceptance of the general proposition that what one Parliament makes another can unmake, either expressly or by implication.[50] Again, however, the question whether Parliament can bind its successors requires more precise phrasing before an adequate answer can be given. Limitations upon future legislative activity may be of several kinds, they may be as to the form or method of legislation, or as to subject-matter, or as to time or space. Some of these kinds of limitations may more correctly

[46] Inst. IV, 1, 61, and Erskine, Inst. I, 1, 19, where he relies on Justinian for authority. This is not merely a question of power. It may also be a question of necessity. To the objection "Who then should punish and coerce the Parliament in case of exorbitance?" Samuel Rutherford answered: "Posterior Parliaments," and when it was urged that they too might err he gave the ultimate cure: "God must remedy that": *Rex lex*, Q. 38.

[47] Such considerations clearly underlay the statement on the binding effect of precedent in the House of Lords on July 26, 1966: [1966] 3 All E.R. 77.

[48] Taylor Innes, in his *Law of Creeds in Scotland* at p. 63 applies this reasoning to the Union legislation itself, yet it seems that, granted the interpretation given above, it is possible to accept a view that some portions of that are fundamental and at the same time allow adequate freedom to future generations.

[49] *Ante*, p. 70, Erskine founds this (Inst. I, 1, 45) on will or consent and thus equates this to desuetude, which he regarded as a revocation of consent. Some statutes went far in an attempt to bind Parliament; see Hope, *Major Practicks*, I, 1, 15. For a clear illustration of such disobedience which was upheld by the courts see *Duke of Douglas* v. *King's Advocate* (1748) Mor. 7695.

[50] The courts may not readily concede a repeal by implication; see *Bain* v. *Mackay* (1875) 2 R.(J.) 32 at 36, and in applying the doctrine the courts may apply a doctrine very close to that of "Occupying the field" common in constitutions where there is a distribution of legislative power: *Arthur* v. *Lord Advocate* (1895) 22 R. 382. The English authorities, *Vauxhall Estates Ltd.* v. *Liverpool Corporation* [1932] 1 K.B. 733 and *Ellen Street Estates Ltd.* v. *Minister of Health* [1934] 1 K.B. 590, are familiar enough in this area of law.

provoke a different question—whether Parliament may redefine itself.[51] It does not follow that the same answer would be given to all types of limitation as is given to one particular type, nor, if the question is put in a different form, that the usual answer to the usual form of question would be as readily given. The fact that the question is posed with greater precision may provoke doubt or hesitation. Thus, for example, the case for the martyrdom of which Lord Mackenzie spoke in the *Culsalmond* case,[52] when he said that judges must obey Parliament or resign, does not arise until they have satisfied themselves that the question Has Parliament spoken? must be answered in the affirmative. This point is clearly made by Lord Pearce delivering the opinion of the Judicial Committee in *The Bribery Commissioner* v. *Ranasinghe*.[53]

If examined, the older cases, with few possible exceptions, go very little way to answering, in an authoritative manner, the question when it is put in any of these more detailed ways, instead of being put in the customary more generalised way, simply because the real point of the question was not an issue in the cases. The more recent cases suggest that the traditional answers are doubtful. The cases of implied repeal prove little. First because the repealed statute did not attempt to limit future legislation, and secondly because the rule is treated as having the same foundation as the rule of interpretation which decrees that the latter part of a statute shall prevail over an earlier part,[54] a rule which is equally applicable to private documents. Even where phraseology is found which might be construed as a limitation, such as the reference in the Acquisition of Land (Assessment of Compensation) Act 1919 to " any statute whether passed before or after the passing of this Act," [55] upon proper examination and construction the words have a much more limited significance, hardly more than the such older phrases as " in all time coming " as used in the Acts of the Parliament of Scotland, which did not even prevent a statute in which they were used from falling into desuetude.[56] Neither the *Vauxhall Estates* case [57] nor the *Ellen Street*

---

[51] See Marshall, " What is Parliament? " (1954) *Political Studies* 193 and " Parliamentary Supremacy and the Language of Constitutional Limitation " (1955) 67 J.R. 62. " Sovereignty in Theory and Practice " by Sheriff K. W. B. Middleton (1952) 64 J.R. 134 at 144; and see his " New Thoughts on the Union " (1954) 66 J.R. 37.

[52] (1842) 4 D. 957 at 1010.

[53] [1965] A.C. 172; and see Sir Owen Dixon, " The Common Law as the Ultimate Constitutional Foundation " (1957) 31 A.L.J. at p. 244, and Marshall, " Parliamentary Sovereignty: A Recent Development " (1967) 12 McGill L.J. 523.

[54] Compare *Bain* v. *Mackay* (1875) 2 R.(J.) 32 and *Moss' Empires Ltd.* v. *Assessor for Glasgow*, 1917 S.C.(H.L.) 1.

[55] s. 1 (dealing with the appointment of official arbitrators). S. 7, which was involved in both the *Vauxhall Estates* case and the *Ellen Street Estates* case, was not so strong, and it is not clear, though it was argued, that that section was bound up with s. 1. For another view on these cases see H. W. R. Wade, " The Basis of Legal Sovereignty " [1955] C.L.J. 172 at 174; and compare Jennings, *Law and the Constitution*, 5th ed., at pp. 162–163.

[56] The wording of the Act of 1592 (A.P.S. III, 579), prohibiting the exercise of crafts in the suburbs of burghs, so held in *Paterson* v. *Just*, Dec. 6, 1810, F.C.

[57] [1932] 1 K.B. 733.

Estates case [58] go very far, despite some dicta contained in the judgments. In the first, of three judges, only one, Avory J., was prepared to construe section 7, and he held that it only applied to statutes existing in 1919. In the *Ellen Street Estates* case, Talbot J. inclined to that view. Scrutton L.J. found, in effect, a direct amendment of the Act of 1919 by a later Act and it was conceded that a direct repeal was effective. Maugham L.J. held that one Parliament could not bind another as to form, but it was not demonstrated that in 1919 Parliament had attempted to do so.[59]

Certainly there are other strong judicial assertions that no Parliament can bind another. Notable among them is that of Lord Sankey L.C. in *British Coal Corporation* v. *The King*.[60] Speaking of section 4 of the Statute of Westminster 1931, he said: " indeed, the Imperial Parliament could, as a matter of abstract law, repeal or disregard section 4 of the Statute. But that is theory and has no relation to realities." [61] On the other hand, Parliament persists in putting purported limitations on the Statute Book. Apart from section 4 of the Statute of Westminster 1931, there is section 4 (2) of the Regency Act 1937 [62] and section 1 (2) of the Ireland Act 1949.[63] There remain, then, several possibilities; either, for example, Parliament believes that there is some force in these provisions, or else it is content to enact what is in effect a sham (and to continue so to do), or again, it may be that there is a greater connection between theory and reality than Lord Sankey suggested.

The objections in principle. The real objection, in principle, is to the total renunciation of legislative competence in any field in a manner which leaves a vacuum. Proponents of the classical view of the sovereignty of Parliament have asserted that Parliament can abdicate its power to another legislature,[64] and this is acceptable since a legislative

---

58 [1934] 1 K.B. 590.

59 But compare H. W. R. Wade, " The Basis of Legal Sovereignty " [1955] C.L.J. 172 at 175–176.

60 [1935] A.C. 500. S. 4 runs: " No Act of Parliament of the United Kingdom passed after the commencement of this Act shall extend, or be deemed to extend, to a Dominion as part of the law of that Dominion, unless it is expressly declared in that Act that that Dominion has requested, and consented to, the enactment thereof." This section should not be regarded as standing alone, but must be regarded as the prototype of a whole series of provisions in later Independence Acts; see, *e.g.*, Barbados Independence Act 1966, s. 1 (2).

61 At p. 520.

62 " The Regent shall not have power to assent to any Bill for changing the order of succession to the Crown or for repealing or altering an Act of the fifth year of the reign of Queen Anne made in Scotland entitled ' An Act for Securing the Protestant Religion and Presbyterian Church Government '."

63 " It is hereby affirmed that in no event will Northern Ireland or any part thereof cease to be part of His Majesty's dominions and of the United Kingdom without the consent of the Parliament of Northern Ireland." The phraseology of this part of the subsection presents difficulties of interpretation. It is phrased as an " affirmation " and could therefore be construed as being merely a declaration of intent included in a statute as distinct from an enactment. The whole circumstances seem, however, to point to greater force than that being intended.

64 Anson, " The Government of Ireland Bill and the Sovereignty of Parliament " (1886) 2 L.Q.R. 426 at 440; Dicey, *Law of the Constitution*, 10th ed., pp. 68–69; and see Cowen, " Legislature and Judiciary " (1953) 15 M.L.R. 282 and 16 M.L.R. 273; but compare Wade, *op. cit.* [1955] C.L.J. 192 *et seq.* On any other assumption,

vacuum does not then arise.[65]   On somewhat similar arguments there does not, subject to qualifications, appear to be any objection in principle to a limitation in time or form.   A parliament which must, for certain purposes, observe particular forms, or procedures, but which has, nevertheless, a full competence as to subject-matter, may nevertheless be regarded as " sovereign." [66]   It has here been accepted that Parliament may make rules governing the legislative process, so that primary legislation may be made in several ways.   This is done by the Parliament Act 1911, which means that, in effect in certain circumstances, Parliament means the Sovereign and the Commons to the exclusion of the House of Lords.[67]   It is equally clear that Parliament can, as by the Life Peerages Act 1958, alter its own composition.   It is true that neither of the measures cited are expressed to be eternal, but for the time being they are accepted as effective law.   That being so it is difficult to see why a parliament should not impose legislative forms or procedures upon itself, and if it so wishes " entrench " such provisions so as to prevent the possibility of any argument about implied repeal.   Indeed Parliament does provide such forms in measures such as the Consolidation of Enactments (Procedure) Act 1949.

The types of limitation

(a) *The Statute of Westminster.*   If against this background we turn once again to the purported self-limitations of Parliament we see that they present various problems.   Section 4 of the Statute of Westminster is the most complex.   It can be construed as imposing a limitation upon Parliament.   It can be construed not as a restriction upon legislative

granted that either the English or Scottish Parliament or both was, or were, sovereign in 1706 the Union of 1707 could not have come about.   Those who deny this proposition tend to do so because of fear of a particular consequence of admitting it.   Compare Sir George Mackenzie arguing, in the *Jus Regium*, against the power of the King to abdicate (which, on his hypothesis, is the same argument) when he says: " nor could [the King] in law consent to an Act of Parliament declaring that he should be the last King.   And if such consents and Acts had been sufficient to bind Successors, many silly Kings in several parts of Europe had long since been prevailed upon to alter the Monarchy from hereditary to elective " (*Works*, Vol. II, p. 474).

65 See *Ibralebbe* v. *The Queen* [1964] A.C. 900 at 924.
66 *Harris* v. *Donges*, 1952 (2) S.A. 428 (A.D.).   It is true that the limitations were imposed by the statute creating the Parliament, and thus the case is not exactly in point.   Nevertheless the propositions on the topic of limitations and sovereignty are general and do reflect on the weight to be attached to considerations of whether a Parliament is sovereign or subordinate which affect the weight to be given to *Att.-Gen. for N.S.W.* v. *Trethowan* (1931) 44 C.L.R. 394.   The same point is made with force in *Bribery Commissioner* v. *Ranasinghe* [1965] A.C. 172 at 200.   In fact the principle may be a quite general one aimed against the creation of impotence; see Mitchell, *The Contracts of Public Authorities*, Chap. I.
67 The Parliament Act 1911 (as amended by the Act of 1949) must, it seems, be regarded as a statute laying down rules for the legislative process, or alternatively as a redefinition of Parliament for particular purposes.   Legislation resulting from it, such as the Parliament Act 1949, cannot be regarded as a form of delegated legislation, though see H. W. R. Wade, *op. cit.*   Consider, *inter alia*, s. 4 of the 1911 Act; and see generally Marshall, " What is Parliament? " (1954) *Political Studies* 193.

competence, but as a rule of construction directed to the courts.[68] Further, its effect may differ if looked at from the point of view of the law of the United Kingdom, or from that of the law of one of the members of the Commonwealth. Neglecting this last possibility, the first two raise issues here relevant. If it be regarded as a rule of construction, then, at first sight, no difficulties arise,[69] there has been no limitation upon Parliament. Nevertheless, the issue of an implied repeal could arise in relation to a subsequent statute and thus the problem of a formal limitation would be provoked. On the other construction there is quite clearly a purported limitation of the United Kingdom Parliament. If, however, the whole statute is looked at, section 4 does not create the abhorrent vacuum, since by other parts of the statute full powers of ordinary legislation are given.[70] Thus it seems that section 4 can be regarded as part of a whole scheme of transference of legal power, intended to make law and fact coincide, and as such capable of being effective, even on the classical theory. This view finds clear support in *Ibralebbe* v. *The Queen*.[71] There Lord Radcliffe clearly regarded an equivalent provision in the legislation establishing the independence of Ceylon as part of such a transfer. It was this that led him to conclude: "There is no power [*scil.* of the United Kingdom] to legislate for Ceylon, to do so would be wholly inconsistent with the unqualified powers of legislation conceded." The same conclusion may be reached even on the alternative construction. The rules governing the legislative process are, in the main, customary. This results simply from the course of history, and does not give to those rules any particular sanctity. It is clear that they may be altered by legislation passed in the ordinary way, and that that legislation is valid until repealed. It is true that the only example of such legislation at present is an Act which excludes a certain stage. If this can be done, there seems to be no reason why, subject to limitations which will appear, an additional stage should not be added as a prerequisite for validity. This, on the alternative construction, section 4 may be regarded as doing—by adding an extraparliamentary stage. No question of implied repeal here arises. If the prerequisites of legislation are laid down, material which does not comply with them is not legislation.[72] It would, however, remain true that on the wording

---

[68] Wheare, *The Statute of Westminster*, 5th ed., p. 153. Support for this view may be found in *Copyright Owners' Reproduction Society Ltd.* v. *E.M.I. (Australia) Pty. Ltd.* (1958) 100 C.L.R. 597 at 612 and 613.

[69] It is upon such a theory that the Canadian Bill of Rights appears to have been drafted, which is much more clearly directed to the courts. See Laskin, *Constitutional Law*, 3rd ed., p. 976, and (1962) 11 I.C.L.Q. 519; and compare the National Insurance Act 1965, s. 116 (2), which, as will be seen, contains the seed of considerable development.

[70] See ss. 2 (2) and 3; the limitations upon legislative competence of the then Dominions related to constitutional legislation.

[71] [1964] A.C. 900.

[72] The suggestion in argument in the *E.M.I.* case (*supra*) that a United Kingdom Act of 1956 could, without compliance with s. 4, be treated as operative in Australia was said by Menzies J. " to attribute an *impossible* intent to the Imperial Parliament " (italics supplied); and see Dixon J. in *Trethowan's Case* (1931) 44 C.L.R. 394 at

of section 4 alone that section 4 could possibly be repealed exclusively *vis-à-vis* the United Kingdom courts by ordinary legislation which did not comply with the terms of that section. That statement, however, is itself to be understood as being subject to the " conventional " rules set out in the preamble to the statute.[73] A full discussion of their impact would involve the arguments on the nature of conventions which have already been rehearsed and need not be repeated. In any case, the effect of even such repeal is uncertain. It would, it seems, amount to no more than a statutory reaffirmation of a power to legislate with extraterritorial effect, and thus would change nothing.

Thus, in the absence of any such repeal it seems that, on any interpretation, section 4 should be regarded as effective. As a redefinition of Parliament for certain purposes it may effectively operate upon the activities of a body which, while for other purposes it is a parliament, is not one for those certain purposes. As imposing a rule of construction, the whole circumstances give to that rule such force that recognition by the courts of a chance repeal by implication is, to use Lord Sankey's words (though not in his sense), unthinkable. A direct or explicit repeal involves the matters which have already been discussed.

(b) *The Ireland Act.* In a similar way section 1 (2) of the Ireland Act 1949 may be regarded, if it be taken as legislative in effect and not merely declaratory of an intent, as redefining Parliament to make it a more widely based body, or as requiring an additional stage for certain legislation. It would follow from the preceding argument that a case can be made for the validity and effectiveness of such legislation, and that that case is not destroyed by any existing authority in whichever way the section be construed.

(c) *The Regency Act.* There remain the provisions of the Regency Act. These undoubtedly exclude the possibility of legislation on certain topics. Again, however, if rightly regarded they do not create the legislative vacuum. That part of the subsection dealing with the Act for Securing the Protestant Religion may be left on one side.[74] Properly

426, where he suggests that in such a case " the courts might be called upon to consider whether the supreme legislative power in respect of the matter had in truth been exercised in the manner required for its authentic expression, and by the elements in which it had come to reside." See also Rand, " Some Aspects of Canadian Constitutionalism " (1960) 38 Can.B.R. 135. In *Bribery Commissioner* v. *Ranasinghe* [1965] A.C. 172 it is re-emphasised that these questions of the definition of a parliament or of what is necessary for an Act have, essentially, nothing to do with the question of whether or not that parliament is sovereign.

73 In the *E.M.I.* case (*supra*) these conventional rules as they existed before incorporation in the preamble were referred to as " strong and unbending " (at p. 612), and as " a rule of construction which this court would be expected to apply " (at p. 613).

74 The insertion of this provision is curious and ambiguous. The fact that the Scottish Act is thus protected and not the English one is consistent with the history of both. The Scottish Act was the result of deep-felt emotions, the English was rather an afterthought, the product of political and ecclesiastical " me-tooism." The provision in relation to the Scottish Act is, however, ambiguous, in that while it prefers that Act above all other legislation, by implication it suggests that that Act is not protected except during a regency.

that part must be looked at in the light of the earlier argument upon the Union legislation, at least so far as repeal of the 1707 Act is concerned. So far as the subsection deals with " alteration " of the Act of Anne it must either be treated on the same footing or else it falls to be dealt with in the same way as the other limitations upon the Regent. So far as the succession to the Crown is concerned the limitation is one in time. There is no total exclusion of legislative competence, and there are conceivable circumstances in which such a limitation would be desirable. It seems, therefore, that arguments of principle should lead to the conclusion that this, too, must be treated like a formal limitation and thus to be rated as potentially valid.

The possible state of the law. The distinction which, it is suggested, must be made is one between Parliament incapacitating itself and Parliament imposing limitations which do not incapacitate. The first is clearly obnoxious in principle, and is opposed by the authoritative writers. The second is not obnoxious in principle and may well, in particular circumstances, be desirable. The possibility that Parliament may effectively limit itself is thus consistent with parliamentary practice, is consistent with relevant, but not binding, modern authority elsewhere,[75] and is not precluded by any domestic authority. Indeed support can be found in parliamentary practice for the view that at one stage Parliament conceived itself to be bound by formal limitations which it had imposed upon itself.[76] Thus, on balance, since the law is not clear, it seems at present possible to assert that Parliament may have thus effectively limited itself. That solution, while untraditional, is strongly supported by modern cases. It is true that, even if they are cases reported in British law reports, they are not strictly related to the United Kingdom jurisdiction (though in this, of course, they differ in no way from the source of the oft-cited dictum of Lord Sankey); nevertheless, they are cases dealing with general principle. The same solution is supported by extra-judicial, but weighty, assertions of a subsequent Lord Chancellor.[77] Moreover, there is, as far as provisions of the type of the Statute of Westminster are concerned, the attraction that this solution is the only one which coincides both with political reality and political morality, with both of which law should have some contact. There is no logical or jurisprudential reason why any other solution should be accepted. So far as formal, procedural or temporal limitations are concerned, again

---

[75] It seems to be the principle upon which the Canadian Bill of Rights was drafted; see particularly s. 2, which is addressed to both Parliament and to the courts imposing rules of draftsmanship on the former and rules of construction on the latter.

[76] By 1 Geo. 1, Stat. 2, c. 4, any naturalisation Bill had to have a clause excluding the person concerned from Parliament, when it was desired to provide particular exemption from this that Act was first repealed and then the conflicting measure was introduced; see the illustration in Hatsell, *Precedents*, relating to the Prince of Brunswick, Vol. II, p. 6.

[77] Lord Gardiner (282 H.L.Deb. 1203): " Several Acts of Parliament have reduced *for all time* vast territorial areas of our sovereignty " (italics supplied).

reason is on the side of the solutions outlined above, and there is again no authority which, when properly examined, stands in the path of the acceptance of a rational solution. In relation to the latter group of restrictions, it is, of course, true that there remains a difficult distinction to be drawn between the limitations which are apparently exclusively formal or procedural and those which amount to the creation of an unacceptable legislative vacuum. The distinction between the two types of limitation may be easier to write than to discern in particular cases. A limitation in form could be so phrased that, in substance, it amounted to a deprivation of power. Such a limitation would, it seems, be invalid,[78] but none of the instances at present upon the Statute Book amount to a deprivation; they go no further than imposing limited conditions.

THE COURTS AND THE VALIDITY OF STATUTES

The problems hitherto discussed might have no more than a theoretical interest. Whether the interest is greater depends to a large extent upon the answer to the question whether or not judicial review of the validity of statutes is possible with us. If it is not, that conflict between academic logic and political reality to which (in a slightly different sense) Lord President Cooper drew attention[79] remains. Again the traditional answer is that no such review is possible. " We sit here as a Court created by Parliament, the organ of Parliament, and must judge according to what appears to be the will of Parliament, or resign our office. I have felt no call to any such martyrdom and shall certainly adhere to my duty of obedience to Parliament," said Lord Mackenzie in 1842.[80]

---

[78] See the doubts of Lord Haldane in *Re The Initiative and Referendum Act* [1919] A.C. 935 at 945, and compare the limitations upon the power of the states to refer matters to the Commonwealth in Australia under s. 51, *placitum*, xxxviii, which were envisaged in *Graham* v. *Paterson* (1950) 81 C.L.R. 1 at 37 and the *Uniform Tax Case* (1942) 65 C.L.R. 373 at 416. In this last instance the problem is complicated by the necessity of maintaining a federal structure, which introduces other considerations. On a much lower plane the same sort of considerations are operative; see *The Magistrates of Crail, Petitioners*, 1947 S.L.T.(Sh.Ct.) 81. The principle that a body cannot disable itself from performing public functions is close to that which insists that the body must itself perform those functions. This or cognate problems arise in several forms; see Laskin, *Canadian Constitutional Law*, 2nd ed., p. 41, and Jaffé, " Delegation of the Legislative Power " (1947) 47 Col.L.R. 359 at 561.

[79] *MacCormick* v. *Lord Advocate*, 1953 S.C. 396 at 412. Lord Cooper was there referring to the " academic logic " which denied any validity to s. 4 of the Statute of Westminster and the political realism which so clearly recognised the validity of the same section.

[80] *Middleton* v. *Anderson* (1842) 4 D. 957 (*The Culsalmond Case*) at 1010. The statement ante-dates the equally forceful question of Willes J. as to whether the courts were to sit as regents over what is done in Parliament; see *Lee* v. *Bude and Torrington Junction Ry.* (1871) L.R. 6 C.P. 576 at 582. Lord Cooper in *MacCormick's* case was at first sight of the same opinion when he said: " This at least is plain, that there is neither precedent nor authority of any kind for the view that the domestic courts of either Scotland or England have jurisdiction to determine whether a governmental act of the type here in controversy is or is not conform to the provisions of a treaty." But his declaration is less plain on examination. The " governmental act " could bear reference to the Royal Proclamation and thus be irrelevant to the present purpose. Moreover, he added, with careful specification,

Once again support for this view can be, or has been, found both in the cases and in the writers.[81]

On the other hand, weight must be given to more recent patterns of thought. It is by no means clear that exclusive reliance on " political " machinery is satisfactory. The role of the Supreme Court in the United States of America as the stimulus to the latent conscience of the United States has, in modern times, had a considerable importance. Equally, experience in continental Europe has shown that constitutional courts have a major part to play in the preservation of essential democratic principles. While the British may be a peculiar people, one of their peculiarities is not necessarily a monopoly of constitutional or political virtue or rectitude. Experience elsewhere is not irrelevant. Thus at the most general level the exclusion of judicial review is not a constitutional prerequisite. It must also be remembered that if some limitations are accepted the terms of debate are changed, as is shown by all the recent cases. The dilemma of Chief Justice Marshall becomes real. Either the rules imposed with all the solemnity of law are real and have juridical value, in which case the courts must pluck up courage and take notice of them,[82] or they are shams and are accepted as such, in which case the whole place of a rule of law is put in question, and political expediency becomes the rule.

Moreover, the authorities are not all on one side, or consistent with themselves. Coke, in *Bonham's Case*,[83] spoke with a different voice, and in *The Prince's Case* [84] the validity of a statute was examined. There are suggestions of judicial review in *Queensberry* v. *Officers of State*,[85]

that " I am constrained to hold that the action as laid is incompetent in respect that it has not been shown that the Court of Session has authority to entertain the issue sought to be raised." The narrowness of this formulation makes it difficult to construe the whole passage as a general denial of possibility of judicial review, particularly if regard is had to some of the authorities cited. Lord Guthrie in the Outer House was more explicit: see p. 403. Lord Russell in the Inner House expressly reserved his opinion on this point (see p. 417).

[81] *Edinburgh and Dalkeith Ry.* v. *Wauchope* (1842) 1 Bell's App.Cas. 252 at 279, *per* Lord Campbell; *Mortensen* v. *Peters* (1906) 8 F.(J.) 93 at 100, *per* Lord Dunedin; *Hoani Te Heuheu Tukino* v. *Aotea District Maori Land Board* [1941] A.C. 308 at 322, *per* Lord Simon; citing *Labrador Co.* v. *The Queen* [1893] A.C. 104. Among the older Scottish authorities see *Mags. of Dumbarton* v. *Mags. of Glasgow*, Nov. 19, 1771, F.C., where a statute was challenged, but the Lords held " though they could explain an act of the legislature, they had no power to supply or correct it; and could even give it no other interpretation than the precise terms used naturally and positively authorised." Yet earlier in *Stuart* v. *Wedderburn* (1627) Durie 301 it is said: " The said Act of Parliament could not be drawn in dispute before the Session, if it was formally or well done or not, they not being judges thereto." Among the writers see Dicey, *Law of the Constitution*, 10th ed., p. 40; Blackstone, 1 Comm. 160 refers to the uncontrollable power of Parliament; Sir George Mackenzie based this upon an idea of a hierarchy of institutions: *Jus Regium* (*Works*, Vol. II, pp. 472–473); see too his *Criminal Law*, Tit. III. The sense of Bankton I, 1, 66 would deny any possibility of judicial review.

[82] *Bribery Commissioners* v. *Ranasinghe* [1965] A.C. 172.

[83] (1610) 8 Co.Rep. 113b at 118; and see Plucknett, " *Bonham's Case* and Judicial Review " (1926) 40 H.L.R. 30.

[84] (1606) 8 Co.Rep. 1a.

[85] (1807) Mor.App.Juris. 19.

See now Pickin

and in *Mackenzie* v. *Stewart* [86] a private statute was set aside on grounds of fraud. It must be remembered that the Scottish background is here somewhat different. So far as public general statutes were concerned the doctrine of desuetude, while it did not amount to judicial review of the initial validity of a statute (which is here in question), did amount to a judicial review of the continuing validity of statutes. So far as private Acts were concerned (and *Wauchope's* case involved such a statute), the Court of Session was given specific jurisdiction to reduce them,[87] and the effect of the various Acts *salvo jure cujuslibet* was to re-emphasise this jurisdiction, and also to emphasise the uncertain status of such private Acts and ratifications.[88] This difference of background makes understandable both the decision of the Scottish courts and the surprise and dismay of the House of Lords in *Wauchope*.

The contrast between jurisdictions should not be overemphasised. An appeal in some form ran from Session to Parliament and had its influence; " and in case the Lords had decided against the Act of Parliament, which no man will suppose, yet their decision would not take away the force from the Act of Parliament but that decreet might be reduced in Parliament," runs the report in *Officers of State* v. *Cowtie*.[89] Such statements are echoed in England,[90] so also are there statements in both jurisdictions emphasising the inferiority of judges—cases of difficulty are not to be settled by them but by Parliament.[91] Sir George Mackenzie based a like view on a hierarchical idea of law, and when he says: " And then, if the Judges of England should publish Edicts contrary to the Acts of Parliament, or if a Justice of the Peace should ranverse a decree of the Judges of Westminster, these their Endeavours would be void and ineffectual." [92] he would doubtless have said the

---

[86] (1754) 1 Pat.App. 578, where it was argued that an Act of Parliament obtained upon a recital of fictitious debts barred the setting up of the true state of affairs but this argument was rejected in the House of Lords (reversing the Inner House); Lord Kames (Sel.Dec. 13) was strongly of opinion that the courts must afford a remedy even against an Act of Parliament in such a case. See too *Donald* v. *Mags. of Anderston* (1832) 11 S. 119, but contrast *Threshie* v. *Gordon* (1841) 3 D. 450.

[87] Act of 1567, A.P.S. III, 29; *cf.* National Insurance Act 1965, s. 116 (2).

[88] See Ersk. I, 1, 39; Hope, *Major Practicks* V, 4, 14; Dirleton, *Doubts*, Tit. *Salvo Jure*. Steuart in his *Answers* indicates sufficiently clearly, though, that if Parliament specifically excluded the courts the exclusion was effective because of the mastery of Parliament. For an example of challenge see *Inglis* v. *Balfour* (1668) 1 Stair Dec. 544 (Mor.Supp.) II, 142. *The Duke of Douglas* v. *King's Advocate* (1748) Mor. 7695 is really in this tradition though not expressly so.

[89] (1611) Mor. 7327, a case of the conflicts of later and earlier statutes. See too *Murray* v. *Bailie of Torwoodhead* (1683) Harc. 13, holding that decreets of Parliament are not to be quarrelled by inferior judges, and Mackenzie, *Criminal Law*, Tit. III.

[90] See, *e.g.*, Petty, *Jurisdiction of Parliament*, Chaps. III and IV. See especially *Streater's Case* (1653) 5 St.Tr. 366 at 386. " If Parliament should do one thing and we do the contrary here things would run around."

[91] Balfour, *Practicks*—Of Law—" na jugeis within this realme has power to mak any lawis or statutis except the Parliament allanerlie "; and see Petty, *op. cit.* Chap. V. At times steps were taken to re-emphasise this inferiority; see Dirleton's *Doubts* and Steuart's *Answers* thereto, *s.v.* Impugning Parliament, and *Kennedy* v. *M'Lellan* (1534) Mor. 7320.

[92] *Jus Regium*; and see note 81, *supra.*

same of Scotland. These older statements do something more. They show the interplay of political ideas and political facts in the creation of ideas or rules of law. The proclamation of the subservience of courts to Parliament after 1688 was necessary since in the years immediately before the parliamentary revolution the courts had not proved themselves strong bulwarks against prerogative claims. This interplay persists,[93] and, in a slightly different way, again creates (as will appear) a feeling of subservience. The emergence of universal adult franchise and the resultant changes of attitudes to Parliament have also their effects upon courts.

The strength of the authorities. Just as it is necessary to look at some of the declarations (including those of Coke and Blackstone) against their political background, so also is it necessary to look at some of the more modern declarations more closely if their proper meaning is to be appreciated. Their generality should often be limited by the particularity of the circumstances of each of the cases. Some turn upon other general principles, such as that international law is not the system administered by domestic courts, and thus treaties cannot there be debated.[94] Most of the others turn simply upon a general need for finality, which operates in law far outside the narrow confines of the debate on the sovereignty of Parliament. Both *Wauchope's* case and the *Bude and Torrington Railway* case are concerned with private legislation and a procedure which approximates to a trial. What is there conceded is that Parliament is master of its own procedure, a concession which would be made to the judgment of any supreme court,[95] and is consistent with the treatment of other aspects of parliamentary life.[96] Equally the general common sense principle, which appears elsewhere in rules relating to the finality of judgments, here appears in the rule that the factual or legal assumptions upon which legislation is founded cannot subsequently be challenged in a court of law.[97] It is as true under our system as it is elsewhere that, upon general political principles, the courts cannot set themselves up as judges of the appropriateness or expediency of legislative action. The matter is put into its proper perspective by Lord Wright in *Co-operative Committee on Japanese*

---

[93] Thus Hume bases his idea of the overwhelming power of Parliament upon a concept of representative government: *Criminal Law*, Chap. XVIII. Speaking of the making of an Act of Indemnity against civil as well as criminal consequences he says: " and this though beyond the power of royal pardon is however lawful to be done in Parliament, because all the lieges are represented there."

[94] *Mortensen* v. *Peters* (1906) 8 F.(J.) 93 at 100–101; *The Aotea Case* [1941] A.C. 308 at 327; *I.R.C.* v. *Collco Dealings Ltd.* [1959] 3 All E.R. 351 at 355 (affirmed [1960] 2 All E.R. 44).

[95] Compare the discussion in Cheshire, *Private International Law*, 7th ed., p. 565 *et seq.*

[96] *Bradlaugh* v. *Gossett* (1884) 12 Q.B.D. 271; and Lord Jeffrey in the *Auchterarder Case*, Robertson's Report, Vol. II, p. 374.

[97] *Mags. of Dumbarton* v. *Mags. of Glasgow*, Nov. 19, 1771, F.C.; *Labrador Co.* v. *The Queen* [1893] A.C. 104 at 123; *The Aotea Case* [1941] A.C. 308 at 322.

Canadians v. *Att.-Gen. for Canada.*[98] Thus, if these cases are looked at in their context, either the generality of particular passages contained in the judgments tends to disappear, or else those passages point to a general principle which has no necessary connection with any doctrine of the sovereignty of Parliament.

Something more must be said of the latest of the United Kingdom cases, *MacCormick* v. *Lord Advocate,*[99] in which the most deliberate attempt so far was made to secure judicial review of a statute. It must be said at the outset that the greater part of the opinions there given consists of *obiter dicta.* The statutes possibly involved were the Crown Proceedings Act 1947 and the Royal Titles Act 1953. The challenge to the first (in so far as it removed the possibility of obtaining an interdict against the Crown), as being inconsistent with Article 19 of the Act of Union, was not pressed. Any challenge to the second disappeared once it was held that that statute was quite irrelevant to the question of the Royal numeral.[1] Nevertheless, the issue of judicial review was fully dealt with in the opinions, and Lord Cooper said: " This at least is plain, that there is neither precedent nor authority of any kind for the view that the domestic courts of either Scotland or England have jurisdiction to determine whether governmental acts of the type here in controversy is or is not conform to the provisions of a Treaty . . . and I am constrained to hold that the action as laid is incompetent in that it has not been shown that the Court of Session has authority to entertain the issue sought to be raised." [2] Lord Russell added, however: " On the hypothetical question as to the power that might be exercised by this Court in relation to an Act passed which infringed such provisions as Article 19 or Article 25 of the Treaty of Union I desire to reserve my opinion." [3] This echoed a similar reservation by Lord Cooper: " I

---

[98] [1947] A.C. 87 at 102. It must be remembered that even where judicial review of legislation is generally operative this same principle is continually reiterated, though the line between legality and expediency is often not easily drawn. The point is most clearly made by the type of problem which is regarded in the U.S.A. as being non-justiciable because it is a " political question "—see the references in Corwin, *The Constitution and What it Means Today,* 11th ed., p. 138 *et seq.,* and particularly the opinions in *Baker* v. *Carr,* 369 U.S. 186 (1962). With us the deference of the courts in matters of foreign affairs has a somewhat similar origin to these American rules and to the domestic rules now under discussion; see, *e.g., R.* v. *Bottrill, ex p. Kuechenmeister* [1947] K.B. 41. Even this line of cases is put in question by *Liyanage* v. *The Queen* [1967] 1 A.C. 259. The doctrine of the separation of powers could be said to have been " read into " the constitution by the Judicial Committee because of its intrinsic importance. If that can be done the same process of implication could do more.

[99] 1953 S.C. 396.

[1] See Lord President Cooper at p. 410; he added that had he had to construe that statute its form made that task impossible.

[2] At p. 413. It may be noted that none of the earlier Scottish authorities, such as they are (and which have been referred to above), appear to have been cited in argument.

[3] At p. 417. It may be noted that immediately before this passage Lord Russell had referred to the process of denationalising what had shortly before been nationalised as illustrating the supremacy of Parliament. With respect the illustration was inapt, the nationalising statutes having no purported fetters upon their repeal, and a proved ability to puff down a house of cards does not demonstrate an ability to blow down a brick wall.

reserve my opinion with regard to the provisions relating expressly to this Court, and to the laws which concern 'private right' which are administered here."[4] The opinions, then, speak with a double voice, while rejecting judicial review in a particular case, they deliberately express reservations about possible future and different cases.

Possible solutions. Perhaps this ambiguity itself suggests solutions. First, the question of title to sue is of great importance. Here the pursuer was seeking general political redress. It is clear that in modern times the courts are not the appropriate forum for the ventilation of general political grievances, and that fact alone may impose a substantial limitation upon any general judicial review.[5] Second, there is an emphasis on the fact that the traditional answer denying judicial review was to a large extent dependent on the traditional view of the sovereignty of Parliament. If that view of sovereignty be not accepted, views on judicial review are affected.[6] Thus if it is accepted that the Acts of Union are constituent documents containing some, if few, fundamental provisions the argument for possible judicial review is greatly strengthened. Indeed, all the implications of the modern cases, especially from Ceylon, are that as a matter of legal logic such review should exist. The foundation of the distinction drawn in *Trethowan* v. *Att.-Gen. for N.S.W.*[7] between the legislature that was born fettered and one born unfettered then disappears, and thus the weight of the case in the British context is changed. Similar arguments apply in other instances if one looks closely at the processes which Sir Owen Dixon describes as "the identification of the source of a purported enactment with the body established by law as the supreme legislature, and the fulfilment of the conditions prescribed by the law for the time being in force for the authentic expression of the supreme will."[8] If those matters are looked at and it is assumed, or accepted, that the definition of that source and the prescription of those conditions are matters of law (which appear to be the case), then again the argument for some form of judicial examination or review is strong. In that form "review" amounts to no more

[4] At p. 412.
[5] Compare *Minister of Interior* v. *Harris,* 1952 (4) S.A. 769 (A.D.) and *Collins* v. *Minister of Interior,* 1957 (1) S.A. 552 (A.D.).
[6] Here notice Lord Cooper's reference to *Harris* v. *Minister of Interior,* 1952 (2) S.A. 428 (A.D.), where, granted the existence of entrenched clauses, judicial review was held to follow. "To hold otherwise would mean that courts of law would be powerless to protect the rights of individuals which were specially protected in the constitution of this country": *per* Centlivres C.J. at p. 470. There is here an echo of the principle upon which Marshall C.J. wrote judicial review into the constitution of the U.S.A.: *Marbury* v. *Madison* (1803) 1 Cranch 137. The conclusion does not necessarily follow; see *Min. of Interior* v. *Harris,* 1952 (4) S.A. 769 at 780 (A.D.), but seems to do so logically in the absence of any express provision. The matter is admirably ventilated in an address, which reasonably stopped short of firm conclusions, by Sir Owen Dixon, "The Common Law as an Ultimate Constitutional Foundation" (1957) 31 A.L.J. 240.
[7] (1932) 44 C.L.R. 394.
[8] (1957) 31 A.L.J. at p. 245.

than ascertaining that an instrument said to be a statute is one. The realisation of the possibility of review would admittedly demand able argument and judicial courage, starting perhaps from that close examination of existing authorities which shows their limited effect.

In considering this possibility it must be remembered that courts have in the past considered such an issue,[9] and Parliament itself has taken steps to validate "Acts" which suffered from any substantial procedural defect [10]; moreover, presence on or absence from the Parliament Roll has been said to be inconclusive as to the existence of a statute.[11] The cases and the statutes are, however, old, and it may well be that if it appears on the face of the statute that all necessary steps, such as obtaining the normal threefold consent, have been taken, then the courts would not inquire further. There seems, however, to be no authority for the proposition that if it appeared from the statute that it had not been passed according to the appropriate forms of law, or that in some other way a rule of law had been broken, the courts would be powerless to question the validity. The arguments which lead to acceptance of the record do not carry this further proposition, and it must be remembered that preambles have not been treated as unchallengeable.[12] Moreover, the supposed "untouchability" of parliamentary activities must be scrutinised. Sometimes this quality in this context is over-emphasised and is regarded as peculiar, when it is not,[13] and in every case the quality of the defect would require careful analysis. The dichotomy of "formal" and "substantive" limitations is probably too rough and ready. Even the supposed rule that the internal actions of either House are no concern of the courts may be too broadly phrased.[14] Finally, other factors must be taken into consideration. Two questions are involved, the validity of a statute and, if invalidity, or the possibility of invalidity, be conceded, the existence of a remedy. As Lord Cooper emphasised, these questions are separate,[15] but they are not entirely

---

9 *The Prince's Case* (1606) 8 Co.Rep. 1a; the old Scottish doctrine of desuetude went even further by inquiring whether an admitted statute was still valid. The strength of these cases is, however, affected by the arguments above set forth. See, too, Lord Pearce in *Bribery Commissioner* v. *Ranasinghe* [1965] A.C. 172 at 195, and the comments by Gray in (196*5*) 27 M.L.R. 705.

10 May, *Parliamentary Practice*, 17th ed., pp. 598–599; and see Cowen, "Legislature and Judiciary" (1953) 16 M.L.R. at p. 275.

11 Craies' *Statutes*, 5th ed., pp. 34 and 50; Heuston, *Essays in Constitutional Law*, 2nd ed., p. 16 *et seq.*; and Gray, "The Sovereignty of Parliament and the Entrenchment of the Legislative Process" (1965) 27 M.L.R. 705 *et seq.*, commenting on the *Bribery Commissioner* case.

12 *Mackenzie* v. *Stewart* (1754) 1 Pat. 578 and the cases cited in Craies' *Statutes*, 5th ed., p. 38 *et seq.*

13 The modern rules about how obviously inappropriate words in a statute are to be dealt with in the courts scarcely differ from similar rules governing the construction of wills.

14 In effect a conflict of opinion between the two Houses on this question underlies the Laying of Documents before Parliament (Interpretation) Act 1948, and the Act assumes limits to the proposition that courts cannot consider procedure in Parliament, as also does the Royal Assent Act 1967.

15 1953 S.C. at pp. 412–413.

independent. Once the possibility of invalidity is clearly recognised the compulsions to find a remedy are greatly increased. Moreover, as the National Insurance Act 1965, s. 116 (2), demonstrates, there is no radical inconsistency between the British habits of legislation and the existence of a power of judicial review even of primary legislation. Indeed, by a suitable combination of drafting techniques, it would be perfectly simple to build in an express Bill of Rights and an enduring power of judicial review by using that subsection as a precedent and combining it with a suitably drafted general enactment.

The issue of remedy. The problems of remedy are varied. Some remedies, interdict or injunction, for example, may involve a direct interference with the internal operations of Parliament, and there is a growing reluctance to grant such remedies, which, being discretionary, are much affected by subtle changes of attitude. Thus, success in *Trethowan* v. *Att.-Gen. for N.S.W.*[16] does not necessarily indicate a certainty of success elsewhere. Account must be taken in assessing probabilities not merely of the deference of one court for another, but also of the possibility of any post-enactment remedy. If that may exist the court may be much less ready to interfere in earlier stages, and vice versa.[17] Above all, account must be taken of the background of general theory against which judges must now work. The place of Parliament in legal thinking cannot be divorced from the place of Parliament in current political thinking. Political decisions are as far as possible to be taken in Parliament, and the growth of the democratic process since 1832 has obviously affected the attitude of the courts.[18] It equally must

---

[16] The ebb and flow in opinion in cases such as *Glasgow Insurance Committee* v. *Scottish Insurance Commissioners*, 1915 S.C. 504; *Russell* v. *Mags. of Hamilton* (1897) 25 R. 350; *Bell* v. *S. of S. for Scotland*, 1933 S.L.T. 519 indicates how variable opinion can be. See too *Harper* v. *Home Secretary* [1955] Ch. 238; *Merricks* v. *Heathcoat-Amory* [1955] Ch. 567 at 576; and *Bilston Corporation* v. *Wolverhampton Corporation* [1942] Ch. 391, and the cases referred to there and in (1943) 59 L.Q.R. 4; and also Sawer, "Injunction, Parliamentary Process and the Restriction of Parliamentary Competence" (1944) 60 L.Q.R. 83, and Cowen, "The Injunction and Parliamentary Process" (1955) 71 L.Q.R. 336. Compare with *Trethowan's* case *MacDonald* v. *Cain* [1953] V.L.R. 411 and *Hughes and Vale Pty. Co. Ltd.* v. *Gair* (1954) 90 C.L.R. 203. In the former the principle of respect of one court for another in this parliamentary context is evident in the opinion of Gavan Duffy J. The questions are further refined in *Clayton* v. *Heffron* (1960) 105 C.L.R. 214, where among other matters emphasis is placed on the importance of the concept of matters internal to Parliament.

[17] *Glasgow Insurance Committee* v. *Scottish Insurance Commissioners*, 1915 S.C. 504 at 511; *Hughes and Vale Pty. Co. Ltd.* v. *Gair* (1954) 90 C.L.R. 203; and *Clayton* v. *Heffron* (1960) 105 C.L.R. 214.

[18] This is clearly reflected in such opinions as that of Lord Normand in *Pollok School* v. *Glasgow Town Clerk*, 1946 S.C. 373 at 386, and though, in the same litigation, Lord Cooper thought that some of the earlier expressions might have gone too far (1947 S.C. 605 at 620) it is evident that such general constitutional changes have a pervasive influence on the law, and clearly influenced such writers as Hearn (who in turn affected Dicey). See his *Government in England*, particularly the first and last chapters. Earlier still this attitude is reflected in Brodie's note to Stair I, 1, 16 on

be remembered that the Acts of Union date from a different period, when natural law elements or the primacy of the common law were much stronger. Thus, despite what is said in *MacCormick's* case,[19] it seems highly doubtful whether the courts today either could or should set themselves up as an appellate court from Parliament to judge whether any alteration of the laws which concern private right is for the evident utility of the subjects within Scotland. Whether for good or ill modern constitutional thinking would regard such decisions as appropriate to a political arena. That was one of the difficulties facing the pursuer in *MacCormick's* case, and it is reflected in the argument about a title to sue. Where review at large of " governmental " statutes is concerned, as in a hypothetical case of a disregard of the provisions of the Ireland Act 1949, these difficulties may well be so great as to prevent any review. Where, however, challenge is more specific and individual [20] the authorities do not, when viewed in the light of modern trends, conclusively rule out any possibility of review. The possibility is perhaps stronger when the challenge is oblique, *e.g.*, it arises in an attempt to enforce upon an individual an Act which may be claimed to offend against some fundamental or limiting provision. Such a conflict of statutes is not inconceivable in relation, for example, to any future measure which might conflict with the Act for Securing the Protestant Religion in the limited sphere in which, it has been suggested, that Act is to be treated as fundamental.

Summary. The argument may, then, be summarised thus. A conjunction of influences produced at one time the concept of an unlimited Parliament, incapable of limiting itself. Since that time events and ideas have caused a reconsideration of this concept and of the authorities upon which it was based. These latter do not perhaps go as far as was at one time thought. Similarly, close examination of the problem of limitation has emphasised distinctions between the Acts of Union and subsequent Acts of the Union Parliament. Events elsewhere, notably in Australia, Canada, South Africa and Ceylon, have also prompted reconsideration of the issues raised by both initial and subsequent limitations

Desuetude: " It just amounts to this that though the Lords of Session derive all their authority from the legislature *as the supreme power*, they are entitled at their discretion to give effect to or disregard the very statutes devised by the power whence their own authority proceeds . . . at this rate the legislature is an absolute mockery " (italics supplied).

[19] 1953 S.C. 396 at 412.

[20] An individual interest was present, *e.g.*, in *MacDonald* v. *Cain* [1953] V.L.R. 411, but was closely scrutinised. In the *Senate* case (*Collins* v. *Minister of Interior*, 1957 (1) S.A. 552 (A.D.)), the most general of the South African cases, an individual interest was present since the challenge to the Senate Act was linked inseparably with the challenge to the South Africa Act Amendment Act which affected the appellants' right to vote. The changing pattern of thought in the United States, resulting in a restriction of the scope of the idea of what is a political question, should here be noticed; see, *e.g.*, *Baker* v. *Carr*, 369 U.S. 186 (1962). Those changes have not been without opposition, yet the Supreme Court has thus provided impulses which could not be provided by the purely political parts of the constitutional machinery.

upon Parliament. Patterns of evolution in continental Europe and the United States of America tend to the same effect. Indeed, one writer has commented of those states which have no judicial review: " They deprive themselves of the sobering and ennobling experience that befalls those who check their acts against their principles, and strive in performing the former never to lose sight of the latter." [21] Indeed, the United Kingdom, having accepted (albeit for a limited period) the compulsory jurisdiction of the European Court of Human Rights and the right of individuals to petition the European Commission of Human Rights, has already subjected domestic legislation to the possibility of judicial review, and in view of Article 26 of the Convention a good case could be made on grounds of convenience alone to consider a domestic tribunal which could effectively exercise functions in this field. These considerations coupled with continuing parliamentary practices make it impossible to adhere with certainty to the older principles in their simple form.

Correspondingly and consequentially the problem of judicial review has been reopened. It has been reopened because any shift in theory on the question of limitation necessarily requires a reconsideration of the problem of judicial review. That reconsideration is also prompted by changes in general thought on the place of parliamentary checks and on the role of judicial checks in the system of government. The system of government has grown so complex that parliamentary checks may not in a modern state have the perfection which was once attributed to them. Further, it has been shown in other countries that those checks alone may not, even leaving the complexity of the state aside, have the strength that was at one time thought. So again much more tentative answers must be given on judicial review, though it is believed that, if earlier authorities are examined critically, the possibility of such review is much stronger than would formerly have been allowed. In view of the lack of modern authority and of the shifts of opinion no concluded answer can be given. Such uncertainty need not excite surprise in this area of constitutional law since a like uncertainty exists in relation to many other of our central rules and institutions. Somewhat similar uncertainty exists, for example, about the position of the Cabinet, or the doctrines affecting it. Moreover, it appears that the accepted doctrines in relation to Parliament have, essentially, grown up as beliefs founded upon assertion rather more than upon proof. At lowest, therefore, they require reconsideration from time to time.

21 Cappelletti (1966) 79 Harvard L.R. 1224.

CHAPTER 5

THE LEGAL SETTING

WHAT has been discussed hitherto is the framework of general ideas. Before turning to the main institutions something must be said of the legal framework within which they operate. Two subjects fall under that head, the Acts of Union and the question of nationality.

THE ACTS OF UNION

It must be emphasised at the outset that the Union was a parliamentary one. The foundation consists of the two Acts of Union, the first passed by the Parliament of Scotland,[1] the second passed by the Parliament of England. The Parliament of Scotland had amended the Articles of Union as they had been agreed on by the Commissioners in minor ways and had added, as a fundamental part, the Act for Securing the Protestant Religion (since the question of the church was excluded from the remit of the Parliamentary Commissioners who negotiated the Union). The Scottish Act was not of itself operative, it only became so when the same terms were agreed to by the Parliament of England. That agreement followed without any amendment to the Scottish Act, save the addition of the Act for Securing the Church of England, the addition of which had been foreseen by the Parliament of Scotland. Thus the Union ultimately took effect on May 1, 1707. The process of inaugurating the new Kingdom was completed by the Act of the Parliament of Scotland settling the manner of electing the representative peers and the forty-five members of the new House of Commons in the Parliament of Great Britain,[2] and in England by the proclamation continuing the existing members for the new Parliament.

For the purposes of law it is these Acts which must be looked at. Not merely were the Articles of Union amended, but those Articles were of no effect unless absorbed in this legislative compact.[3] This is, more-

---

[1] A.P.S. XI, 414. For the history of these events see Dicey and Rait, *Thoughts on the Scottish Union*; Matheson, *Scotland and the Union*; Pryde, *The Treaty of Union*. The Minutes of the Proceedings of the Commissioners were separately printed by order of the House of Commons together with the original Articles of Union, and the Scottish Act which approved them as amended.

[2] A.P.S. XI, 425.

[3] See, however, T. B. Smith, "The Union of 1707 as Fundamental Law" [1957] *Public Law* 99, and his *Short Commentary on the Laws of Scotland*, where he treats this aspect of the agreement as a treaty; and see Sheriff K. W. B. Middleton, "New Thoughts on the Union" (1954) 66 J.R. 37, and J. T. Cameron, "Summoning the Estates," 1961 S.L.T.(News) 98.

over, consistent with a general treatment of treaties in our law. As has already been indicated, it is conceived that these Acts must be regarded as constituent documents, and that attitude is consistent both with their terminology, and with contemporaneous ideas. The constitutional framework which was thus established was, however, skeletal. This was inevitable. The art of drawing constitutions was still young, and indeed scarcely born. The circumstances of the Union made it desirable that the Commissioners should thus limit themselves. They confessed, when presenting their labours to the Queen, that " In these we have come to an agreement on every point we judged necessary to effect and complete a lasting Union, and we have endeavoured not to stir into any matter we had reason to think was not so." It was the intention that thereafter the Union should develop.

For the moment it must suffice to indicate the main parts of that skeleton. To a considerable extent the importance of the Union and its consequences must be judged in the non-legal worlds of economics, politics and sociology, and the present concern is not with them. Within the realm of law, many of the effects of the Union are incidental to the development which followed the Union. Those effects are to be seen in the fields of private as well as public law, and again the effects upon private law do not fall to be discussed here.[4] In the field of public law the consequences of the Union have been many and detailed, and a full examination of them would be out of place at this point, and confusing.[5] These effects, coupled with the problem of how united is the United Kingdom established in 1707, can only be studied as they arise over the whole field of law.

The Union. What must here be looked at is the framework which was established in 1707. The Acts established (Arts. I and II) the new Kingdom by the name of Great Britain with one Crown to descend according to the rules of the Act of Settlement, and by Article III established the one Parliament. By Article IV there was conferred upon all subjects full freedom of trade and equal privileges throughout the whole Kingdom and annexed dominions. Just as the political union in Articles I to III was regarded as of the utmost importance by the English Commissioners, so was the free trade provision of Article IV

---

[4] Frequent references to these effects are to be found in T. B. Smith, *Short Commentary on the Laws of Scotland*, and in the same author's Hamlyn Lectures, *British Justice: the Scottish Contribution*, and his *Studies Critical and Comparative*. It must, however, be remembered that the effects are not all on one side. Few English lawyers remember that (in these references) *Donoghue* v. *Stevenson* [1932] A.C. 562 or *Institute of Patent Agents* v. *Lockwood* [1894] A.C. 347 were Scottish cases. See too, *e.g.*, *Abbott* v. *Philbin* [1960] Ch. 27; [1961] A.C. 352; and 76 L.Q.R. 182.

[5] See, as one example only, Mitchell, " The Royal Prerogative in Modern Scots Law " [1957] *Public Law* 304. The influence of the Union working through the new Court of Exchequer (which was itself a consequence of the Union) had, it is believed, a marked effect upon prerogative rules. As to the economic background and consequences see Smout, " The Anglo-Scottish Union of 1707," *Economic History Review* (1964), p. 454, and Campbell in the same number at p. 468.

similarly regarded by the Scots. That general provision was supplemented by others. Article VI provided that for ever after all parts of
the Kingdom should have the same allowances, encouragements and
drawbacks, and be under the same prohibitions, restrictions and regulations of trade and liable to the same customs and duties, as well as (Art.
VII) the same excises. Thus the free trade provisions were backed by
provisions for equal treatment in trading matters.[6] One provision in
particular had curious effects. Article XVIII provided that the laws
concerning the regulation of trade, customs and such excises to which
Scotland was by virtue of the Treaty to be liable should be the same in
Scotland from and after the Union as in England. This provision led
to the uniformity of patent law, and some expressions in the cases imply
that it was intended to make uniform all mercantile law.[7] It is now
clear that such an interpretation is no longer possible.

This group of provisions did provoke some litigation, particularly in
the context of the rights of royal burghs,[8] but it is on the whole surprising
that more was not provoked, since they contain the germs of such litigation as has flourished upon like provisions in the constitutions of either
Australia or the United States. One reason may be the ambiguities of
drafting. Despite the provision for uniformity of "encouragements
and drawbacks" and regulation in Article VI, a lack of uniformity was
elsewhere either provided for or contemplated as a possibility. In some
cases the provisions were temporary, notably the transitional provisions
as to various duties.[9] Similarly, Article XV, dealing with the Equivalent
(essentially the sum due to Scotland by reason of the fact that from the
Union Scotland would assume the burden of servicing a "united"
national debt of which proportionately the much greater part would be
attributable to the former English national debt), provided for special
investment in Scotland. That Article provided that a portion of the
Equivalent should be used for the encouragement of the manufacture of
coarse wool and for encouraging and promoting fisheries and such other
manufactures in Scotland as would be conducive to the general good.
However, subsequent legislation, starting with the Fisheries (Scotland)
Act 1726, establishing Commissioners to manage those funds, provided
too that they should also manage any other sums which might thereafter be provided, thus contemplating further payments for the benefit

---

6 These provisions, which endure, were supported by other transitional provisions, *e.g.*,
 as to the taxes upon meat and salt, and other matters in Arts. X–XIV. Some of
 these provisions were of immediate consequence, *e.g.*, as to the Malt Tax; see Dicey
 and Rait, *op. cit.* p. 284 *et seq.*
7 *Nielson* v. *Househill Coal and Iron Co.* (1842) 4 D. 470.
8 *Smith* v. *Guildry of Inverness* (1757) Mor. 1952; *Aboyne* v. *Magistrates of Edinburgh*
 (1774) Mor. 1972; *Morison* v. *Connell*, June 24, 1801, F.C.; but see *Incorporated
 Trades of Aberdeen* v. *Magistrates of Aberdeen*, May 28, 1793, F.C., in which it is
 said that the Articles of Union were not intended to affect the rights of private parties.
9 *e.g.*, Arts. IX, X, XI.

of Scotland.[10] Moreover, Article XIV (dealing with the issue of exemptions from duties) runs: " Seeing it cannot be supposed that the Parliament of Great Britain will ever lay any sorts of burthens upon the United Kingdom, but what they shall find of necessity at that time for the preservation and good of the whole, and with due regard to the circumstances and abilities of every part of the United Kingdom," and thus appears to contemplate a differentiation according to need of parts considered as parts of the whole Kingdom. This attitude is reflected in the Manufactures Improvement Fund (Scotland) Act 1847. What appears to be ruled out is differentiation based simply upon the fact that a preference is given for or against a particular area as being Scotland or England. It would thus be difficult to challenge, *e.g.*, the element of subsidy in dealing with the air services in the Highlands and Islands, since this is dictated by the peculiarities of the region and not by the fact that those areas are Scottish. On this basis any challenge to economic legislation as being discriminatory, while not impossible, is difficult to conceive.[11]

These economic provisions were backed by revenue provisions designed to produce a uniformity in revenue law, and (Art. XIX) a uniform system of enforcement. That Article contemplated the establishment of a new Court of Exchequer in Scotland having the same power and authority as the same court in England. The intent of this Article was carried out by the Exchequer Court (Scotland) Act 1707, creating the new court and directing it (with certain exceptions) to proceed upon the basis of the Court of Exchequer in England.[12] These provisions, particularly when coupled with measures to increase the efficiency of the collection of the revenue, inevitably produced unrest, and yet they were the necessary complement of the " free trade " provisions.[13]

The institutional provisions. Apart from establishing the common institutions to which reference has already been made, the Acts provided (Art. XXIV) for a Great Seal of the United Kingdom and a Seal of Scotland for use in connection with private rights or grants applicable within Scotland. More importantly Article XIX provided that the Court of Session and the Court of Justiciary should remain in all time coming within Scotland with their existing authority and privileges, subject to regulation by Parliament for the better administration of

[10] For an outline of the development of these Commissioners embracing fish and fine art see the appendix to Milne, *The Scottish Office*. For arguments about the use of these funds see Ferguson, " The Making of the Treaty of Union 1707," Scot.Hist.Rev., XLIII, p. 89.

[11] The general economic consequences of the Union cannot here be discussed; see Pryde, *A New History of Scotland*, Vol. II, and Report on Scottish Financial and Trade Statistics (1952) Cmd. 8609.

[12] A provision still capable of producing uncertainty: *Barrs* v. *I.R.C.*, 1961 S.C.(H.L.) 22.

[13] See too Art. XVII, standardising weights and measures, and Art. XVI, standardising coinage; as to banknotes, see Holden, *History of Negotiable Instruments*, and 461 H.C.Deb. 178–179.

justice. The Court of Admiralty was preserved for the time being,[14] as were other courts in Scotland. By Article XX heritable offices and jurisdictions were preserved in the same manner as they were then enjoyed, and (Art. XXI) the rights and privileges of the royal burghs were to remain, notwithstanding the Treaty. These latter privileges have been greatly abbreviated and, in any important sense, abolished. The heritable jurisdictions were abolished (by means of purchase) in 1746. These last two provisions lack the eternal element that is to be seen in Article XIX, and it was inevitable that the changing patterns of government should be reflected in their amendment or repeal, just as changing conditions have been reflected in reforms of the Court of Session and Court of Justiciary. The preservation of these courts, which implied the preservation of a system of law, was further protected by the provision in Article XIX that no causes in Scotland should be cognoscible by the Courts of Chancery, Queen's Bench, Common Pleas or any other court in Westminster Hall, and that those English courts should have no power to review the sentences of any judicatures within Scotland. It is in these provisions that the federal desires of the Scottish Commissioners appear and survive. The protection of this system of courts was undoubtedly essential to the approval of the Union Agreement in the Parliament of Scotland, and, as has been seen, that protection (in principle though not in detail) has been treated as of particular significance.[15]

The provisions relating to the new Parliament are significant in that Article XXII ensured a bicameral legislature, in which Scottish representation was fixed in both Houses. The number of members of the House of Commons was one of the matters which caused most dispute between the Commissioners and after a conference the Scottish proposal of forty-five was accepted. The number of representative peers was fixed as a proportion of the number of members of the Commons.[16] Other stipulations were included in Articles XXII and XXIII governing the privileges of both the representative peers and other peers of Scotland but the manner of election was left to be regulated by the Parliament of Scotland. It appears, therefore, that the essential element in these Articles is merely the principle of adequate representation. The number of representatives in the House of Commons has been increased, and under the House of Commons (Redistribution of Seats) Acts 1949–58 is not to be less than seventy-one. Nor does it appear that the machinery for the election of the representative peers is to be regarded as essential to the Union Agreement. Thus, although the contrary has been argued,[17]

---

[14] See Walker, *Introduction to the Scottish Legal System.*
[15] See, *e.g.,* the reservations of Lord Russell in *MacCormick* v. *Lord Advocate*, 1953 S.C. 396 at 417, and Chap. 4, *ante.* As to the evolution of the courts, see Chap. 14, *post.*
[16] See proceedings on June 15, 1706.
[17] See the opinion of the Lord Lyon (1962–63) H.C. 38, H.L. 23, App. 14. As to the admission of these peers see First and Second Reports from the Committee for Privileges (1964–65) H.L. 11 at 33.

the abolition of these elections with the admission of all peers of Scotland to the House of Lords by the Peerage Act 1963, s. 4, cannot be regarded as a breach of the Acts of Union. The provisions as to the church were marked out in a particular way in the Acts, and may properly be regarded as fundamental to the Union scheme at least in so far as the Church of Scotland is concerned, and the sense in which this entrenchment should, it is thought, be read has already been discussed.[18]

The provision as to law. The Scottish Commissioners had insisted upon the maintenance of a distinct system of law, and although (as has been seen) provision was made for the uniformity of the laws concerning the regulation of trade, the laws contemplated by that provision do not comprise the whole of mercantile law, but are rather those concerning the regulation of exports and imports. All other laws of either Kingdom were by Article XVIII to remain in force, save such as were inconsistent with the Treaty, but they were to be alterable by the new Parliament. Some of the difficulties of this provision have already been noted in the context of the sources of law. It should here be again noted that this attribution of legislative competence is modified by the provisions in Article XVIII which contemplated the possibility of the unification of the laws concerning " publick right policy and civil government," but which provided that " no alteration be made in the laws which concern private right, except for evident utility of the subjects within Scotland." The definitions of what is public right and what is private right must, it seems, be taken to be those which would be acceptable today (such an interpretation follows from the acceptance of the Acts as constituent documents). It is to be doubted whether the issue of " evident utility " can be debated anywhere outside Parliament. Such a question would fall within the category of " political issues " with which courts have an almost overwhelming reluctance to meddle.[19]

Later legislative history. The Acts of Union have not remained untouched by Parliament.[20] Immediately after the Union, a series of measures, notably the Toleration Act 1711,[21] the Yule Vacance Act 1711, the Patronage Act 1711, the imposition of the Malt Tax, the

---

[18] *Ante*, p. 72.

[19] See, however, T. B. Smith, *Studies Critical and Comparative* at p. 18. The machinery for dealing with Scottish legislation in the House of Commons to be discussed later should be borne in mind.

[20] A current text taken from the Statutes Revised is presented in the Appendix to T. B. Smith, *Short Commentary*. The process of amendment has been inelegant to say the least. With the exception of the Statute Law Revision (Scotland) Act 1906, the Statute Law Revision Acts have referred to the English Act, and not to the Scots Act. This process has produced minor variations in the provisions of the respective Acts which are still extant, but these variations do not appear to be constitutionally significant. The Statute Law Revision (Scotland) Act 1964 has produced uniformity.

[21] For views on this see Burleigh, *A Church History of Scotland*, pp. 277–279; and see Pryde, *The Treaty of Union*, Chap. IV, and *A New History of Scotland*, Vol. II, Chap. V, and Dicey and Rait, *Thoughts on the Union*, Chap. VII.

introduction of the English law of treason, and the abolition of the Scottish Privy Council, all combined to create a dislike of the Union, and some went near to conflicting with the terms (as well as the spirit) of the Union compact, but it is doubtful if any can legally be regarded as a breach. For reasons given earlier, it is doubtful if the abolition of the tests prescribed in the Act for Securing the Protestant Religion can be regarded as a breach.

Those provisions which have been repealed consist of the transitional provisions, mainly of a fiscal nature, those which are spent such as the greater part of Article XXII dealing with the first meeting of the new Parliament, and others such as that part of Article XVI dealing with the maintenance of the Mint in Scotland which were caused by changed circumstances. Alteration of the effect of some of those provisions which remain is contemplated as with Article XXIII (the privileges of peers) or Article XXIV (the Seals). Other provisions such as those providing for the uniformity of coinage or excise in no way inhibit alterations of the law, and in other cases such as the preservation of the rights of royal burghs or of heritable offices it is clear from a reading of the negotiations that the provisions were not intended to be unalterable. What remain are the provisions relating to the courts and the church and the counterbalancing provisions relating to the unitary institutions of Crown and Parliament and those relating to freedom and equality of trade. In relation to the former group the element of entrenchment is apparent.[22] In relation to the second group it is clear from a reading of the Union compact and its negotiations that they form the foundation of the new Kingdom proposed in 1706, and that consequently any alteration in respect of them would amount to the substitution of a new constitutional foundation.

NATIONALITY [23]

The Acts of Union did not themselves deal with the issue of nationality, speaking simply of the subjects of the United Kingdom, since the new Kingdom necessarily involved a new nationality. Under the Union of the Crowns from 1603 to 1707 the position of those born owing allegiance to the common sovereign was that they were not to be treated as aliens in either Kingdom.[24] After the Union of 1707 the citizens of each of the former Kingdoms were citizens of the new United Kingdom. Difficulties, however, arose from the existence of pre-Union statutes which opened up possibilities of limited or more general naturalisation of foreigners. The effect of Article XXV of the Acts of Union upon these

---

22 Thus in relation to the courts some matters are marked off as capable of alteration, and the implication as to other parts has been accepted. See Chap. 4, *ante*.

23 See, generally, Clive Parry, *Nationality and Citizenship Laws*. What follows here is merely an outline, the detailed complexities may be pursued in that exhaustive work.

24 *Calvin's Case* (1608) 7 Co.Rep. 1a; and A.P.S. IV, 366.

is not clear. On the one hand, it was held in a Scottish case that Acts such as that which naturalised partners in the Bank of Scotland were repealed as inconsistent with the Act of Union.[25] On the other, it was held in *Att.-Gen.* v. *Ernest Augustus Prince of Hanover* [26] that the Act of 1705 naturalising the descendants of the Electress Sophia (which was not expressly repealed until 1948) had the effect of making the respondent a British subject, even though the Act, being a pre-Union statute, was couched in terms of English nationality. The Act of 1705 had certain peculiarities not shared by the other legislation, and may, in any event, be regarded as exceptional.[27]

After the Union, the concept of a universal nationality based upon allegiance to a common sovereign continued to operate in the expanding Empire and Commonwealth until the development of the Common-wealth showed that that concept without further addition could cause inconvenience and was inconsistent with the idea of member states in the Commonwealth. It was reasonable that the new member states of the Commonwealth should control their own citizenship laws.[28] In 1947 a Commonwealth conference recommended [29] that each member state should have the right of defining its own citizens, but that an element of universality should be preserved by means of the concept of a British subject or Commonwealth citizen. The status of British subject or Commonwealth citizenship would follow automatically from the grant of local citizenship, and would confer advantages in each state, in that the citizen of another Commonwealth state would have a higher status than an alien.

This plan was only partially implemented because of subsequent events, notably the departure of the Republic of Ireland from the Commonwealth. As a result of that and of other events there emerged the concept of reciprocal citizenship, which appealed more strongly than did the 1947 scheme to some members of the Commonwealth, particu-larly to the new republics. Any discussion of the citizenship laws of the individual states of the Commonwealth would be out of place here. What follows is an outline of the law as it operates in the United Kingdom.

The basis of that law is the British Nationality Act 1948.[30] That Act created the citizenship of the United Kingdom and Colonies,[31]

---

[25] *Macao* v. *Officers of State* (1822) 1 Shaw App. 138. On this and the following case see T. B. Smith, *Studies Critical and Comparative*, p. 21 *et seq.*, and the authorities there cited.   [26] [1957] A.C. 436.

[27] It should, however, be noted that, in the House of Lords, it was made clear that no opinion was there expressed on the effect of the Acts of Union on the Act of 1705: see [1957] A.C. 436 at 464 and 472.

[28] This had already been recognised by the Imperial Conference of 1930; see Cmd. 3479.

[29] Cmd. 7326.

[30] Which is amended by the British Nationality Act 1958 and the subsequent Acts of 1964 and 1965, the whole forming the British Nationality Acts 1948 to 1965, to take account of further developments in the Commonwealth.

[31] In the case of Channel Islanders and Manxmen the term " citizens of the United Kingdom Islands and Colonies " may be used.

which is at the same time the local citizenship of the United Kingdom
and the residual citizenship in the Commonwealth, that is to say, it is a
citizenship possessed by those British subjects who do not have another
" local " citizenship. It was the generality of this citizenship which in
part caused the difficulties lying behind the Commonwealth Immigrants
Act 1968. Such citizenship may under the terms of the 1948 Act be
acquired by birth, by descent, by naturalisation or by registration.
Registration was a new procedure to enable citizens of a Commonwealth
country or of the Republic of Ireland to acquire this local citizenship,
and (in the great majority of cases) such registration is a matter of right,
not of discretion as is naturalisation. The original conditions for the
acquisition of citizenship by registration contained in the 1948 Act (s. 6)
were increased and made somewhat more onerous by the Commonwealth
Immigrants Act 1962 (s. 12), and in one case a discretionary element was
introduced by that Act.[32] Similarly, the grounds for the revocation of
registration are much more limited than those for the revocation of
naturalisation.

The detailed conditions governing the acquisition and loss of citizenship should be sought in the Acts, but it may be noted that the Act of
1948 aided the acquisition of double nationality. Naturalisation in a
foreign country does not of itself cause loss of United Kingdom citizenship or British nationality. That effect only follows if a declaration of
renunciation is made under section 19. Similarly, a woman on marriage
to an alien does not lose her British nationality, but may renounce it.

So far as our constitutional law is concerned British nationality (or
Commonwealth citizenship) is a concept of greater importance than
citizenship of the United Kingdom and Colonies. Under Part I of the
1948 Act all citizens of the United Kingdom and Colonies together with
the citizens of all countries mentioned in section 1 (3) of the Act (i.e., the
member states of the Commonwealth) are British subjects. That list of
countries serves a double purpose. It carries out the 1947 scheme for
those Commonwealth countries which adhered to it and carries out
the reciprocal scheme as far as the United Kingdom is concerned in
relation to appropriate countries. As new members of the Commonwealth emerge the list is amended.[33] Our own important legislation
is drawn in terms of British nationality and not of United Kingdom
citizenship. Thus section 1 of the Representation of the People Act
1949 confers the right to vote (subject to the qualifications of the general
electoral scheme) upon British subjects, and the same qualification
applies to Members of Parliament. The surviving limitations in the
Aliens Act 1914 and the Aliens Restriction (Amendment) Act 1919 have,

---

32 See note 41 below.
33 See, e.g., s. 2 of the Uganda Independence Act 1962 and s. 1 of the South Africa
Act 1962 to delete the mention of South Africa by reason of that country leaving the
Commonwealth.

of course, no application.[34] Hence a British subject as defined in the 1948 Act has all the civic rights of a citizen of the United Kingdom.

The civic rights are somewhat further extended. Although the Republic of Ireland has left the Commonwealth, neither history nor current feelings made that break easy to achieve. The break occurred after the 1948 Act (which had continued certain citizens of Eire as British subjects and for the rest had provided that other citizens of Eire should not be treated as aliens) and the Ireland Act 1949 attempted to regulate the situation as far as this country is concerned; section 5 of the Ireland Act contains particular provisions as to the operation of the British Nationality Act. These were, however, inadequate to deal with the complex situation which was made yet more complex by the 1949 Act. On the one hand it provided that that part of Ireland formerly known as Eire was no longer part of Her Majesty's dominions, but on the other it was also declared by section 2 that the Republic of Ireland was not a foreign country. Thus, citizens of that Republic are in a twilight world, being neither aliens [35] nor British subjects, and they may acquire citizenship of the United Kingdom by registration. The Ireland Act continued existing legislation in force as if the Act had not been passed, and so citizens of the Irish Republic were held to fall under the National Service legislation.[36] Continuing this somewhat ambiguous but convenient legislative policy section 1 of the Representation of the People Act 1949 gives the right to vote to citizens of the Republic of Ireland who, since they are not aliens, may also be elected to the House of Commons and be members of the House of Lords if they hold a peerage other than an Irish one.[37]

The Commonwealth Immigrants Act. One result of the adherence of the United Kingdom to the theory of universal nationality in the Commonwealth [38] was that no British subject could be refused admission to, or deported from, the United Kingdom [39] even though that was not his country of origin. This situation was altered by the Commonwealth

---

[34] The limitations on the civil employment under the Crown of aliens contained in that Act and s. 6 of the Act of Settlement 1700 are made less rigid by the Aliens Employment Act 1955.

[35] See the definition of aliens: s. 32 of the British Nationality Act 1948, which is continued in force by the Ireland Act 1949.

[36] *Bicknell* v. *Brosnan* [1953] 2 Q.B. 77.

[37] The story is made more complicated by the fact that the Republic does not recognise the division of Ireland, and by reason of the relationship of Northern Ireland to the Republic special rules are made by the Ireland Act 1949, s. 6, as to the qualifications of electors in constituencies in Northern Ireland. Such matters should be pursued in Clive Parry, *op. cit.*

[38] This adherence was much firmer than it was elsewhere in the Commonwealth.

[39] Certain accused persons can be dealt with under the Fugitive Offenders Act. The Act of 1881 caused difficulty in recent times; see 674 H.C.Deb. 581 and *Armah* v. *Government of Ghana* [1966] 3 All E.R. 117. It has been replaced by the Fugitive Offenders Act 1967, based on an agreement of the Commonwealth Law Ministers; see Cmnd. 3008.

Immigrants Act 1962. Part I, which (in the first instance) was to continue in force only until December 31, 1963, unless extended, as it has
been by subsequent Expiring Laws Continuance Acts, rendered possible
the exclusion of Commonwealth citizens other than those born in the
United Kingdom or those holding a United Kingdom passport and
who are citizens of the United Kingdom and Colonies, or who hold
such a passport issued in the United Kingdom or Republic of Ireland.
This provision, relating to citizens of the United Kingdom and Colonies
and those who hold a United Kingdom passport, was thought to create
difficulties in the case of inhabitants of a new member state of the
Commonwealth who could not take, or did not choose to take, citizenship of that state and thus retained both United Kingdom citizenship
and passport. Under the Act of 1962 no control could be exercised
over the immigration to the United Kingdom of such persons. So, the
Commonwealth Immigrants Act 1968 extended control to such persons
unless there was a link with the United Kingdom, *i.e.,* that he or one of
his parents or grandparents was born in the United Kingdom or was
naturalised or adopted there, or became a citizen of the United Kingdom
by registration in the United Kingdom or one of the countries in section
1 (3) of the British Nationality Act 1948. The power to refuse admission
is further limited in the case of those who are ordinarily resident in the
United Kingdom, or have been so resident in the past two years, or
those who hold an employment voucher or wish to enter for the purpose
of study,[40] and the Act of 1968 has also limited the power to refuse
entry to persons under sixteen whose parents are resident in the United
Kingdom or are seeking entry with him. Thus although citizenship of
the United Kingdom and Colonies became an important factor (and of
increased importance when coupled with the element of locality under
the 1968 Act), it has not become the exclusive governing factor. Part II
of the Act (which is permanent) authorises the deportation of Commonwealth citizens who have been convicted of criminal offences punishable
by imprisonment and who are recommended for deportation by a
court.[41] The power does not apply to a person born in the United
Kingdom, or whose father was so born or whose parents were ordinarily
resident in the United Kingdom at the time of his birth. Nor does it

---

[40] See s. 2. The Act is supplemented by the instructions to Immigration Officers
published as (1962) Cmnd. 1716 which were replaced by new instructions in 1966
(Cmnd. 3064). For its general operation see the *Report of the Committee on
Immigration Appeals* (1967) Cmnd. 3387. Fresh instructions (Cmnd. 3552) are being
issued under the 1968 Act. That Act strengthened various aspects of the control
introduced in 1962, *e.g.,* as to health under s. 2, or as to those who gain unauthorised
entry (s. 4).

[41] It may be noted that this question of deportation is decided by the Home Secretary,
who has general control over aliens and over immigration. The conditions under
which a recommendation or deportation order may be made are given in ss. 7–10.
Where a recommendation for deportation or a deportation order is in force the right
of a Commonwealth citizen to be registered as a citizen of the United Kingdom is
suspended though the Secretary of State *may* nevertheless so register. See generally
Rogerson, " Deportation " [1963] *Public Law* 305, and (1962–63) H.C. 293.

apply to a citizen of the United Kingdom who becomes such by naturalisation here, by being adopted, or by registration, or is the wife of any such person.[42] General principles have been enunciated (at any rate as far as England is concerned) by the Court of Criminal Appeal on the application of the Act.[43]

Protected persons. There is one further group which should be noted of those who are, in strictness, neither aliens nor British subjects. By section 32 of the British Nationality Act 1948, British protected persons are declared not to be aliens for the purpose of the Act. The British Protectorates, Protected States and Protected Persons Order 1949 [44] defines those who, by reason of their connection with protectorates or protected states or trust territory, are British protected persons. Such persons are by the Aliens Employment Act 1955 exempted from the limitation in civil employment under the Crown contained in the Aliens Restriction (Amendment) Act 1919. Under the British Nationality Act 1948, protected persons may apply for naturalisation if they comply with the conditions applicable to registration by Commonwealth citizens,[45] and to that extent they are preferred to aliens, but their position resembles that of aliens in that naturalisation remains discretionary. Under the Commonwealth Immigrants Act 1962, both Part I and Part II (dealing with immigrants and deportation) apply to British protected persons, as they do to Commonwealth citizens. British protected persons do not, however, have the right to vote in United Kingdom elections; in that they are farther from being British subjects than citizens of the Republic of Ireland.

[42] s. 6.

[43] *R.* v. *Edgehill* [1963] 1 Q.B. 593; see, too, *R.* v. *Kelly* [1966] 3 All E.R. 282 and *R.* v. *Lynch* [1965] 3 All E.R. 925.

[44] S.I. 1949 No. 140.

[45] The conditions are amended by, and set out in, Commonwealth Immigrants Act 1962, s. 12.

Part Two

THE INSTITUTIONS

CHAPTER 6

PARLIAMENT—THE STRUCTURE

Introduction. It is reasonable to take 1707 as the starting-point, since
it is evident that the authors of the Union settlement conceived of the
first Union Parliament as something new and distinct, a view which
was shared by those concerned with its working.[1] In its working it was
natural that, for many reasons, the new Parliament should inherit much
from the English Parliament. Most obviously the locality of the new
Parliament and the fact that the majority of its members were familiar
with the ways of the old English Parliament were strong inducements.[2]
There were other reasons. While the Parliament of Scotland had grown
in stature very rapidly between 1688 and 1707 and the practices of the
two Parliaments had tended to grow alike,[3] it was true that privileges of
Parliament *vis-à-vis* both Crown and courts were stronger and more
deeply rooted in England than in Scotland. It was, then, natural that
the more extensive of the old rules of privilege should be taken as the
basis of the new rules,[4] just as it was natural that the more highly
developed procedure of the English Parliament should continue.[5] The
bicameral nature of the new Parliament (which was envisaged by the
Acts of Union), as compared with the unicameral character of the Parliament of Scotland, made the break clear to the Scottish members, but
held no novelty for the English. The result was that to a large extent
Parliament in its internal aspects presented an appearance of continuity
with the English Parliaments.[6] Outside the House there were of course

[1] See Hatsell, *Precedents*, 3rd ed., II, p. 41, the case of Asgill, and the tenor of the
Royal Proclamation relating to the new Parliament, and the terms of the Acts of
Union themselves.

[2] This was strengthened by the fact that the members of the last pre-Union English
Parliament were continued as members of the first post-Union Parliament. Thus,
on the first day, reference was made to earlier English precedents; see *House of
Commons Journal*, Oct. 23, 1707, in relation to the election of the Speaker.

[3] See, *e.g.*, on the methods of determining disputed elections Rait, *Parliaments of
Scotland*, pp. 309–312; Terry, *The Scottish Parliament*, p. 125.

[4] The wider extent was apparent in two ways. The individual member was in England
better protected from his creditors; see *Molison* v. *Clarke* (1707) Mor. 10398,
Stair III, 1, 37, and members were better protected against the Crown: Rait, *op. cit.*
p. 525; Lockhart, *Disquisition upon Peerage*, p. 12. Both extensions might be
welcome to members: *Livingston* v. *Morison* (1710) Mor. 8565, II Fount 526 and
Lady Greenock v. *Sir John Shaw* (1709) Mor. 8563.

[5] These procedural points were important. The relative lack of procedural development
had been one of the great causes of weakness in the Parliament of Scotland.

[6] Aided by statutes which extended older English rules to the new Parliament such as
the Succession to the Crown Act 1707, s. 29 (membership) and s. 7 extending to the
United Kingdom the Triennial Act 1694 (6 & 7 Will. 3, c. 2). These extensions
were liberally treated: see *Connell on Elections*, p. 287, which takes the former

differences. The elections of the Scottish representative peers distinguished them from their fellows, and the old Scottish electoral system
continued until 1832 for the Commons. Slowly a degree of uniformity
has been established, partly as a result of legislation, but also as a
result of judicial action. This change is not solely attributable to the
Union. In the years immediately before the Union the Parliament of
Scotland had greatly developed. It had used effectively such weapons
as the denial of supply [7] in an assertion of its independence, and by
other means had sought to increase its power over the executive.
Equally it had asserted stronger claims to the control of its own
privileges. It was then natural to adopt the habits of a Parliament in
which these matters had been pushed still further and in so doing there
was a continuity with the later years of the Parliament of Scotland. It is
thus understandable that the law of the United Kingdom Parliament
should draw heavily on English pre-Union precedents, though the scope
of application of some may have to be examined.

It will be convenient if Parliament is discussed under the headings
of Composition, Privileges, Functions and that thereafter its relationship
to the executive be examined.

THE HOUSE OF LORDS

The House of Lords now consists of five groups: (1) peers of the United
Kingdom; (2) the peers of Scotland; (3) peers spiritual; (4) Lords of
Appeal in Ordinary; (5) life peers. Formerly there were also representative peers of Ireland, but after 1922 there was no machinery for the
election of such representatives. Since formerly they had been elected
for life the then members of the House continued, the last, Lord
Kilmorey, dying in 1961, and the report in 1962 on reform of the House
did not recommend the admission of peers of Ireland and the Peerage
Act 1963 did not alter their situation. Subsequently the House of Lords
rejected a petition from certain Irish peers asking that the system of
representation be reactivated, and held that the right to elect no longer
exists. Thus doubts as to the position of Irish peers seem to have been
finally put to rest.[8]

Peers of the United Kingdom. The largest group is that of peers
of the United Kingdom (including peeresses in their own right), under
which title may be comprised the holders of peerages of England (whose
rights to sit in the House of Lords of the Parliament of Great Britain

provision as including the English pre-Union legislation on bribery. These first
provisions have not always been noticed by the House of Commons: Report of
Select Committee on Elections (1955) H.C.P. 35.
[7] It was thus that the Act for Security of the Kingdom (A.P.S. XI, 130, 136) was
forced through.
[8] See 278 H.L.Deb. 363 and the Report of the Committee for Privileges (1966–67) H.L.
53. See too Lord Dunboyne, " Irish Representative Peers: Counsel's Opinion 1924 "
[1967] *Public Law* 314.

were continued by Article XXII of the Acts of Union 1707), of peerages of Great Britain created between 1707 and the Union with Ireland in 1800, and of peerages of the United Kingdom created thereafter, all of whom are entitled to a writ of summons unless disqualified. The modern method of creating a peer is by letters patent, but the most ancient peerages may owe their origin to a writ of summons. Provided that the summons was to a full Parliament and that the seat was taken thereunder,[9] it came to be accepted that there was a hereditary right to receive such a writ vested in the heirs at common law of the original recipient. Under the more modern form of creation by letters patent, the critical date at which a peerage becomes fully effective is the indorsement of the Lord Chancellor.[10] The letters patent, in the normal form, equally create an inheritable right to a writ of summons, but they may designate a particular line of succession, e.g., including heirs female, provided that the designation would be valid as a limitation of real property in England at common law.[11] The modern cases in which this proposition is asserted have, however, involved English pre-Union peerages, and the effect of the Union is not entirely clear. The rules for the descent of Scottish peerages are many and varied,[12] and differ substantially from the English ones, and limitations exist which would be invalid by the latter rules.[13] It is not clear whether the pre-Union English rules have now become universal or whether a grant in appropriate terms of art to a person domiciled in Scotland (or where for other reasons there are particular Scottish connections), might not be valid if it would be good by Scots law. If so the rule in the *Buckhurst* case may be of a more limited application than appears at first sight.[14]

Whilst, in origin, peerage was linked with tenure, peerage by tenure was rejected from fairly early times.[15] Moreover, while at one time the Crown, as the fountain of honour, had full liberty in the grant of peerages, it is now recognised that " by a firmly based constitutional convention " letters patent may only issue to a consenting party.[16] Once

---

[9] The *St. John Peerage Case* [1915] A.C. 282 and the *Clifton Peerage Case* (1673) Collins' *Claims* 291.

[10] Hatsell, *Precedents*, II, p. 392 *et seq.*

[11] *Buckhurst Peerage Case* (1876) 2 App.Cas. 1; *Wiltes Peerage Case* (1869) L.R. 4 H.L. 126.

[12] See *post*, p. 112.

[13] *e.g.*, those relating to the Earldom of Selkirk or in modern times the grant in 1861 of the dignity of Countess of Cromarty to the Duchess of Sutherland. See, too, Lord Colonsay in the *Wiltes Peerage Case* (1869) L.R. 4 H.L. at p. 169 and Riddell's *Peerage Law*, I, pp. 184 *et seq.*, 561 *et seq.*; and see Lord Hughes, 287 H.L.Deb. 1392.

[14] It must be remembered that the Committee for Privileges tendering advice is not bound by precedent in the way in which the House is when sitting as a court: (1869) L.R. 4 H.L. at p. 147, *per* Lord Chelmsford.

[15] The *Berkeley Peerage Case* (1861) 8 H.L.Cas. 21 at 83; the *Fitzwalter Peerage Case* (1669) Collins' *Claims* 268. In Scotland elements of the concept of peerage by tenure endured, for a variety of reasons, rather longer and more strongly than was the case in England; see Rait, *Parliaments of Scotland*, p. 177.

[16] *Re Bristol S.E. Election* [1961] 3 All E.R. 354 at 370.

created, however, a peerage by English law could not be surrendered [17] (though Scottish peerages were capable of surrender, either *in favorem* or *ad remanientiam*) and it seems that this doctrine applies to peerages of Great Britain or of the United Kingdom.[18] Now, by the Peerage Act 1963, anyone inheriting a peerage may disclaim it within twelve months of inheritance or of attaining full age (or within one month if he is a member of the Commons or a parliamentary candidate). Such disclaimer divests that person (and his wife) of all rights, and relieves from any disabilities, flowing from peerage; but it does not affect the right of his heir to inherit in due time.

Issues of peerage are determined by the Committee for Privileges of the House of Lords upon a reference by the Crown. It is that body which will in effect determine (though the " decision " will take the form of advice) a claim by any individual to a peerage. Such claims, it should be noticed, are not barred by any lapse of time.[19] This type of claim should be distinguished from the claim that the abeyance affecting a peerage should be terminated, for in such a case it has been resolved that abeyance should not be terminated after the lapse of a hundred years.[20] A distinction must also be drawn between peerage and lordship of Parliament; the latter need not follow as a necessary consequence of the former, but both issues are tried by the same body, which thus determined that peeresses in their own right were not entitled to a seat in Parliament,[21] or that one to whom letters patent had been issued specifically granting him a peerage for life was not entitled to a seat, under the law as it then was.[22] It may here be mentioned that after the Union this jurisdiction of the House of Lords was extended to the determination of entitlement to a peerage of Scotland or to the right to vote at the election of the representative peers of Scotland. Formerly this jurisdiction was exercised by the Court of Session,[23] but it has been

[17] The *Berkeley Peerage Case* (1861) 8 H.L.Cas. 21 at 81.
[18] It was accepted as the basis for putting forward the Wedgwood Benn (Renunciation) Bill (1954–55) H.L. Papers 23; as to Scottish peerages see note 43 below, and the Report on House of Lords Reform (1962–63) H.L.P. 23, upon which the Peerage Act 1963 was based. The report doubted if the surrender of Scottish peerages was still possible.
[19] *Hastings Peerage Case* (1841) 8 Cl. & F. 144.
[20] *Report on Peerages in Abeyance*, 1927. Abeyance means that a peerage goes into suspense when there is a co-heirship. This can arise under English law; it does not, in relation to a peerage, under Scots law: Stair III, 5, 11; Ersk. III, 8, 13; and see the *Herries Peerage Claim* (1858) 3 Macq. 585. Its effect on United Kingdom peerages might depend on the argument above at note 14 and related text.
[21] *Lady Rhondda's Case* [1922] 2 A.C. 339; but see now Peerage Act 1963, s. 6, which confers a right to a seat.
[22] The *Wensleydale Peerage Case* (1856) 5 H.L.C. 958. In this case the House seized itself of the matter on its own motion, and here it is most clearly dealing, as a House, with its own composition.
[23] This was done even after the Union; see the cases referred to in Riddell, *Peerage Law*, pp. 285–292. This jurisdiction was attacked by Lord Kames' *Historical Law Tracts*, Tit. " Courts," and by Lord Hailes (as he became); see Lockhart, *Disquisition on the Right of Jurisdiction in Peerage Successions*.

assumed in both respects by the House of Lords, and now appears to be unchallengeable.[24]

It has from time to time been asserted that the House of Lords alone could determine any peerage issue. This statement goes too far. It is clear that the House has a right to determine its own composition, but where a question of peerage arises incidentally in other litigation the appropriate court has power to determine this matter for its own purposes.[25]

There are legal disqualifications, apart from those which have been mentioned, which will debar a peer from taking his seat, these are minority,[26] bankruptcy[27] and conviction for treason.[28] Apart from these there are conventional limitations. Civil servants are restrained from taking part in the political activities of the House,[29] there are conventional restraints upon the participation of the judicial members of the House,[30] and it seems that those peers who are involved in the running of nationalised industries do not take part in the relevant debates.[31]

The Scottish representative peers. The sixteen representative peers of Scotland were elected under the provisions of the Act of 1707 (as amended) until the Peerage Act 1963 (s. 4) admitted all Scottish peers (not otherwise disqualified) to the House. Proof of the matriculation of relevant arms before the Court of the Lord Lyon was declared acceptable (in the absence of any other circumstances) as sufficient evidence of entitlement to a peerage,[32] and the peers thus admitted took their seats without formality.[33] There thus ended a system of representation the details of which had been established by one of the last

[24] See the speech of Lord St. Leonards in the *Montrose Peerage Case* (1853) 1 Macq. 401 at 439–441 and *Barclay-Allardice* v. *Duke of Montrose* (1872) 10 M. 774 at 777; the situation which resulted was not, in the past, an entirely happy one, because of differences in peerage law which were not always fully appreciated.

[25] *Alexander* v. *Officers of State* (1868) 6 M.(H.L.) 54; *Dunbar* v. *Sinclair*, Feb. 2, 1790, F.C.; *Re Bristol S.E. Election* [1961] 3 All E.R. 354 at 373.

[26] Standing Order of 1685, and the Act of Parliament of Scotland 1707, governing election of representative peers.

[27] Bankruptcy Act 1883, s. 32; Bankruptcy Disqualification Act 1871; Bankruptcy (Scotland) Act 1913. The disqualification terminates if the bankruptcy is annulled or if, in England, he is discharged with a certificate that bankruptcy was due to misfortune, not misconduct; and see Goudy, *Bankruptcy*, 4th ed., p. 361.

[28] Disqualification following conviction for treason under the Forfeiture Act 1870 appears to remain. Formerly conviction for felony could disqualify. The distinction between felonies and misdemeanours was not current in Scots law, and is abolished by the Criminal Law Act 1967 in England and Wales. Disqualification is excluded by s. 1 (2) of that Act. It would seem that the House has power to exclude those committing offences of which it disapproves; see Lord Herschell in 334 H.L.Deb. 3 s., col. 357. Presumably lunatics may be dealt with under the same power.

[29] By Treasury Circular of 1928.

[30] Bromhead, *The House of Lords and Contemporary Politics*, pp. 67–72.

[31] See, *e.g.*, the debates on the Air Corporations Bill 1960, 220 H.L.Deb., and the solitary intervention of Lord Douglas of Kirtleside at col. 1202. This restraint is necessary to avoid the creation of another form of responsibility to the House.

[32] H.L. 33 (1963–64).

[33] H.L. 11 (1963–64).

Acts of the Parliament of Scotland.[34] The change was not momentous. Few peers in the peerage of Scotland who wished for a political career were in fact excluded. Factors such as minorities and the possession of additional peerages of Great Britain reduced the apparent gap between the total number of peers in the peerage of Scotland and the number of representatives. Some, indeed, who had the right to vote had little or no real connection with Scotland. While the system endured it produced two Acts (limiting the right to vote in respect of peerages by virtue of which votes were not cast) which might have proved to be models for dealing with the problem of " backwoodsmen." [35] In the years immediately after the Union, the restriction of the meeting of peers exclusively to elections was probably significant in preventing the emergence of a parliament in a different guise. At the same time disputes about the right to vote [36] and the right to seats in the House [37] were signs that the Union itself was not immediately acceptable to all, but of this there were other indications, and these matters are now of historical interest rather than of interest as current constitutional law.[38]

The right to vote, as well as other questions relating to election, was determined by the House of Lords and the absorption of the peers of Scotland into the House in 1963 was easy. That absorption has not, however, caused the disappearance of a separate peerage of Scotland. That continues and is still capable of expansion if the House should accept a new claim to a pre-Union peerage. This should be noted for the rules for the descent of Scottish peerages are many and varied [39] and in many cases do not correspond to those permitted in English law. This question could perhaps still be important if an attempt were made in a suitable case to create a peerage with a limitation not acceptable under the English rules. While such a limitation may well be possible [40] it would seem that the peerage would have to be in the peerage of the United Kingdom. While the Act of Union did not in terms make it impossible to create new peers of Scotland,[41] the general tenor of the Act when coupled with the general viewpoint of the times (there was a contemporary desire to close the ranks of the peerage)

---

[34] For a general account see Fergusson, *The Sixteen Peers of Scotland*.

[35] The Representative Peers (Scotland) Acts of 1847 and 1851. In fact these were little used in their own context.

[36] The Duke of Hamilton's protest against the Duke of Queensberry; see Robertson's *Peerage Proceedings*.

[37] The case of the Duke of Hamilton and Brandon: Robertson, *op. cit.*

[38] Some further detail of these elections is given in the first edition of this book.

[39] When in 1740 the House of Lords asked the Court of Session what the general rules were, that court could only supply a list of peerages but no general rules which would have been helpful; see Islay Campbell, *Acts of Sederunt*.

[40] See note 13, *ante*, p. 109.

[41] Riddell's *Peerage Law*, pp. 269–270; *cf.* Anson, *Law and Custom of the Constitution*, Vol. I, p. 211. It may be noted that the Act of Union with Ireland contained provisions for the limited creation in the future of peers of Ireland.

makes it probable that that was the intention of the framers. That view has also judicial support,[42] and must, it seems, be now accepted.

Apart from questions which related to the representative peers of Scotland there are now few constitutional issues which arise in connection with the peerage of Scotland. The Act of Union (Art. XXIII) settled matters of precedence and conferred upon that peerage all privileges (save those dependent upon membership of the House) which might be enjoyed by the peers of England or of Great Britain, but from the point of view of the working constitution these have ceased to be important.[43]

The peers spiritual. The origin of the bishops in the House of Lords is imprecise. The position of some as tenants in chief had its influence, as did their spiritual capacity.[44] They consist of bishops of the Church of England only, bishops of the Church of Ireland and the Church in Wales being excluded by the Acts disestablishing those churches. From 1847, at the time of the creation of the bishopric of Manchester, the number of lords spiritual has been fixed and that bench now consists of the two Archbishops of Canterbury and York, the Bishops of London, Durham and Winchester and twenty-one others according to their seniority of appointment. At one time both the appointment of bishops and the part played by them in the House had considerable political importance, but the first has ceased to have any such significance, and the part played by the bishops in the activities of the House even in non-political matters has now very greatly diminished.[45]

A claim was advanced in 1953 on behalf of the Church of Scotland for representation in the House by analogy with this representation of the Church of England.[46] Apart from doctrinal difficulties, it is difficult to see how such representation could be arranged, though it is to be noted that among the appointments to life peerages there has been one distinguished elder of the church.

---

[42] *Walker Trustees* v. *Lord Advocate*, 1912 S.C.(H.L.) 12; 1910 S.C. 1037, in which case, however, the Lord Advocate argued that a Scottish peerage could still be granted. It is arguable whether the point was essential to the decision. The Report (1962–63) H.L.P. 23 recommends legislation to put this beyond doubt.

[43] Questions of the trial of peers ceased to be important after the Criminal Justice Act 1948. The former disability of eldest sons from standing for a Scottish constituency or voting (as to which see *Daer* v. *Stewart*, Jan. 24, 1792, F.C.) ceased to be important after 1832. Other matters, which were argued after the Union, have ceased to be important, such as the form of oath of a peer in the ordinary courts; see, *e.g.*, *Duke of Montrose* v. *M'Auley* (1711) Mor. 10029. Doubtless the old incidents of Scottish peerages such as the possibility of surrender (see *Lady Mary Bruce* v. *Earl of Kincardine* (1707) Fount. II, 367 and More's Stair, cclxiv, and Riddell's *Peerage Law*, p. 34) continue.

[44] See Pollard, *Evolution of Parliament*; Anson, *Law and Custom of the Constitution*, Vol. I, pp. 236–237.

[45] Their votes were important in relation to the passage of the Parliament Act 1911; for the modern position see Bromhead, *op. cit.* p. 53 *et seq.*

[46] Royal Commission on Scottish Affairs (Cmd. 9212), § 106.

Lords of Appeal in Ordinary. There was difficulty in securing the services of a sufficient number of persons to discharge the judicial functions of the House, and there was the more serious difficulty of ensuring that such persons were properly qualified. After the failure to solve these difficulties by means of life peerages as a result of the *Wensleydale* case,[47] some relief was found in elevations to the peerage, such as that of Lord Colonsay, but the real reform came with the Appellate Jurisdiction Act 1876, authorising the appointment of Lords of Appeal in Ordinary with life peerages and a seat in the House. Their judicial office is held upon the normal terms of judicial tenure, but their membership of the House continues after retirement from that office.[48]

Life peers. Most proposals for the reform of the House of Lords have involved suggestions of life peerages in one form or another which would carry the right to a seat in the House of Lords, and, in the Queen's Speech in October 1967, it was proposed to bring in legislation which would eliminate the hereditary basis of the House, and make some form of life peerage the universal basis for membership. This follows earlier declarations of the Government, indicating an intent not to create new hereditary peerages. Under the Life Peerages Act 1958 it became possible to confer a life peerage which would also (subject to the disqualifications of general law) carry the right to receive a writ of summons. Such peerages might be conferred upon women, though the disabilities affecting peeresses in their own right remained until 1963.[49] The number of appointments under this head has been limited (amounting to some 160 so far) and is almost insignificant in relationship to the total number of the House. It is not, however, insignificant in relation to the normal " working " membership. Appointments have been varied, a relatively high number have been made among those who have followed a political career,[50] but there have also been appointments from among men of distinction in other walks of life. The first list and that in 1962 contained names of persons designated as being appointed after consultation with the Leader of the Opposition, and the practice has been continued, and extended beyond the official Opposition. While members of the opposition party have at other times been appointed this phrase has not been used, and it is probable that the Leader of the Opposition was not consulted. It is clear from the separation of these lists from the ordinary Honours Lists that elevations to the peerage under this head are, at present, somewhat differently regarded from those under the traditional heads. In particular

47 (1856) 5 H.L.C. 958.
48 Appellate Jurisdiction Act 1887; Judicial Pensions Act 1959. Thus they may, even after retirement, sit for the purposes of hearing appeals in a different capacity, namely, as peers who have held high judicial office—see *post*, pp. 138 and 258.
49 Peerage Act 1963, s. 6.
50 Nearly two-thirds of the first 36 nominations might be classed as " political."

some attempt is made by this method to "balance" the composition of the House in a variety of ways.[51] It is as yet too early to say much of the constitutional significance of this device, or perhaps the phase after 1958 will be too short to have great significance. It seems possible to assert, though, that it had the effect of enlivening the House. Regularity of attendance has increased, not only among the life peers, but at the same time there was an accentuation of the political character of the House, partly because within the number of regular attenders the number of life peers was significant and within that group there was a significant number who felt most at home in a House of Commons atmosphere. Moreover, this accentuation was the natural and inevitable consequence of using life peerages as a balancing factor. One consequence of this increased political atmosphere (which was marked by the provision for payment of salaries to the Chief Whip and Leader of the Opposition in the Ministerial Salaries Consolidation Act 1965) was probably to increase the pressure to further reform.

Some general characteristics of the House. The composition of the House is varied. Members have expertise in a wide range of subjects. Others have the invaluable quality (in a legislative assembly) of ordinariness, but the size and general political bias of the House present difficulties. While the number of "working" members may be relatively small, the threat of the "backwoodsmen" exists, at least on paper.[52] On the other hand neither wealth nor leisure necessarily accompanies nobility today. Hence, in this century there have been many proposals for reform, these have involved modifications of the hereditary principle, life peerages, indirect elections and arrangements to ensure a representation of non-political bodies.[53] Fresh conversations were announced in November 1961 between the major parties and the reforms of 1963 can be regarded as partially the result, being changes which were acceptable, even if they were not agreed. Further and more substantial reforms were foreshadowed in the Queen's Speech in October 1967. The difficulty in the past has been that whereas there was broad agreement on the elements of the reform of composition such agreement has been

---

[51] These lists are normally kept apart from the "Honours List" and appointments to achieve the similar objects to those desired at the time of the elevation of the first Lord Stansgate (see *The Times*, Dec. 23, 1941) are now made by this means. It must be remembered that heirship to a peerage can substantially limit or injure a career in the House of Commons, and the use of a life peerage as an honour should not be precluded, though such consequences are lessened by the Peerage Act 1963. The list of life peers created on August 8, 1967, is a clear example of a "political" list, intended to have this balancing effect.

[52] The largest number voting in a division in modern times is 333 in 1956 on the issue of the abolition of capital punishment. See Bromhead, *op. cit.* Chap. III.

[53] Apart from the two Command Papers (1918) Cd. 9038 and (1948) Cmd. 7380, see the summaries in Bailey, *The Future of the House of Lords* (Hansard Society) and *Parliamentary Reform 1933–58* issued by that Society; Bromhead, *op. cit.*, and Jennings, *Parliament*, Chap. XI; Morrison, *Government and Parliament from Within*, Chap. IX; Lord Chorley, "The House of Lords Controversy" [1958] *Public Law* 216; Crick, *The Reform of Parliament*.

lacking on the question of function. This disagreement is only one sign of a basic uncertainty about the House of Lords. At one time there was, or could be, a coherent theory about the House. Aristocracy was thought to have a specific place in the constitutional scheme of things.[54] That was a theory that could not endure, partly because British aristocracy was not always very aristocratic. The general background of the ballad *The Laird of Cockpen* had more to do with it than the themes underlying the Almanach de Gotha. There has been little general attempt even to produce a specific theory of bicameralism in the United Kingdom. So reform has been of a random and piecemeal nature.

Hence the reforms promised in the preamble to the Parliament Act 1911 have only taken shape in the Act of 1958 (which was not an agreed measure) and the Peerage Act 1963, and in certain modifications in the practice of the House.[54] Under resolutions of the House, peers are entitled to claim the cost of railway fares between their homes and London incurred in performing their parliamentary duties, if they are in regular attendance, and to recover expenses similarly incurred up to a maximum of four-and-a-half guineas a day.[55] The modification of greater constitutional significance is the Standing Order relating to leave of absence.[56] Under this members are invited at the beginning of each Parliament to apply for leave of absence, and any peer who does not reply and does not attend within the first month is deemed to have so applied. Members who are granted leave of absence on either ground are not expected to attend, unless they terminate that leave by notice. This attempt to control any sudden emergence of the backwoodsmen depends for its force on purely moral sanctions, the House having concluded that it had no power to deprive a member of his right to attend, a deprivation which would amount to an interference with general legal rights. The shape of the rule thus indicates a clear view of the limits of the privilege of the House in controlling its own composition.

THE HOUSE OF COMMONS

Constituencies. A convenient starting-point is to be found in the constituencies now regulated by the House of Commons (Redistribution of Seats) Acts 1949 and 1958. The combined effect of this legislation is that the Boundary Commissioners, set up by those Acts, are directed to aim at achieving a House of approximately 613 members, not less than seventy-one of whom shall come from Scottish constituencies and

---

[54] See, *e.g.*, Weston, *English Constitutional Theory and the House of Lords.*

[55] The sums are governed by resolutions of the House and are provided by the Appropriation Acts.

[56] S.O. 21. For the report leading up to the adoption of this, see *Report on the Powers of the House in Relation to the Attendance of its Members* (1956) H.L.P. 66–1 and the debate in H.L.Deb. 206.

not less than thirty-five from Welsh ones, and twelve from Northern Ireland.[57] Under the Acts there are four commissions, for England, Scotland, Wales and Northern Ireland, each with the Speaker as Chairman and a judge as Deputy Chairman,[58] which are to report on each constituency at intervals of not less than ten and not more than fifteen years. Their object is to achieve rough uniformity of constituencies by finding the appropriate electoral quota for an "average" constituency by dividing the electorate of that part of the United Kingdom by the number of constituencies therein.[59] Provisions are made to ensure a degree of unity in constituencies, or rather to avoid too sharp a disunity, and the whole rules are a compromise between cold analysis and community sentiments. Thus the interval of review was extended by the 1958 Act to preserve continuity of feeling in a constituency, even though mathematical equality may suffer, and the discretion conferred upon the Commissions by section 2 (2) of the 1958 Act emphasises this compromise.[60] It is to be noted that the starting-point is number of electors; this factor combined with the absence of any residence rule for candidates emphasises the fact that members represent national parties much more than localities.

The franchise. The basis of the franchise is now "one man, one vote," which is the result of a long period of reform and simplification,[61] and which adds importance to the equalisation of constituencies. Those entitled to vote at any election are British subjects (or citizens of the Republic of Ireland) who are of full age, not subject to any legal disqualification, and are upon the operative register.[62] Registration depends upon residence in a particular constituency on the qualifying date, which is now October 10 in any year.[63] The fact that residence is the test makes it possible to be on the register for one or more constituencies, but a vote can be cast in only one. The register, which is created by a canvass, is the responsibility of the registration officer,[64] who determines

---

[57] The present house numbers 630. Monmouthshire is here part of Wales. For an account of the Acts see Craig, "Parliament and the Boundary Commission" [1959] *Public Law*, and generally Jennings, *Party Politics*, Vol. I, *Appeal to the People*.

[58] There are two other members of each with the appropriate Registrar General and the Director of Ordnance Survey as Assessors.

[59] The detailed rules are to be found in the Schedules to the 1949 Act, as amended by the Act of 1958.

[60] The original rules had proved too rigid in practice; see *Harper* v. *S. of S. for Home Department* [1955] Ch. 238, a case which, in substance, demonstrates the modern reluctance of courts to interfere in what might be looked upon as parliamentary matters.

[61] Keir, *Constitutional History of Modern Britain*, Chap. VIII, and Butler, *The Electoral System in Britain since 1918*.

[62] Representation of the People Act 1949, s. 1.

[63] Electoral Registers Act 1953, s. 1. The date is September 15 for Northern Ireland. As to the conclusiveness of the register, see *Marr* v. *Robertson*, 1964 S.C. 448. The economy measure which reduced a six-monthly register to an annual register has become permanent.

[64] The assessor of a county or large burgh in Scotland, the clerk of an appropriate authority elsewhere: Representation of the People Act 1949, s. 6.

in the first instance claims and objections to registration, and similarly decides on claims to vote by post or by proxy, or to be registered as a service voter.[65] From this decision appeal lies in Scotland to the sheriff and thence to a special court of three judges of the Court of Session.[66] The disqualifications from voting (which will apply even though an individual's name is on the register) are infancy, alienage, peerage (unless the peerage has been disclaimed), conviction for corrupt or illegal practices,[67] insanity.

Voting and the conduct of an election. The basic rule is, of course, the secrecy of the ballot which was established in 1872, and is now protected by detailed rules.[68] Provision is made for voting by proxy (mainly for servicemen and Crown servants abroad), and by post (for those unable to get to the poll) in exceptional cases.[69] There is equally a large body of legislation aimed against corrupt and illegal practice at elections,[70] which hits at the more obvious forms of corruption, but which, by rigid rules as to expenses and as to who may authorise expenditure, also goes much further. Some provisions should be noted as affecting the general conduct of an election. The aim is not merely to keep the election clean, but within limits to keep it calm. Thus, the use of bands, banners and torches is prohibited, as is the use of wireless broadcasts from abroad, domestic broadcasting being regulated by conventional rules to maintain a rough balance among parties. Moreover, a deliberate attempt is made to " close the ring " and keep election activity to the contestants and their authorised supporters. No one other than the candidate's agent may lawfully incur expenditure on certain major things with a view to promoting the election of a candidate.[71] These provisions may, as they stand, be difficult to enforce since they envisage particular campaigns in particular constituencies, whereas to a steadily increasing extent campaigns have become national, financed out of central party funds, thus difficulties

---

[65] See Representation of the People Act 1949, ss. 12 and 13, and, as an illustration, *Daly* v. *Watson*, 1960 S.C. 216, or *Donnelly* v. *Edinburgh Electoral Registration Officer*, 1964 S.L.T.(Sh.Ct.) 80 (the latter as to those in prison).

[66] In England appeal lies to the county court (see, *e.g.*, *R.* v. *Hurst, ex p. Smith* [1960] 2 Q.B. 133) and thence to the Court of Appeal; and see generally for detailed rules Schofield, *Parliamentary Elections.*

[67] Representation of the People Act 1949, s. 40. This includes disqualification under the Public Bodies Corrupt Practices Act 1889, s. 2, arising from corruption not connected with elections. It should be noted that the Forfeiture Act 1870, disqualifying convicted felons, did not apply to Scotland.

[68] See the election rules scheduled to the Representation of the People Act 1949.

[69] See Representation of the People Act 1949, s. 13.

[70] It has been said that " A corrupt practice is a thing which the mind goes along with. An illegal practice is a thing the legislature is determined to prevent whether it is done honestly or dishonestly ": *Barrow in Furness Case* (1886) 4 O'M. & H. 76. The main body of law is now contained in the Representation of the People Act 1949. For its evolution see O'Leary, *The Elimination of Corrupt Practices in British Elections, 1868–1911.*

[71] Representation of the People Act 1949, s. 63. It has been also proposed to limit opinion polls immediately before the close of poll: Cmnd. 3550.

have arisen about accounting for the expenses of the leader of a party.[72] Moreover, as they stand the rules give rise to difficulties of interpretation.[73] These latter difficulties are inherent in the subject-matter and in some cases their existence enhances the deterrent effect of legislation rather than detracting from it.

The character of an election is also strongly influenced by the electoral timetable. The proclamation dissolving the old Parliament directs an election for the new. Nominations must be made not later than the eighth day after the proclamation summoning a new Parliament and polling is on the ninth day thereafter.[74] When it is remembered that it is extremely rare for a Parliament to run its full course, and that the date of dissolution is at the choice of a Prime Minister, it is clear that intense political activity is concentrated into a relatively short period, which cannot be predicted long in advance with any degree of accuracy. This concentration is probably desirable. The abnormal situation which can arise with a government having a very small majority, when there is in effect a continuing long-drawn-out electoral campaign, emphasises this.

The conduct of the election is the responsibility of the returning officer (who, in Scotland, is the sheriff[75]), who will decide by lot in case of equality of votes. Candidates must be nominated by a proposer and seconder supported by eight other electors. Nomination must be accompanied by a deposit of £150 to be forfeited if the candidate does not poll one-eighth of the votes cast, and the candidates consent (incorporating a declaration of his belief that he is not disqualified). It may be noticed that neither on the nomination paper nor on the polling paper may there be any reference to a political party. The result of an election may be challenged by an election petition,[76] heard by an election court consisting of two judges of the Court of Session (or of the High Court elsewhere). The trial may occur in the constituency. The petition in modern times is most commonly a challenge

---

[72] *Grieve* v. *Douglas-Home*, 1965 S.L.T. 186; and see *R.* v. *Tronoh Mines Ltd.* [1952] 1 All E.R. 697, which shows that generalised intervention will be outside the Act; for other examples see Butler, *The British General Election of 1951*, pp. 31–34, and Gwyn, *Democracy and the Cost of Politics*. In 1965 a Speaker's Conference on Electoral Law, covering this and other matters, was announced: 712 H.C.Deb. 520, and has now reported—Cmnd. 3550. For the evolution of the system see Butler, *The Electoral System in Britain since 1918*.

[73] *e.g.*, the period covered by s. 48 limiting expenses is not entirely certain. It is in fact rare for the allowed amount to be expended; see the figures in Butler, *op. cit.* p. 139.

[74] Representation of the People Act 1949, Sched. II. By Representation of the People Act 1918, s. 21 (3), the interval between the proclamation and the meeting of the new Parliament must not be less than 20 days.

[75] The sheriff (in the different, non-judicial sense) is the returning officer in an English county constituency; in boroughs, etc., the returning officer is the mayor or chairman.

[76] See generally the Representation of the People Act 1949, Part III. Allegations of corruption, etc., may be investigated under the alternative procedure of the Election Commissioners Act 1949. Reports of such Commissioners under earlier legislation led, even in the nineteenth century, to the temporary disfranchisement of constituencies.

to the capacity of the elected candidate, but it may refer to any matter which could affect the validity of an election.[77]   The court reports to the House of Commons, and, in cases where there have been malpractices, to the appropriate authority with a view to prosecution.   In particular the court may, where the first candidate has been found to be disqualified and the disqualification was well known at the time of the election, declare the second candidate (even though he received fewer votes) elected on the grounds that votes cast for his rival were thrown away.[78] The report to the House of the result of the election must, it seems, be accepted without debate.[79]   This procedure is a mark of the claim of the House to regulate its own composition.   The trial of election petitions having been in the past of considerable political importance, and being often formerly determined in the House on political grounds, the matter was eventually, after a series of attempts to secure neutrality in the House,[80] handed over to the courts.   The place of the House is preserved by the reporting procedure, and by the fact that the House retains power to determine questions of qualification, where, for example, the time for presenting a petition has expired.[81]

Candidates and members.   By law all that is required is that a candidate shall be a British subject of full age not suffering from any legal disability.   Neither by law nor convention is there any requirement of residence, so that the " locality " of the member's interest may again be limited.   The disabilities are similar to those discussed in relation to peers, subject to the addition of peerage, and of those arising from having been convicted of corrupt or illegal practices.   Further there are the rules of disqualification from membership of the House which will be discussed below.   It is to be noted, however, that the returning officer is not entitled to reject a nomination on the ground that the candidate is disqualified.   Such matters are, as has been indicated, to be tried either by election petition or by the House itself.

The main disqualifications of constitutional importance are now contained in the House of Commons Disqualification Act 1957.   The history of disqualifications indicates both the evolution of our constitutional institutions and the varied purposes that the rules are designed to serve.   In Scotland the Officers of State had long (though not without interruption) been present in Parliament *ex officio*, and indeed for long played a dominant role in the Committee of Articles which itself often

---

[77] See, *e.g.*, *Grieve* v. *Douglas-Home*, 1965 S.L.T. 186; *Re Kensington North Parliamentary Election* [1960] 2 All E.R. 150.

[78] *Beresford-Hope* v. *Lady Sandhurst* (1889) 23 Q.B.D. 79; *Re Bristol S.E. Election* [1961] 3 All E.R. 354.

[79] Representation of the People Act 1949, s. 124 (3), and 545 H.C.Deb. 41.

[80] See *post*, p. 129.

[81] See, *e.g.*, the proceedings in 1955 in the constituencies of Fermanagh and S. Tyrone and of Mid-Ulster: 543 H.C.Deb. 1305; 545 H.C.Deb. 41 and 55; and 546 H.C.Deb. 1504.

ruled Parliament.[82] In the years before the Union, however, the growing strength of Parliament was reflected in practices affecting their position. A commissioner appointed to one of the great offices lost his seat as commissioner, though retaining his place as officer.[83] In England events went further. The Act of Settlement of 1700 would, by excluding all placemen, had that provision come into force, have excluded all office holders, and thus frustrated any development of cabinet government. Underlying this were theories of the separation of powers, discontent with the attempt at a diarchical system under the earlier Stuarts, and a desire for the independence of Parliament from the executive.[84] That provision was repealed by the Regency Act 1705,[85] which substituted a distinction between " old " (pre-1705) and new offices, a distinction which in time was translated into one between political and other offices. The process of change was slow and accompanied by many inconveniences [86]—particularly those arising from the necessity of re-election on nomination to an old office, a requirement that was first modified and then repealed.[87] There were not only inconveniences, but also uncertainties in the working of the system. It was doubtful how ancient offices in Scotland fitted into the scheme,[88] it was often doubtful what was an office of profit since the profit could be purely hypothetical. Moreover, as time passed, provisions became inappropriate; the development of corporate firms had that effect upon the exclusion of Crown contractors.[89] Other matters became important in relation to the House such as the isolation of the boards of nationalised industries. The process of piecemeal reform continued,[90] but after a flurry of validation and indemnity legislation in 1955–56 an attempt was made by the House of Commons Disqualification Act 1957 to reform and consolidate the law.

This Act incorporates several principles. There is first the traditional one of the independence of the House from the Crown or, in modern times, the Government. A Government today may have close on 130 ministers of varying grades, if Parliamentary Private Secretaries are included. If to that number is added a number of would-be ministers

[82] Though in 1689 Parliament excluded the Officers from all Committees unless elected thereto (A.P.S. IX, App. 128), by an Act of 1690 their power was substantially restored (A.P.S. IX, 113).
[83] A.P.S. X, 11.
[84] See Dodd, *The Growth of Responsible Government from James I to Victoria*, for a general account.
[85] Which was extended to the United Kingdom by the Succession to the Crown Act 1707.
[86] See Alphaeus Todd, *Parliamentary Government in England*, II, p. 27.
[87] Re-election of Ministers Acts 1919 and 1926.
[88] *The Case of Maitland*, Wight, *Election Laws*, p. 298; Bell, *Election Laws*, p. 452.
[89] It was only those who contracted personally who were excluded, and with the evolution of government contracts made by individuals which were quite insignificant could disqualify; those made by companies did not disqualify directors.
[90] Including the House of Commons Disqualification (Declaration of Law) Acts 1931 and 1935; Ministers of the Crown Act 1937; Ministers of the Crown (Parliamentary Secretaries) Act 1951. So far as these Acts, as amended, regulate numbers, *e.g.*, of Secretaries of State, they must be read with the 1957 Act.

their influence in a House of 630 could be substantial. There is also, granted a bicameral Parliament, the necessity of having the Government represented in both Houses. So, based on such theories, section 2 (1) of the Act limited the number of holders of ministerial office who might have seats in the House to seventy in all, with not more than twenty-seven holders of the offices listed in Part I of the Second Schedule (which includes all the senior ministers with the exception of the Law Officers).[91] Those limitations were repealed by the Ministers of the Crown Act 1964, s. 3, which has the effect of removing the limit on the number of senior ministers who can sit in the House of Commons at any one time, and of raising the maximum number of office holders who can sit in the House to ninety-one. Thus the change not only affected the House of Lords, but also the position of the Government in the Commons. For different reasons, those of neutrality, there are excluded by the Act of 1957 civil servants,[92] members of the regular forces and the holders of judicial offices strictly defined,[93] as well as members of various tribunals in which neutrality is particularly important.[94] Equally full-time police are excluded in the same interest. Outside these large groups there are set out in Parts II and III of the First Schedule a large list of disqualifying offices. Some of the disqualifications, like membership of the board of a nationalised industry, are intended to keep lines of constitutional responsibility clear, others, such as the disqualification of town clerks, exist because of the incompatibility of the two offices. Again, however, principles interlock. Advocates depute are not excluded from the House, probably on the grounds that parliamentary experience is desirable for some who might become Lord Advocate. Further, where suspicion of local influence might arise, holders of particular offices are excluded by Part IV of that Schedule from the constituencies likely to be affected by such influences. Finally, there is a provision against combining membership of the House and membership of any legislature outside the Commonwealth, to prevent double membership of the parliaments at Westminster and Dublin which would otherwise be possible, since, as has already been seen, citizens of the Republic of Ireland are eligible to stand.

It is clear that some provisions are inserted with an eye to the interest of the House, some to the world outside. The Act is not, however, complete. It repealed (s. 9) the disqualification of Crown pensioners

[91] Part II of that Schedule has already been amended by the addition of a further office—Ministers of the Crown (Parliamentary Secretaries) Act 1960. In the debates preceding that Act the problem of governmental influence was raised: 630 H.C.Deb. 700.

[92] s. 1 (i) (b). In addition civil servants are restricted from standing for Parliament without resigning.

[93] See Part I of Sched. I, which covers all normal judicial offices; but it may be noticed that honorary sheriff substitutes are not included. The origin of the exclusion of Senators of the College of Justice by the Act of 1733 had a strong political background. See 1957 S.L.T.(News) 134.

[94] Part II of Sched. II.

and Crown contractors. The former had become insignificant, the position of the latter, it was concluded, was best regulated by the House itself in the form of privilege.[95] Control of the House over its own membership is to an extent increased, since amendments to the First Schedule may be made by Order in Council,[96] and the House has, under section 6 (2), power to waive a disqualification where the grounds for it have ceased, but without prejudice to any election petition. Such a waiver will, however, prevent a petition (under section 7) to Her Majesty in Council, to be referred to the Judicial Committee, claiming that a person is disqualified from membership under the Act.[97] Traditional disqualifying offices, such as the Stewardship of the Chiltern Hundreds, are preserved to make it possible for members to resign, but it is specifically provided (s. 8) that no member or candidate can be required to accept a disqualifying office.[98]

---

[95] See [1957] *Public Law* 340 *et seq*. Privilege may well afford a more flexible method of regulating the matter.

[96] See, *e.g.*, S.I. 1960 No. 2468, adding among other disqualifying offices the government director of MacBraynes Ltd. Subsequent amendments arising from the creation of new boards, etc., conform to the original pattern; see, *e.g.*, the list of 22 new offices added in January 1967: 756 H.C.Deb. 2163.

[97] Such a petition, while serving the same purpose as an election petition, could be presented after time, for the latter had expired.

[98] At one time such devices were used to get rid of inconvenient members. The section is to be confined to its proper context: *Re Bristol S.E. Parliamentary Election Petition* [1961] 3 All E.R. 354.

CHAPTER 7

PARLIAMENTARY PRIVILEGES

Introduction. Before turning to the functions of Parliament, something should be said of parliamentary privilege. The basic concept of privilege is a very common one, which appears under different names. Prerogative is in this sense a variant of privilege, and essentially the word covers those special rules which enable a public body to perform its proper task. Redlich's definition of the privileges of the Commons, "The sum of the fundamental rights of the House and of its individual members as against the prerogatives of the Crown, the authority of the ordinary Courts of Law, and the special rights of the House of Lords," [1] while being in a sense accurate, is deficient unless allowance is made for this element of purpose, and also for the rights which one House claims against the other.[2] It is this element of purpose which gives both historical and continuing importance to the topic, but it must be remembered that, while the general purpose of maintaining the independence of Parliament has been constant, the particular purposes have varied from time to time, and thus inconsistency may appear in the authorities. Privilege fed upon, and was fed by, the general growth of Parliament.[3] At one period the struggle in relation to privilege was with the Crown, at another with the courts, today the struggle is sometimes with various private or unofficial bodies outside Parliament, but at no time has any particular conflict ceased to be important.

Further, the whole discussion of privilege is important in a more general way. The doctrines upon which claims to privilege are founded, and upon which the jurisdiction of the courts is admitted or restricted, have much in common with those which underlie other issues, such as the sovereignty of Parliament.[4] Underlying all these disputes is the argument whether or not the law and custom of Parliament is something distinct from the general law of the land, for upon that turns much of the argument about the place of the courts in relation to privilege. Because of the fundamental nature of privilege such questions cannot,

---

[1] Redlich and Ilbert, *Procedure of the House of Commons*, I, p. 46.

[2] These, such as the Commons privileges in finance, are most conveniently dealt with under the powers or functions of the House.

[3] In Scotland the rise of Parliament is marked by the growth of its control over its own privileges in relation to the elections: see Rait, *Parliaments of Scotland*, p. 309 *et seq.* In England this double growth is reflected in the attitude of the courts, which, once Parliament had established its place, watched more closely the claims to privilege.

[4] In particular there is a resemblance between such cases as *Wauchope's Case* (1842) 1 Bell's App. 252 and the rules about the internal affairs of Parliament in the privilege cases.

with us, often be answered with precision, but they must be borne in mind in any reading upon the subject.

To a great extent the particular origins of many of the rules may be said to be English. For this there are two main reasons. The fact that the Union Parliament met in London meant that there was a natural tendency to refer to precedents which were there familiar. Secondly, in 1707, doctrines of parliamentary privilege were more fully developed in England, and it was, therefore, natural that the greater should be accepted as the basis, since the major rules which had been established were those strengthening Parliament against the Crown. Nevertheless, privilege had been developing in Scotland in much the same way as in England. The Act of 1701 [5] had declared that members were not to be imprisoned on any account whatever during the session of Parliament without a warrant from Parliament; the Claim of Right claimed freedom of speech and debate (though the terms of the Claim of Right and other instances can be used to show that privilege was not yet firmly established). [6] The differences of origin were not therefore generally important [7] since the aims in England and Scotland were identical. Moreover, to a large extent the principles of privilege may be universal, [8] and thus the assignment of particular local origin may on the most general level be unimportant. From 1707 the process of unification continued as a result both of legislation and of decision [9] and as a general rule the law must be taken as uniform, though in particular cases where procedural rules of general law are important there may still be differences. There is, however, little modern authority in Scotland, and the weight of English authority as forming a pattern of thought must be regarded as substantial.

---

[5] Act for preventing wrongous imprisonment, etc., A.P.S. X, 272.

[6] See the case of Lord Belhaven, 1702, A.P.S. XI, 65b and 66a; and earlier see A.P.S. VIII, 247a. Parliamentary privilege was not a new-found thing in Scotland. In 1587 the King had promised to do nothing to prejudice free voting and reasoning of the Estates (A.P.S. III, 443), but the history of the country had prevented any steady evolution; compare, e.g., the case in 1663, A.P.S. VII, App. 101b, though see as to England the Case of Sir William Williams (1684) 13 St.Tr. 1370.

[7] Though the claim that the member was absens reipublicae causa, which was the basis of some privileges in Scotland, made some consequences of " privilege " somewhat broader in scope and less peculiar to Parliament than did the basis in England. Moreover, the Scottish basis left no doubt that the rules of privilege were part of the ordinary law of the land. On occasion the Scottish courts would concede greater privilege than would be allowed in England; see Mackintosh v. Dempster (1767) Macl.Rem.Cas. 383 (No. 79). Such cases indicate the uncertainties about privilege in Scotland.

[8] Compare Methodist Federation for Social Action v. Eastland, 141 F.Supp. 729 (1957), where a result which could here be reached on grounds of privilege was reached by way of the doctrine of the separation of powers.

[9] The Parliamentary Privilege Act 1770 extended the Act 12 & 13 Will. 3 to Scotland; and more generally see Hume, Criminal Law, Vol. II, Chap. I. Uncertainty can arise even in modern times; see (1955) H.C.P. 35, though in that particular case there need have been no uncertainty.

THE PRIVILEGES OF THE HOUSE OF COMMONS

The traditional claim. It will be convenient to deal in the first place
with the privileges of the House of Commons. By custom the Speaker
claims certain privileges at the beginning of each Parliament.[10] These
cover freedom of the person of members, liberty of speech, access to the
Sovereign, and the claim that the proceedings of the Commons shall
receive the most favourable construction. The last, which has reference
to early struggles of the House and to early forms of legislation, is now
of little importance. The right of access is a corporate right exercised
through the Speaker, and again was at one time important in relation
to petitions for the redress of grievances, and important for the evolution
of the House, as under Speaker Lenthall in his passage with Charles I,
but it is now mainly used for formal purposes only. Nevertheless it is
of some continuing importance since the right is a one-way right. It thus
excludes the Sovereign from taking current official interest in matters
pending in the House. Hence, officially, the Queen receives only
decisions of the House as a whole,[11] and in this respect that traditional
claim could have a continuing importance.

The first of the privileges thus claimed is, in its present form, much
more limited than was once the case. At one stage it covered members,
their goods and their servants, but the extent of the privilege thus defined,
having provoked protests,[12] was whittled away [13] so that it now only
confers immunity from civil arrest for forty days before and forty days
after the meeting of Parliament, and, with the diminution in the
significance of imprisonment as a means of enforcing a debt,[14] this
aspect of the privilege has lost much importance. The privilege does
not extend to arrest in respect of criminal offences,[15] and the House in
the case of *Wilkes* declared that it did not extend to imprisonment for
seditious libel. Generally the privilege does not affect imprisonment for
contempt of court, at least where that contempt has a quasi-criminal

---

10 For the form in which they are claimed see Erskine May, 17th ed., pp. 44–45.
11 Mr. Baldwin, in a not very serious matter, seriously reminded George V of the
constitutional position: Nicholson, *George V*, pp. 428–429.
12 *Livingston* v. *Morison* (1710) Fount. II, 526. In Scotland this privilege rests on the
Act for preventing wrongous imprisonment 1701 (A.P.S. X, 272).
13 Parliamentary Privilege Act 1770.
14 The Debtors Act 1880 and the Civil Imprisonment Act 1882, and as to England the
Debtors Act 1869. Members were subject to the Act of 1772 in relation to
sequestration, and to the modern form of bankruptcy under the Act of 1856. As to
England see now the Bankruptcy Act 1914, s. 128. For the protection under the old
law see *Molison* v. *Clark* (1707) Mor. 10398 and A.P.S. V, 614a.
15 The Act of 1701 for preventing wrongous imprisonment provided that if a member
committed a capital crime or a manifest breach of the peace he was to be secured
and delivered to the High Constable until Parliament decide what should be done,
and that provision remains in force. In general the House is informed of the arrest
of any member. It may be noted that in *Mackintosh* v. *Dempster* (1767)
Macl.Rem.Cas. 383, the Court of Justiciary was prepared to allow a plea of
privilege in some criminal matters. Detention under Defence Regulations is not
prevented by this privilege: (1939–40) H.C. 164.

aspect, but it seems that it will protect where the contempt is civil.[16] It seems, however, that the House can insist on release in a suitable case.

This privilege is based upon the theory that the House has a prior claim upon its members' services, and on that basis no citation or subpoena can be issued to a member to appear as a witness without leave of the House, and members are immune from jury service.[17] It was at one stage maintained that this privilege created an immunity from being impleaded, but the Parliamentary Privilege Act 1770 excludes the claim of privilege as a bar to the prosecution of an action.[18]

Freedom of speech. In practice the most important of these traditional privileges today is that of freedom of speech. Originally this privilege was of the greatest importance in establishing the position of the House as against the Crown. It was with this aspect that many of the great cases, such as *Haxey's Case*[19] or *The Case of Hollis, Valentine and Eliot*,[20] were concerned, as also were the Commons Protest of 1621 and the claims to freedom of speech in both the Bill of Rights and Claim of Right.[21] The right as against the Crown was effectively established at the Revolution. Freedom of speech as against others outside Parliament is equally important, and must be taken to be similarly established. The Bill of Rights is much more specific than is the Claim of Right, providing that " Freedom of speech and debates or proceedings in Parliament ought not to be impeached or questioned in any court or place out of Parliament."[22] Thus no action will lie for defamatory words spoken in Parliament, but the privilege related to internal proceedings, and a report ordered to be published by the House was held not to be privileged.[23] Legislation was accordingly passed conferring absolute privilege in relation to papers published by order of either House, and qualified privilege upon those who print extracts

---

[16] The *Case of Long Wellesley* (1831) 2 Russ. & M. 639 (C.J. (1830–31) 701); compare on the civil side *Stourton* v. *Stourton* [1963] 1 All E.R. 606; and see Goudy, *Bankruptcy*, 4th ed., p. 71.

[17] In England by the Juries Act 1922; in Scotland the exemption is a common law one.

[18] As to the scope of this Act see *Re Parliamentary Privilege Act 1770* [1958] A.C. 331, to be discussed subsequently. In Scotland the effect on actions was not clear; see *Lady Greenock* v. *Sir John Shaw* (1709) Mor. 8563 and *Middleton—Suppliant* (1713) Mor. 8569, where the court would allow the action to continue but suspended diligence; and see A.P.S. VII, App. 101b, and R.P.C. (2S) III, 623. The service of process within the confines of the House still probably amounts to contempt: see (1950–51) H.C. 244.

[19] (1397) Rot.Parl. iii, 434.

[20] (1629) 3 St.Tr. 294. The proceedings in relation to Lord Belhaven in 1681 demonstrate the importance of this aspect of privilege; A.P.S. VIII, 242a and 247b; and see A.P.S. XI, App. 139a.

[21] The motion for a protest against an adjournment in 1703 (A.P.S. XI, App. 65, 66) related to a more generalised freedom of debate.

[22] The Act of 1770 had no effect upon this provision: see *Re Parliamentary Privilege Act 1770* [1958] A.C. 331.

[23] *Stockdale* v. *Hansard* (1839) 9 A. & E. 1. For a discussion of the other points in this case see *post*, p. 131 *et seq.*

from or abstracts of such papers.[24] Unofficial reports in newspapers of either House receive the limited protection of qualified privilege under the Defamation Act 1952, s. 7.[25]

In modern times yet another aspect of this freedom has become apparent. It is common for members to owe some form of allegiance to associations of various types outside Parliament. The House will regard as a breach of privilege any case where such allegiance improperly influences a member in speaking or voting, but the point at which impropriety begins is by no means clear.[26] This freedom is circumscribed. The Bill of Rights runs: " That the freedom of speech and debates or proceedings in Parliament ought not to be impeached or questioned in any court." It is therefore fundamental to know what is a proceeding in Parliament. Clearly speeches in the House are covered.[27] That phrase was at one stage treated as covering anything which a member " might say or do within the scope of his duties in the course of Parliamentary duties." [28] But this seems too broad. When Mr. Strauss raised in a letter to a Minister the methods by which the London Electricity Board disposed of scrap (a matter which he might have ventilated in the House, but for which the Minister was probably not responsible) it was held by the House that sending this letter did not amount to a " proceeding in Parliament," [29] and thus the House rejected the report of the Committee of Privileges.[30] The limits of the term are thus uncertain, and there is the possibility that the courts and Parliament might take different views upon this matter,[31] but that issue must be discussed, together with others, in the context of the whole relationship of the courts to Parliament over privilege.

Control over membership and strangers. Apart from these major privileges there are others of less practical importance today. The House claims control over its own membership and, even though, as has been seen, disputed elections are normally determined outside the House

---

[24] Parliamentary Papers Act 1840, the relevant provisions of which are by the Defamation Act 1952, s. 9, extended to broadcasting.

[25] In England the law formerly depended upon *Wason* v. *Walter* (1868) L.R. 4 Q.B. 73 and the Law of Libel Amendment Act 1888. This Act did not apply to Scotland. It seems that qualified privilege would, in Scotland, attach by commmon law; see *Shaw* v. *Morgan* (1888) 15 R. 865. Now it would seem that newspapers in Scotland are protected by Part II (para. 8) of the Schedule to, and s. 7 of, the Defamation Act 1952. However, the Act of 1888 as amended by the Act of 1952 still does not apply to Scotland.

[26] See particularly (1946–47) H.C. 118 and (1943–44) H.C. 85. It is clear that the machinery of the party Whips, being parliamentary, is outside these rules.

[27] See, *e.g.*, *Dillon* v. *Balfour* (1887) 20 L.R.Ir. 600; but not everything which occurs in the precincts of Westminster is privileged: *Rivlin* v. *Bilainkin* [1953] 1 Q.B. 485.

[28] (1939) H.C. 101.

[29] (1957–58) 570 H.C.Deb. 208–346. See too *Att.-Gen. for Ceylon* v. *de Livera* [1963] A.C. 103, where in a different context a somewhat similar issue arose.

[30] (1956–57) H.C. 305. For a discussion of these events see Thomson, " Letters to Ministers and Parliamentary Privilege " [1958] *Public Law* 10, and de Smith, " Parliamentary Privilege and the Bill of Rights " (1958) 21 M.L.R. 465. It may be noted that such letters would in any event be covered by qualified privilege.

[31] [1958] A.C. at pp. 353–354.

by way of election petitions, the form of privilege is preserved in these cases. Nevertheless the House still retains power to exclude a member who is disqualified,[32] or to expel or otherwise discipline a member for offences against the House. It is on this foundation that the power of the House to direct the issue of writs for by-elections rests. The House, too, claims the right to exclude strangers, and to restrain the publication of debates. The former (now embodied in S.O. No. 110) may be used as a tactic in party warfare, and may also be used to secure a secret session, though the secrecy of the latter was, in wartime, substantially reinforced by Defence Regulations.[33] The latter privilege was used to restrain partial reporting but, from the time of Wilkes, has not been insisted on save in the interests of secrecy. From 1908 *Hansard*, the official report of debates, has been under the control of the House.[34] One element of this privilege remains important: leave of the House is necessary before evidence may be given of proceedings therein.[35]

Exclusive jurisdiction and contempt. Further the House makes two important claims. First, it claims exclusive jurisdiction over proceedings within its walls. This claim has many aspects, some of which affect the privileges already mentioned, but above all this claim affects relationships with the courts, and it will be there discussed. Second, the House claims the right to punish both members and non-members for contempt. Contempt is a concept somewhat broader than privilege. While a breach of privilege may be punished by the House as contempt, not all contempts can be assigned to any specific head of privilege. Generally it suffices to say that this power will be used to protect the dignity and effectiveness of the House. Thus, interfering with witnesses before Committees of the House, or obstructing members, or abusing or pillorying them, will be regarded as contempt.[36] It is this power which can be used to protect growing institutions, such as the meetings of the parliamentary parties, and to protect the dignity and probity of the House against modern attacks upon it.[37] So broad a power is undoubtedly necessary, but it can also be dangerous to the rest of the community, and as a result the Committee of Privileges has frequently urged restraint upon members.[38] When, however, issue is joined with the courts the House is not so diffident in advancing its claims.

The punishments which the House can inflict for breach of privilege are varied. So far as members are concerned the House can expel,

---

[32] See, too, House of Commons Disqualification Act 1957, ss. 6 and 7.
[33] *e.g.*, reg. 3 (2) of the Defence (General) Regulations 1939.
[34] See for the history of this matter Trewin, *Printer to the House.*
[35] See, *e.g.*, 486 H.C.Deb. 1973 and *Dingle* v. *Assoc. Newspapers Ltd.* [1960] 2 Q.B. 405; the subsequent proceedings ([1961] 2 Q.B. 162) are not here relevant.
[36] See, *e.g.*, the instances given in Erskine May, 17th ed., p. 109 *et seq.*
[37] See (1946–47) H.C. 138 and the debate thereon: 443 H.C.Deb. 1096–1200; see too the resolution passed in 1947: 445 H.C.Deb. 1095–1159.
[38] *e.g.* (1950–51) H.C. 244; or as to the give and take of political debate see (1963–64) H.C. 247 (Mr. Quintin Hogg) and (1964–65) H.C. 269 (Mr. Callaghan).

suspend, reprimand or admonish; so far as others are concerned the House can imprison (as presumably it could in an extreme case of a member) or reprimand or admonish. Imprisonment is during the pleasure of the House and prorogation causes the release of the contemnor, who could, however, be rearrested if the House saw fit. At one time the House claimed the right to fine for contempt but this claim must now be regarded as abandoned.[39] The fit punishment in any particular case is determined by the House as a whole, which does not always follow the recommendations of the Committee of Privileges.[40]

The courts and privilege. Historically privilege has tended to grow, indeed the nature of privilege requires that it should both grow and change, to meet changing circumstances. The extended role of Parliament and the emergence of new forces of many kinds, from broadcasting or nationalised industries to trade unions, require at least a reinterpretation of traditional rules. Thus the struggles in relation to privilege are not concluded, the more so since past conflicts have often ended in an inconclusive manner and there thus remains an uncertainty even in fundamentals.[41] So far as conclusions have been reached they are often couched in terms which conceal rather than solve the real difficulties. Some of the oldest pronouncements upon the relationship of the courts to privilege must be rejected as based upon a confusion between one House, and the whole of Parliament acting in a legislative capacity.[42] At other times the attitude of the Commons to the courts was affected by the fact that, in England, the House of Lords was the ultimate court of appeal, and to that extent an admission of the jurisdiction of the courts could mean a subjection of one House to another.[43] In Scotland political evolution had not created the same stress,[44] though similar issues were emerging at the time of the Union. In consequence, the beginning of the eighteenth century may be taken as the starting-point for the modern law of privilege, and for the reasons already discussed the Union did not substantially affect the development of doctrines.

39 The last case when a fine was imposed was in 1666, and the power was denied by Lord Mansfield in the course of argument in *R.* v. *Pitt* (1762) 3 Burr. 1335.
40 See, *e.g.*, 443 H.C.Deb. 1096–1200. For the procedure where contempt is alleged see Erskine May, *Parliamentary Practice*, Chap. VIII.
41 *Re Parliamentary Privilege Act 1770* [1958] A.C. at p. 354, *per* Lord Simonds. The process of reconsideration is perhaps continuing; in 1965 a Select Committee was established to review the law: 731 H.C.Deb. 368. The report has now been published: (1967–68) H.C. 34.
42 In particular *Thorpe's Case* (1452) 5 Rot.Parl. 240, *per* Fortescue C.J. The fallacy was often exposed, notably in *Stockdale* v. *Hansard* (1839) 9 A. & E. 1, yet it persists—see *Bowles* v. *Bank of England* [1913] 1 Ch. 57.
43 This is apparent in the account of the proceedings in the *Case of the Men of Aylesbury*: Hatsell, *Precedents*, Vol. III. The jealousy on the part of the Commons of any interference by a peer in an election, and of the Lords in matters of finance, must be remembered.
44 Compare A.P.S. VII, App. 101b.

Ashby v. *White*, and its sequel the *Case of the Men of Aylesbury* (*or Paty's Case*),[45] are the real starting-point. The first involved the action of a burgess against a returning officer who had refused his vote. The Court of Queen's Bench held (Holt C.J. dissenting) that the action could not be maintained. Holt C.J., while recognising a jurisdiction in the Commons, maintained that here was an issue of property fit to be tried in the courts. It was his view which was upheld by the Lords on an appeal by writ of error. When others sued, they were imprisoned for contempt by the Commons, and their efforts to secure release produced the second case. Again Holt C.J. dissented. The majority of judges would not examine claims to privilege but, in the view of the Chief Justice, privilege being a matter of law, the courts must decide upon claims to it when the issue was properly raised. Again there was an appeal to the Lords, but this time, despite conferences between the Houses, no agreed solution was reached, so that no final answer was then given on the fundamental matters raised by Holt C.J. His views later received support in *Burdett* v. *Abbott*,[46] though the course which that case took provoked no crisis. That crisis came with the *Stockdale* v. *Hansard* complex of litigation. The House having ordered a report to be printed and Stockdale having thought himself libelled in it, Stockdale raised an action. In that Hansard pleaded the defence of justification with success. In a second action,[47] on the direction of the Commons, the defence rested upon the order of the House for publication, and upon the plea of privilege. As to the first plea the answer was short, the resolution of one House cannot alter the law. To a certain extent that point also arose on the second plea for, said Patteson J., the House could not by simple declaration give to itself new privileges. Privilege was a matter of law, and there was nothing mysterious in the laws and customs of Parliament. Thus, applying the law, the courts would determine whether or not a privilege existed. Subject to this, so far as the internal regulation and proceedings of either House were concerned the courts would not inquire further.

What is noticeable, apart from this insistence that privilege was a matter of law, is the analogy drawn with other courts—this is particularly clear in the passages wherein Patteson J. dealt with commitment for contempt, but it runs through all the cases from Holt C.J. in *Ashby* v. *White* to Lord Ellenborough in *Burdett* v. *Abbott*. This aspect of privilege is common to both jurisdictions and was strongly emphasised by Lord Jeffrey.[48] Equally the Court of Session showed a readiness to

---

[45] (1703) 2 Ld.Raym. 938; (1704) 3 Ld.Raym. 320; *Paty's Case* (1705) 2 Ld.Raym. 1105.
[46] (1811) 14 East 1.
[47] (1839) 9 A. & E. 1; the whole background is related in Trewin, *Printer to the House*.
[48] The *Auchterarder Case* (Robertson's Report, Vol. II, p. 374); and see Lord Gillies at p. 34 *et seq.*, fully accepting the authority of *Stockdale* v. *Hansard*.

determine within these limits the scope of privilege.[49]   In Scotland as in
England the courts regarded privilege as a matter of law, and indeed the
supposed basis of some privileges—that the member was *absens
reipublicae causa*, or alternatively held a *munus publicum*, reinforces
this.[50]   Yet this equation, in dealing with the exercise of privilege by
the Commons, with the exercise of jurisdiction by another superior
court, had a consequence in England which could, in practice, take away
much of the protection conferred in *Stockdale* v. *Hansard*.   When
Stockdale brought yet another action (which was allowed to go by
default) and the Sheriff of Middlesex attempted to levy execution, the
latter was committed by the House for contempt.   When he sought his
liberty by habeas corpus proceedings, the return to the writ was simply
that he was held for contempt of the House.   Such a return was in the
Case of the Sheriff of Middlesex[51] held to be sufficient.   Had a particular
ground of contempt been specified the court could have looked at that
and judged its validity.   As it was, since the return to the writ merely
stated that those concerned were held under warrant from the Speaker
for contempt of the House, and such was a good ground for detention if
true, the court would go no further into the matter.   To some extent the
case may turn upon procedural peculiarities relating to that writ.   If that
were so the case might be of limited authority where, as in Scotland,
habeas corpus does not, for these purposes, exist.   Essentially, however,
the opinions turn upon the deference which one superior court owes to
another which is acting within its jurisdiction.[52]   This fact makes the
general acceptance of the principle of the case more likely.[53]   Once it is
conceded that any court must have power to commit for contempt for its
own protection,[54] then, if it be also accepted, as it seems it must be, that
in the case of a superior court or its equivalent another court will not
normally inquire into justification,[55] the same answer will be given in
Scotland as was given in England, despite the fact that procedure by
petition (which is necessary in Scotland) might at first sight seem to
open up a wider possibility of debate on facts than does the English

49 *Lady Greenock* v. *Sir John Shaw* (1709) Mor. 8563 and 9166; *Livingston* v. *Morison*
(1709) Mor. 8565; (1710) Fount. II, 526; *Lord Lyon's Case* (1753) Elch. *sub. tit.*
Member No. 59; see also the High Court, *Mackintosh* v. *Dempster* (1767)
Macl.Rem.Cas. 383.
50 See Stair, III, 1, 37, and *Molison* v. *Clark* (1707) Mor. 10398, and *Lady Greenock* v.
Sir John Shaw (1709) Mor. 8563.
51 (1840) 11 A. & E. 273.
52 Though in *Gosset* v. *Howard* (1845) 10 Q.B. 411 at 456 Parke B. put the House
somewhat higher.   See also *The Queen* v. *Richards, ex p. Fitzpatrick and Browne*
(1954) 92 C.L.R. 157, where the power to commit is regarded as an essential for
Parliament, and where this same element of respect is apparent.
53 See the summary of the case in *Middleton* v. *Anderson* (1842) 4 D. 957 at 1016,
per Lord Mackenzie, and Lord Jeffrey in the *Auchterarder Case* (Robertson's Report,
Vol. II, p. 374).
54 *Hamilton* v. *Anderson* (1858) 3 MacQ. 368.
55 *Macleod* v. *Spiers* (1884) 11 R.(J.) 26 at 32.   In other cases, such as *Milburn*, 1946
S.C. 301, where justification for committal was inquired into, the circumstances
were upon the record and, because of the form of procedure, were properly debated.

procedure. This result is all the more likely when allowance is made for the deference customarily paid by courts to Parliament or either of its Houses.[56] Therefore, although the courts might appear to have given away in practice in the *Case of the Sheriff of Middlesex* all that they had claimed in *Stockdale* v. *Hansard*, in truth the two cases go upon the same theory, and both are equally consistent with the doctrine upheld in the courts that privileges are part of the law of the land.

The generalities of that complex of litigation do not, however, conclude the matter without further possibility of dispute. " When," said Lord Denman C.J. in *Stockdale* v. *Hansard*, " the subject-matter falls within their jurisdiction, no doubt we cannot question their judgment," but he would question whether a particular matter did so fall or not. This is the question which harks back to *Ashby* v. *White* and is echoed in later cases such as *Bradlaugh* v. *Gossett*.[57] There the distinction, inherent in all the above cases, is drawn between a right to be exercised within the House itself, such as a right of sitting, and a right to be exercised out of and independently of the House. On the former the judgment of the House would be final. On the latter the courts would judge for themselves independently of what the House might say.[58] The exact scope of what is an internal proceeding or a proceeding in Parliament is by no means clear. The House may, as it did in the proceedings relating to Mr. Strauss, change its mind, and its view need not coincide with that of the courts.[59] It is on the whole likely that the courts today will concede rather more, as being the " internal " affairs of Parliament, than was at one time the case,[60] and to that extent the possibility of conflict may be diminished. While it may be that, in effect, privilege is now recognised as a matter of general law, and to that extent the duality which provoked *Stockdale* v. *Hansard* is no longer strongly felt, the possibility of conflict nevertheless exists by reason of this room for divergent interpretations of certain important phrases.

This whole story and the underlying theory have an importance which goes beyond the confines of privilege. As has been emphasised,

[56] Without going to the extreme of Lord Coalston in *Mackintosh* v. *Dempster* (1767) Macl.Rem.Cas. 383, where he said: " for how would it look, if our judgment this day shall differ from that of the House of Commons," it is clear that such bodies must be normally allowed to be masters of their own affairs.

[57] (1884) 12 Q.B.D. 271; see particularly Stephen J. at p. 278: " I think the House of Commons is not subject to the control of Her Majesty's Courts in its administration of that part of the statute law which has relation to its own internal proceedings." For a general account of the background to all the *Bradlaugh* litigation see Armstein, " Gladstone and the *Bradlaugh* Case " (1962) 6 *Victorian Studies* 303.

[58] *Cf. Bradlaugh* v. *Clarke* (1883) 8 App.Cas. 354; and see *Wellesley* v. *Duke of Beaufort* (1831) 2 Russ. & M. 639 at 660.

[59] In *Re Parliamentary Privilege Act 1770* [1958] A.C. 331 at 353 the court studiously avoided interpreting that phrase in the particular context in question. Compare, however, *Rivlin* v. *Bilainkin* [1953] 1 Q.B. 485.

[60] Compare the general tenor of *Harper* v. *Home Secretary* [1955] Ch. 238, though it must be noted that the treatment of the validity of the Boundary Commissioners' Report as being for Parliament alone was in that case arrived at on the basis of statutory construction, not of privilege. See too *Dingle* v. *Associated Newspapers Ltd.* [1960] 2 Q.B. 405, where possible difficulties were avoided.

privilege was important in the general growth of Parliament, and on the other side claims to privilege are affected by that growth.[61] Even more broadly, these cases should be borne in mind in any discussion of the sovereignty of Parliament and judicial review. These cases make clear both the grounds for, and the limits of, the deference of courts to Parliament. The same sort of reasoning is applicable in cases such as *Edinburgh and Dalkeith Ry.* v. *Wauchope*.[62] These are essentially concerned with the internal proceedings of Parliament, which the courts refuse to examine. To the extent, however, that their basis is not peculiar to legislation it may be that their weight in the argument about the sovereignty of Parliament is correspondingly reduced. Certainly the two lines of authority should be considered together.

PRIVILEGE IN THE HOUSE OF LORDS

The main controversies about privilege have centred upon the Commons, and to a large extent the privileges of the two Houses are similar, hence only the major points of difference will be here noted. At the outset privileges of Parliament must be distinguished from privileges of peerage. The latter inhere in a peer whether he be a peer of Parliament or not. All peers are immune from jury service,[63] or from arrest in civil process.[64] In judicial proceedings they take the oath in ordinary form.[65] At the Union all the privileges of the peers of England were communicated to the peers of Scotland under Article XXIII. The privilege most emphasised in that Article, trial by peers, was abolished by the Criminal Justice Act 1948, s. 30. The privileges of peers of Parliament were communicated and made uniform by the same Article at the Union. The House of Lords claims freedom from arrest for its members as peers of Parliament, though the claim is limited,[66] and in regard to that House the claim of a right of access to the Sovereign is an individual right, not a corporate one. There is also an individual right to have a protest entered in the *Journal* of the House. Freedom of speech, and in one sense of opinion, is insisted on.[67] Like the House of Commons the House claims a right to regulate its own composition, and it has gone so

---

[61] In a different way the general growth in the status and significance of Parliament perhaps affected the court in *Harper* v. *Home Secretary* [1955] Ch. 238, and because on that score more was accorded to Parliament than would once have been the case, the issue of privilege did not arise for decision.

[62] (1842) 1 Bell's App.Cas. 252. In contrast the House of Lords was not certain how far a somewhat similar principle would go in relation to delegated legislation. See 153 H.L.Deb. 331–352, the debate preceding the Laying of Documents before Parliament (Interpretation) Act 1948.

[63] Jurors (Scotland) Act 1825, s. 2; Juries Act 1870, s. 9.

[64] *Stourton* v. *Stourton* [1963] 1 All E.R. 606; but see *Young* v. *Earl of Bute* (1716) Mor. 10030 for alternative remedies.

[65] *Brysson* v. *Duke of Athol* (1710) Mor. 10028, which is concerned with the position immediately after the Union, and *Campbell* v. *Countess of Fife* (1772) Mor. 9404.

[66] By S.O.s 71, 72.

[67] See S.O. 74.

far, in the *Wensleydale Peerage* case, as determining whether or not a particular form of peerage entitles the holder to a seat in Parliament.

The position with regard to suspension or disqualification of a member is not clear. It seems that the House could not impose any disqualification upon its members which did not exist in the general law for itself or other similar bodies. Thus the House could exclude on the ground of conviction in Scotland for offences where such convictions would in England disqualify from membership by statute. Suspension presents different issues, and, on the analogy of the outcome of the *Wilkes* case, it seems likely that such a power exists, a likelihood which is increased by reason of the admitted ability of the House to imprison a member of it. Nevertheless, the House, and a committee of it, have recently expressed doubt whether even such a limited power exists.[68] The difficulty arises from the fact that the " external " right of standing and the " internal " right of membership, which were distinct in the *Wilkes* case, are rolled together in the case of a peer. Like the House of Commons the House has also a generalised power to commit for contempt, though it has been much more rarely used, and the House may punish by fine, or by imprisonment for a fixed time, in addition to other methods. The power of the House to summon by writs of assistance the judges and the Law Officers may also be ranked among its privileges,[69] but it is one which has substantially declined in importance, at least so far as the judges are concerned.

The link between privilege and the evolution of Parliament is clear. The decay of certain privileges of the Lords is one indication, the heat with which certain privileges of the Commons were insisted upon is another. Each rule tends to be marked by an era. In those circumstances, without denying the continuing importance of privilege to protect Parliament, questions may still be asked about the rules as they are. Whether, for example, the immunity in respect of words spoken in Parliament should be as absolute as it is, or whether it should be capable of being lifted by either House, or whether each House should remain sole judge of offence and punishment without any appeal,[70] are among the questions which can be raised. It is then to be hoped that the moves to consider this branch of law will bear fruit.

---

[68] See Report on the Powers of the House in relation to the attendance of its members (1955–56) H.L. (7) (66–1) (67) and the debate thereon: 206 H.L.Deb. 987; and see 209 H.L.Deb. 891–950.

[69] See 206 H.L.Deb. 337–382. This related to the common law judges in England. The Scottish judges were, for obvious historical reasons, differently treated, but after the Union the House adopted the practice of requiring their attendance or advice on occasion. See *Lords Journal*, XXV, p. 99 *et seq.*

[70] The position of the courts (in England at least), which was formerly similar, has after all been radically changed by the Administration of Justice Act 1960. The recommendations of the Report of the Select Committee (1967–68) H.C. 34, if adopted, could go far to modernise and clarify the law of privilege, and would also increase the protections afforded to those charged with a breach of privilege.

CHAPTER 8

THE FUNCTIONING OF PARLIAMENT

THE FRAMEWORK

ANY Parliament has now a maximum life of five years from the day
on which it was appointed to meet by the writ of summons, though its
life may be prolonged by a statute passed in the ordinary way,[1] and
it may be cut short at any time by an earlier dissolution. The statutory
maximum life of a Parliament has some important practical consequences, but the ability of the executive to cause an earlier dissolution is
of far greater importance, being fundamental to the relationship of the
government to Parliament. It is upon that that the predominance of the
government greatly depends. A session of any Parliament is brought
to an end by prorogation, a prerogative act done upon ministerial advice.
In law there is no necessary duration for a session, and, while for practical reasons annual meetings of Parliament are now necessary, the only
requirement in the Bill of Rights and the Claim of Right is that
Parliament should meet frequently. Prorogation puts an end to all
uncompleted business then before Parliament. Within a session each
House controls adjournments for appropriate recesses, the major ones in
fact coinciding.[2] The duration of Parliament is now independent of the
life of the Sovereign, and if the Sovereign should die after a dissolution
and before the date of a new Parliament, then the old Parliament revives
for a maximum period of six months.[3] Arrangements are made for the
earlier recall of Parliament when it stands adjourned or prorogued,
should circumstances so require.[4]

The principal officers are, in the House of Commons, the Speaker
elected by the House and approved by the Sovereign,[5] and the Chairman

---

[1] The Septennial Act 1715, as amended by the Parliament Act 1911. The Parliament
which was elected in 1935 was continued until 1945.

[2] Exceptionally the House of Lords has resumed sitting before the House of Commons,
e.g., in September 1947, though it is symptomatic of the standing of the two Houses
that the government refused to make any statement since the Commons was not
sitting: 151 H.L.Deb. 1410.

[3] Representation of the People Act 1867, s. 51; Succession to the Crown Act 1707,
ss. 4 and 5.

[4] By the Standing Orders of the House of Commons and a resolution of the House of
Lords; and see Meeting of Parliament Acts 1797, 1799, 1870 and the Parliament
(Elections and Meeting) Act 1943. In certain circumstances in an emergency
Parliament must be recalled: see, e.g., Emergency Powers Act 1920, s. 1, and the
Reserve Forces Act 1966, s. 5 (2). See, too, the Prorogation Act 1867.

[5] By custom, the Speaker, once elected, is normally not opposed in his constituency,
nor in successive Parliaments. His actions cannot be challenged except on a
substantive motion. In contrast the Chairman of Ways and Means (in effect the
Deputy Speaker) is likely to change with the government. See as to his office

of Ways and Means, who presides over the committees of the whole House and is Deputy Speaker. The choice of these officers is, so far as is possible, made by agreement between the parties, though failing such agreement the issue is decided in the House. Outside the House the Speaker is its representative, inside it he presides over it, and complete impartiality is expected of him. Thus, in modern times he does not participate in debates, nor does he vote, save in a case of equality, and then casts his vote so that the House may consider the matter again. The Chairman of Ways and Means is not so isolated from politics, though while he holds office he is expected not to participate in debates or divisions. In the Lords the presiding officer is the Lord Chancellor (with, as his first deputy, the Lord Chairman of Committees) but the burden and the nature of his duties is very different from those of the Speaker. He is a member of the Cabinet, speaks for (and changes with) the government, and thus is no neutral figure, as is the Speaker. The Leader of the House is, in each case, a member of the Cabinet, but while he has, with the aid of the Whips, the control of government business in the House, he is, particularly in the Commons, a guardian of the rights of the House as a whole, and as such has distinct obligations.[6]

JUDICIAL FUNCTIONS

The judicial functions of Parliament are now primarily the concern of the House of Lords. The Commons try their own issues of contempt, have nominally the right to impeach, but any claims to any general jurisdictions would not now be advanced.[7]

The House of Lords has, as a result of the Criminal Justice Act 1948, lost any original criminal jurisdiction, and claims, earlier advanced, to original civil jurisdiction [8] have now been abandoned. Any original jurisdiction is now limited to peerage claims. It has appellate jurisdiction in civil matters from England, Scotland and Northern Ireland, and in criminal matters from England and Northern Ireland.[9] The civil appellate jurisdiction is founded upon the right to petition Parliament or the King in Council,[10] and will hereafter be discussed in the context of

Laundy, *The Office of Speaker*, and for the general organisation Marsden, *The Officers of the Commons*, and as a background Roskell, *The Commons and their Speakers 1376–1523*.

[6] See Morrison, *Government and Parliament*, 3rd ed., p. 130 *et seq.*; and see p. 199, *post*.

[7] The last case when the House stretched out in this way was in 1721.

[8] *Skinner* v. *E. India Co.* (1666) 6 St.Tr. 710.

[9] The limited nature of this appeal was broadened by the Administration of Justice Act 1960, which now regulates the matter. Appeal lies on a point of law of general public importance at the instance of the defence or prosecution. A like appeal lies from the Courts-Martial Appeal Court, a United Kingdom court. Any criminal appellate jurisdiction from Scotland was rejected in *Mackintosh* v. *L.A.* (1876) 3 R.(H.L.) 34.

[10] See Richardson and Sayles, *Parliaments and Great Councils in Mediaeval England*; and see *Introduction to Scottish Legal History* (the Stair Society), Chap. XXIII.

the courts.[11]   It may, however, here be noted that the character of the
House as a court of appeal may differ from its character in other
respects.   To some extent when acting as such a court it must, in strict
law, be regarded as an extension of the jurisdiction whence comes the
appeal in question.[12]   When dealing with United Kingdom statutes,
particularly in the field of taxation, the United Kingdom character is
more obvious and in any event practice may on this matter give a
somewhat different answer to that given by legal theory.

The obviously technical nature of its work as a court presented
difficulties over membership.   The first patent for Lord Wensleydale,
which the House rejected,[13] was one attempt at a solution, as was the
elevation of Lord Colonsay.   After the inoperative attempt to abolish
all appeals to the House, the Appellate Jurisdiction Act 1876 confirmed
the jurisdiction and authorised the appointment of Lords of Appeal in
Ordinary who, together with peers who have held high judicial office,[14]
make up the House when it sits as a court.   Since lay peers are effectively
excluded from participation in judicial proceedings [15] the House has a
distinct character when sitting as a court.   Though this exclusion of lay
peers may be regarded as conventional it has certainly been recognised
in law.[16]   This distinctiveness has been further emphasised since as a
result of temporary measures taken during and after the war, which
appear to have become permanent, an Appellate Committee [17] was
established on a sessional basis.   It consists of peers qualified by statute
and its function is to hear appeals and to report to the House.   Thus
legislative business need not interrupt judicial business.[18]

11 See p. 259, post.
12 Thus, while Lord Brougham in Att.-Gen. v. Lord Advocate (1834) 2 Cl. & F. 481
   refers to it as an Imperial court, he also refers to it as a court of Scotch and
   English appeals; and compare Duncan v. Cammell Laird & Co. Ltd. [1942] A.C.
   624 and Glasgow Corporation v. Central Land Board, 1956 S.C.(H.L.) 1; though
   see I.R.C. v. City of Glasgow Police Athletic Association, 1953 S.C.(H.L.) 13; and
   generally on the point see T. B. Smith, Judicial Precedent in Scots Law; and for an
   account of the consequences of the appeal Dewar Gibb, Law from Over the Border;
   and post, p. 259.   For a general assessment see Stevens, " The Role of a Final
   Appeal Court in a Democracy: the Role of the House of Lords Today " (1965)
   28 M.L.R. 509.
13 The Wensleydale Peerage Case (1856) 5 H.L.Cas. 958.
14 Normally a Lord of Appeal in Ordinary who has retired would be able to sit in this
   second capacity, though exceptional cases appear possible where this would not be
   so.   Subsequent legislation has increased the authorised number of Lords of Appeal
   to 11: Administration of Justice Act 1968.
15 O'Connell v. The Queen (1844) 11 Cl. & F. 155; Bradlaugh v. Clarke (1883) 8
   App.Cas. 354, although in the past it seems that lay peers have been used to make
   up a quorum; see 63 L.Q.R. 151 and 65 L.Q.R. 22.
16 Re Lord Kinross (1905) 7 F.(H.L.) 138.
17 To distinguish from the older Appeal Committee which considers questions of leave
   to appeal and interlocutory matters, as to which see Johnston v. Johnston (1859) 3
   Macq. 619 at 640.   For a general description see the Introduction to Heuston,
   Lives of the Chancellors.
18 Distinctiveness in a different sense had earlier established that English judges should
   not be consulted on Scots appeals: Edinburgh and Glasgow Ry. v. Mags. of
   Linlithgow (1861) 3 Macq. 691.

LEGISLATIVE BUSINESS

Legislative business has become mainly, but by no means exclusively, the concern of the Commons as a result of general constitutional changes which were confirmed in certain respects by the Parliament Act 1911, and as a result of the Commons' claims to privilege in relation to finance, which, granted the content of modern legislation, limits the possibility of introducing many Bills in the House of Lords, despite various devices which soften the effect of the Commons' claims.[19] Attention will therefore be given in the first place to legislative procedure in the Commons.

The classification of Bills. Different types of legislation must first be distinguished. Public Bills are those affecting the community at large, and may be introduced by the government or by private members. Private Bills, initiated by petition, are for the benefit of particular persons [20] or bodies. A third category—hybrid Bills—must be distinguished. These are either Bills which could otherwise be private, but which are desired by a government department, and, on the argument that the Crown cannot petition, are introduced as public Bills, or they are Bills with a substantial public interest which nevertheless affect particular bodies.[21] The lines between each type cannot be drawn with precision, and in any particular case a decision is taken by officials of the House. Public Bills must be further distinguished. The annual financial legislation (and particularly the Appropriation Bill) though public in form is distinct in character, and Money Bills,[22] which are public Bills whose main object is to authorise expenditure or impose taxation, are again specially treated. Formerly they were required to be founded upon a resolution of a Committee of the Whole, but since 1938, when presented by a minister, they may be treated as a Bill, the financial provisions of which are subsidiary, and the necessary financial resolutions may be obtained before the Committee stage of the Bill. One rule of major importance is that the House insists that any charge upon moneys to be provided by Parliament must be recommended by the Crown—that is to say, the government. This rule has had a great

---

[19] The Commons' claims are based on resolutions of 1671 and 1678 and reaffirmed in 1860. See Erskine May, *Parliamentary Practice*, Chap. XXIX. Bills may be introduced into the Lords with the financial clauses sidelined, so that they do not formally form part of the Bill, or with bogus clauses that the measure imposes no charge. There are limits to the use of these devices, and a procedural proposal which would have let the House of Lords debate a Bill, but not as a Bill, was rejected in relation to the Legal Aid Bill 1963; see 248 H.L.Deb. 663 and 801; but *cf.* the Prices and Incomes Bill, 276 H.L.Deb., col. 1765, which was introduced as a Paper (1965–66) No. 8. Where speed is vital the device of concurrent introduction has been used, as with the Commonwealth Immigrants Act 1968.

[20] Personal Bills are introduced in the House of Lords.

[21] The Bank of England and the Cable and Wireless Bills 1946 are examples. For a typical reference to a Committee of such Bills see 631 H.C.Deb. 1397.

[22] The same term is used in the Parliament Act with a somewhat different meaning; *post*, p. 150.

influence upon the evolution of the House, and today continues to restrict the scope of legislative proposals by private members, except those supported by the government. It thus contributes to the control of the House by the government.

Public legislation

The legislative stages. Public Bills are now introduced either upon an order of the House, a method applicable to financial legislation or to Bills introduced under the so-called " Ten-Minute Rule " (S.O. 13), by which a private member may sometimes successfully launch a non-contentious Bill, or by presentation after notice, a method which covers the great majority of Bills. After a formal first reading the stages are: Second Reading, Committee, Report and Third Reading. Each stage has a particular purpose, and although there is room for repetition in debate, this specialisation is important to the efficiency of a legislature.[23] Formerly, the Second Reading was always (except for Scottish Bills) taken on the floor of the House, but now, under S.O. 60A, may be taken in Committee, as may be the Report under S.O. 62A.

The Second Reading is a debate in principle. Rejection is moved by proposing that the motion read: " That the Bill be read upon this day six months " or by a reasoned amendment, which at one time had not the finality of the more usual form, but is, it seems, acquiring it. The Committee stage may be taken in a Committee of the Whole, in a Standing Committee, or in a Select Committee or under the procedure appropriate to Welsh or Scottish Bills. Normally a Bill will be referred to a Standing Committee unless it is of major constitutional impor-tance [24] and a resolution is passed for consideration to be given in a Committee of the Whole. There are, however, no absolute rules, and practice may depend upon the state of the House and of the legislative programme, but it is likely that the pattern of recent events will mean that a Committee stage taken on the floor of the House will be increasingly rare.

There is now no limit to the number of Standing Committees, which are a relatively modern device, dating from 1882. Each now consists of a minimum of twenty members, and a maximum of fifty, and will more or less reflect the composition of the House. The Committees, although membership will vary according to the subject-matter of the Bill under consideration, are in effect not specialised, and they examine the Bill in detail upon the basis of information available to the members of the Committee for the time being. Under the Standing Order 56 adopted in 1967 ministers may speak, but not vote, in Committees of which they

---

23 The resolution of 1696 (A.P.S. X, 35) imposing delays on the passing of legislation was part of the process of Parliament asserting its rights.

24 A term of imprecise content. The Immigration Bill 1961 was, for example, thus treated.

are not members, and which are considering (broadly) government Bills. If the Bill is referred to a Select Committee,[25] then evidence may be heard. In the case of Scotland special arrangements are made by Standing Orders 61 and 62. Bills relating exclusively to Scotland are referred to the Scottish Standing Committee consisting of thirty members from Scottish constituencies to whom additions may be made of up to twenty members. This Committee must be distinguished from the Scottish Grand Committee which consists of all the Scottish members and ten to fifteen others. The Grand Committee may consider a Bill as to principle at what would otherwise be the Second Reading stage unless ten or more members object, and thereafter unless six members object, the House will not consider the Bill for the purposes of that stage.[26] Under new arrangements adopted in November 1961 a Welsh Grand Committee was created with more limited powers,[27] and additionally any Bill relating exclusively to Wales is to be considered by a Committee which includes all the members from Welsh constituencies.

The Report stage follows, at which amendments similar to those which could be put in Committee may be moved, but there can be no wrecking amendments. The last stage—Third Reading—permits only verbal amendments, so an intervening stage of recommittal is possible to enable substantial amendments to be made.

Thereafter the Bill goes, in the case of one starting in the Commons, to the Lords where the same stages occur, though in that House the substance of each stage may be somewhat different. There is a greater degree of informality, there are no Standing Committees, and little use is made of Select Committees. There is, moreover, substantially greater possibility of consultation with outside experts.[28] The amendments made by one House to a Bill starting in the other have then to be considered by the original House. This process may involve a series of references between the Houses,[29] as a result of which either agreement is reached, or disagreement remains, and if there is no agreement either the Bill must be dropped or the Parliament Act procedure must be invoked.

It is clear that to a great extent the House of Lords is now concerned mainly with revising and improving legislation sent up by the Commons, and to its work in that respect tribute has been paid. The bicameral nature of Parliament has also certain technical advantages in the

---

[25] As was the Defamation Bill 1952.

[26] The Scottish Grand Committee may also deal with the Scottish Estimates, and any specific matter concerning Scotland which is referred to it. Originally there was only one Scottish Standing Committee. A second was created in March 1963 for the remainder of the then current session; see 674 H.C.Deb. 1657.

[27] The Committee consists of the Welsh members and not more than 25 others. It has no powers over the Second Reading stage of a Bill, or over estimates. See 650 H.C.Deb. 197.

[28] See Lord Chorley, " The House of Lords Controversy " [1958] Public Law 216.

[29] See Erskine May, Parliamentary Practice, Chap. XXIX. When agreement is reached the formality of the Royal Assent follows. The Royal Assent Act 1967 provides a procedure for giving the Assent which does not disrupt business.

mechanics of legislation.[30] The Lords may, as with the Criminal Justice Bill 1948, go considerably beyond revision, but as a result of the Parliament Acts, to be discussed later, their opposition can be surmounted if that is desired.

Public Bills introduced by private members go through the same stages. While these are a valuable source of minor changes in the law, and more rarely of wider " social " changes in the law (of a type which would divide a party), limitations on the time available for such Bills, and the difficulty facing a member of " managing " such a Bill through the House, mean that they produce only a minor part of legislation as a whole. There is, moreover, the limitation that if the Bill involves a charge, government backing is essential. This situation is consistent with constitutional theory, for it has become recognised that legislation is the affair of government. It was noticeable that the Leader of the House, putting forward the procedural reforms in November 1967, gave as the first aim that of ensuring that the legislative process enabled policies to be translated into law at the speed required by the tempo of modern industrial change. Hence, despite the increased time offered for Private Members' Bills in November 1967, it seems likely that the general situation of Private Members' Bills will remain unchanged, and that those Bills which receive government backing, such as the Abortion Bill 1967, will be those that will profit.[31]

The legislative process. It would be a mistake to assume that the procedure once a Bill has been introduced is the whole of what could properly be called the legislative process. Debates upon White Papers are often significant in affecting both the time of introducing measures and their shape. These debates are to some extent a substitute for the older debates upon the resolutions to bring in a Bill. Apart from such preliminaries, legislation owes much to Reports of Royal Commissions and other bodies and to the consultative process which follows such reports before a Bill is produced. The parliamentary stages will only be seen in the right perspective if set against this background.[32] Pressures arising from the nature of a modern state have not merely forced the government to assume responsibility for the great bulk of legislation, so that we have, in effect, returned to the position that the King makes the laws in Parliament (with the substitution of responsible ministers for a personal King), but these pressures have also caused a great growth

[30] As to both points see, *e.g.*, Morrison, *Government and Parliament*, Chap. IX.

[31] See Bromhead, *Private Members Bills*, and A. P. Herbert, *The Ayes Have It.* For the present position, see 753 H.C.Deb. 155. The quotation from the Leader of the House is at 753 H.C.Deb. 246.

[32] See Griffith, " The Place of Parliament in the Legislative Process " (1951) 14 M.L.R. 279 and 425. It must be remembered that Maitland said of the eighteenth-century Parliament that " It seems afraid to rise to the dignity of a general proposition." See also Jennings, *Parliament*; Thring, *Practical Legislation*; and Ilbert, *Legislative Methods and Forms.* The flavour of proceedings can be gained from Hanson and Wiseman, *Parliament at Work*, and see Lord Chorley [1968] *Public Law*, p. 52.

in the amount of legislation. The emergence of Standing Committees, the provisions for taking the Second Reading in Committee, and changes in the procedure for financial legislation, are all marks of this growth and are designed to speed the legislative process. Other devices now play an important part in meeting that pressure. Some, such as the Consolidation of Enactments (Procedure) Act 1949, attempt to simplify procedure. Other devices are aimed at shortening and concentrating debates. The earliest of these, the Closure, originated by Speaker Brand in 1881, enables the debate to be ended if, in his discretion, the Speaker will accept a motion to that effect, and provided that, in the House, at least 100 members vote in its favour.[33] Another—the Kangaroo—enables (S.O. 33) the Speaker or Chairman of Ways and Means, in order to avoid repetition, to select amendments to be discussed.[34] The most important of these devices is probably the Guillotine, an Allocation of Time Order, under which, by order of the House, a timetable is set for the progress of a Bill.[35] Such an order, by ensuring a proper distribution of time, may in fact assist parliamentary scrutiny of legislation, though proposals to make such orders common form have been rejected, perhaps because the process of obstruction which may lead to such orders has a legitimate place in other aspects of parliamentary life.

The whole flow of legislation is regulated by two Cabinet Committees, the Future Legislation Committee and the Legislation Committee, which determine the content of the legislative programme for any session and survey progress during the session.[36] It is only when legislation has found a place in the programme that the parliamentary draftsmen (who are under the Treasury or, for Scotland, in the Lord Advocate's Office) can start work upon the Bill. Thus, at times, pressure upon them is extreme. All these factors, coupled with the fact that growing international organisation in trade or transport and the continuing evolution of the Commonwealth produce a quantity of inescapable legislation, must be borne in mind when such matters as delegated legislation are considered.

Two other considerations must also be borne in mind in considering that part of the legislative process which occurs in Parliament. The first is that increasingly law is technical and made for technicians. The

[33] The device has been extended to Standing Committees, the relevant figure being reduced to the quorum for the Committee fixed under S.O. 9.

[34] This power was extended in 1934 to Chairmen of Committees (S.O. 59 (5)).

[35] Sample Allocation of Time Orders are set out in Morrison, *Government and Parliament*, App. B. The details of orders are as far as possible worked out between the party Whips. A voluntary time-table for Committee and Report stages was agreed in November 1967: 754 H.C.Deb. 247 *et seq.* In an emergency the whole procedure can be got through in a very short time, as with the Southern Rhodesia Act 1965; see 270 H.L.Deb. 373 and 720 H.C.Deb. 687, when all substantial stages were taken quickly on November 15.

[36] See Morrison, *Government and Parliament*, 3rd ed., Chap. XI, and Sir Granville Ram, "The Improvement of the Statute Book" (1951) J.S.P.T.L. 442.

techniques involved may be those relating to radioactive substances, food and drugs in their chemical aspects, town planning, company law, or indeed any branch of the complexities of modern life. Detailed criticism of legislative proposals requires an expert knowledge, and essentially the House of Commons is not an expert House. The member is chosen to stand not so much because of any expertise he may have, but because he will be a good candidate. Moreover, so far as there is any particular expertise in the House it tends to be maldistributed between the parties. These factors, no matter how well briefed members may be, affect the detailed criticism to which a measure may be subjected. The second consideration, which affects the same matter, is that the House is above all (and properly so) a political arena, and that, since legislation (in so far as it is not purely technical) is a reflection of government policy, the House will tend to debate it (especially in those proceedings which are in the whole House) in political terms. Thus the effective criticism in the House must be limited by the relationship of government to Parliament which will be discussed later. Such considerations may enhance the importance of the non-parliamentary stages of legislation, of the revising functions of the House of Lords (where the political battle is not of such significance) and of other forms of legislation. They do not, however, diminish the importance of parliamentary criticism from the point of view of the struggle between government and alternative government.

Private legislation

In regard to private legislation Parliament is as much concerned with the protection of individual rights as with conferring new powers. In both jurisdictions this form of legislation has a long history.[37] Its importance may have declined for a variety of reasons. More general empowering Acts are now passed and Divorce and Naturalisation Bills, which at one time were numerous, are now superseded by other means to the same ends, but local Acts continue to be important as a source of power and, particularly in Scotland, as regulating the lives of citizens of particular areas. This form of legislation also remains important since it gives Parliament an immediate contact with local administration and affords a method of experimenting with new forms of public services. It seems likely, however, that this second aspect has declined. It is being increasingly expected that much of what was once done by private legislation should now be done by public Acts. To a certain extent such an attitude is a reflection of changes which have been noted under public legislation, but it is arguable how far such an attitude should prevail,

---

37 See Clifford, *History of Private Bill Legislation*; Williams, *History of Private Bill Procedure*; and Terry, *The Scottish Parliament*. In 1645 a special committee was appointed by the Parliament of Scotland for this purpose (A.P.S. VI, 288) and later particular times were set aside for such legislation in Parliament as a whole.

in the context.[38] In modern times disadvantages have been found in the procedure for private legislation. Its adversary character, although valuable, has limiting effects, since a choice has to be made between alternatives, neither of which may, on examination, offer the best solution.

General procedure. Two forms must be distinguished, the one applicable to England and Wales, and occasionally to Scotland, the other applicable to Scotland. Bills are initiated by petition, and the general form requires the deposit and advertisement of the Bill, and that individual notice should be given to those particularly affected. Opponents of the measure may petition against it. The promoters' petition is considered by Examiners (one appointed by the Lords and one by the Speaker) to ensure that Standing Orders have been complied with, and any non-compliance is further considered by the Standing Orders Committee. Thereafter it is determined in which House the Bill shall originate, this being purely a matter of convenience. At that stage petitions against the measure are considered by the Court of Referees where the *locus standi* of the petitioners may be objected to. It is only where he has a particular interest that an opponent will be heard. Thus, individual ratepayers will not be heard as such, though representative organisations of interests may be.[39]

The stages of a private Bill are similar in name to those of a public Bill, but differ in substance. The Bill is deemed to have been read a first time once it is laid on the Table. The Second Reading is normally also a formality unless objection is raised, which is infrequent. " Instructions " to the Committee to deal with particular matters in a particular way may be moved at this stage. In the case of Bills promoted by nationalised industries it has, however, come to be recognised that the debate may be more general upon that industry.[40] Thus the Second Reading is not, as in the case of public and hybrid Bills, taken as establishing the principle of the Bill, and at the Committee stage the promoters will be put to proof of the need for the proposed Bill.[41] If that be proved, then the Bill is considered in detail. Throughout, the proceedings at the Committee stage are judicial in character. Counsel are heard, and witnesses examined for both promoters and opponents and the views of government departments are considered. Thereafter

---

[38] Some of the arguments are discussed in the *Report of the Joint Committee on Promotion of Private Bills* (1958–59) H.C.P. 262. There are also procedural factors which required that the Pipe-lines Act 1962 should be public, rather than that the same objects be attained by private Bills.

[39] See, *e.g.*, the cases reported in the various series of *Locus Standi Reports.* A convenient summary is to be found in the supplement to the *Encyclopaedia of the Laws of Scotland*, Tit. *Private Legislation*. In the case of urban authorities in England ratepayers may, but often do not, express their views in town meetings under the Local Government Act 1933, s. 255.

[40] *Report of Joint Committee on Private Bill Procedure* (1955–56) H.C. 139, § 15.

[41] See for a good account of the procedure Hanson, " The Leeds Private Bill " (1957) 35 *Public Administration* 45.

the Report and Third Reading stages follow in the original House and a like procedure will be followed in the other House. There may be thus two " hearings " before Committees, but frequently adjustment and compromise are made before the first House so that the second hearing may be less contentious.[42] This requirement of proof of need means that even unopposed Bills must be referred to a committee, though in this case one which is especially composed.

Scottish procedure. It is evident that the procedure may be lengthy and expensive particularly if two full hearings are involved. It is one of the advantages of the Scottish procedure that expense is mitigated. That procedure originating in the Act of 1899 is now governed by the Private Legislation (Scotland) Act 1936. Under that Act, with the exception of estate Bills, all matters which would otherwise be dealt with by private Bill must, in relation to Scotland, be dealt with by the Provisional Order procedure. Objection was taken to the original proposals on the grounds that this excluded the citizen's right to petition Parliament. The procedure has, however, in its present form, similarities to the procedure by way of Bill. Petitions are made to the Secretary of State to make a Provisional Order in the terms of a draft.[43] Preliminary advertisement and notice are equally necessary. The petition is considered by the Chairman of Ways and Means and the Chairman of Committees of the Lords, who report to the Secretary of State. If they report that the measure relates to matters outside Scotland to such an extent, or raises questions of public policy of such novelty and importance " that they should be dealt with by Bill," then the Secretary of State must refuse the order.[44] Similarly if a promoter with diverse interests wishes to promote a measure having effect inside and outside Scotland the 1936 Act provides a method by which procedure by Bill may be substituted, in whole or part, for procedure by Provisional Order and under modern practice a fairly wide use has been made of this power. Compliance with General Orders is examined, and if there is opposition to the Order the Secretary of State directs an inquiry before Commissioners. The latter are chosen from panels, two parliamentary panels being made up from members of each House, and one panel being non-parliamentary. Normally two Commissioners are chosen from each parliamentary panel, but all may be chosen from one. If four members cannot be obtained from the parliamentary panels resort is had to the non-parliamentary panel, which is made up of citizens of distinction. Such a situation is relatively uncommon. These Commissioners hold the inquiry into the Order, normally in Edinburgh or Glasgow, but it

[42] A Bill may in the first instance be referred to a Joint Committee.
[43] Such petitions may be made twice a year, and not once only as with Bills.
[44] The proposal to remove the *ex officio* members from the Glasgow Town Council was thus taken and the proposal to alter the status of Grangemouth was regarded as requiring a Bill. In one case, the Church of Scotland (Property and Endowments) Act 1933, what started as a Provisional Order ended as a public Act.

may be held anywhere that is convenient in Scotland. The procedure before the Commissioners is similar to that before a committee at Westminster, save that the Commissioners determine questions of *locus standi* as part of the inquiry.

The report of the Commissioners is final if it is against the Order, for the Secretary of State may not make it in the face of an adverse report. If, however, the Commissioners report that the Order should be made, with or without modifications, this report does not bind him. He may issue the Order with such modifications as appear to him to be necessary, having regard to the report and to the recommendations of the chairman or of government departments. To be valid the Order still requires confirmation by a Bill. If at this stage there is still opposition and petitions have been lodged against the Confirmation Bill a member may move that it be referred to a Joint Committee of both Houses which will operate as in other private legislation. If such a motion is not carried the Bill is deemed to have passed all stages up to and including the Committee stage. Only one measure has been thus referred, and it is clear that great weight is given in Parliament to the Commissioners' report. Thus, in practice, there is, under this system, only one inquiry, which, being local, involves a substantial saving. Some saving is certain even if there are two hearings since one will be local before the Commissioners.[45]

Where there is no opposition in the first place, the Secretary of State may, and at times does, order a local inquiry (which will be held as above) and in any event he may himself modify the Order in the light of any comments of the chairman or government departments. Again the submission of a Confirmation Bill to Parliament is required.

Other legislative forms. Although the Scottish procedure has not been extended, Provisional Order procedure, which contains an element of parliamentary control, has to a certain extent displaced private legislation. The latest form, under the Statutory Orders (Special Procedure) Act 1945, was intended to produce a unified system, but has not had that effect. Under that Act, the Order after inquiry is laid before Parliament. At that stage an attempt is made to divide petitions against the Order into those of amendment and those of general objection. The former are always referred to a Joint Committee of both Houses, the latter are not unless one House so directs. If the Committee reports the Order with amendments which are not acceptable to the minister he may either withdraw it, or schedule the original Order to a Bill, which is treated as a public Bill which has passed the Committee stage. On the whole this amalgam of procedures has not proved successful.[46]

---

[45] Despite the advantages of locality and of reducing expense, suggestions to make the procedure more generally applicable have been rejected (1955–56) H.C. 139.
[46] See (1950) 3 *Parliamentary Affairs* 458.

It is thus evident that there is a spectrum of private legislation both as to degree of parliamentary control and as to content. At times such legislation is particular, at times it resembles public legislation. This ambiguity of character is reflected in the uncertainty of the attitude of the courts. As has been indicated such legislation was, even apart from the Acts *salvo jure cujuslibet*, treated as distinct from public legislation,[47] and private Acts were, until the Interpretation Act 1850, required to be specially pleaded,[48] and today the construction of private Acts still differs from that of public Acts.[49] Moreover, the courts have in this context indicated an ability to interfere. The courts have claimed a jurisdiction to restrain a party from petitioning against a Bill,[50] even though more recently the jurisdiction has been doubted.[51] It must be remarked that a like jurisdiction exists, and has been exercised, where a parliamentary stage is the final stage in making an Order.[52] It seems likely therefore that the jurisdiction exists, but that in so far as the remedy sought is a discretionary one, the courts will normally not interfere since the substantial matter at issue is one of general public interest and thus one which in principle should be ventilated in Parliament. Where that element of public interest is not present there seems to be no sound reason why the courts should not intervene. The argument that they cannot appears to deny to the courts their proper function, and also to involve an improper extension of any doctrine of the sovereignty of Parliament. It is, however, now clear that once a Bill or Confirmation Bill has received the Royal Assent the courts will not investigate the preliminary procedure to ensure that all proper steps have been taken.[53] The distinction is a rational one since such an investigation as would be involved in the latter case would be inconsistent with the normal attitude of one superior court to another. Procedure must properly be regarded as internal to Parliament, and thus the concern of Parliament. Petitioning for or against Bills is external and thus is a proper matter for consideration in the courts.

THE LORDS AND COMMONS IN CONFLICT

Introduction. Legislation is not the only field in which the two Houses might come into conflict, but it is the main one, and the matter is most

---

47 Ersk. I, 1, 39. This attitude was common to both jurisdictions: Craies' *Statute Law*, Part I, Chap. I.
48 See now the Interpretation Act 1889, s. 9.
49 See Craies, *op. cit.*
50 *Stockton and Hartlepool Ry.* v. *Leeds and Thirsk, etc., Ry.* (1848) 2 Ph. 669; *Heathcote* v. *North Staffordshire Ry.* (1850) Mac. & G. 100.
51 *Bilston Corporation* v. *Wolverhampton Corporation* [1942] Ch. 391; and see (1943) 59 L.Q.R. 2. Agreements of the type here in question have been condemned in Parliament as undesirable.
52 *Bell* v. *S. of S. for Scotland*, 1933 S.L.T. 519; *R.* v. *Electricity Commissioners* [1924] 1 K.B. 171 at 192; *Russell* v. *Mags. of Hamilton* (1897) 25 R. 350; though contrast *Harper* v. *Home Secretary* [1955] Ch. 238 at 251.
53 *Edinburgh and Dalkeith Ry.* v. *Wauchope* (1842) 8 Cl. & F. 710.

conveniently discussed here. Throughout the nineteenth century the increasing reliance of a government upon the Commons had its effect on the place of the Lords in relation to general legislation. Earlier, claims of the Commons to a monopoly of power as to taxation had been advanced in 1671 and 1678, and had, to some extent, been conceded by the Lords in 1702. The claims of the Commons in this matter were vigorously reaffirmed in 1860, after the House of Lords had rejected the Paper Duties Bill. Friction over general legislation existed between the two Houses throughout the nineteenth century, and became evident in relation to particular measures. Once, however, it had become clear and accepted that legislation was the business of the government, and that the government was dependent for its existence on the good will of the Commons (but could treat with contempt a vote of no confidence in the Lords), then some regulation of the role of the House of Lords in the legislative process became necessary. The full impact of these considerations was felt only towards the end of the nineteenth century. The necessary regulation could have come about by conventional means, as in the case of the financial privileges of the Commons, but a combination of events and personalities made more formal regulation inevitable.

A fresh crisis arose in 1909 with the rejection of the Finance Bill by the Lords. This in itself was the culmination of disputes between the Houses which had continued since 1906. After an intervening election the Finance Bill was passed by the Lords, but as a result of past events attention was centred on the Parliament Bill, intended to reduce the powers of the House of Lords, which was founded upon Resolutions passed in the new House of Commons. That Bill eventually reached the Statute Book as the Parliament Act 1911, which, subject to amendment by the Act of 1949, still regulates in law the relationship between the Houses in the legislative field.[54] The Act, while at the time being a matter of great controversy, probaby only codified what would have been, in normal times, acceptable doctrine, as being consonant with the principles, mentioned above, which had emerged as a result of developments starting with the Reform Act 1832.

The Parliament Act procedure. Under the ordinary legislative procedure, assuming a Bill to have started in the Commons, the Lords amendments are considered in the Commons, and either accepted, or, if they be not accepted, they are returned to the Lords with a message indicating reasons for the disagreement. If the Lords insist upon their amendments the process of the exchange of reasons can continue. Normally a compromise is sought and obtained, but this method provides no solution if the Lords will neither agree nor give way. The possibility

---

[54] For an outline of these events see Anson, *Constitutional Law*, Vol. I, Chap. VI; and see Nicholson, *George V*, Chap. X, and Jenkins, *Asquith*, Chap. XV.

of a solution is provided by the Parliament Acts. The Act of 1911 divided Bills with which it was concerned into Money Bills and others. The definition of Money Bills in section 1 (2) is narrow; in effect they are those which deal exclusively with fiscal matters. A Bill which establishes an important new scheme or machinery, even though it is of great financial importance, could not thus be certified by the Speaker under the Act as a Money Bill.[55] If a Money Bill is passed by the Commons and sent up to the Lords at least one month before the end of a session, then, if it is not passed by the Lords without amendment within one month, it may be presented for the Royal Assent without passing the House of Lords, unless the House of Commons otherwise direct. Other Bills might, under the 1911 Act, be similarly presented if passed in three successive sessions in the House of Commons, and rejected by the House of Lords in each of those sessions, provided that two years had elapsed between the Second Reading in the first session and the date of passing the Commons in the third. A Bill is treated as rejected if not passed without amendment, or with such amendments only as are agreed by both Houses. This two-year period was thought to be too long, and so the Parliament Act 1949 reduced the number of sessions to two, and the period of delay to one year,[56] but apart from this the provisions of the 1911 Act remain in force.

These provisions require the Speaker to certify a Money Bill, and to certify that the only amendments to the Bill finally presented to the Lords are those made necessary by the passage of time, or are amendments proposed by the Lords and agreed to by the Commons. No such certificates can, under section 3, be challenged in any court, so that such matters of parliamentary procedure are reserved for decision by parliamentary machinery.[57] It is possible for the Commons when sending a Bill to the Lords for the second time to suggest amendments, without inserting them in the Bill, and if they are accepted by the Lords they may be incorporated in the Bill as presented for the Royal Assent.

---

55 The definition runs: " A Money Bill means a Public Bill which in the opinion of the Speaker of the House of Commons contains only provisions dealing with all or any of the following subjects, namely, the imposition, repeal, remission, alteration, or regulation of taxation; the imposition for the payment of debt or other financial purposes of charges on the Consolidated Fund, or on money provided by Parliament, or the variation or repeal of any such charges; supply; the appropriation, receipt, custody, issue or audit of accounts of public money; the raising or guarantee of any loan or the repayment thereof; or subordinate matters incidental to those subjects or any of them. In this subsection the expressions ' taxation ', ' public money ', and ' loan ' respectively do not include any taxation, money or loan raised by local authorities or bodies for local purposes." It is doubtful if the Finance Bill of 1909 could have been so certified, and relatively frequently the Finance Bill is not so certified; see Jennings, *Parliament*, Chap. XI.

56 This Act, which was passed under the procedure of the 1911 Act, contained a provision for a retrospective application, which was not in fact used. For the preliminary consultation between the parties see Cmd. 7380, *Agreed Statement on Conclusion of the Conference of Party Leaders, 1948.*

57 It is to be noted that this provision does not exclude the possibility of challenge if an attempt were made, without more, to use this procedure to secure the passage of a Bill which was outside the scope of the Parliament Acts.

The Parliament Act procedure applies only to public Bills [58] and thus has no application to delegated legislation which requires parliamentary approval. Moreover, it cannot (s. 7) be used to extend the life of Parliament beyond five years. The Acts appear to be regarded as intended to protect government legislation as much as to protect the House of Commons. This view is supported by the genesis of the Acts, the general position of the government in relation to legislation today, and practice under the Acts.[59] The procedure does not avoid all possibilities of conflict between the Houses and the provisions relating to the identity of the last Bill with the first Bill are sufficiently rigid to present some difficulty in applying the procedure in particular cases.

The general significance of the Acts. In fact the Parliament Act 1949 is the only Act to reach the Statute Book which has been passed under the Parliament Act procedure and which has entered into force in the way intended.[60] This fact does not, however, mean that the Act is without influence. The bargaining position of the government may be greatly strengthened by its existence. On the other hand it should not be thought that the existence of the legislation has made opposition from the House of Lords either meaningless or ineffective. It is difficult, however, to judge at this time the effect of the 1911 Act in this respect, since a degree of subservience of the House of Lords was in any event normally accepted even before 1911 and that subservience would tend to increase. It is to be noted that the Act of 1911 did not delimit the relationship of the two Houses, even in the legislative field, with rigidity. The basis of privilege was expressly preserved (s. 6), and with it, implicitly, the possibility of further change. In particular that provision made it impossible for the Lords to claim that the Act was intended to be a conclusive delimitation of the role of the House in legislation. It is clear, on the contrary, that attitudes have continued to change. Lord Carrington, in the context of the London Government Bill 1967, indicated [61] that the view of the Opposition (Conservative) peers was " that there could arise a matter of great constitutional and national importance on which there was known to be a deep division of opinion in the country or perhaps on which the people's opinion was not

---

[58] The possibility of challenge in the courts of a statute improperly brought within the procedure of the Act is not excluded by the Acts themselves, nor, it seems, by any principle of law.

[59] See the proceedings in relation to the Private Member's Capital Punishment Bill in 1956. This proposition is not falsified by arguments raised about the possible use of these provisions in the context of the Abortion Bill 1967. By the time that that Bill was in its final stages the Government had effectively made it its own or had become politically committed to it, and thus this instance falls within the text above.

[60] The Government of Ireland Act 1914 and the Welsh Church Act 1914 passed under this procedure; the former never came into force, the latter was substantially amended before it did.

[61] 280 H.L.Deb. 420; and see 285 H.L.Deb. 1459–1460. See generally, on changing attitudes to the House, Bromhead, *The House of Lords and Contemporary Politics*, Chap. IX, and Jennings, *Parliament*, Chap. XI.

known " and in such a case there could be a right or duty in the House of Lords to use its powers. By implication this was the only case in which those powers could properly be used to the full. While this statement did not command universal support, it would appear to be generally acceptable as a rough definition of the powers which the House could use and expect to survive their use. This suggests a contraction since 1911 of what would conventionally be understood to be the real power of the House.

The Acts raise more general questions of constitutional theory. It has been argued that legislation passed under them is in truth a species of delegated legislation.[62]   Others have regarded the Acts as amounting to a redefinition of Parliament for certain purposes and in certain circumstances,[63] or it may be that the Acts redefine for particular purposes what the courts must recognise as law. It seems that either of the latter alternatives are to be preferred, but if they are preferred, the issue of other methods of redefinition must be considered.[64]   Finally it may be observed that the preamble to the Parliament Act 1911 recited that the Act was intended as a prelude to further reform of the House of Lords. That process has been a halting one. The only substantial measures of reform, the Life Peerages Act 1958 and the Peerage Act 1963, were not entirely agreed measures, and any reform of the House of Lords bearing upon function is likely to meet with substantial political opposition. Membership and function are linked. A powerless House of Lords would have little attraction for members. Any reform which substantially limited the nominal powers of the House could adversely affect its work as a revising chamber. Equally, any increase in power, even over delegated legislation, would clearly provoke political opposition. Further reforms of membership pose problems of political imagination to see how the House may be made more representative or more lively and without exciting the enmity of the Commons; since reforms which had the effect of increasing the powers of the House or of increasing its readiness to use its powers by reason of the fact that it felt more secure in public repute would clearly meet with opposition from the House of Commons and could reintroduce a dangerous rivalry between the Houses.[65]   Since the presently proposed reforms have been neither elaborated nor enacted, the present is not the time to pursue this matter.

---

[62] H. W. R. Wade, " The Basis of Legal Sovereignty " [1955] C.L.J. 172 at 193.

[63] G. Marshall, " What is Parliament? " (1954) *Political Studies* 193.

[64] *Ante*, Chap. 4. The provisions of the Ireland Act 1949, s. 1 (2), may be so regarded, for if Parliament may be redefined by subtraction, may it not also be redefined by addition?

[65] See also p. 115, *ante*; and see *Report of Joint Committee on House of Lords Reform* (1962–63) H.C. 38, leading to the 1963 Act. It will be noted that the reforms presently proposed embrace both function and composition. The House of Lords considered its own reform in 281 H.L.Deb. 1287–1396; and see Bromhead and Shell, " The Lords and their House " (1967) 20 *Parliamentary Affairs* 337.

FINANCIAL LEGISLATION

Financial legislation has hitherto been left on one side. Much of it is concerned with administration, and so it forms a convenient link between the legislative and administrative aspects of the work of Parliament. This type of legislation is peculiarly the concern of the House of Commons. Parliamentary control of finance is fundamental to the evolution of the present constitutional position of Parliament, but its roots run deep. Craig insisted on the necessity for the consent of the people and of the estates for taxation,[66] and much of the seventeenth-century constitutional struggles were concerned with establishing this proposition,[67] which was prominent in the Bill of Rights and Claim of Right. Historical causes gave emphasis to the control of taxation and also aided a separation between Supply and Appropriation, control over the former being established before control over the latter. The idea of control over appropriation is also ancient,[68] but practical realisation of it on any large scale did not come about until the nineteenth century, and of that the Exchequer and Audit Departments Act 1866 is a mark.

The modern system is, then, based upon this dichotomy, the two main annual Acts being the Appropriation Act and the Finance Act. Within the House the procedure was based upon two Committees of the Whole House, the Committee of Supply and the Committee of Ways and Means, and it is in these that those measures had to originate. The Committee of Supply was abolished in 1966.

Appropriation. Parliamentary procedure still reflects an annual basis for national accounting. The financial year begins on April 1. Hence before that date estimates are introduced into the House, the process of formulating estimates within departments having started in the preceding year. These estimates show expenditure in considerable detail and form the foundation for the Schedules to the Appropriation Act. The shape of estimates is of considerable importance to the subsequent control of expenditure by the House and is governed by the House and by the Committee on Public Accounts and the Select Committee on Estimates.[69] The estimates were considered over twenty-six Supply Days, but though these days were spread out as far as possible, they had to be taken before the end of July, in order that the Appropriation Act might reach the Statute Book in due season. The choice of subject-matter for debate upon these days was recognised as being the right of

66 *Jus Feudale* I, 1, 16.
67 The Act Anent Peace and War 1703, A.P.S. XI, 107, was forced upon the King by withholding supplies; and see A.P.S. XI, 112.
68 See Chubb, *Control of Public Expenditure.* Early attempts were not always successful; the Act of 1698, A.P.S. X, 175, appropriating money to a Chair of Law in Edinburgh, proved abortive.
69 The form of estimates was substantially simplified in the interest of greater clarity in 1962. See (1960–61) H.C. 252 and (1960–61) H.C. 184 (Select Committee on Estimates); and as to the Supplementary Estimates, see (1962–63) H.C. 41.

the Opposition. Thus the estimate chosen merely provided a convenient peg for a debate which was generally upon policy and not upon detail. If these days were so used, it is clear that the Appropriation Act would not reach the Statute Book before the beginning of the financial year. Thus it was necessary to provide money for immediate needs of the public services. This was and is done in a Consolidated Fund (No. 1) Act, which authorises sums of money on account of votes which will later appear in the Appropriation Act. Since *virement* (the transfer of money voted for one purpose to another) is much more freely possible with the Service Estimates, a sum on account of one vote will normally suffice for them, but for the Civil Estimates sums on account must be authorised in respect of each vote. At the same time it is necessary to deal with Supplementary Estimates. Where the sums voted for one year prove to be insufficient, the additional sums had to be sanctioned in the Committee of Supply and finally the issue of money for this purpose is authorised by the same Act.[70] Procedure was simplified in December 1966, when the Supply or Allotted Days were increased to twenty-nine, and the matter to be debated on those days, while remaining the choice of the Opposition, was detached from the necessity of finding a vote or estimate on which to hang the debate, or else of going through a procedural ritual. The Allotted Days could thus be spread out yet more effectively.

It is to be noticed that the whole of the legislation is concerned with the expenditure of money and not with incurring liabilities, and although it has been said that the validity of contracts depends upon voting of supply, this is doubtful.[71] In effect the Appropriation Act lays down a framework of law for the administration, but that law has only an " internal " character, that is to say, the inclusion of an item gives no individual a necessary right to claim payment of sums due, the exclusion of an item does not deny his right to claim.[72] This procedure applies to the Supply Services, for which expenditure must be authorised annually, and not to the Consolidated Fund Services, which include such matters as judicial salaries, and which are a standing charge upon the Consolidated Fund. The second group is not then open to annual debate. In practice the Estimates have, overall, lost a great deal of flexibility. Out of the total amount of government expenditure a substantial amount is

---

[70] It may be necessary to take up variations between estimates and expenditure for several years back. The appropriation of these sums is contained in the Appropriation Act. That Act also authorises Treasury borrowing. For further details, see Campion, *Introduction to the Procedure of the House of Commons*; and see the modifications made in (1960) 627 H.C.Deb., col. 2255 *et seq.* See, too, Brittain, *The British Budgetary System*, and Bridges, *The Treasury*. The sums involved in the Supplementary Estimates remain very considerable—£562m. in 1968—and, as will be seen, they are reported on by the Select Committee on Estimates. To an extent variations are mainly due to subsequent government decision; see (1967–68) H.C. 56. The debate on the procedural reforms of 1966 is to be found in 738 H.C.Deb. 470 *et seq.*

[71] See *Churchward* v. *The Queen* (1865) L.R. 1 Q.B. 173; and Mitchell, *The Contracts of Public Authorities*, p. 68 *et seq.*

[72] *R.* v. *Fisher* [1903] A.C. 158; and Street, " The Provision of Funds in Satisfaction of Government Liabilities " (1949) 8 Univ. Toronto L.J. 32.

committed by rates determined by such Acts as the National Insurance Acts.[73] The Estimates procedure must then be looked at against this much broader background, and against that background it has lost much of the significance which it once had.

Supply. Supply is the process by which, to a great extent, the pool of the Consolidated Fund is filled.[74] Here all is dependent upon the Budget, which is opened in the Committee of Ways and Means,[75] and on the first day all the Budget resolutions, with the exception of one necessary to keep the debate alive, are passed. Statutory force is given, provided that certain conditions are fulfilled, to the resolutions which vary or reimpose or renew an existing tax (but not to new taxes) by the Provisional Collection of Taxes Act 1913.[76] The Finance Bill is founded upon the resolutions of the Committee of Ways and Means, but it is by no means unusual for its provisions to vary from the proposals originally put forward by the Chancellor of the Exchequer. These variations may often be the consequence of considerations brought out in the Budget debate, or as a result of it. The whole parliamentary procedure could, if it followed strictly the pattern of other public legislation, give rise to considerable duplication of debate, and some stages have therefore become formalised,[77] and as a further step the Committee stage of the Finance Bill may now, from 1968, be taken in a Standing Committee rather than upon the floor of the House. Nevertheless, the procedure has the disadvantages of rigidity in a situation in which the Budget is not merely the means of raising necessary money, but also a means of regulating the national economy.[78] Hence, in the Finance Act 1961, power was taken (and has since been renewed) to change or institute certain duties by statutory instrument. Moreover, increasing concern over the efficiency of the system led to changes of method. Provision was made in 1960 for a debate upon a White Paper on Public Invest-ment, and for the Select Committee on Estimates to report on the

---

[73] In 1958–59 charges on the Consolidated Fund amounted to £819m. " Fixed " charges (*i.e.*, those determined by other legislation) amounted to well over half of the total of the Civil Estimates.

[74] Money earned by revenue-earning departments is dealt with by appropriations in aid.

[75] The Committee has confusingly also the function of authorising payment of sums voted for Supplementary Estimates and Votes on Account.

[76] The Act was made necessary by the successful challenge to the habit of collecting taxes on the basis of the resolutions in *Bowles* v. *Bank of England* [1913] 1 Ch. 57. It requires among other things that the Bill confirming the resolutions becomes law within four months after the passing of the resolutions. This and other conditions impose substantial restrictions on the legislative programme; indeed it has been said that that timetable can only be justified in terms of the corn king and spring queen. New taxes may be made retrospective, and the Act is reinforced as to customs by the Finance Act 1926, s. 6. The Act of 1913 is repealed and consolidated with other equivalent measures by the Provisional Collection of Taxes Act 1968.

[77] See Morrison, *Government and Parliament*, 3rd ed., pp. 229–230; and (1962–63) H.C. 190; and now S.O. 40, which allows the Bill to be sent to a Standing Committee. See the debate in 755 H.C.Deb. 1445 *et seq.*

[78] Prest, *Public Finance*, Chap. 8. The theories of Lord Keynes, while reflected in budgetary practice, are not reflected in parliamentary procedure.

Supplementary Estimates and upon the variations in the Estimates for one year as compared with those of the preceding year.[79] These changes were intended both to increase the efficiency of the whole budgetary process, and also to make it easier for the House to take greater account of the changing role of the Budget and of public expenditure in the general economic life of the country. It nevertheless remains true that the procedure connected with the major financial Bills is more closely linked with the role of Parliament in controlling or criticising the conduct of administration. On the one hand, this appears in the use to which the Supply Days were put and in the procedural changes in 1966 which have been referred to above, and on the other, in the work of two committees, the Select Committee on Estimates and the Public Accounts Committee, and their work is particularly dependent on the shape of the Appropriation Act. It seems that without a radical change in the relationship of government to Parliament the House could not reasonably be expected to deal with Estimates in detail. That task would require very different procedure in the House if the Estimates were to be passed by the necessary time. Even if such changes were made, such detailed scrutiny of Estimates might, it seems, involve a major alteration in the theory of parliamentary control of the administration. Thus it could provoke a substantial shift in the origination or choice of policy from the government to Parliament, since the priorities of expenditure depend upon policy. It is therefore necessary to consider the general role of Parliament in relation to the administration. It follows, therefore, that the procedural change of 1966 even though they affected certain historic aspects of the House were merely recognising realities and this relationship of government to Parliament.

THE ADMINISTRATIVE FUNCTIONS OF PARLIAMENT

It is evident that Parliament does not concern itself exclusively with legislation, and, from what has been said, it is clear that debates which may have a legislative context are frequently concerned with parliamentary control of the administration. The words " administrative functions " are in a sense inapt. It remains true, as Mr. Gladstone asserted, that the business of the Commons or of Parliament " is not to govern the country, but it is, if you think fit, to call to account those who do govern it." In minor ways, as through private legislation, Parliament may have a direct hand in administration, and in the past, particularly, in revolutionary times Parliament has directly administered [80]; and at times in the early nineteenth century showed a tendency to concern itself in ways which could have had that effect.[81] Nevertheless, the evolution of doctrines of ministerial responsibility prevented

79 See the debate in (1960) 627 H.C.Deb. 2255 et seq.
80 See, e.g., A.P.S. IX, 11 et seq., concerned with the Revolution of 1688–89.
81 For examples, see Williams, The Clerical Organisation of the House of Commons.

any real development on these lines, so that the general principle may now be set out as above.[82] The methods of parliamentary control must be reviewed against this background, and against the general principles of the relationship of government to Parliament, to be discussed subsequently.

Parliamentary questions and related devices. The most obvious and most praised method is the Parliamentary question. Questions are limited by the fact that their subject-matter must engage ministerial responsibility, and by the fact that no minister can be compelled to answer, though clearly a minister will, normally, be reluctant to refuse to do so. Because of their popularity it has become necessary increasingly to regulate questions. Thus, substantial notice came to be required as a normal rule, subject to the exception of the Private Notice questions used in particular by the Leader of the Opposition. Further, it has been necessary to limit the number of questions requiring an oral answer any one member can ask on any one day,[83] and to limit the number of supplementary questions. Other devices, such as the " Rota System " as to subject-matter, have been adopted in an attempt to preserve the efficiency of this device, and in particular special arrangements have been made for questions addressed to the Prime Minister.[84] The latter is a change which reflects the changing position of the Prime Minister (and his dominant position), the former, while administratively convenient, has meant that much of the immediacy has gone out of questions, when allowance is made for the number of ministers, and for such things as parliamentary recesses. In the House of Lords, where the device originated, " starred " questions, seeking only information, are a modern device, and are limited. The older form, also requiring an oral answer, normally receives a much longer reply than is customary in the Commons and may in fact initiate a brief debate.

In the Commons an unsatisfactory answer may lead to a longer debate if the questioner can succeed in moving the adjournment of the House to discuss a " specific and important matter that should have urgent consideration." [85] The Speaker must first be satisfied that each part of the phrase is applicable and that the matter involves ministerial

---

[82] See, too, Maitland, *Constitutional History*, pp. 284–285, and Alphaeus Todd, *Parliamentary Government*, Vol. I, p. 235, and Vol. II, Pt. V. A good general account of the relationship is given in Butt, *The Power of Parliament*, which covers the legislative and " administrative " aspects from many angles. For a particular aspect, see Richards, *Parliament and Foreign Affairs*.

[83] The number is now two: see 617 H.C.Deb. 33–186. Written answers are printed in *Hansard* and are often lengthy and detailed. As an example of a refusal to answer see 736 H.C.Deb. *351*, where Mr. Jenkins refused any information on safeguards against unauthorised " wire-tapping."

[84] July 18, 1961, 644 H.C.Deb. 1052. A change which marks the changing role of the Prime Minister. Some changes, such as the Rota System, are also administratively necessary. A minister must have reasonable time for his departmental duties.

[85] Under S.O. 9, see Greenleaf, " Urgency Motions in the Commons " [1960] *Public Law* 270, as to the old style. These motions are not, of course, limited to matters raised in questions.

responsibility. The criteria by which under the older form of words, "a definite matter of urgent public importance," such matters were judged had become so strict that it was said that the only interest in attempting such a motion was to see if the Speaker would invent a new reason for rejecting it. Although, as a result of the Report of the Select Committee on Procedure of 1959,[86] some relaxation had occurred, rigidity remained and the new formulation was adopted in the hope of breaking the established pattern, though certainly weight will continue to be given to the need for the regularity of business. It is then possible that this new form may add urgency to questions, just as the existence of parliamentary questions adds weight to the letters written by members to ministers. The letter contains the unwritten threat of a question. While the importance of questions as a device for controlling the administration may be exaggerated, nevertheless, the possibility of questions has a substantial influence on the conduct of administration. The existence of that possibility can have an effect upon the taking of decisions, which may be more important than the actual challenge of decisions once taken. The doctrine of a " Fleet in being " has more than one application. Questions also remain important constitutionally as giving a particular opportunity to backbenchers, and as a constant reminder of the doctrine of ministerial responsibility.[87] As such they do much to preserve the ministerial system. In their absence a similar process to that by which ministers took effective and, eventually, nominal power also from the Crown might have been repeated in the case of ministers and civil servants. The latter exercise power in fact, but, among other things, questions prevent the overt assumption of power.

Adjournment debates and related devices. Apart from the " urgency " motions mentioned above, which now may become more common, somewhat longer and more general are debates upon the adjournment. Half an hour is allotted at the end of each day from Monday to Friday when private members may raise matters, the subject being either balloted for by members or chosen by the Speaker.[88] The subject-matter of such debates must involve ministerial responsibility, but the form of debate (which is obviously on the motion to adjourn) prevents any specific resolution, thus the opportunity is one for the ventilation of grievances. Somewhat similar in type are the debates upon the four annual " holiday " adjournments. Rather more general

---

[86] (1959) H.C.P. 92. Questions may be combined with other parliamentary devices to produce a campaign; for an illustration see Hanson, *Parliament at Work*; and as an illustration of the particular failure of the device, but of its general use, see 753 H.C.Deb. 1029–1035.

[87] See generally the very valuable survey by Chester and Bowring, *Questions in Parliament*, and Howarth, *Questions in the House*; and see the Report of the Select Committee on Procedure (1964–65) H.C. 188 and (1966–67) H.C. 410.

[88] See the arrangements accepted on Feb. 8, 1960, 617 H.C.Deb. 34 *et seq.* It is sometimes said that giving notice of an unsatisfactory answer to a question can affect the Speaker in his choice.

are the days allocated to private members' motions,[89] and somewhat more specific were the debates upon the motion for going into the Committee of Supply at the opening of the Civil and Service Estimates.[90] Debates upon amendments to the motion for the address at the beginning of the session are varied, but all these afford opportunities for criticism.[91] Much more specific are the opportunities afforded by the Estimate Procedure. By convention the Supply Days were used to debate matters chosen by the Opposition, and, reshaped, afford opportunities for more serious and sustained attacks upon the government.[92] Thus, what are nominally debates upon Estimates are in reality debates upon administration. There are then numerous possibilities of debating the activities of the administration, and the examples given do not exhaust the list. Prayers against statutory instruments may, for example, serve that purpose rather than a purpose more closely linked with the statutory instrument. Nevertheless, these opportunities do not provide a sustained and planned surveillance of the administration—to a large extent their effectiveness depends upon their random quality. Moreover, they are opportunities for debate, and do not involve the House in any direct participation in the administrative process.

Such direct participation does in fact exist. S.O. 92 (relating to mail and telegraphic contracts) is a long-standing minor example, but, in modern times, just as private Bill legislation gives Parliament a direct interest in local administration, so also does public legislation give it such an interest in the conduct of the central government. Often legislation, either in its primary or in its delegated form,[93] is today only a facet of administration, and thus to the extent that Parliament influences legislation it is in such cases affecting administration. Such opportunities, however, necessarily also occur in a random way. More regular surveillance is provided by the two committees dependent on financial procedure, the Public Accounts Committee and the Select Committee on Estimates.[94]

Detailed controls. The Public Accounts Committee is established under S.O. 79 to examine the appropriation accounts, and other accounts laid before Parliament. The Chairman is, by convention, an Opposition

89 *Ibid.* The time for these was cut down in 1967 to increase time for Private Members' Bills: 753 H.C.Deb. 156.
90 See Erskine May, *Parliamentary Practice*, 16th ed., pp. 726–727.
91 The shape of these debates can be readily gathered from Hanson, *Parliament at Work*.
92 As a result of the Select Committee on Procedure, steps were taken to increase their efficiency in this respect by loosening the rules governing them: see 718 H.C.Deb. 204 and 738 H.C.Deb. 470–612.
93 See, *e.g.*, the debate in 658 H.C.Deb. 395 *et seq.*
94 See Chubb, *The Control of Public Expenditure.* Something of the manner of working of the Committee can be seen more shortly in the debate in 650 H.C.Deb. 637–762, and that beginning at 652 H.C.Deb. 208. See too 754 H.C.Deb. 36 *et seq.*, where the current working of the P.A.C. is described. More generally see Normanton, *The Accountability and Audit of Governments*, and the good detailed survey, Johnson, *Parliament and Administration.*

member who normally has held office at the Treasury. The Committee is assisted by the Comptroller and Auditor-General, who, while being technically a witness before the Committee, is in fact its principal *aide*, other assistance being provided by two Treasury Officers of Accounts who are in attendance. The Committee, having power to send for persons and papers, deals with the Accounting Officers (normally the permanent heads of departments) and may be in effect a court to which they are answerable.[95] So far as accounts are concerned the work of the Committee (and of the Comptroller) reaches far beyond consideration of narrow accountancy questions into questions of administrative efficiency, and in relation to the Defence Estimates its powers in relation to *virement* give to it a considerable potential interest in detail.

The operation of the Committee is intimately connected with the shape of the Estimates and the Schedules to the Appropriation Act. As a consequence it is established that the Committee has a voice upon proposed alterations in the shape of the Estimates.[96] The two facts, that the Committee receives expert help from the Comptroller and Auditor-General and that it deals with senior officials, mark the work of the Committee, and give to it both effectiveness and weight. On the other hand, the fact that it is dealing with the made-up accounts means that a Report may lose in topicality. The Third Report adopted in July 1961 dealt with accounts for 1959–60, and with events running back to 1955. Nevertheless, it is clear that the Committee's Reports (upon which the Treasury comments are published) do have a substantial effect upon government activity and organisation. The Comptroller and Auditor-General, whose salary is charged upon the Consolidated Fund, and who is only removable on an address by the two Houses of Parliament,[97] holds an office of great independence, enhanced by the fact that he is regarded as a servant of Parliament and of the House of Commons in particular. Over the years he has built up a peculiar position in relation to the civil service,[98] being at the same time an inspector and a collaborator, and having many of the requisite facilities to survey the administration from a broad point of view. Thus this Committee has both the opportunity and the means of surveying the governmental machine and reporting to Parliament, and its strength is perhaps increased by the fact that so far as is possible it does not trench upon policy. It is probably also helped by the fact that it takes evidence from senior civil servants, whose views take account of the general picture of the governmental machine.

A somewhat similar function is performed by the Select Committee

---

[95] See the appropriate heading in the *Epitome of Reports of the Public Accounts Committee* and Brittain, *British Budgetary System*, pp. 248–250.
[96] See (1960–61) H.C. 252–1.
[97] Exchequer and Audit Departments Act 1866, ss. 3 and 4. While his functions as Comptroller are important from the point of view of the regularity of financial administration, those as Auditor have assumed an even greater importance.
[98] See, *e.g.*, the description in (1952–53) H.C. 235 in the evidence of Sir Frank Tribe.

on Estimates. This Committee has sprung into importance after 1945 as a result of experience gained by the Select Committee on National Expenditure in the war years. Its predecessors before the war had met with little success. They concerned themselves with money, whereas Supply debates are concerned with policy, and for this, among other reasons, the work of the Committee had little effect.[99] During the war the Committee on National Expenditure had concentrated upon particular problems of expenditure, and had operated through sub-committees. This model was adopted for the reconstituted Select Committee on Estimates, and in 1960 its membership was increased to give greater scope for the appointment of sub-committees.[1] The Chairman is a government backbencher. While its function is to examine the Estimates it is supposed not to trench upon policy. In effect in these aspects its work bears a close resemblance to that of the Public Accounts Committee and it also surveys the administrative machine.[2] But to it are entrusted certain specific tasks, in particular the examination of the spring Supplementary Estimates. It is also required to report to the House upon the principal variations between the Estimates and those of the preceding year before the autumn debate on public expenditure. These tasks were added in 1960 in an effort to increase parliamentary control of expenditure.

The methods of operation of the Committee differ in two important ways from those of the Select Committee on Public Accounts. Its sub-committees may investigate on the spot, and it lacks the expert advice given to the Public Accounts Committee. While the first of these differences does give the Committee advantages, there is also the danger that the evidence which it receives may be given by persons not fully aware of the whole departmental situation, and also that the smaller sub-committees may be heavily influenced by the views of particular members. These risks are not diminished by the second difference, which means that the Committee and its sub-committees rely almost entirely on their own resources, though this factor can also work in both directions. These differences have resulted in the work of the Committee being subjected to more criticism than that of the Public Accounts Committee.[3] Despite criticism it is clear that the Committee has been much more successful after the war than it was before, though it is also evident that except in relation to the matters added to its terms of reference in

[99] See Chubb, op. cit. Chap. VIII, and Jennings, Parliament, Chap. IX.
[1] 627 H.C.Deb. 1292 and, e.g. (1966–67) H.C. 327.
[2] See, e.g., the report upon Treasury control (1957–58) H.C. 254 and 254–1 or the report on O. and M. (1946–47) H.C. 143. For its work on Supplementary Estimates see, e.g. (1966–67) H.C. 83 and 257 or (1967–68) H.C. 56 or (1967–68) H.C. 89. For the " cycle " of its work in recent years see (1964–65) H.C. 303.
[3] See, e.g., the criticism contained in J. D. B. Miller's " The Colonial Office and the Estimates Committee " (1961) Public Administration 173 et seq.; and for a general account see Johnson, Parliament and Administration, The Estimates Committee 1945–1965.

1960 its work tends, in substance, to resemble that of the Public Accounts Committee.

Added time was provided from 1960 for debating the reports of these Committees; but, apart from such debates, the fact that the reports of these Committees are answered by the Treasury or the relevant department means that they are capable of influencing administrative structures and practices. The work of these Committees is, however, to some extent generalised, retrospective and episodic, and does not amount to a continuing current scrutiny of administrative activity. This remains true despite the fact that their work is so arranged that their visitations upon major departments arrive in a relatively small cycle of time. The episodic character is then apparent in the aspects which are examined. It is, moreover, limited by the fact that neither Committee may, by its terms of reference, trench upon policy, though that is a word which is difficult to define in this context.

Apart from these Committees, the Select Committee on Statutory Instruments [4] does affect and to some extent scrutinises administration, since statutory instruments even more than statutes may reflect the current needs and intentions of departments. Once again, however, this Committee is formally excluded from the field of policy, and once again the success of the Committee is perhaps attributable to the expert assistance which it receives from counsel to the Speaker. The Select Committee on Nationalised Industries discharges, in substance though not in form, somewhat similar functions in its own field to those of the two financial Committees. This Committee, too, has asked, but in vain, for expert assistance.[5]

Partly as a result of the form of the debates upon the Supply Days, and partly springing from the limitations upon the work of these Committees as well as from other causes (especially the explosion of governmental activity which increased the feeling of the impotence of Parliament in the face of the executive, a feeling of its inability to fulfil the task which even Gladstone had left to it), there arose a demand for a larger part in controlling the executive for the House of Commons and for backbenchers in particular. It was argued that committees of the House could ascertain the price of maintaining a guard dog in the base at Singapore, but could not effectively argue why the base was there at all. The feeling was understandable, not only because of that explosion of business, but also because the backbencher had lost, and was not likely to regain, the place in legislative business which rightly or wrongly it was felt should be his. There was also operative a confusion of thought. Except for rare and special periods the British tradition had

---

[4] As to which see *post*, Chap. 15.
[5] See Special Report (1959–60) H.C. 276; and on this and similar topics Wheare, *Government by Committee*, Chap. VIII; for a survey of the work of the Committee see (1961–62) H.C. 116.

never been one of parliamentary government (in the sense in which
" parliamentary " is substituted for " congressional "). It had been a
tradition of cabinet government. The tendency was, however, to talk
as if the former had been the case. More or less concurrently there
arose proposals for specialised committees after the congressional model
and for the Parliamentary Commissioner for Administration (the British
translation of Ombudsman). Thus, two " specialised " committees were
created, one for agriculture, with the remit " to consider the activities in
England and Wales of the Ministry of Agriculture and Fisheries," and
the other for science and technology, with a more general remit related
to its subject-matter, which from 1968 specifically includes Scotland.

An extension of these committees was proposed by the Leader of the
House in 1967. It is arguable that the choice of subject-matter for these
experimental committees was largely determined by the fact that the
respective ministers at the time were those who were prepared to accept
these committees. It is too early to assert with any degree of confidence
whether or not the experiment will be successful. It is evident that on
the one hand the Select Committee on Agriculture did, in fact, whatever
the appearance may be, stumble early on the rock of " policy "—in the
particular context of the proposed British negotiations to adhere to the
Treaty of Rome its investigations crossed the boundary of agriculture
and entered the field of the Foreign Office [6] (and the absence of a Select
Committee on Foreign Affairs among the experimental ones is note-
worthy). It is evident, too, that the committees have suffered from the
lack of expert staffing which is common to the majority of House of
Commons committees. The latter is not, in the long run, of vital concern.
It is easily capable of remedy, if the conflict of principle between parliamentary and cabinet government be resolved. The committees pose that
question, which is, as earlier references to Alphaeus Todd show, an old
one. Whether this generation will give the answers which he gave
remains to be seen. The probability is that it will, and, while these
committees will considerably expand the amount of information available, they will not substantially alter the processes of decision-taking.
They will in a different form carry out the sort of work done more
generally by the two older financial committees.

The third committee—the Select Committee to which the Parliamentary Commissioner is answerable—poses different issues. His role
is much to be disputed, but must be considered against a background
of administrative law, and discussion may, therefore, be postponed. On
the other hand, this complex of committees raises a more general issue,
whether it is desirable that an attempt should be made to cumulate so
much detailed work in Parliament. A strong case can be made for
decentralising by institutional means. It is probable that the work of

[6] See (1966–67) H.C. 378—XVII. The departmental replies are given in Cmnd.
3479 (1967).

the Comptroller and Auditor-General might be more effectively done in a framework akin to the Cour des Comptes producing effectively and overtly the material upon which a Public Accounts Committee could then work.[7] This would be no more than a rationalisation of the present situation. It is a mistake, as will later be argued, in the context of the Parliamentary Commissioner, to build institutions upon the hypothesis that Parliament in general and the House of Commons in particular should effectively be the only controlling mechanism in constitutional law.

Thus it is that these committees pose, by implication, major questions about certain principles hitherto accepted as basic constitutional thought and about institutional structures within a modern highly developed state. Certainly the value of such committees as controlling devices should perhaps not be estimated merely by the extent to which they discover faults. Their existence and the implication of potential scrutiny has its effect throughout the administration. Moreover, their activity is circumscribed by general doctrines, both administrative and constitutional. So long as the doctrine of ministerial responsibility exists limits are imposed upon the questions which can properly be put to, and the answers which can properly be given by, civil servants. If such bodies are to operate impartially, then many points must be reserved for the House itself. Equally it is likely that the House would be jealous of any growth of the powers of such committees, since such growth would be likely to be at the expense of the House as a whole. It is true that ministers have been prepared to meet the new committees, and that those committees have opened their proceedings to the public and that thus established patterns have been broken. Yet, it is likely that, until such committees are numerous and powerful enough to cause a fundamental rethinking of the role of Parliament in the formation of policy, their functions are likely to remain as they now are, namely, informing the House, informing individual members, and providing some, but limited, contact between administration and members. Any other role would have major consequences upon the role of the House of Commons itself. Administratively it may, in any event, be unsatisfactory for those limits to be greatly exceeded. Too detailed investigation can both disrupt and delay the administrative process, and produce the wrong attitude of mind for efficient administration. Finally, the whole of this question must be viewed against the more general background of the relationship of government to Parliament, which is discussed hereafter.

Conclusion. Overall it is, however, clear that there is a concentration of activity upon the floor of the House. The proceedings of the committees being, for the most part, private until their reports are published,

---

[7] Here see generally Normanton, *The Accountability and Audit of Governments.*

their activities do not attract current attention. When published the reports tend to be overshadowed in the public mind by other business, though their effect inside the administration is not thus limited. It is also clear that the work of these committees looks to the past and not to the future. It does not amount to a current supervision, although recent changes in relation to the Select Committee on Estimates have slightly altered that condition, and the influence of some reports upon the future shape of administrative structures should not be underrated. The fusion of the Diplomatic and Commonwealth Services can, for example, be attributed to the report earlier cited. In the House, where controls over the administration may have a greater impact on current activities, the operation of many of the mechanisms is necessarily affected by the political character of the House. This is by no means exclusively so, any member accepts readily the obligations which he has to protect the interests of his constituency and of all his constituents. The general establishment of " clinics " at which the member is available to hear complaints from his constituents is evidence of that acceptance, and the obligation which is felt is not simply one of party politics. Many of the grievances felt by ordinary citizens are thus heard and are dealt with, where appropriate, in correspondence with the relevant minister. Weight is added to such letters by the fact of being a member and by the backing of the parliamentary opportunities to raise grievances. Such activities attract little publicity, though achieving much good, and by filtering off the less controversial matters tend again to cause those matters with a more political character to be reserved for discussion in the House. These circumstances may cause the influence of members in individual cases to be underrated because that influence is not always publicised. There are other faces to the coin. There is an impermanence about a parliamentary answer or debate which is inevitably accepted by and acceptable to members, being politicians. Redress may be a function of the pertinacity, nuisance value or standing of the member. There are more serious issues. At the more general level there is the question of the relationship of government to Parliament, to which attention has been drawn. At the level of detail, of individual grievance, it is the relative place of Parliament and the courts, of the place of politics and of law in society, which are in issue. Most noticeably there has been, in the context of the detailed issues, the argument that the backbencher needs to be restored to his place in the sun. A case can be made for some restoration, but what that place should be is still an open question. If the House is to be the great forum for political debate, wherein the debate is often as much intended for the ears of the electorate as for those of the opposing party, all questions which can appropriately be argued within the House must be those which are suited to that highly charged political forum.[8]   Some issues of administration are so suited, as rarely may be some individual cases, but the whole of this recent evolution should be considered against a background of a definition of what is the real function of the House, and must be limited by that definition.

As is to be expected, if the relative position of the government to each House is considered, the House of Lords is much more concerned in this matter with issues of general principle.   The virtual exclusion of that House from the field of finance has the effect under the existing system of largely excluding it also from many opportunities of controlling administrative activity.   The absence of many senior ministers from the House has also its effect in limiting the activities of the House in this respect.   In more general debates the experience of some of its members may be valuable in moulding the pattern of administration.   It is even possible that these limitations may have certain advantages.   The task of answering in the House of Commons for a busy department which may be at the centre of controversy is a heavy one, and the absence of such demands in the House of Lords may in the case of some departments aid their administration, if it prove politically possible for the minister in charge to be in the House of Lords.   The result is then that in so far as there is parliamentary control or supervision of the administration, that control is predominantly exercised by the House of Commons.   Granted the present composition of the two Houses, no other result would be reconcilable with current theories of government.

[8] This political character is illustrated by the failure of the experimental morning sittings in the Session 1967–68.   Business was to be non-controversial.   Divisions were to be postponed till the afternoons, but the House rejected these de-politicised sittings, and the experiment was not renewed in 1968–69.   Instead a morning sitting can be held to avoid an all-night sitting.

CHAPTER 9

THE EXECUTIVE—I

THE CROWN

IT is convenient to treat the Crown first of all under this heading, since it is in the name of the Crown that the central government operates. Further, the concept of the Crown dominates much of our constitutional thinking and continues to affect even detailed rules.[1]   This domination produces both advantages and disadvantages.   Some of the advantages may be psychological, but nevertheless important, such as the feeling of continuity or stability, others may be practical,[2] and both may be dependent upon a lack of precision in ideas about the Crown.   The disadvantages flow, in part, from the same imprecision.   To a large extent the existence of the concept of the Crown has provided an excuse for a failure to produce a theory of the state, the absence of which may create difficulties in modern times.   There may well be an unrealistic dichotomy in the treatment of the machinery of government because of the need to determine which parts of that machinery are, and which parts are not, to be regarded as " the Crown." [3]   Further dependent terminology—such words as " prerogative "—may in modern conditions acquire distorted significance because of the connection with " the Crown."   In many cases powers would be better seen for what they are if they were regarded as belonging to the government.

The Sovereign—title and succession.   The simplest meaning of the word " Crown " is that given by the Interpretation Act 1889, s. 30—the Sovereign for the time being.   That Sovereign is determined by rules of succession laid down in the Act of Settlement 1700 and incorporated in the Acts of Union (such incorporation being one of the main objectives of the English Commissioners).   By the Act of 1700 the succession is settled upon the heirs of the body (being Protestant) of the Princess Sophia.[4]   The title descends lineally according to the old feudal rules, males being preferred to females, with the rule of primogeniture

---

[1] Consider the different remedies sought against the various defenders in *Adams* v. *S. of S. for Scotland*, 1958 S.C. 279 even though they were all engaged in a common enterprise.

[2] The separation of the " dignified capacity " of which Bagehot spoke in his *English Constitution* remains important.

[3] Maitland, *Constitutional History*, p. 417, and *The Crown as a Corporation* in his *Selected Essays*; and consider the interplay of terminology in *Chandler* v. *D.P.P.* [1962] 3 All E.R. 142 at 156.

[4] By H.M. Declaration of Abdication Act 1936, the Duke of Windsor and his issue are excluded.

applying equally among males and females.[5]   By the Bill of Rights,
again incorporated (to this extent) in the Acts of Union, any person who
becomes a Roman Catholic or marries a Roman Catholic forfeits all
right to the throne and is treated as if dead.[6]   Any person succeeding to
the throne is required to take the coronation oath,[7] to declare himself a
faithful Protestant,[8] to swear to maintain the Church of Scotland and
the Church of England [9] and to enter into communion with the Church
of England.[10]   It will be seen that the title is a parliamentary one, and it
is only Parliament that can alter the succession.[11]   In this respect Parliament is now limited by the Statute of Westminster 1931.   The preamble
requires the consent of the parliaments of the dominions to any law
touching the succession and the royal style and titles, and any such law
intended to have effect within a dominion would also be affected by
section 4.   The present title is regulated under the Royal Titles Act
1953.[12] The Commonwealth agreement which underlies this Act demonstrated the two ideas of unity and independence which mark the theory
of the Commonwealth.   Each member was free to choose a title appropriate to its own circumstances, but all should include the description
of the Queen as Queen of Her other Realms and Territories and Head
of the Commonwealth.   Thus the Act of 1953 authorises the adoption of
a title for the purposes of the United Kingdom and the territories

5 This matter possibly admitted argument until the accession of the present Queen,
  proclaimed as solely entitled.   Though Coke and Blackstone asserted that the eldest
  daughter succeeded solely, and in 1937 the Law Officers regarded legislative clarification as unnecessary, the matter was perhaps not beyond dispute.   For the arguments
  see Farran, " The Law of Accession " (1953) 16 M.L.R. 140.   For the older Scots
  law, which Craig asserted depended upon universal public laws (*Jus Feudale* 1,
  14, 8), see the sources referred to in *Sources and Literature of Scots Law* (the Stair
  Society) at p. 360.   It seems that Art. II of the Act of Union by implication made
  all the rules applicable to the Crown of England apply after the Union.
6 The appropriate provisions of the Bill of Rights and the Act of Settlement were
  also extended as United Kingdom law by the Succession to the Crown Act 1707;
  and see the Claim of Right.
7 The Coronation Oath Act 1688.   Despite the terms of this Act the oath taken has
  been varied without statutory approval.   See 511 H.C.Deb. at 2099–2100 for the
  last form.
8 Bill of Rights 1688; the Act of Settlement.   The terms of the declaration were
  amended by the Accession Declaration Act 1910 at the instigation of Edward VII.
9 The Acts for the Security of the Church of Scotland, and for the Security of the
  Church of England, incorporated in the Union Settlement.
10 The Act of Settlement.
11 Thus H.M. Declaration of Abdication Act 1936 was necessary to give effect to the
  declaration itself.   Parliamentary control is expressly affirmed, and denial of it made
  treason by the Succession to the Crown Act 1707; compare the Declaration of the
  Parliament of Scotland 1685, A.P.S. IX, 459, accepting the ideas of Mackenzie in his
  Jus Regium.
12 The Act emerged as a result of the agreement reached by Commonwealth ministers
  in 1953 (Cmd. 8748).   Although this agreement is referred to in the preamble to this
  Act it is not scheduled to it, so that Lord President Cooper regarded the Act as
  incomprehensible according to the ordinary rules of interpretation in *MacCormick* v.
  Lord Advocate, 1953 S.C. 396 at 411.   The title adopted under the Act was
  " Elizabeth the Second, by the Grace of God of the United Kingdom of Great
  Britain and Northern Ireland and of Her other Realms and Territories Queen, Head
  of the Commonwealth, Defender of the Faith."   See generally de Smith, " The
  Royal Style and Titles " (1953) 2 I.C.L.Q. 263, and Mansergh, *Documents and
  Speeches on British Commonwealth Affairs 1931–1952*, Vol. II, p. 1289.

dependent on it. Objection was taken in Scotland to the adoption of the numeral II, which was first used in the proclamation, but the action was held to be incompetent,[13] and the numeral was subsequently justified on the grounds that it was the custom to use the lowest numeral not yet used in England or Scotland. The changes in the royal title are significant as marking changes in the constitution of the Commonwealth,[14] and should be studied in that context.

The accession of a new Sovereign is marked by the proclamation authorised by an Accession Council, an assembly of notables, which in 1952 included representatives of the members of the Commonwealth. Proclamation is not essential in law since it has come to be accepted doctrine that the King never dies and that succession is instantaneous upon the death of the former Sovereign, assuming that the statutory conditions are fulfilled. In relation to matters of government, statute has provided for continuity, particularly the Demise of the Crown Act 1901 in relation to office holders.[15] In due course the coronation follows, the service again tending to illustrate current constitutional facts. Thus, in 1953, apart from the Moderator of the General Assembly of the Church of Scotland having a part in the service, the Prime Ministers of member states of the Commonwealth were present.

Minority and illness. In England minority was no bar to reigning and in Scotland the position had been variously regulated at different times.[16] *Ad hoc* arrangements were made, often with great difficulty, to deal with the minority, absence or incapacity of the King and in 1937 standing legislation was first introduced. This has required subsequent amendment, and the Regency Acts of 1937, 1943 and 1953 still retain certain *ad hoc* characteristics.

The Regency Act 1937 provides for the discharge of the royal functions by a Regent when the Sovereign is under eighteen,[17] or where the Sovereign is incapable by reason of infirmity of mind or body of discharging such functions, or where the Sovereign is for some definite

[13] *MacCormick* v. *Lord Advocate*, 1953 S.C. 396.

[14] Notably the adoption of the title Head of the Commonwealth in 1949 which marked the acceptance of republics within the Commonwealth. See Mansergh, *op. cit.* Vol. II, p. 846, and de Smith, *The Vocabulary of Commonwealth Relations.*

[15] This is to be contrasted with the older rules limiting the grant of offices to the life of the Sovereign; see the rules discussed in *Officers of State* v. *Lord Dunglas* (1838) 1 D. 300. In part these rules were to protect the royal revenues in part to protect the independence of action of each Sovereign. See, *e.g.,* Fount. I, 339 on the danger of a Parliament surviving a King, and compare the modern rules contained in the Act of Succession 1707; the Meeting of Parliament Act 1797 and the Representation of the People Act 1867, which ensure the rapid meeting of Parliament (even of a dissolved one) on the death of a Sovereign.

[16] See *The Queen and Her Comptroller* v. *Hamilton* (1557) Mor. 7855 and the various Acts in 1526 (A.P.S. II, 301), 1564 (A.P.S. II, 545), 1567 (A.P.S. III, 13 and 429) and 1704 (A.P.S. XI, 136). For the English rule see Co.Litt. 43a, b; and see Farran, "The Regency Act" (1954) 17 M.L.R. 146. This legislation applies only to the U.K. and its dependent colonies.

[17] S. 1 (2) makes the eighteenth birthday the appropriate date for making any necessary oath or declaration by the Sovereign.

cause not available for such functions.[18]   Normally, the Regent is the person next in succession who is a British subject of full age (which by the Act of 1953, s. 1 (1), here means eighteen), domiciled in the United Kingdom.[19]   The Regent is subject to the excluding rules in the Act of Settlement and is required to take the oath of allegiance.   Temporarily, however, by the Act of 1953, s. 1 (2), should a regency become necessary, either on the death or incapacity of the present Queen before any child or grandchild of hers attains eighteen, the Duke of Edinburgh becomes Regent and Guardian.   The Regent has all the royal powers, save that, by section 4 (2) of the Act of 1937, he cannot assent to any Bill altering the order of succession to the throne, or altering the Act for the Security of the Church of Scotland.[20]

Apart from regencies difficulties had also arisen in other cases of illness, and the Act of 1937 makes provision for the appointment of Counsellors of State in the case of illness not amounting to incapacity or where the Sovereign is to be absent from the United Kingdom.   The Counsellors of State are the spouse of the Sovereign, the present Queen Mother and the four persons next in succession (not being disqualified),[21] subject to the possible omission under the Act of 1943 of persons who will also be absent.   The Counsellors of State can exercise such functions as are delegated to them by Letters Patent, but no power to dissolve Parliament save on express instruction or to grant any honours may be delegated.[22]

The Royal Family.   The eldest son of the Sovereign is, from birth, Prince and Steward of Scotland, and Duke of Rothesay.[23]   He is similarly Duke of Cornwall in the peerage of England and is created Prince of Wales.   The law of treason protects a Queen Consort and the heir, but without special legislation the husband of a Queen is not so protected.   Special privileges and precedence are conferred upon such a husband but the details may vary in each case.[24]   Marriages in the Royal Family are restricted by the Royal Marriages Act 1772.   For this purpose the Royal Family is defined as the descendants of George II other than the issues of princesses who have married into foreign families. Such persons if under twenty-five require the consent of the Sovereign to

---

18 These last two conditions are to be established to the satisfaction of three or more of the following, the spouse of the Sovereign, the Lord Chancellor, the Speaker, the Lord Chief Justice and the Master of the Rolls.   What amounts to non-availability is not clear.

19 Regency Act 1937, s. 3.

20 As to these provisions, see p. 80, *ante.*

21 The limitation to members of the Royal Family dates back in practice to 1936. See Tom Jones, *Diary with Letters*, p. 63.

22 In practice an equivalent protection of the Church of Scotland to the statutory one in the case of a regency is included.

23 And the Earl of Carrick, Baron of Renfrew, Lord of the Isles. As Duke of Rothesay he voted in the elections of representative peers up to 1807; for its history see " A Short Account of the Principality of Scotland " by Lord Dunedin; and see Croft Dickinson in (1924) *Economica.*

24 See, *e.g., London Gazette*, Sept. 30, 1952.

their marriage or if over twenty-five must obtain such consent or give notice to the Privy Council.[25] For most purposes, however, the other members of the Royal Family are treated as ordinary subjects.

The royal revenues. By a steady process, starting from the accession of George III the majority of the hereditary revenues of the Crown have been surrendered by each Sovereign at the beginning of the reign in exchange for the Civil List—sums appropriated by Parliament.[26] The Civil List Act makes provision for the Sovereign and for such other members of the Royal Family as may be appropriate. The sums payable to the Queen are appropriated under five heads. The revenues not surrendered are those of the Duchies of Cornwall and Lancaster and of the Principality of Scotland, the first and the last belonging to the heir apparent,[27] and while the heir apparent is a minor the Civil List is abated. The surrendered lands and land revenues are now managed by the Crown Estate Commissioners under the Crown Estate Acts 1956 and 1961.[28] A distinction must be drawn between the Crown Estate which is thus managed, and the private estates of the Crown which are separately regulated, notably by the Crown Private Estates Act 1862 and the Conveyancing (Scotland) Act 1874. The latter estates are treated as private property, and bear appropriate fiscal burdens. At the back of this division lies a long history, especially in Scotland. There was for long a determined effort to annexe lands and revenue to the Crown, and to prevent their alienation, in order to preserve the national revenue. The distinction also appeared in cases where it was argued that the Crown, acquiring from a subject superior, *utitur jure communi.*[29]

In a strict form these arguments have ceased to be important because of fundamental changes in the nature of government and of government finance. Nevertheless, some of the principles which underlie the older cases remain of importance when the terminology is translated into appropriate modern words. Thus, the Regalia, the proprietary rights adhering to the Crown by virtue of the prerogative, are divided into

[25] See Farran, " The Royal Marriages Act " (1951) 14 M.L.R. 56; this Act, coupled with the Act 4 Anne, c. 1, conferring English nationality on the lineal descendants of the Princess Sophia, creates many uncertainties; see Clive Parry, " Further Considerations upon the *Prince of Hanover's* Case " (1956) 5 I.C.L.Q. 61. The latter Act, repealed by the British Nationality Act 1948, was held in *Att.-Gen.* v. *Ernest Augustus Prince of Hanover* [1957] A.C. 436 to have conferred British nationality upon that Prince.

[26] See Civil List Act 1952.

[27] *Purves* v. *Laird of Luss* (1680) Mor. 8542; *Johnston* v. *Riccarton* (1608) Mor. 11685; and see Bell, Princ. 672 and 674. The lands fall to be managed by the Crown Estate Commissioners.

[28] In effect the Crown Estate is regarded as held upon trust: see (1955) Cmd. 9483.

[29] *e.g., Bruce* v. *Veitch*, Nov. 28, 1810, F.C.; and see " The Royal Prerogative in Modern Scots Law " [1957] *Public Law* 304, though for a rather fuller account and a slightly different view see Cameron, " Crown Exemption from Statute and Tax in Scotland," 1962 J.R. 191. Among the institutional writers see Stair, Inst. II, 3, 35; Ersk. Inst. II, 3, 15; Craig, *Jus Feudale*, 1, 15, 17.

regalia majora and *regalia minora*,[30] the former being inalienable, the latter capable of alienation. The former, in particular, were regarded as being held upon trust for the people,[31] and as belonging to the Crown as representing the state, and as existing for the protection of subjects.[32] Generalised ideas, such as the idea of *res extra commercium* or of *res publicum*, also played their part.[33] The functional aspects of these rights, as necessarily belonging to a government irrespective of its form, were also emphasised.[34] These proprietary rights have then their importance for an understanding of the theory of prerogative, for they have developed from the period when jurisdiction was property,[35] and they thus form a necessary link with the discussion of prerogative which is inseparable from a discussion of the royal functions.

THE PREROGATIVE

Introduction. Public right, said Figgis, shapes itself out of private right. The powers of modern governments run back to the proprietary rights and jurisdictions of particular persons. Pre-eminent among these was the Sovereign, and with the evolution of modern and responsible government these powers, and their derivatives, have in fact become the attributes of government, but their discussion is still obscured by the almost mystical aura of majesty which, because of their origin, still surrounds them. Maitland's warning [36] to observe how the new wants of a new age were being met is still neglected by governments and institutional writers, though there was a time when the courts in Scotland took a more realistic view.[37] Essentially, prerogative powers are those which, of necessity, inhere in governments.

---

[30] The details of the rights comprised under these heads are not appropriate to the present work, and for them the curious reader is referred to the Title *Crown* in the *Encyclopaedia of the Laws of Scotland*, and to Fraser, *Constitutional Law*, p. 99 *et seq.*; Rankine, *Land Ownership*, Chap. XIV; and McMillan, *Bona Vacantia*. While in general the rights correspond to those in England there are differences: see, *e.g.*, *Henderson* v. *Scott* (1793) Mor. 17072 in relation to waifs; and see now *Lord Advocate* v. *Aberdeen University*, 1963 S.C. 533.

[31] *Marquess of Bute* v. *McKirdy*, 1937 S.C. 93; *Smith* v. *Lerwick Harbour Trustees* (1903) 5 F. 680; *Burnet* v. *Barclay*, 1955 J.C. 34.

[32] See the authorities cited by Craig, *Jus Feudale*; Ersk. Inst. II, 6, 17; and *Smith's* case, *supra*; *Cruickshank* v. *Gordon* (1843) 5 D. 909 at 962. This was also the foundation of Montrose's famous letter upon prerogative.

[33] Such ideas ran through the treatment of public bodies: *Wotherspoon* v. *Mags. of Linlithgow* (1863) 2 M. 348; but *cf. Western Heritable Investment Co.* v. *Glasgow Corporation*, 1956 S.L.T. 2 (affirmed 1956 S.C.(H.L.) 64).

[34] *King's Printers* v. *Buchan* (1826) 4 S. 559; and see the *Aberdeen University* case, *supra*, note 30.

[35] This idea underlay the provisions in the Act of Union for the benefit of royal burghs and the owners of the heritable jurisdictions. Its persistence caused considerable inconvenience: see Kames' *Law Tracts* on the Heritable Jurisdictions and Innes' *Legal Antiquities*.

[36] *Constitutional History*, p. 417.

[37] See *Lord Advocate* v. *Galbraith* (1910) 47 S.L.R. 529 and the cases cited in [1957] *Public Law* 304 *et seq.*; (1962) 7 J.R. 191 *et seq.* The view was charmingly and forcefully put in the Appendix on the indefeasible rights of Kings in Kames' *Essays*. It is accepted in *Burmah Oil Co. (Burma Trading) Ltd.* v. *Lord Advocate*, 1964

The use of the word " prerogative " with us is confusing. It meant to Blackstone the special pre-eminence of the King, to Dicey the residue of the discretionary or arbitrary power legally left at any time in the hands of the Crown,[38] to Lord Haldane it meant the common law as distinct from the statutory powers of the Crown.[39] There is also the obvious distinction between the prerogative powers which remain personal to the Sovereign and those which have been transferred to the government, and there is another complication, since terminology, such as the words " Order in Council," may have a prerogative appearance which conceals the fact that an institution is statutory. Hence the basic ideas underlying the concept of prerogative separate out or coalesce in different ways in different situations. Thus, the idea of discretionary power sometimes refers to those powers which can be exercised by the government without the prior consent of Parliament. Such powers exist pre-eminently in the field of foreign affairs, and in effect these are common law powers, in the sense that they are powers which tend to inhere in any government.[40] At other times the discretionary powers exercised by a government are in origin statutory, yet they attract the attributes of prerogative powers of the common law type, despite the fact that it has been declared by the House of Lords that a statute operating in the field of prerogative excludes the possibility of exercising the old prerogative powers.[41] This rule, which in some areas is applied with strictness,[42] could have surprising effects if applied with logical firmness to the departments of the central government. In relation to them, it is not uniformly applied so that the lines of division are blurred. There may be from the point of view of the government both practical and psychological advantages in using the word " prerogative," but this imprecision, while it has to be accepted, must also be watched.[43]

This imprecision is perhaps attributable to the fact that disputes about prerogative have always been at the centre of constitutional law,

S.C.(H.L.) 117, where, however, Lord Reid appears to accept that the rules had somehow crystallised at a date (uncertain) in the past, and Lord Radcliffe (at p. 150) almost confessed an inability of the common law to match necessities which were felt and seen, whereas all the cases which he discussed were in the past doing precisely that. The case as a whole is unsatisfactory. Argument suffered from a pre-litigation letter from the Treasury Solicitor's Office. It suffered from the shape of the pleadings (1964 S.C.(H.L.) at p. 140). It was reversed by the War Damage Act 1965. It should perhaps be regarded as an example of the confusion into which the law now falls when dealing with essential matters of government. The best account of the background is in 79 Harvard L.R. 614 *et seq.*

[38] Dicey's view runs through the opinions in *Chandler* v. *D.P.P.* [1962] 3 All E.R. 142, though in the *Burmah Oil* case Lord Radcliffe, rightly, criticises this definition.

[39] *Theodore* v. *Duncan* [1919] A.C. 696.

[40] Thus the constitutional limitations upon the powers of the President of the U.S.A. to declare war in practice give way before other powers of a President to take action in such a field, as the events of 1940–41 demonstrate.

[41] *Att.-Gen.* v. *De Keyser's Royal Hotel* [1920] A.C. 508. The rule thus expressed may require some refinement and lack the certainty which it once had; see *Sabally* v. *Att.-Gen.* [1965] 1 Q.B. 273 at 299, *per* Russell L.J.

[42] *Re Mitchell* [1954] Ch. 525.

[43] See especially the *Report on the Interception of Communications* (1957) Cmd. 283; and compare *Re K. (Infants)* [1962] 3 All E.R. 1000 at 1014.

but the disputes have never been settled in detail. Even beyond that these uncertainties exist, above all, because of the way in which we have thought about these questions. It does not follow (as Lord Reid suggested that it did in the *Burmah Oil* case), that the only or proper approach is the historical one. That may be far from the case, for as Lord Reid himself admitted, history gave one uncertain answers which themselves needed reinterpretation. A more satisfactory approach would be a functional one, regarding the essential nature and purpose of the state, but it is just that approach which is either precluded or made much more difficult by the terminology of " Crown," etc., in which these matters are discussed.

At least one historical lesson remains true, however. What is clear is that prerogative cannot mean a power above the law. The view of Berkeley J. in the *Case of Ship Money* [44] or of Sir George Mackenzie in the *Jus Regium* that " It was fit for the people that Kings should be above the Law " was no longer tenable after the Civil War and the events of 1688–89. It was these events which secured victory for the views of George Buchanan, Coke C.J. and Lord President Seton. [45] The victory was secured with difficulty. Steuart in his *Answers*, while agreeing that law is the great *litus* of prerogative, was unwilling to discuss in detail the limits which the law might set to prerogative, advancing the matter little further than Dirleton's *Doubts*. *Godden* v. *Hales* and the Act of 1685 for the Security of the Officers of State supported the other view. [46] Moreover, when won, the victory was not certain. Principles have had to be reasserted since. [47] In effect the events of 1688–89 only settled the relationship of law to prerogative at the highest and most general levels. The law could determine the existence of a prerogative power, but the courts could not enter into a discussion of the rightness of the exercise of an admitted power. Thus further controls were needed to supplement the control by law. These controls had, of necessity, to be political. Thus, the system of responsible government (the form which these controls eventually took) must be looked at as the necessary complement to the solution, in respect of legal controls, which was sketched by the Revolution. There was, thus, created a diarchy, which still exists and is most clearly seen operating in cases involving foreign relations in war and peace [48] and in statutes in the same field such as

[44] (1637) 3 St.Tr. 825 at 1098. See, too, *Bate's Case* (1606) 2 St.Tr. 371. For the background to this case and to the subject see Keir and Lawson, *Cases on Constitutional Law*, and (1953) 69 L.Q.R. 200.

[45] In the *Case of Prohibitions* (1607) 12 Co.Rep. 63 and *Bruce* v. *Hamilton*; see (1952) 58 J.R. 83. Contrast Hope, *Major Practicks*, I, p. 13.

[46] (1686) 11 St.Tr. 1166; A.P.S. VIII, 484. Not all lawyers would speak out. Fountainhall, as his *Memorials* show, could connive in illegality; Stair, though he claimed to have written upon prerogative, never published the work.

[47] *Entick* v. *Carrington* (1765) 19 St.Tr. 1029. That argument continues: see Cmd. 283, above, note 43.

[48] In such cases as *R.* v. *Bottrill, ex p. Kuechenmeister* [1947] K.B. 41; *Mighell* v. *Sultan of Johore* [1894] 1 Q.B. 149; *Government of the Republic of Spain* v.

the International Organisations (Immunities and Privileges) Act 1950, which, in any event, imposes limitations upon the activities of the courts. The determination and control of decisions which are essentially political are left to political mechanisms. The shape which the political controls took have, perhaps, over the years, increased the limitations upon the sphere of operation of the courts. What is understood by a " political " matter has in an internal sense become wider and the diarchy, in so far as it continues to exist, has become ill-balanced. It is that proposition which underlies the arguments about administrative law and the appropriateness of the Parliamentary Commissioner.

It is at lower levels than matters of foreign affairs that the continuance of the diarchy is not clear, and in part this is because of the ambiguity of the word " prerogative." Cases such as *Liversidge* v. *Anderson*,[49] which fundamentally involve the same issues as those which formerly underlay the dispute about prerogative, tend to be looked upon as distinct because of a statutory background. In fact the issue of the scope of the proper limits of judicial review of governmental acts remains a live and critical one. This background of " prerogative " should be remembered in that context for in both the questions involved are the place of the courts in the machinery of government and the limits and effectiveness of other controlling mechanisms. It is dangerous to assume that the issues of prerogative have been finally settled either in their traditional or newer forms.

The personal prerogatives. Traditional prerogative powers may most conveniently be discussed under two heads: those which remain personal to the Queen, and those that are exercised by the government. The former are obviously limited in modern times. It is said that the Sovereign has merely the right to be consulted, the right to warn, and the right to encourage, and in normal times this is true. In exceptional circumstances more effective power still remains. There is, however, one governing consideration—that the Sovereign should remain neutral in politics and should appear so. Power has steadily been transferred to ministers, a transference which owes much to the growth of the idea of ministerial responsibility but which owes something also to much older doctrines, and institutions, such as the evolution of the various seals,[50] which, when coupled with the human desire of any office holder to aggrandise his office, can operate in much the same direction. The whole process of transference has in modern times also been aided by the attitude of the Sovereign for the time being.[51] As a result the personal

---

National Bank of Scotland, 1939 S.C. 413; and see *Chandler* v. *D.P.P.* [1962] 3 All E.R. 142, especially at pp. 158–159.
[49] [1942] A.C. 206.
[50] Such institutions were also a means of subjecting the King to law; see, *e.g.*, *A.* v. *B.* (1538) Mor. 7854.
[51] See Mackintosh, *The British Cabinet*, particularly Chaps. 9 and 16, which should be generally referred to, together with Jennings, *Cabinet Government*. Earlier, see Roberts, *The Growth of Responsible Government in Stuart England*.

prerogatives are limited in scope. The Sovereign, it is said,[52] acts personally in relation to certain Orders, the Order of Merit, the Garter, the Thistle and the Royal Victorian Order, but with the probable exception of the last two it is likely that ministerial advice will more and more predominate, since appointments may well take on a political significance. Indeed, on occasion they may be intended to have, as with the grant of a K.C.V.O. to Sir Humphrey Gibbs in 1965; though such episodes are rare.

Apart from such rights the Sovereign retains the traditional rights, to advise, to warn and to encourage the government, and to be informed by it. These functions must be seen in proper perspective. They can be overemphasised or underrated. It is clear that no Sovereign can overrule a government or force it to take action against its will.[53] Instances of " warning " were relatively common under George V, and existed under George VI also, though, since the crises of that reign were not so much of a political kind, there was less opportunity for it.[54] It is not easy to determine the weight that these interventions have had. Sometimes there is a conflict of evidence [55] but there certainly appear to be cases when the intervention of the King has been valuable, as in relation to Ireland in 1921–22.[56] Moreover, the weight of any intervention by the Sovereign is not constant, depending as it does on many factors such as the experience of Sovereign or minister. The interventions can particularly after a long reign be backed by a very full knowledge. The Sovereign receives Cabinet minutes and has frequent meetings with the Prime Minister, the political members of the household provide links with the party in power, and unofficial occasions allow contact with the Opposition. It is one of the functions of the Private Secretary to ensure a store of political information.[57] Thus over the years a considerable experience could be built up. Perhaps for that reason George V was particularly insistent on his right to be informed. Clearly, however, any royal interventions cannot be made public at the time, nor can they be made from the standpoint of party politics, and ultimately the Sovereign, though he may warn, must give way to his government.

Just as important can be the right to " encourage " a government. Encouragement may amount to no more than a sympathetic reception, but that can be significant. The manner of the reception by George V

52 Morrison, *Government and Parliament*, 3rd ed., p. 99. The present Government has announced (734 H.C.Deb. 1301) that it would recommend no more hereditary honours, and, further, that it would discontinue the practice of the award of honours for political services (though this may turn out to affect mainly the terms in which an award is announced). It has also attempted to limit the growth of the Honours List. See generally Richards, *Patronage in British Government*.
53 Morrison, *op. cit.* p. 94 *et seq.*
54 See Nicholson, *George V*; Wheeler-Bennett, *George VI*; and Mackintosh, *op. cit.*
55 As in the appointment of Mr. Bevin as Foreign Secretary which the King claimed was due to his suggestion but which is denied by Lord Attlee, a denial which seems to fit the facts.
56 Or in relation to the Parliament Act 1911.
57 The office can be one of importance; see the Appendix to Wheeler-Bennett, *op. cit.*

of the first Labour government probably helped that government to assume office and helped the country at large to accept that government. In this field, too, as that episode emphasised, any activity of the Sovereign must be founded upon a spirit of impartiality. This necessity marks even more strongly the use of the residual political powers which upon occasion a Sovereign may have to exercise.

It is arguable whether or not a Sovereign has a right to refuse a dissolution requested by a Prime Minister.[58] There is no modern instance of a refusal, though George V was reluctant to grant a dissolution to Mr. Ramsay MacDonald in 1924. A refusal is likely to bring the monarchy into the centre of political controversy, as is shown by the experience of Lord Byng in Canada in 1926,[59] and while it seems that the power may exist it is one which would only be exercised in extreme, and virtually revolutionary, circumstances to preserve the constitution. The same is true of the " right " to dismiss a ministry. Again there are no modern precedents, though modern authorities assert the right.[60] Its exercise would be so dangerous to the monarchy that its use could only be justified in like extreme circumstances, and history alone would decide the appropriateness of the decision. More real is the personal prerogative in relation to the choice of Prime Minister. In normal circumstances the issue does not arise. It can do where there is no party with a clear majority, or where, because of the death or resignation of a Prime Minister during the currency of a Parliament, a choice has to be made in the absence of an election. Such a choice has had to be made in 1923, 1931, 1940 and 1957. On such occasions the Sovereign has not always had the advice of the outgoing Prime Minister, and, while the advice of elder statesmen is taken, there remains a personal responsibility of the Sovereign, the burden of which is increased by the fact that though the office of Deputy Prime Minister exists, it is not formally recognised (and in any event the Deputy is not necessarily heir apparent). Further, it was said in 1922 that the King would not wait upon a party choosing a leader, though in 1957 the Labour Party indicated that that was the acceptable procedure as far as it was concerned.[61] Since, thereafter, the Conservative Party has also (from 1965) adopted an electoral system, it seems likely that normally the results of an election would now be awaited. A choice might still have to be made in a variety of hypotheses. The result of an election in either party might so divide the party that it ceased to command the House. In a crisis time might not permit the slow electoral processes, or the House may be so divided that a choice must be made. Such a choice is often difficult, and capable of

[58] The authorities are discussed in Jennings, *Cabinet Government*.
[59] Forsey, *Dissolution of Parliament*.
[60] See Jennings, *Cabinet Government*; Amery, *Thoughts on the Constitution*; Marshall and Moodie, *Some Problems of the Constitution*.
[61] For details of these events see Jennings, Mackintosh and Marshall and Moodie in the works already cited, and Bassett, *1931 Political Crisis*.

arousing controversy, as did the action of George V in 1931 in relation to the formation of the National Government, even though it is accepted as constitutionally correct. It is, however, difficult to provide by rules for such cases (even the electoral rules of both parties, designed to aid the Sovereign in remaining above politics, could, as has been suggested, cause further difficulties), and it is perhaps inevitable that a residual power should exist to meet such situations. The existence of that power re-emphasises the necessity for the continuous political education of the Sovereign. The effectiveness of a constitutional long-stop can be important even if his services are rarely needed.

The political powers exercised by a Sovereign have then been reduced to a minimum. With that reduction the possibility of a Sovereign exercising a more general influence upon the life of the community has perhaps increased, and such influence should be allowed for in any calculation about the importance of the monarchy in the constitution. Royal interest can give " respectability " to new institutions; such things as the interest which George V demonstrated in industrial society can be important. The exploration of these questions would go too far into the realms of sociology, but they must be mentioned in this context.[62] It must also be emphasised that in the wider sphere of the Commonwealth the institution of monarchy and the prerogative may have an even greater importance. The element of neutrality which in this country enables persons who dislike the government for the time being to serve the Crown with equanimity assumes a greater importance. Monarchical members of the Commonwealth are prepared to give to the Crown an allegiance which they would not give to the United Kingdom, and for the republican members the title Head of the Commonwealth can achieve some of the same results. Aided by these shadowy and ill-defined concepts practical co-operation can develop through many agencies in ways which would otherwise be much more difficult. It should, moreover, be remembered that as a result of the resolutions of the imperial Conference of 1930, the Sovereign has, in a sense, an independent existence in relation to the other member states. Each has a right of direct access to the Sovereign, not through the United Kingdom government.

As has been seen this Commonwealth interest in the Crown is reflected in, among others, the rules governing changes in the royal titles, and it must be remembered that the rules here discussed are United Kingdom rules. Because of this Commonwealth interest debate has arisen whether the Crown is one or several. Older cases tended to emphasise unity,[63] but subsequent events, in particular the abdication of Edward VIII, made it difficult to maintain a theory of indivisibility since

---

[62] Books such as Petrie, *The Modern British Monarchy*, or Kingsley Martin, *The Crown and the Establishment*, can be starting-points for further inquiry.
[63] *Williams* v. *Howarth* [1905] A.C. 551.

he ceased to be King in different parts of the Commonwealth on different days. Nevertheless, an element of unity remains in the agreement which preceded the Royal Titles Act 1953, and at times is operative in United Kingdom law,[64] though at others it is rejected.[65] This uncertainty is understandable, but it must be remembered that when the Crown is here referred to it is the Queen in the right of the United Kingdom to which reference is made, and the prerogative rules discussed are those in relation to that Kingdom.

POLITICAL OR GOVERNMENTAL PREROGATIVES

This group of powers and immunities consists of those which have been transferred to or affect the central government. They do not unfortunately fall into tidy categories. They may be discussed under the following heads:

The prerogatives connected with foreign affairs. These are perhaps the widest. The Crown by virtue of the prerogative in foreign affairs is master of the sending and receipt of ambassadors, of the recognition of foreign states as independent or sovereign,[66] and of the recognition of persons or bodies as having diplomatic status.[67] Similar powers are conferred by statute in other like cases.[68] The existence of a state of war is determined by prerogative declarations.[69] So far as treaties are concerned the Crown has, by virtue of the prerogative, a power to enter into any treaty, but where a treaty requires any alteration of domestic law to become effective that must be done by Parliament. Similarly, it is probably true that any treaty involving the cession of British territory requires parliamentary approval for its effectiveness.[70] By convention, under the so-called Ponsonby Rules, other treaties, particularly those imposing obligations, are to be laid before Parliament, though the exact scope of these rules is a matter of dispute. For political reasons Parliament may often be involved in the treaty-making process even where there is no legal or conventional obligation, for, while the power to act may exist, the actings may later be reviewed in Parliament and the support which is politically necessary may then be found to be lacking

---

64 In the case of Mr. Holland Martin in 1955 disqualification from the House of Commons was founded upon this theory of unity.

65 See generally de Smith, "The Royal Style and Titles" (1953) 2 I.C.L.Q. 263.

66 *Duff Development Co. Ltd.* v. *Govt. of Kelantan* [1924] A.C. 797; *Govt. of the Republic of Spain* v. *National Bank of Scotland*, 1939 S.C. 413; *Owners of S.S. Victoria* v. *Owners of S.S. Quillwark*, 1922 S.L.T. 68.

67 *Engelke* v. *Musmann* [1928] A.C. 433; and see Dykes and Oswald, *Principles of Civil Jurisdiction*, and the Diplomatic Privileges Act 1708.

68 The law on this matter is now contained in the Diplomatic Privileges Act 1964, carrying out the Vienna Convention of 1961.

69 *R.* v. *Bottrill, ex p. Kuechenmeister* [1947] K.B. 41.

70 This applies even within the Commonwealth; see, *e.g.*, Christmas Island Act 1958. Details upon this whole subject should be sought in appropriate books on international law.

without prior discussion. By an extension of these principles it has been said that the interpretation of treaties is a matter for the executive,[71] and it may be noted that treaties, since they operate in the spheres of international law, do not confer enforceable rights on particular subjects.[72]

Within the field of international affairs there is also a power to take executive action. The plea of act of state will be a good defence in any action founded upon acts done upon the authority of the Crown, or subsequently ratified by it, where the act is under a general discretionary power and where the act is done to an alien outside British territory,[73] though it will not be so where the act is against a British subject anywhere in the world,[74] nor against a friendly alien here.[75] There are suggestions, notably in *Poll* v. *Lord Advocate*,[76] that the plea is of somewhat wider operation in Scotland, but in view of the authorities there cited (which would not support the broader statements in the opinion) and of the whole circumstances of the case it seems that these suggestions should be disregarded. What was in issue in that case was the right of the Crown to exclude any alien,[77] a right which is generally admitted.

The prerogative in an emergency. It is to be noted that in general the prerogative here looks outward. Internally (a word which in this context must be held to include dealings with British subjects) a different view is taken, in the interest of subjecting governmental acts to legal controls. The plea of act of state or state necessity is normally rejected. The contrast is made by Lord Camden C.J. in *Entick* v. *Carrington*[78]; " And with respect to the argument of State necessity, or a distinction which has been arrived at between State offences and others, the common law does not understand that kind of reasoning, nor do our books take notice of any such distinction." So equally in *Smith* v. *Jeffrey*[79] there is an insistence that the courts must determine the validity of the exercise of claimed prerogative powers, and that legal authority for all

---

[71] *Cook* v. *Sprigg* [1899] A.C. 572; *Oyekan* v. *Adele* [1957] 2 All E.R. 785.
[72] *Hoani Te Heuheu Tukino* v. *Aotea District Maori Land Board* [1941] A.C. 308; *Civilian War Claimants* v. *The King* [1932] A.C. 14; and *Nissan* v. *Att.-Gen.* [1967] 2 All E.R. 1238 at 1242.
[73] *Buron* v. *Denman* (1848) 2 Exch. 167; and see *Sec. of State in Council of India* v. *Kamachee Boye Sahaba* (1859) 13 Moo.P.C. 22; Wade, " Act of State in English Law," 15 B.Y.I.L. 94.
[74] *Walker* v. *Baird* [1892] A.C. 491. This appears to be confirmed by the Court of Appeal in *Nissan* v. *Att.-Gen.* [1967] 2 All E.R. 1238; reversing on this point the court below: [1967] 2 All E.R. 200. The case is under appeal to the House of Lords.
[75] *Johnstone* v. *Pedlar* [1921] 2 A.C. 262; as to enemy aliens see *R.* v. *Bottrill* (*supra*) and *Commercial Estates Co. of Egypt* v. *B.O.T.* [1925] 1 K.B. 271.
[76] (1899) 1 F. 823 (discussed [1921] 2 A.C. at p. 289); and see *Boyesen* v. *Nixon*, Jan. 16, 1813, F.C., and the remarks of Stephenson J. in *R.* v. *Governor of Brixton Prison, ex p. Soblen* [1963] 2 Q.B. 243 at 282.
[77] And see *Musgrove* v. *Toy* [1891] A.C. 272. Where, however, instead of using prerogative powers, the Crown uses somewhat similar statutory powers, but errs in so doing, liability may arise; *Kuechenmeister* v. *The Home Office* [1958] 1 Q.B. 496.
[78] (1765) 19 St.Tr. 1029.
[79] Jan. 24, 1817, F.C.

acts must be demonstrated, an insistence more recently emphasised in *Glasgow Corporation* v. *Central Land Board.*[80]

Nevertheless, the existence of a state of war brings in its train enlarged prerogative powers in which the plea of state necessity plays a larger part. In 1914 the Trading with the Enemy Proclamation was made under the prerogative,[81] and there arise rights to interfere with both persons and property. The right to impressment[82] or to quarter troops[83] is admitted[84] as is a right to requisition property. Such rights were treated by Hume[85] as depending upon necessity and as being possessed by other governmental bodies as well as the Crown. The scope of such rights in modern conditions is not entirely certain,[86] wars have changed their character since the doctrines were recognised. Such special rights as do emerge are, however, controlled by the courts as to their scope and existence; a plea of state necessity cannot exclude the jurisdiction of the courts. There was uncertainty about how far compensation was due for interference with property, but it now appears that in an emergency, whether warlike or not, compensation is due as a matter of general principle at common law.[87] This general rule has been severely affected by the War Damage Act 1965, excluding any common law claims for acts done within or without the United Kingdom during or in contemplation of the outbreak of war. Thus, although passed because of a particular decision—the *Burmah Oil* case—the Act has very wide effects. The general principle is also excluded in these cases where the defence of " act of state " can be pleaded. The rules governing the quantum of compensation remain entirely obscure, and it is customary to regulate such matters by legislation when occasion demands.

Martial law. For convenience another power to deal with emergencies may be mentioned here, since it is sometimes treated as a prerogative power, that is, the power to govern by martial law. The

[80] 1956 S.C.(H.L.) 1.
[81] Hankey, *Supreme Command*, p. 92; though as to the operation of such proclamations in relation to prize see *The Zamora* [1916] 2 A.C. 77.
[82] *Smith* v. *Jeffrey, supra.*
[83] *Boswell* v. *Mags. of Cupar*, July 10, 1804, F.C.
[84] *The Case of Saltpetre* (1606) 12 Co.Rep. 12; *Moffat Hydropathic Co. Ltd.* v. *Lord Advocate*, 1919, 1 S.L.T. 82.
[85] *Lectures*, III, 205. In the *Burmah Oil* case Lord Kilbrandon, in the Outer House (1962 S.L.T. 347), who had admitted the possibility of compensation, rejected a distinction between prerogative acts and acts of necessity in the context, holding the act a prerogative one; and see Prosser [1963] *Public Law* 12; and Glanville Williams, " The Defence of Necessity " (1953) 6 *Current Legal Problems* 216.
[86] See Scott and Hildesley, *The Case of Requisition.*
[87] The case for compensation may be stronger in Scotland than England and may turn upon a distinction between taking and destruction; but compare *The Moffat Hydropathic Co., supra*, and *Carlton Hotel* v. *L.A.*, 1921 S.C. 237 with *Att.-Gen.* v. *De Keyser's Royal Hotel* [1920] A.C. 508; and see note 85, above; but, subject to the limitations suggested above, *The Burmah Oil Case* [1965] A.C. 75 and *Nissan* v. *Att.-Gen.* [1967] 2 All E.R. 1238 appear to admit a general right to compensation. Much of the argument in these cases is an example of the difficulties which flow from treating " prerogative " as an historical, and not a functional, concept.

Bill of Rights prohibited trying civilians by martial law in time of peace, and, in effect, the Claim of Right contains similar provisions. Though the prohibition of the use of officers is more general, the provision in relation to the use of the army in time of peace is to a like effect. In substance it seems that when invasion or rebellion has caused such interruption of government that the courts cannot operate normally, then their powers are suspended and special tribunals may operate.[88] It is, however, for the courts to determine whether such a state of affairs exists.[89] The power of the courts is only suspended, and once normality is restored they may, in theory, review the legality of acts done meantime. In practice an Act of Indemnity would generally prevent such review. The obscurities of the common law on this subject are likely to remain, since it is customary to make statutory provision, as under the Emergency Powers (Defence) Act 1939.[90] Other aspects of these emergency powers, such as billeting, are also covered by legislation. Issues relating to the overlap of prerogative and statutory powers will be discussed later, as will be lesser powers to deal with lesser emergencies.

Prerogative rules and immunities. Other prerogative powers are of continuing significance. These powers were substantially diminished in the seventeenth century, when any general power to legislate by prerogative was excluded,[91] the suspending and dispensing powers were denied by the Claim of Right (more clearly)[92] and by the Bill of Rights, as were powers of taxation or of imposing customs by prerogative act. The erecting of courts where others already existed was excluded by the Claim of Right, and any prerogative power to create new courts is in England negligible because of limitations upon it.[93] Thus any power to govern by prerogative is excluded. Existing prerogatives do, however, aid government. Formerly the Crown had a complete immunity from suits in tort in England, and in contract could only be sued by the cumbrous method of a Petition of Right.[94] In Scotland the situation was

---

88 *Re Clifford and O'Sullivan* [1921] 2 A.C. 570.
89 *R.* v. *Allen* [1921] 2 Ir.R. 241; *R.* v. *Strickland* [1921] 2 Ir.R. 317; and see generally *Ex p. Marais* [1902] A.C. 109; *Tilonko* v. *Att.-Gen. of Natal* [1907] A.C. 93, and the articles in (1902) 18 L.Q.R. Martial law in this sense must be contrasted with military law governing service discipline, and the government of occupied territory overseas by the military forces.
90 Though such provisions existed in a curious half-world. The powers there given were (by s. 9) expressly granted in addition to and not in derogation from prerogative powers. What, therefore, was the effect of a statutory right to compensation if the exercise of the prerogative gave none is not easy to determine; see, too, Naval Discipline Act 1957, s. 138 (1).
91 *Case of Proclamations* (1611) 12 Co.Rep. 74; no equivalent explicitly Scottish authority exists until *Grieve* v. *Edinburgh & District Water Trustees*, 1918 S.C. 700.
92 This condemnation occurred shortly after the University of St. Andrews had been prevailed upon to send an address maintaining their rightness (Fount. I, 503).
93 *Re Lord Bishop of Natal* (1865) 3 Moo.P.C.(N.S.) 115. Though the Criminal Injuries Compensation Board appears to be recognised as a " court " of some sort created by a White Paper: *R.* v. *Criminal Injuries Compensation Board, ex p. Lain* [1967] 2 All E.R. 770.
94 See, generally, Robertson, *Civil Proceedings against the Crown*.

different. Without doubt the Crown could be sued in contract, and for long could be sued for other civil wrongs, though in respect of actions of reparation the English rule came to be accepted.[95] This immunity has been largely removed by the Crown Proceedings Act 1947 (which will be discussed later), though important procedural advantages still remain with the Crown.[96]

The Crown has also an immunity from statute unless the statute is made expressly or by implication binding upon it. Again this rule did not exist in the old Scots law and appears to have come in after the Union through the Court of Exchequer.[97] Even today there is probably a difference between the two jurisdictions in the scope of the immunity. The view of Lord Dunedin in *Magistrates of Edinburgh* v. *Lord Advocate*[98] is entirely consistent with Scots law, and the rejection of that view in *Province of Bombay* v. *Bombay Corporation*[99] should not, it seems, be taken as applicable to Scotland. Lord Dunedin's view (which echoes yet older English views) was summarised by him when he said: " While I do not doubt that there are certain provisions by which the Crown never would be bound—such, for instance, as the provisions of a taxing statute or certain enactments with penal clauses adjected—yet when you come to a set of provisions in a statute having for its object the benefit of the public generally there is not an antecedent unlikelihood that the Crown will consent to be bound, and this, I think, would be so in the case of regulations which are meant to apply to all land in the city, and where the Crown's property is not property held *jure coronae*." [1] This view, which narrows the Crown immunity, commends itself as being rational.

The evolution of the Crown's immunity from taxation has a somewhat similar history. Unless expressly granted, it did not exist before the Union,[2] but it came to be accepted as a consequence of the Exchequer Court (Scotland) Act 1707, and includes immunity from local

---

[95] *MacGregor* v. *L.A.*, 1921 S.C. 847; *Somerville* v. *L.A.* (1893) 20 R. 1050 at 1075. See, generally, Sir Randall Philip, " Crown as Litigant in Scotland " (1928) 40 J.R. 238, and Mitchell, " The Royal Prerogative in Modern Scots Law " [1957] *Public Law* 304.

[96] *Duncan* v. *Cammell Laird Ltd.* [1942] A.C. 624; *Glasgow Corporation* v. *Central Land Board*, 1956 S.C.(H.L.) 1. These matters are discussed in Chap. 17, *post*.

[97] See the discussion in the article in [1957] *Public Law* referred to above, and contrast Cameron, " Crown Exemption from Statute and Tax in Scotland," 1962 7 J.R. 191, where he argues that the absence of a clear Scottish doctrine rather than the presence of a distinct one is material. While this view is not accepted, the results may not be very different in that both views lead to distinctions between English and Scots law.

[98] 1912 S.C. 1085.

[99] [1947] A.C. 58; and see Street, *Governmental Liability*. *Re M.* (*an Infant*) [1961] Ch. 81 and 328 seems more consistent with the former case, though *Minister of Agriculture, etc.* v. *Jenkins* [1963] 2 All E.R. 147 is not. See, generally, Maxwell, *Interpretation of Statutes*, and the articles referred to in notes 95 and 97, above.

[1] This distinction as to property may yet be important, though see *Burnet* v. *Barclay*, 1955 J.C. 34.

[2] *Bruce* v. *Veitch*, Nov. 28, 1810, F.C. For the evolution of the doctrine, see [1957] *Public Law* 304 and (1962) 7 J.R. 191.

taxation. In its modern form this immunity operates even if it does so to the detriment of the public.[3]

Other prerogative rules. Apart from these general prerogative immunities, there are other more detailed powers and privileges. The prerogative of mercy is exercised by either the Home Secretary or the Secretary of State for Scotland.[4] Further, the interests of the Crown are protected by special rules, in particular the King's interest cannot be adversely affected by the neglect of his servants,[5] a rule which can be of importance,[6] serving as it does to preserve the revenue. That rule, or others like it, prevents, in certain circumstances, the interests of the Crown being hampered by contractual obligations.[7] Yet other rules, particularly in relation to land, exist to aid the protection of those interests.[8]

General considerations. It will be seen, then, that prerogative rules are capable of affecting all operations of the Crown and its servants. This fact makes it important to ascertain who may be said to be a servant of the Crown. A variety of criteria have, from time to time, been suggested and applied by which this question may be determined in the absence of any statutory clarification. At times function has been important, at others the method of creation of the body concerned, but most recently the test of control has predominated,[9] and in modern statutes the tendency has been to define more clearly those bodies which are to be treated as Crown servants, or those to which prerogative attributes are to attach.

This clarification and slightly increased certainty in the law are to be welcomed, but there remain fundamental difficulties caused by the present shape of the law. Chief among them is the resultant dichotomy, in law, of the machinery of government, which contrasts with increasing unification in practice. In a functional sense it never did matter whether

---

3 *Bank voor Handel en Scheepvaart N.V.* v. *Administrator of Hungarian Property* [1954] A.C. 584. In view of the context there does not seem to be any room for any difference between the jurisdictions (*I.R.C.* v. *Glasgow Police Athletic Assoc.*, 1953 S.C.(H.L.) 13), even though this case appears to be inconsistent with the reasoning of other Scots cases, *e.g.*, *Salt* v. *McKnight*, 1947 J.C. 99. The immunity may also have incidental effects: *Re Automatic Telephone, etc., Co. Ltd.'s Application* [1963] 2 All E.R. 302.

4 It extends only to penal consequences: Ersk. IV, 4, 105; Hume, *Criminal Law*, II, p. 496.

5 A rule founded on the Act of 1600, A.P.S. IV, 231; Stair IV, 35, 11; Ersk. II, 2, 27.

6 *L.A.* v. *Mirrielee's Trs.*, 1943 S.C. 587; 1945 S.C.(H.L.) 1. The rule is probably better founded than was allowed for by some members of the House of Lords there.

7 *Rederiaktiebolaget Amphitrite* v. *The King* [1921] 3 K.B. 500; *Commissioners for Crown Lands* v. *Page* [1960] 2 Q.B. 274. This whole subject has many aspects, including the operation of personal bar or estoppel: see Mitchell, *The Contracts of Public Authorities.*

8 [1957] *Public Law, loc. cit.,* note 95.

9 See the *Bank voor Handel* case, *supra,* and the discussion in Glanville Williams, *Crown Proceedings,* Griffith and Street, *Principles of Administrative Law,* and 9 Univ. Toronto L.J. 169. See, too, *British Broadcasting Corporation* v. *Johns* [1965] Ch. 32.

Commissioners of Sewers or like bodies were servants of the Crown. At a lower level, and in a different form of emergency, it may be as important that a local authority should have a governmental power to act as it is that the central government should have such powers in relation to great affairs of state. The need for the powers springs from the governmental character of both authorities. For technical reasons it always has mattered in law and perhaps now tends to matter more. Yet what should be significant about a highway authority, to take another example, is its public character, not its character as being or as not being a Crown servant.[10] To some extent this modern division is attributable to the nineteenth-century uncertainty about the state, and public authorities, and to a concern to limit the operation of certain privileges, notably fiscal immunities.[11] The division of public authorities, which in the nineteenth century produced beneficial results, may in a modern and more complex state produce severe inconveniences to litigants and distort the law. It should be noted that these detailed rules or attributes, particularly those discussed under the last two heads, apply to the Crown irrespective of the source of power for the act in question. For these purposes it does not matter whether the Crown is performing an act justified by common law or one justified by statute. The special attributes are related to the doer of the act, not to the kind of act done. It is this which gives importance to the classification of persons or bodies as being Crown servants. Nevertheless, the source of a power may matter. It has been held that where a statute occupies the same field as common law prerogative powers, the statutory powers, in the absence of any provision to the contrary, prevail in the sense that the Crown does not have the option of choosing between alternative justifications. Thus the conditions imposed upon the exercise of the statutory powers will apply even if the common law power was unconditional.[12] Such a solution is a necessary consequence of the ultimate supremacy of statutes, but it means that in such circumstances a distinction has to be drawn between prerogative powers in the sense of common law powers, and statutory powers which may be of a like kind exercised by the Crown and to which, in consequence, some general prerogative rules may apply. Yet both sets of power are essentially of the same

---

[10] To circumvent some of the difficulties that face a litigant raising an action against a Crown servant attempts have been made to distinguish the character in which such persons act, or to distinguish their functions as statutory or prerogative. Such attempts have met with little success: *Merricks* v. *Heathcoat-Amory and the Minister of Agriculture and Fisheries* [1955] Ch. 567; *Harper* v. *S. of S. for the Home Department* [1955] Ch. 238; *Griffin* v. *L.A.*, 1950 S.C. 448.

[11] See, *e.g.*, *Greig* v. *The University of Edinburgh* (1868) 6 M.(H.L.) 97, and the docks and harbour cases therein referred to which, among many others, illustrate both these aspects.

[12] See *Att.-Gen.* v. *De Keyser's Royal Hotel* [1920] A.C. 508. The exact operation of the statute is not clear. Lord Atkin (at p. 540) refers to the prerogative as abridged or in abeyance. Lord Parmoor (at p. 554) says the Crown must be presumed to act under the statutory powers. *Sabally* v. *Att.-Gen.* [1965] 1 Q.B. 273 appears to support the above formulation. *Cf.* Emergency Powers (Defence) Act 1939, s. 9.

order. Frequently the statutory powers are created because of uncertainties about the common law powers, but the statutory intent is not to create powers essentially different. In practice, whatever the powers are called, the body exercising them attracts to itself other " prerogative " attributes, examples of which have just been given, and thus further confusion arises from confused terminology.

Two further (and perhaps consequential) difficulties should be noted. First, this concentration of attention upon the Crown may provoke misconceptions about many rules. Many of the rules (and perhaps all of the most important ones) have nothing to do with the Crown in the sense of monarchy, they are simply the attributes of the Crown in the sense of government. Failure to notice this may make the student unaware of their universality,[13] and that failure lies at the root of many of the irrationalities of the modern law.[14] In this matter the older treatment in Scots law was much more rational, and elements of this still remain. The old concern was with powers which must belong to a government [15]; looked at in that way and shorn of false feudalism, many of the rules can be better understood and applied. In the second place, and conversely, this overconcern with the Crown and with words like " prerogative " has tended to cause the neglect, and sometimes the disappearance, of somewhat similar rules (though differently named) which were applicable to other governmental bodies which could not be classified as the Crown.[16] Both these aspects are important, for it remains true, as Montrose asserted, that prerogative, in the sense of essential governmental power, is often fundamental to the existence of the subjects' liberty. It exists, if properly regarded, as much for the subjects as for rulers. It should, therefore, be looked at from a functional point of view, which has too often been neglected in modern cases.

Mention has already been made of differences between the law of Scotland and the law of England on this subject. At one time they were much greater than they are now. The mere existence of the Union would in any event produce pressure towards a standardisation of the law. That pressure was greatly increased by the Exchequer Court (Scotland) Act 1707, which, in effect, directed the re-formed court to apply the same law as would be applied in Exchequer cases in England.[17]

---

[13] Compare, for example, Auby and Drago, *Traité de Contentieux Administratif*, Vol. I, wherein are treated similar rules and institutions, but from a quite general standpoint. Similar instances could be cited from the U.S.A.; see the discussion in *Baker* v. *Carr*, 369 U.S. 186 (1962).

[14] Consider the evolution from *Farrier* v. *Elder and Scott*, June 21, 1799, F.C., to the acceptance of *Bainbridge* v. *P.M.G.* [1906] 1 K.B. 178. This confusion of thought may even be dangerous at a time when there is nothing to fear from the Crown in the sense of the Sovereign.

[15] See, *e.g.*, *King's Printers* v. *Buchan* (1826) 4 S. 559 and " The Royal Prerogative in Modern Scots Law " [1957] *Public Law* 304. The wording of the Crown Suits (Scotland) Act 1857 was perhaps more in accord with tradition than was its interpretation in *MacGregor* v. *L.A.*, 1921 S.C. 847.

[16] Compare the underlying thought in *Phin* v. *Mags. of Auchtermuchty* (1827) 5 S. 690 and *Western Heritable Investment Co.* v. *Glasgow Corp.*, 1956 S.C.(H.L.) 64.

[17] See Clerk and Scrope, *The Court of Exchequer*.

This had the effect of bringing into operation in Scotland all the prerogative rules which affected the Crown in relation to the revenue.[18] The peculiarity of Exchequer causes tended not to be sufficiently observed, and the influence of the Act spread beyond those confines, in part as a result of a desire for uniformity.[19] Against this process protests were raised,[20] and as has been shown the House of Lords has held that prerogative rules may differ in the two jurisdictions.[21] Hence the tendency in this context, which existed at the beginning of this century, to follow (almost automatically) English authority in Scotland may no longer hold, where, as with the applicability of statutes to the Crown, reason and convenience do not add their weight to the law.

[18] *Advocate General* v. *Garioch* (1850) 12 D. 447.
[19] *Moffat Hydropathic Co. Ltd.* v. *L.A.*, 1918, 2 S.L.T. 220.
[20] *Admiralty Commissioners* v. *Blair's Trs.*, 1916 S.C. 247 at 260 and 266; *Somerville* v. *L.A.* (1893) 20 R. 1050 at 1075.
[21] *Glasgow Corporation* v. *Central Land Board*, 1956 S.C.(H.L.) 1. This evolution is discussed in [1957] *Public Law* 303 *et seq.*

CHAPTER 10

THE EXECUTIVE—II

GOVERNMENT AND CABINET

General. Government is conducted in the name of the Crown, and there has already been discussed both the titular head of state, and some of the legal rules which concern the operations of the central government. There must now be discussed the effective machinery of government. At the outset two terms must be distinguished, government and Cabinet. At one stage these terms could be treated as virtually synonymous. With the growth of governmental activity and the consequential growth in the number of ministers a distinction has to be made. By the term " government " is meant the whole body of ministers, including junior ministers, by the term " Cabinet " is meant the central group of ministers who are constantly concerned with the general policy of the government; in effect the Cabinet lies at the centre of the government. Terminology is not always exact; often the phrase " The government has decided " should more accurately be " The Cabinet has decided," and, as will appear, it is often neither possible nor desirable to distinguish the two. Nevertheless, the existence of both the macrocosm and the microcosm must be remembered if a true picture of the operation of the governmental machine is to be gained.

It is impossible within the compass of this work to give a full account of the evolution of the modern machine or of its operation. For that the reader must turn to the specialised texts.[1] All that can be emphasised here are the general basic principles which must, in short compass, be set out somewhat dogmatically. The system as it has evolved is a highly centralised one. Just as the Cabinet has to some extent separated itself from the government (and dominates it), so within the Cabinet there is a dominance of the Prime Minister, who has ceased to be merely *primus inter pares.* It is with reason that one speaks of " Mr. X's Government." [2] Moreover, the system is one in which power flows from the top or centre, it is not delegated from the larger to the smaller bodies.[3]

---

[1] Notably Jennings, *Cabinet Government and Parliament,* and Mackintosh, *The British Cabinet* (which is much broader in scope than its title suggests). Morrison, *Government and Parliament,* gives an admirable picture of the working of the institutions. For the earlier history see particularly Aspinall, *Cabinet Council.* The contrast between the text of Bagehot's *English Constitution* exposing a classical view and the views in Crossman's critical introduction to the Fontana edition of that book will show the changes over a hundred years.

[2] See particularly Mackintosh, *op. cit.,* and his short Appendix on this topic.

[3] Sir Ernest Barker's pyramid of delegation, from the nation through Parliament to the Cabinet (*Reflections on Government,* Chap. II), to a large extent inverts the

Our system is properly called one of Cabinet government rather than parliamentary government. To emphasise this is not to underrate the importance of other bodies, but if it is remembered from the outset that Parliament is not so much the source of power, but the forum wherein power is exercised many misconceptions about the relationship of government to Parliament may be avoided.

This centralised quality of the government is obviously closely related to another quality, which is its cohesiveness. The mere existence of a pyramid of power dependent on the Prime Minister would not necessarily imply the degree of cohesiveness which marks our system. This second quality owes a great deal also to the party system, which is not so much a consequence as a cause of the present constitutional system, being fundamental to it. Dependence, in normal times, upon one party, of which the Prime Minister is leader, gives that cohesion. It must be noticed that primarily this is a dependence upon a parliamentary party rather than upon a party at large.[4] This enhances the cohesiveness. Not only have ministers common beliefs (so far as there is unity in any party), but they have a common background, which is parliamentary. Moreover, their allegiance is in the first instance to a relatively defined body, the parliamentary party, and to that extent there is some immunity from the influence of pressure groups of varying kinds,[5] influences which could tend to be schismatic in effect. These characteristics are bound up with a further principle of our government. The system is designed to produce a strong government bounded by certain checks, legal, conventional or institutional, rather than a completely representative government. In a changed form, with a substitution of Cabinet for King there has been a return (after no great interruption) to the old principle that the King makes the laws in Parliament.

Two further points should be mentioned at the outset. There is both an independence of the Sovereign, and a dependence on, or answerability[6] to, Parliament, though words like " dependence " and " independence " must always be taken in a relative sense. Reliance upon parliamentary majorities in the years following 1832 enabled ministries to establish that independence, which was, however, established without giving to Parliament a mastery. In the process of the transfer of power much remained in the hands of Prime Minister and Cabinet, and did not pass from Sovereign to Parliament.

true position, as did Bagehot in regarding the Cabinet as a Committee of the Commons (*English Constitution*, Chap. I); *cf.* Amery, *Thoughts on the Constitution*, and Crossman's introduction to the Fontana edition of Bagehot.
[4] See Mr. Attlee's declaration in 1945, quoted in Morrison, *op. cit.*, 3rd ed., p. 155. Thus there is no room for the caucus system. The same principles operate in Opposition. Even if there is election to a Shadow Cabinet, the distribution of functions is left to the Leader, and membership of the Shadow Cabinet does not guarantee membership of the Cabinet.
[5] Such influences do exist; see Potter, *Organised Groups in British National Politics*.
[6] The apparent inconsistency of this word with what has gone before will be resolved when the relationship of government to Parliament is discussed.

All these factors must be borne in mind. The roots of the Cabinet system go deep.[7] Impeachment can be seen as the start of responsibility to Parliament. The doctrine of the Seals necessarily produced a small body of men who between them controlled the sources of power. In any institution there tends to be an inner ring which controls. Cabinets in one form or another are universal, but certain historical and political factors have moulded our Cabinet into a particular shape and given it a distinctiveness. Thus, although the Lords of the Articles had many qualities of a Cabinet, and could properly be so called, the absence of other qualities make them entirely distinct. The modern British Cabinet can only be understood as an institution if it is seen as the seat of controlled power, and it is the forms of the controls (which are themselves the product of local politics and history) which mark it out as distinct among the many " Cabinets " which exist.[8]

From these general principles flow many of the detailed rules which are accepted in the interest of the system as a whole. The doctrine of collective responsibility is fundamental to cohesion; Cabinet secrecy follows as a matter of common necessity.[9] The legal rules by which it is backed are not the true compulsion.

The Cabinet. It will be seen that the Cabinet is one of the parts of the governmental machinery least governed by law. Nearly all the important rules regulating its formation and relations with the Crown, Parliament and the Prime Minister are conventional.[10] This situation exists because the evolution of the Cabinet is continuing, and its method of operation is, to some extent, dependent upon the character of each Prime Minister. Flexibility is preserved by retaining the conventional basis. That flexibility is restricted not merely by the forces which, in general, ensure observance of conventions, but also by a generally felt belief that an " ideal " Cabinet system had evolved by the early years of this century. Respect for this " ideal " has the effect of slowing down reaction to the pressure of current conditions. It must, however, be emphasised that because of the secrecy which surrounds Cabinet operations anything which is written may have already been overtaken by practice.[11]

While logically a start should be made with the Prime Minister, it is convenient to start with the Cabinet itself. The Cabinet is, then, a

---

[7] What could be taken to be the rudiments of a Cabinet system can be found in George Buchanan's *De Jure Regni.*

[8] Compare, *e.g.,* Sawer, " Councils, Ministers and Cabinets in Australia " [1956] *Public Law* 110, to see the effect of slightly differing conditions.

[9] The common sense, rather than the mysticism, of our government can best be understood by reading Massigli, *Sur Quelques Maladies de l'Etat,* one of the best introductions to our system, though not written about it.

[10] The split between government and Cabinet is recognised by the Ministers of the Crown Act 1937, s. 3.

[11] Mackintosh in his work has by various methods attempted to ensure that his account is as modern as possible, but his reliance on interview emphasises this point.

group of senior ministers, many of whom can by virtue of their office claim a seat in the Cabinet; the Chancellor of the Exchequer, the Foreign and Home Secretaries, and the Secretary of State for Scotland, are obvious examples. The inclusion or exclusion of any particular minister is (as is the allocation of ministries) a matter for the Prime Minister's discretion, limited albeit by political considerations, and will depend upon the current importance of particular branches of government business. There is always included a number of ministers whose departmental functions are not onerous, such as the Paymaster-General, but to whom particular tasks, which may be heavy, can be entrusted. Membership is very flexible. Mr. Casey was, for example, a member of the War Cabinet in the Second World War, as was General Smuts in the First. The number in the Cabinet has in recent times tended to be about twenty, sometimes rising to twenty-five. Although in both world wars small War Cabinets have been formed, it was found that in practice such bodies rarely met without additional members. This size has an effect upon theory and operation. It results in the paradox that the bulk of the Cabinet, a body which determines general policy, consists of those ministers whose departmental duties are heaviest. It means also that, even at its relatively large modern size, a substantial number of ministers in charge of major departments is excluded from the Cabinet. There are then the problems of co-ordination and the proper formulation of policy, even though non-Cabinet Ministers may be summoned to particular meetings.

Arguments have been advanced for small policy-making Cabinets [12] but experience has shown that such bodies cannot in fact work within the limits of size envisaged. Moreover, experience has shown that "operational" responsibilities are important. The "high brooding" minister can get out of touch with the realities of political life. Moreover, under our system, policy and administration cannot be separated. Small matters may suddenly become matters of great political importance in the Commons. Experiments by Mr. Churchill with Co-ordinating Ministers—the Overlords—failed. Not merely were lines of responsibility blurred, but the system coupled with our forms of parliamentary attack made it too easy for the Opposition to divide and conquer.[13] Instead relief has been found by other means. Assistants have been found for some ministers by the appointment of Ministers of State (first used in connection with the Scottish Office), or by the invention of offices such as that of Chief Secretary to the Treasury.

---

[12] Notably by Amery, *Thoughts on the Constitution*.

[13] See Morrison, *op. cit.* p. 45. The survivor, the Minister of Defence, is a special case, and under the arrangements forecast in 672 H.C.Deb. 40 *et seq.* his position *vis-à-vis* the Service Ministers will come close to that of the Secretary of State for Scotland *vis-à-vis* his Under-Secretaries of State; see Central Organisation for Defence (1963) Cmnd. 2097. These proposals have been carried out in the Defence (Transfer of Functions) Act 1964.

Such appointments are possible where a block of business or activity is reasonably severable (as, for example, in the 1968 arrangements in the Foreign Office), and the difficulties of the Overlord system are thus avoided.

Cabinet committees. Above all, the related problems of co-ordination and the pressures of business have been met by the evolution of Cabinet committees. The existence of some, though not all, of such committees is known, as may also, from time to time, be the name of the chairman. Some of the committees appear to exist regularly despite changes of government, such as the Defence Committee, the Legislation Committee and the Future Legislation Committee, others are dependent upon the philosophy of a particular government or the run of events,[14] such as the committee in 1962 concerned with the negotiations over the then proposed entry of the United Kingdom into EEC. Such committees enable non-Cabinet Ministers (who are members) to work on the formulation of general policy, and also enable much business to reach the Cabinet in a pre-digested form. They are consistent with general constitutional theory, for they do not affect responsibility to Parliament. To the extent that the chairman of such committees performs the co-ordinating functions of an " Overlord " the difficulties inherent in that system (when such functions are overt) are avoided, since his functions are carried out behind the curtain.

The existence of such committees may have consequences upon the place of the Cabinet and Prime Minister. In the pressure of business it is likely that a report from such committees will be accepted in the Cabinet, thus placing the real decision elsewhere. It has generally been denied that a real Inner Cabinet exists, except in the sense that there will inevitably be a certain group of ministers to whom a Prime Minister will talk more readily than to others, or in the sense of a committee of the Cabinet.[14] It is possible that the group of chairmen could become such an Inner Cabinet. Since the Prime Minister is master of which committee shall be appointed, of their membership and of the chairmanship, it is also possible that, granted the other conditions in which a Cabinet works, the influence of a Prime Minister could be enhanced.

All accounts make it clear that the method of operation of a Cabinet, its discursiveness or brevity, is to a large extent a reflection of the personality of the Prime Minister. Equally the Prime Minister is the master of summoning Cabinets and of the business to be discussed.[15] He controls the agenda[16] and the debate. It is clear that a vote or

---

14 Mackintosh, *op. cit.* p. 437 *et seq.* In 1960, for example, the Lord Chancellor was a member of 23 Cabinet committees: Coldstream, " The Lord Chancellor's Office " (1962) *Graya* 13.

15 Jennings, *Cabinet Government*, Chap. IX; Mackintosh, p. 429 *et seq.*

16 Subject to this, or to the Cabinet requiring a report upon a particular subject, it is for the minister concerned to determine whether or not to submit any question for Cabinet decision, a determination which may often require a nice balance of independence and subservience.

anything approaching it is a rarity in the Cabinet; the Cabinet should be a united body and anything which would tend to disrupt that unity, such as vote-taking, is to be avoided if at all possible. Hence decisions will normally be taken by the Prime Minister gathering the sense of the meeting.

Cabinet machinery. The Cabinet has evolved from highly informal meetings. The informality of its origin continues to mark its methods, and until modern times decisions were taken and recorded in a thoroughly unbusinesslike way. There were frequent incidents demonstrating the confusion and uncertainty which might exist in consequence. Reform, which was strongly opposed in some quarters,[17] came about through Mr. Lloyd George's reorganisation of the War Cabinet in 1916 which resulted in Lt.-Col. Hankey, the Secretary to the Committee of Imperial Defence, becoming also Secretary to the Cabinet.[18] After the war the two offices continued to be combined until 1938. In 1956 the office of Secretary to the Cabinet was joined to that of one of the Joint Secretaries to the Treasury, and in 1962 a separate appointment to the post of Secretary to the Cabinet was made. The Secretariat is intended to be no more than that, it is concerned with the preparation of Cabinet papers, the circulation of minutes and decisions. It is not an advisory body.[19] It seems that the minutes contain no more than is necessary to record the heads of argument and conclusions. Individual views are not recorded as such, so that ministers retain a freedom of action, and so that unity can be preserved by denying them an opportunity to " Hansardise " each other.

It must be emphasised that the office remains small in size and limited in scope. Between 1939 and 1945 its functions expanded with an Economic Section and a Central Statistical Office as well as the Prime Minister's Statistical Section.[20] After the war the Economic Section had a varied career, finally ending in the Treasury, and the Prime Minister's Statistical Office disappeared. Some of these changes were due to particular circumstances, and thus were not of general importance, but the scope of the functions of the Cabinet Secretariat is of constitutional importance. The limitation of that scope affords an institutional check upon the growth of the power of the Prime Minister. The availability of

---

[17] In fact, Cabinet minutes were not a novelty; see Aspinall, *Cabinet Councils*, though the word had varying uses; see Mackintosh, *op. cit.*

[18] See Hankey, *Diplomacy by Conference.*

[19] For an account of how the office works see Hewison, " The Organisation of the Cabinet Secretariat " (1952) 30 *Public Administration* 221. The Cabinet minutes of one government are not, as such, available to its successor. Copies are currently transmitted to the Sovereign. There has recently been, however, a tendency to increase the number of advisers within the Cabinet office generally.

[20] *The Organisation of British Central Government 1914–1956* (ed. Chester), Chap. IX.

independent sources of information, in contrast to reliance upon
ministers, could greatly enhance that power.[21]

By these methods the capacity of the Cabinet to deal with the
increased business and its general efficiency have been improved.
Difficulties remain. It is clear on the one hand that decisions which
would formerly have been taken by Cabinets are now taken by civil
servants, and on the other that matters which in themselves are not of
fundamental importance and do not raise great principles are referred to
the Cabinet because they may have political repercussions. While there
is probably room for a better organisation of business it must be
remembered that the Cabinet is a political body, it is not merely an
administrative mechanism, and this fact governs alike its composition
and work.

The Prime Minister. At the heart of the Cabinet is the Prime
Minister. Again the office is recognised by law,[22] but all the important
rules which regulate it are conventional. As has already been seen there
may, exceptionally, be an element of personal discretion in the selection
by the Sovereign of a Prime Minister. The person chosen must be one
who is capable of forming a government acceptable to the House of
Commons, and hence acceptable to the dominant party or combination
of parties in that House. Although in 1940 there was some talk of Lord
Halifax becoming Prime Minister,[23] and even though an element of
ambiguity about the generality of the precedent of 1923 when Mr.
Baldwin was chosen in place of Lord Curzon,[24] it must now be taken as
settled that the Prime Minister must have a seat in the House of
Commons. The renunciation of his peerage by Sir Alec Douglas-Home
was a constitutional as much as a political necessity. There has also
grown up a direct relationship with the electorate. Where the result
of a General Election is clear, a Prime Minister is no longer expected
to meet the new Parliament before resigning. On the other hand there
is no rule which requires that a Prime Minister who assumes office
during the life of a Parliament should seek a mandate from the electorate
as soon as is practicable.

Once installed a Prime Minister has the right to choose his colleagues
(and a use of the House of Lords may enable him to bring in ministers
from outside Parliament either directly or by promoting to the House
a member who holds a safe seat, which can be taken by the desired
minister). During the life of a ministry he has the right to promote

---

21 Compare the growth of the White House Office: Hobbs, *Behind the President*. In
wartime the staffs of Prime Ministers have increased, and this has contributed to the
increased pre-eminence of the latter.

22 Notably by the Ministers of the Crown Act 1937, which, as amended, provides for a
salary, and in effect annexes the office to that of First Lord of the Treasury.

23 Wheeler-Bennett, *George VI*, p. 441 *et seq.*

24 The considerations given in Nicholson, *George V* at pp. 376–377, have an element of
particularity.

or dismiss ministers and to determine the scope of ministries. Such rights can of course only be exercised within the limits imposed by political considerations. On the surface dismissals appear to be rare, they are couched in the terms of resignations.[25] Moreover, the Prime Minister's powers are not only in respect of individuals. He can, as in 1947 and in 1962, carry through a major reconstruction of the government. Even greater power is given to him by his control of the time of a dissolution, or of the resignation of a government. There is some consultation with colleagues in the former case, but the matter is not one for Cabinet decision.[26] As to the latter, it seems to follow from the former.[27] It is this power of choosing the time for a dissolution which perhaps more than anything else has given the government control in Parliament and the Prime Minister control in government. Apart from such extreme instances it is recognised that, in the conduct of a government, a Prime Minister has a right of independent action.[28] He may either openly or less obviously take control of particular branches of government. Mr. Ramsay MacDonald was his own Foreign Secretary. Other Prime Ministers have (sometimes harmoniously) assumed a joint direction of foreign affairs with the Foreign Secretary, and indeed the place of the Prime Minister in that field has been advanced, among other justifications for having a Foreign Secretary in the House of Lords in modern times. More recently the Prime Minister assumed a direct relationship with the Department of Economic Affairs.

To these powers must be added the Prime Minister's control of Cabinet business, already referred to. It is then clear that a modern Prime Minister has come to occupy much of the position of a governing President.[29] Perhaps the greatest checks which remain to the growth of his powers are institutional, chief among them being the nature of the Cabinet office and the place of the Treasury in the governmental machine. This pre-eminence is not perhaps affected by the nomination of a Deputy Prime Minister. That office is a long time being born. Attempts have been made to nominate persons to it, and despite refusals

[25] For such a dismissal see Blake, *The Unknown Prime Minister*, p. 383. The Cabinet reconstruction of 1962 affords examples of the varied shades of meaning in the customary letters.

[26] Mackintosh, *op. cit.* pp. 386–387; Laski, *Reflections on the Constitution*, pp. 102–103.

[27] In 1931 the Cabinet had, it seems, authorised a resignation, but Mr. Ramsay Mac-Donald's agreement to the formation of a new government under him was given without consultation: see Morrison, *op. cit.* p. 77 *et seq.*; Bassett, *1931 Political Crisis*; Jennings, *Cabinet Government*, pp. 48–49.

[28] Mr. Churchill's (and after him Mr. Attlee's) agreements in relation to atom bombs are outstanding examples, as is Sir Anthony Eden's initiative over Suez, but many others are given in Jennings. A more restrained view of the powers of the Prime Minister is given in Jones, " The Prime Minister's Powers," 18 *Parliamentary Affairs* 167. For an account of differing styles, see Mallaby, *From My Level*.

[29] See, generally, Carter, *The Office of Prime Minister*.

to recognise the office,[30] the attempts continue.[31] Whatever the outcome, such an office is not likely to govern succession to the premiership.

Cabinet and government. Beyond the inner ring of the Cabinet lies the larger group of non-Cabinet Ministers. Something must be said later of the role of particular ministers and of the operation of ministries, but at this stage the rules which govern the relationship of the Cabinet to the larger whole and those which govern both may be conveniently discussed. As has been said, it is for a minister to select in the first instance matters affecting his department which should be decided by the Cabinet. It is for the Prime Minister and Cabinet to control the general conduct of affairs. From this flows the general doctrine of collective responsibility—a doctrine which, it must be emphasised, applies to the government as a whole and not only to the members of the Cabinet. Special circumstances, such as the existence of a War Cabinet, have been thought to modify the vigour of the doctrine, but in normal times it binds all, including junior ministers.[32] It means that, in one direction, any minister, in the broad sense, must accept government decisions and policy or resign office. In the other direction the " collective " quality is in effect optional. A government does not have to support a minister who has made a mistake or whose acts prove to be unpopular. It may disown him.[33] In the first sense the tendency has been for the doctrine to become more vigorous,[34] and to extend not only as to the persons which it covers, but also as to the questions and actions which will be affected by it. Junior ministers have been dismissed for speeches both inside and outside Parliament. Inside Parliament this growth is significant in relation to the control by the government over Parliament.

The doctrine is not, however, exclusive. A blending of collective and individual responsibility marks many of the practices of the central government. Even though a policy may have been determined by the Cabinet, a minister remains individually responsible for the manner in which it is carried out and for the working of his own department. He cannot rely exclusively on the more general responsibility. The limits of this personal responsibility (which requires a minister to accept responsibility for the faults of his subordinates, and which in extreme cases, requires his resignation) are not precise. For any major fault, whether of commission or omission, these consequences should follow,

---

30 Wheeler-Bennett, *King George VI*, p. 797; and see 680 H.C.Deb. 582–583.
31 Mr. R. A. Butler was, in July 1962, named as Deputy Prime Minister and designated First Secretary of State, a novel designation for which a variety of reasons might exist. The two titles do not now necessarily coincide in the same person.
32 Morrison, *op. cit.* p. 60.
33 The case of Sir Samuel Hoare in 1935 is perhaps extreme. It is possible that Sir Samuel Hoare was in fact carrying out Cabinet policy.
34 Jennings, *Parliament*, Chap. V. Its vigour must be looked at in a general political context. From time to time dissent is known to exist, but for political convenience the dissentient is retained meanwhile. Such a situation cannot long endure without gravely weakening a government.

for lesser faults confession and repentance may suffice.[35] This individual responsibility, while it is maintained in theory, has recently been weakened in fact. Relatively frequent movements among ministerial posts, or the transfer of functions between departments, may mean that the minister in charge, and thus responsible, at the time of the discovery of the fault is not the same as the one who was in charge at the time of its commission, which has an effect of lessening the responsibility of each. There may too be an increased tendency to " close the ranks," and for the government to accept general responsibility, which may to some extent relieve an individual minister.[36] In the sense that a minister must answer to Parliament for the actions of his department, there remains a reality in the doctrine. In the sense that resignation may now normally be expected to follow upon departmental errors, there is little reality left in the doctrine and thus it is no longer a doctrine backed by real sanctions. Concentration upon the rare occasions upon which the major consequences of responsibility have been exacted should not, however, obscure the importance of its continuous reflection in smaller matters through parliamentary questions. Nor should it be forgotten that constitutional doctrines have a negative effect. The existence of this doctrine, and the continued belief in it (even though it had ceased to be fully effective in the way that was believed to be true), had, as will be seen, inhibiting effects on the evolution of the law and of constitutional machinery.

The nature of the rules. In particular instances an admixture of functions makes the application of these rules difficult. This is so in relation to the Law Officers and to the exercise of the prerogative of mercy. The Law Officers, apart from their political functions, have also functions related to the administration of justice, especially in Scotland, which must be separated, as far as is possible, from political considerations. Because of this situation the general rules of responsibility are, in these cases, eased, and also a separation from the government in those respects is recognised.[37] Equally in relation to the exercise of the prerogative of mercy answerability to Parliament has, in effect, been limited, in modern times.[38]

---

[35] Again a civil servant cannot rely on avoiding all consequences of his acts by reason of the minister taking all blame. For the rules here, see particularly 530 H.C.Deb. 1286.

[36] See 642 H.C.Deb. 211–217 and [1961] *Public Law* 228–229. See especially Finer, " The Individual Responsibility of Ministers " (1956) 34 *Public Administration* 377, and Alderman and Cross, *The Tactics of Resignation*. A good account of the problem as seen from the inside is to be found in Mayhew, *Britain's Role Tomorrow*, Chap. 12.

[37] See Marshall and Moodie, *Some Problems of the Constitution*, 4th ed., p. 144 *et seq.* Such modifications are no doubt necessary, even though, as Sir Ilay Campbell emphasised, constitutional checks upon the Law Officers are desirable; and compare *Hester* v. *Macdonald*, 1961 S.L.T. 414 on the attitude of the courts.

[38] See [1961] *Public Law* 8 *et seq.*

These doctrines are, as has been said, conventional. This conventional nature involves their fluidity. They can be tailored to particular circumstances, such as the position of particular ministers, or the emergence of a temporary institution such as a War Cabinet or to other special circumstances. The existence of a minority or coalition government may require an adaptation of the normal rules.[39] Such fluidity is necessary in practice, but rules which have that fluidity have also their dangers. The protections against abuse are to be found almost entirely in parliamentary traditions.

The rules and the general law. Despite this conventional nature, the rules are capable of having their reflection in law in matters of practice.[40] They do, in matters of principle, have even wider effects. One of the factors which has limited judicial control of administrative actions has been the existence of parliamentary responsibility.[41] Within limits that reticence is justified. It is a mark of the diarchy to which reference has already been made. It is also true that there are " political " issues which are, as Lord Normand emphasised, more appropriate to Parliament than to courts. Indeed, it is by no means certain that the line between the two jurisdictions has always been drawn at an appropriate place. Judgment upon that issue, which is important in any assessment of the efficiency of the whole machinery of the constitution, must be a matter of individual determination after a study of the effectiveness of parliamentary control.

The relationship of government to Parliament. That issue raises the whole problem of the relationship of government to Parliament. There is a dominance of government over Parliament which, as has been suggested, is consistent with our constitutional theory. It is consistent with the facts of political life. Often only a government has the knowledge essential for decision. This dominance manifests itself in many ways. It is possible for the government to monopolise the legislative time available. Government business has priority. In many matters Parliament can only criticise after the event, when it may be too late. This dominance is aided by many things. Above all there is the party system and the fact that the government party has its majority in the House of Commons and the means of maintaining that majority. For that task (among others) the Whips, the Junior Lords of the Treasury, exist,

---

39 See Mr. Ramsay MacDonald's declaration in 1924 (Jennings, *Cabinet Government,* p. 494), or the agreement to differ: Jennings, *op. cit.* p. 280.

40 *Adair* v. *Hill,* 1943 J.C. 9 at 15, where the Lord Justice-Clerk (Cooper), an ex-Law Officer, recognises the existence of the responsibility of the Lord Advocate to Parliament for his actions. See, too, *Dalziel School Board* v. *Scotch Education Department,* 1915 S.C. 234; *Griffin* v. *L.A.,* 1950 S.C. 448; and *Ryder* v. *Foley* (1906) 4 C.L.R. 422.

41 *Pollok School Co. Ltd.* v. *Glasgow T.C.,* 1946 S.C. 373 at 386, *per* Lord President Normand; *Liversidge* v. *Anderson* [1942] A.C. 206 at 222; or *Carltona Ltd.* v. *Commissioner of Works* [1943] 2 All E.R. 560 suffice as examples.

and have at their disposal a number of weapons. A potent one is the threat of a dissolution which, apart from the uncertainty with which it faces a member, also makes him consider whether, although he may disapprove of a government decision, he does not on the whole prefer a government of that party to the alternative. Lesser weapons, such as the withdrawal of the Whip (in the sense of exclusion from the party), are reinforced by the fact that disapproval by a party may have the consequence of excluding a member from committees or delegations on which he is anxious to serve,[42] as well as prejudicing his political future.

It should not, however, be taken that the dominance is complete. The Leader of the House, who regulates its business on behalf of the government, owes allegiance to the House as well as to the government. The Whips are as much channels of communication between back-benchers and government as they are controllers.[43] Indeed, the influence of Parliament upon both government policy and legislative proposals can be underrated. Sometimes this influence is observable in changes in a measure on its way through Parliament [44]; at other times the influence delays or prevents the introduction of measures.[45] In this last case the influence may not be seen until long after the event. In other cases such as debates upon White Papers (which have to a great extent taken the place of bringing in a Bill upon Resolutions) a careful comparison of the debate and the measure as subsequently brought in can reveal the operation of the influence.

Further, the methods by which opposition makes itself felt must be observed. There is the " official " Opposition, whose Leader is recognised and paid out of public funds.[46] That Opposition has its conventional rights, the right, for example, to choose the subject-matter of Supply debates, or the right to move a motion of no confidence on occasions of its choosing. Hence, on major issues the theoretical govern-ment monopoly of parliamentary time is limited by conventional rules, as is its control of subject-matter of debate. That Opposition is limited also by similar conventional rules, by responsibility in the ordinary sense of the word.[47] The effort and tactics of the official Opposition are largely dominated by the desire of that party to demonstrate, as the alternative government, its fitness to be the government. Thus much of its activities are directed to the electorate rather than to the

[42] See, e.g., 660 H.C.Deb. 221–222. Exclusion at the time of an election is all the more serious since the virtual disappearance of the independent member. The candidate needs the party machine.

[43] This interplay of dominance and subservience is illustrated in many of the books cited. Its substance is perhaps best conveyed in Morrison, Government and Parliament, or Butt, The Power of Parliament.

[44] See generally Mackintosh, op. cit. Chap. XV; Jennings, Parliament, Chaps. V and VI.

[45] See, e.g., Tom Jones, Diary with Letters, p. 161 (the Hoare-Laval Pact) and p. 368 on the prelude to the Public Order Act 1936.

[46] Ministerial Salaries Consolidation Act 1965, which also provides salaries for the Chief Opposition Whips.

[47] Amery, Thoughts on the Constitution.

government. When formal battle is joined in the House and the Whips are on, it has little, if any, chance of defeating a government. "It is the government's job to say what the policy should be and it is for the government's supporters to support the government, the choice having been made "[48] was a recent ministerial assessment of the position which could be regarded as typical. This being so, great importance must be attached to the opposition within the government ranks, which operates to a great extent through the meetings of backbenchers, the "1922 Committee" on one side, and of the Parliamentary Labour Party on the other. As has been seen, these party meetings have already been constitutionally recognised in the rules of privilege, and it is in them that the most effective opposition may be felt. There a government can change its plans the more easily since it does so without public loss of face.

It is these conditions which give substance to the assertion that Parliament is the forum wherein power is exercised. The importance of the fact that power is there exercised should not be underrated because of all the other elements which combine to produce a complex and subtle result, and which obscure the clear perception of each separate element. Influences which are not glaringly obvious may nevertheless be real and significant.

It is, indeed, possible to assert that there is no modern instance of a defeat in the House causing the fall of a government. In 1940 Mr. Chamberlain, in fact, secured a majority in the Narvik debate. The Labour Government of 1931 fell in the Cabinet, not the House. In 1924, when the Labour Government was defeated over the Campbell case and resigned, it had already become clear that the government lacked the necessary solidarity of support. The effective causes of the fall of governments in 1916 and 1922 are to be found outside the House of Commons. Nevertheless, the House of Commons is significant in the death as in the life of governments. Even without an actual defeat it is pressures and reactions in the House which demonstrate that a government has lost cohesion and confidence and the ability to govern. It is in the House that divisions inside a government, which cause its fall, become apparent. Ministers bred in parliamentary traditions accept the consequences without forcing an issue. If they did not, the power to defeat a government remains and would no doubt, in the last resort, be exercised.

All this may be called the positive side of ministerial responsibility, that is to say, the way in which the doctrines operate to achieve their intended purposes. There is another side to their constitutional effects which may be loosely called negative. The existence of these doctrines,

---

[48] Mr. Callaghan: 742 H.C.Deb. 1242. Point is added to the citation when it is realised that it comes from the debate on so politically inert a matter as the base figure for a decimal currency.

coupled with their historical background has effects upon constitutional growth, since a pattern of thought about the control of governmental activity, outside the field of specifically local government, has been set. The pre-eminence which Parliament has attained in the legislative field finds some counterpart in this other side of its activities, and in a growing belief in the necessary universality of parliamentary control, in the sense that that control tends to be regarded as the only appropriate method where traditional judicial controls are not available. The latter have tended to contract in favour of Parliament. Thus, as will be seen, the tendency has, for several reasons, been to bring the control of nationalised industries more and more in line with traditional methods even though, as originally conceived, they were intended to break with that pattern. Again it is difficult for newly established bodies to take root, if they do not fit that pattern. The relative ineffectiveness of the forerunners of the National Prices and Incomes Board, such as the Council on Prices, Productivity and Income, is in part attributable to this, just as some of the proposals of the Franks Committee on Tribunals and Inquiries foundered upon the rock of ministerial responsibility. The problem is an enduring one. The Prices and Incomes Board has pointed to the unresolved problems of its relationship to the Government,[49] and those problems when analysed come back to the doctrine of ministerial responsibility, and to the fears of breaking with the present pattern. Similarly, in despair, the Select Committee on Nationalised Industries in effect recommends the dismantling of alternative controls over air-lines and a return to straightforward ministerial control.[50] Perhaps rightly, since compromise solutions have demonstrated their inadequacy. Yet to give way to this despair is of necessity to bring back into a political arena problems which are not essentially political in the sense of the political nature of the House of Commons.

There are more serious consequences which flow from an over-reliance on the doctrine of ministerial responsibility as the primary means of control. It must be remembered that even in the traditional fields for which the doctrine arose the range of matters over which supervision should be exercised has increased vastly. An overloaded machine is inefficient. Theoretical virtues, and past virtues in a simpler society, should not be allowed to obscure the real problems of working the system in a changed society, nor to prevent the evolution of new techniques to deal with new and expanding fields of government activity. Not merely because of congestion of business should a deconcentration of the mechanisms of control be contemplated. In itself, because of the arena within which it operates the doctrine has been responsible for much of the secretiveness of government.[51] Other institutions can force

---

[49] Second General Report, Chap. 6.
[50] Second Report, on B.E.A. (1966–67) H.C. 673.
[51] See, e.g., Mr. Crosland, 751 H.C.Deb. 751: " It is not the custom under any Government for the Government to quote the advice they have received from the

greater openness, which is a desirable part of democratic government. Further, the doctrine has the effect of increasing pressures to centralisation. The machine that is to be controlled must be adapted to the mechanism of control. If the latter is a centralised one the machine must have the same characteristic. The Cabinet system, as has been seen, necessarily produces a high degree of centralisation in the areas of activity for which it operates. Matters which come under parliamentary review must, under our system, also come under the Cabinet machinery and there thus results a steady concentration of the decision-making process over an increased range of subject-matter in one relatively small body, originally conceived as operating for a much narrower range of decisions.[52] Without this deconcentration of controlling mechanisms any attempts at devolution are unlikely to have any real success, while the dangers of over-centralisation are admitted and real. Even within Parliament the limiting effects of the doctrine are likely to be felt. As has already been seen, the new Select Committees, while they may increase the amount of information available, especially that on Science and Technology, are unlikely to achieve the hopes of some of their sponsors, precisely because of the limitations imposed by the doctrine of ministerial responsibility. Any evaluation of this doctrine must therefore take into account these negative aspects as well as the positive ones, which in themselves may be less effective than is generally believed.

U.G.C." See also The Answer to the Estimates Committee (1966–67) H.C. 246 and 1380, cited in Shonfield, " The Pragmatic Illusion," *Encounter*, June 1967.

[52] One consequence of this concentration may paradoxically be a weakening in fact of control. See the earlier discussion of ministerial responsibility in recent years, and see Davis, " English Administrative Law " [1962] *Public Law* 139. Consider also the general criticisms in Shonfield, *Modern Capitalism*, which demonstrates that we do not have all the virtues in government, and perhaps do not have many which we believe we have.

CHAPTER 11

THE EXECUTIVE—III

THE STRUCTURE OF THE CENTRAL GOVERNMENT

THERE is little need to describe in detail the structure and functions of
each ministry. One or two only need be discussed as having particular
constitutional importance.

The general framework. In general the structure of a department
conforms to the pattern of a minister supported by one or more political [1]
colleagues, an Under-Secretary of State in the case of a Secretary of
State, or a Parliamentary Secretary in the case of other ministers. Under
them are the permanent staff of the department spreading down from
a Permanent Under-Secretary of State or Permanent Secretary, as the
case may be.[2] Except where distinct attributions of functions are made
(as with the Under-Secretaries of State of the Scottish Office), the powers
of Parliamentary Secretaries may be very varied according to the
dispositions of their masters, who remain responsible for their departments. It is one of the advantages of the doctrine of parliamentary
responsibility that the public appearance of a rigid separation of the
government from the administration is maintained. Subject to overriding statutes such as the House of Commons Disqualification Act 1957,
which by its Schedules regulates the number of ministers who may be
members of that House, there is a considerable flexibility in the structure
of the central government, which enables the pressures of events and the
ideas of Prime Ministers to be reflected in it.[3] The Ministers of the
Crown (Transfer of Functions) Act 1946 enables the transfer of functions
on the dissolution of a ministry to be easily accomplished in law.[4] The
creation of a new ministry, if staff are to be directly employed, and not
lent by other departments, requires statutory authority, but such statutes
are short and stylised.[5] Other administrative changes of major
importance, such as those affecting the Joint Permanent Secretaries to
the Treasury, can be made with little formality.

The creation of new ministries cannot entirely solve the problem of
the increasing burden of work falling upon the government as a whole.

---

[1] Details are readily available in, *e.g., The Whitehall* and *The New Whitehall* Series.
[2] Nomenclature may vary in particular departments, *e.g.,* the Post Office.
[3] See, *e.g.,* " Organisation of British Central Government 1956–62," by F. M. G.
Willson (1962) 40 *Public Administration* 159, and *Organisation of British Central
Government 1914–56,* ed. Chester and Willson.
[4] See for a case study [1961] *Public Law* 150 *et seq.*
[5] The assumption of a title does not so require, *e.g.,* Mr. Churchill's assumption of
the title of Minister of Defence in 1940.

Such creations increase the problem of co-ordinating activity within the government, particularly if a demarcation of function cannot easily be made. Relief has been found for the most heavily burdened ministers through the appointment of Ministers of State or their equivalent. They may increase the burden at the centre. If there has to be a reconciliation of views between ministries, ultimately that reconciliation must be done in the Cabinet. Differences of views within a large ministry can be resolved at a lower level within the ministry itself. Thus the emergence of Ministers of State within ministries should be observed since their efficient use could have the effect of slowing down the creation of new ministries. This was not their original purpose, and probably is still not so. Such appointments may be made where it is desirable that a particular facet of the work of a ministry should receive particular attention, but separation into a separate ministry is thought undesirable either because of the temporary nature of the problems involved, or because the work should not (for administrative reasons) be thus detached from the parent ministry. They may also be made, as in the case of the Minister of State for Scotland where it is thought desirable that someone of ministerial rank, but free of many parliamentary duties, should be available. Other Ministers of State have distinct responsibilities, for which they are answerable to Parliament, as is the Chief Secretary to the Treasury (an office which is currently combined with the office of Paymaster-General), who is a colleague, but not the subordinate, of the Chancellor of the Exchequer and has a seat in the Cabinet. It is this latter group which suggests the possibility of limiting the growth of the number of ministries. The office of Minister of State and those offices akin to it thus afford added flexibility.

The unity of government. All departments of the central government operate in the name of the Crown, but questions arise as to how far the administration must be regarded as a unitary whole. So far as Secretaries of State are concerned it is said that, each discharging part of what was once a single office, any Secretary of State can act for another.[6] This may well be so, even though specific functions are conferred upon a specific Secretary *nominatim.* The argument, if sound, would cover that case as well as the exercise of more general powers. In other cases the specific functions of a minister may, at first sight, be designated with a degree of precision.[7] Ambiguity may arise as to whether a particular matter falls within a certain description, or it may arise in cases where one minister acts on behalf of another. It has been said that the assumption of authority by a department, albeit *ultra vires,* will bind.[8] It seems, however, that such assertions go too far,[9] and that for most purposes

---

[6] *Harrison* v. *Bush* (1855) 5 E. & B. 344.
[7] See, *e.g.,* Minister of Aviation Order 1959, S.I. 1959 No. 1768.
[8] *Robertson* v. *Minister of Pensions* [1949] 1 K.B. 227; *Alsager U.D.C.* v. *Barratt and Others* [1965] 2 Q.B. 343.
[9] *Howell* v. *Falmouth Boat Construction Co.* [1951] A.C. 837.

each department must be treated as a separate entity [10] (with the exception of the departments of the Scottish Office, to be discussed later), though where cases of personal bar or estoppel arise it may be necessary to distinguish between simple attributions of power, and the power given to one minister to act with the approval of another. In the second case the qualification may be regarded as being a matter of internal law not affecting persons outside the government.[11]

The Treasury. The particular functions of the Junior Lords of the Treasury as Whips (in which capacity they are aided by unpaid Whips) have already been noticed. Otherwise function is sufficiently indicated by the name of the ministry, save that the offices of Paymaster-General, Lord Privy Seal, Chancellor of the Duchy of Lancaster and Lord President of the Council frequently have particular other responsibilities added to their light departmental duties. Something must, however, be said of the Treasury. Traditionally its power rested upon the patronage which it controlled, which was of the utmost value to governments, and upon its control of finance.[12] While the former basis has declined in importance, the latter has increased. Treasury control operates not only at the stage of Estimates, when it is the function of the Chancellor of the Exchequer (the effective political head of the Treasury), in conjunction with the Chief Secretary to the Treasury to keep departmental expenditure in line with general government policy, but also to some degree at the stage of administration, notably in relation to *virement*, and at the stage of ultimate accounting.[13] The nature of Treasury control changes. Just as it was affected by the Gladstonian reforms, so also the generalised acceptance of Keynesian economics and of economic planning alters and extends its role in respect of forward planning,[14] though these changes are only slowly being absorbed. The Treasury is, however, much more than a Ministry of Finance, even in the widest sense of that term. It is also responsible for a large number of managerial services in relation to the civil service, notably through its Organisation and Methods Division, but also in relation to recruitment, training, discipline and payment of <u>civil servants</u>. In recognition of this aspect of the work the Permanent Secretary to the Treasury was, in 1919, given the title of Head of the Civil Service, a title which was carried by one of the Joint Permanent Secretaries when the office was divided. The

1968

[10] The Crown Proceedings Act 1947 operates upon that assumption, though, by admission, the unitary theory was accepted in *Commissioners for Crown Lands* v. *Page* [1960] 2 Q.B. 274 at 290.

[11] Mitchell, *Contracts of Public Authorities*, p. 234 *et seq.*

[12] Heath, *The Treasury*; Beer, *Treasury Control* and the sources therein referred to. For the modern aspects, see Bridges, *The Treasury* (2nd ed.).

[13] See, generally, Sixth Report of the Select Committee on Estimates (1957–58) H.C. 254.

[14] The Plowden Report 1961 (Cmnd. 1432). The appointment in October 1961 of the Paymaster-General as Chief Secretary to the Treasury with particular responsibility for estimates, public investment and forward planning was one mark of this. See generally the articles in (1963) 41 *Public Administration* 1–50.

rearrangement of functions in July 1962 was in part intended to underline the importance of these tasks.[15] Thereafter the creation of the Department of Economic Affairs has removed many questions of economic planning from the jurisdiction of the Treasury.

The Law Officers. Constitutionally the position of the Law Officers has also its peculiarities. They are the Attorney- and Solicitor-General for England and the Lord Advocate and Solicitor-General for Scotland. The Attorney-General takes precedence,[16] and the discharge of functions among the two pairs of Law Officers is now regulated by the Law Officers Act 1944. They are the legal advisers of the government, though the Attorney-General assumes also the more general advisory functions not limited to a particular jurisdiction. By custom the Attorney-General and the Lord Advocate have recognised claims to judicial office, and in particular to the Lord Chief Justiceship or to one of the Chairs of the Divisions in Scotland respectively, should a suitable vacancy occur. Each of these Law Officers has a certain precedence at their respective Bars. By reason of the existence of the office of Dean of the Faculty of Advocates the Lord Advocate cannot be said to be head of the Scots Bar, as the Attorney-General is in respect of the English Bar; in contrast, however, the place of the Lord Advocate within the Bar when he appears in court reflects the fact that in the past he was entitled to a seat upon the Bench.

Despite this general identification there are significant differences. The Lord Advocate controls the system of public prosecution in Scotland, a system which does not exist universally in England.[17] On the other hand he lacks the special place in relation to charities held by the Attorney-General, though in other cases the Advocate may be required to be served to represent the public interest. In relation to numerous appointments which in England would be controlled by the Lord Chancellor's department it is the Lord Advocate who in Scotland has the effective voice.[18] The parliamentary draftsmen for Scotland are to be found in the Lord Advocate's department, whereas the office of parliamentary counsel falls under the Treasury. Formerly the Lord Advocate had extensive privileges as representing the Crown, including a right to sit upon the Bench particularly when the interests of the

---

[15] *Ante*, p. 193. The distinctive purposes of the Department of Economic Affairs, and its intended relationship to the Treasury, are given by Sir Douglas Allen, " The Department of Economic Affairs " (1967) 38 *Political Quarterly* 351.

[16] *Att.-Gen.* v. *Lord Advocate* (1834) 2 Cl. & Fin. 481.

[17] It has been asserted that the Lord Advocate has complete immunity from legal proceedings arising out of the discharge of his duties in this respect: *Hester* v. *MacDonald*, 1961 S.L.T. 414. *Sed quaere. Cf. Henderson* v. *Robertson* (1853) 15 D. 290. The views there expressed appear to go beyond what was necessary for the decision of that case or for the proper protection of the Lord Advocate. See, generally, as to his position, *D. and J. Nicol* v. *Dundee Harbour Trustees*, 1915 S.C.(H.L.) 7 and *King's Advocate* v. *Lord Dunglas* (1836) 15 S. 314.

[18] 623 H.C.Deb. 172–173.

Crown were involved.[19] His office is one of great historical importance. He was one of the great officers of state and for long periods, even after the Union, the Lord Advocate was the effective government of Scotland. Those privileges and his effective position have declined, but marks of them are to be found in the present position as, for example, in the patronage vested in him. His advisory capacity is not limited to those of legal adviser and other functions such as membership of the Scottish Universities Committee of the Privy Council adhere to the office.

The offices normally follow the ordinary ministerial pattern, though exceptionally a Law Officer may not be of the Government party, or he may not have a seat in the Commons. Normally, however, a Law Officer is at the same time minister (and thus bound by the ordinary political rules) and also an officer of the law in the sense that he is concerned with the neutral administration of justice. He is thus called upon to distinguish his functions, and on occasion to act in the interest of justice against what might be thought to be his political interests.[20] This duality of interest causes difficulties in working the rules of ministerial responsibility, and, in practice, also causes their modification.[21]

The service departments. At one time questions of the existence of a standing army were of considerable constitutional importance, as is made clear by both the Claim of Right and the Bill of Rights. So, from 1715, military law was sanctioned each year by the annual Mutiny Act. From the Army Act 1881 a standing code was enacted which was renewed in vigour each year by the Army Act. The Royal Air Force was brought under this system and the Act became the Army and Air Force (Annual) Act. These annual Acts were concerned with the continuation of the code of military (or air force) law. Though they recited the concurrence of Parliament to the maintenance of land and air forces, nothing was said on this in the enacted portion, and it appears that the parliamentary authority for the actual forces was, and is, the votes in respect of men in the Appropriation Act. In 1955 the system was changed, partly because it was found that the old procedure could provide fruitful opportunities for parliamentary obstruction, but also for other reasons.[22] The Army Act (and the Air Force Act) of that year provided for a similar code of military law, and a mechanism for enforcing it. The Act was to last for one year, with the possibility of annual renewal by Order in Council up to a total period of five years. In 1961 similar legislation amended and renewed the 1955 legislation.

[19] See, generally, Omond, *Lord Advocates of Scotland*; Milne, *The Scottish Office*; and the article in *A Source Book of Administrative Law in Scotland.*
[20] Shawcross, "The Office of Attorney-General," *Parliamentary Affairs*, 1953–54.
[21] Marshall and Moodie, *Some Problems of the Constitution*, 4th ed., p. 144 *et seq.* For the best general account of the Law Officers in England see Edwards, *Law Officers of the Crown.*
[22] (1951–52) H.C. 241, 331; (1952–53) H.C. 140, 289; (1953–54) H.C. 223.

Thus there is the opportunity every five years for a substantial review of military law.

Naval forces did not present the same threat to liberty as did land forces and annual legislation was theoretically not required for the maintenance of the navy. In practice the navy as much as the army depended on the annual Appropriation Act. The code of naval discipline is now contained in the Naval Discipline Act 1957, which moves towards a common code of service law, but which unlike the other legislation is permanent.

Constitutionally ultimate control is vested in the civilian heads of the service departments. Collective service advice was given through the Chiefs of Staff Committee. Since 1955 there has been a separate Chairman of the Committee who is Chief of Defence Staff to the Minister of Defence. In 1962 this process was carried further by the proposal that the Ministry of Defence should, in effect, absorb the service departments, the three ministers becoming Minister of State subordinated to the Minister of Defence.[23] It was these arrangements that were carried into force by the Defence (Transfer of Functions) Act 1964.

The Scottish Office. Mention must also be made of the Scottish Office. For a substantial period after the Union the Lord Advocate was to a great extent the government of Scotland. The present office springs from the Secretary for Scotland Act 1885,[24] which was extended in 1887. The Secretary became a Secretary of State in 1926 under the Secretaries of State Act. Despite the Reorganisation of Offices (Scotland) Act 1928, the board system continued to have a wide operation in Scotland. That system was condemned in the Gilmour Report,[25] and the Reorganisation of Offices (Scotland) Act 1939 carried out the recommendations of the Report, removed some anomalies created by the 1928 Act, and made the Scottish Office resemble a normal department. There remained, however, a considerable number of government functions in Scotland which were not formally under the control of the Secretary of State. As a result of the Report of the Royal Commission on Scottish Affairs,[26] many functions were transferred from " United Kingdom " departments to the Scottish Office, *e.g.,* in relation to roads. The result is that the Secretary of State has more diversified functions than any other minister, many of which he exercises jointly or in parallel with another minister, *e.g.,* of Agriculture. Partly, but not entirely, because

23 672 H.C.Deb. 31 *et seq.* The new arrangements were outlined in Central Organisation for Defence (1963) Cmnd. 2097.
24 A Secretary of State existed intermittently until 1746. Thereafter the Lord Advocate was minister for Scotland (as far as there was one) until this Act. For the history of the Office see Milne, *The Scottish Office.* More recently see particularly Hanham, " The Creation of the Scottish Office 1881–87," 1965 J.R. 205 *et seq.* For an assessment see Mackintosh, " Regional Administration: Has it Worked in Scotland?" (1964) 41 *Public Administration* 253.
25 (1937) Cmd. 5563.
26 (1954) Cmd. 9212.

of this he has a distinct character as "Scotland's Minister," and is expected to represent Scottish interests and feeling generally in the Cabinet, and also, in Scotland, to concern himself beyond statutory functions with Scottish life and economy. The difficulties of combining these functions, some of which must be performed in London and others in Scotland, led to the appointment in 1951 of a Minister of State, who has until the present time been a peer, and hence freed for performing duties in Scotland. This diversity of function also affects the structure of the Office. There are three Parliamentary Under-Secretaries of State, each of whom is responsible for an area of activity. The departments of the Scottish Office are each headed by a Secretary, who has many of the attributes of a Permanent Under-Secretary of State in ordinary departments.[27] The Permanent Under-Secretary of State, while having a general oversight of the whole work of the Office, has no specific departmental duties and is an adviser to the Secretary of State.

The general Scottish position. The organisation of the Scottish Office is peculiar in that it is the one department which is defined by geography rather than by function. It is the result of past history, as well as of other factors which mark off Scotland as an entity. That country is distinguished by the existence there of a separate jurisdiction, and a separate church, and these things combined with other factors produce solid differences which also distinguish the country as a unit. The organisation of the Scottish Office is a reflection of this. That organisation, taken alone, suggests nothing more than a partial adminis-trative devolution, partial since many governmental functions necessarily continue to be carried out on a United Kingdom basis, and in particular the jurisdiction of the Treasury is universal. Nevertheless, the whole constitutional position of Scotland can only be gathered if this organisa-tion is seen in the context of the other distinguishing factors, which have been mentioned, and of the particular arrangements made for Scottish legislation and affairs in Parliament. To all these must be added such matters as the Electricity Reorganisation (Scotland) Act 1954, which both in its transfer of responsibility from the Minister of Fuel and Power to the Secretary of State and in the exclusion of the Scottish electricity boards from the general scheme is an example of how this pattern of activity affects the whole of the machinery of government in Scotland. Thus, practical devolution may overall be greater than is apparent at first sight. This reality of the devolution may be obscured because of the piecemeal method by which it has been created.

[27] Since 1939 the Secretary of State has a free hand in the reorganisation of the work in the Office. In June 1962 the Office was reorganised. There are four main departments, the Home and Health Department (which includes national health and local health and welfare services), the Scottish Development Department (covering housing, planning and electricity among other things), the Department of Agriculture and Fisheries, and the Scottish Education Department.

Northern Ireland and Wales. More extreme conditions and a different history have produced a greater and more formalised devolution in respect of Northern Ireland, which can be said to have a semi-federal relationship with Great Britain.[28] Elsewhere in Great Britain particular arrangements have been made in relation to Wales. The Statute of Wales 1284 and the Law in Wales Act 1536 incorporated Wales into England, and until recent times no special measures had, in general, been taken in relation to the government of Wales, the most notable exceptions being the Welsh Board of Health and the administration of education in Wales. In 1951 the Home Secretary was also named as Minister for Welsh Affairs, having a general rather than departmental interest. That responsibility was in 1957 transferred to the Minister of Housing and Local Government, and a Minister of State for Wales was appointed. In the same year the Council for Wales and Monmouthshire was established as an advisory body. There had been development in the Welsh offices of various of the central departments, and the Council pressed for the appointment of a Secretary of State for Wales after the manner of the Secretary of State for Scotland, a solution which was at first rejected, but was eventually accepted in a modified form and a Secretary of State for Wales was appointed, but still with more limited powers (especially in regard to agriculture and education) than those possessed by the Secretary of State for Scotland.[29] Similarly, the arrangements in Parliament for Wales are, as has already been noted, more limited than those made in relation to Scotland.

Decentralisation in general. Apart from Scotland and Wales, there exists administrative decentralisation in departments where that is possible, such as in the Ministry of Pensions and National Insurance, and in advisory bodies such as Regional Boards for Industry. On any substantial scale this decentralisation is only possible where the service is essentially local, or where there is much detailed administration not involving major policy decisions. Something approaching a regional organisation had existed during the war of 1939–45, but while pressures towards decentralisation exist, other factors, above all the general doctrine of parliamentary responsibility, and simple geographical

---

28 For a description of that and of the organisation of government in the Isle of Man and the Channel Islands see the two volumes on the United Kingdom in Stevens' *British Commonwealth Series*; and see Queckett, *The Constitution of Northern Ireland*, and Barrett and Carter, *The Northern Ireland Problem*. For an assessment see Wallace, " Home Rule in Northern Ireland; Anomalies of Devolution " (1967) 18 N.I.L.Q. 159.

29 See particularly the Council's Third (1957) and Fourth (1959) Memoranda (Cmnd. 53 and 631) and the earlier reply of the Prime Minister (1957) Cmnd. 334. Those disputes led to a reconstruction of the Council (see 595 H.C.Deb. 1323–1324) and point to the difficulties of combining a system of ministerial responsibility with other devices. For the division of responsibilities see 663 H.C.Deb. 1277. The functions of the Secretary of State are set out in 636 H.C.Deb. 623–626. The Welsh language has received specific protection by the Welsh Language Act 1967.

considerations have militated against the emergence of any system of regional government based upon these foundations.[30]

The administration: the civil service. Within this general administrative framework, and under ministerial control, the work of administration is carried out by the civil service staffs. Two aspects of their position should be noticed, their relationship to the minister and their general position in law. All functions are carried out in the name of the appropriate minister, but, since clearly the minister cannot do everything, the civil servants have authority to act, and the act is accepted as that of the minister.[31] This legal responsibility is balanced by a similar political responsibility. The minister is responsible for what his servants have done or might have done, and for organising " a safe system of work " in his department.[32] The maintenance of these responsibilities, particularly the second, is an important element in the maintenance of the neutrality of the civil service. Despite this, there is also importance in retaining some element of individual responsibility on the part of the particular servant. It should, therefore, be noted that neither the responsibility which the department has in law for the acts of its servants (the enforcement of which was facilitated or created by the Crown Proceedings Act 1947, to be discussed hereafter) nor the political responsibility to Parliament borne by the minister is entirely exclusive of any personal responsibility of the individual civil servant.

Recruitment to the civil service is controlled by the Civil Service Commission.[33] Once engaged, in law, the civil servant holds his position at pleasure.[34] In practice he has a high degree of security of tenure, and an elaborate system of internal tribunals exists. These must be regarded as part of a system of internal administrative law. Conditions of employment are regulated by the Treasury and a system of collective bargaining exists through the Whitley Councils.[35] Somewhat similarly

[30] See particularly Sixth Report Select Committee on Estimates (1953–54) H.C. 233 and the Acton Society Trust, *Studies on Regionalism*, as well as the debate in 271 H.L.Deb. 706–794.

[31] *Carltona Ltd.* v. *Commissioner of Works* [1943] 2 All E.R. 560; *Adair* v. *Hill*, 1943 J.C. 9; *Dalziel School Board* v. *Scotch Education Department*, 1915 S.C. 234. There are probably limits to this doctrine. In some cases the court may require the minister to act personally: *Duncan* v. *Cammell Laird & Co. Ltd.* [1942] A.C. 624 at 638. Moreover, a minister is not bound by a representation of authority made by one of his servants in excess of real authority.

[32] This responsibility is also not without limit. See *ante*, pp. 196–197.

[33] See, generally, Mustoe, *Law and Organisation of the Civil Service*; *The Civil Service in Britain and France*, ed. Robson. Perhaps the best account and criticism of recruitment in relation to function is given in the Sixth Report of the Estimates Committee (1964–65) H.C. 308, and particularly in the memorandum of Professor Mackenzie, there printed.

[34] *Riordan* v. *The War Office* [1959] 3 All E.R. 552; [1960] 3 All E.R. 774n. (C.A.); and see the older cases discussed in Mitchell, *The Contracts of Public Authorities*. The legal nature of the civil servant's engagement is ambiguous. See the arguments therein, and *I.R.C.* v. *Hambrook* [1956] 2 Q.B. 641, and the cases there cited; *Marks* v. *The Commonwealth* (1964) 111 C.L.R. 549; and Blair (1958) 21 M.L.R. 265.

[35] The restrictive provisions in the Trade Disputes and Trade Unions Act 1927 were repealed in 1946.

the denial at law of a right to sue for his salary does not represent the true position of the civil servant.[36] Because of the nature of his employment the civil servant is subjected to some unusual limitations. Certain grades are free from restrictions on political activities, others, particularly higher grades concerned with policy and those where the work is local and hence difficulty might arise, are restricted in their participation in national politics, and in particular cases in participation in local politics.[37] Further, the standards of conduct required may be higher than those exacted by the ordinary law,[38] and in particular special security checks may be made, under the system established in 1948, and enlarged in scope thereafter.[39] Here once again the element of " internal law " is apparent. Appeals run to the Three Advisers—former senior civil servants who act as a court of appeal.

To a large extent the regulation of the civil service remains, in form, on a prerogative basis.[40] The service is governed by Orders in Council, or by Treasury circulars. The Civil Service Commissioners were established by Order in Council and continue upon that basis. In effect, this basis preserves a discretionary element which is required for the running of the public service. It is probable that the exclusion of the general law is carried further than is necessary, and causes once again a sharp distinction between the servants of central government departments and other public servants which is not wholly justified.

In general the importance of the place of the civil service in the machinery of the government should not be underestimated. The civil service reforms which followed the Northcote-Trevelyan Report of 1854 should be rated as constitutional reforms. In particular the retention of the theory of civil service anonymity is of the greatest importance in working our system. It is upon that anonymity that the doctrine of ministerial responsibility depends, and the maintenance of a barrier between the political element, which must exist somewhere in a government department, and the administrative side is of great importance in the public administration. In this respect the doctrine of ministerial responsibility had been of major importance, though even in this context

---

36 Thus the Superannuation Acts preserve the "discretionary" element in pensions, although the existence of these is taken into account, together with security of employment in calculating salaries; see generally Blair, " The Civil Servant " [1958] Public Law 32; and see Bankruptcy Act 1914, s. 51 (1); and Bankruptcy (Scotland) Act 1913, s. 148; Law Reform (Miscellaneous Provisions) (Scotland) Act 1966, s. 1.

37 See Servants of the Crown (Parliamentary Candidature) Order 1950 and the Masterman Report 1949 (Cmd. 7718) and the White Paper of 1953 indicating the government's policy arrived at after consultation with the Whitley Council (Cmd. 8783): over 60 per cent. of the service is completely free politically.

38 (1937) Cmd. 5517, Acceptance of Business Appointments by Officers of the Crown.

39 See the Report on Security Procedures in the Public Services 1962 (Cmnd. 1681), which summarises past developments; see also Jackson, " Individual Rights and National Security " (1957) 20 M.L.R. 364; and Jackson, " The Dismissal of Civil Servants in the Interests of National Security " [1963] Public Law 51.

40 The justification of this may be doubtful. The differentiation from other forms of service is much more justifiable. The mere fact that an office was a munus publicum entailed many similar consequences (Ersk. III, 6, 7) and perhaps all that are desirable.

Joelson/

it is observable how much more publicity is given to individual civil servants, and it is probable that that tendency may be enhanced if the new specialised committees develop. Moreover, while rivalry will exist in any large-scale enterprise, in a governmental enterprise this anonymity *vis-à-vis* the public does much to ensure that the rivalry is a professional one, and to that extent the civil service can more easily remain and be accepted as politically neutral in its operation. The creation and maintenance of such a service in modern times might indeed be rated as one of the major constitutional achievements.[41]

[41] The foundation of the modern civil service is to be found in the Northcote-Trevelyan Report of 1854 (Paper 1713) (reprinted (1954) 32 *Public Administration* 1). See, too, Wheare, *The Civil Service in the Constitution*, and Wyn Griffith, *The British Civil Service, 1854–1954*. The whole structure of our central government is best considered against the background of Shonfield, *Modern Capitalism*, an excellent survey of techniques and purposes.

CHAPTER 12

PUBLIC BOARDS AND CORPORATIONS

Introduction. The modern creation of public boards is the result of several causes.[1] Changing conceptions of the functions of the state result in an expansion of the areas of state activity, and in an expansion of the activities of traditional departments. If all new activities were to be carried out by traditional ministerial methods the consequence of the centralisation, which necessarily follows both in the administration and in Parliament, would overload existing machinery. Other considerations may suggest that the conduct of some governmental activities be isolated (to a greater or lesser degree) from Parliament. Quite apart from pressure on parliamentary time, the possibility of close parliamentary questioning dictates administrative procedures and attitudes which may not be appropriate where procedures should be closer to those of large-scale business. Again, such isolation may be desirable to exclude political pressures, where those would be inappropriate, as, for example, with the B.B.C., and a greater freedom of action (including a freedom to make mistakes) than traditional methods will allow may also be desirable. Moreover, the board form may facilitate the desirable participation of persons not normally engaged in government service in the management of the enterprise.[2] The weight of such considerations is not uniformly felt, for the choice of ministerial or board form will be greatly influenced by the inclination of the government for the time being.

The pattern of creation of public boards is no more uniform. Economic or purely political considerations may cause a particular government to concern itself more immediately with a particular industry or activity rather than with others like it. Even if it be determined that government interest should be close, and that a board be preferred to a department, the nature of the activity may cause considerable variation in the method of intervention. The National Health Service is run through boards and committees created *ad hoc*. The Legal Aid Scheme is run through ordinary professional bodies. The different qualities of gas and electricity cause differences in the organisation of those nationalised industries. Thus there is no uniformity of pattern any more than

---

[1] In small compass many of the reasons are seen operating in the Report on Crown Lands (1955) Cmd. 9483. More generally, see Robson, *Nationalised Industry and Public Ownership*. Barry, *Nationalisation in British Politics*, gives an account of the modern political background.
[2] See the Rochdale Report (1962) Cmnd. 1824, § 147, and 616 H.C.Deb. 33–35, on part-time directors of the Bank of England, and Cmnd. 350, and 631 H.C.Deb. 200.

there is of legal structure. Cable and Wireless Ltd. exists under the Companies Acts, the Bank of England is a chartered corporation, the National Coal Board a statutory one.

Nor are distinctions clear-cut. The Post Office, which had long existed as a department, has, since 1961, been steadily undergoing a process of change which will leave it with, at any rate, the appearance of a board.[3] Parts of the Atomic Energy Authority resemble closely institutions run in departmental form. At the other end of the spectrum there is a graduation upwards from the private enterprise village shop (which is nevertheless state-regulated in some respects, e.g., as to hours of opening or commodities sold) through increasing degrees of regulation to the exclusive conduct of an activity under a public board, an operational board which may have emerged as the only convenient method of regulating an activity. Coal-mining, with immaterial exceptions, is exclusively in the hands of a public board. Iron and steel were " denationalised," [4] but the Iron and Steel Board continued to have regulatory powers over the industry, until steel was again nationalised by the Iron and Steel Act 1967. Parts of air transport are in the hands of a public board, but aircraft construction, although it remains in the hands of private industry, is heavily influenced by governmental policies, practices and suggestions, and government investment in that industry (e.g., in bearing development costs of aircraft) affects decisions on proposals of the nationalised air-lines. While British European Airways are expected to provide uneconomic services in the Highlands and Islands, MacBraynes Ltd., an ordinary company, is subsidised to provide like services in other fields of transport.[5] Public investment exists in private companies through the National Research Development Corporation. The same gradations exist within the field of regulation narrowly so called. Nurses are governed by a state-created body, advocates or barristers by private corporations acting in the public interest.

Historical background. Public corporations must therefore be looked at against a broad background,[6] and history must find its place in that background. There is nothing new about a public board, in the sense of a body which has some governmental attributes, but which also operates as might a private corporation. The Bank of Scotland [7] was

---

[3] The Post Office Act 1961 and Report on the Status of the Post Office (1960) Cmnd. 989; and now see *The Reorganisation of the Post Office* (1967) Cmnd. 3233.
[4] Iron and Steel Act 1953.
[5] Highlands and Islands Shipping Services Act 1960. The share capital in that company is, however, half-owned by the B.T.C., acquired on the take-over from the L.M.S. Railway.
[6] The extension of that background to include experience with boards in Australia and the U.S.A. is desirable to break ideas of any necessary connection with certain political views, which may exist if only the local scene is regarded.
[7] See the Act of 1695 (A.P.S. IX, 494).

such a body, as were the Darien Company,[8] the East India Company and the Hudson's Bay Company, among many other examples. More recently the boards like the Poor Law Commission of 1835 were created to run what had come to be regarded as distinctively governmental services. These should perhaps not be regarded as the predominant stream in the ancestry of the present boards. Steadily they were reduced to the ministerial pattern, and, although the name board might continue, as with the Local Government Board, in reality they had, for the most part, become, by the end of the nineteenth century, traditional ministerial departments. It should, moreover, be noted that in one sense they were almost " accidental " in the way in which modern boards are " deliberate." They were created before modern doctrines of ministerial responsibility had been worked out with all their consequences, and the decline in these early boards corresponds to the growth of these doctrines. Whereas the newer boards are deliberately intended to breach these doctrines, the former were not so conceived. They were, moreover, early experiments based upon a simple theory that, once a policy had been determined, able and upright men, like Chadwick, could administer, and nothing more was required. That theory proved to be inconsistent with doctrines of ministerial responsibility, and without some other mechanism for control which was effective, the dichotomy which it contained proved unworkable. The theory remains alive, but without the evolution of appropriate institutions continues to present difficulties.

There is, however, another strain of boards, related perhaps to the nineteenth-century *ad hoc* commissions in local government for lighting, paving, etc., which can be said to start with the Mersey Docks and Harbour Board of 1857 and to run through the Port of London Authority and the London Passenger Transport Board. These were operational boards performing a commercial service with governmental interest strongly marked in financial controls, in appointments to the controlling board, and in general regulation, but having also a degree of independence from the government, and having representatives of consumers and operators also upon that board. A degree of governmental regulation of such enterprises was no novelty. The idea of a public utility is of long standing traceable back to the old common law regulation of common carriers, innkeepers and the like, and continuing through the regulation of railways under such bodies as the Railway and Canal Commission or the Railway Rates Tribunal[9] and of other public utilities. These bodies had special rights and privileges, *e.g.*, powers of compulsory purchase, etc., but they had also special liabilities in that they were subjected to varying degrees of regulation in the public interest. Thus, the new boards can be regarded as merely an accentuation of governmental interest, and it was through them, and in particular

---

[8] See the Act of 1695 (A.P.S. IX, 377).
[9] See, generally, Kahn-Freund, *The Law of Inland Transport*, Chap. 4.

the Port of London Authority, that a renewed interest was shown in the idea of public boards in this century.

General difficulties. The pressures which stimulated that interest have been indicated. There are also matters in present circumstances which militate against the success of such boards. It has been found that the division between "policy" and "administration" is not, in general, a happy or workable one within the existing institutional pattern, particularly when the board is concerned with an essential service or product. Isolation from Parliament means, on one side, a diminution in parliamentary control but, on the other, it means a denial of the possibility of using the parliamentary forum to explain the hopes and intentions of the board, and reports of public boards, no matter how well produced, tend to reach only those readers who are prepared to venture into the lowest and darkest parts of libraries. Compromise solutions, such as that of having a member of the board who is also a member of the House of Commons, were bound to fail. The member might answer for the board, but could not control it.[10] Hence, with the rise of the doctrine of ministerial responsibility, as the dominant mechanism for control, the board system was heavily condemned [11] and in the more purely governmental fields of activity (of which the poor law stream is typical) declined, though somewhat unevenly, throughout the Kingdom as a whole.[12] The forced decline of the "poor law stream" almost coincides with the vigorous expansion of the "Mersey stream." Once again it was hoped that if general policy had been determined these quasi-commercial ventures could largely be left to run themselves. So there emerged the London Passenger Transport Board, 1933, the Central Electricity Board, 1926, British Overseas Airways, 1939, the North of Scotland Hydro-Electric Board, 1943. Nevertheless, in these new

[10] The Forestry Commission had such an arrangement until 1945, and it is for the reasons given above, rather than for any others, that the House of Commons Disqualification Act 1957 excluded members of the boards of public corporations from the House. For a general account of the nineteenth-century decline of boards, see F. M. G. Willson, "Ministries and Boards" (1955) 33 *Public Administration* 43.

[11] In particular by the Royal Commission on the Civil Service, Fourth Report (1914) Cd. 7338, Chap. IX; the Report of the (Haldane) Machinery of Government Committee (1918) Cd. 9230, §§ 31–33; and the Report of the Gilmour Committee (1937) Cmd. 5563.

[12] The chronology here is interesting. The board system continued in full vigour in Scotland long after its decline had become marked in England. By the time the Scottish boards were just reaching a stage of absorption into the ministerial form, as the English ones had earlier, the new stream of boards springing from the Mersey Docks and Harbour Board were appearing. At the time of the abolition of the Scottish boards great energy was being devoted to the creation of newer United Kingdom boards in the "Mersey stream." These boards and their post-war fellows show signs of repeating only rather more rapidly the nineteenth-century cycle of development. It must be noted that the creation of local boards has not stopped; see the Covent Garden Market Act 1961, and despite uncertainties about the mechanisms for controlling the newer national boards, others are being created on the old pattern; see Report on Civil Aerodromes and Air Navigational Services (1961) Cmnd. 1457, now the Airports Authority Act 1965. On the other hand, the Second Report of the Select Committee on Nationalised Industries (1966–67) H.C. 673 advocates a greater return to direct ministerial control.

creations ministerial control was strongly marked, and persisted in the post-war creations. Thus, the inconsistencies condemned by the Gilmour Report were put once again upon the Statute Book.

These creations of the years between the wars should be noted, for they tended to become models, both in form and in other ways, particularly the B.B.C., created in 1926. The need to secure political neutrality for that body was evident, and hence, although a ministerial power of direction existed, there was a refusal to answer parliamentary questions on the day-to-day affairs of the Corporation,[13] a refusal which set a subsequent pattern.

General problems. This outline and genealogy are a necessary prelude to any discussion of the constitutional position, since they make clear the facts that the creation of boards has not been based upon any consistent theory, that no continuous effort has been made to fit boards into the general machinery, or to adjust that machinery to increase the chances of fitting them in. That outline also emphasises the ambiguous character of many of these boards, being on the one hand in some ways an extension of government,[14] and on the other hand being in different ways not distinct in kind from private organisations. These conditions make it difficult to define their constitutional position in law with precision. An effort must be made towards such definition, since the existence of these bodies creates constitutional problems. Lines of responsibility may become dangerously blurred if the relationship of boards to ministers is not clear. The relationship of boards to Parliament and the functions of Parliament in respect of boards are important, as are other methods of control; and these matters depend, to some extent, on that definition. Apart from these almost technical issues, there are the broader ones (which increase the importance of the narrower) resulting from the existence of these agglomerations of power. The fiscal and economic significance of their operations is so great that they could affect the economic life of the nation as a whole.[15] Moreover, the monopolistic character of many, whether of a commercial type or not, makes possible the existence in an accentuated form of problems of

13 See Report of Select Committee on Nationalised Industries (1951–52) H.C. 332. The action of the Assistance Board was also influential here, this being a board in relation to which it was most easy to divide policy and administration.
14 See particularly Sir James Bowman (1956–57) H.C. 304, Q. 911, and report of B.O.A.C. for 1961. At one extreme the Bank of England can be properly described as the City branch of the Treasury.
15 See, for example, the figures given in relation to nationalised industries in the White Paper *The Financial and Economic Obligations of Nationalised Industries* (1961) Cmnd. 1337. The significance of these bodies is enhanced by the fact that they tend to exist at key points in the economy, and that the conditions which govern the methods of raising capital for them cause that operation to have a heavy impact on a particular capital market. Investment in nationalised industries amounts to almost half the national investment in the public sector, estimated at £965m. out of a total of £2,060m. for 1963–64; see (1962) Cmnd. 1849.

abuse of power,[16] which may affect citizens or firms in their lives or livelihood.

The general character of boards. Before approaching these problems some description must be given of the modern boards, though within the scope of this work that description must be generalised.[17] There must be put on one side boards which are either ministerial departments, or parts of such departments such as the Board of Inland Revenue. There must also be discarded bodies such as the Air Licensing Board or the Service Committees under the National Health Service, which, as regulatory bodies, will be discussed with administrative tribunals. Of the rest, there are two broad groups, a social service or administrative group, and an operational group, though the division is not a clear one. In the former group may be placed the New Towns Commission (for England and Wales), the Development Corporations for New Towns, the Regional Hospital Boards (and their subordinates, the Hospital Management Committees), Supplementary Benefits Commission, or the Land Commission. Such bodies are administering services on behalf of the government in a relatively direct manner.[18] They are bodies corporate, the members of the corporations being appointed by the minister, who is sometimes bound by a requirement of consultation (before appointing) with local authorities or other appropriate bodies,[19] but the minister nevertheless retains a very considerable discretion. Each corporation is entrusted with a relatively narrow field of administration and their finance is derived primarily from sums provided by the minister. Thus, the sums required for the hospital boards are contained in the ordinary Estimates. Critical matters, such as the rates of National Assistance, are determined by general law or by the minister, and it is generally true that the powers of overt control by ministers tend to be somewhat larger in relation to this group than they are in relation to the second.

The second group, that here called "operational," includes the large nationalised industries, coal, electricity, gas, railways and the air corporations. These have the appearance, at first sight, of being commercial undertakings, in that they sell a product and thus have independent sources of revenue. Their apparent charter may be large, "securing the efficient development of the coal-mining industry," for example. Again, the boards are bodies corporate, consisting of members appointed by the minister (sometimes there is a generalised requirement

---

[16] Consider the general situation in such cases as *Eric Gnapp* v. *Petroleum Board* [1949] 1 All E.R. 980; *Barber* v. *Manchester R.H.B.* [1958] 1 All E.R. 322; *Palmer* v. *Inverness Hospitals Board*, 1963 S.L.T. 124.

[17] For more detail, see Griffith and Street, *Administrative Law*, and Robson, *Nationalised Industries and Public Ownership*.

[18] The relationship can in effect be one of agency, as with the Agricultural Land Commission in England.

[19] New Towns Act 1946; National Health Service Act 1946, Sched. 3; N.H.S. (Scotland) Act 1947, Sched. 4.

that a member should have a particular skill),[20] but here too the terms
are so broad that the minister has an abundant discretion. The board
may itself be centralised, as with the National Coal Board, or the
industry may be organised on a regional basis. Thus the area gas boards
can be regarded as the basic units, the Gas Council, the central body,
having fewer functions, that structure having been at the time thought
to be appropriate to the technical conditions of the industry.[21] In
regard to electricity, while generation is, in principle centralised under
the Central Electricity Generating Board, and distribution is in the hands
of the area boards (who thus have a degree of autonomy), general policy
is determined by the Electricity Council, composed mainly of the chairmen of the various boards. These arrangements for the electricity
industry operate only in England and Wales. In Scotland with two
boards, the South of Scotland Electricity Board and the North of
Scotland Hydro-Electric Board, each combines generation and distribution.[22] Where the structure is thus decentralised the minister has direct
links with the areas. The structure of the Transport Commission under
the Reorganisation Scheme 1954 [23] was something of a compromise
between the two forms. Under the Transport Act 1962 an entirely new
structure was created, which imposes decentralisation by region and by
function. It created four boards, the British Railways Board, the
London Transport Board (which has powers over both rail and road
transport in the London Passenger Transport Area), the British Transport Docks Board and the British Waterways Board. In addition the
British Transport Holding Company was created to hold and manage
securities formerly vested in the Transport Commission, and to control
any wholly owned subsidiaries. Apart from the structure, in which
(outside London) divisions are based on function, a regional structure
is provided for in section 2 in relation to railways, these being in six
Regional Railway Boards in the first instance, the members of the
Regional Boards being appointed by the Railways Board with the
approval of the minister. Under the proposed scheme the Regional
Boards will disappear, as will the Holding Company, and a new National
Freight Corporation will emerge with powers to carry goods by road,
and a duty to help the integration of road and rail transport.

In relation to this second group the term " operational " has been
used rather than industrial or commercial, for there is written into the
terms of reference of the corporations an element of public interest,[24]

---

[20] e.g., Coal Industry Act 1949, s. 1; Transport Act 1962, s. 1 (3). Throughout it
must be remembered that anything said on transport is subject to the Transport
Bill now before Parliament.

[21] Gas Act 1948.

[22] See Electricity Reorganisation (Scotland) Act 1954 and Electricity Act 1957; but see
the Mackenzie Report, "Electricity in Scotland" (1962) Cmnd. 1859, § 186 et seq.

[23] See Cmd. 9191.

[24] e.g., Hydro-Electric Development (Scotland) Act 1943, where it is most explicit; but
it exists elsewhere, e.g., Transport Act 1962, s. 7 (1).

either explicitly or implicitly, and this element is often of great significance.

As will appear, the distinction between the two groups is not as clear as might appear at first sight, and in between them lie the Atomic Energy Authority, whose commercial activities may be said to be limited (with the Central Electricity Generating Board as its main customer), the B.B.C., the Independent Television Authority and the Bank of England. While the B.B.C. is primarily operational, but dependent on public funds, I.T.A. (although it may be operational) is intended to be mainly regulatory and to negotiate with the programme contractors, from whom it receives its revenues. The Bank of England cannot be regarded as providing a service in the sense of the first group, but is perhaps a necessary halfway house between the Treasury and the world of business.

Relationship to the government. The relationship of the boards to the government is complex. In all the Acts there are powers conferred on the minister to give directions to the corporation as there are by the Charter of the B.B.C. (though, for historical and other reasons, these latter must be somewhat differently regarded). These powers may be merely to give directions, as in relation to regional hospital boards, or to give directions of a general character, as in relation to the National Coal Board. This distinction can well be overemphasised. There is no clarity about the meaning of the word " general," which may well vary according to circumstances, and moreover it is clear that directions will be rarely used, and, if used, are a mark of the breakdown of the system. Ministerial influence pervades both groups equally.[25] This influence exists not merely because of the intimacy of the board staffs with ministerial staffs, but even more because of other reasons. Ministerial control over accounting dealings with surpluses can be important, and the regulation of appointments to the boards and conditions of tenure enhance this influence. Perhaps most important of all, the methods of raising capital which, because of the nature of the boards, involve the Treasury afford many opportunities for influence.[26]

[25] The Reports of the Select Committee on Nationalised Industries on both the Air Corporations ((1958–59) H.C. 213) and British Railways ((1959–60) H.C. 254) make this abundantly clear. The figure of £250,000 at which ministerial approval was required for a capital project of the latter is well below the figure at which the approval of the central board might be requested in industries of a comparable size. The Transport Act 1962, s. 27, continues a tight ministerial control; and see 682 H.C.Deb. 441–452. The Report of the Select Committee on Nationalised Industries (1966–67) H.C. 673 continues the series. The Select Committee is examining this issue but its report has not yet been issued. The Minutes of Evidence appear in the series (1966–67) H.C. 440, and typical answers in 678 H.C.Deb. 9–10 and 687 H.C.Deb. 168.

[26] " Government Control of the Capital Expenditure of the Nationalised Industries " by S. Please (1955) 33 *Public Administration* 31; and see " The Financial and Economic Obligations of Nationalised Industries " (1961) Cmnd. 1337. The relationship has been described as that of banker and customer: 668 H.C.Deb. 214. That Paper is carried further by the *Review of Economic and Financial Objectives* (1967) Cmnd. 3437.

Granted the nature and purpose of these boards, it cannot be said that this influence is in any way improper. What may be asked is whether lines of responsibility are obscured or, alternatively, whether real responsibility corresponds with legal appearance. In effect, it must be asked whether as now organised a board system does not embody all the defects which were condemned in the context of a slightly different system by the Gilmour Committee. The answer to these questions involves the scope of parliamentary and other controls.

Parliamentary controls. Parliamentary questions remain limited but significant in number and scope. Theoretically, a minister being responsible for what he could do but has not done as well as for what he has done, the scope of the ministerial directing power opens up a wide field for parliamentary questioning. Such questioning would be inconsistent with the intentions in establishing the boards; moreover, the precedent of the B.B.C., as has already been mentioned, imposed a limitation. Nevertheless, the desire for questioning exists. In relation to some bodies, such as Regional Hospital Boards, where the Acts and orders made thereunder give considerable responsibility to ministers, there is little difficulty. Difficulty does arise in connection with nationalised industries. Initial uncertainty was ultimately settled by a ruling of the Speaker that he would allow questions upon matters involving ministerial responsibility to stand upon the Order Paper which, in his opinion, were of sufficient public importance, despite the fact that answers to questions of like type had previously been refused and, thus, under the normal rules the question would not have been accepted. Questions involving the " day-to-day " administration of the nationalised industries are normally excluded. Subsequently the Select Committee on Nationalised Industries which examined the problem, did not urge any alteration of the rules.[27] In this connection it must be remembered that a minister cannot be compelled to answer a question, but also that with sufficient ingenuity it is normally possible to circumvent the rules if it is desired so to do in a particular case.

Other opportunities for discussing nationalised industries exist. Supply Days may be used for this purpose, as may debates upon capital investment. Moreover, three days are normally allocated for discussion of the annual reports of public boards, with the choice of report lying with the Opposition. Apart from these routine opportunities others exist. Since the establishment of nationalised industries, reports such

---

27 For the normal rule see 449 H.C.Deb. 172, and for the Report see (1951–52) H.C. 332. The limitations can perhaps cause difficulty in relation to privilege; see the discussion of the *Strauss* case, *ante*, p. 128, and the importance there of the definition of " a proceeding in Parliament." For the present position see 682 H.C.Deb. 449–455. For questions on broadcasting see 702 H.C.Deb. 185. In general a debate can be quickly mounted; see, *e.g.*, 757 H.C.Deb. 110 *et seq.*, dealing with the proposed contract between the N.C.B. and Alcan which had only just become public.

as the Herbert Committee on Electricity,[28] the Fleck Committee on Coal, the Guillebaud Report on Railway Pay, reports such as the Programme of Nuclear Power,[29] or the Pilkington Report on Broadcasting,[30] have been sufficiently numerous to afford opportunities for fundamental review. Equally, the changes in the original structure in railways or electricity, for example, have served the same purpose. (It is almost true to say that the railways have never yet operated under an Act the amendment of which was not under consideration, and thus they have been under continuous scrutiny.) So, too, have private Bills promoted by the corporations, the Second Reading of which affords an opportunity for surveying the work of the board in question. Again, the financial structure of nationalised industries affords recurrent opportunities for discussing them. Authorisation of borrowing, such as the Air Corporations Act 1960, or of advances, such as the Coal Industry Act 1960, is given with a relatively low ceiling, so that a return to Parliament is inevitable, and as a further means to the same end in 1960, arrangements were improved for giving information about capital investment in nationalised industries.[31]

Many of these opportunities for parliamentary discussion have a random quality. Moreover, in so far as they occur when changes are being discussed, the emphasis is upon the merits of the change rather than on general performance. Thus they do not afford an opportunity for continuous scrutiny, as far as that is consistent with the intended purposes of establishing the boards. A distinction must, however, be drawn which corresponds roughly to the broad division which has been made. Where the board, as with Regional Hospital Boards or the Atomic Energy Authority, is primarily financed out of moneys supplied by Parliament, then the mechanism of the two financial Select Committees (or the new Committee on Science and Technology in the latter case) can operate, and the Comptroller and Auditor-General can act in his customary way. In the case of the ordinary run of nationalised industries the accounts are audited by ordinary accountants appointed by the appropriate minister, and the final accounts and auditors' reports are placed before Parliament. Under this procedure the scope for the intervention of the Comptroller and Auditor-General, and thus for the effective use of the Public Accounts Committee, is very severely limited.[32] These difficulties, combined with others about parliamentary questioning, caused pressure for the appointment of a particular Select Committee.

[28] (1956) Cmd. 9672.
[29] (1955) Cmd. 9389.
[30] (1962) Cmnd. 1753.
[31] See 619 H.C.Deb. 1113–1114. From 1956 the financing of gas, electricity and transport was withdrawn from the market to the Exchequer: (1961) Cmnd. 1337. The reconstruction of the capital structure of B.O.A.C. under the Air Corporations Act 1966 can also help.
[32] Chubb, *The Control of Public Expenditure*, p. 145 et seq., and H.C. 235 of 1952–53. The Select Committee on Estimates has no foothold.

The present Select Committee on Nationalised Industries emerged from the proposals of a Select Committee appointed to consider this issue of accountability.[33] The recommendations were not fully accepted, for no specific officer was appointed to help the committee, which was established in 1955. The terms of reference of that committee excluded, *inter alia*, matters which had been decided by or clearly engaged the responsibility of a minister. This exclusion, together with others, left in the opinion of the committee too little room to work.[34] Thereafter new terms of reference were devised, and the committee was established in 1956.[35] That committee (and its successors) has in a series of major reports surveyed the operation of the main nationalised industries, and the reports have produced much valuable material. It has further surveyed its own work, and the report [36] shows that the particular reports have had results in practice beyond this informative function, though they have influenced the boards rather than governments. To some extent it is clear that the existence of this Select Committee has, by affording an opportunity for explanation, lessened the distrust of boards springing from their isolation. Its work remains limited by reason of the limited staff available to it, and a plea for further specialised staff [37] has not been acted upon, except to the limited extent of making available some economic advice.

There exists therefore adequate machinery for periodic review in depth of public boards, which in the case of the B.B.C. is supplemented by the fact that hitherto the charter of the Corporation has always been of limited duration. Thus periodic review by a committee or Royal Commission is ensured. What does not exist in Parliament is machinery for regular supervision. Such machinery would be inconsistent with the aims which led to the establishment of those boards, and it must be remembered that parliamentary time is not infinitely expandable. Each new task that Parliament assumes can only be performed at the cost of some sacrifice of time which would otherwise be available for performing its functions in traditional fields. This position makes it necessary, however, to look at the other controlling devices.

Other administrative controls. As has been indicated, it is clear that internally particular ministries and the Treasury do exercise a supervision which is closer than the statutes might suggest on first-reading.

33 (1952–53) H.C. 235.
34 (1955–56) H.C. 120.
35 Having as its terms of reference " To examine the Reports and Accounts of the Nationalised Industries established by Statute whose controlling Boards are appointed by Ministers of the Crown and whose annual receipts are not wholly or mainly derived from moneys provided by Parliament or advanced from the Exchequer."
36 (1961–62) H.C. 116. Coombes, *The Member of Parliament and the Administration*, surveys the work of this committee, and Hanson, *Parliament and Public Ownership*, sets out good examples of the types of parliamentary intervention.
37 (1958–59) H.C. 276.

Since, however, this supervision is conducted in the form of consultation, and not direction, particular instances of its operation may well not be apparent at the time, in relation to the second group of boards. The first being much more closely connected with ministries, and thus with traditional methods of regulation there is little need for special machinery. The fact that the members of Regional Hospital Boards or of development corporations are chosen from outside the civil service causes a dispersal of power and representation of other interests which may suffice, granted the nature of the service with which they are concerned. In the case of the second group different arrangements exist. For coal, there are under the relevant statutes two central bodies, the Domestic Coal Consumers' Council and the Industrial Coal Consumers' Council, whose functions include considering any representation made by a consumer, and considering anything referred to them by the minister. For steel the Consultative Council abolished in 1953 is revived and can notify its conclusions on matters considered by it (including prices) to the Corporation. From their centralised character and the nature of the trade the activities of these bodies tend to be somewhat general and precatory. For gas and electricity there exist consultative councils for each area, the chairmen being also members of the area boards. The change of name is probably significant [38]; they are much more links than merely complaint-receiving bodies, though on the latter side their activities are somewhat more formalised. Machinery exists whereby failing a suitable response from an area board, the Consultative Council may report to the Electricity Council,[39] or to the minister, as the case may be, and those authorities may intervene with the board.

In relation to air transport the Air Transport Advisory Council formerly existed both to receive complaints, and in its latter days to perform licensing functions. It has been succeeded by the Air Transport Licensing Board, established under the Civil Aviation (Licensing) Act 1960, which is primarily a licensing body, though (under section 4) it has advisory functions. In addition B.E.A. has itself established advisory councils for particular parts of Great Britain, including one for Scotland. In relation to railways there was a dual system. So far as rates were concerned the Transport Tribunal was required to approve and review charges schemes, and to determine any question of reasonableness where a maximum charge had not been fixed.[40] Apart from

[38] The London Electricity Consultative Council in 1962 said that it had three objectives: (1) to encourage the consumer to assist in the more economic use of generating plant, etc.; (2) to obtain the consumer's co-operation in the search for economies in administration; and (3) to secure a fair deal for the consumer.

[39] The individual who is discontented with the response of the Council may also appeal.

[40] The Transport Act 1953 gave to the Commission in general a much greater freedom in relation to charges which it could move within the limits of a charges scheme. This freedom has, outside London, been very greatly increased by the Transport Act 1962. See, generally, Kahn-Freund, *The Law of Inland Transport*; and for the working of the 1947 and 1953 Acts, see Milne and Laing, *The Obligation to Carry*. Typically,

that there were erected under the Transport Act 1947 the Consultative Committees, of which there is a central one, and area committees established by the minister, one of which must be for Scotland and another for Wales and Monmouthshire, both of which annually reported direct to the minister. These bodies could hear complaints, and in particular have been much concerned with problems of closing branch lines. On such issues the committees in effect held public inquiries.

The Transport Act 1962 substantially altered these arrangements. The Transport Tribunal sits in two divisions, the Road Haulage Appeals Division (which is not of present concern) and the London Fares and Miscellaneous Charges Division. This latter division has jurisdiction to make orders in relation to passenger railway fares where the journey is wholly within the London Passenger Area, and road passenger fares within the London Special Area. Such orders are to fix maximum fares. It has a general jurisdiction as to the carriage of mail, and members of the armed forces or police. Apart from these limitations the Railways Board can charge such fares as it thinks fit (s. 43 (3)). Under the Act there is also to be established the Nationalised Transport Advisory Council, consisting of the chairman of the Board and of the Holding Company, a chairman and Vice-chairman of the Council, and not more than five other persons. Its function is to advise the minister, particularly upon co-ordination. The Transport Consultative Committees are continued on the former pattern (s. 56), to consider representations made to them by members of the public, matters referred to them by the minister, or matters which one of the committees may itself raise. The central committee and the area committees for Scotland and for Wales must report annually to the minister. Under this Act the functions of the area committees as respects railway closures are strengthened, and the procedure is formalised (s. 56). Except in this matter the movement, since 1947, has been to free the railways, to a greater or lesser extent, from the controls then established.

It may be noted that the affairs of nationalised industries and of hospitals are outside the jurisdiction of the Parliamentary Commissioner for Administration. On the other hand, while nationalised industries were within the so-called " early-warning system " of the first White Paper on Prices and Incomes, they were brought under the potential jurisdiction of the Prices and Incomes Board, and from September 1967, the Government decided to refer all major increases by those industries to the Board, and the White Paper on Economic and Financial Objectives of 1967 proposes to strengthen that Board so that it could perform functions in relation to these industries akin to those performed by the Comptroller and Auditor-General in relation to central departments.

s. 30 of the Iron and Steel Act 1967 enables a steel producer who is not nationalised to complain to the minister of unfair practices by the Corporation, even though the concept of unfair competition is one which presents a justiciable issue.

Thus the special mechanisms outside Parliament for regulating or controlling the second group of boards are varied in nature and purpose. Sometimes the machinery exists as much to explain the board to the public as for any other purpose, sometimes the machinery can control effectively. At other times it is only advisory. In many cases, especially with the consultative committees, the machinery is probably less effective than was intended, because it is distinct from the ordinary machinery of local or central government, and its existence is too little known.[41] In other cases, where control was originally close, as with the Transport Tribunal, the scope of those controls has been substantially reduced since the original schemes were enacted.

Judicial control. The full position of these boards can only be judged by considering also the role of the court, since in effect each regulator has an effect on each other one. The limits of parliamentary control may have been affected by the existence of the special mechanisms just discussed. Judicial controls are affected by the existence of them, and of parliamentary controls.[42]

Judicial control must clearly exist, but its scope is both affected by, and forms, ideas about the nature of these corporations. What is said here must be linked with what is said later about the general problems of judicial control. The " Charters " of the boards are broadly drawn, and hedged with provisos. It is the " duty " of the Hydro-Electric Board to provide supplies of electricity to meet demands, so far as is practicable, and the board shall, so far as its powers and duties permit, collaborate in carrying out any measures for the economic development and social improvement in its area. Such a formulation, which is not untypical, gives legal power but leaves its scope largely undefined, unless the courts are to assume a capacity to judge what is practicable; and the expertise of courts lies in law, not electrical generation and distribution.[43] Obligations to balance the books and the like may be regarded as obligations which, except in extreme cases, are to be enforced by political means,[44] particularly where, as with the air corporations, the statutory powers of the boards are controllable by the minister. In the most recent statute, the Transport Act 1962, this is made clear by those provisions which direct that particular sections shall not be construed as imposing any

41 The report of the London Electricity Board for 1962 is here significant. Some bodies like the North of Scotland Hydro-Electricity Board have made very considerable use of local authorities to overcome this difficulty.

42 Compare *Fife C.C.* v. *Railway Executive*, 1951 S.C. 499 and *British Oxygen Co. Ltd.* v. *S.W. Scotland Electricity Board*, 1955 S.C. 440 at 457.

43 *Magistrates of Paisley* v. *S. of Scotland Electricity Board*, 1956 S.C. 502; though contrast *Adams* v. *S. of S. for Scotland*, 1958 S.C. 279. A reluctance of the courts to intermeddle is apparent in *Charles Roberts and Co.* v. *British Railways Board* [1964] 3 All E.R. 651.

44 The whole complex of litigation by the British Oxygen Company ending in 1956 S.C.(H.L.) 112 and 1959 S.C.(H.L.) 17 emphasises this point. It is to be noted that that litigation reserved a place for the courts; *cf.* the Report on Railway Wages (1955) Cmd. 9372 and 9352.

form of duty or liability enforceable in any court.[45] In addition to these generalised powers and duties there are others which are more specific, and in relation to these the courts may be more able to intervene. All that can here be indicated are what are thought to be the relevant general principles.

At the most general level, as in relation to the duty to supply electricity quoted above, it seems doubtful if the courts can intervene even in the absence of provisions such as those in the Transport Act. Such matters must be controlled by the minister. This is clear when the minister has specific statutory powers of supervision,[46] hence the default powers of the minister under the National Health Service Act 1946 and the National Health Service (Scotland) Act 1947 (s. 56) would preclude the courts from passing upon the suitability of the general hospital scheme for an area. On the other hand where a particular individual or group is particularly affected as a result of a failure to observe some general principle he may have a remedy in the courts.[47] What interest will suffice is not clear. In effect the dispute is about the scope of the *actio popularis*, and the existing rules (which in themselves are imprecise) were worked out in relation to rather different authorities,[48] and may not be entirely suitable. In particular the definition of the " proprietary " interest which will suffice may require adjustment. Although these generalised duties may not in themselves be capable of enforcement by an individual they may nevertheless influence a court when it is dealing with a more specific problem.[49] Thus it cannot be said that courts are in no way concerned even with these general duties. Where the duties are individualised a remedy may lie,[50] but a different problem of alternative remedies may arise. The relevant statutes may provide for enforcement by prosecution,[51] and in such cases, in the absence of particular damage, this may be the only remedy available.[52]

To some extent the phraseology which makes it difficult to enforce duties has also the effect of making difficult the application of the *ultra vires* principle. At first sight the principle is applicable, since normally a section of each statute prohibits the corporation from disregarding any rule of law. Difficulty arises, however, where, as is customary with

45 See ss. 3 (4), 7 (9), 9 (3) and 10 (4). Similar provisions are contained in the current Transport Bill.
46 *Watt* v. *Kesteven C.C.* [1955] 1 Q.B. 408; and it is made explicit in the Transport Act 1947, s. 3 (5). See generally on the effect of alternative remedies Griffith and Street, *Administrative Law.*
47 *Adams* v. *S. of S. for Scotland*, 1958 S.C. 279. The element of particularity existed as a result of the terms of a former endowment.
48 *D. & J. Nicol* v. *Dundee Harbour Trustees*, 1915 S.C.(H.L.) 7; *Conn* v. *Magistrates of Renfrew* (1906) 8 F. 905.
49 *British Oxygen Co. Ltd.* v. *S.W. Scotland Electricity Board*, 1955 S.C. 440 at 462.
50 *British Oxygen Co. Ltd.* v. *S.W. Scotland Electricity Board*, 1956 S.C.(H.L.) 112.
51 As is done in the Gas and Electricity Acts.
52 For instances of such prosecution, see Report of the Northern Gas Board, 1962, § 166. The arguments here on the exclusion of other remedies are general.

the second group of corporations, a "general powers" clause is added. In such cases it has been said that a power to carry on activities incidental to the primary purpose is not without limit, even though the activities claimed to be incidental would be convenient.[53] However, except where express prohibitions are incorporated into the statutes,[54] or where it can be shown that there is an improper motive, it is difficult to see how the courts could apply the doctrine in relation to general activities. Control must here lie primarily with the minister, as it is made to do expressly by the Air Corporations Act 1949, s. 3 (2). The invalidation of acts on grounds of an improper motive (i.e., détournement rather than excès de pouvoir) presents its own difficulties. Where the act was clearly and exclusively directed by "malice" or by a wrongful purpose no doubt it may be overturned.[55] Where, however, there is a mixture of motives, good and bad, the answer is not clear, but it would seem to require a very strong case before the courts would intervene, and in many cases, granted the rules of recovery of documents, it may well be impossible to get sufficient proof.

It is in regard to such matters, which may well be of the greatest importance to individuals, that the exercise of judicial control is most difficult,[56] though it is often also in relation to them that other controls may also be relatively ineffective. In the more straightforward matters of contractual and delictual liability the courts are free to intervene,[57] subject to the general rules about the interplay of statutory powers and duties and private rights and to a possible adjustment of remedies.[58]

The general constitutional position. Generally it may be said that these new institutions have not been properly absorbed into our constitutional system. The intention was to break, on a national scale, with traditional methods by using mechanisms which had formerly only been used (save for untypical examples) on a local scale. The successful accomplishment of that intention required a greater adjustment of the traditional machinery of government than has hitherto proved to be acceptable to governments. The result has been that while new boards are created, and the constitutional theory of the boards has remained unchanged, in practice there has been, behind these forms, something of a repetition of the nineteenth-century process, that is to say, ministerial influence has tended if anything to increase, so that substantial

---

[53] D. & J. Nicol v. Dundee Harbour Trustees, 1915 S.C.(H.L.) 7; Charles Roberts and Co. v. British Railways Board [1964] 3 All E.R. 651. Considerable difficulty will be found in controlling the Steel Corporation as a result of the Iron and Steel Act 1967, s. 2.

[54] e.g., Electricity Act 1947, s. 2 (3).

[55] Compare Earl Fitzwilliam's Wentworth Estates Co. v. Min. of Town and Country Planning [1951] 2 K.B. 284 (affirmed [1952] A.C. 362) and Iveagh v. Minister of Housing and Local Government [1961] 3 All E.R. 98.

[56] Part of the difficulty may lie in the absence of a specific jurisprudence of public law.

[57] Virtue v. Police Commissioners of Alloa (1873) 1 R. 285, where a former rule, once rejected, was reapplied. See, too, Mersey Docks and Harbour Board v. Gibbs (1866) L.R. 1 H.L. 93.   [58] Mitchell, The Contracts of Public Authorities.

differences from organisation on a ministerial form have tended to diminish.[59] This tendency has probably been more marked in fact than it has been in law, though Acts such as the Transport Act 1962 increase the recognition in law of this tendency. Such a situation provokes constitutional problems, since true lines of responsibility do not accord with appearances, and these problems still require to be resolved.

Interwoven with this uncertainty is another uncertainty, namely, as to the classification in law of these boards. Initially there could be substantial dispute about whether or not the boards were Crown servants.[60] While this argument can continue, and can on occasion be important,[61] it is to a large extent excluded in modern statutes by a clear provision on this point.[62] What is of continuing importance is the uncertainty about the treatment in law of these bodies. Whereas some may be declared to be " public authorities," the extent to which such a declaration is significant is not clear. Little difficulty arises in relation to boards of the first group. A regional hospital board is a public authority, in the sense that it is created by an official act and is primarily financed from national revenues. It is also a public authority in the sense that it is providing a social service in the national interest, and the character of a " service " may have its effects on ordinary rules of law,[63] and upon normal remedies. So far as the second group is concerned they are clearly public authorities judged by the criteria of methods of creation and to a considerable extent in relation to finance. Even if the fact that their deficits are met from national revenues is disregarded, their purposes and circumstances prevent capital being raised for them by means appropriate to private corporations.[64] They are also public authorities in that they are intended to serve, to some extent, public purposes as distinct from purely economic purposes, and in their actings it is clear that such public or national considerations rather than purely economic ones have on occasion been dominant. These characteristics are again capable of affecting legal obligations and remedies.[65] Nevertheless, this public character is not always apparent,

---

[59] See particularly Special Report of the Select Committee on Nationalised Industries (1955–56) H.C. 120, and for further examples, the report of that Committee on the Air Corporations (1958–59) H.C. 213. Consider in relation to B.E.A. 756 H.C.Deb. 779 and the evidence to the Select Committee (1966–67) H.C. 673.

[60] Griffith and Street, *op. cit.* Chap. VII, and the authorities there referred to.

[61] *Adams* v. *S. of S. for Scotland*, 1958 S.C. 279 appears to be fundamentally in conflict with *Nottingham No. 1 Area H.M.C.* v. *Owen* [1958] 1 Q.B. 50. *Cf. Launceston Corporation* v. *Hydro-Electric Commission* (1959) 100 C.L.R. 654 at 662 and Friedman and Benjafield, *Administrative Law*, 2nd ed., pp. 125–128.

[62] *e.g.*, s. 2 (8) of the New Towns Act 1959; Transport Act 1962, s. 30.

[63] See the argument of Lord President Cooper in *Hayward* v. *Edinburgh Royal Infirmary*, 1954 S.C. 453 at 478; *cf. Barber* v. *Manchester Regional Hospital Board* [1958] 1 All E.R. 322. In contrast to *Barber's* case the full consequences of the nature of the employment are emphasised in *Palmer* v. *Inverness Hospitals Board of Management*, 1963 S.L.T. 124 at 125.

[64] See the Herbert Report on Electricity Supply (1956) Cmd. 9672; and see (1961) Cmnd. 1337, § 13.

[65] *B.T.C.* v. *Westmorland C.C.* [1958] A.C. 126 recognises this in principle.

and the effects of its existence are not universal, either because logically the liability in particular circumstances is not, or should not be, affected by the public character of one of the actors,[66] or because, in relation to the facts in question, the corporation may be carrying out a purely business transaction as would a purely private body. Just as the public service character may be overemphasised so may be the commercial character, and just as uncertainty about the nature of these bodies is at present reflected in general constitutional controls, so also is it reflected in more detailed rules of law.[67]

It is probably a mistake, in this context, to attempt to classify these bodies for all purposes; what must be looked to is the particular function, or the manner in which the public purposes of the body will be affected.[68] Thus concentration upon the idea of public duties may aid in determining the extent to which ordinary rules of law may require variation. This concentration and the resultant increased segregation of these duties (which resembles, but does not coincide with, the classification into " day-to-day " activities and others) is likely to help a rationalisation of the broader constitutional controls. This process will be all the more difficult since unfortunately the idea of public utility, which marked so strongly one group of institutions and which influenced the conception of these newer boards, has tended to disappear,[69] at a time when it would have been helpful to expand it. The classification into governmental and private bodies (which is all that then remains) is too rough and ready to be useful for a modern complex state, and attempts to use it have tended, it seems, to produce constitutional anomalies and inadequacies. Here the proper treatment of these hybrid bodies has, it seems, yet to be worked out. That process may require a rejection of Dicey's concept of a uniform system of law,[70] for it is that concept which may underlie much of the uncertainty of the present rules of law, which by hindering one form of control, through the courts, makes all the more difficult the application of other methods of constitutional regulation.

[66] *Edwards* v. *N.C.B.* [1949] 1 K.B. 704.
[67] As, for example, in the decisions of the Air Licensing Board dealing with conflicting applications from private air-lines and nationalised corporations.
[68] Mitchell, *The Contracts of Public Authorities*, Chap. V.
[69] *Marshall* v. *Scottish Milk Marketing Board*, 1956 S.C.(H.L.) 37; *Western Heritable Investment Co. Ltd.* v. *Glasgow Corporation*, 1956 S.C.(H.L.) 64. At one time these ideas, and those of a public service, were the formative ideas: *Farrier* v. *Elder and Scott*, June 21, 1799, F.C.; *Whitfield* v. *Lord Despencer* (1778) 2 Cowp. 754.
[70] See *ante*, p. 57, and *post*, p. 320.

CHAPTER 13

LOCAL GOVERNMENT

A FULL discussion of local government would be beyond the range of the present volume, and for an exploration of all the intricacies of that important branch of law the reader must look elsewhere.[1] The present purpose is merely to complete a sketch of the major institutions as part of the constitutional framework of our society. In that sketch particular emphasis will be placed upon the Scottish system.[2] Although there are broad similarities in the evolution of local government in Scotland and England there are nevertheless substantial but sometimes subtle differences between the two systems; hence an equal treatment of both might lead to too much detail.

Historical. As in England, the foundation of local government in Scotland is to be found in the burgh.[3] In Scotland a distinction must be drawn between royal burghs and burghs of barony and of regality, the first having superior status and privileges (particularly in monopolistic trading rights) and also heavier burdens, in that they bore the burghal share of land tax. The burghs became closed corporations, with the merchants holding a dominant position within them. Neither in this nor in the abuse of burgh property is their history distinctive. This situation endured until 1833.[4] The organisation of the royal burghs in the Convention of Royal Burghs [5] had broader constitutional effects. In so far as it could act as a burghal Parliament it detracted from the Parliament of Scotland and its existence tended to isolate the burghal

---

1 See Whyte, *Local Government in Scotland*; Bennett Miller, *An Outline of Administrative and Local Government Law in Scotland*; McLarty, *A Source Book of Administrative Law in Scotland*; Campbell, *The District Councillor*. There is added reason for brevity since both in Scotland and in England local government is being examined by Royal Commissions, which it is hoped will recommend major changes. Some of the elements of the problem can be seen in Robson, *Local Government in Crisis.*

2 For England and Wales, see Robson, *Development of Local Government*, Hart, *Introduction to the Law of Local Government*, and Jennings, *Principles of Local Government Law.*

3 Dickinson, *The Sheriff Court Book of Fife*; *Early Records of the Burgh of Aberdeen* and *The Court Book of the Barony of Carnwath*. More shortly see Pryde, *Central and Local Government in Scotland since 1707*, *The Scottish Burgh in Decline*, and Pryde and Mackie, *Local Government in Scotland.*

4 As good a picture as any of their working is to be found in John Galt, *The Provost*, a book which is not entirely out of date, and see Dickinson, *John Galt, The Provost and the Burgh* (the John Galt Lecture, 1954).

5 Pagan, *The Convention of Royal Burghs.* This body, which was once of considerable legislative and administrative importance, declined after the Union, particularly after the Reform Act 1832. It remains of greater importance than the modern associations of local authorities since it cuts across classifications based on size or interest and is thus capable of producing a national viewpoint, since it now comprises all burghs.

members from others. Apart from these "governmental" bodies it must be remembered that the church was carrying out what have become to be regarded as local government functions. This factor contributed to the delayed evolution of local government organisations outside the burghs, which began with the establishment of the Commissioners of Supply by the Act of 1667.[6] These were initially solely concerned with the land tax, but to them were subsequently added local government functions. Thus, in Scotland, as in England, the "system" of local government was in origin a dual one,[7] distinguishing between burghs and counties. The fact that in Scotland the "judicial" element (which was apparent in England because of the use of quarter sessions) was much less [8] has left its mark on the general control of local government. This duality has continued to mark the organisation of local government in England to a far greater extent than it does in Scotland.[9]

In Scotland reform of the burghs started in 1833, both as to franchise and function. In that year there was introduced, as a result of the Burghs and Police (Scotland) Act, a new important category of burgh—police burghs (the word "police" having the significance of the word when used in the phrase "the police power" in the U.S.A., and embracing watching, lighting and sanitary functions). These police burghs could be separate bodies or an historic burgh could adopt the Police Acts, in which case there would exist a dual system of administration within its boundaries. That duality endured until the Burgh Police (Scotland) Act 1892 and the Town Councils (Scotland) Act 1900, which produced a degree of uniformity. County councils had emerged with the Local Government (Scotland) Act 1889, though not to the entire exclusion of other bodies,[10] and ultimately a general framework was established by the Local Government (Scotland) Act 1929, which, as amended by the Local Government (Scotland) Act of 1947, still provides the framework of the administrative structure. In the course of this development there had been absorbed into the system various *ad hoc* boards.[11]

The administrative framework. The authorities for the purposes of local government consist of counties, counties of cities, large burghs and

---

[6] A.P.S. VII, 540 (an Act of the Convention of the Estates).

[7] In England the distinction was between the borough system and that of government through quarter sessions in the counties. The significant role of the sheriff in Scotland has not affected the question of judicial review in the same way.

[8] The justices of the peace, never as important in Scotland as in England, had some local government functions but tended to give ground before the Commissioners of Supply.

[9] The Local Government Act 1933 was the first universal Act, but it preserved elements of the differences, which still have their effect upon boundary problems.

[10] Over 1,300 authorities were concerned with local government in Scotland before the Act of 1929.

[11] Most notably the school boards established under the Education (Scotland) Act 1872, which were abolished by the Education (Scotland) Act 1918, being replaced by *ad hoc* education authorities, which survived until the Local Government (Scotland) Act 1929, when counties and the counties of cities became education authorities.

small burghs. These bodies are scheduled to the 1947 Act,[12] and except as to small burghs there is thus imparted a certain rigidity. County councils consist of members elected directly for the landward areas, *i.e.*, those areas not comprised within a burgh, and of members representing the burghs who are indirectly elected, being elected by the town councils to serve on the county council.[13] The whole council is renewable every third year (but a member of the second group ceases to hold office on ceasing to be a town councillor). Each council elects its own convener and vice-convener. Within the area of a county council there exist, for the landward areas, district councils, established under a scheme made by the county. (These district councils are by no means equal in status or powers to the English county district councils.) The district council consists of the county councillors for the district, together with members specifically elected to it, though contested elections are rare. To these bodies are given few and minor functions (which may account for the lack of electoral interest), but the county may appoint the district council its agent to discharge other functions.

Town councils, whether for large or small burghs, consist of members elected either on a ward basis or on a burgh basis. These councils are renewable by thirds, one-third of the members retiring each year.[14] The council elects its provost, honorary treasurer and bailies. The provost and treasurer hold office for three years from their election, the bailies until they are due to retire as councillors.[15] Large and small burghs are not, in structure distinct one from the other. The distinction is in function. Whereas large burghs exercise a wide variety of functions, the most important function left with small burghs is probably housing. Similarly, the counties of cities are not, in general, distinctive in composition,[16] in function they are all-purpose authorities combining the functions of counties and burghs. Apart from these primary authorities, local authorities may establish joint committees or boards for specific purposes, or the Secretary of State may under section 120 of the 1947 Act compel the combination of particular authorities for specific purposes. A county council may establish special districts for administration in a particular area. Such special districts are not autonomous authorities as are district councils.

12 Though it must be noted that by s. 118 the counties of Perth and Kinross, and those of Moray and Nairn, are combined for many purposes.
13 These members have limited voting rights; s. 72 of the 1947 Act.
14 The strict rotation of members may be upset by various factors; see s. 17 of the 1947 Act.
15 In contrast to the position of aldermen in England the election of a councillor as bailee does not cause a vacancy as councillor. Provost, treasurer and bailies are all elected from among the councillors, whereas a mayor or alderman need not be. The election of a provost or treasurer may have the effect of extending his term and of accelerating the retiral of another councillor from the same ward.
16 But see s. 330 of the 1947 Act. That section incorporated in the councils of the four cities and of Perth contain *ex officio* members. By the Local Government (Scotland) Act 1947 (Amendment) Act 1965 these members were deprived of their right to vote in council, etc., meetings.

Alteration of areas. Very limited powers exist to alter county boundaries. Burgh boundaries may, subject to an appeal to the Court of Session, be altered by the sheriff (s. 131 of the 1947 Act). There is no machinery (save an Act of Parliament, and for this purpose the Scottish private legislation procedure is inappropriate) which can create a new large burgh, but the sheriff may, after inquiry, create a new small burgh out of any populous place, with a population of at least 2,000, on the application of twelve or more persons. A small burgh may enter into an agreement with the county for its dissolution. Thus, while at the top of the scale of local authorities there is considerable rigidity in the machinery, at the bottom there is considerable potential flexibility.

Elections. The franchise for local elections, in addition to the requirement of British nationality (or citizenship of the Republic of Ireland) and the absence of disqualifications similar to those operative in parliamentary elections, depends upon residence or the occupation of any rateable heritage of the yearly value of not less than £10. Peers are, of course, entitled to vote in such elections. Members of a local authority, in addition to being British subjects of full age, must be either registered as local government electors, or have resided in the area of the authority for the twelve months preceding nomination.[17] Disqualification, in addition to those also operative for parliamentary elections, arises from holding either by himself or through a partner any place of profit in the gift of the authority or of any relevant joint board. In general, elections are regulated in a like manner to parliamentary elections, but no deposit is required. An obligation to appoint an agent was imposed by section 55 of the Representation of the People Act 1949, and he may now be paid. The regulations limiting expenses are applicable with necessary modifications; thus a much lower limit is fixed for total permissible expenses. Clearly the regulations relating to corrupt and illegal practices apply.[18]

Functions. Normally functions are allocated to local authorities according to type of authority. Thus, counties are exclusively responsible for education within their areas, and they have responsibility for health, housing and highways. These last functions are, however, shared with other authorities on differing bases. While the county is responsible under the Public Health (Scotland) Acts for all public health services in the landward areas, in small burghs lesser functions are entrusted to the burgh. Under the National Health Service (Scotland)

[17] For qualification of electors see Representation of the People Act 1949, s. 21; as to councillors see the Act of 1947, Part II.

[18] The general rules for the conduct of elections are now contained in the Representation of the People Act 1949, Sched. III (Scotland) and Sched. II (England). The law relating to corrupt and illegal practices was amended and consolidated by the 1949 Act, Parts II and III. For a commentary on this and a comparison with the older Law see Schofield, *Local Government Elections* (4th ed.).

Act 1947, local health authorities are the county councils and the town councils of large burghs. So far as roads are concerned the county is again similarly responsible for all roads in the landward areas (with the exception of trunk roads which are the responsibility of the central government—*i.e.*, the Secretary of State for Scotland) and for classified roads in small burghs, the town councils of which are responsible for public streets. For planning, the county has (with minor exceptions), authority for the whole area, with the exception of large burghs (and the small burghs of St. Andrews and Thurso). Housing is the responsibility of the burghs, the county being concerned only with the landward areas. Thus large burghs are entrusted with classified roads within their boundaries, public health functions and those under the National Health Service, and planning functions in addition to the functions which can be exercised by a small burgh. This distribution is theoretically accounted for by the size and probable wealth of authorities. Nevertheless, variations in size of population and wealth of authorities of any one group create difficulties.[19] To some extent, as with planning, the major consideration may be appropriateness of area, but again, like variations cause similar difficulties. The counties of cities, being all-purpose authorities, combine within their areas the functions of large burghs and of counties. This modern statutory classification of authorities appears to be critical in relation to powers. While there are suggestions that the royal burghs may have additional powers by virtue of that character, it is doubtful how extensive those are,[20] and, with the exception of the possible enlargement of powers by local legislation (a process which has been extensive in the counties of cities), the powers of local authorities are those given by general legislation and are determined by this grouping.

Three services should be mentioned specifically. Under the Fire Services Act 1947, the pattern of organisation of the service in Scotland departed from that then established in England. Under that Act eleven combined areas were established for running the service, so that it was removed from the immediate control of any one type of local authority. In relation to police there has again been a process of concentration. Police authorities are, subject to amalgamation, counties and the four counties of cities, and the large burghs scheduled to the Police (Scotland)

---

[19] Among the counties, Sutherland has a population of 12,281, an area of 1,297,914 acres and a rateable value of £188,000. Lanark has a population of 572,102, an area of 535,792 acres and a rateable value of £9,834,733. Among small burghs there are New Galloway, population 323, rateable value, £5,012, and Grangemouth, population 18,924 and rateable value £940,237. East Kilbride, a small burgh until 1967, had a larger population than over half the large burghs. The White Paper, *The Modernisation of Local Government in Scotland* (Cmnd. 2067), proposed adjustments in structure and function to overcome those difficulties.

[20] See *Graham* v. *Glasgow Corporation*, 1936 S.C. 108; and compare *Att.-Gen.* v. *Leicester Corporation* [1943] Ch. 86. The preservation of the rights and privileges of the royal burghs by the Act of Union is not to be construed as a permanent provision, many of these rights could not stand against a changing society.

Act 1967.[21] In relation to this service the pressures are towards larger areas. This was also true in relation to water supply. The Water (Scotland) Act 1967 contains provision for thirteen regions, one of which somewhat inconveniently includes Orkney and Zetland with a mainland area. In addition to the ordinary regions there exists the Central Scotland Water Development Board to co-ordinate the activities of the Regional Boards within its area.

The functions discussed are those which can be called administrative. There are others, which are regulatory or legislative. Under the Building (Scotland) Act 1959, for example, a dean of guild court or, outside burghs, a building authority composed of members of the local authority can regulate buildings under the Building Standards (Scotland) Regulations which replace local by-laws. Among this group of functions may also be put those which can be regarded as policing in a civil sense. The inspection of such things as day nurseries or nursing homes may be as important as older inspecting functions such as those related to weights and measures. Recent legislation, such as the Weights and Measures Act 1963, can increase the importance of some of these functions. To get all these manifold functions in perspective it may be noted that in the City of Edinburgh, as an example, expenditure on education and highways exceeds half the total expenditure, and those items with expenditure of police and housing amount to over two-thirds of the total. Expenditure on education alone comes to close on half the total expenditure. There is, further, a general power conferred by the Local Government (Scotland) Act 1947 on counties and burghs to make by-laws for good rule and government, and in addition many other statutes have conferred legislative powers in relation to specific matters upon local authorities.[22] The power is exercised subject to a confirming authority, normally the Secretary of State or the sheriff.

This power of making by-laws is limited, but, nevertheless, deserves further attention, since the cases show the attitude of courts to local authorities. It should be noticed that the mere fact of confirmation does not prevent any subsequent challenge to validity in law, since the confirming authority is as much concerned with the expediency of the by-law in all the circumstances as it is with questions of law in the

---

[21] In fact by 1962 amalgamations had reduced the forces to 19 county forces, and 14 forces in the burghs and counties of cities. The Royal Commission on the Police envisaged an extension of this process (see the Report (1962) Cmnd. 1728). Under the Police (Scotland) Act 1966, consolidated by the Act of 1967, the process of amalgamation was facilitated. The total number of forces is now 18 county forces and seven others.

[22] A county council has by s. 300 of the Act of 1947 powers in relation to vagrancy and nuisances. That Act lays down a general procedural code for by-laws. Royal burghs have probably some non-statutory powers of making by-laws, but these have ceased to be significant. The Building (Scotland) Act 1959 authorises the Secretary of State to replace by-laws by regulations.

sense of *vires*.[23] By-laws must be *intra vires*; those words mean not merely that the by-law must be within the terms of the authorising statute, but also that the power is exercised for the proper purposes, and not for collateral ones.[24] Moreover, it is said that the by-law must not be in conflict with the general law. That phrasing is inelegant, since if the by-law is to do anything it must of necessity alter the pre-existing law. What appears to be intended is that the by-law must not make lawful anything declared unlawful by general law, and must not take away any right specifically given.[25] It is also said that by-laws must not be unreasonable or uncertain. Unreasonableness here goes beyond the question of expediency, it must in effect amount to oppression,[26] and the courts will be extremely reluctant to interfere with the exercise of a discretion of this type by an elected body.[27] It is difficult clearly to distinguish cases of uncertainty from those of unreasonableness. Uncertainty may be an aspect of unreasonableness, where, for example, the by-law is not precise in its terms but merely confers too wide a discretion upon a local authority.[28] It may, however, be an independent head of validity, since a breach of a by-law being punishable as a crime, any one is entitled to reasonable notice of an offence.[29] It is a commonplace in England to obtain an injunction against a person who persistently breaks a by-law.[30] This process has met with criticism on the grounds that it can involve an increased penalty (as a result of proceedings for contempt

23 *David Lawson Ltd.* v. *Torrance*, 1929 J.C. 119; *Glasgow Corporation* v. *Glasgow Churches Council*, 1944 S.C. 97, a good authority on the issue of confirmation; and see *Burgh of Dunblane, Petitioners*, 1947 S.L.T.(Sh.Ct.) 27. It was at one stage suggested that confirmation by the Secretary of State would exclude subsequent judicial review: *Crichton* v. *Forfar Road Trustees* (1886) 13 R.(J.) 99. It is now clear that this is not so, and the case is typical of an era of uncertainty as to how courts should deal with the emerging phenomena of a modern state. The doubts expressed in *Stewart* v. *Todrick*, 1908 S.C.(J.) 8 are indicative of the same uncertainty. For English law see Hart, *op. cit.* Uncertainty about the effect of judicial review can persist: *Rossi* v. *Magistrates of Edinburgh* (1903) 5 F. 480 at 584 was said to be "a simple case." The House of Lords in (1904) 7 F.(H.L.) 85 reversed the decision in the Outer House and Second Division.

24 *Somerville* v. *Lord Advocate*, 1933 S.L.T. 48; *Brock* v. *Forth Pilotage*, 1947 S.N. 41. While chartered corporations have certain non-statutory powers of making by-laws (*University of Glasgow* v. *Faculty of Physicians and Surgeons* (1837) 15 S. 736), it is doubtful if, in the field of local government, great reliance could be placed upon these; *cf. Graham* v. *Glasgow Corporation*, 1936 S.C. 108.

25 *Rae* v. *Hamilton* (1904) 6 F.(J.) 42 and *Aldred* v. *Miller*, 1925 J.C. 21 at 27. In general the rules as to validity are uniform throughout the kingdom; compare the reliance on *Kruse* v. *Johnston* [1898] 2 Q.B. 91 in these cases. "Unreasonableness" and *ultra vires* may coalesce: *Mixnam Properties Ltd.* v. *Chertsey U.D.C.* [1965] A.C. 735.

26 *Glasgow Corporation* v. *Glasgow Churches Council, supra*, note 23.

27 *Robt. Baird Ltd.* v. *Glasgow Corporation*, 1935 S.C.(H.L.) 21. It is probable that the reluctance is increased where the order has been made or confirmed by a minister as a result of the doctrine of ministerial responsibility: *cf. Crichton* v. *Forfar Road Trustees, supra*, note 23. It is also probable that it is now more difficult to establish unreasonableness than was formerly the case.

28 *McGregor* v. *Disselduff*, 1907 S.C.(J.) 21.

29 *Allan* v. *Howman*, 1918 J.C. 50 and *Herkes* v. *Dickie*, 1958 J.C. 51; but see *Marshall* v. *Clarke*, 1957 J.C. 68 as to what is uncertainty of standard.

30 *Att.-Gen.* v. *Harris* [1961] 1 W.L.R. 1200; [1961] 1 Q.B. 74; and see 77 L.Q.R. 25 and [1960] *Public Law* 415.

of court) beyond that contemplated by legislation. It is asserted that the remedy of interdict in like circumstances is not available in Scotland. It seems probable, however, that the assertion goes beyond the present state of the authorities.[31]

One difficulty, in Scotland, in describing the powers of local authorities lies in the fact that local legislation is there much more significant than is usually the case in England. This is especially true in the case of the counties of cities, and reference to the Dundee Corporation (Consolidated Powers) Order Confirmation Act 1957, or the Edinburgh Corporation Order Confirmation Act 1967, will make apparent the scope of these special powers. They substantially extend or otherwise vary the powers available under the general law even in such matters as powers of arrest and search or rights of public meeting. In any particular case, reference must therefore be made to local legislation, and the significance of the Private Legislation Procedure (Scotland) Act 1936 must be judged against this background.

Method of operation. It will be observed that functions are entrusted to county councils, town councils, etc. In theory of law it is, in general, the council which administers or decides. In practice councils work through a committee system, which may, with smaller authorities, not be significant in one sense, since all, or virtually all, the council may make up a committee. Committees may have matters referred to them, or may have delegated powers (except the power to borrow or levy a rate), the education committee in particular having a high degree of autonomy. That committee is also distinguished by the fact that since it is established under distinct legislation it often includes co-opted members, in contrast to the general rule for committees under section 116 of the 1947 Act, which provides that they shall consist of members of the authority only. Some committees, such as the finance committee, are mandatory. The distinction between the council sitting as such, and sitting as a committee of the whole, was at one stage of importance, since the Press and the public had no right to be present at a meeting in committee, but under the Public Bodies (Admission to Meetings) Act 1960, this rule has been altered.[32] There is then a marked difference from the working of the central government. There can be no Cabinet system nor ministerial responsibility, though in practice the chairmen of

---

[31] *Mags. of Buckhaven, etc.* v. *Wemyss Coal Co.*, 1932 S.C. 201. It seems that the Lord President's judgment relies too heavily on *Tay District Fishery Board* v. *Robertson* (1887) 15 R. 40, and upon assumptions about the position of the Attorney-General in England which are not entirely borne out by cases such as *Att.-Gen.* v. *Harris (supra).* In any event the case turned primarily on a question of title to sue. It is to be noted that Lord Sands very clearly reserved his opinion on the point of the availability of an interdict.

[32] Subject to reservations, where confidentiality in administration is required, this Act confers on the Press and public a right to be present at meetings of local authorities, local water authorities and education committees, but not at committee meetings, unless the committee consists of the authority. The Act can be circumvented if the committee consists of all but one of the members of the authority.

committees are recognised as having distinct responsibilities (above all in the case of the treasurer), and the party system exists in a more rudimentary form.[33]

These differences in method are apparent in much of the law. So far as membership is concerned, there is an insistence on locality for candidature, and since the operation of the system involves a heavy expenditure of time, members are entitled to certain allowances to compensate for loss.[34] Above all, the conduct of members is much more strictly regulated by law in relation to disabilities arising from financial interests,[35] and to the personal responsibility of members for wrongful expenditure through the mechanism of surcharge, which will be subsequently discussed. Similarly, there is a tight regulation of the officers of local authorities. There is regulation of the officers who must be appointed,[36] and regulation of the qualifications which must be held by officers, as well as of questions of administrative morality.[37] It has, moreover, long been recognised that the relationship of a local authority to its officers is not the usual master-and-servant relationship,[38] and in certain circumstances an officer has a right or obligation of independent action, since he is regarded as also being a servant of the public.[39] Further, as will appear, there is often a tight control exercised by the central government in relation to officers.

Finance. Apart from the fund known as the common good in the burghs, which is the residue of the ancient burgh properties, local authorities rely on two sources of revenue, rates, and grants from the central government. The income derived from the common good has become insignificant in relation to general local government expenditure and it is used to supplement the main sources of revenue in minor

---

33 Though in the larger authorities nevertheless in a significant form, party meetings outside the council chamber may determine conduct within it, and a system of whips exists.

34 Public Authorities (Allowances) Act 1961, and the legislation there referred to, and the Local Government (Scotland) Act 1966, s. 36.

35 Local Government (Scotland) Act 1947, ss. 73, 101 and 126; Local Government Act 1948, s. 131; Local Government (Miscellaneous Provisions) Act 1953, s. 16; Local Government Act 1933, s. 76 (as amended). The Local Government (Pecuniary Interests) (Scotland) Act 1966 and the Local Government (Pecuniary Interests) Act 1964 have removed the disabilities when the interest is remote. Standing Orders or local legislation may increase the strictness of these provisions, as is the case in Edinburgh.

36 See, *e.g.,* Part IV of the 1947 Act. By s. 85 the town clerk must, save with the consent of the Secretary of State, be distinct from the town chamberlain. Offices such as those of medical officer of health or sanitary inspector are also closely regulated.

37 ss. 101 and 102 of the 1947 Act.

38 *Mags. of Montrose* v. *Strachan* (1710) Mor. 13118; *Simpson* v. *Todd* (1824) 3 S. 150; *Morrison* v. *Abernethy School Board* (1876) 3 R. 945; and s. 100 of the 1947 Act. Unlike the position in England the provisions in s. 39 of the Police (Scotland) Act 1967 making the chief constable the appropriate defender are not yet in force.

39 Consider the implications of s. 201 (1), proviso (*b*), of the 1947 Act.

ways.[40] Rates are a local tax upon the occupiers of heritable property,[41] based upon a notional annual value, which is determined upon a rather different basis for dwelling-houses and non-industrial hereditaments and for other properties.[42] This annual value is determined in a variety of ways, too complex to be here discussed.[43] The effect of valuation is complicated by the process of derating. Agricultural lands are entirely derated, industrial and freight transport lands and heritages are, under the Local Government and Miscellaneous Financial Provisions (Scotland) Act 1958, derated up to 50 per cent., but this benefit was intended to go as from 1966–67 under the Local Government (Financial Provisions) (Scotland) Act 1963; it has, however, now been extended by the Rating of Industry (Scotland) Order 1965 to 1970–71. There are also other relatively minor exemptions, such as churches and lands held for charitable purposes.[44] Valuations are made by the assessor of a county or of one of the counties of cities, in contrast to the position in England where valuation is made by an officer chosen by the Commissioners of Inland Revenue. In practice the assessor has a considerable degree of independence. It is his responsibility to draw up the valuation roll, and, apart from an administrative appeal to him, appeal lies to the valuation appeal committee for the area, which committee is appointed by the sheriff. Thence appeal lies to the Lands Valuation Appeal Court, consisting of three judges of the Court of Session, from which there is no appeal.[45] The raising of money by the actual levy of a rate is the function of rating authorities which are county councils for the landward areas, and town councils for burghs. Other authorities obtain their necessary funds by requisitioning (precepting in England) on the rating authority. The latter must thus levy a rate sufficient to meet its own requirements as well as those of appropriate requisitioning authorities. This system produces a consolidated rate demand, but has the disadvantage of dividing the odium of collecting from the pleasure of spending. It is evident that this system of annual finance requires to

[40] *Graham* v. *Glasgow Corporation*, 1936 S.C. 108. Expenditure is regulated in that it must be for purposes consistent with the public good, and for the general benefit: *Kemp* v. *Glasgow Corporation*, 1920 S.C.(H.L.) 73; and see s. 183 of the 1947 Act. Formerly the common good was a fund often much abused, and sometimes dissipated; see Royal Commission on Municipal Corporations (Scotland) 1835.

[41] Until the Valuation and Rating (Scotland) Act 1956, they were also levied upon owners. See the Sorn Committee Report (1954) Cmd. 9244.

[42] Valuation and Rating (Scotland) Act 1956, s. 6. The law in Scotland was thus brought much closer to that of England.

[43] For details see Armour's *Valuation* (3rd ed.).

[44] The main exemptions had their origin in economic measures to stimulate or subsidise particular areas of activity. Railway and electricity hereditaments are exempt, but make contributions to local authorities on the basis of their own legislation. For the exemption of charities see s. 4 of the 1962 Act. See now " Recent Reforms and the Ratepayer," 1967 S.L.T.(News) 125–130. The equivalent section in the English Rating and Valuation (Miscellaneous Provisions) Act 1955 has been a fruitful source of litigation; see Bean and Lockwood, *Rating and Valuation Practice*.

[45] In England appeals run through local appeal courts to the Lands Tribunal from which, through the machinery of a case stated, the matter may reach the House of Lords. The effect of House of Lords decisions in Scotland was discussed in *Assessor for Aberdeen* v. *Collie*, 1932 S.C. 304.

be supplemented by long-term borrowing for capital purposes, as well as short-term borrowing for current needs. Such borrowing is authorised, subject, in most cases, to ministerial control, by section 258 of the 1947 Act, as well as by other particular statutes.[46]

Local authority grants. This system of dependence on one local tax is a rigid one, and the fact of this dependence necessarily gives the central government a major place in the system of local government. The deficiencies of the system, even if there were not other causes, would lead to the intervention by, or participation of, the central government. It is evident that there is no necessary equation of the needs of a district and its ability to raise money through rates. Very often the greater the needs, the less that ability. This and other factors make government grants essential,[47] together with some redistribution of rating wealth. Specific grants had for long been made, but from 1929 block grants (which were made to the authority at large, and covered a range of services) began to be introduced. Today central government grants now fall into two main categories, general and specific. A new system of central government grants came into operation in the local authority financial year 1967–68, under the Local Government (Scotland) Act 1966. These grants, known as rate support grants, replace the former Exchequer equalisation grants and the general grant, and in addition take a further step in shifting the burden of local authority expenditure onto the shoulders of the general body of taxpayers.

The rate support grants are divided into three elements, the needs element, which corresponds with the former general grant, the resources element, which corresponds with the former Exchequer equalisation grant, and the domestic element, which is a new conception, amounting to a measure of derating of dwelling-houses (but not of private garages). Whereas previously the total amount paid in grants was merely the sum of all the parts, now the Secretary of State is required to determine the total amount of money that will be available for grants towards the reckonable expenditure of local authorities.[48] From this sum there

---

46 See generally Doodson and others, *Local Authority Borrowing* (the Institute of Municipal Treasurers). Government control is in gross (with the annual White Paper on Capital Investment) and in detail, when a particular request for loan sanction is made.

47 These grants are not new. In 1858 grants were made available for police purposes in order to stimulate local activity. In other forms this stimulus from the centre is as old as the burgh itself.

48 See generally "Recent Reforms and the Ratepayer," 1967 S.L.T.(News) 125–130. The needs element takes up 75 per cent. of the rate support grants for the periods 1967–68 and 1968–69. In contrast with England (where the formula is statutory) the basic apportionment of this element is left to be prescribed by the Secretary of State. Consultation with the appropriate associations of local authorities may be assumed. It has been calculated that in 1967–68, the total assistance will amount to 62½ per cent. of reckonable expenditure, and in 1968–69, 63½ per cent. Housing subsidies are not included in these sums, being covered by the Housing (Financial Provisions, etc.) (Scotland) Act 1967. The specific grants include grants under the Rating Act 1966, which provides for a rating rebate scheme to relieve persons with small incomes of some of the burden of rates.

must be deducted the total of the various specific grants payable. The balance is the total of the rate support grants available. Education which now falls within the " needs element " first came under the general grants in 1958. Police remain outside these general grants and a number of new specific grants have been introduced, relating to redevelopment, the provision of public open spaces, reclamation of derelict land, and any special provisions which a local authority may have to make for Commonwealth immigrants.

All these grant systems contain elements of control by the Secretary of State, enabling him to reduce grants where services are not of a reasonable level, and further the calculations of relevant expenditure which enter into the determination of the grants also contain an element of approval of expenditure. This element was enhanced by the Local Government (Financial Provisions) (Scotland) Act 1963 (particularly section 3 (1)) and continues in its strengthened state.

Local government audits. It is not merely in the financing of local government that the central government plays a large part. The Secretary of State has also a role in accountability (apart from the general supervisory controls vested in him which will be discussed later). In this there is nothing new. There was theoretically some royal control over the funds of royal burghs. An Act of 1693 of the Parliament of Scotland attempted more, and an Act of 1822 subjected burgh accounts to the scrutiny of the Exchequer. The system is now regulated by Part X of the 1947 Act. It requires the appointment of auditors by the Secretary of State, the deposit of an abstract of the accounts of the authority, and the publication of a notice indicating the right of a ratepayer to object to the accounts and indicating where the auditor will hear such objections. Where the auditor considers that any payment is contrary to law, or that a loss or deficiency has been incurred owing to the negligence or misconduct of any persons, he reports to the Secretary of State. The Secretary of State, after intimation to the persons affected, and after holding a local inquiry (if requested), may, as he thinks fit, surcharge the amounts upon those responsible. The Secretary of State may, however, refrain from making a surcharge if satisfied that those persons acted reasonably, or in the belief that their action was authorised by law, or if he thinks relief fair and reasonable. His decision, unless he has clearly gone outside the law, is final.[49] This procedure gives to ratepayers a possibility of intimate control or questioning, and to the Secretary of State a considerable opportunity for surveillance. The system is in important ways in contrast with that operating in England under the Local Government Act 1933. Under that Act the district auditors (the most general system of audit) are appointed by the Minister

---

[49] *County Auditor of Lanark* v. *Lambie* (1905) 7 F. 1049. Though he may earlier be required to state a case for the opinion of the court.

of Housing and Local Government, and are on the staff of his department. They have themselves the power of surcharge, with the minister
acting as a court of appeal. Alternatively appeal may be, subject to
conditions, to the courts. Both the appeal bodies may themselves grant
relief. The Scottish system concentrates power in the Secretary of
State.[49] Both systems theoretically enable a control to be exercised over
the way in which local authorities exercise their discretion, but perhaps
because the Scottish auditors do not form a distinct and expert corps,
as do the English ones (who are, as has been mentioned, upon the staff
of the ministry though enjoying a degree of independence), this aspect
has never been so prominent in Scotland as in England.[50] Both systems,
it must be noted, are capable of producing an individual liability of
either members or officials of local authorities, which can be important.[51]

General relationship with the central government. Historically local
authorities are autonomous bodies. In current practice this theory does
not correspond with reality. For this there are many reasons. The
former corruption in the burghs has left its mark, not merely in the
provisions for audit. Modern tendencies towards centralisation, and
the tendency to regard essential services as national obligations, have
contributed to the same end. Equally important is the fact that the
system is founded upon authorities which owe much to older history,
whereas the needs of modern local government spring from the more
recent industrialisation of the country. Thus areas are not necessarily
functional and in the case of the all-purpose or most-purpose authorities
their areas are often inappropriate for many of their functions.[52] Whilst
the classification of authorities for workaday purposes has, of necessity,
had to break with historical classifications (thus a royal burgh may be a
county of a city, a large or a small burgh), the same process has not
been operative throughout local government.[51] This inappropriateness
of area combined with limitation of financial resources have caused
reliance upon central government support. It must, however, be

[50] Though prior ministerial approval of expenditure does not, by the 1947 Act, exclude
surcharge as it does in England, this would no doubt be an element in the
determination of reasonableness by the Secretary of State.
[51] No case akin to *Roberts* v. *Hopwood* [1925] A.C. 578 has arisen in Scotland, and
the report in 1961 on rents of houses in Dunbartonshire, which emerged as a result
of a separate inquiry, would in England in all probability have emerged through the
action of the district auditor and surcharge by him. See also *Taylor* v. *Munrow*
[1960] 1 All E.R. 455. Compare with *Roberts* v. *Hopwood, Re Walker's Decision*
[1944] K.B. 644; and see [1962] *Public Law* 52. For the conditions of relief see
Local Government Act 1933, s. 230, and *Annison* v. *St. Pancras Auditor* [1961] 3
W.L.R. 650. See generally Helmore, *The District Auditor.*
[52] This problem has become much more acute in England, and standing machinery has
existed for some years to review areas which in its present form consists of the
Local Government Commissioners for England and for Wales, established under the
Local Government Act 1958, and the obligation upon counties to review the areas
of county districts. The proposed reorganisation of local government in London
by the London Government Act 1963 is prompted by the same causes which there
have an accentuated effect. The Housing and Town Development (Scotland) Act
1957 is one sign of this problem.

emphasised that this strong element of central control is only the accentuation of a factor which has always existed in the modern local government system. The Board of Supervision was created to exercise central control in poor law matters, and from that Board (through the addition to it of public health functions and its change into the Local Government Board) has come the modern central department concerned with local government matters. A similar history exists in England; the Poor Law Commissioners exercising central control and eventually becoming a department of state, now the Ministry of Housing and Local Government.

Moreover, within the most modern fields of state activity—economic planning—local authorities do not play a prominent part. It will have been noticed that essentially the traditional functions of local government authorities are those of administration within a framework of various schemes established by the central government. The role of these authorities within this important new field of economic and regional planning is even more limited. The designation of development areas is probably inevitably a function of the central government, and under the present financial system it is clear the control of the means of influencing regional growth will also belong primarily to that body. The regional development even within a general plan follows the same pattern. The Regional Economic Planning Boards charged with the co-ordination of government activity are composed of civil servants. They are advised by Economic Planning Councils, the members of which are, in Scotland, appointed by the Secretary of State, and the membership includes some members drawn from local government. The Chairman of the Council in Scotland is a minister. In addition, there are operational bodies such as the Highlands and Islands Development Board established under the Highlands and Islands Development (Scotland) Act 1965, which is again a nominated body. It has a range of powers the exercise of which has, however, to be fitted into the powers of local authorities underneath and the powers of the central government overhead. The result has perhaps been a dispersal of effort which has been unhelpful, and a further decline in the public image of local government, which is felt to play a minor role in this new and important area of activity. This problem relates back to the ideas dominating the structure of the present system of local government. The position could be changed if the proposals for the reform of local government which emerged from the Royal Commission turn out to be major ones.

In the traditional field of local government activity mechanisms of central control are varied. Where grants are payable, they are accompanied by default powers.[53] In relation to most essential social

---

[53] *i.e.*, powers of the central government to act in default of action by local authorities. These powers are a last resort and are rarely used. In relation to housing they were

services, such as education or health, the functions of the authority are
to be carried out in accordance with an administrative scheme which
requires the approval of the Secretary of State. Specialised officials,
such as the medical officer of health or sanitary inspector, must have
qualifications prescribed by general legislation or by the Secretary of
State, who can also control the duties entrusted to them, and whose
sanction is required for their dismissal. In other fields, such as
education, recruitment of staffs and methods of operation may be
tightly regulated by the Secretary of State.[54] In many services a system
of inspection, which may be linked with grants, provides continuing
control, and section 356 of the 1947 Act provides general machinery for
complaint to the minister and inquiry by him as to any default of
a local authority in carrying out its function. Even outside such extreme
provisions the Secretary of State is often, as in planning matters, the
responsible authority to hear appeals from decisions of local authorities,
so that those authorities in taking decisions are likely to make them
accord with his known policies. The power or influence of the Secretary
of State is increased by two considerations. First there may exist, even
where qualifications may be laid down, a discretionary area in which
some other policy of the Scottish Office may operate,[55] which will allow
further scope for control. Second, it is clear that local and central
government cannot operate in a spirit of rivalry, and, granted the area
where co-operation is compulsory, it is probable that the area of
voluntary collaboration with, or of influence by, the central government
is more extensive than was formerly the case. It is also probably true
that experimentation (which is an aspect of autonomy of local authorities) is now less acceptable in certain fields than it was formerly.[56] It
is also clear that the central government exercises a supervisory
jurisdiction not merely as to policy, but as to questions of law also.
As has been seen this is more evident in the auditing procedure in
England than in Scotland. Default powers straddle issues of policy and
of law, and provisions such as section 30 of the Local Government
Superannuation (Scotland) Act 1937, or section 16 of the Housing and
Town Development (Scotland) Act 1957, give to the minister powers of
determining issues of law. There is thus a substantial administrative

considerably increased by the Local Government (Financial Provisions) (Scotland)
Act 1963, s. 3. The best general account of the relationship is Griffith, *Central
Departments and Local Authorities.* Although written primarily from the standpoint
of England and Wales, the pattern there described is general.
54 Thus, although education now falls within the general grant, conditions of employment
of teachers, or standards of school construction, are thus regulated, and an extensive
system of inspection exists. In effect control through a specific grant was super-
fluous and in giving it up the Secretary of State lost little if anything.
55 *Mags. of Kilmarnock* v. *S. of S. for Scotland,* 1961 S.C. 350.
56 *Prescott* v. *Birmingham Corporation* [1955] Ch. 210 at 225, which had its repercussions in Scotland. Public Service Vehicles (Travel Concessions) Act 1955, as
amended by the Local Government Act 1958 and the Local Government and Miscellaneous Provisions (Scotland) Act 1958. There has probably been a contraction
in what is regarded as the proper scope of private legislation.

tutelage, though much of the law remains based upon the theory of autonomy. Here, as elsewhere, a maladjustment between law and reality is unhealthy for society.

Police. One service, police, must be mentioned specifically, since constitutionally it has anomalous features. Regulations made by the Secretary of State, especially the grant regulations and the definition of the efficiency therein, give to the central government operating through H.M. Inspectors of Constabulary the possibility of close control in many respects, though not in the actual day-to-day operation of the force. At the same time, the control exercised by local authorities (where they are police authorities) is limited. Under the Police (Scotland) Act 1967 (a consolidating Act) the Secretary of State has acquired wider powers in relation to the appointment and dismissal of chief constables, and in relation to the provision of central services as well as other matters. In law the police authority is little more than a paymaster.[57]   Police are then neither the servants of local authorities nor of the Crown.[58] In some respects the police must observe directions of the Lord Advocate, but it must be noted that the existence of the system of public prosecution in Scotland materially affects their position. They are an investigatory body as far as crime is concerned and not a prosecuting one. It is possible to regard the relatively autonomous position of the police and the dispersal of control over them as a sound constitutional safeguard. Others may regard this situation as producing a constitutional weakness.[59] The question is one of balance. Too strong and too centralised police forces can be a danger, as can too weak forces, or forces over which too much political control can be exercised.

The general character of local authorities and their servants. While it is true that each local authority is, in law, the employer of its own officials, it is not unreasonable to speak, in fact, of a local government service. To a great extent fundamental matters are dealt with on a national basis. Superannuation (under the English and Scottish Acts of 1937) is an obvious example, and brings many consequences in its train. Of equal importance is the fact that national schemes governing conditions of service were agreed in 1946 for England and Wales and in

[57] See Mitchell, " The Constitutional Position of the Police in Scotland," 1962 J.R. 1.
[58] *Girdwood* v. *Midlothian Standing Joint Committee* (1894) 22 R. 11; *Muir* v. *Mags. of Hamilton,* 1910, 1 S.L.T. 164. The background to *Fisher* v. *Oldham Corporation* [1930] 2 K.B. 364 does not really exist in Scotland. See, too, Report of Royal Commission on the Police (1962) Cmnd. 1728, Chap. IV, and now see s. 39 of the Police (Scotland) Act 1967, which, however (unlike the corresponding English provisions), is not yet in force.
[59] Compare the vigorous dissent to the Report of the Royal Commission by Prof. Goodhart with the views expressed in the article referred to in note 57, above.

1947 for Scotland.[60] Thus the area of discretion left to any individual
authority is substantially diminished. The effect of these schemes is
also to reinforce, in the field of internal administrative law, general
principles which have long been established marking off at least some
local government service from the ordinary rules of master/servant
relationship.[61] Apart from these general conditions of appointment
the conduct of officers is specifically regulated in sections 97 to 103
of the 1947 Act. Section 103, it is to be noted, confers a personal
immunity upon officers who in the course of their functions act reasonably and in an honest belief that their actions were justified in law, even
though the latter should prove not to be the case.

Just as the public character of their functions marks the position of
local government officers, so also this character marks the treatment
in law of the authorities themselves, it imposes standards of conduct
upon them in regard to their actions and imposes limitation upon their
freedom of action,[62] and for some purposes the distinction between their
activities for public purposes and their other activities is important,[63]
though the distinction is not uniformly made.[64]

Judicial control. It is evident that there exists a substantial judicial
control over local authorities and of this the control over by-laws which
has been discussed is a fair example. This is exercised to restrain authorities within the limits of their lawful powers, but it is also exercised to
control the propriety of their actions,[65] and in this respect it seems that
in Scotland the courts will be less concerned than they are in England
with the question of whether the actions can be classed as quasi-judicial
or not, and to that extent the powers of the courts are, perhaps, more
general.[66] The difference may be attributable to two things. First to

---

[60] These two " Charters " were the culmination of a process started by the Hadow
Report 1934 (and see Royal Commission on Local Government (1936) Cmd. 3436).
They are not identical in terms, though they are in general spirit. See Robson,
Development of Local Government, and Warren, *The Local Government Service.*
[61] *Simpson* v. *Todd* (1824) 3 S. 150; *Farish* v. *Mags. of Annan* (1836) 15 S. 107;
Mags. of Rothesay v. *Carse* (1903) 5 F. 383; *Lord Advocate* v. *Ayr District Board
of Control*, 1927 S.L.T. 337. The fact that an officer holds " during pleasure " does
not, however, deprive him of a right to reasonable notice; *Board of Supervision* v.
Old Monkland Board (1880) 7 R. 469 and s. 100 of the 1947 Act. *Cf.* Local
Government Act 1933, s. 121, reversing *Brown* v. *Dagenham U.D.C.* [1929] 1 K.B.
737. Similarly, it is thought that the principles involved in cases such as *Re Magrath*
[1934] 2 K.B. 415 would be applicable.
[62] *Mags. of Kirkcaldy* v. *Marks & Spencer Ltd.*, 1937 S.L.T. 574; *Paterson* v. *Mags.
of St. Andrews* (1881) 8 R.(H.L.) 117; and see Ersk. II, 1, 7. The fundamental
issues here resemble, and are perhaps identical with, those which underlie *The
Amphitrite Case* [1921] 3 K.B. 500; see Mitchell, *The Contracts of Public Authorities.*
[63] *Glasgow Corporation* v. *I.R.C.*, 1959 S.C. 203.
[64] *Western Heritable Investment Co.* v. *Glasgow Corporation*, 1956 S.C.(H.L.) 64, where
it is probable that because of a neglect of this distinction the purposes of the statute
in question were frustrated.
[65] *Moss' Empires Ltd.* v. *Assessor of Glasgow*, 1917 S.C.(H.L.) 1; *Nicol* v. *Mags. of
Aberdeen* (1870) 9 M. 306; *Caledonian Ry.* v. *Glasgow Corporation* (1905) 7 F. 1020.
[66] *McDonald* v. *Lanarkshire Fire Brigade Joint Committee*, 1959 S.C. 141; and see
Mitchell, " The Scope of Judicial Review," 1959 J.R. 197, and Bennett Miller,
" Quasi-Judicial Decisions in Scots Law," 1958 J.R. 39. To some extent this

the "formlessness" or generality of the remedy of reduction, which contrasts with the formalism and particularity of remedy through the prerogative writs, and their successors the prerogative orders. Second to the differences in history. Courts played a much smaller part in the working of local government in Scotland than did quarter sessions in England. Similarly, the Court of Session had a more general jurisdiction than did the Court of Queen's Bench whose control was linked to its jurisdiction to control inferior courts. There is thus, perhaps, a greater readiness or ability, if required, to use particular powers to prevent oppression by public authorities.[67] It has, indeed, long been asserted that there exists in the Court of Session a general power to redress administrative wrongs.[68] This generality may affect the weight to be given to some English authorities. Thus, it is perhaps doubtful if *Smith* v. *East Elloe R.D.C.*[69] would be accepted as a sound authority, granted this background. Nevertheless, it has also been long accepted that the court must impose some limitation upon its control, if it were not effectively to determine policy. This problem was seen at the very beginnings of the modern state in cases such as *Pryde* v. *The Heritors and the Kirk Session of Ceres.*[70] It is as a consequence of that that the courts accept within broad limits the bona fide exercise of a discretion by public authorities.[71] As these authorities have become more democratic this acceptance has become somewhat broader,[72] and the control more restrained. Moreover, since the duties upon local authorities have become more general, the question of a title to sue has become more important, and limitations on that right have contributed also to restricting the scope of judicial review. The right to challenge illegal payments exists, as has been seen, as also does the right to challenge any *ultra vires* activity which would involve the expenditure of money from the rates. Much more difficulty arises in relation to raising a challenge to a failure to act, or to an unreasonable action within the

difference is attributable to the history of local government in the two jurisdictions. In England, courts, acting in one way or another, were much more prominent.

[67] See, *e.g.*, the use of powers in relation to expenses in *Marshall* v. *School Board of Ardrossan* (1879) 7 R. 359; *Love* v. *Lang* (1872) 10 M. 782; *Liddall* v. *Ballingry Parish Council*, 1908 S.C. 1082.

[68] *Ross* v. *Findlater* (1826) 4 S. 514 at 518; and see Kames, *Historical Law Tracts*, 4th ed., p. 228, where he speaks of this power as being necessarily assumed by the Court of Session after the abolition of the Privy Council in Scotland. That assumption was one of a generalised power of control. It is one of the continuing uses, and perhaps the main one, of the *nobile officium* to overcome administrative difficulties, and this is another aspect of this jurisdiction.

[69] [1956] A.C. 736.

[70] (1843) 5 D. 552; *Dawson* v. *Allardyce*, Feb. 18, 1809, F.C.; and see Lord Cockburn's comments in the *Journal*, Vol. II, pp. 1 and 257. This problem is a facet of the fundamental issue which also appears in the argument about the relationship of courts to prerogatives.

[71] *Guthrie* v. *Miller* (1827) 5 S. 711.

[72] *Sommerville* v. *Langmuir*, 1932 J.C. 55; *cf. Sommerville* v. *Lord Advocate*, 1933 S.L.T. 48; *Parlane* v. *Perth and Kinross Joint C.C.*, 1954 S.L.T.(Sh.Ct.) 95.

ambit of admitted powers. Review of the general administration of
burgh funds has been refused.[73]

The older cases tended to rest the title to sue upon injury to a
patrimonial right, which was one method of securing the necessary
limitation. That foundation may today be inadequate with the changed
nature of many of the duties of local authorities, particularly when
allowance is made for the differences between the position of Lord
Advocate and Attorney-General, and the absence in Scotland of the
equivalent of the English relator actions.[74] Because of these circumstances the administrative supervision by the central government departments assumes greater importance, and is seen to have an additional
function. It is arguable, however, whether, under the law as it now
stands, a right balance has been struck between these two methods of
regulation. Included in that argument is the question whether, as at
present organised, the relationship *inter se* of administrative bodies is
sufficiently regulated by law in order to preserve the distribution of
powers which underlies the legal structure. These issues are, however,
wide, stretching beyond the field of local government, and can best be
discussed in the context of the general scope of judicial review which
will be dealt with subsequently.

---

[73] *Conn* v. *Magistrates of Renfrew* (1906) 8 F. 905, though Lord Dunedin was hesitant
about specific *ultra vires* acts: 1915 S.C.(H.L.) at p. 17. See now *Innes* v. *Royal
Burgh of Kirkcaldy*, 1963 S.L.T. 325, where, exceptionally, an interdict was granted
to prevent a reduction of local authority rents.

[74] See the discussion of this problem in *D. & J. Nicol* v. *Dundee Harbour Trustees*,
1914 S.C. 374 and 1915 S.C.(H.L.) 7. Compare *Watt* v. *Kesteven C.C.* [1955] 1
Q.B. 408. In early cases, such as *Guild* v. *Scott*, Dec. 21, 1809, F.C., although there
is the appearance of the enforcement of a general duty the patrimonial interest was
present.

CHAPTER 14

THE COURTS

Introduction. The place of the courts in the modern constitution is one of the major current issues. That subject, however, arises in the discussion of almost every institution or major rule. The present chapter is only concerned with an outline of the structure of the courts, and with the main rules which govern their constitutional position. The story of the evolution of the main courts is, in one sense, more straightforward in Scotland than it is in England.[1] Instead of the struggles of distinct courts for jurisdiction (which led to complexities in the forms of action and to complications derived from fictions), and instead of the double stream of law and equity up to the reforms of 1875, the story in Scotland on the civil side is of the evolution of the one central court, the Court of Session, which from its origin in 1532[2] can be said to have had a general jurisdiction, and which over the years has absorbed other courts of a more specialised type. Clearly, the development since 1532 was not entirely smooth, but this generality of jurisdiction, and the idea of a centralised civil court,[3] have left their marks on the attitude of courts to government. On the criminal side justiciars had existed in Scotland since about 1166 and the office of Lord Justice General had existed since 1524, but justices of the peace never took root, and the justice ayres never had the qualities of the justices in eyre in England. Any really effective circuit system had to await the abolition in 1747 of the heritable jurisdictions.[4] From 1836 (under the Court of Session Act 1830), the offices of Lord President and Lord Justice General were conjoined and from the Criminal Procedure (Scotland) Act 1887 the Senators of the College of Justice became also Lords Commissioners

---

[1] See, on the one hand, Plucknett, *Concise History of the Common Law*, and on the other, Hannay, *The College of Justice*, and the articles in the Stair Society publications, Vols. 1 and 20. For accounts of the modern jurisdiction see Walker, *The Scottish Legal System*; Smith, *Short Commentary on the Law of Scotland*; Gloag and Henderson, *Introduction to the Law of Scotland*; and M'Millan, *Evolution of the Scottish Judiciary*.

[2] A.P.S. II, 335. The court did not, of course, spring new-born from the statute. Behind the statute lay the history of the Lords Auditors and of the Lords of Council and Session; see Duncan, *The Central Courts before 1532* (the Stair Society, Vol. 20).

[3] The full centralisation was not established until relatively recently. In 1830 the civil jurisdiction of the Admiralty Court was transferred to the Court of Session and to sheriffs. The jury court, established in 1815, was absorbed in 1830. The Court of Exchequer, which was reconstituted immediately after the Union, was finally merged with the Court of Session by the Court of Exchequer Act 1856. Between 1823 and 1836 the jurisdiction of the commissary courts was transferred to the sheriffs or the Court of Session.

[4] See the articles in Vols. 1 and 20 of the Stair Society publications; Hume, *Criminal Law*. For the modern system, see Renton and Brown, *Criminal Procedure*, and Smith, *Short Commentary on the Law of Scotland*.

of Justiciary, and the modern pattern was thus established for the High
Court of Justiciary.   From the abolition of the heritable jurisdictions
in 1747, the modern sheriff courts began to evolve, and it was the Sheriff
Courts (Scotland) Act 1825 which provided that sheriff substitutes
should have legal qualifications, which is, perhaps, the most significant
point in that evolution.

In essence, therefore, the present system of major courts was
established by the middle of the nineteenth century.

The modern system. The central courts.   At the heart of the modern
system is the Court of Session, consisting of nineteen judges including
the Lord President and the Lord Justice-Clerk,[5] and evenly divided
between the Outer and Inner House.   The Inner House sits in two
Divisions, the First presided over by the Lord President, the Second by
the Lord Justice-Clerk.   The court retains something of its collegiate
character in that a Lord Ordinary may make up a quorum in the Inner
House or a judge of the Division can sit in the Outer House.   Membership of the Inner House is governed by seniority, and appointments are
not made to it directly as they are to the Court of Appeal.   The
Ordinary Lords of Session are appointed by the Queen upon the
nomination of the Secretary of State for Scotland, who receives the
advice of the Lord Advocate.[6]   Appointments to the two chairs are
normally made from the Law Officers or ex-Law Officers.

In principle the Outer House is a court of first instance, the Inner
House a court of appeal, though the distinction is not absolute.   Certain
matters, notably the exercise of the *nobile officium,* are reserved to the
Inner House, as also are special cases for the opinion of the court and
special cases for opinion and judgment (appeal lying to the House of
Lords in this second form of special case).   In its appellate jurisdiction
the Inner House hears appeals both from Outer House decisions and
from sheriff courts.   Either Division may in a case of difficulty consult
other judges or summon three others to make a court of seven judges or
may consult all the judges or have a hearing before the whole court.
These thus constitute useful mechanisms for the reconsideration of points
of law though problems can arise in their operation.[7]   Such courts have

---

5 Sixteen was the number authorised by the Restrictive Trade Practices Act 1956, s. 32.
  Under s. 49 of the Criminal Justice (Scotland) Act 1963, the authorised number was
  increased to 17, and the Resale Prices Act 1964 added yet one more.   The Administration of Justice Act 1968 authorises 19, with the possibility of further increase by
  Order in Council.   For the sake of brevity what follows is mainly concerned with
  the Scottish judicial system; for the English system, see Hood Phillips, *First Book
  of English Law*; Jackson, *Machinery of Justice in England*; Kiralfy, *The English
  Legal System.*
6 623 H.C.Deb. 172–173, where the general patronage of the Lord Advocate is
  indicated.   As a sample of English practice, see Heuston, " Lord Halsbury's Judicial
  Appointments " (1962) 78 L.Q.R. 504.
7 The collegiate character of the court raises argument about the effect of decisions
  reached by a court of seven.   See Smith, *Judicial Precedent in Scots Law*, p. 28
  et seq.   Until 1808, the court sat as a whole, further reforms, notably the Act of

THE MODERN SYSTEM. THE CENTRAL COURTS

power to overrule an earlier decision of the Inner House, to resolve
conflicts of decisions, or to overrule a decision that has come to be
regarded as erroneous. As has been indicated, the Court of Exchequer
has now been absorbed in the Court of Session, though Exchequer
business is still marked by peculiarities of procedure and remedy.[8] In
addition, certain special jurisdictions have been conferred upon the
Senators, the Lands Valuation Appeal Court consisting of three Senators
hears appeals from local valuation appeal committees. The Registration
Court of Appeal under section 45 (9) of the Representation of the People
Act 1949 consists of three Senators, and election petitions under section
110 of the same Act are to be heard in the Election Petition Court by
two Senators.

The High Court of Justiciary. The High Court, the criminal counterpart of the Court of Session, has many equivalent attributes, such as a
power equivalent to the *nobile officium.*[9] It has exclusive jurisdiction
in the most serious crimes,[10] and for criminal trials circuit courts are
held. Appeals from the High Court and from proceedings on indictment
in sheriff courts lie, under the Criminal Appeal (Scotland) Act 1926,
to the Court of Criminal Appeal.[11] In contrast to hearing appeals,
properly so called, the High Court has also power to review the proceedings of the lower courts. This power may be exercised through the
mechanism of a stated case, under the Summary Jurisdiction (Scotland)
Act 1954, which can be used in cases where allegations of corruption,
malice or oppression are made, apart from normal questions of law.
Review is also possible through the common law means of suspension or
advocation, both of which are parts of a very long-established supervisory jurisdiction.[12] It has also jurisdiction in the limited civil appeals
from the Small Debt Court.

Sheriff courts. In the ordinary life of the country the system of
sheriff courts is of as great importance as any other system of courts.
The fact that this system, which emerged from the destruction of the
heritable jurisdictions, provided the machinery for regular administration
of justice at a local level is the justification for Cosmo Innes's assertion

1830, produced the modern arrangement. In *Carron Co.* v. *Hislop,* 1930 S.C. 1050,
the full court considered the issue of who could judge the validity of an Act of
Sederunt. This issue was not debated in the House of Lords; 1931 S.C.(H.L.) 75.
[8] *Barrs* v. *I.R.C.,* 1961 S.C.(H.L.) 22; and see 1960 S.L.T.(News) 46, " Habeas Corpus
in Scotland."
[9] *Milne* v. *M'Nicol,* 1944 J.C. 151. It has, too, the same power of convening a larger
court than is normal for particular purposes: Renton and Brown, *Criminal Procedure.*
[10] As well as in relation to charges of wilful neglect, corruption or malversation of office
by public officials: Hume, *Criminal Law,* II, p. 58; Alison, *Criminal Law,* p. 633.
[11] No appeal lies to the House of Lords: *Mackintosh* v. *Lord Advocate* (1876) 3
R.(H.L.) 34; *cf.* as to England, where criminal appeals are now governed by the
Administration of Justice Act 1960.
[12] The details of these procedures are inappropriate here; see Moncrieff, *Review in
Criminal Cases,* and such modern works as Renton and Brown, *op. cit.*

that that destruction is one of the cornerstones of liberty.[13] For the hereditary sheriffs were substituted sheriffs-depute (now sheriff-principals) as the effective judges.[14] The substitutes which the latter appointed were, from 1825, required to have legal qualifications, and there thus emerged the position where full-time, legally qualified judges were readily available in any locality. The offices of sheriff-principal, which remain part-time offices (except in Lanarkshire and the Lothians and Peebles), not only provide a local method of appeal, but also provide the machinery for training or testing those who may be made judges of the Court of Session. In ordinary civil actions there is no upper pecuniary limit to the sheriff's jurisdiction, but below £50 his jurisdiction is exclusive and his decision final. The main limitations upon the jurisdiction are the exclusion of actions concerning status, and many company matters where the paid-up capital of the company exceeds £10,000, actions for reduction and actions of proving the tenor.[15] Appeal from the sheriff-substitute lies to the sheriff-principal, and thence to the Inner House, or alternatively direct to the Inner House. As a criminal court the sheriff court has full jurisdiction, with the exception of the crimes of treason, murder (and attempts thereat), incest and rape, but since the powers of sentencing are limited many of the more serious offences tend to be taken to the High Court. As has already been noted, the sheriff has many administrative functions as well as his judicial ones.[16]

The Court of the Lord Lyon. This court retains an active jurisdiction in matters of heraldry, being concerned with questions of the grant or of the abuse of arms, and on its criminal side has its own procurator-fiscal.[17] The jurisdiction, which has a common law origin, was confirmed by the Lyon King of Arms Act 1867. The court was formerly subject to the Privy Council in Scotland, and after the Union this power of review passed to the Court of Session [18] from which appeal lies to the

---

13 *Scotch Legal Antiquities,* p. 149, and Ilay Campbell, *Scottish Judicatures.*

14 For the peculiarities of terminology, see 1952 S.L.T.(News) 121. The fact that a sheriff-substitute is normally expected to live in his sheriffdom is of considerable social importance, and some provision to that effect is generally included in his commission. At one time, residence elsewhere was inconceivable in law: *Smith* v. *Falconer* (1890) 18 R. 343.

15 See, generally, Smith, *Short Commentary on the Law of Scotland,* and Gloag and Henderson, *Introduction to the Law of Scotland,* and Sheriff Courts (Civil Jurisdiction and Procedure) (Scotland) Act 1963.

16 In all respects the sheriff court is to be contrasted with the county courts in England which have a limited civil jurisdiction, no criminal jurisdiction, and fewer administrative functions. On the criminal side quarter sessions have wider powers of punishment than have sheriffs. For the present limits for county courts see the County Courts Act 1959 and the County Courts (Jurisdiction) Act 1963.

17 Innes of Learney, *Scots Heraldry.* Cf. *Manchester Corporation* v. *Manchester Palace of Varieties* [1955] P. 133 and 71 L.Q.R. 187.

18 *Procurator Fiscal of the Lyon Court* (1778) Mor. 7656; and it seems that ultimately the decrees of the court are only enforceable through the Court of Session: *Macraes' Trs.* v. *Lord Lyon King-of-Arms,* 1927 S.L.T. 285.

House of Lords.[19] The court has no jurisdiction to determine questions either of precedence or of chieftainship.[20]

The Scottish Land Court was established by the Small Landholders (Scotland) Act 1911,[21] having as its chairman an advocate who enjoys the rank and tenure of a Senator of the College of Justice. The other members have a more limited tenure.[22] Its jurisdiction, which is important, and has increased with recent agricultural legislation, is now concerned with agricultural problems going far beyond those of small land-holding.[23] No appeal lies to the Court of Session, but the court may be required to state a case on a question of law for either Division of that court, and it is subject to the more general supervisory control of that court.[24] The position of the Land Court has certain peculiarities. While it has many of the attributes of an ordinary court it lacks others, for example, while being a court of law it is doubtful if it is a court of record or superior court,[25] and it lacks the power to enforce its own orders.

The Restrictive Practices Court. Among these specialised courts should be noted the Restrictive Practices Court, established under the Restrictive Trade Practices Act 1956. This court has several notable features. Like the Land Court it could be regarded as the most highly judicialised form of administrative tribunal though by the Act it is declared to be a superior court of record, even though for some purposes it has to rely on the aid of the ordinary established courts. Its principal peculiarity is, however, that it is a United Kingdom court. Judges nominated to it are three from the High Court in England, one from the Court of Session and one from the Supreme Court of Northern Ireland. Whereas the court can sit anywhere in the United Kingdom, none of these judges can be required to sit outside their jurisdiction of origin, but there is nothing to debar them from so doing by consent. Whether the court is sitting in England or Scotland a member of either Bar has a right of audience (Northern Ireland is specially treated). Orders of the court are by section 20 (3) made effective throughout the

---

19 *Stewart Mackenzie* v. *Fraser Mackenzie*, 1922 S.C.(H.L.) 39.

20 *Royal College of Surgeons of Edinburgh* v. *Royal College of Physicians of Edinburgh*, 1911 S.C. 1054; *Maclean of Ardgour* v. *Maclean*, 1938 S.L.T. 49; *Maclean of Ardgour* v. *Maclean*, 1941 S.C. 613. Compare the operation of this court and of the Court of Session in *Munro's Trs.* v. *Monson*, 1965 S.L.T. 314 and *Sir Hugh Munro-Lucas-Tooth, Petitioner*, 1965 S.L.T. (Lyon Court) 2.

21 See 1958 S.L.T.(News) 129 and 1956 S.L.T.(News) 65; and see Connell and Johnston, *Agricultural Holdings (Scotland) Act.*

22 See Scottish Land Court Act 1938.

23 The main extensions are to be found in the Agriculture (Scotland) Act 1948 and the Agricultural Holdings (Scotland) Act 1949. Administrative functions relating to crofters were transferred under the Crofters (Scotland) Act 1955 to the Crofters Commission.

24 *Kennedy* v. *Johnstone*, 1956 S.L.T. 73.

25 *Mackay and Esselmont* v. *Lord Advocate*, 1937 S.C. 860; *Milburn*, 1946 S.C. 301. The term " court of record " though used in *Milburn* has probably no precise meaning in Scotland.

United Kingdom. Thus there has emerged (perhaps for the first time) a United Kingdom court.[26] Appeals on points of law from the court are fitted into the appellate system of the jurisdiction in which it sits. The jurisdiction of the court is concerned with the validity of agreements which restrict trading (s. 6), and is of considerable economic significance. To its original jurisdiction has been added that under the Resale Prices Act 1964, s. 5, to exempt goods of any particular class from the general effect of s. 1 of the Act which avoids all conditions maintaining resale prices. In addition to the judicial members of the court, others, experienced in industry, commerce or public affairs, are appointed on the recommendation of the Lord Chancellor, and for any hearing the court must consist of the presiding judge and at least two other members. The presiding judge (who delivers the judgment of the court) has special prerogatives in relation to the operation of the court.

Local courts. Some local courts of limited jurisdiction should also be noted. The justices of the peace have some jurisdiction in civil matters in the small debt court under the Small Debt (Scotland) Act 1825. The jurisdiction is limited to £5, and, subject to reduction by the Court of Session, the decision is final. In the counties the justice of the peace court is concerned with breaches of the peace and petty offences. From it appeal lies to quarter sessions and to the High Court of Justiciary by way of a stated case. The jurisdiction is limited by the fact that penalties imposed cannot exceed a £10 fine or imprisonment for sixty days,[27] and it is concurrent with the jurisdiction of the sheriff. In burghs a similar minor criminal jurisdiction exists in the police or burgh court. In both cases the system of public prosecution in use in higher courts is operative, each court having its own fiscal.[28]

Church courts. Among the other courts in Scotland must be noted those of the Church of Scotland. With the abolition of Papal jurisdiction in 1560 [29] there was immediate confusion; the Reformed Church and the Court of Session exercised consistorial jurisdiction until the Commissary Courts were established in 1563. The jurisdiction of those

---

26 This United Kingdom character is capable of having certain inconveniences as to the law administered by the court; see, *e.g.*, 1959 S.L.T.(News) 13 *et seq.*; and generally see Wilberforce, *Restrictive Trade Practices*. An understanding of this sort of litigation (as distinct from an understanding simply of the rules of law) can be got from Barker and Davies, *Books are Different*, dealing with the case involving the net-book agreement. See, on its general economics, Stevens and Yamey, *The Restrictive Practices Court*, and Hunter, *Competition and the Law*.
27 Summary Jurisdiction (Scotland) Act 1954, s. 3.
28 The origin of the burghal jurisdictions is partly common law. The Act of Union had preserved the rights and privileges of the royal burghs, and the Heritable Jurisdictions Act 1746 had continued their powers, but from 1813 processes of reform produced more standardisation, and the Burgh Police Act 1892, in particular, defined the jurisdiction of these courts (see now the Summary Jurisdiction (Scotland) Act 1954). For an outline history of these courts, see *Introduction to Scottish Legal History* (the Stair Society, Vol. 20) and for details of their jurisdiction see Smith, *op. cit.*, and Renton and Brown, *op. cit.*
29 A.P.S. II, 534. See, generally, *Introduction to Scottish Legal History*, Chap. 27.

courts was eventually absorbed, in the nineteenth century, by the Court of Session and the sheriff courts. Thus the church courts of the Reformed Church never really exercised this jurisdiction. These courts, however, continued to operate both to maintain discipline within the church and to punish moral offences [30] which fell outside the criminal law, and effectively their jurisdiction is today exercised only within the first field, though that may have consequential effects upon civil rights. Within their jurisdiction it was recognised by the Court of Session that they were supreme—" within their spiritual province the church courts are as supreme as we are within the civil," said Lord Justice-Clerk Moncreiff.[31] This jurisdiction (and its pre-eminence) is recognised by the Church of Scotland Act 1921,[32] and is exclusive. The ultimate court of appeal within the system of church courts is the General Assembly of the Church of Scotland.[33]

The matters thus baldly stated were at one time a matter of heated argument and of deep significance in the history of the country, underlying, as they do, the disruption cases, and in particular the Strathbogie cases.[34] It was the object of the Declaratory Articles to close that unhappy chapter and to declare " the right of the church to self-government in all that concerned its own life and activity." [35] The result is to produce a marked contrast to the practice of the Church of England, in relation to which the Sovereign is, under the Submission of the Clergy Act 1533 and the Act of Supremacy 1558, the supreme governor of the church. In consequence the ultimate court of appeal for that church is now the Judicial Committee of the Privy Council, and parliamentary control over the legislation of the church is preserved under the Church of England Assembly (Powers) Act 1919, which, nevertheless, permits a large element of practical devolution to the Assembly.[36]

In relation to both Scotland and England the above statements apply to the courts of the established churches. Jurisdiction in other voluntary

---

[30] Ersk. I, 5, 35. At one time the jurisdiction extended over parochial schooling.
[31] Wight v. Presbytery of Dunkeld (1870) 8 M. 921 at 925. As courts they receive the customary protections: Sturrock v. Greig (1849) 11 D. 1220, and there is an obligation on lay courts to lend their aid: Presbytery of Lewis v. Fraser (1874) 1 R. 888.
[32] See Ballantyne v. Presbytery of Wigtown, 1936 S.C. 625 at 657: " the right claimed by the Church of Scotland to legislate and adjudicate finally in all matters of government is now the law of the Church, declared by the Church itself, and recognised by Parliament." Arts. IV and V of the Declaratory Articles scheduled to the Church of Scotland Act 1921 are of particular importance. Art. VIII recognises that " The Church has the right to interpret these articles."
[33] As to the constitution and procedure of the courts see Cox, Practice and Procedure in the Church of Scotland.
[34] See particularly The Presbytery of Strathbogie (1840) 2 D. 585.
[35] 1936 S.C. 625 at 654, per Lord Justice-Clerk Aitchison. See, too, Sir Thomas Taylor, " Church and State in Scotland," 1957 J.R. 121; and for the background, Taylor Innes, The Law of Creeds, and Stölinder, Presbyterian Union in Scotland 1907–1921.
[36] See generally Halsbury's Laws of England, sub tit. Ecclesiastical Law; and for discussion see Dr. Garbett, Church and State in England; and for the system of courts, Ecclesiastical Jurisdiction Measure (No. 1) 1963.

churches depends upon contract or trust,[37] and even where similar particular rules may apparently apply to both established and voluntary churches the basis for that application differs.[38]

The House of Lords. The courts hitherto described have been those which have their seat in Scotland. Apart from these there are others which affect Scotland, chief among them being the House of Lords, the ultimate court of appeal in civil matters. The Acts of Union contained what was, perhaps, a deliberate ambiguity. It was provided that no cause in Scotland should be heard in certain named courts or those sitting in Westminster Hall. The House of Lords answered to neither description, and from the Union appeals started to run to that House. There was considerable uncertainty about that jurisdiction.[39] The appeal for remeid of law to the Parliament of Scotland had itself been a matter of dispute,[40] and in any event appeal to the House of Lords was of a somewhat different order from the appeal for remeid. On the other hand, the right to petition Parliament was, however, specifically inserted in the Claim of Right. The jurisdiction of the House was not at first challenged and when it was, in somewhat exceptional circumstances, was upheld.[41] In effect, however, this jurisdiction simply grew and became accepted.[42] This appellate jurisdiction exists, with few exceptions, in civil matters.[43] It does not in criminal matters.[44]

The difficulties which the House of Lords encountered in acting as a court of appeal in England were accentuated as far as Scotland was concerned.[45] Even when lawyers were available, they were not familiar with Scots law, nor, for many years, were judgments in the Court of Session given in a form which might aid the House. Substantial relief came with the Appellate Jurisdiction Act 1876, authorising the appointment of Lords of Appeal in Ordinary, and from that time there has always been one Scots lawyer in the House,[46] and by convention there

37 *McMillan* v. *General Assembly of the Free Church* (1859) 22 D. 290; *Skerrett* v. *Oliver* (1896) 23 R. 468.
38 *Presbytery of Lewis* v. *Fraser* (1874) 1 R. 888.
39 *Lady Mary Bruce* v. *Earl of Kincardine* (1707) II Fount. 367.
40 *The Earl of Callander's Case* (1674) Stair's Dec. II 262 and Mor. 2991; and Sir George MacKenzie's *Memoirs of the Affairs of Scotland*, and Stair, Inst. IV, 1, 56.
41 *Greenshields* v. *Mags. of Edinburgh* (1709) 1 Rob. 12. The point there was a very narrow one, but if appeals were there accepted they must also be on more general matters. By 1712 Fountainhall was already complaining of this growth: Fount. II, 7, 34; and see the introduction to Robertson's *Appeals*; Malcolm, "The House of Lords and Appeals from Scotland" (1910) 22 J.R. 295; Beven, "Appellate Jurisdiction of the House of Lords" (1901) 17 L.Q.R. 357 *et seq.* and 11 Macq. 577.
42 See MacQueen, *Appellate Jurisdiction of the House of Lords.* By 1709 the House of Lords regulated appeals to bring them into conformity with English ones.
43 Even when it does not exist, the weight of a House of Lords decision was elegantly described by Lord Sands in *Assessor for Aberdeen* v. *Collie*, 1932 S.C. 304 at 312.
44 *Mackintosh* v. *L.A.* (1876) 3 R.(H.L.) 34. Though the House of Lords has heard such appeals: Kames, *Historical Law Tracts, sub tit.* Courts.
45 "The House of Lords as a Court of Law" (1936) 52 L.Q.R. 186 at 205 *et seq.*
46 For the list see Walker, *Scottish Legal System*, 2nd ed., p. 179. The total number currently approved (subject to increase by Order in Council) is 11: Administration of Justice Act 1968.

are now at least two. For judicial purposes the House now consists of the Lord Chancellor, the Lords of Appeal in Ordinary and other peers who have held high judicial office.[47] Lay peers do not sit, or, if they do, their votes are not counted,[48] and the conventional separation of the House has long been recognised,[49] and from 1949 an Appellate Committee has been constituted, though upon a sessional basis to preserve constitutional proprieties.[50] The existence of the House as the final court of appeal has had a considerable effect upon private law in both jurisdictions, producing an influence of one upon the other (though probably in the main of English upon Scots law), which has at times been beneficial but has at other times been much criticised.[51] It seems, however, that the House cannot, when acting in this capacity, be properly regarded as a United Kingdom body for all purposes, and decisions are technically only binding on the House itself in the same way, that is to say, that a decision in an English appeal does not absolutely preclude a conflicting decision in a Scottish appeal. Judgments are only binding in the jurisdiction whence came the appeal, and the order of the House is directed specifically to the Court of Session, or as the case may be.[52]

Judicial Committee of the Privy Council. Somewhat similar is the position of the Judicial Committee of the Privy Council, established under the Judicial Committee Act 1833, and composed of persons with like qualifications to those who make up the House of Lords acting as a court, together with members from Commonwealth countries.[53] In the main its jurisdiction is to hear appeals by right, or by special leave, from those parts of the Commonwealth which have not abolished such appeals. In addition, it hears appeals from ecclesiastical courts in England, and in prize. Matters may also be referred to the Judicial Committee for its opinion under section 4 of the Act of 1833, and these may often be matters of considerable constitutional importance.[54] It

---

[47] A term which will include Lords of Appeal who have retired on reaching the age limit.
[48] *O'Connell* v. *The Queen* (1844) 11 Cl. & F. 155; *Bradlaugh* v. *Clarke* (1883) 8 App.Cas. 354; and see *Current Legal Problems* (1949), p. 1.
[49] *Re Lord Kinross* (1905) 7 F.(H.L.) 138.
[50] Bromhead, *House of Lords in Contemporary Politics*, p. 83 *et seq.*; and see *ante*, Chap. 8.
[51] See, *e.g.*, Dewar Gibb, *Law from over the Border*; Smith, *British Justice, the Scottish Contribution*.
[52] See *Glasgow Corporation* v. *Central Land Board*, 1956 S.C.(H.L.) 1 and the authorities quoted in Smith, *Judicial Precedent in Scots Law*, p. 48 *et seq.* Where the House is, as with revenue law, dealing with United Kingdom law the binding force is enlarged: *I.R.C.* v. *City of Glasgow Police Athletic Association*, 1953 S.C.(H.L.) 13. The binding force of decisions of the House is affected by the statement issued on July 26, 1966 ([1966] 3 All E.R. 77), indicating that the House would in appropriate cases depart from previous decisions. As to the difficulties of the system of law applicable, see *Burmah Oil Co. (Burma Trading)* v. *Lord Advocate*, 1964 S.C.(H.L.) 117.
[53] See 503 H.L.Deb. 273.
[54] *e.g.*, *Re Parliamentary Privilege Act 1770* [1958] A.C. 331. A like jurisdiction exists under the House of Commons Disqualification Act 1957; and see *Government of Ireland Act 1920*, ss. 51–53.

further hears appeals from the Medical Disciplinary Committee of the General Medical Council under the Medical Act 1950, and from certain other similar medical bodies.

Courts-Martial Appeal Court. Courts-martial, which are concerned with offences against discipline in the armed services, present some peculiarities. Irrespective of the place of trial, a Scottish advocate or solicitor (or their English counterpart) has a right of audience and, under the Courts-Martial (Appeals) Act 1951, there is established a Courts-Martial Appeal Court, consisting of judges from England, Scotland and Northern Ireland, which can sit in Divisions in any place within or without the United Kingdom. In practice, when sitting in Scotland, it consists of such Lords Commissioners of Justiciary as have been nominated to it, but, wherever sitting, the law applied by the court is English criminal law, by reason of the Army Act 1955, s. 70.

General considerations. The whole structure of the judicial system thus discloses both unity and separation. Some courts are purely local, others are clearly United Kingdom courts, others are partly one and partly the other. It must, however, be emphasised that the preservation by the Acts of Union of the Court of Session preserved a separate and distinct jurisdiction and system of law.[55] This fact, while its effects are limited by a variety of statutes, can nevertheless in particular areas of the law produce inconvenience, unless there is further regulation.[56]

The tenure of judges. In England the Supreme Court of Judicature (Consolidation) Act 1925, s. 12, provides that, with the exception of the Lord Chancellor, all judges of the Supreme Court hold office during good behaviour, subject to removal by His Majesty on an address presented by both Houses. This and equivalent provisions in the Appellate Jurisdiction Act 1876 repeat the provision of the Act of Settlement. There are thus two methods of removal, since removal by the Crown for official misconduct is not ruled out. Other judges are specifically regulated. Under the County Courts Act 1959, county court judges may be removed by the Lord Chancellor for inability or misbehaviour. The Lord Chancellor's powers to remove, while rarely used, are much less limited in respect of justices of the peace.[57] In Scotland the same abuses of power by the Stuarts produced a reaction like that which occurred in England.[58] The Claim of Right recited as a grievance the changing of judges' commissions *ad vitam aut culpam* into commissions *durante*

---

55 See particularly Lord President Inglis in *Orr Ewing's Trs.* v. *Orr Ewing* (1884) 11 R. 606; and see (1885) 13 R.(H.L.) 1; (1886) 2 L.Q.R. 111. More recently the detailed consequences of this separation were emphasised in *McCullie* v. *Butler* [1961] 2 All E.R. 554.

56 *Stuart* v. *Stuart and Moore* (1861) 4 Macq. 1; and the Report on Conflicts of Jurisdiction affecting Children (1959) Cmnd. 842.

57 Colonial judges hold at pleasure: *Terrell* v. *S. of S. for the Colonies* [1953] 2 Q.B. 482.

58 See McNeil, "The Independence of the Scottish Judiciary," 1958 J.R. 132.

beneplacito. Before the Union, control over judges could have been exercised by the Scottish Privy Council, but that body ceased to exist after 1707 and there is no equivalent provision to that contained in the Act of Settlement applicable to Scotland. It seems, therefore, that removal for misconduct can only be by the Crown. There are suggestions that redress lies through Parliament. " If any judge, either judicially or not, should commit a wrong, God forbid there should be no remedy; but then the redress does not lie with us; it is by application to the King in Council or to Parliament," said Lord Robertson.[59] Other suggestions are more specific that the machinery of an address moved in both Houses is appropriate.[60] It seem, however, that there is no obligation in law to pursue such a course, though it might well, should occasion ever arise, be the most convenient method.

This tenure, *ad vitam aut culpam,* is in Scotland regarded as the natural consequence of judicial office,[61] unless specific provision is made to the contrary, and it is noticeable that the Judicial Pensions Act 1959, imposing an age limit of seventy-five upon all judges in the Court of Session, Supreme Court or House of Lords, did not alter the position of existing judges. Specific provision is made in relation to sheriffs by the Sheriff Courts (Scotland) Act 1907. Section 13 provides for removal, on grounds of inability, neglect of duty [62] or misbehaviour, by the Secretary of State acting on the report of the Lord President and the Lord Justice-Clerk, though in the case of a sheriff-principal the order of removal requires to lie before Parliament for four weeks. An arguable case can be made for the assertion that these formal methods of removal of judges should be the only means (except in cases of sickness, etc.) as a safeguard against induced retirements. Sheriffs and sheriffs-substitute and county court judges are required to retire at the age of seventy-two.[63]

The protections of independence. Certainty of tenure does not alone ensure independence. The insistence on the separation of courts from government, already noted,[64] must also be observed. So, too, must the earlier rules about declinature,[65] which were at one time of importance in ensuring the neutrality of judges as between parties. Further, it was

[59] *Haggart's Trs.* v. *Hope* (1824) 2 Shaw App. 125 at 135.
[60] *Cruickshank* v. *Gordon* (1843) 5 D. at p. 963, *per* Lord Medwyn; *MacMurchy* v. *Campbell* (1887) 14 R. 725; *M'Creadie* v. *Thomson*, 1907 S.C. 1176 at 1182. There have also been suggestions that use might be made of the Judicial Committee of the Privy Council.
[61] Ersk. I, 2, 32, and *Mackay & Esselmont* v. *L.A.*, 1937 S.C. 860.
[62] These words are omitted as to sheriffs-substitute. Justices of the peace may be removed by the Secretary of State.
[63] Sheriffs' Pensions (Scotland) Act 1961, s. 6, which did not affect existing holders of office, and the County Courts Act 1934, s. 7.
[64] In cases such as *Earl of Morton* v. *Fleming* (1569) Mor. 7325; Lord Cooper's note on *Bruce* v. *Hamilton* in (1946) 58 J.R. 83 and the *Case of Prohibitions* (1607) 12 Co.Rep. 12.
[65] Ersk. I, 2, 25 and 26.

once the rule under Acts of 1424 and 1457 that judges must have a sufficient personal fortune so that they could be made to suffer for wrongdoing. Political neutrality is ensured by exclusion from the House of Commons,[66] and by the fact that their salaries are charged upon the Consolidated Fund, thus removing an opportunity for annual debate. The House of Commons will not discuss the conduct of a judge save on a substantive motion. Independence requires protection in other ways. A degree of immunity from criticism is necessary, though that can be carried to extremes. Murmuring the judges was a crime capable of too wide an application,[67] and the protection of judges in this respect is now normally the province of the law of contempt,[68] a power which will also protect the court in the sense of excluding influences calculated to affect the administration of justice.[69]

Immunity from suit is also required, or, said Stair, none but a fool or a pauper would become a judge. So far as the Court of Session and High Court of Justiciary are concerned this immunity is absolute,[70] as it is in England in respect of judges of superior courts.[71] As to other judges the law is not clear. It is said that the sheriff is in a like position,[72] and granted the position and jurisdiction of a sheriff (at any rate in civil matters), the proposition is a reasonable one. As to inferior

---

[66] House of Commons Disqualification Act 1957, Sched. II, excludes judges of the Supreme Court in England, of the Court of Session, sheriffs and salaried sheriffs-substitute, and county court judges among others. As to the origin of this rule in Scotland see 1957 S.L.T.(News) 134. As to Lords of Appeal in Ordinary, see *ante*, p. 114.

[67] See the Act of 1540, A.P.S. II, 374, and *H.M. Advocate* v. *Robertson* (1870) 1 Coup. 404; Hume, *Criminal Law*, Chap. X; but consider Kennedy, " The Second Division's Progress " (1896) 8 J.R. 268. As to other protections see Ersk. I, 2, 36. For these offences against judges and justice, see Gordon, *Criminal Law*, Chaps. 49 and 50.

[68] As to the principles that govern, see *Milburn*, 1946 S.C. 301. It is there emphasised that contempt can also be too broadly interpreted. See, too, *Ambard* v. *Att.-Gen. for Trinidad and Tobago* [1936] A.C. 322 at 335 : " Justice is not a cloistered virtue : she must be allowed to suffer the scrutiny and respectful, even though outspoken, comments of ordinary man."

[69] *Stirling* v. *Associated Newspapers*, 1960 J.C. 5; and see Gordon, *Criminal Law*, pp. 1020–1022. It should be noted that s. 11 of the Administration of Justice Act 1960, extending the defences in cases of contempt, does not apply to Scotland. The rules exemplified in *Stirling's* case are more rigorous than equivalent rules in England. This is partly attributable to the public character of preliminary proceedings in England, as against the privacy in Scotland and this difference sets a different pattern of thought. For the subtlety of the rules to take account of the nature of the court, see *R.* v. *Duffy, ex p. Nash* [1960] 2 Q.B. 188.

[70] *M'Creadie* v. *Thomson*, 1907 S.C. 1176, and the cases there referred to; *cf.* the older rule in *Band* v. *Clerk and Scott*, May 31, 1797, F.C.

[71] *Anderson* v. *Gorrie* [1895] 1 Q.B. 668.

[72] *Harvey* v. *Dyce* (1876) 4 R. 265, though it must be noted that the case was one of alleged slander, and in this field the law confers much broader protection than in others. *Cf. Watt* v. *Thomson* (1869) 8 M.(H.L.) 77. As to administrative acts, see *Beaton* v. *Ivory* (1887) 14 R. 1057. The position of the sheriff in criminal matters is not quite so clear. It is true s. 75 of the Summary Jurisdiction (Scotland) Act 1954 excludes sheriffs from its scope. But the penalties under the Act of 1701 anent Wrongous Imprisonment were, it seems, recoverable from sheriffs: *Andrews* v. *Murdoch* (1814) 2 Dow. 401. The arguments based on scope of jurisdiction which are emphasised in *Hamilton* v. *Anderson* (1856) 18 D. 1003 do not carry the same weight on the criminal side; and see the hesitation in *Watt* v. *Thomson* (1868) 6 M. 1112 at 1120. See also Glegg, *Reparation*, 4th ed., pp. 163–164.

judges, it seems that liability attaches for acts which are outside their jurisdiction, and probably for acts done within their jurisdiction where malice and want of probable cause can be shown, though it is arguable whether liability will arise from *culpa levissima*.[73] In criminal matters the situation is regulated by the Summary Jurisdiction (Scotland) Act 1954 (s. 75).[74] Strict conditions are laid down before any suit for damages can be brought for any action done under that Act, conditions which support the above views and suggest that a mere misconstruction of powers will not result in liability. In England there is also uncertainty, but it seems that there is liability on the part of judges of inferior courts for acts done without or in excess of jurisdiction, though again the concept of reasonableness enters in.[75]

It has been said that this immunity is based on the fact that the judges are the Queen's judges, and to allow liability to exist would be to substitute responsibility to subjects for that to the Queen.[76] The argument is, however, a weak one. How far it is correct to treat judges as Crown servants is debatable,[77] the more so in Scotland where many incidents of their office have been attributed to the fact that that office is a *munus publicum*. The foundation of the principle appears to be the simple fact that it is one necessary for the administration of justice. This is reflected in a variety of rules. The exception in section 2 (5) (which of itself proves nothing about the position of the judges in this respect) to the generality of the Crown Proceedings Act 1947 (whereby it is provided that no action shall lie against the Crown by reason of anything done or omitted in the discharge or purported discharge of judicial responsibilities or in connection with the execution of judicial process) is one application of this principle. Such a rule is also needed to prevent the retrial of decided issues by a collateral attack. So, too, is the immunity of prosecutors in Scotland,[78] and the immunities of those

---

[73] *M'Creadie* v. *Thomson*, 1907 S.C. 1176; *Murray* v. *Allan* (1872) 11 M. 147.

[74] Replacing earlier legislation. As to the effect of this section, see Renton and Brown, *Criminal Procedure*, pp. 449–452.

[75] *Houlden* v. *Smith* (1850) 14 Q.B. 841; *Calder* v. *Halket* (1839) 3 Moo.P.C. 28. County court judges are in this category, and the difference between them and sheriffs is explicable when their jurisdictions are compared. For the equivalent to the 1954 Act, see the Justices' Protection Act 1848; and Thomson, " Judicial Immunity and the Protection of Justices " (1958) 21 M.L.R. 517; and Sheridan, " The Protection of Justices " (1951) 14 M.L.R. 267. For administrative acts, see *O'Connor* v. *Isaacs* [1956] 2 Q.B. 288; and for domestic tribunals, see *Abbott* v. *Sullivan* [1952] 1 K.B. 189.

[76] *M'Creadie* v. *Thomson*, 1907 S.C. 1176; a further difficulty is suggested in *Haggart's Trustees* v. *Hope* (1824) 2 Shaw App. 125 of one judge sitting judgment on another.

[77] Holdsworth (1932) 48 L.Q.R. 25 and Glanville Williams, *Crown Proceedings*, p. 38. For purposes of National Insurance they are treated as self-employed.

[78] *Henderson* v. *Robertson* (1853) 15 D. 292; *Graham* v. *Strathern*, 1924 S.C. 699; and *Hester* v. *MacDonald*, 1961 S.C. 370. The older cases (if *obiter*) allowed an absolute privilege to the Lord Advocate, and more limited protection to other prosecutors. The last case, if it be correctly decided on this branch of the argument, extends an absolute privilege to all. *Sed quaere*, compare *Rae* v. *Strathern*, 1924 S.C. 147. The terms of s. 75 of the Summary Jurisdiction (Scotland) Act 1954 appear to be inconsistent with the broad proposition.

taking part in judicial proceedings.[79] The special privileges of the police which have been noted spring from the same stock. This general principle is one dictated by necessity and has nothing to do with Crown service. It will be noted that in most of its applications there is a gradation in the absolute quality of the immunity so that its application is confined within the scope necessary to achieve the desired end. So it is that the central privilege, that of judges, is graded downwards from that of superior judges. The cases have tended to increase protection.[80] Perhaps the warnings which the courts have sounded in relation to the power to commit for contempt,[81] which has a certain similarity in purpose with the rules now in issue, are also relevant in this context, where the absence of the restraints imposed by a separation of powers should be noted. It must, however, be noted that here again institutional checks are operative. The organisation of the respective Bars affords a check (and in Scotland the role of the Dean of the Faculty of Advocates is to be particularly noted) as does the rule of publicity.[82] Above all the techniques of recruitment to and traditions of the Bench are of great importance.

What has been described is the formal structure of the courts, together with the rules which establish the independence of courts and judges. The operation of the courts, and thus their true constitutional significance, cannot be so easily described, and yet that is, perhaps, one of the most important subjects in constitutional law today. It is evident that the rudimentary and traditional role—the administration of justice in a civil or criminal sense—continues as before. It is, though, also evident that in other respects the role of the courts has changed. The extent to which courts are law-makers has diminished, though clearly it persists.[83] For this change there are many reasons. The rules which the courts themselves evolved, such as the doctrines of precedent, have had a confining influence. The rise of Parliament, both in stature and in scope of operation in regard to legislation and the control of the administration, clearly has its effect, especially when coupled with the growth of ideas of democratic government in restraining courts. There

---

[79] *Williamson* v. *Umphray* (1890) 17 R. 905, though the limits there stated should be noted, and *Marrinan* v. *Vibart* [1962] 3 All E.R. 380. On this matter, generally, see Glegg, *Reparation*, 4th ed., pp. 165–169. These cases emphasise the element of public policy which also underlies the cases on judicial immunities.

[80] *Hester* v. *MacDonald*, 1961 S.C. 370; and compare the old general rules as to judges in *Band* v. *Clerk and Scott*, May 31, 1797, F.C. and Ersk. I, 2, 32.

[81] Note 68, *supra*. As to tribunals of inquiry, see the Report of the Royal Commission (Cmnd. 3121), Chap. VII. *Cf.* the provisions for appeal contained in the Administration of Justice Act 1960 in England.

[82] *Riddell* v. *Clydesdale Horse Society* (1885) 12 R. 976.

[83] Lord Devlin confesses that he doubts " if judges will now of their own motion contribute much more to the development of law," and considers that " The work done by the judges of England is not now as glorious as it was "—*Samples of Law Making*, pp. 23 and 6. In effect the courts are confined to the process of refinement. Earlier the efforts of courts were more fundamental; see, *e.g.*, Fifoot, *Judge and Jurist in the Reign of Queen Victoria*.

has grown up a reliance upon other forms of control to the exclusion of judicial controls, even though the practical working of those other forms may not accord with the assumed manner of their working. Moreover, the issues of public policy have become more obvious and at the same time more political. The development of ideas of corporate personality during and after the Industrial Revolution, which was largely the work of the courts, had considerable social implications, but these were not so generally obvious as are similar implications of litigation concerning the activity of a modern state. Law, in modern statutory forms, is more than ever an instrument of policy, and of policy upon which opinion may be sharply divided, and this fact may again provoke judicial reticence.[84] All the difficulties which surround courts are aggravated by the fact that the law in many important areas is changing from a law of obligations to a law of standards. Questions of land-use are, for example, today as important as questions of land-ownership, yet they cannot be decided by similarly objective rules. Hence, as will appear, many matters of vital concern to particular citizens have been withdrawn from the ordinary courts and entrusted to administrative tribunals. Thus courts do not assume the dominant place in the thoughts of citizens (other than criminals) that they once did. Issues which concern citizens are determined elsewhere, either in the first instance or finally. This fact, too, has its influence upon the place of courts. These matters will be elaborated in the following chapters, but in assessing the constitutional position of the courts allowance must also be made for what has already been said in relation, for example, to prerogative or local government. The general decline of the courts in the field of public law, or their failure to maintain their place in this expanding field, has major constitutional implications, and it may be that, for reasons that will be more apparent after certain aspects of administrative law have been discussed, the correction of this imbalance will require the creation of an appropriate specialised court.[85] For the moment it suffices to say that the doctrine of the separation of powers, if it is to have value, must involve more than a formal separation. There must also be a distribution or balance of power. While the formal separation has been preserved, it is doubtful, to say the least, whether the distribution or balance is correct at the moment.

---

[84] For some illustrations of this tendency, see Mitchell, " The Flexible Constitution " [1960] *Public Law* 321. The narrowness of the boundary between law and policy is illustrated by *Adams* v. *S. of S. for Scotland*, 1958 S.C. 279. In the end of the day the field of policy may for the reasons suggested in the text have expanded at the expense of the field of law.

[85] See Mitchell, " The Constitutional Implications of Judicial Control of the Administration in the United Kingdom " [1967] C.L.J. 46 and " Administrative Law and Parliamentary Control " (1967) 38 *Political Quarterly* 360.

Part Three

THE INTERLOCKING OF INSTITUTIONS
AND CONSTITUTIONAL BALANCE

CHAPTER 15

DELEGATED OR SUBORDINATE LEGISLATION

Introduction. As has been shown, with minor exceptions, whatever arguments may exist about other meanings of the sovereignty or supremacy of Parliament, there can be none about that meaning of those phrases which implies that Parliament is the sole source of legislative power. It is evident that all legislation necessary for the community cannot be made by Parliament. Hence powers of legislation are conferred by Parliament on other bodies, ministers, town councils, universities, and many others. In some of these cases the word " delegation " may be accurately used, in the sense that the power of law-making is conferred upon the other body to act (within limits) without reference to Parliament, and by-laws may be taken as an example of this form of delegation. In other cases legislation may result from processes by which most of the formal legislative stages occur outside Parliament, but some stages occur or may occur inside Parliament. When the term " delegated legislation " is used to describe such legislation the phrase " subordinate legislation " might be more accurate, since the final power of making the law is not delegated by Parliament, but is retained by it or alternatively a right of veto is reserved to Parliament and to that extent a residual power is retained by Parliament. Parliament is simply relieved to a greater or lesser extent in the preliminary stages, and the ultimate parliamentary stage may be more or less of a formality. Such legislation is subordinate in the sense that the provisions governing it are contained in an ordinary statute, and in the sense that it is of more limited scope than primary legislation made by means of an ordinary statute. The Scottish private legislation procedure, which has already been noted, may be taken as an example. In most cases, under that procedure the most important stages occur outside Parliament, but parliamentary stages remain, and the procedure is considered to be inappropriate for major issues of principle, for which primary legislation should be used. This second type of subordinate legislation appears in many forms, the Provisional Orders arising from the general procedure or Special Procedure Orders are examples, as are statutory instruments, and procedures such as those under the Consolidation of Enactments (Procedure) Act 1949 are not clearly distinguishable. It may be possible by formal definition to distinguish these two broad types of delegated or subordinate legislation, but if substance rather than form be looked at it is difficult to distinguish them in many cases, and the term " subordinate legislation " will be used to cover both types.

Development of subordinate legislation. In one sense there is nothing new about subordinate legislation. The Statute of Proclamations 1539 conferred law-making powers upon Henry VIII. In Scotland delegations to conventions, to the Privy Council or to commissions were common and apparently exhibit many modern characteristics.[1] These early delegations are not, however, true examples of what we would now recognise as subordinate legislation. They differ in that ideas of parliamentary supremacy in the legislative field had not then been fully developed. The breach with exclusively parliamentary methods of legislation was not then as conscious as it now is. Moreover, they belong to a different period of legislative draftsmanship, when the respective Parliaments were only just assuming control of the final shape of legislation.[2] Modern subordinate legislation is the result not of accident or oversight, but of principle and necessity. In the years following 1832 the idea that administration, including administrative regulation, could safely be left to others played its part,[3] but the necessity of adjusting legislative methods to the requirements of a new industralised society, coupled with the importance of focusing (whenever possible) parliamentary attention on matters of principle, thereafter ensured that subordinate legislation would grow in size and bulk.[4] That, as Maitland observed, we became a much governed nation was a condition forced upon us rather than chosen by us. To some extent the legislative needs could be met by improvements in legislative procedure,[5] but, whatever improvements were made, difficulties remained. Pressure on parliamentary time became steadily greater despite the evolution of the committee system and of closure devices, and without undesirable inroads into time available for other necessary parliamentary purposes time could not be found for the necessary quantity of legislation unless relief was sought and found outside Parliament.[6]

Further, the House of Commons is not a technical house. Candidates are chosen for their ability as candidates, not for their technical skills,

---

[1] See, *e.g.,* A.P.S. II, 10, the Act of 1425 giving powers to the King and a commission to amend the laws that need amending, the statute of 1685, A.P.S. VIII, 494, giving power to Commissioners to regulate inferior courts and " to make orders to have the samen force and effect as if they were past into a law by ane Act of Parliament in all time thereafter, and to be printed and published as ane Act of Parliament," or the Act Anent the Poor of 1698, A.P.S. X, 177, giving powers to Commissioners to make orders not inconsistent with the standing laws.

[2] Rait, *Parliaments of Scotland,* Chap. VI; Plucknett, *Concise History of English Law,* p. 324.

[3] *e.g.,* the Poor Law Amendment Act 1834, s. 15. The problems of the poor seem always to have influenced constitutional developments.

[4] See Ilbert, *Legislative Methods and Forms;* Thring, *Practical Legislation;* Willis, *The Parliamentary Powers of English Government Departments;* Allen, *Law and Orders;* Sieghart, *Government by Decree;* and for the general background Maitland, *Constitutional History;* Lowell, *Government of England,* Chap. XIX.

[5] Ilbert, *op. cit.* Chap. IV; and Chap. 8, *ante.*

[6] The point is made by a simple comparison of the annual volume of statutes and statutory instruments. In statistical terms the growth of legislation is set out in the *Minutes of Evidence to the Third Report from the Select Committee on Procedure,* the Appendices to the evidence of Sir Gilbert Campion (H.C. 189–1 of 1945–46).

and where there is expertise in the House it is often maldistributed between government and opposition; yet increasingly law is technical, and is made not for the lawyer so much as for the chemist or the engineer. Thus, the floor of the House is not always the appropriate place for criticism. Again, there is a need for flexibility in law to meet changing conditions, and a need to experiment, and a need to act quickly in an emergency.[7] These needs cannot be met within the limits of the ordinary parliamentary timetable.

For these reasons subordinate legislation became increasingly important in practice, and was accepted in theory. Mill, in his *Representative Government*, wrote of the unsuitability of a numerous assembly for the business of legislation [8]; Lord Thring wrote of the necessity of confining parliamentary attention to principle and leaving the details to departments [9]; Sir Courtenay Ilbert indicated the necessity for some delegation,[10] a necessity accepted by Maitland [11] and Dicey.[12] The virtue of delegated legislation is not that it takes something from Parliament, but that it enables Parliament to do better the task for which it is fitted.[13] In fact, delegated legislation is a universal phenomenon. Sometimes attempts are made (with indifferent success) to formalise it and define its scope.[14] Elsewhere, as with us, it breaks through constitutional machinery, even where it might be thought that a monopoly of legislative power was given to one body.[15] It should not, however, be thought that the constitutional merits of subordinate legislation are only of this almost technical order. Government is a rational art, and requires the co-operation of the governed. Delegated legislation can help to win that co-operation and to produce more sensible rules than would otherwise be made. It has these effects since it enables the process of legislation to be spread much more widely through the community. As has already been indicated the legislative process in the sense of primary legislation involves consultation with outside interests. That

[7] Consider Rating and Valuation Act 1961, s. 2; Civil Defence Act 1948; Emergency Powers (Defence) Act 1939; Finance Act 1961, s. 9 (as amended by the Finance Act 1962, s. 34 and Sched. XI); Road Traffic Act 1960, s. 46, or among statutory instruments the trades dealt with in any wages council Order or the permitted emulsifiers in S.I. 1962 No. 720, to take two simple and common-place examples; and see Carr, *Concerning English Administrative Law*, Chap. II, and *Delegated Legislation*, Chap. II.

[8] The " management " of a modern Parliament modifies but does not remove this unsuitability.

[9] *Practical Legislation*, 2nd ed., pp. 44–45.

[10] *Legislative Methods and Forms*, Chap. III.

[11] *Constitutional History*, p. 415 et seq.

[12] *Law of the Constitution*, Chap. I, where, indeed, he urges the extension of the practice.

[13] Griffith, " The Place of Parliament in the Legislative Process " (1951) 14 M.L.R. 279 and 425.

[14] See the French Constitution of 1958; and see P.-M. Gaudemet, " La Loi dans la Constitution de 1958 " [1961] *Public Law* 386, and the sources there referred to.

[15] See particularly *Yakus* v. *U.S.*, 321 U.S. 414 (1944); and compare *Panama Refining Co.* v. *Ryan*, 293 U.S. 388 (1934). Constitutional necessities have everywhere a way of defeating neat semantic arguments.

consultation must be limited in certain ways out of respect for Parliament, which could well resent being faced with what might appear to be a " negotiated " Bill, or with one which because of the nature of the preliminary consultation it would be difficult to change at the parliamentary stage. Such Bills do exist; any multiplication of them could be injurious to Parliament. In the case of subordinate legislation, when principles have already been supposedly determined by Parliament, difficulties in consultation are not so great. It is possible by that means to secure the effective advice of those most knowledgeable in a particular field, and it is indeed possible for such persons to have the feeling that they are effectively part of the legislative process, with consequences upon their acceptance of the rules which emerge. This generalised participation in the legislative process is in itself a valuable element in government.[16]

Yet, while the merits and universality of the institution may be admitted, there are dangers in it; and virtues in parliamentary legislation which Ilbert, among others, emphasised in the passages above referred to. It is possible that too broad powers could be conferred, that matters of principle could be concealed behind the guise of detail and improperly kept from Parliament, or that there should be too little scrutiny of the use made of powers conferred by Parliament. Above all, there is the danger of " hip-pocket " law, law which may vitally affect a citizen but of which, by reason of defects of publicity in its making or promulgation, he could not be reasonably aware.[17] These dangers gave rise to exaggerated fears,[18] which prompted the appointment in 1929 of the Committee on Ministers' Powers. The report of that Committee [19] accepted, within limits and subject to safeguards, that delegated legislation was constitutionally legitimate and necessary, but recommended a greater systematisation, and certain safeguards. In particular, it was concerned that powers should be clearly defined, that judicial review should not be excluded, that measures should be taken to increase intelligibility and publicity, and it was proposed that a special supervisory committee of the House of Commons should be established. The report had little immediate effect, but since 1944 a Select Committee has

16 There are obvious dangers of syndicalism if the process is carried too far, but the process as now organised ensures that the government is involved and should, therefore, be able to judge where the general interest lies and protect that. Moreover, the process of legislation requires degrees of refinement or specification. The legislative process initiated by the Commonwealth Immigrants Act 1962 was completed by a variety of statutory instruments made under it (e.g., S.I. 863, 1316, 1340, 1341, 1342, all of 1962), by the instructions to immigration officers and by R. v. Edgehill [1963] 1 All E.R. 181, at least as far as England is concerned.

17 This danger does not only exist in subordinate legislation; it can equally exist in private legislation; see Mitchell, " Reflections on Law and Orders," 1958 J.R. 19.

18 Which found expression in Lord Hewart's New Despotism. It remains highly inconvenient that on the day on which an Act receives the Royal Assent it should be amended substantially by an instrument made under it, e.g., the Building Control (Cost Limit Exemption) Order, S.I. 1966 No. 997 or S.I. 1966 No. 1021.

19 (1932) Cmd. 4060.

been set up by the House of Commons in each session.[20] In the House of Lords a too-little-observed Special Orders Committee had existed since 1925.[21] Major legislative reform did not result from the report of the Committee on Ministers' Powers until the Statutory Instruments Act 1946, which replaced, and improved on, the earlier Rules Publication Act 1893.

It must be noticed, however, that these reforms are concerned, in the main, with one form of subordinate legislation—that made by ministers. Other forms remain to a large extent in an unregulated state, and what has earlier been said about the by-laws of local authorities is to a large extent applicable to these other forms.[22]

The formal framework of modern subordinate legislation. Powers having been conferred by statute, they are normally today exercised by statutory instrument. That term is defined by section 1 of the Act of 1946.[23] It is a term of art in that its use (or the use of the phrase " Order in Council ") in a statute brings into operation the provisions of the 1946 Act, which has thus to be invoked by post-1947 statutes. There are excluded from the Act such things as Provisional Orders, or such things as " rules " to be made by ministers, where the power of making them is not cast in the appropriate terms. Delegated legislation exists, however, at several levels. It is possible for the exercise of delegated legislative power to confer a further power of law-making, thus there

---

[20] As to the origin of this, see Morrison, *Government and Parliament*, 3rd ed., p. 330 *et seq.* Its terms of reference are to consider all general statutory instruments " with a view to determining whether the special attention of the House should be drawn to it on any of the following grounds: (i) that it imposes a charge on the public revenues or contains provisions requiring payments to be made to the Exchequer or any government department or to any local or public authority in consideration of any licence or consent, or of any services to be rendered, or prescribes the amount of any such charge or payments; (ii) that it is made in pursuance of an enactment containing specific provisions excluding it from challenge in the courts, either at all times or after the expiration of a specified period; (iii) that it appears to make some unusual or unexpected use of the powers conferred by the statute under which it is made; (iv) that it purports to have retrospective effect where the parent statute confers no express authority so to provide; (v) that there appears to have been unjustifiable delay in the publication or in the laying of it before Parliament; (vi) that there appears to have been unjustifiable delay in sending a notification to Mr. Speaker under the proviso to subs. (1) of s. 4 of the Statutory Instruments Act 1946, where an instrument has come into operation before it has laid before Parliament; (vii) that for any special reason its form or purport calls for elucidation; (viii) that the drafting of it appears to be defective." This last head was added in 1967.
[21] Carr, " Parliamentary Control of Delegated Legislation " [1956] *Public Law* 200, and Kersell, " Upper Chamber Scrutiny of Delegated Legislation " [1959] *Public Law* 46.
[22] See, *e.g.,* the Universities (Scotland) Act 1889, s. 21, giving rise to university ordinances upon which regulations and rules of senates and faculties depend.
[23] As explained by the Statutory Instruments Regulations 1947 (S.I. 1948 No. 1) and the following regulations, S.I. 1948 No. 2. The point of technicality as a justification for delegated legislation is made by this start to the new Act. Under s. 1 rules, etc., which are to be made by a power expressed to be exercisable by statutory instrument are statutory instruments, and orders made under a power conferred on Her Majesty to be exercisable by Order in Council also fall within the definition. For some difficulties, see 1960 S.L.T.(News) 173; and for detailed discussion, see Griffith and Street, *Principles of Administrative Law*, particularly for the arrangements for bringing the provisions in pre-1948 Acts into the general scheme.

arises what is termed subdelegated legislation. It has been suggested that this falls outside the scope of the Act,[24] but the government view and the general practice appear to be that subdelegated legislation falls within the Act.[25] It should, however, be noted that the power to subdelegate in that manner is not readily conceded.[26]

The fact that the Act is applicable causes (s. 2) the instrument to be numbered and printed, and under the Act the procedure for laying instruments before Parliament is standardised (ss. 4, 5, 6 and 7). Thus where the instrument is subject to annulment following a resolution of either House it must be laid for forty days,[27] and the consequences of annulment are defined. These provisions are subject to escape clauses. Thus, if it be essential that an instrument come into operation before copies are laid, provision is made for this in section 4 and for an explanation being given to the Speaker and Lord Chancellor. Under the regulations exemptions from the existing requirements are made for, e.g., bulky schedules, temporary or local instruments, or instruments otherwise normally published.[28] Force is given to the requirement of publicity by section 3 (2) of the Act, which provides that in any proceedings for any contravention of an instrument it shall be a defence to prove that at the date of the contravention the instrument had not been published, unless it can be shown that reasonable steps had been taken to bring the instrument to the notice of the public or of persons likely to be affected by it.[29] The exact force of these requirements is uncertain. They may be mandatory, or they may be directory only, in the sense that failure to observe some of them will not involve the invalidity of the instrument in question. On the one hand, the existence of the National Fire Service Regulations (Indemnity) Act 1944 might suggest that such provisions as those relating to laying are mandatory (though such Acts may be passed *ob majorem cautelam*); on the other hand, there is judicial authority for the view that such provisions are directory only.[30] It is clear that where further positive parliamentary action is contemplated the provisions are more than directory, and it may be that no

---

24 *Blackpool Corporation* v. *Locker* [1948] 1 K.B. 349. It may be noted that in *Palmer* v. *Inverness Hospitals Board of Management*, 1963 S.L.T. 124 at 128, a circular from the Secretary of State under the N.H.S. Acts was treated as legislative, at least as far as the hospital board was concerned.

25 Griffith and Street, *op. cit*, 4th ed., pp. 52–55; and see reg. 2 (1) (*a*) of the Statutory Instruments Regulations 1947 (S.I. 1948 No. 1). There may, as the *Blackpool* case indicates, be substantial difficulty in distinguishing genuine subdelegated legislation and ministerial circulars, etc.; and consider the treatment of the circular in *Palmer's Case*, 1963 S.L.T. 124. For an example of express powers to subdelegate, see Southern Rhodesia Act 1965, s. 2 (3).

26 *e.g.*, H.C. 5–III (1958–59).

27 See, too, Laying of Documents before Parliament (Interpretation) Act 1948. There is no absolute uniformity of timetable; see Finance Act 1961, s. 9 and Sched. III.

28 S.I. 1948 No. 1, regs. 5 to 8.

29 See *Defiant Cycle Co. Ltd.* v. *Newell* [1953] 1 W.L.R. 826; *R.* v. *Sheer Metalcraft Ltd.* [1954] 1 Q.B. 586.

30 *R.* v. *Sheer Metalcraft Ltd.* [1954] 1 Q.B. 586 at 590.

universal classification is possible.[31]   In any event, the provisions relating to publicity avoid this difficulty, at least in regard to any criminal prosecution, though the issue could still arise in a civil cause, *e.g.*, in relation to contract, when questions of illegality of the contract could arise.

The controls of subordinate legislation. The Statutory Instruments Act 1946 goes some way to meeting criticism in relation to publicity. There is a well-ordered system of publication of one form of delegated legislation to which resort can be had. The extent to which use is made of this facility is not a matter of legislative regulation. The value of that publicity is perhaps diminished by drafting techniques which do not always aid comprehension by the uninitiated,[32] though these difficulties are in part met by the explanatory note which now accompanies each instrument. Apart from that the main importance of the Act may well be that it provides a framework within which other controls may work.

Parliamentary controls[33] present the greatest difficulties of balance. If they are too light it is said that Parliament is being robbed of its functions; if they are too heavy the essential objectives of the whole system are frustrated. In effect they are of three main types. There is, first, control of the nature and scope of the power delegated at the time that the parent Act is before Parliament as a Bill. On the whole it may be said that greater attention is now paid to this element of control. In the second place, there is the control of the exercise of the power granted. It must be emphasised that this is restrained by the fact that, as now organised, Parliament can only accept or reject an instrument even where it has a positive role to play. It cannot amend, after the manner of a Bill, and this limits parliamentary control to a significant extent. The formal control arises as a result of the mechanism of laying. Laying may take a variety of forms. The instrument may be required to be laid, either before or after it becomes operative, without anything more. In effect this procedure is informative only. Secondly, the instrument may be laid and made subject to annulment, the so-called negative procedure. If a prayer is successfully moved against an instrument, then it may be revoked by an Order in Council.[34] Such revocation does not affect the validity of anything done under the instrument, nor does it prevent another instrument in identical terms being put before the House, even before the revocation takes effect.[35]

---

[31] *Hepburn* v. *Wilson* (1901) 4 F.(J.) 18.

[32] In particular, legislation by reference is unhelpful, though such techniques may be required to make the law as watertight or " rogue-tight " as is possible.

[33] See generally Kersell, *Parliamentary Supervision of Delegated Legislation*, and Carr [1956] *Public Law* 200.

[34] Statutory Instruments Act 1946, s. 5.

[35] See, *e.g.*, S.I.s 315 and 845 of 1951. For an example of the alternatives, see the Building Control Act 1966, s. 8 (5) and (7). Tighter controls need affirmative resolutions in both Houses. Relaxation is subject to a negative vote in either.

Moving for such an address became at one stage a major tactic in party warfare, but that harassing quality has been much diminished by S.O. 100.[36] Frequently the debates upon such motions are not so much specifically directed to the terms of the Order in question as to the general issues which can reasonably be raised on its terms. Sometimes the debate may be merely seeking information, and it is rare for an instrument to be entirely rejected, though a minister may withdraw it in order to put forward an amended version. Thirdly, laying may take the form of laying subject to an affirmative resolution. Without that resolution the instrument has no force or ceases to have force. In practice the main difference between this and the preceding form is that here it is the government which has to make time and keep a House for the debate. In the former case such matters are the concern of those moving the prayer, but overall there is little difference in time occupied by the positive and negative forms.[37] A fourth possibility is laying in draft subject either to an affirmative or negative resolution.[38] These opportunities for parliamentary control are important, but they must remain controls much more of principle than of detail, and their value is affected by the fact that the use made of them is frequently (and properly) political, for the House of Commons is a political body.

The third form of parliamentary control through the Select Committee on Statutory Instruments, commonly called the Scrutiny Committee, is perhaps the most important. The terms of reference of this Committee, which is a sessional one, have already been given,[39] but the importance of " laying " might, formerly, simply be that as a necessary consequence the instrument comes under consideration of the Committee, but as has been seen the remit of the Committee was enlarged in 1968 and this element of the importance of " laying " has diminished. That Committee, like the Public Accounts Committee, receives expert advice, in this case from counsel to the Speaker.[40] In the first fifteen years of its existence the Committee considered 10,232 instruments of which it reported 120 to the House, most falling fairly equally between the heads

---

[36] See, e.g., 561 H.C.Deb. 187–190. The Standing Order provides that on a motion for a prayer against a statutory instrument, the Speaker may adjourn the debate at 11.30 p.m. if he thinks that because of the time of starting the debate and because of the importance of the matter, the time for debate has not been adequate. This removes much of the " harrying " quality of such motions (leading to all-night sittings) which they formerly had. A proposal in 1967 to extend these time-limits to affirmative resolutions was not carried into effect.

[37] See Report of the Select Committee on Delegated Legislation (1952–53) H.C. 310. It should be noted that under this positive form the instrument may either never have effect until approved or may cease to have effect unless approved within a limited period.

[38] As to the use of these, see Griffith and Street, op. cit. For an example of inconsistency, compare S.I. 1959 No. 1975 with S.I. 1959 No. 1827; and as a recent example of the " draft " procedure, see the Monopolies and Mergers Act 1965, s. 3 (11) and Sched. 2.

[39] Note 20, supra.

[40] Who at the establishment of the committee was Sir Cecil Carr, whose works have been referred to above.

of "unusual or unexpected use of power," "delay in publication or laying" or "need of elucidation." Its importance should not be judged by a simple comparison of these figures. The mere existence of the Committee is important as a potential check, particularly since it has the power to require explanations from the departments concerned, and in a variety of ways, especially as to clarity, its influence has been noticeable. The special reports produced by the Committee have drawn useful attention to general problems.[41] The work of this Committee is to a large extent dissociated from the challenge by way of motion. Often, since the Committee requires written explanations, its reports may be too late for such a motion, and furthermore, the purposes of the two techniques of control differ. The motion, if it is not simply intended to seek information, is generally an attack on government policy, whereas the Committee is not intended to consider the merits and policy of an instrument.[42] In the House of Lords instruments which require an affirmative resolution are referred to the Special Orders Committee which may, according to the circumstances, report that the House should examine by a Select Committee,[43] and until a report is received from the Special Orders Committee this affirmative motion is not moved.

Institutional controls. What may generally be called institutional controls are perhaps as important as any, since they operate at the stage before the instrument is made, and at a stage, therefore, where amendment is relatively easy. They include the process of consultation, which may be informal or may be much more formalised. Even apart from any special provision the general convention of consultation in relation to legislative proposals is here operative, and perhaps more effectively so than in relation to primary legislation.[44] Special provisions take many forms. They may require consultation with an *ad hoc* body (as under the Protection of Birds Act 1954, s. 13) or with a particular body which exists for more general purposes (as under the Police Act 1919, s. 4, or more importantly with the Council on Tribunals under section 8 of the Tribunals and Inquiries Act 1958 as to procedural rules made for tribunals falling under the supervision of the Council) or with bodies which are approved or accepted for the purposes of the parent legislation

---

[41] See, as to its working, Report of the Select Committee on Delegated Legislation (1952–53) H.C. 310. From 1957–65 the figures are 5,171 examined and 36 reported on; see (1966–67) H.C. 266, a subsequent survey of its work.

[42] The difference between this and an unusual use of the power is not easy to draw; see Sir Cecil Carr, *Third Report of Select Committee on Procedure*—Minutes (1945–46) H.C. 189–1, Q. 4669. There is, perhaps, some tendency for the Committee to come closer to questions of *vires*; see, *e.g.* (1966–67) H.C. 661–1 or (1967–68) H.C. 9 (iv)—the Second Report from the Select Committee.

[43] The procedure of the Special Orders Committee (see [1956] *Public Law* 207) makes its work particularly useful.

[44] At its most extreme it may, as under the Dock Workers (Regulation of Employment) Act 1946, amount to preparation of the subordinate legislation by affected interests. Too widespread a use of such devices could be, it seems, constitutionally dangerous.

(as under the Education (Scotland) Act 1946, s. 59).[45] The operation of the Council on Tribunals may be of particular importance both in producing a desirable degree of uniformity, and in drawing the attention of departments to the need to maintain certain standards, since it is well possible that a department being primarily concerned with substance might not give equal attention to procedure. The more general these provisions, the more difficult they may, theoretically, be of enforcement, but in practice little difficulty arises.[46]

One particular instance may be noted, namely, the National Insurance Advisory Committee created under section 41 of the National Insurance Act 1946, and continued under section 88 of the National Insurance Act 1965. That Committee has the function of advising the minister and, in general, under section 77 of the 1946 Act (now section 108 of the 1965 Act), the right to see all draft regulations, upon which it reports, having made such inquiry or taken such evidence as it thinks appropriate. Its position is particularly strong since the Committee's Report and the minister's reasons for not accepting any of the recommendations in the former must be laid before Parliament. The Committee itself is a strong one and its work has been invaluable. It is, however, to be doubted whether a widespread use of such a device would not unduly impede governmental action. While the process of consultation, in whatever form, has the democratic virtue of bringing informed opinion to bear,[47] it has also possible disadvantages. If too elaborate it may impose delay, and provoke resistance,[48] or erode both parliamentary control and doctrines of ministerial responsibility. While some erosion may well be acceptable, the process could go too far. The value of this control must, therefore, be judged in a quite general setting.

A second group of what one may call institutional safeguards exists within the administration itself. Subordinate legislation is not taken lightly by the civil service. Internal committees exist to consider drafts, considerable weight being given both to ministerial approval and where possible to ministerial signature. The form of power asked for, whether it is to be subject to positive or negative procedure, is carefully considered

---

45 The Educational Institute for Scotland has, for example, by its charter, particular rights to be consulted.

46 *Thorneloe and Clarkson Ltd.* v. *B.O.T.* [1950] 2 All E.R. 245; and as to the meaning of consultation and advice, see *Rollo* v. *Minister of Town and Country Planning* [1948] 1 All E.R. 13; *Hayman* v. *Lord Advocate*, 1951 S.C. 621. The question arises here, too, whether or not such provisions are mandatory or not: *May* v. *Beattie* [1927] 2 K.B. 353. In *Cannon & Ors.* v. *S. of S. for Scotland*, 1964 S.L.T. 91 the question arose of the situation where the body consulted was improperly composed. The question of the mandatory/directory distinction was not fully argued. It may be noted that the greater part of the Report of the Council on Tribunals for 1966 was taken up with an account of " consultations " which appear to form the greater part of its work. The scope of consultation was enlarged slightly by the Tribunals and Inquiries Act 1966.

47 *Cf.* Circular 21/61 of the Ministry of Housing and Local Government.

48 On the first point, see the debate in 650 H.C.Deb., col. 771; on the second compare Jaffé, " The American Administrative Procedure Act " [1956] *Public Law* 218.

as is draftsmanship itself.[49] All these devices may be conventional, but do not for that reason lack force, and the necessary or desirable scope of other forms of control should be calculated against the background of their existence.

Judicial control. It is evident that the controls hitherto discussed have each a slightly different object. One form of parliamentary control is concerned with policy, a second with technical regularity and general observance of parliamentary intent. Among the institutional controls one is greatly concerned with content, another with administrative morality. None of these classifications is absolute, but the degree of specialisation is useful. None of these controls is primarily concerned with legality, though clearly that is an important element of administrative morality, and equally the House of Commons Committee when it is considering an unusual or unexpected use of the power given is very close to the question of *ultra vires.* In the main, however, control of legality must properly be left to the courts. Concern for the preservation of this element of control is evident in the report of the Committee on Ministers' Powers, and in the terms of reference of the Scrutiny Committee of the House of Commons. It is also evident in the attitude of the courts themselves.

The role of the courts is at the centre of the debate about the effect of provisions such as one that the orders " shall have effect as if they were contained in this Act." Assuming the inability to challenge a statute it was argued that such provisions also made subordinate legislation unchallengeable. It was mistakenly thought that such provisions were modern, whereas they were ancient, running back to a time of uncertainty about the nature of both primary and secondary legislation.[50] In origin such provisions probably meant little more than that the rules were to be observed as law. One result of this misconception was that there were suggestions that such provision did effectively exclude judicial review,[51] though these suggestions did not form part of the *ratio* of the decision. In later years, in England, considerable doubt has been cast upon such suggestions, particularly in *Minister of Health* v. *The King (on the prosecution of Yaffé)*[52] though it cannot yet be said that the widest interpretation (which would exclude judicial review) will not sometimes be there accepted.[53] In Scotland substantial uncertainty existed,[54] and was not quietened by *Lockwood's* case, but it has finally

---

[49] See particularly *Minutes of Evidence, Select Committee on Delegated Legislation* (1952–53) H.C. 310–1, especially the evidence of Sir Frank Newsam and Sir David Milne: and see Mitchell " Reflections on Law and Orders," 1958 J.R. 19.
[50] See the examples in note 1, *supra.*
[51] *Institute of Patent Agents* v. *Lockwood* (1894) 21 R.(H.L.) 61 at 67; [1894] A.C. 347 at 360, *per* Lord Herschell.
[52] [1931] A.C. 494; see particularly at p. 503, *per* Lord Dunedin. The rejection of *Lockwood's* case is not as clear as might have been wished.
[53] *Bankes* v. *Salisbury Diocesan Council & Ors.* [1960] Ch. 631 at 656.
[54] *Crichton* v. *Forfar County Road Trs.* (1886) 13 R.(J.) 99; *Glasgow Insurance Committee* v. *Scottish Insurance Commissioners*, 1915 S.C. 504; *Shepherd* v. *Howman*,

been asserted that even a provision in the form "as if enacted in the Act" will not entirely exclude judicial review.[55]

The argument is, however, not entirely simple. Judicial review may be concerned with procedural or with substantive regularity, and the attitude of the courts, reflected in the cases referred to above, may affect the interpretation of the sections conferring legislative power. So far as procedural irregularities are concerned, where these do not go to matters of substance, and the order has been made, the courts may more readily accept its finality,[56] though they are prepared to intervene in the preliminary stages.[57] It is clear that in matters of substance the courts are prepared to consider whether or not an order is *ultra vires* in the simpler sense of that phrase, but the exercise of the power to review in that sense depends upon the phraseology of the Act conferring the legislative power. Where that conferment is either in very broad terms, or in terms which largely involve elements of policy, judicial review may be effectively excluded, even though it is not expressly excluded. The wording of the power may be such that the courts are incompetent to determine whether the exercise of it is properly to be regarded as ancillary to the primary purpose,[58] or, where the ambit of the power is defined by such phrases as "for purposes of maintaining services essential to the life of the community," the courts may feel that the interpretation of these phrases is not for them.[59] Again, a power conferred upon Commissioners of Customs and Excise to make regulations for matters for which provision "appears to them to be necessary" does not in terms exclude judicial review, but makes its exercise very difficult.[60] In practice it is in relation to such provisions that debate as to the exclusion of the courts now mainly centres. Provisions of the type "as if contained in the Act" are now rare, and provisions of the type now under discussion (*i.e.*, provisions which do not, in terms, exclude judicial review, but which by their breadth make it difficult) are much

1918 J.C. 78; *David Lawson Ltd.* v. *Torrance*, 1929 J.C. 119; *Bell* v. *S. of S. for Scotland*, 1933 S.L.T. 519.

55 *M'Ewan's Trs.* v. *Church of Scotland General Trs.*, 1940 S.L.T. 356 at 359. It seems that, interpreted in the light of Lord Robertson's remarks, such phrases add little to the strength of the order when made. This interpretation is probably consistent with the history of these provisions.

56 *Hepburn* v. *Wilson* (1901) 4 F.(J.) 18; *R.* v. *Sheer Metalcraft Ltd.* [1954] 1 Q.B. 586.

57 *Bell* v. *S. of S. for Scotland*, 1933 S.L.T. 519.

58 *Demetriades* v. *Glasgow Corporation* [1951] 1 All E.R. 457.

59 *Pollok School* v. *Glasgow Town Clerk*, 1946 S.C. 373.

60 *Commissioners of Customs & Excise* v. *Cure & Deeley Ltd.* [1961] 3 All E.R. 641. The difficulty is probably enhanced by the fact that constitutional cases not being clearly separated from others, the influence of some, decided in special circumstances, such as *Liversidge* v. *Anderson* [1942] A.C. 206, lingers on too strongly in changed circumstances. The particular case of *Cure & Deeley Ltd.* may, however, be of limited application since it involves taxation where rules of construction are more strict. It is to be noticed that, perhaps for the first time, in *Ridge* v. *Baldwin* [1964] A.C. 40 at 72, *per* Lord Reid, full weight is given to such special circumstances. An example of a wide-ranging provision (including the amendment of a statute) which would give powers virtually immune from judicial control is to be found in cl. 61 (5) of the Transport Bill 1968.

more common. Yet their full implication for judicial review may escape the attention of the Scrutiny Committee. In assessing the scope of judicial review allowance must be made for the deference of courts to Parliament, and of the reliance which is placed upon the effectiveness of the doctrine of ministerial responsibility. Such deference has the effect of still further increasing the scope of broad provisions, since their exercise will clearly involve considerations of policy which will make the courts reluctant to intervene.

One further factor should be considered in relation to the possibility of a real or effective exclusion of judicial review. That is the existence of provisions which allow a short period for challenge, but once that period has elapsed it is declared that " the Order shall not be challenged in any legal proceedings whatsoever." Such provisions are useful in limiting challenge upon procedural grounds or based upon straight-forward issues of *vires*, which was probably their original purpose. They may work hardship where the challenge is based upon bad faith, since the grounds for such a challenge might not be discernible within the limited period. It has been held in England that such provisions would operate to exclude challenges to validity based upon assertions of bad faith, where the challenge is made outside the short period of time.[61] It is, however, doubtful whether such provisions would be similarly interpreted in Scotland.[62] The element of general principle in the judicial control of public bodies which marked the growth of Scots law in this context would appear to be inconsistent with such a result.

Subject to these reservations judicial control can ensure that proper procedures are followed,[63] that the order, as made, is squarely within the terms of the power and is not achieving some oblique purpose.[64] The courts will also concern themselves with the form of orders, particularly where there is the possibility of a prosecution in the event of breach, and will thus insist upon a minimum degree of certainty and clarity.[65] Thus there exists a sufficient framework for judicial control.[66]

---

[61] *Smith* v. *East Elloe R.D.C.* [1956] A.C. 736.

[62] See, *e.g.*, the reservations in *Pollok School* v. *Glasgow Town Clerk*, 1946 S.C. 373 and *Demetriades* v. *Glasgow Corporation* [1951] 1 All E.R. 457. See, too, *Caledonian Ry.* v. *Glasgow Corporation* (1905) 7 F. 1020 at 1027, *per* Lord President Dunedin.

[63] *Magistrates of Ayr* v. *Lord Advocate*, 1950 S.C. 102; *Kerr* v. *Hood*, 1907 S.C. 895.

[64] *Caledonian Ry.* v. *Glasgow Corporation* (1905) 7 F. 1020; *Rossi* v. *Magistrates of Edinburgh*, 1904 7 F.(H.L.) 87; *Brock* v. *Forth Pilotage Authority*, 1947 S.N. 41; *London and Westcliff Properties Ltd.* v. *Minister of Housing and Local Government* [1961] 1 All E.R. 610.

[65] *Marshall* v. *Clark*, 1957 J.C. 68; *Tuker* v. *Minister of Agriculture* [1960] 2 All E.R. 834. It should, however, be noted that in the former case the suggestion is not that the regulations would be invalid, but that they would be unenforceable; moreover, the attitude of the court in the former case emphasises the importance of the operation of the Scrutiny Committee in relation to clarity.

[66] It must be emphasised that the framework only is here discussed. The detailed application of the rules gives rise to many difficult questions, including such matters as the relationship of subordinate to primary legislation; see, for example, among recent illustrations *Bingham* v. *Bruce* [1962] 1 All E.R. 136; *Canadian Pacific Steamships* v. *Bryers* [1958] A.C. 485; *Stephens* v. *Cuckfield R.D.C.* [1960] 2 Q.B. 373;

The operation of that control is, it must be emphasised, affected by many of the considerations indicated above. It is probable that subordinate legislation made by bodies other than ministers will be more closely scrutinised (though the tests may formally be the same) than will be ministerial subordinate legislation.[67] It is at such points that the theoretical effectiveness of conventional doctrines such as those of ministerial responsibility have effect in determining the attitude of the courts. Moreover, while principles may still be formulated in traditional words it may also be true that the practical application of these principles has changed.[68] Judicial control must be looked at against the background of the whole complex of controls. That complex is necessary because of the different elements of subordinate legislation which require surveillance, not all of which could be overseen by one body.

Thus the sufficiency of the present system of surveillance cannot be judged from the point of view of any one method of control. The operation of each is to a certain extent determined by views which are held of the operation of others, and these views may amount to little more than an acceptance of traditional phraseology, or they may be determined by a realistic assessment of the operation of other controls. It is for the student to determine for himself whether an appropriate balance is now struck, particularly in relation to judicial control, though it must be emphasised that all the difficulties which face courts when they reach out into the realms of policy (albeit through the mechanism of " reasonableness "), and which have already been noted,[69] are here as great as anywhere else.

Boddington v. *Wisson* [1951] 1 K.B. 606. The proper explanation of these aspects is more appropriate to books on administrative law, and the reader is referred to Griffith and Street, *op. cit.*; Wade, *Administrative Law*; and Bennett Miller, *Local Government and Administrative Law*.

67 See *Marshall* v. *Clark*, 1957 J.C. 68; *Pollok School* v. *Glasgow Town Clerk*, 1946 S.C. 373; or *Sparks* v. *Edward Ash Ltd.* [1943] K.B. 223.

68 Consider, *e.g.*, the modern application of the principles enunciated by Lord President Inglis in *Nicol* v. *Magistrates of Aberdeen* (1870) 9 M. 306 at 308 in the light of *Blair* v. *Smith*, 1924 J.C. 24; and compare *Sommerville* v. *Langmuir*, 1932 J.C. 55 with *Magistrates of Ayr* v. *S. of S. for Scotland*, 1950 S.C. 102 at 106–107, or the weight attributed to laying before Parliament in either *Lockwood's* case or (more particularly) *Yaffé's* case, note 52, above.

69 *Ante*, p. 265.

CHAPTER 16

ADMINISTRATIVE TRIBUNALS

Introduction. The changing role of government had its effects on the machinery for adjudication, just as it had upon the machinery for legislation. The introduction of a system of National Insurance, for example, brought with it a vast increase in the number of issues upon which adjudication was necessary. Similarly, the changing nature of law had its effects. In many important fields, such as property, law was changing from a law of obligation to a law of standards; questions of land-use, for example, became almost as important as questions of land-ownership. Thus new issues arose for decision, or old issues arose in greater quantity or in more significant forms.[1] Coupled with such developments was the development of the courts themselves. The process of the refinement of the judicial process involved an increasing rigidity in courts, and in their procedures, which reduced the suitability of courts for the more modern forms of adjudication which were required. A specialised machine designed for making a precision product is expensive to run and relatively inflexible. Thus superior courts were unsuited for the determination of many issues, because of expense and slowness, qualities which, within limits, were necessary consequences of their other functions.[2] Lower courts could equally be overwhelmed by the mass of these newer disputes,[3] and even if they were not overwhelmed the ordinary administration of justice could suffer insupportable delays. In neither set of courts may the judge have the necessary expertise in the qualities of good farming or good town planning, and in both, the procedures and rules of evidence, designed for dealing with issues of fact, may well be inappropriate or too complex for the matters involved, and may well increase the expense of securing a determination.[4]

Other reasons contributed to these developments. In its expanded scope efficient administration required new methods for reaching

---

[1] The aedilic jurisdiction of the Dean of Guild Court, and the concern of that court for neighbourhood questions, are sufficient examples.

[2] See, *e.g.,* Lord Cooper, " The Defects in the British Judicial Machine," 2 J.S.P.T.L.(N.S.) 91, and his views in " Administrative Justice " (1954) 32 *Public Administration* 165.

[3] Local appeal tribunals under the National Insurance (Industrial Injuries) Act heard in 1961 7,006 cases, claims determined under that and the National Insurance Acts in that year numbered some 15,000,000 (Report of the Ministry of Pensions and National Insurance for 1961). The industrial injuries jurisdiction was transferred from sheriff and county courts as possible and usual tribunals of first instance. The jurisdiction was to a great extent arbitral. The litigious element in the Workmen's Compensation Scheme was one of the points of criticism of it.

[4] The Small Debt Court exists to overcome somewhat similar difficulties.

decisions. The necessary information upon which to formulate a decision might most easily be acquired by means of a local inquiry, at which adversary procedures could be important in testing the weight of evidence. Moreover, with the advent of an " open " society, administration must itself, if its results are to be generally acceptable, become more open in its processes. One consequence of this pressure is the development of consultation in the legislative process, another is the development of local inquiries to which reference has already been made. Again, as law developed in the ways that have been indicated it became, in one sense, less pure. The element of policy in any decision tended to grow and to be more obvious,[5] and thus it was felt that decisions should be taken by bodies other than the ordinary courts, a feeling which increased as respect for the neutrality of those courts developed. It must be emphasised that the evolution was, until recent years, slow, but that there is nothing new in administrative tribunals. The Commissioners for the Plantation of Kirks and Valuation of Teinds [6] were such, and met with all the criticisms of modern administrative tribunals. Correspondingly, because of the length of that development the courts are not without the marks of administrative tribunals.[7] Just as the evolution of delegated legislation gave rise to problems and to disquiet so too did the rise of administrative tribunals. Informality and speed can prejudice justice, in the administration of which the courts had an expertise, even if they were not expert on other aspects of the disputes. The expert may be too enthusiastic, and give too little weight to other considerations. The creation of administrative tribunals can be carried too far, so that the process of administration becomes too judicialised,[8] and other constitutional doctrines, such as ministerial responsibility, are eroded. Here, as elsewhere, the problem is one of finding the right balance of controlling techniques.[9]

Types of tribunal. It is impossible to separate by any clear and meaningful test administrative tribunals from courts properly so called.[10]

---

5 See, *e.g., General Poster & Publicity Co. Ltd.* v. *S. of S. for Scotland*, 1960 S.C. 266 at 275. It must be remembered that an element of policy has always been present (*cf.* the history of the doctrine of common employment), but the nature of " policy " in the cases now under discussion is sharper and more debatable.

6 A.P.S. V, 35.

7 *e.g.,* in questions such as the appointment of *curators,* or in questions of guardianship, see the discussion in *Re K. (Infants)* [1962] 3 All E.R. 1000; *Fowler* v. *Fowler and Sines* [1963] 1 All E.R. 119.

8 *Cf. M'Millan* v. *Inverness C.C.,* 1949 S.C. 77, *per* Lord President Cooper.

9 See, generally, Allen, *Law and Orders*; Griffith and Street, *Principles of Administrative Law*; de Smith, *Judicial Review of Administrative Action*; Wade, *Administrative Law*; Dicey's article " The Development of Administrative Law in England " (1915) 31 L.Q.R. 148 should be noted for his reaction to the growth of administrative tribunals.

10 The attempt was made in the *Report of the Committee on Ministers' Powers* (1932) Cmd. 4060, §§ 73–74, to isolate the so-called quasi-judicial function; that attempt has often been attacked; see, *e.g.,* Robson, *op. cit.,* and de Smith, *op. cit.,* and the *Report of the Committee on Administrative Tribunals and Enquiries* (1957) Cmnd. 218 (the Franks Report). Chap. 3 commends an empirical approach.

There is a gradation from what could be called a typical judicial process to a typical administrative process. One useful distinction may, however, be made between administrative tribunals and inquiries. Proceedings in the former result in a decision, those in the latter normally result in a recommendation, the final decision being taken by or on behalf of the minister. The two types of proceedings are distinguished in the Tribunals and Inquiries Act 1958, s. 1.[11] All that here can be done is to indicate the range of tribunals and the sort of decision with which they are concerned. A detailed survey of all tribunals would only serve to obscure a picture which is in any event sufficiently difficult to comprehend.

It would be reasonable to regard both the Restrictive Practices Court and the Scottish Land Court, to which reference has already been made, as administrative tribunals of a highly formalised type. In both cases the element of policy or discretion can be great, involving non-legal considerations in a way which distinguishes the operation of such courts from that of a court concerned with an ordinary civil cause.[12] Although both have marked judicial characteristics, the " administrative " quality of both is indicated by the sharing of related functions with administrative bodies. Thus, in the case of the Restrictive Practices Court the related problem of monopolies is entrusted to the minister and the Monopolies Commission (since questions of policy or politics assume in that context a greater significance). So, too, in relation to crofting, policy, in a slightly different sense, requires a sharing of functions between the Land Court and the Crofters Commission.[13] In this same

---

[11] The distinction there made is useful, because it affects the operation of the Council on Tribunals. It may not be as " real " as it appears. Of the 6,500 inquiries in 1960 under the Minister of Housing, the Minister accepted the inspector's recommendation in 93 per cent. of the cases (641 H.C.Deb., col. 5). This situation led to the proposal in the White Paper (Cmnd. 3333) and in the Town and Country Planning Bill now before Parliament to delegate these decisions. Although in Scotland the term " reporter " suggests a concern with fact only, the St. Andrews House Circular of May 12, 1958, says the report will normally lead up to recommendations. A fair idea of the range of the first group of tribunals can be gained from a scrutiny of Parts I and II of Sched. I to the Act of 1958. The lists there given cannot be taken as generally exhaustive, being only for the purposes of the Act and also being liable to amendment as new tribunals are created. The distinction between the tribunals and inquiries is based on the Franks Report, Chap. 3, emphasising the weight of rules of law in relation to the decisions of administrative tribunals. It should be noted that all inquiries referred to in this chapter are part of the normal machinery of government and are distinct from those held under the Tribunals of Inquiry (Evidence) Act 1921, which are for the most part established to deal with allegations of a " scandal " in government and which were simply intended to overcome the " political " tendency of Select Committees. As to these, see the Report of the Royal Commission on Tribunals of Inquiry (1966) Cmnd. 3121.

[12] S. 21 of the Restrictive Trade Practices Act 1956 sets out the grounds upon which the court may hold a registered agreement not to be contrary to the public interest. These grounds involve the assessment of economic and other considerations quite outside the range of law. See, too, the considerations which must govern the Land Court in determining whether or not to uphold a notice to quit: Agricultural Holdings (Scotland) Act 1949, s. 25 (as amended).

[13] Restrictive Trade Practices Act 1956, ss. 28 and 29, and the Crofters (Scotland) Acts 1955 and 1961. Storing and Self, " The Birch in the Cupboard " [1960] Public Law 367, should be considered in this context: and see The Farmer and the State by the same authors.

group must be placed certain other tribunals. The Lands Tribunal, operating in England and Wales,[14] is a tribunal dealing very broadly with problems of valuation and compensation, so that there can be built up both expertise and uniformity, but its aspect as a court is emphasised by the fact that its president must either have held judicial office or be a barrister of seven years' standing. From it appeal lies by way of case stated to the Court of Appeal. In relation to inland transport, the Transport Tribunal operates both as a court of first instance in relation to charges schemes in London, and as a court of appeal from licensing authorities for goods vehicles, and for its different purposes is now organised in two divisions.[15] It has marked characteristics as a court, the president, a lawyer, holds office during good behaviour, and from it appeals on questions of law lie to the Court of Session or Court of Appeal, depending upon the venue of the original hearing.[16] The Special Commissioners of Income Tax [17] form in effect a court of a similar specialised type, but in that case, and in relation to the Air Transport Licensing Board,[18] the strong " judicial " element in the presidency which has been noticed in relation to the bodies just discussed is not so apparent, or is absent. The Special Commissioners are civil servants, the chairman of the Air Transport Licensing Board holds office according to the terms of the instrument of his appointment. Somewhat in between these two groups are the industrial tribunals first established under the Redundancy Payments Act 1965, which have since had powers under the Contracts of Employment Act 1963 and the Industrial Training Act 1964 transferred to them, and new powers given by the Selective Employment Payments Act 1966 and the Docks and Harbours Act 1966. Thus there has emerged a series of tribunals which is capable of having major effects in the field of industrial law, and there is evident in these transfers an attempt at grouping functions which is a hopeful indication of a desire to secure an element of the system within the range of tribunals.

Apart from such specialised tribunals the curial character of administrative tribunals varies greatly. Where tribunals concerned with a particular subject-matter are organised in a hierarchy that character is often marked in the higher tribunals, whereas the lower ones may merge with the administration. Thus in the field of National Insurance, the initial decision is taken by an insurance officer who is a civil servant

---

14 Established under the Lands Tribunal Act 1949; see, generally, Van Oss and Mac-Dermot, *The Lands Tribunal*. Its functions as an appeal court in the rating system are performed by the Valuation Appeals Court in Scotland. Compensation, failing agreement, on a compulsory purchase is there dealt with by arbitration.

15 See, generally, for the history of this body, Kahn-Freund, *The Law of Inland Transport*, and for the present structure, see Transport Act 1962, s. 57.

16 As to appeals, see *British Transport Commission* v. *L.C.C.* [1953] 1 Q.B. 736 and *Merchandise Transport Ltd.* v. *B.T.C.* [1962] 2 Q.B. 173.

17 Income Tax Act 1952, s. 8; the legal qualifications of the Special Commissioners are markedly different from those of the General Commissioners.

18 Civil Aviation (Licensing) Act 1960, s. 1 and Sched. I.

chosen by the minister. Thence appeal lies to a local tribunal of three members; a paid chairman, and one chosen from a panel of employers and self-employed persons, the third from an employed persons panel.[19] All are part-time appointees and have no real long-term security of tenure. From this body appeals lie to the Commissioner (or Industrial Injuries Commissioner in the case of the parallel scheme), who is required to be an advocate or barrister of not less than ten years' standing, who holds office during good behaviour.[20] Somewhat similarly, under the National Health Services Acts,[21] there is an increase in formality from the service committees which investigate alleged breaches of service by National Health Service staffs, and report to the Executive Council which decides upon a recommendation to the minister. Anyone aggrieved by the decision of the Executive Council may appeal to the minister, who may (and sometimes must) hold a local inquiry, at which procedure becomes much more formal.

In other cases administrative tribunals are not thus part of a system. Of this group there are many examples, and the independent schools tribunals,[22] or rent tribunals,[23] can serve as examples. Among this group, where appellate procedures are provided, appeal may lie to the minister, as in the system of licensing public services by road transport.[24]

Types of inquiry. Inquiries are as varied in form and purpose as are tribunals. The Tribunals and Inquiries Act 1958, s. 1, speaks of them in the context of " administrative procedures involving . . . the holding by or on behalf of a minister of a statutory inquiry." That context is broad enough. It can cover inquiries which precede decisions about the designation of a new town, those which precede the confirmation of a compulsory purchase order, or approval of a planning scheme. They may be concerned with the enlargement of a burgh, the alterations

---

[19] For a good factual analysis of the staffing of administrative tribunals, see McCorquodale, " The Composition of Administrative Tribunals " [1962] *Public Law* 298.

[20] The term " Commissioner " includes Deputy Commissioners. In case of difficulty a tribunal consisting of the Commissioner and two Deputies may be convened. For operation, see Safford, " The Creation of Case-Law under the National Insurance and National Insurance (Industrial Injuries) Acts " (1954) 17 M.L.R. 197. In 1961 the Commissioner decided 1,544 National Insurance appeals, 773 under the industrial injuries scheme, 80 family allowance appeals. Seven appeals were heard by tribunals, being appeals which involved questions of law of special difficulty.

[21] National Health Service Act 1946 and National Health Service (Scotland) Act 1947. In 1966, 1,006 decisions were issued by the minister. Out of 85 appeals against decisions of Executive Councils, 37 were allowed. Out of 208 decisions to withhold remuneration, only 32 related to the General Medical Services.

[22] Education (Scotland) Act 1962, s. 113; Education Act 1944, s. 72.

[23] Rent of Furnished Houses Control (Scotland) Act 1943, s. 1, or the English Act of 1946. Under the Rent Act 1965 a system of local rent assessment committees is established.

[24] In contrast to the system in relation to goods vehicles (note 15, *supra*) the Transport Tribunal has jurisdiction as to road transport in the London area: Transport Act 1962, s. 45. The route of appeal is not uniform. The Caravan Sites and Control of Development Act 1960, s. 33, gives an appeal against a planning enforcement notice to the minister in England and Wales. In Scotland such appeals still run to the sheriff, as they have since 1947.

of ward boundaries within a burgh, the reorganisation of local government areas. They may be established primarily for the ascertainment of facts, as in connection with accidents on the railways, in the air or at sea, or mining accidents. In such cases they may, either originally, or as the inquiry progresses, become concerned with the attribution of blame or the ascertainment of fault. In such cases, when the inquiry becomes thus centred upon an individual it is noticeable that the procedure becomes more formalised in relation to that individual.[25] Just as the subject-matter of inquiries is varied, so is the type of person who holds the inquiry. He may hold such inquiries as part of his normal duties. A sheriff is responsible, for example, for inquiries in connection with the extension of a burgh, and that administrative function is part of the standing obligations of the office. He may hold a specialised appointment such as that of the Commissioner of Wrecks (when the inquiry into marine accidents is most formal). The person presiding may, as with the inspectors on the staff of the Ministry of Housing and Local Government, be a civil servant responsible for holding inquiries into a large range of matters related to local government, or he may, as is frequently the case in such cases in Scotland, be a " reporter " named *ad hoc* for the purposes of the particular inquiry, who is otherwise a practising member of the Bar. At one time the appointment of advocates was almost automatic, though recently there has been an increasing tendency to appoint former civil servants of distinction, or other similar persons.

The inquiry may then be primarily fact-finding; it may be primarily concerned with governmental matters. Even these last may affect individuals in a variety of generalised ways, as, for example, in connection with the adjustment of burgh boundaries. The inquiry may affect an individual much more directly and closely in relation to his property, as, for example, where the inquiry is in relation to a compulsory purchase order, or upon a planning matter. Except where the revocation of a licence is involved (as may be the case with pilots of aircraft, officers of the Merchant Navy or mining officials) there is always a substantial element of policy involved in the final decision even when individual property rights are most immediately affected (as in the case of a compulsory purchase order). Considerations of the location of population, of public investment, or even of the desirability of the project for which the order is required, may all be involved. All of these may be matters of argument rather than of proof. Thus, it is clear that in these cases although there may be a dispute, there is much less of a *lis* or specific claim than in those matters which are normally dealt with by tribunals.

On the whole, questions have arisen largely in connection with inquiries arising from proposals for compulsory purchase orders, or from

---

[25] The Report of the Committee on Civil Aircraft Accident Investigation 1961 (C.A.P. 169) will give an indication of the techniques and difficulties.

inquiries relating to planning matters, and it is these which will be mainly discussed here.

The problem of administrative tribunals and inquiries. It is apparent that among administrative tribunals there is no uniformity as to structure, nor as to their relationship with the ordinary courts. From some appeals lie to the ordinary courts, from others appeal is to another administrative tribunal or to an administrative body. Some closely resemble courts in composition, and, in operation, are simply specialised courts. In other cases the resemblance is much more to an administrative body. Yet others resemble more closely bodies which are halfway between public and private bodies. Under the Police Acts, and the disciplinary regulations made thereunder, tribunals are constituted for hearing allegations of offences against those regulations.[26] Such bodies closely resemble in function professional disciplinary bodies such as the Disciplinary Committee of the General Medical Council from which, under the Medical Act 1956, appeal lies to the Judicial Committee of the Privy Council.[27] There is a further shading from such bodies to the disciplinary organs of private bodies, such as trade unions, whose operations can have consequences of which the state must take notice.[28] Because of this variability and of these gradations there are obvious difficulties in formulating general rules of law for controlling all such bodies.

Inquiries. These difficulties are enhanced when inquiries are considered. The device of an inquiry (which, when that course is suitable and convenient, is held locally) is an obvious one, serving the useful purpose of gathering information and permitting objectors to proposals to formulate their objections. Most frequently the device was (and still is) used in circumstances which involved the compulsory purchase of land. The system could conveniently be worked so long as local authorities were originators, and had a relatively high degree of autonomy in such matters as slum clearance, building lines or housing. In such circumstances the minister could appear as the *deus ex machina*, hold an inquiry, and issue a determination. Once, however, it was common for the proposals to originate with the minister (as they must under the New Towns Act 1946) or it was common for the minister to be in close contact with a local authority at all stages in a proposal (so that he could not suddenly appear as a neutral) the situation was

---

[26] See Police Act 1964, s. 37, s. 49 and Sched. 5, and see Police (Scotland) Act 1967; and as to fire services, see *McDonald* v. *Lanarkshire Fire Brigade Joint Committee*, 1959 S.C. 141.

[27] As to such appeals, see *McCoan* v. *General Medical Council* [1964] 3 All E.R. 143. The public character of similar bodies is reflected in the *Report of the Committee on Powers of Subpoena* (1960) Cmnd. 1033. These medical tribunals are concerned with the profession generally, those above referred to are concerned with policing the National Health Service.

[28] e.g., *Barnard* v. *National Dock Labour Board* [1953] 2 Q.B. 18; *Lee* v. *Showmen's Guild* [1952] 2 Q.B. 329.

altered.[29] In any event, other doctrines come into play in relation to many such inquiries. If the theory of ministerial responsibility is to be maintained the person holding the inquiry cannot formally decide in his own name.[30] Moreover, the element of policy involved in the decisions in question was such that ultimately the controlling voice had to be administrative. Individual disquiet was therefore inevitable. The individual, rightly or wrongly, might assume that he was in the face of a judge, who was not neutral, and he would see overridden arguments, which were to him convincing.

The process of reform. The haphazard growth of tribunals and inquiries meant that there were faults in the system. Reasons might not be given for a decision, and there was no clear feeling that justice was done. The feeling of malaise grew, and was emphasised in the same way as was that in relation to delegated legislation. The Committee on Ministers' Powers therefore considered administrative adjudication as well as administrative legislation. The misfortune of the report was that it attempted to separate, by definition, judicial, administrative and quasi-judicial decisions, but in practice these definitions proved inadequate as a basis for legislative reform.[31] While therefore the Committee recommended minor reforms no action was taken. Interest was renewed particularly as a result of *Franklin* v. *Minister of Town and Country Planning*,[32] and of unhappy events at Crichel Down[33] (even though the latter were, in truth, distinct from the issue of administrative adjudication). In consequence a Committee (commonly called the Franks Committee) on Administrative Tribunals and Enquiries was established.[34] The report of that Committee adopted an empirical approach,[35] and proposed detailed reforms in procedure, as well as the general reform of the establishment of a supervisory body. As a result

---

29 This alteration in England provoked all the argument about a *lis* or a *quasi-lis*: *Board of Education* v. *Rice* [1911] A.C. 179; *Errington* v. *Minister of Health* [1935] 1 K.B. 249, leading up to *Franklin* v. *Minister of Town and Country Planning* [1948] A.C. 87. In England the position was aggravated by the fact that the inquiry was normally held by an inspector who was on the staff of the minister. In Scotland it was held (as has been indicated above) by a reporter, normally a member of the Bar.

30 In fact, it was, however, said that of 6,500 inquiries under the Minister of Housing the inspector's report was accepted in 93 per cent. of the cases and in the balance of cases the departure from the report was not always substantial (641 H.C.Deb., col. 5). Now, however, see the proposals in Cmnd. 3333 and the Town and Country Planning Bill 1967 delegating the power of decision.

31 For criticism of these definitions, see *Ridge* v. *Baldwin* [1963] 2 All E.R. 66, *per* Lord Reid; and in the books, see Robson, *Justice and Administrative Law*; and Griffith and Street, *op. cit.* Chap. IV; and see, generally, Wade, *Administrative Law*; and de Smith, *Judicial Review of Administrative Action*, Chap. II.

32 [1948] A.C. 87.

33 Report of the Public Inquiry on the Disposal of Land at Crichel Down (1954) Cmd. 9176.

34 The report (the Franks Report) was published in 1957 as Cmnd. 218. The report and the minutes of evidence are to be commended as a mine of information on administrative adjudication.

35 Though at points the semantic approach was not absent; see particularly § 40 and Chap. 4.

of the consideration of the report, the Tribunals and Inquiries Act 1958 was passed carrying out those of the proposals of the Committee which were acceptable to the government. Yet others, *e.g.*, in relation to procedures at inquiries, were implemented by administrative means. While the Report is of general importance, it seems most suitable to consider its consequences in the context of the various controls of administrative tribunals.

Institutional controls. Attention has already been drawn to the requirement that the president of certain tribunals should have legal qualifications. By section 6 of the Tribunals and Inquiries Act there was an extension of this requirement to certain tribunals under the National Service Acts. More importantly by section 3 the chairmen of certain tribunals established under the National Assistance Act, or National Insurance Act, and of rent tribunals under the Furnished Houses (Rent Control) legislation, shall now be selected from panels appointed by the Lord Chancellor or the Lord President or Lord Chief Justice of Northern Ireland, as the case may be, for tribunals operating in England and Wales, in Scotland, or in Northern Ireland. Further, by section 5, no power to terminate a person's membership of any of the tribunals listed in the First Schedule to the Act (with few exceptions) can be exercised without the approval of the Lord Chancellor, Lord President or Lord Chief Justice of Northern Ireland, according to where the tribunal sits. If it sits in more than one jurisdiction each appropriate person must consent. Thus there is some buttress for independence, but where appointments are for limited terms, as is normal, this provision does not affect the question of renewal of appointment, so that its effect can be overemphasised. Probably the most important provision in the Act is section 1 establishing the Council on Tribunals with a specific Scottish Committee (some of whose members are, and others of whom are not, members of the General Council). Under the Act the Scottish Committee must be consulted where appropriate and it may of its own motion report on a matter to the Council. The Parliamentary Commissioner for Administration was made a member of the Council and of the Scottish Committee by the Parliamentary Commissioner Act 1967.

The charter of the Council is a broad one. It is charged with keeping under review the constitution and working of the tribunals listed in the First Schedule to the Act [36]; with reporting on such matters as may be referred to it concerning any tribunal (other than a court of law); and with reporting on matters referred to it or which it may consider to be of special importance with respect to administrative procedures which involve the holding of an inquiry. Originally the definition of a statutory inquiry was a narrow one, and included only

---

[36] Under s. 10 additional tribunals may be added to the Schedule as was, for example, the Registrar under s. 13 of the National Insurance Act 1959.

those which were obligatory under statutes. By the Tribunals and
Inquiries Act 1966 others of a discretionary character may be brought
within the scope of the Council. Further, by section 8 of the Act, no
power to make procedural rules for any of the scheduled tribunals
may be exercised by any appropriate authority without consultation
with the Council. As a result of a somewhat inelegant process of
amendment a new section, 7A, is inserted by section 33 of the Town and
Country Planning Act 1959, and of the Scottish Act of the same year,
giving to the Lord Chancellor and the Lord President the power to make
rules (after consultation with the Council) regulating procedure at
inquiries. By section 4, the Council is given the specific task of making
general recommendations on appointments to tribunals or to the panel
from which they are formed.

There is thus constituted for the first time a body capable of keeping
under continuous review the system of administrative adjudication, and
the performance of that function will be aided by the practice of the
Council of making on-the-spot inspections of tribunals. It is likely that,
as a result of the operations of the Council, greater uniformity of practice
will arise, and that newly created tribunals will conform to an established
pattern.[37] It must, however, be emphasised that the Council is an
advisory body. Recommendations which it makes, while having great
weight, are not binding upon ministers.[38] It is in such matters that
the weight of the doctrine of ministerial responsibility is seen, as it is
also in a comparison between the recommendations contained in the
Franks Report and the ensuing Act. A choice has to be made between
different methods of control, and if a choice is made to maintain the
system of ministerial responsibility the ultimate effectiveness of such
institutional controls as the Council must be thus limited. It must
equally be emphasised that the Council is supervisory. It is not an

---

[37] See Wade, " The Council on Tribunals " [1960] *Public Law* 351; and for a factual
account of its working, Garner, " The Council on Tribunals " [1965] *Public Law*
321. Unfortunately, the Tribunals and Inquiries Act is in one sense not complete
in itself. Further amendments to the law which resulted from the Franks Report are
to be found, *e.g.*, ss. 179, 181 of the Town and Country Planning Act 1962 and ss.
31, 32 of the Town and Country Planning (Scotland) Act 1959. In both cases s. 32
(or 181) extends s. 9 of the Tribunals and Inquiries Act to inquiries, the original
section having been limited to tribunals, and s. 31 (or 179) extends forms of procedure applicable in cases of compulsory purchase to planning. By the Tribunals
and Inquiries (Discretionary Inquiries) Order 1967 (S.I. 1967 No. 451) some 65 new
classes of inquiry were brought under the Council. See, too, p. 298, *post*.
[38] Second Report of the Council on Tribunals, § 46; and compare the report of the
Council on the Rights of Third Parties at Inquiries (Cmnd. 1787) and the subsequent
regulations, S.I. 1962 Nos. 1424 and 1425 (made, for England and Wales, under the
new s. 7A above referred to), and the correspondence between the Chairman and the
Lord Chancellor reported in [1962] *Public Law* 392 *et seq.* and 239 H.L.Deb. 1149;
664 H.C.Deb., cols. 726–752. As an example of the rejection of recommendations
as to rules, see the Report for 1961, § 33. The Report on the Award of Costs 1964
has been followed by circulars from the Ministry of Housing and Local Government
(No. 73/65), the Welsh Office (No. 35/65) and by the Scottish Development Department (No. 25/66) drawing attention to the Report. In other cases it is difficult to
know what weight to attach to the " exchanges of views " with ministers which appear
regularly in the Annual Reports of the Council.

appellate body. Though it receives complaints from individuals it can, it seems, only concern itself with the general principles involved.[39] In effect, therefore, its concern is primarily with procedure, and in operation it in no way derogates from other controls. In that field it can produce a useful degree of standardisation (if that is not pushed too far) and prevent new tribunals having too much of a random quality. Complaints to the Council are numerically static, and thus when allowance is made for the increase of tribunals under its control are, in one sense, decreasing.

Judicial control. The other main control over administrative adjudication is of necessity judicial. In relation to the most highly judicialised tribunals, parliamentary control would be inappropriate, as it would be in relation to those tribunals organised on a hierarchic basis. Where ultimately, as from the Air Transport Licensing Board, appeal lies to the minister the ordinary rules of answerability to Parliament are applicable. Those rules also apply in relation to inquiries, and there with particular force. The decision is that of the minister, the procedure is designed to preserve that situation and therefore his responsibility remains. There is, however, nothing particular to observe about parliamentary control in this context. The existence of that control does not exclude judicial control, for example, over procedural matters in relation to inquiries,[40] but, as has already been indicated, the two methods react upon each other. If parliamentary controls are to be maintained they will relate to substance. That being so, judicial control will be primarily concerned with procedural and not substantive due process.

There are other reasons which lead to the same conclusion. In the same way that the reasons for the existence of delegated legislation impose limitations upon the controls, so also do the reasons for creating administrative tribunals have a like effect. An appeal upon the subject-matter of the expertise from an expert body to a less expert body is generally inappropriate. The expertise of the courts lies in law and the administration of justice and it is therefore largely upon these matters that judicial control is focused. The topic cannot here be explored in the detail which is appropriate to a work of administrative law, and what follows will be largely concerned with general principles.

A distinction must be made at the outset between appeal and judicial review. Where an appeal exists it may be on a question of fact or of law, or of both. Appeals where they lie to the ordinary courts from administrative tribunals are normally only upon law, and the normal mechanism is by way of stating a case for the opinion of the court. Such

---

[39] Third Report of the Council for 1961, §§ 12, 13 and 63–70; *cf.* Report for 1962, § 62.

[40] *e.g., Magistrates of Ayr* v. *S. of S. for Scotland,* 1950 S.C. 102. The immediate effect of that decision was subsequently removed by statute. As to the effect of this ministerial control, see Report of the Select Committee on Nationalised Industries on British European Airways (1966–67) H.C. 673, paras. IV. 1–56.

proceedings are concerned with the substance of the dispute, and the appellate tribunal may substitute its own decision for that of the inferior tribunal. The Tribunals and Inquiries Act 1958, s. 9, extended the range of tribunals from which such appeals might lie.[41] By the Town and Country Planning legislation of 1959 this section is extended to specified ministerial decisions following inquiries. From many important tribunals, such as the Lands Tribunal, such an appeal already lay. In other cases, notably the National Insurance tribunals, it was considered that the system of tribunals was itself so strong that the addition of an appeal was unnecessary, and might indeed impede.[42] Judicial review on the other hand is concerned with the regularity of proceedings, and so the consequence is that the superior tribunal exercising its power to review will reduce or quash the decision of the inferior tribunal or, if the inferior has not acted, direct it to act. It is in connection with judicial review that most problems arise.

In England the scope of judicial review was, until recently, largely determined by the forms of action, which survived in the field of public law long after private law had been freed from all save their ghosts. The prerogative orders (formerly writs) of mandamus, certiorari or prohibition (these being the most important here) which were the means by which review was sought also dictated its limits. Mandamus existed to compel a tribunal to act, certiorari to quash a decision, and prohibition to prevent a tribunal acting wrongfully. Of them all certiorari was the most important, and since it turned upon the " record " of the proceedings its effectiveness might be limited by the silence of the record as to reasons.[43] The formalism of judicial review has in recent years somewhat abated as a result of the evolution of the more generalised remedy by way of a declaratory order, but it remains important for the influence it has had upon modes of thought,[44] in particular the classification of a function as being judicial or quasi-judicial as against administrative may assume undue importance.[45] In contrast judicial review in Scotland has, it seems, a much more generalised basis, and to a large extent lacks specialised procedures, those available for reducing (or quashing) a

[41] S. 13 also removed some limitations on appeal to the House of Lords.

[42] Under the National Insurance Act the minister determines some issues, and from his decisions appeal lies to the courts. The factor of efficiency should be noted. Control may lead to inertia or to delay, and thus absolute regularity may be bought at too high a price. See, however, *Punton* v. *Ministry of Pensions and National Insurance* [1963] 1 All E.R. 275.

[43] *R.* v. *Northumberland Compensation Tribunals, ex p. Shaw* [1952] 1 K.B. 338.

[44] For details of these techniques the reader should refer to de Smith, *Judicial Review of Administrative Action*; Griffith and Street, *op. cit.*; Wade, *Administrative Law*; and Zamir, *The Declaratory Judgment*.

[45] Compare *R.* v. *Central Professional Committee for Opticians, ex p. Brown* [1949] 2 All E.R. 519 and *Hayman* v. *Lord Advocate*, 1951 S.C. 621; and compare the speech of Lord Reid with those of the other members of the House of Lords in *Ridge* v. *Baldwin* [1963] 2 All E.R. 66; and see, too, Mitchell, " Reflections on Law and Orders," 1958 J.R. 19, and Bennett Miller, " The Place of Quasi-Judicial Decisions in Scots Law," in the same volume.

quasi-judicial act are often the same as those which would be used for
a like purpose in relation to administrative acts.[46] Thus, there has been
an insistence that the Court of Session must be open to those who
complain of a wrong done by an inferior body,[47] and in this respect
the abolition of the Scottish Privy Council had the consequence of
enlarging the jurisdiction of the Court of Session,[48] and while limitations
have, by statute, been placed upon that review, the court is reluctant to
admit limitations upon its powers,[49] and it is probable that the Tribunals
and Inquiries Act was of less significance in Scotland than in England.

The grounds of review. Broadly speaking, the grounds for judicial
review are first that the tribunal has acted improperly. Here, above all,
the rules of natural justice are of importance.[50] These rules involve
that no man shall be a judge in his own cause, and that the judge shall
be without bias. They also imply an obligation to hear both sides,
which itself involves the proposition that each side shall know the case
he has to meet. Clearly, within the bounds of the ordinary courts these
rules are rigidly adhered to. Within the scope of administrative tribunals
some require modification if the purpose of creating the tribunals is not
to be frustrated. The impartiality of the tribunal will be safeguarded,[51]
and there is also insistence upon the absence of such an interest of the
judge as may create bias,[52] but while the fact of a " hearing " will be
insisted on,[53] the form of " hearing " need not involve the submission of
oral evidence. These rules are insisted upon not merely where injustice
may have been done, but where a suspicion could arise that justice may
not have been done. Improper action may cover more than this
insistence on a reasonable standard of conduct. Thus, the tribunal
must itself decide and cannot delegate that function.[54] It must, too,

---

[46] This formlessness, unless observed, can lead to mistakes about the scope of judicial
review in Scotland, as it did in the Franks Report, § 107. See generally Mitchell,
" The Scope of Judicial Review," 1959 J.R. 197.

[47] *Jeffray* v. *Angus*, 1909 S.C. 400 at 402, *per* Lord Justice-Clerk MacDonald; *Ross* v.
Findlater (1826) 4 S. 514 at 518, *per* Lord Pitmilly.

[48] Kames, *Historical Law Tracts*, 4th ed., p. 228.

[49] *Guthrie* v. *Cowan*, Dec. 10, 1807, F.C.; *Guthrie* v. *Miller* (1827) 5 S. 711; *Lord
Advocate* v. *Police Commissioners of Perth* (1869) 8 M. 244; *Sitwell* v. *McLeod*
(1899) 1 F. 950; *Kerr* v. *Hood*, 1907 S.C. 895; *Royal Victoria Hospital* v. *Lord
Advocate*, 1950 S.C. 511 among many cases.

[50] See the formulation in *Local Government Board* v. *Arlidge* [1915] A.C. 120; and
Board of Education v. *Rice* [1911] A.C. 179; *Ridge* v. *Baldwin* [1963] 2 All E.R. 66.

[51] *Lockhart* v. *Irving*, 1936 S.L.T. 567. The principle is of long standing; in *Gray* v.
Earl of Lauderdale (1685) Mor. 16497 it was argued: " Judges must be like Caesar's
wife, not only chaste but void of all suspicion, debent et mentis et manusque puras
habere." More recently, see *Barrs* v. *British Wool Marketing Board*, 1957 S.C. 72.

[52] *University of Edinburgh* v. *Craik*, 1954 S.C. 190; *Moore* v. *Clyde Pilotage Authority*,
1943 S.C. 457; *Walsh* v. *Magistrates of Pollokshaws*, 1907 S.C.(H.L.) 1, though the
rules as to a disqualifying interest are complex and should be pursued in the books
referred to.

[53] This insistence is also of long standing—*Earl of Roxburgh* v. *A Minister* (1683) Mor.
7328; *Brown* v. *Heritors of Kilberry* (1825) 4 S. 174. For recent illustrations, see
Barrs v. *I.R.C.*, 1961 S.C.(H.L.) 22 and *Ridge* v. *Baldwin* [1964] A.C. 40; *Jeffs* v.
New Zealand Dairy Production, etc., Board [1966] 3 All E.R. 863.

[54] *Thomson* v. *Dundee Police Commissioners* (1887) 15 R. 164; *Brown* v. *Minister of
Pensions*, 1946 S.C. 471.

decide upon the facts and evidence, and cannot simply decide either by general principles which it applies automatically, or by its own unaided knowledge.[55] The contrasts thus drawn are not easily applied. Clearly the tribunal must have general principles, or else the random quality of its decisions provokes criticism; clearly, too, it must use expert knowledge. It was created for that purpose, but the borderline between correct and incorrect methods of decision may perhaps be easier sensed than described.

In the second place judicial review will ensure that the inferior tribunal has acted within its jurisdiction.[56] Again, it is not easy on the borderlines to separate issues which go to jurisdiction from those which go to the substance of the decision.[57] While clearly a tribunal cannot give itself a jurisdiction, where properly it should have none, by a finding of fact, those facts which go to jurisdiction may also be the facts which are involved in the merits. Similarly, this element of control implies that, within limits, the courts should scrutinise the principles applied by the inferior tribunal, for a gross error can amount to an excess of jurisdiction, yet, if the courts carry this control too far the distinction between review and appeal (which is valuable) largely disappears.[58] Under this same head could be placed the control of the motives of the tribunal, for a wrongful motive could carry the tribunal beyond its allotted function, and this issue is involved in many of the cases already referred to.[59] In the main it is evident that judicial review is concerned with questions of law, but it is not easy to distinguish these from issues of fact. At a certain point a misconstruction of fact may involve an excess of jurisdiction, since the legal definition of jurisdiction only has significance once it is interpreted in a factual situation.[60]

There remains a discretionary element in judicial review. That element arises not merely from the uncertainty of many of the boundaries which have been discussed, but from other causes also. Normally where appellate procedures are available and have not been exhausted the courts will not intervene, but they will where there are sound reasons why resort should not be had to those procedures.[61]

---

55 Compare *M'Lean* v. *Paterson*, 1939 J.C. 52 or *M'Callum* v. *Arthur*, 1955 S.C. 188 with *Alexander & Son Ltd.* v. *Minister of Transport*, 1936 S.L.T. 553; *Buchan* v. *Stephen's Reps.*, 1946 S.C. 39; and *Cotton* v. *Assessor for Dumbarton*, 1936 S.C. 279; again it is difficult to define with precision the exact limits imposed upon the tribunals.
56 *Lord Prestongrange* v. *Justices of Haddington* (1756) Mor. 7350; *Cheyne* v. *Architects' Registration Council*, 1943 S.C. 468. Note that in *Robb* v. *School Board of Logiealmond* (1875) 2 R. 698 the court required reasons to be adduced.
57 *Patullo* v. *Sir Wm. Maxwell*, June 25, 1779, F.C. is a good example; compare *Foote & Marshall* v. *Stewart*, Aug. 9, 1778, F.C.
58 This was early perceived: *Pryde* v. *Heritors and the Kirk Session of Ceres* (1843) 5 D. 552; *Guthrie* v. *Miller* (1827) 5 S. 711; *Barrs* v. *I.R.C.*, 1961 S.C.(H.L.) 22; *Hayman* v. *Lord Advocate*, 1951 S.C. 621; *Ashbridge Investments Ltd.* v. *Ministry of Housing and Local Government* [1965] 3 All E.R. 371.
59 *Caledonian Ry.* v. *Glasgow Corporation* (1905) 7 F. 1020 is one example.
60 Consider, *e.g.*, *Bennett* v. *Scottish Board of Health*, 1921 S.C. 772.
61 *Adair* v. *Colville*, 1926 S.C.(H.L.) 51.

Further, many of the matters which might be used in seeking review of the decisions of the inferior body involve, or may involve, questions of policy. That fact inhibits courts, and may itself add an element of discretion or uncertainty, since the inhibiting effect may be outweighed by other considerations. A degree of uncertainty is probably inevitable and perhaps provoked much of the malaise about such tribunals.

The procedural reforms contained in the Tribunals and Inquiries Act 1958 have helped. Their mere existence may well prove to be as important as any use that is made of them. That is to say, that in so far as the possibility of judicial review was enlarged as a result of them, there will be a reflection in the attitude and actions of inferior tribunals irrespective of the use that is made of that possibility. In particular section 12 requires that the tribunals specified in the First Schedule to the Act must, subject to limited and reasonable exceptions if requested, give reasons for the decision. The section is particularly important in England as opening up a possibility of review by certiorari, which would not exist in the absence of reasons but would exist where it can be said that the order is a speaking order. It also probably facilitates review in Scotland, even though the Court of Session had power to require reasons to be given.[62] That power of the court could nevertheless still be important, for the reasons stated in accordance with a request under section 12 may be inadequate in their vagueness or in their formulation,[63] and this older power could be used to require them to be supplemented. Moreover, under section 11, any provision that any order shall not be challenged in any court contained in Acts passed before the commencement of the Tribunals and Inquiries Act shall not have the effect of excluding review by reduction or suspension (or certiorari or mandamus, as the case may be). The importance of this section can be over-emphasised since such provisions were rare, and it was uncertain how effective they were, particularly on jurisdictional matters.[64] Moreover, the force of the common provision which excludes review after a limited period of time is not affected by this section. As to future legislation, no doubt the Council on Tribunals would make representations should a Bill contain an absolute finality clause.

What has been said hitherto upon the topic of judicial review applies in the main to administrative tribunals properly so called, in relation to which the problems were not acute. As has been indicated above,

---

[62] *Robb* v. *School Board of Logiealmond* (1875) 2 R. 698. It has been asserted that a similar power exists in England: *R.* v. *Northumberland Compensation Appeal Tribunal* [1952] 1 K.B. 338. *Sed quaere.*

[63] *Ex p. Woodhouse, The Times,* June 18 and 28 and Dec. 16, 1960, and Second Report of the Council on Tribunals (1960), § 105, and Third Report (for 1961), § 44. See also *Benjamin* v. *Minister of Pensions* [1960] 2 Q.B. 519; *Re Poyser and Mills Arbitration* [1964] 2 Q.B. 467; and Report for 1962, § 44. The clearest instance is *Givaudan and Co.* v. *Minister of Housing and Local Government* [1966] 3 All E.R. 696.

[64] De Smith, *Judicial Review of Administrative Action,* p. 226 *et seq.*; and *Punton* v. *Minister of Pensions* [1963] 1 All E.R. 275.

greater dissatisfaction was felt with inquiries. In relation to them the element of policy which enters into the final decision is greater, and may outweigh, in the minister's mind, arguments which appeared convincing to an opponent of a proposal. Thus, particular decisions can provoke discontent. There was, too, difficulty arising from the fact that in England (though not in Scotland) [65] the great majority of inquiries were held by departmental officials. Thus a suspicion of bias, whether well or ill founded, inevitably arose. The fact that the report on the inquiry was not made public, out of deference to the doctrine of ministerial responsibility, increased doubts about this procedure. Secrecy heightened suspicion. In the inter-war years an attempt had been made in law to " judicialise " these inquiries, but it had broken down because of the compulsions arising from the mechanics of government. By reason of the structure of local government the minister was increasingly concerned with the matters covered by the inquiry before the stage of inquiry was reached and thereafter had to gather departmental views upon the report. The application of rules requiring a neutral judge became therefore increasingly difficult. It was sometimes thought, though probably inaccurately, that any judicial element in this process of inquiry and decision had been largely removed by *Franklin* v. *Minister of Town and Country Planning*,[66] in which the proposal had in the first instance necessarily come from the minister, who was also responsible for the inquiry. This view of the case is probably unjustified, and the judicial element of the inquiry stage was unaffected by it.[67]

The Franks Committee, whose report covered both tribunals and inquiries, recommended a variety of reforms, some designed to make the inquiry more open and others to increase the judicial air of the inquiry. Not all of these were accepted. The Tribunals and Inquiries Act (as amended) enabled rules to be made (after consultation with the Council) governing procedure at inquiries, and by section 12 required that where a minister notifies a decision after holding an inquiry, he shall if requested give reasons therefor, thus opening up wider possibilities of review.[68] These rules [69] are designed to improve the quality of the

---

65 The use of reporters in Scotland could make a significant difference to the approach of the courts; see *Magistrates of Ayr* v. *S. of S. for Scotland*, 1950 S.C. 102, where it helped the court to distinguish *Franklin's* case (note 66, below).

66 [1948] A.C. 87. *Ridge* v. *Baldwin* [1964] A.C. 40 could be taken as an indication to the contrary. The current of opinion runs in a confusing way, however. Thereafter consider *Vidyodaya University Council* v. *Silva* [1964] 3 All E.R. 865; *Peter Holmes Ltd.* v. *S. of S. for Scotland*, 1965 S.L.T. 41. See also Bradley, " A Failure of Justice and Defect of Police " [1964] C.L.J. 83.

67 See Griffith and Street, *op. cit.* pp. 179–180, and the Franks Report, Part IV.

68 This provision does not apply s. 12 (2) to ministerial decisions which are legislative and not executive in character, and this distinction may be difficult. Nor does the provision apply where there are other statutory provisions requiring that reasons should be given.

69 See S.I. 1962 Nos. 1424 and 1425. Now replaced by S.I. 1965 No. 473 and S.I. 1965 No. 1453 for England and Wales. The original Scottish rules lagged behind for reasons set out in the Reports of the Council on Tribunals for 1962 and 1963. See also S.I. 1964 No. 181. By the 1966 Act the Secretary of State makes rules.

inquiry by giving each side greater information of the arguments of the other, as well as by ensuring that government views are put upon record to a greater extent than was formerly the case. In particular, provision is made, in certain circumstances, for a government department, which has expressed views upon the proposal in dispute, to send a representative to the inquiry, who may be examined as a witness. He may be asked questions upon fact though he cannot be asked questions on government policy. The conduct of the inquiry is, subject to certain general principles, largely in the hands of the person holding it. By earlier circulars (which do not appear to be entirely displaced by the new regulations) [70] he was required, if so requested, to make available to parties his findings of fact before they were submitted to the minister, so that parties may comment on them. The recommendations of the reporter do not bind the minister, but, under the new regulations, where he differs from the reporter on a finding of fact or after the closing of the inquiry receives any new evidence, including expert opinion on a matter of fact, or takes into consideration any new issue of fact (not being a matter of government policy), and for any of these reasons is disposed to disagree with a recommendation, he must notify the parties of the new material and give an opportunity to them of making representations or of asking for the inquiry to be reopened. These rules are intended to strike a balance between the administrative and the judicial aspects of the inquiry system, and are the result of considerable debates. [71] It is too early to forecast their results, but they will not be easy of application, " fact " and " policy " are not always clearly distinguishable, nor is " expert opinion on a matter of fact " a phrase which rules out all doubt. It seems that the rules have the defects of a compromise (perhaps necessary) between pressures to judicialise the process and pressures to maintain ministerial responsibility.

The rules must be considered in the light of the obligation (referred to above) of the minister to give reasons. In that context it is evident that the control of *vires* is, or may be, enhanced if full and explicit reasons are given. [72] Judicial control of procedure is not increased to the same extent, since many of the rules governing the inquiry stage confer a discretion, the exercise of which would be difficult to challenge. It is at that stage that the more generalised approach of Scots law is significant. In the matters with which inquiries are normally concerned

[70] *e.g.*, Department of Health for Scotland Circular of May 12, 1958.
[71] See [1962] *Public Law* 125–129, 254–256 and 392–394 and the references there given. See *Lord Luke of Pavenham* v. *Minister of Housing and Local Government* [1967] 2 All E.R. 1066.
[72] *London & Westcliff Properties Ltd.* v. *Minister of Housing and Local Government* [1961] 1 All E.R. 610, although the power will not be easy to exercise in all areas; see, *e.g.*, *Hanks* v. *Minister of Housing and Local Government* [1963] 1 All E.R. 47; and see Mandelker, " Planning Appeals and the Adjudication of Policy " [1960] *Public Law* 257 and his *Greenbelts and Urban Growth*.

there is a limit beyond which they cannot be made to resemble judicial proceedings. On the other hand a concern for their effectiveness, even if they are accepted as part of the administrative processes, may enable the court to control procedures where otherwise it could not. It was such a concern which enabled the court to intervene in *Magistrates of Ayr* v. *S. of S. for Scotland*,[73] and it is perhaps that approach which enables a nicer balance to be struck between the administrative needs and the aspirations of affected citizens.[74] Thus the differences in the general legal background of judicial review in England and Scotland may still be important.

Difficulties remain which spring from the concept of a " *lis*." In particular, third parties who may be adversely affected by the decision in planning matters are, by the rules, given the possibility (but not the right) of appearing at the inquiry; but their rights at later stages are even more limited,[75] and they will not normally be able to avail themselves of statutory appeal procedures, which are generally limited to " persons aggrieved," a highly technical phrase which often excludes both those who are disappointed by a decision and those who may be adversely affected by it,[76] and such persons may also find that they have no such title to sue as would enable them to pursue alternative remedies.[77] Some of these difficulties may be said to result from a formalistic approach. Others are perhaps the consequence of a failure to evolve concepts and techniques appropriate to the present scope of public law.[78]

" We do not have a developed system of administrative law—perhaps because until fairly recently we did not need it," said Lord Reid in a slightly (but not essentially) different context.[79] The need is now pressing, and it remains to be seen how far the adaptation of traditional techniques will suffice to meet that need. Two examples of the sort of problem may indicate the difficulties. On the one hand, concepts such as that of title to sue were developed in a different context, and may not be entirely appropriate in this one. On the other hand, the elaboration of control, either by procedural rules or by extending judicial review, can unduly retard government action.[80] It is possible that the search

---

73 1950 S.C. 102 at 110.
74 *General Poster & Publicity Co. Ltd.* v. *S. of S. for Scotland*, 1960 S.C. 266, though the procedure adopted in that case could substantially affect the operation of the " new evidence " provisions in the new rules.
75 [1962] *Public Law* 392–394; and Report of the Council on Tribunals on the position of " Third Parties " at Planning Appeal Inquiries (1962) Cmnd. 1787. These matters continue to give difficulty. See the Report of the Council on Tribunals for 1966 and case C. 473/67 referred to the Parliamentary Commissioner in his report of Nov. 30, 1967.
76 *Magistrates of Kilsyth* v. *Stirling C.C.*, 1936 S.C. 149; *Buxton* v. *Minister of Housing and Local Government* [1961] 1 Q.B. 278.
77 *Simpson* v. *Edinburgh Corporation*, 1960 S.C. 313.
78 The courts have regretted their impotence in this field: *Buxton* v. *Minister of Housing and Local Government, supra,* note 76.
79 *Ridge* v. *Baldwin* [1963] 2 All E.R. 66 at 76.
80 Consider *M'Millan* v. *Inverness-shire C.C.*, 1949 S.C. 77.

for a solution which involves the separation of inquiries from the rest of the administrative machinery is not entirely helpful. The essential problem is a broader one, namely, that of judicial control of administrative activities more generally conceived. The real issue is, as the Franks Committee emphasised, one of policing administrative morality.[81] Judicial control of decisions taken following upon inquiry should be looked at in this broader setting, and against a background of other controls. Those controls must include the simple element of openness which has increased after the Franks Report. To the extent that judicial control, however extended, must remain largely a control of form, it must be considered whether such controls by reason of their technicality are always satisfactory.[82] To the extent that controls of substance or policy are reserved to Parliament, out of respect for the doctrine of ministerial responsibility, it must be considered how real is parliamentary control. It is thought that the proper balance has not yet been found and that solutions may have to be found through other administrative devices or through a slightly different use of courts.[83] These issues are, then, related to the general questions of the courts in relation to public authorities, and they should then be looked at in the light of the considerations raised in the following chapter.[84]

[81] " We wish to emphasise that, whatever our recommendations under either part of our terms of reference may be, nothing can make up for a wrong approach to administrative activity by the administration's servants ": Report, § 405. It might be added that it is considered that concern for this morality is felt as much in the civil service as it is elsewhere.

[82] A minor change in wording in *R.* v. *Minister of Housing and Local Government, ex p. Chichester R.D.C.* [1960] 2 All E.R. 407 would have made the order unassailable, and have carried out the intent of the Act and the minister. See, too, *R.* v. *Agricultural Land Tribunal (S.W. Province), ex p. Benny* [1955] 2 Q.B. 140. Some degree of flexibility can exist, *e.g., Kay* v. *Perth County Council,* 1959 S.C. 132.

[83] See the discussion in Mitchell, " The Flexible Constitution " [1960] *Public Law* 332; " The Causes and Consequences of the Absence of a System of Public Law " [1965] *Public Law* 95; and " The State of Public Law in the United Kingdom " (1966) 15 I.C.L.Q. 133.

[84] In particular the question of the creation of a Parliamentary Commissioner or Ombudsman as against a broader use of courts is here relevant. This subject cannot, however, be dealt with until further aspects of law are considered in the next chapter. His role can only be properly considered against a full background of administrative law.

CHAPTER 17

PUBLIC AUTHORITIES IN THE COURTS

Introduction. The scope and availability of actions against public
authorities lie at the heart of any discussion of the rule of law. The place
of the courts in the framework of the state can only be assessed after a
consideration of such matters. While the subject of remedies against
public authorities is therefore of great importance, too detailed an
exploration of the subject would advance too far into the field
appropriate to administrative law, and what follows will be concerned
with general principles. There is no necessary harm in that; many
of these general principles have tended of late to be overlooked. To
a great extent it will also be concerned with the remedies available to
private individuals against public authorities. As has already been
indicated the control exercised by superior administrative bodies over
inferior is normally exercised by administrative means, such as directions
which are frequently backed by financial sanctions.[1] It is possible that
the superior authority may enforce obligations through the courts,[2]
though this is rare. On broader questions it is also rare that an inferior
administrative body should challenge the actings of the superior in the
courts. A challenge to a ministerial direction by a nationalised industry
on the grounds that it lacks sufficient generality is almost inconceivable
in practice, though theoretically possible. On more detailed matters
such challenges exist, the appeals by local authorities from ministerial
decisions in town planning matters are examples.[3] So, too, as between
equal authorities, the tendency is for disputes to be determined elsewhere
than in the ordinary courts,[4] and frequently by a minister. For such
a tendency there are good reasons, including cost and the need for
administrative harmony. Nevertheless these conditions mean that the
courts do not play the part in policing the administrative structure of
the state that they do elsewhere,[5] and where, as in planning appeals, the
local authority does challenge a decision it does so in the same way

---

[1] See, *e.g.*, Town Development Act 1952, s. 3; Housing and Town Development (Scotland) Act 1957, s. 16; Local Government (Scotland) Act 1947, s. 356. Where, as in
that case, provision is made for an ultimate appeal to the courts for an order that
functions shall be performed, the courts are placed in a difficult and almost impossible
position: *Board of Supervision* v. *Local Authority of Lochmaben* (1893) 20 R. 434.
It is certainly undesirable that the courts should claim to review all matters
de novo as in *Madras College Trustees* v. *S. of S. for Scotland*, 1959 S.C. 335.
To do that is to substitute for the administration.
[2] *S. of S. for Scotland* v. *Fife C.C.*, 1953 S.C. 257; *S. of S. for Scotland* v. *Fife C.C.*,
1957 S.C. 261.
[3] Or see *Fife C.C.* v. *Lord Advocate*, 1950 S.C. 314.
[4] *e.g.*, S.I. 1958 No. 1486, Coal Mining (Subsidence) (Land Drainage) Regulations.
[5] See generally Mitchell, " The Flexible Constitution " [1960] *Public Law* 332.

and on the same footing as would a private individual, and a neglect of the " public " character of the disputants may, on occasion, have its inconveniences.[6] This situation means also that one check to the tendencies to centralisation is missing, and it is doubtful if any enduring devolution is possible without a change in the role of law in government.

It is in this area of law that the belief that public law is not something distinct has had its greatest influence. The insistence upon the ordinary law and the ordinary courts has, it is believed, been a limiting factor upon the operation of the courts, since rules which work justly between individuals do not necessarily do so between an individual and a public authority, nor always are remedies appropriate.[7] This insistence neglects the distinctive character of the state and of government, and as a result government is hampered unnecessarily (so that the community suffers) and the individual is denied protections from the law which should rightly be his. It may also be true that the concentration upon delegated legislation and administrative tribunals has distracted attention from the more generalised questions of the judicial control of administrative action. Those two matters are, it is believed, simply facets of a more general problem of the appropriate control of government, and what has been said in the preceding chapters must be borne in mind in reading the present one.

While the problem of that control is essentially one, it is with us fragmented, for reasons which have already appeared. The machinery of government, the administration, cannot for many purposes be regarded as one. That part of it which can be regarded as the Crown, or as servants of the Crown, must often be isolated, since different rules are applicable to the Crown, even though the distribution of functions between the Crown and other public authorities is often a matter of historical chance. Although that distribution has consequences in law, those consequences may be justifiable only upon historical and not upon rational grounds.[8] One other general point must be made here. While the word " control " has been used, it must also be remembered that government exists to act on behalf of the community, and it must be allowed to act with a speed which matches the needs of the modern world. It should be one of the objects of the law to enable it so to

---

[6] *Magor & St. Mellons R.D.C.* v. *Newport Corporation* [1952] A.C. 189.

[7] Consider, *e.g.*, the consequences of a refusal to consider the purposive element in a statute in *Western Heritable Investment Co.* v. *Glasgow Corporation,* 1956 S.C.(H.L.) 64; and Mitchell, " *Contrats Administratifs en Grande Bretagne* " (1959) R.D.P. 491 and " The Causes and Consequences of the Absence of a System of Public Law in the United Kingdom " [1965] *Public Law* 95. For a background to the ideas of public law, see Sandevoir, *Etudes sur le Recours de Pleine Juridiction.*

[8] Thus the ability to get an injunction or interdict depends not on the character of the function performed but upon the chance circumstance of whether it is performed by a local authority or a Crown servant. Compare *Nottingham No. 1 Area Hospital Management Committee* v. *Owen* [1958] 1 Q.B. 50 and *Adams* v. *S. of S. for Scotland,* 1958 S.C. 279.

act with safety for individuals. Law which creates too many obstacles to action creates incentives to evade the law itself.

Remedies against the Crown. The dominant piece of legislation today is the Crown Proceedings Act 1947; though that Act has to be seen against a rather different historical background in England and Scotland. In England, it was not possible to sue the Crown in tort, and in contract resort had to be had to the cumbrous procedure of a petition of right.[9] To some extent deficiencies in the law could be overcome by fictions such as the nominated defendant,[10] but such devices met with opposition in the courts which in turn led to mounting pressure for proper regulation. In Scotland, on the other hand, it had always been possible to sue the Crown in contract, and it seems that it was clearly possible at one stage to raise an action for reparation against the Crown,[11] though in later years it came to be accepted, but not without objection, that the English rule as to actions in tort applied in similar circumstances in Scotland.[12] Even when that stage had been reached remedies were more readily available against the Crown in Scotland than they were in England.[13] An earlier statute, the Crown Suits (Scotland) Act 1857, which as amended remains in force, had regulated procedure, but the apparent generality of its words was restrictively construed.[14]

The Crown Proceedings Act 1947 was intended, in principle, to equate civil liability of the Crown to that of private individuals. The substitution of an action for a petition of right (s. 1) enabled actions in contract to be brought in England, and sections 2 and 43 subjected the Crown to liability in reparation (or tort) in respect of acts committed by its servants or agents where, apart from the Act, a cause of action would have existed against the servant or agent, or in respect of duties owed as an employer to servants or agents, or in respect of common

---

9 See Robertson, *Civil Proceedings by and against the Crown*; Robinson, *Public Authorities and Legal Liability*; Street, *Governmental Liability*.

10 *Adams* v. *Naylor* [1946] A.C. 543; *Royster* v. *Cavey* [1947] K.B. 204.

11 *Earl of Morton* v. *Lochleven* (1543) Mor. 16479; and see Sir Randall Philip, " The Crown as Litigant in Scotland " (1928) 40 J.R. 238.

12 Perhaps the final acceptance may be said to have been *MacGregor* v. *Lord Advocate*, 1921 S.C. 847; for earlier protests, see, *e.g.*, Lord M'Laren in *Somerville* v. *Lord Advocate* (1893) 20 R. 1050 at 1075. See generally Philip, " The Crown as Litigant in Scotland " (1928) 40 J.R. 238, and Lord Murray, " *Rex non Potest Peccare*," 55 S.L.R. 1 and 40.

13 *Bell* v. *S. of S. for Scotland*, 1933 S.L.T. 519, where an interdict was readily granted; and see generally Mitchell, " The Royal Prerogative in Modern Scots Law " [1957] *Public Law* 38; see, however, Cameron, " Crown Exemption from Statute and Tax in Scotland," 1962 J.R. 191, where he suggests a somewhat different basis for the rules.

14 The Act authorised all actions brought on behalf of or against Her Majesty, or in the interest of the Crown, or on behalf of or against any public department, to be raised by or against the Lord Advocate. The Act, which is primarily of procedural importance, was held in *MacGregor* v. *Lord Advocate*, 1921 S.C. 847 not to enable actions of reparation against the Lord Advocate. The description of the bodies which the Lord Advocate may represent is of interest as showing uncertainties about " The Crown " and " Public Authorities." See now *Forestry Commission* v. *Argyll C.C.*, 1950 S.C. 304.

law obligations arising from the ownership, possession or control of property. Similarly (s. 2 (2)) liability for breach of statutory duty is imposed where a private person would be liable,[15] and the general rules as to indemnity and contribution are made applicable. The generality of the liability thus imposed is, however, limited in a variety of ways. Some are necessary concessions to the position of government, others have an historical explanation. So the Act does not (s. 1 (5)) extend liability in respect of matters arising from the discharge of judicial functions or the execution of judicial process, and while salvage claims may now be made against the Crown, actions *in rem* are incompetent. By section 9 certain immunities in relation to postal packets are continued,[16] by section 3 the special rights of the Crown to use patented inventions are preserved,[17] and by section 10 the position of persons in the armed forces is so regulated that service injuries can only be dealt with under the pension warrants. More generally by section 11 all powers and authorities of a prerogative type, particularly those connected with defence, are specifically preserved.

In procedural matters the position of the Crown as government comes out more clearly. While the old rule that the Crown can only be convened in the supreme courts has been abrogated and actions can now be raised in county or sheriff courts, the Crown may still require the proceedings to be transferred to the supreme court. More importantly a pecuniary judgment against the Crown cannot be enforced against the Crown, and remedies which could particularly interfere with the administrative process, interdict or injunction or an order for specific implement or specific performance are excluded (ss. 21 and 43) and the appropriate court can only make a declaratory order.[18] While it must be expected that in all ordinary cases the executive will obey any order of a court these provisions are necessary concessions to the needs of governments, though they are perhaps somewhat more broadly phrased than is necessary. Concessions are similarly made to the executive in sections 28 and 47, which first apparently enable a litigant

[15] The phraseology of the section can give rise to difficulty, *e.g.*, arising from the nature of vicarious liability, or consider *The Truculent* [1952] P. 1. Only general principles can here be discussed; for details see Glanville Williams, *Crown Proceedings*; Bell, *Crown Proceedings*; Griffith and Street, *Principles of Administrative Law*; and Street, *Governmental Liability*; Wade, *Administrative Law*; Treitel [1957] *Public Law* 321.
[16] *Triefus & Co.* v. *Post Office* [1957] 2 Q.B. 352; and Post Office Act 1961.
[17] See, too, Patents Act 1949; and Meinhardt (1949) 12 M.L.R. 112. For an application of this, see *Pfizer Corporation* v. *Ministry of Health* [1965] A.C. 512.
[18] As to which, see *Griffin* v. *Lord Advocate*, 1950 S.C. 448. Formerly, see the principle underlying *Lord Advocate* v. *Matheson* (1866) 1 S.L.R. 174 and *Carlton Hotel Co.* v. *Lord Advocate*, 1921 S.C. 237. This provision has the inconvenience (perhaps unforeseen) of denying interim relief: *International G.E.C., etc., Ltd.* v. *Commissioners of Customs & Excise* [1962] Ch. 784, the principles of which seem to be logically equally applicable in Scotland, though the matter is open; see *Magistrates of Ayr* v. *Secretary of State*, 1966 S.L.T. 16. This rule may point to a general principle. The direct intervention of the courts in the administrative process can be unhelpful, and a much greater use may have to be made of remedies which do not have that effect.

to secure disclosure [19] of documents by the Crown, but proceed to maintain the vigour of any rule which " authorises or requires the withholding of any document " where disclosure would be injurious to the public interest.[20] These two sections, though similar in wording, may be markedly different in effect, since it has been held, in England, that a minister's declaration that disclosure would be contrary to the public interest cannot be overridden,[21] although the fact that the principle thus stated is modified by administrative action [22] appears to show that it is wider than is necessary. In Scotland it has been held that the Court of Session retains an inherent power to override such declarations in the interest of justice,[23] though that affirmation of principle has not been followed by any instances in which it has been put into effect. In England the fumblings have continued. Discontent has been expressed with the existing rules, and finally the House of Lords, in *Conway* v. *Rimmer* (of which only a newspaper report is available at the moment of writing), has attempted a resolution of the problem in a review of the authorities. It is true that in that decision the element of finality of the Minister's certificate has been much reduced, but the problem of overriding it (which was not attacked in detail in the Scottish case) remains unresolved in any way which is acceptable and efficient. Indeed a solution is propounded which involves a judge in examining a document produced by one party and which is unseen by the other. Such a solution is doubly objectionable. On a technical level it transfers an administrative decision to a judge, which is inappropriate, and since he is untrained in such a matter it is likely that he will lean too far in favour of the administration. Much more seriously, on the level of principle, it is in the ordinary way inconceivable that a judge should be placed in a position of seeing and

---

[19] A term intended to bridge English discovery and Scots recovery of documents.

[20] The two sections differ as to oral answers, but, subject to what is said about the general differences in law in the two jurisdictions, it is doubtful whether this particular difference is important in practice.

[21] *Duncan* v. *Cammell Laird & Co. Ltd.* [1942] A.C. 624.

[22] 197 H.L.Deb. 741–748; 237 H.L.Deb. 1191. The constitutional desirability of creating this form of sub-law is debatable to say the least; it would certainly not have commended itself to Dicey.

[23] *Glasgow Corporation* v. *Central Land Board*, 1956 S.C.(H.L.) 1; *Whitehall* v. *Whitehall*, 1957 S.C. 30. The English story starts with *Duncan* v. *Cammell, Laird & Co. Ltd.* [1942] A.C. 624, which gave rise to many expressions of discontent; see *Re Grosvenor Hotel, London* [1964] Ch. 464; *Re Grosvenor Hotel (No. 2)* [1965] Ch. 1210; *Merricks* v. *Nott Bower* [1965] 1 Q.B. 57; *Wednesbury Corporation* v. *Ministry of Housing and Local Government* [1965] 1 All E.R. 186; and *Conway* v. *Rimmer* [1967] 2 All E.R. 1260. The last is the decision in the Court of Appeal which was reversed in the House of Lords in the decision referred to in the text above (*The Times*, Feb. 29, 1968). The solutions which can be found may be said to start with *Barel*, C.E., May 28, 1954, R.D.P. 509, and continue through *Houhou*, C.E., May 11, 1962, R. 319; *Foucher Crétau*, C.E., Oct. 2, 1963, R. 468, and may be said for the moment to rest with the *conclusions* of M. Galmot in *Tochou*, C.E., April 22, 1966, R.D.P. 584, which demonstrate what can be achieved by a continuous intelligent application of a coherent philosophy. The apparent proposal of the House of Lords in *Conway* v. *Rimmer* was rejected by the Conseil d'Etat in *Houhou* as unthinkable for a judge.

deciding on material produced by one side only. There are techniques which are capable of solving both difficulties, which appear to have been entirely unexplored by the House. They are the techniques of a true system of administrative law, evolved in the Conseil d'Etat. This matter should be borne in mind in relation to the discussion in the next chapter of the need for a real system of administrative law. The need relates to procedure as well as substance, and both these fumblings over procedure and their sad conclusion point to that need.

It is thus evident that there are substantial limitations upon the equiparation of the Crown and individuals contained in the Act itself. These are made the more significant by various finality provisions contained in it,[24] and by the consideration that the prerogative rules—such as that the Crown is not necessarily bound by statutes—which have been discussed, are also applicable. Moreover, the terminology of the Act may conceal difficulties. References to " a contract " must be read in the light of the supposed rule that the Crown cannot fetter its future executive action,[25] or that in certain instances estoppel or personal bar does not operate against the Crown,[26] or that other necessary acts by the Crown may entirely alter the relationship of the parties.[27] In the same way, the existence of governmental powers may render lawful acts which would otherwise be delictual.[28] Thus essentially the Crown Proceedings Act is concerned with ordinary civil wrongs, and even in that context has to make concessions to the necessities of a government. What it does not deal with in any satisfactory way are what may be called governmental wrongs, or the problems of abuse of power.[29]

Certain other constitutional matters arise in relation to the Act. There is ambiguity in the use of the word " Crown " since there is uncertainty about the nature of the Crown, or about what it is. The Act makes clear (s. 40 (1)) that it speaks only of the Crown in a political or governmental sense, and in no way affects the law in relation to the sovereign in a private capacity. There are, however, other uncertainties inherent in the word " Crown." It was at one time thought that the Crown was one and indivisible,[30] but for most purposes that theory must be now abandoned, and the Crown Proceedings Act makes this explicit.

---

[24] ss. 10 (2), 11 (2), 40 (3); and see *Adams* v. *The War Office* [1955] 1 W.L.R. 1116.

[25] *Rederiaktiebolaget Amphitrite* v. *The King* [1921] 3 K.B. 500. The formulation of this rule there should not be taken at its face value. See the discussion in Mitchell, *The Contracts of Public Authorities.*

[26] *Lord Advocate* v. *Mirrielees' Trs.*, 1943 S.C. 587, *per* Lord Keith. The doubts in the House of Lords (1945 S.C.(H.L.) 1) on the origin of this doctrine are perhaps unfounded.

[27] *Commissioners for Crown Lands* v. *Page* [1960] 2 Q.B. 274.

[28] *Burmah Oil Co.* (*Burma Trading*) *Ltd.* v. *Lord Advocate*, 1964 S.C.(H.L.) 117. Whether in that case the right consequences were derived from this finding as to the legality of the act in question may be debated, but this does not affect the present point. The decision has, of course, been nullified by the War Damage Act 1965.

[29] Consider the difficulties indicated in *R.* v. *Governor of Brixton Prison, ex p. Soblen* [1962] 3 All E.R. 641 at 661 and 664.

[30] *Williams* v. *Howarth* [1905] A.C. 551.

The operation of the Act is confined to liabilities arising in respect of the Crown as being the government in the United Kingdom, and does not affect proceedings by the Crown in any other capacity. Again provision is made for conclusive certification by a Secretary of State as to the capacity in which the Crown did a particular act.[31] Within the United Kingdom itself there are problems of the extent to which the administration should be regarded as an entity. The Act assumes a unity, or else provides, for greater caution, that no set-off or counterclaim shall be available in any action by the Crown for taxes, duties or penalties, and that otherwise set-off or counterclaim shall not be available by or against the Crown (except with leave of the court) unless the transactions in question relate to the same department.[32] Again, this segregation of departments is probably necessary for administrative reasons.

The Act speaks of delictual liability arising by reason of things done or omitted by the servants or agents of the Crown. In the general law the problem of determining who is a Crown servant is a difficult one, but for the purposes of the Act there is a specific definition of the persons through whom liability may attach for the purposes of section 2. These are defined as officers directly or indirectly appointed by the Crown and who were at the material time paid wholly out of the Consolidated Fund moneys provided by Parliament, or other fund certified by the Treasury.[33] It seems then that for liability to attach it must be shown that the wrongdoer was a servant in the ordinary sense, and fulfils the above conditions. The definition has a restrictive effect on the liability of the Crown. Under the general law the master may be responsible for the servant who is " borrowed," not hired. Such liability appears to be excluded by the payment provisions.[34] Liability can also attach to the Crown for the acts of agents (which appears to mean independent contractors) and who are not affected by the limitations in section 2 (6).

The problems do not, however, end there. The particular definition of servants refers only to the liabilities arising under section 2. Other parts of the Act refer simply to the Crown, notably the provisions relating to the disclosure of documents.[35] Similarly in any litigation

---

[31] In the absence of such certification, problems of some complexity could arise: *Reardon Smith Line Ltd.* v. *Ministry of Agriculture, etc.* [1962] 1 Q.B. 42 and [1960] 1 Q.B. 439 at 467.

[32] ss. 35 (2) (g) and 50; *Atlantic Engine Co. (1920) Ltd.* v. *Lord Advocate*, 1955 S.L.T. 17; and see pp. 204–205, *ante*.

[33] s. 2 (6). Although this subsection uses the term " officer," and s. 2 (1) (a) uses the term " servant," it seems that the two are synonymous. This could otherwise bring within the scope of the Act Regius Professors where it can be established that their stipend comes entirely from the University Grants Committee. Even if it could be shown that police are Crown servants, any act by them could not give rise to liability on the part of the Crown by reason of s. 2 (6).

[34] Other difficulties arise, particularly as to the servants of boards which are themselves Crown servants. See Glanville Williams, *Crown Proceedings*, Chap. 2; and Griffith and Street, *op. cit.*, 4th ed., pp. 259–261.

[35] It must be noted, however, that the plea by the Lord Advocate to prevent recovery of documents is more general, and is made in the public interest: *M'Kie* v. *Western S.M.T.*, 1952 S.C. 206. The power of the Court of Session to overrule such a plea

against the Crown, prerogative rules such as the immunity from statute, or the rules as to personal bar, may be relevant. For these purposes the general tests of Crown service are appropriate,[36] and it must be remembered that the peculiar rules relating to the Crown may be applied even though that application is not for the benefit of the Crown.[37] It is these rules which, in litigation, give particular importance to the segregation of the Crown.

Further issues arise. The Act deals with proceedings against the Crown, and provides (s. 21 (2)) that no order shall be made against an officer of the Crown if the effect would be to grant any relief against the Crown which could not have been obtained in an action against the Crown. The purpose of this provision is simply to prevent circumvention of the Act by raising actions against officers of the Crown as individuals, and not against the Crown itself. Attempts have, however, been made to distinguish the character in which a particular officer has operated, and, where a particular duty has been cast on him by statute, to assert that in performing that duty he is carrying out a duty independent of the Crown, and hence any action relating to it would fall outside the scope of the Act. It seems, however, that such attempts will not normally be successful.[38] To that extent it is clear that the courts will not distinguish between the common law and the statutory duties of the Crown, but that all governmental powers will be treated as a unity, and the distinction sometimes drawn between the prerogative powers (in this sense of common law powers) and statutory powers or duties is not here of significance.[39]

While the 1947 Act enables an action for breach of statutory duty to be raised against the Crown, it does so (s. 2 (2)) only where that duty is also binding upon persons other than the Crown. That limitation does not affect the possibility of enforcing statutory duties against the Crown by a declaratory order (as limited by the Act), but such enforcement is difficult. Statutory or other duties are normally generally phrased, and it is frequently said in one formulation that the duty resting upon the Crown does not confer any enforceable right upon a particular

---

was reaffirmed in *Glasgow Corporation* v. *Central Land Board*, 1956 S.C.(H.L.) 1 at 16; and any interpretation of the opinions in *M'Kie* suggesting a weakening of that power was firmly rebutted by Lord Normand.

[36] See p. 185, *ante*, and the authorities there referred to. For the application of the rules see *Glasgow Corporation* v. *Central Land Board*, 1956 S.C.(H.L.) 1; 1955 S.C. 64. Such cases are cases of Crown privileges properly so called. In *B.B.C.* v. *Johns* [1965] Ch. 32 the B.B.C. was not regarded as having " Crown " status since it did not perform functions of the executive government. The issue can arise in a wide range of contexts—consider *Pfizer Corporation* v. *Ministry of Health* [1965] A.C. 512.

[37] *Bank voor Handel en Scheepvaart N.V.* v. *Administrator of Hungarian Property* [1954] A.C. 584.

[38] *Griffin* v. *Lord Advocate*, 1950 S.C. 448; *Merricks* v. *Heathcoat-Amory, etc.* [1955] Ch. 567.

[39] *Theodore* v. *Duncan* [1919] A.C. 696, *per* Lord Haldane.

individual who is within its ambit.[40] That is to say that, in effect, a title to sue is denied, and this may be so where the duty is either common law or statutory. Alternatively it may be said (which comes to the same thing) that the duty so far as one exists is one owed to the Crown and only enforceable in Parliament.[41] Thus it is that only where the duty is specific and any discretionary element is lacking that it is at all easy to enforce obligations through the courts.[42] It is possible that the courts may be somewhat more liberal in this respect in Scotland than in England, and rather more willing to approach the boundary of what must be left to the administration.[43] On the other hand, restraining the wrongful acts of the Crown is somewhat easier where the authority to act is statutory and it can be shown that the proposed act is *ultra vires*.[44] Where, however, the claim to restrain is based upon an assertion of improper motive, once again the tendency is to rely upon parliamentary controls to the exclusion of judicial ones. Again the problems of the admixture of motives arise.[45] These problems are not unlike those which have already been discussed in the context of administrative tribunals and inquiries; and while the control of motive is preserved in theory,[46] its practical application remains difficult.

Procedural aspects. Something must be added on the mechanism of the Act. In Scotland proceedings may be brought against the Lord Advocate, by virtue of the Crown Suits Act 1857, which (s. 1) authorises such a course in actions against the Crown, or against any public department. The latter phrase is partially defined by the Act (s. 4) but it seems that it must be limited under the *ejusdem generis* rule to those departments and authorities which would be regarded as the Crown or as

---

40 *Civilian War Claimants Assoc.* v. *R.* [1932] A.C. 14; *China Navigation Co. Ltd.* v. *Att.-Gen.* [1932] 2 K.B. 197; *Griffin* v. *Lord Advocate,* 1950 S.C. 448. It was this rule which caused the problem which led to the " Sachsenhausen case " before the Parliamentary Commissioner (1967–68) H.C. 54.

41 *Griffin* v. *L.A.,* 1950 S.C. 448; *Harper* v. *S. of S. for the Home Department* [1955] Ch. 238. There is nothing novel about this idea; see *Grant* v. *Lords of Treasury* (1704) II Fount. 224; *Stewart* v. *Bothwell,* Feb. 26, 1742, F.C.; *Craigie* v. *Hepburn,* Dec. 22, 1809, F.C.

42 *R.* v. *Commissioners of Income Tax* (1881) 21 Q.B.D. 313, where the duty rested upon officials as *personae designatae,* and where the right was equally specific; contrast *R.* v. *S. of S. for War* [1891] 2 Q.B. 376. The principle of these cases, although enunciated in the context of mandamus, is no doubt applicable in the context of declaratory orders; and see de Smith, *Judicial Review of Administrative Action,* Chap. 12. The same principles appear in *Carlton Hotel Co. Ltd.* v. *L.A.,* 1921 S.C. 237 to be accepted by Lord Salvesen at p. 249, and (probably) by Lord Dundas.

43 See, *e.g., Adams* v. *S. of S. for Scotland,* 1958 S.C. 279, wherein the court left a discretion to the Secretary of State, but limited it.

44 The positive and negative aspects may tend to run together: *Mags. of Kilmarnock* v. *S. of S. for Scotland,* 1961 S.C. 350. As to the rules, see subsequently S.I. 1963 No. 2077 (s. 114) and the Police (Scotland) Act 1966.

45 Consider such cases as *Pollok School* v. *Glasgow T.C.,* 1946 S.C. 373; 1947 S.C. 607; and *R.* v. *Governor of Brixton Prison, ex p. Soblen* [1963] 2 Q.B. 243.

46 Even in the most difficult of areas: *Chandler* v. *D.P.P.* [1962] 3 All E.R. 142 at 158, *per* Lord Devlin.

Crown servants,[47] and it seems that in determining who would be so regarded the general test of control will be applied, and that some weight will be given to the English list of "authorised departments." [48] The title of the Lord Advocate to defend extends to agencies of the Crown in right of the United Kingdom, even though the events giving rise to the action occurred outside Scotland.[49] There existed a variety of statutory provisions which authorised government departments to sue and be sued.[50] These were repealed by the Second Schedule to the Crown Proceedings Act 1947, but it seems that, since there is no prohibition of raising an action against such bodies contained in the Crown Proceedings Act, such actions remain competent, although in practice actions will be normally raised against the Lord Advocate. To that general proposition there is one large exception. Section 1 (8) of the Reorganisation of Offices (Scotland) Act 1939 contemplates legal proceedings against the Secretary of State in the name of the "Secretary of State for Scotland," and it is customary, where there is involved any department for which the Secretary of State is responsible, to raise the action in those terms.[51] This position appears to be entirely consistent with the theory of the Act, so far as that theory appears from section 17 (which is applicable to Scotland). It is also consistent with the terminology of the Crown Suits (Scotland) Act 1857. What has been said about raising an action against the Crown applies, subject to necessary modifications, to actions by the Crown, and it may be noted that, under the Crown Suits (Scotland) Act 1857, while the Lord Advocate is required to have the authority of the public department in question (either for instituting or defending actions), no private party can challenge that authority, upon grounds that it has not been given or that evidence of such authority has not been produced. It would, it seems, be competent to challenge on the ground that the public authority in question was not of the type covered by the Crown Suits Act, i.e., was not a Crown servant.

In England the position is differently regulated, since the Attorney-General did not have the representative character of the Lord Advocate. Section 17 of the Act of 1947 provides for the Treasury issuing lists specifying the government departments which are authorised departments

47 *Smith* v. *Lord Advocate*, 1932 S.L.T. 374; *Lord Advocate* v. *Argyll C.C.*, 1950 S.C. 304.

48 *i.e.*, those authorised to sue and be sued under the Crown Proceedings Act 1947, s. 17 (1); *Lord Advocate* v. *Argyll C.C.*, 1950 S.C. 304.

49 *Cameron* v. *Lord Advocate*, 1952 S.C. 165; *Burmah Oil Co. (Burma Trading) Ltd.* v. *Lord Advocate*, 1964 S.C.(H.L.) 117. It may be noted that the House of Lords there concluded that the governing law was English law, on the grounds that it was that law which was transplanted to colonial territories.

50 Provisions which gave rise to certain difficulties; see Glanville Williams, *Crown Proceedings.*

51 For the background of this position, see Fraser, *Outlines of Constitutional Law*, p. 162. The practice of submitting a stated case to the Court of Session in the name of the relevant minister where that is the appropriate appellate procedure from an administrative tribunal continues.

for the purposes of the Act to sue or be sued in their own name. If no authorised department is appropriate, or if there is doubt as to which is appropriate, the action may be raised by or against the Attorney-General. At any stage in the proceedings the Attorney-General may make an application to have himself substituted as defendant in place of an authorised department or have such a department similarly substituted for himself.

Problems can arise as to venue. The jurisdiction to hear actions against the Crown which is conferred upon the sheriff courts by the Act of 1947 is subjected to all the limitations, whether as to subject-matter or otherwise, applicable to those courts. Among the grounds of jurisdiction is the fact that the defender resides, or has a place of business or owns heritable property in the particular sheriffdom. It follows that, since there is a sheriff court house in each sheriffdom, the Crown may be sued in any, irrespective of the local origin of the cause of action. No doubt if the action is raised in a sheriffdom which is inconvenient in the particular case the provisions for transfer to the Court of Session would be invoked. Similarly the jurisdiction of the Court of Session or of the Supreme Court in England does not depend upon the locality of the cause of action. It is theoretically possible, therefore, to raise an action in Scotland although the cause of action arose in England,[52] and there may be reasons of convenience why the action should be raised in one jurisdiction rather than the other. It may be time-barred in one and not the other,[53] or rules of procedure or evidence may be more convenient in one than in the other.[54] It is possible that the pursuer in an action of which the cause was essentially English might be met by a plea of *forum non conveniens*, but it is doubtful how far such a plea, as it is now interpreted,[55] would be successful, and it is to be noticed that there is no provision in the Act of 1947 for any transfer of actions between one jurisdiction and another.

Other public authorities. Formerly, other public authorities were given particular protections under the Public Authorities Protection Act 1893, and these protections were extended to the Crown by the Crown Proceedings Act 1947. Now, however, the Law Reform (Limitation of Actions, etc.) Act 1954 has repealed the Act of 1893, and actions against public authorities are mainly governed by the general law which would be applicable in actions between individuals.[56] In other respects

---

[52] Street (1948) 11 M.L.R. 141.   [53] As was the *Burmah Oil* case, *supra*, note 49.

[54] As in *Glasgow Corporation* v. *Central Land Board*, 1956 S.C.(H.L.) 1.

[55] Duncan and Dykes, *Principles of Civil Jurisdiction.*

[56] Some special periods continue, *e.g.*, Summary Jurisdiction (Scotland) Act 1954, s. 75 (the protection of magistrates), or Law Reform (Limitation of Actions) Act 1954, s. 5 (2) (imposing a 12-month period of limitation in actions against the Crown in respect of registered postal packets), or Licensing (Scotland) Act 1959, s. 195. For a table applicable to Scotland setting out the periods additional to the ordinary prescriptive periods, see Walker (1954) S.L.T.(News) 125; and see Preston and Newsom, *Limitation of Actions.*

it seems at first sight that the ordinary law is applicable to actions against public authorities. On closer examination this is not so, and rules akin to those which have been discussed as prerogative rules emerge. Thus public authorities other than the Crown cannot contract away their public responsibilities,[57] their capacities as proprietors may be affected by statutory or common law restrictions.[58] Liability in reparation (or in tort) may be affected by the governmental or public character of their responsibilities,[59] as it is by the fact that public authorities may be performing statutory functions.[60] Even the relationship of the authority to its servants and the nature of the functions imposed on the latter may affect the law.[61] Those servants themselves by virtue of their public character may receive either at common law, or by statute,[62] particular immunities as a result of the " malice or want of probable cause " rule or its equivalent. Thus the character of public authorities does affect the substantive law as it is applicable to them in ways which are similar in principle if not in phraseology to the rules applicable to the Crown.

In a somewhat similar way the remedies available to an individual are affected. While the Crown Proceedings Act 1947 excludes execution against the Crown, to a large extent the same effect is achieved, either by common law or by statute, in relation to other public authorities.[63] Remedies which directly interfere with the administrative process may be applicable only with modification to local and other public authorities,[64] though, since such interference may not be so critical in

---

[57] *Ayr Harbour Trustees* v. *Oswald* (1883) 10 R.(H.L.) 85; *William Cory & Sons* v. *Corporation of London* [1951] 2 K.B. 476; and see Mitchell, *Contracts of Public Authorities*, Chap. II.

[58] *Magistrates of Kirkcaldy* v. *Marks and Spencer Ltd.*, 1937 S.L.T. 574, in which there are signs of the survival of the idea of the *res extra commercium*.

[59] While the particular point at issue in *Plank* v. *Magistrates of Stirling*, 1956 S.C. 92 is no longer of importance as a result of the Occupiers' Liability (Scotland) Act 1960 and the Occupiers' Liability Act 1957 (applicable to England), the general approach which underlies the opinion in *Plank* may still be important, and questions of " occupation " can still arise. *Cf. M'Phail* v. *Lanarkshire C.C.*, 1951 S.C. 301; and see *Keogh* v. *Edinburgh Corporation*, 1926 S.C. 814.

[60] *East Suffolk Catchment Board* v. *Kent* [1941] A.C. 74, the principles of which seem likely to be applicable in both jurisdictions. The whole question of liability for performing statutory duties is here relevant.

[61] The instance of the police has already been given. Despite the suggestion that the position of the police may be unique (*Kilboy* v. *S.E. Fire Area Joint Committee*, 1952 S.C. 280), this appears not to be so: see *M'Phail* v. *Lanarkshire C.C.*, 1951 S.C. 301 at 313.

[62] *e.g.*, s. 103 of the Local Government (Scotland) Act 1947, which is a commonplace provision.

[63] *Phin* v. *Magistrates of Auchtermuchty* (1827) 5 S. 690; *Kerr* v. *Magistrates of Linlithgow* (1865) 3 M. 370; *Magistrates of Lochmaben* v. *Beck* (1841) 4 D. 16; though compare *Wotherspoon* v. *Magistrates of Linlithgow* (1863) 2 M. 348 and *Macdonald* v. *Reid* (1881) 9 R. 211, which appear to be distinguishable. See, too, *Att.-Gen.* v. *Walthamstow U.D.C.* (1895) 11 T.L.R. 533 and *Stancomb* v. *Trowbridge U.D.C.* [1910] 2 Ch. 190; Local Government Act 1933, s. 211, and Local Government (Scotland) Act 1947, s. 287.

[64] *Pride of Derby and Derbyshire Angling Assoc.* v. *British Celanese & Ors.* [1953] Ch. 149 at 181 and *Att.-Gen.* v. *Colchester Corporation* [1952] Ch. 586, both of which illustrate principles of general application. The problems of remedy where

relation to public authorities other than the Crown, and since the functions of such authorities are much more " mixed " (many not being so marked with public characteristics), the rules are not so absolute as they are in relation to the Crown. Orders ordaining a public authority to perform a specific duty may be obtained, but as has been indicated the rules giving a title to sue have not yet been fully worked out, and the courts carefully, and necessarily, avoid being placed in the position of controlling services,[65] being concerned rather to control only excesses.[66] Further, although a jurisdiction exists to control the propriety of the actings of public authorities[67] it is one sparingly used because of the difficulties of determining questions of motive, and when used the question is in effect posed as one of *ultra vires*.[68] It is probably true here, as in relation to the Crown, that the jurisdiction to restrain is much more effective than the jurisdiction to compel action; the reason for the difference being simply that the latter intermingles the courts much more in the administrative process and therefore is avoided except in extreme cases.

General considerations. Many of the problems of the judicial control of the administrative actions of public authorities are similar to those of the control of the judicial or quasi-judicial actions of such bodies. Administrative morality is equally important in relation to any activity of a public authority. It is probable that the fact that the forms of action which were most commonly used in England until the more recent development of the declaratory order had the consequence of focusing attention on the control of judicial/quasi-judicial action. Indeed, at times, it appeared that a classification of an activity as " administrative " resulted in an absence of judicial control, or in a marked diminution of it.[69] In Scotland the fact that remedies are much more generalised has meant that that effect has been much less marked.[70] This has not

---

public duties are involved remain acute and unsolved; consider, *e.g., Smeaton* v. *Ilford Corporation* [1954] Ch. 450.

65 *Watt* v. *Kesteven C.C.* [1955] 1 Q.B. 408; *Grahame* v. *Magistrates of Kirkcaldy* (1882) 9 R.(H.L.) 91; and see *Oxford Essays in Jurisprudence,* Chap. X.

66 *British Oxygen Co. Ltd.* v. *S. of Scotland Electricity Board,* 1959 S.C.(H.L.) 17 and 1956 S.C.(H.L.) 112; *Parlane* v. *Perth & Kinross Joint C.C.,* 1954 S.L.T.(Sh.Ct.) 95.

67 *Nicol* v. *Magistrates of Aberdeen* (1870) 9 M. 306; *Associated Picture Theatres Ltd.* v. *Wednesbury Corporation* [1948] 1 K.B. 223.

68 As an example of their reluctance, see *Blair* v. *Smith,* 1924 J.C. 24; and for the difficulties of challenge, see Ganz, " A Voyage of Discovery into Administrative Action " [1963] *Public Law* 76.

69 *R.* v. *Metropolitan Police Commissioner, ex p. Parker* [1953] 1 W.L.R. 1150; *Ex p. Fry* [1954] 1 W.L.R. 730; *R.* v. *Central Professional Committee for Opticians, ex p. Brown* [1949] 2 All E.R. 519; *cf. McDonald* v. *Lanarkshire Fire Brigade Joint Committee,* 1959 S.C. 141 or *Hayman* v. *Lord Advocate,* 1951 S.C. 621, and consider the two aspects of *Nakkuda Ali* v. *Jayaratne* [1951] A.C. 66, the insistence on reasonable grounds, but the limitation of procedural due process; and Wade, " The Twilight of Natural Justice " (1951) 67 L.Q.R. 103. These cases should now be considered in the light of the opinions in *Ridge* v. *Baldwin* [1964] A.C. 40. The generality of principle in the opinion of Lord Reid should be particularly observed. See also Bradley, " A Failure of Justice and Defect of Police " [1964] C.L.J. 83.

70 See the cases in note 69; and Mitchell, " The Scope of Judicial Review," 1959 J.R. 197 and " Reflections on Law and Orders," 1958 J.R. 19.

involved any diminution upon the insistence in the principle of natural justice,[71] but it has enabled judicial review to be exercised upon a somewhat more liberal basis. Nevertheless, even in such conditions, the difference is one of degree and not of kind, since many of those conditions which inhibit courts are universal. By reason of their bulk the English decisions help, however, to form a pattern of thought throughout the Kingdom. The whole business of government cannot be transferred to the courts by means of actions purporting to call upon courts to enforce generally phrased statutory duties, and fear of such a consequence induces a judicial reticence.[72] In England this reticence has found expression in the concentration upon the judicial/quasi-judicial questions. In Scotland it exists though not in that form.

One other factor should be noted. The denial of public law as a distinct *corpus* of law, except for teaching purposes, was probably useful in the process of building up a rule of law. In a modern, highly developed society it has had damaging consequences. The departures from the rules of private law, in contract or reparation, are regarded as exceptions, and thus little attempt is made to systematise them. Correspondingly, there is, it seems, an inadequate development of rules and concepts in the courts. Thus the critical concept of a title to sue remains undeveloped,[73] as are others, such as the operation of the *ultra vires* rule in relation to public authorities. Procedural techniques and remedies, it seems, suffer also. The absence of subtlety in the rules about the disclosure of documents has been met by administrative adjustment,[74] which is in itself an unsatisfactory procedure. More seriously, it may be said that other detailed rules of law remain undeveloped, and do not take account of the conditions of a contemporary society. The responsibility of public authorities for statements made by their servants does not, it seems, take proper account of the altered position of those authorities.[75] Similarly, just as certain standards of " reasonableness " as to their rents policy may be enforced by the Secretary of State upon local authorities as housing authorities, so also it may be that the dominant position of local authorities in that capacity, as to certain types of housing, may also require enforcement of

---

[71] *Barrs* v. *British Wool Marketing Board*, 1957 S.C. 72; and Bennett Miller, " Problems of Natural Justice," 1960 J.R. 29.

[72] This fear is evident from *Pryde* v. *Heritors and Kirk Session of Ceres* (1843) 5 D. 552 and Cockburn's *Journal*, II, 1 and 257 to the *British Oxygen* case referred to above, note 66.

[73] Consider the circumstances in *D. & J. Nicol* v. *Dundee Harbour Trustees*, 1915 S.C.(H.L.) 7.

[74] *Ante*, note 22; these adjustments though not as such applicable in Scotland are likely to affect practice there.

[75] Consider *Southend-on-Sea Corporation* v. *Hodgson (Wickford) Ltd.* [1962] 1 Q.B. 416; *Att.-Gen. for Ceylon* v. *A. D. Silva* [1953] A.C. 461 and the problems involved in *Howell* v. *Falmouth Boat Construction Co.* [1951] A.C. 837; and Mitchell, " The Flexible Constitution " [1960] *Public Law* 332. Lord Reid's assertion in *Ridge* v. *Baldwin* (*supra*) that we have no proper system of administrative law is equally true in this context.

standards of reasonableness as to terms and conditions in ways which would be inappropriate in questions between tenant and private land-lord.[76] Indeed, apart from the problems already noted in the discussion of the Crown Proceedings Act 1947, many public contracts pose considerable questions, and are likely to do so more and more in the future. Contracts have become a means of government, they can be an important factor in the execution of a regional policy or in attaining other governmental purposes.[77] Such matters clearly change the way in which they must be regarded. Equally the special problems of accounting, or those which spring either from the peculiar strengths or weaknesses of government, should have their effects in the law, for these are matters which distinguish such contracts from private ones.[78] At an earlier stage such differing standards were enforced in the relation-ship between the emergent public authorities and their officials, as against the rules of private employment. The creative process, however, appears to have stopped.

That is to say that it is arguable that the general isolation of problems relating to quasi-judicial functions and the concentration upon those aspects of judicial review have tended to prevent the proper development of substantive public law, and to limit the proper exercise by courts of their functions in respect of other actions of administrative bodies. That development is also hampered by the dichotomy between the Crown and other parts of government. Increasingly the governmental machine is becoming, in fact if not in law, unitary by the interlocking of its parts, a process which is apparent both in the field of local government and in the field of public corporations. Yet the general law is based on, and greatly influenced by, this theoretical dichotomy. Thus an overall treatment of governmental operations becomes difficult. Specialised terminology, such as the word " prerogative," springs from the same cause, and has like effects. The effects are widespread. By reason of this failure to evolve a coherent system of public law attuned to, and adequate for, the needs of a modern state the courts and law are playing a less significant role in the machinery of government than was once the case. That situation is neither necessary nor desirable. The argument can be carried too far. Government cannot be turned into a judicial process, but, nevertheless, just as there is a place for politics, there is also a place for law. One difficulty has been that administrative law has never been seen in its full scope. A concentration

[76] See *Carleton* v. *Greenock Corporation*, 1962 S.L.T. 35 and Lord Porter's reference to discretion in *Shelley* v. *L.C.C.* [1949] A.C. 56 at 66.

[77] See, *e.g.*, *Public Purchasing and Industrial Efficiency* (1967) Cmnd. 3291.

[78] See the First and Second Lang Reports (Cmnd. 2428 and Cmnd. 2581). These considerations go far beyond defence contracts. They affect as strongly those of the National Health Service or those relating to road construction ; see the N.E.D.C. reports, *Efficiency in Road Construction*. See, too (1964) 29 *Law and Contemporary Problems*, where such contracts are regarded as " quite distinct from their private counterparts," and Maxwell, *Public Sector Purchasing*. The story continues ; see the Wilson Report on aero engines (1967–68) H.C. 129.

upon limited difficulties concerned with delegated legislation and administrative tribunals led to reforms associated with the Statutory Instruments Act 1946 and the Tribunals and Inquiries Act 1958. The reforms were desirable in themselves but, almost at once, it became clear that neither they nor the Crown Proceedings Act 1947, which (late in the day) dealt with another aspect of the problem, had produced any solution. Discontent was not one-sided. In the absence of a distinct corpus of law which allows both for the needs of government and the rights of citizens sometimes the needs of government are recognised without an adequate protection of the citizen. Sometimes the over-elaboration of procedural safeguards has impeded government unreasonably without giving any substantial benefit to the citizen. Sometimes there are violent swings which leave the individual ill-protected or unprotected. The *Burmah Oil* case (the result of which was debatable on grounds of general principle) had its effect in the War Damage Act 1965, which by a violent overcorrection removes all rights past and future for compensation for the damage there in dispute. Thus the malaise continued and became deeper.[79] In time, this feeling coincided with a feeling in the House of Commons that the member (or rather the backbencher) was now impotent against the administration. He had lost his place in the sun.

It was then as a result of a combination of forces that the Parliamentary Commissioner for Administration (P.C.A.) emerged as a proposal, and was accepted. The office was created (or ratified) by the Parliamentary Commissioner Act 1967. The P.C.A. is given equivalent status to that of Comptroller and Auditor-General, and he has power (s. 5) to investigate a complaint by a member of the public that he has " sustained injustice in consequence of maladministration " of a relevant department and the complaint is referred to him by a member. The relevant departments are broadly the departments of the central government. Thus all nationalised industries, however factually close their connection may be with a ministry, are excluded, as are, specifically, hospital boards. Important central agencies (such as the Bank of England, playing a vital role in exchange control) are also, wholly or partially, excluded.[80] Moreover, even within this range of departments important matters are excluded by the Act, *e.g.*, action by the administration of any overseas territory, anything done by the Home Secretary under the Extradition Acts or Fugitive Offenders Acts,

---

[79] One sign of it was the report by Justice—*The Citizen and the Administration* (1961), discussed in a series of articles in [1962] *Public Law* 24–57. See generally Mitchell, " The Ombudsman Fallacy " [1962] *Public Law* 24; " The Causes and Consequences of the Absence of a System of Public Law in the United Kingdom " [1965] *Public Law* 95; " The Present State of Public Law in the United Kingdom " (1966) 15 I.C.L.Q. 133.

[80] It is essentially unhealthy that international trading should be conducted on the basis of discretion and hint. The risks are sufficient in any event and the investor should know the rules clearly.

anything done by a Secretary of State connected with security or the investigation of crime, any action relating to contractual or commercial transactions and anything relating to personnel matters of the civil or armed services.   In principle there are also excluded any matters in respect of which the individual had a right of resort to a tribunal or to a court.   Within the limits of what is left the P.C.A. has powers of summoning witnesses and while the rules of Crown privilege in evidence do not bind in the investigating stage (with the exception of Cabinet proceedings which are protected), nevertheless those rules can all be brought back at the report stage (s. 11 (3)) so that the individual may never know the true grounds upon which his complaint was determined, for the investigation is private, and it is not adversary in form; all that is required is that the department shall have an opportunity to comment upon the complaint.   The outcome is a report which is not necessarily public, and if the P.C.A. believes that injustice done is not likely to be remedied, then he may make a special report to the House.   A Select Committee was established to examine his reports, but the most significant report so far, on the " Sachsenhausen case," [81] by-passed the Committee.   To this should be added his First Report,[82] which indicated that the P.C.A. regarded the Metropolitan Police (as well as other forces) as excluded.   He made it clear also that some members preferred to exhaust their own resources before making any reference. In regard to the critical area of discretionary decisions he indicated a heavy reliance on procedure, to regard " the area of my investigation to be the administrative processes attendant on the decision. . . .   If I find no such defect, then I do not find myself as competent to question the quality of the decision."   The first Annual Report for 1967 makes clear how substantial are the exclusions when coupled with this narrow definition of maladministration.

Before commenting on these provisions three remarks must be made. First, that it is perfectly possible that an Ombudsman can, in some countries, be effective.[83]   The New Zealand Ombudsman has been.[84] It is, however, unreasonable to transplant an institution to another country and expect the same in essential result.   In size of population, in urban congestion, and in the degree of industrialisation (all of which are critical factors in government), the United Kingdom is radically different to New Zealand or Denmark.   Second, there is today a need for a general surveillance of administrative machinery from outside, and this the P.C.A. could do.   Third, the adaptations which

---

[81] (1967–68) H.C. 671.
[82] (1967–68) H.C. 6.
[83] See generally Rowat, *The Ombudsman*, and Gellhorn, *Ombudsmen and Others.*
[84] Sir Guy Powles reflects on the general problem in " Aspects of the Search for Administrative Justice," 9 *Canadian Public Administration* 133.   His concluding passages should, however, be noted.

were made in importing the office to the United Kingdom probably weakened the office.

The main objections to the office are twofold. First, that an inadequate solution to the real problems has been produced, and, second, that the solution has been sought by the wrong means. At the root of present difficulties lay the initial hypothesis of the White Paper [85] which preceded the Bill. " We do not want to create any new institution which would erode the functions of Members of Parliament in this respect [*scil.* in taking up the grievances of constituents], nor to replace remedies which the British Constitution already provides." This sentence was preceded by one indicating that citizens should not suffer injustice and by another invoking (by implication) the virtues of parliamentary questions, adjournment debates, etc. In all of this many fundamental issues were half-glimpsed and then evaded. By all great traditions relief from injustice is a matter for the courts and for the law. It had become generally accepted that parliamentary question had in this sense become ineffective, but the essential distinction between a political forum and a legal one was evaded, as was any deep analysis of the weakness of Parliament on the one hand or of the real problems of law on the other. There was certainly evident the mingling of the two streams of discontent already mentioned, but the possibility that each required distinctive remedies, and the fact that the cause in each case was the inadequacy of the present constitutional mechanisms, were both neglected. It is probable that we have surpassed the limits of capacity of the present constitutional machinery.

The parliamentary problem is one which must find its solution in changed political practices. The remedies were readily available had the political parties wished to resort to them. The problem of finding a place in the sun for the backbench M.P. is essentially different from the problem of finding effective means of redress for the individual who has suffered injustice. As far as that other problem was concerned, the problem of the relationship of individual to the state, the solution adopted of the P.C.A. in the first place kept within a political forum issues which were not by their nature political. Two consequences flow from that. First, that they are debated in false terms, and, secondly, by denying the possibility of other means of relief, the fundamental problem must in time be exacerbated. Indeed the " Sachsenhausen case " [86] demonstrates many of these points. It demonstrates that in the first place traditional parliamentary techniques were inadequate; secondly, that in the background lay serious weaknesses of law. The issue need never have become one of major controversy. In the background there existed what was essentially a " trust fund " for a determinable group. It would have been perfectly simple to

[85] Cmnd. 2767.
[86] (1967–68) H.C. 671.

recognise a right in claimants, and on the basis of established claims
to distribute the fund.   The issues of fact and of interpretation which
were involved are commonplace and could properly and conveniently
have been dealt with by a court.   This method of dealing with the
situation was excluded as a result of rules of law,[87] which themselves
go back to the unreasonably narrow concepts of public law which have
become ingrained but which in themselves are by no means inevitable.
In a wide range of jurisdictions rights of this order are readily
recognised.   In the end the debate [88] that followed showed both that
there were disadvantages in the method of investigation which the
P.C.A. has to use and more seriously the unresolved conflicts (which
still exist and are likely to become more important) with other dominant
constitutional beliefs.

What has happened is that we have allowed the modern revolution
of the active or welfare state to happen and have done little to adjust
law to its needs after the manner in which the Victorians made positive
efforts to absorb the industrial revolution into law.   It is indeed true
that we have never examined in its fullness the problem of administrative law.[89]   Delegated legislation and administrative tribunals did
not lie at the heart of the matter.   They were only signs of the change.
As has been seen, the Crown Proceedings Act 1947 has not solved real
problems.   As has already been noticed in the last chapter, major
procedural matters relating to " Crown privilege," as well as major
matters of substance in contract or reparation, were left untouched by
it, or found no solution in it.   Problems of growing importance, such
as those of the representations of officials which turn out to be false,
cannot find solutions at the present time, because the intellectual
framework of the law is inadequate.   Private rules of personal bar or
estoppel cannot be applied to government.   The first annual report of
the P.C.A. emphasises how, among the matters investigated, this issue
bulks large.   He cannot effectively solve the problem without becoming
a judge, which predicates a system of law.   Therein lies the true
problem.   We lack a real system of public law, and as a result both
individuals (corporate or human) and the state suffer.   The individuals

---

[87] *Civilian War Claimants* v. *The King* [1932] A.C. 14.   The same point could be
illustrated from other reports.   Equivalent weaknesses underlay C703/67 and C473/67
of November 30 and 22.   It is difficult to cite these reports.   They are not published in any regular series and can only be made available, if asked for, if the
member consents.   Summaries are published in the Annual Report of the P.C.A.;
see his report for 1967 (1967–68) H.C. 134.   The first Annual Report of the P.C.A.
(1967–68) H.C. 134 reinforces the point that in many cases it is the weakness of the
law in the background which causes the trouble; consider some of the cases
involving the Ministries of Labour and of Social Security.

[88] 758 H.C.Deb. 107 *et seq.*

[89] In Mitchell, " The Causes and Consequences of the Absence of a System of Public
Law " [1965] *Public Law* 95, these matters are explored at length.   The whole
history is one of patchwork.   We tidied up bits of the prerogative with, *e.g.*, the
Foreign Enlistment Act 1870, but we never cleared our minds; see Holdsworth,
History of English Law, Vol. XIV.

are left increasingly to rely on benevolent discretion and the state is impeded, since our reliance on the cumulation of procedural safeguards has slowed the machinery of society to an unacceptable extent. (It is likely that the definition of " maladministration " adopted by the P.C.A. will accentuate that trend.) All these matters can be effectively safeguarded by a proper system of administrative law.

The problem is indeed one of constitutional significance in two ways. It is wrong that a minister should indicate that irrespective of the terms of a contract the government will reserve an ultimate uncontrollable discretion over sums to be paid.[90] It is wrong that the essential terms governing immigration should be found not in law but in a White Paper. It is wrong that the Iron and Steel Act 1967 should reserve for the minister's political decision questions such as that of unfair competition which is almost universally recognised elsewhere as presenting a justiciable issue. It is wrong that a government department should issue a document appearing to be a contract of employment but which is worthless.[91] It is wrong that the realities of the relationship of minister to nationalised industry bears little relation to that set out in the parent statute. The list could be made much longer.

All these things are marks of the essential problem.[92] None can be effectively met by the P.C.A. He cannot deliver judgment, he cannot evolve law. Not only is he thus limited, but the difficulties spread through the whole of government including local government. Again he can do nothing, and a rash of P.C.A.s could not produce coherent results. A system of administrative law need suffer none of these disadvantages. Beyond that there are other constitutional matters at issue. We have become a highly centralised country, perhaps the most so in Europe. There is a direct relationship between the forms of control and the shape of the thing to be controlled. None of the recent proposals for devolution either in a structural sense or in the sense of the administrative devolution of planning decisions can be successful without this deconcentration of control. Finally, because of our present system we have an administration which, perhaps against its will, is the most secretive in Europe,[93] and in a democracy this is not

---

[90] 273 H.C.Deb. 712.

[91] *Riordan* v. *The War Office* [1959] 3 All E.R. 552. The sad state of the law of tort is illustrated well enough by *Smeaton* v. *Ilford Corporation* [1954] Ch. 450. The over-reliance on procedural devices, which in the end prove both illusory protection to one party and unreasonably cumbersome to the other, is illustrated by *Bradbury* v. *London Borough of Enfield* [1967] 3 All E.R. 434 and its sequels. It is also wrong on constitutional principle that the P.C.A. should have been appointed before the Bill creating his office had even left the Commons. We have made the legislative process insignificant. See generally Mitchell, " The Present State of Public Law " (1966) 15 I.C.L.Q. 133.

[92] It is these matters which are elaborated in " The Constitutional Implications of Judicial Control of the Administration of the United Kingdom " [1967] C.L.J. 46.

[93] See, *e.g.*, 751 H.C.Deb. 751, where the minister refuses to disclose on a major educational matter advice from the University Grants Committee (as indeed all his predecessors would have refused). Yet how then can the people judge?

only unhealthy, but provokes distrust against government which need not exist.[94]

These things can be cured by a real administrative jurisdiction. It remains true, as Montesquieu said, that only power can match power. The power of a court is needed to match the power of government, but the law it administers must be attuned to the needs of a modern state. That is why the specific creation of a new court charged with those purposes is essential. Only a new body can break the established patterns easily enough to establish a coherent and efficient jurisprudence in this vital field of the modern relationship of man and the state. Lord Devlin has rightly remarked: "I believe it to be generally recognised that in many of his dealings with the executive the citizen cannot get justice by process of law. The Common Law has now, I think, no longer the strength to provide any satisfactory solution to the problem of keeping the executive with all the powers which under modern conditions are needed for the efficient conduct of the realm, under proper control."[95] The problems are not insoluble. An administrative jurisdiction can be, and has been proved to be, an effective solution, providing proper protection for the interest of state and individual with all the weight of a judgment while at the same time avoiding the danger of trying to convert government into a judicial process. It must be emphasised that a true administrative court does not enter the field of politics. Policies are left to be decided through Parliament. What it does is to insist that they are carried out with absolute even-handedness. Thus it is immediately apparent that such a body could help us to regain a clearer idea of what is a political matter as well as help us to deal with those that are truly justiciable. Such courts are not strange. They operate by the techniques familiar to any common lawyer; but such an evolution is needed to restore the place of law in government.[96] That restoration is in itself necessary to protect the more modern forms of liberty in a society in which, for example, the control of land-use has become often more important than questions of land-ownership. These new issues result then from an evolution dependent on the traditional liberties which remain to be discussed, but it is they which present the urgent problems. By excluding or postponing the possibility of the emergence of a real system of public law we have cut ourselves off from a richness of ideas and techniques of which we stand greatly in need.

94 Compare 758 H.C.Deb. 14, where the minister admits a readiness to compensate (if he feels like it) in the same way as would be compelled under the doctrines of *imprévision* or *fait du prince* in France. Yet we do not allow this moral obligation, which is admitted, to become a legal one.

95 "The Common Law, Public Policy, and the Executive" (1956) 9 *Current Legal Problems* 1 at 14.

96 That evolution is well illustrated by the *conclusions* of M. Galmot in *Tochou*, C.E., April 22, 1966, R.D.P. 584. Such a court and its consequences are discussed in Mitchell, "Administrative Law and Parliamentary Control" (1967) 38 *Political Quarterly* 360, to which the reader is referred. *De lege ferenda* is an important subject, but here can only have a limited place.

CHAPTER 18

FUNDAMENTAL LIBERTIES

Introduction. The issues raised at the end of the last chapter, and those discussed in the context of delegated legislation and administrative adjudication, are clearly concerned with the liberty of the subject. The expansion of individual liberty (in one sense) as a result of the development of social services and of the acceptance of principles of social security, as well as the general growth of state activity, all create problems of the protection of individuals. Every measure which produces the possibility of beneficent state action necessarily produces at the same time a possibility of the abuse of power. It is probable that the urgent problems of liberty are to be found in the branches of law just discussed. Certainly these developments serve to emphasise that the concept of liberty is neither static nor precise. In all its aspects questions of balance arise since there is a conflict between various desired ends. Any formulation of principle must therefore be in general, or qualified, terms. This consideration may make the fact that internally we lack any specific guarantees of liberty less significant than it is sometimes thought to be. Such guarantees, where they exist, may only be meaningful when read in the context of the constant shifts of judicial decisions, and, even when couched in absolute terms, concealed reservations are always present. On the other hand there are advantages in having clearly declared standards even if the declaration cannot be couched in terms of absolute precision and the absence of such a declaration is attributable to the chronology of our revolutions and the chance pattern of constitutional evolution which has resulted. It is clear that were it now necessary to draw a British Constitution such a declaration would be included. Indeed it can be argued that we now have such a general declaration since the United Kingdom has (for a period of three years in the first instance) recognised the right of individuals to petition the European Commission of Human Rights and subscribed to the compulsory jurisdiction of the European Court of Human Rights.[1] Despite the absence in the past of such general

---

[1] For the relevant texts, see (1966) 15 I.C.L.Q. 539–541 and for the major provisions of Sect. 1 of the Convention see the Appendix hereto. See generally Robertson, *Human Rights in Europe.* The changing pattern of the concern for liberty is most conveniently seen in Aron, *Essai sur les libertés,* and the general case for having a firmer protection of liberties is made in Cappelletti, *Il controlo giudizario di constituzionalità della leggi nel dirito comparato,* where he discusses, among other matters, the post-war evolution in Europe. In a " British " context the problem of the concealed limitations in general declarations can be glimpsed in *The Adelaide Company of Jehovah's Witnesses Incorporated* v. *The Commonwealth* (1943) 67 C.L.R. 116, particularly in the opinion of Williams J. Consider, too, the shape of

guarantees, the background of insistence on fundamental rights should be noted. While the Bill of Rights insists on political liberties and procedural rectitude, the contemporaneous Claim of Right goes somewhat further. In effect it stipulates liberty of opinion, reciting that the opinion of the Lords of Session " that persons refusing to discover their private thoughts and judgments in relation to points of treason, or other men's actions, are guilty of treason " is contrary to law, and that the forcing of the lieges to depone against themselves in capital crimes is contrary to law.[2] Both documents have an underlying insistence upon the freedom of the person, and both too assume the existence of a freedom of property. The former is made more explicit by the special penalties provided in both the Act Anent Wrongous Imprisonment 1701 and the Habeas Corpus Act 1679.

Similar fundamental assumptions are apparent in the cases. They are made sufficiently obvious as to personal liberty in either *Knight* v. *Wedderburn*[3] or *Somersett's Case*,[4] and thereafter in the tenor of the law in many branches, ranging from the Truck Acts to the law regulating contracts in restraint of trade. Similarly, the assumption of a right of property is inherent in *Smellie* v. *Struthers*.[5] The continuing influence of such conceptions can be seen in the presumptions in statutory interpretation. The weight of this tradition should not be underestimated, and it is one which must always be kept alive. The absence of general declarations may make that task more difficult on occasion, though correspondingly the presence of such declarations may produce a sense of false security. In either case the ultimate safeguard remains the outlook of members of society.[6]

FREEDOM OF SPEECH

If a choice had to be made of the most important among fundamental liberties in a modern society perhaps freedom of speech and opinion would be chosen, for upon that depends the ventilation of grievances and

the Canadian Bill of Rights and the comments of Bora Laskin in (1962) 11 I.C.L.Q. 519 and in (1959) 37 Can.B.R. and in his *Constitutional Law*, Chap. XV. The device of " guiding principles " in the Indian Constitution may here be noticed. The question of " balance " runs, of course, most clearly through the opinions of Mr. Justice Holmes.

2 So, too, the Articles of Grievances 1689 recite: " That the obliging the lieges to depone upon crymes against delinquents utherways than when they are adduced in special processes as witnesses is a great grievance."

3 (1778) Mor. 14545. *Cf. Carrington* v. *Geddew* (1632) Mor. 9454. Stair I, 2, 11, could condemn English villeinage, but gloss over the condition of colliers and salters. Fountainhall, in one of his elegant passages (I, 825), at least condemned the institution as contrary " to the mildness of our government." By Erskine's time liberty had risen to be a favourite of the law (Inst. I, 1, 56).

4 (1772) 20 St.Tr. 1.

5 May 12, 1803, F.C. in *The Case of Saltpetre* (1606) 12 Co.Rep. 12, or *The Moffat Hydropathic Co. Ltd.* v. *Lord Advocate*, 1919, 1 S.L.T. 82, or *The Burmah Oil Case*, 1963 S.L.T. 261 ; and see Gough, *Fundamental Law in English Constitutional History*.

6 Compare *Report of the Royal Commission on the Police* (1962) Cmnd. 1728, § 138.

the exposure of abuses. Of necessity the freedom is qualified. It is limited by the law of defamation, which in itself demonstrates the impossibility of absolutes in this area of law. Where other necessities, such as the administration of justice, require it, statements are absolutely privileged.[7] Where the weight of other considerations is not so great qualified privilege may be granted by the law, or no privilege may be given at all. The public interest in the dissemination of news, granted the conditions of publishing newspapers today, may require special rules to be applicable to the Press, and these are provided.[8] In other circumstances, such as an election, particular care must be taken against the making of false statements and the general law is adjusted to make provision for such cases.[9]

Similarly the law at one time was particularly careful of the reputation of those administering it. By common law insulting a judge was a crime, and murmuring a judge contrary to the Act of 1540 was an indictable offence.[10] It is doubtful if any such charge would now be laid, and matters would be dealt with by proceedings for contempt.[11] Such proceedings are also used to limit abuses of the freedom of speech and reporting in the interest of the fairness of a trial.[12] In Scotland the rules in this matter go much farther than they do in England. This is in part accounted for by differences in criminal procedure, notably the absence of a public preliminary hearing, but even apart from that fact the greater strictness is evident. Comment is inhibited not merely from the moment when any charge is made, but the inhibition may also reach back into the stage of investigation.[13] There is a greater strictness for another reason, in that the Administration of Justice Act 1960, ss. 11 and 12, provide special defences (particularly in cases of unintentional contempt), but these sections are not applicable to Scotland. It has, however, been emphasised in Scotland that a rule of law necessary for the proper administration of justice should not be abused or be allowed to degenerate into an instrument of oppression,[14] so it is probable that like considerations would apply. It may be noticed that the provisions in section 13 of that Act for an appeal in cases of

---

[7] *Ante*, p. 263; and see generally works on defamation such as Cooper, Chap. XIV. The existence of verbal injury in Scots law should be noted; see Smith, *Short Commentary on the Law of Scotland*, p. 175; Cooper, *Defamation*, Chap. XI.

[8] Defamation Act 1952, s. 4. See, too, on the confidentiality of the sources of information of the Press, *Att.-Gen.* v. *Clough* [1963] 1 All E.R. 420 and *Att.-Gen.* v. *Mulholland* [1963] 2 W.L.R. 658, wherein the element of judicial control providing a twofold check should be noted. See, too (1963) 79 L.Q.R. 167.

[9] Representation of the People Act 1949, s. 91; Defamation Act 1952, s. 10; and see *Plummer* v. *Charman* [1962] 3 All E.R. 823.

[10] *H.M. Advocate* v. *Robertson* (1870) 1 Coup. 404.

[11] See Macdonald, *Criminal Law*, p. 178, for other like offences; and Gordon, *Criminal Law*, Chap. 50.

[12] Again for the flexibility of the law, see *R.* v. *Duffy, ex p. Nash* [1960] 2 Q.B. 188.

[13] *Stirling* v. *Associated Newspapers*, 1960 J.C. 5 at 10 and *MacAlister* v. *Associated Newspapers*, 1954 S.L.T. 14; and *ante*, p. 262 and Criminal Justice Act 1967, s. 3.

[14] *Milburn, Petitioner*, 1946 S.C. 301. See, however, *Wylie* v. *H.M. Advocate*, 1966 S.L.T. 149 as to an appeal to the *nobile officium*.

contempt do not apply to Scotland, and though appeal would lie from committal in a sheriff court no such appeal lies, it seems, in the case of either the Court of Session or the High Court.

Criminal aspects. The interests of the state impose limitations on any absolute freedom or licence. The crime of sedition consists in inciting violence or illegality against the government. The older definitions of this crime, such as those in Hume,[15] while they may still be acceptable as a formulation, will be applied differently. To Hume, " stirring those foul and mutinous humours in the multitude, which when once set afloat may naturally issue in open violence and insurrection " was sedition and the offence might be constituted by attacking the " settled frame and order of things." In modern practice, without any specific formulation of the principle, a clear and present danger is looked for, and alternative charges of a lesser order are most frequently used.[16]

Other interests of the state are protected by the limitations on free speech based on the rules governing such offences as blasphemy or obscenity. There has, somewhat similarly, been a tendency over the years to liberalise the law. Blasphemy, speech or writing designed to vilify or ridicule the scriptures or the Christian religion no longer inhibits any reasonable criticism,[17] and prosecutions are rare. Prosecutions which might once have been brought for this crime are brought instead for offences against public order. Concern for morals is reflected in the law against obscenity. In Scotland the offence has most recently been defined in *Galletly* v. *Laird*,[18] where Lord Cooper emphasised two elements. The material must be such as is calculated to deprave or corrupt those open to such influences and it must be shown that it is being circulated in such circumstances that it is likely to fall into the hands of those liable to be corrupted. Thus, all is a matter of place and circumstance. In England the definition of the offence (which closely resembles that in Scotland) is given in section 1 of the Obscene Publications Act 1959. That Act, by section 4, admits a defence based on the assertion that publication was for the public good, or the interest of science, literature, art or learning, or other objects of public concern. The Act does not apply to Scotland, and it would seem that such a defence is excluded by Scots law as it now stands. It is uncertain how far this difference will, in practice, be significant. In this context the

15 *Criminal Law,* Chap. XXVII. For the modern law, see Gordon, *Criminal Law,* Chap. 37.
16 See, in particular, the Incitement to Disaffection Act 1934, making it an offence to endeavour to seduce any member of H.M. Forces from his duty or allegiance. Prosecutions in England require the consent of the Director of Public Prosecutions (such a provision being unnecessary in Scotland). S. 2 (2) gives extended powers of search. As to the police, see Police Act 1919, s. 3.
17 *Bowman* v. *Secular Society* [1917] A.C. 406; for an example, see *Paterson* v. *Brown* (1843) 1 Broun 629.
18 1953 J.C. 16.

court has refused to examine the reasons which may have moved the Lord Advocate in refusing to initiate a public prosecution, and has denied that a private prosecutor can have a sufficient interest to be allowed to proceed with a private prosecution.[19] It is then likely that a degree of uniformity will exist despite differences in the law (as the case cited indicates). There is thus a wide discretion, apparently uncontrollable by the courts, vested in the Lord Advocate in this matter as a result of the system of public prosecution. It must, however, be emphasised that this discretion relates only to the initiation of a prosecution.

It may here be noted that in England the courts have claimed a general power to police morality. " In the sphere of criminal law I entertain no doubt that there remains in the courts of law a residual power to enforce the supreme or fundamental purposes of the law, to conserve not only the safety and order but also the moral welfare of the state, and that it is their duty to guard it against attacks which may be the more insidious because they are novel and unprepared for," said Lord Simonds,[20] upholding the relevancy of a charge of " conspiring to corrupt public morals." While this case is authoritative only in England, a like power could exist in Scotland under the doctrine enunciated in *H.M. Advocate* v. *Greenhuff*.[21] The existence of such a jurisdiction poses problems. It fits uneasily with any doctrine of precedent, and calls in any event for a high degree of wise judicial restraint. The abandonment of such a jurisdiction, so that these matters are left exclusively to the control of the legislature, is probably a less happy solution, since these matters fit even less easily into the world of politics.

FREEDOM OF MEETING AND ACTION

Crimes against the state. The conflicts between the need of a state to protect itself and the desire of individuals to change that state provoke,

---

[19] *McBain* v. *Crichton*, 1961 J.C. 25. The book in question had been found to be not obscene in England as a result of the Act: *R.* v. *Penguin Books Ltd.* [1961] Crim.L.R. 690. As to stage plays, a system of licensing under the Lord Chamberlain exists by the Theatres Act 1843. The showing of films is regulated by local authorities under the Cinematograph Act 1909, supplemented by the voluntary British Board of Film Censors. The Television Act 1963 imposes some limit on the programmes of independent television (see earlier the Television Act 1954). See, too, Children and Young Persons (Harmful Publications) Act 1955. The whole question of the censorship of the theatre has been reviewed by a Joint Committee of both Houses ((1966–67) H.C. 503) and the Theatres Bill has subsequently been introduced. The difficult problem of informing the Press, but yet protecting necessary governmental secrecy, is controlled by the difficult system of " D " notices, as to which see the Report of the Committee of Privy Councillors 1967 (Cmnd. 3309), and Williams, *Not in the Public Interest*; and on all these questions, see Street, *Freedom, the Individual and the Law.*

[20] *Shaw* v. *D.P.P.* [1962] A.C. 220 at 267; and see Seaborne Davies, " The House of Lords and the Criminal Law " (1961) 6 J.S.P.T.L.(N.S.) 104; Hart, *Law, Liberty and Morality.*

[21] (1838) 2 Swin. 236; and see Elliott, " Nulla Poena Sine Lege," 1956 J.R. 22, and Gordon, *Criminal Law*, p. 21 *et seq.*

in a slightly different context, similar and related problems of balance. Membership of any society involves obligations and restraints, but the scope of these is not constant. Emergencies involving the defence of the state justify inroads upon property or personal liberty, which would at other times be regarded as unacceptable.[22] Similarly the law of treason, in the interest of maintaining the unity of the state, limits the freedom of action of those to whom it applies. The foundation of this law remains the Statute of Treasons 1351, which, by the Treason Act 1708, was extended to Scotland.[23] Under this Act, high treason consists of (1) compassing or imagining the death of the King, the Queen Consort or their eldest son and heir; (2) violating the King's consort, his eldest daughter unmarried or the wife of the King's eldest son and heir; (3) levying war against the King in his realm; (4) adhering to the King's enemies in his realm, giving them aid and comfort in the realm, or elsewhere; or (5) slaying the Chancellor, Treasurer of the King's justices performing their office, to whom were, by the Act of 1708, added the Lords of Session and Justiciary; or (6) by the Act of 1702, depriving the person next in succession of his right to succeed.

"Imagining" must be accompanied by an overt act, which may, in certain circumstances, include writing.[24] Levying war within the realm can be constituted by any armed rising [25] which has for its object some national political purpose.[26] Adhering to the King's enemies may be constituted by acts done elsewhere.[27] It should be noted that the offence of treason depends upon allegiance, which may be owed by those who are not British subjects.[28] The Treason Act 1945 assimilated procedure in a trial for treason to that in trials for murder, and it seems that that Act, by amending the Act of 1708, has removed the possibility of trial outside Scotland of those who might commit treason in Scotland, a matter which was of considerable consequence after 1745.[29]

In modern times statutes have created special offences with lesser punishments which might have fallen under the heading of treason. The Treason Felony Act 1848 made it an offence (by that name) to compass to depose the sovereign or to wage war in order to make him change his counsel, or to overawe Parliament, or to incite foreigners to invade his realms, and by the Treason Act of 1842 a special offence was created of

---

22 *The Case of Saltpetre* (1606) 12 Co.Rep. 12 ; *The Burmah Oil Case*, 1963 S.L.T. 261 ; *Smith* v. *Jeffrey*, Jan. 24, 1817, F.C., when a common law right of impressment or conscription is admitted in emergencies.
23 An extension which, while no doubt necessary, had all the inconveniences of legislation by reference ; Smith, *Short Commentary on the Law of Scotland*, p. 175. The details of this offence should be sought in appropriate works on criminal law.
24 Hume, I, 517 ; Blackstone, IV, Comm. 74.
25 The case of Sir James Wilson, *Trials for Treason in Scotland*, II, pp. 335, 339.
26 *R.* v. *Dammaree* (1710) 15 St.Tr. 521.
27 *R.* v. *Casement* [1917] 1 K.B. 98.
28 *Joyce* v. *D.P.P.* [1946] A.C. 347 ; *R.* v. *Ahlers* [1915] 1 K.B. 616. Moreover, a British subject cannot shed his nationality in time of war (*R.* v. *Lynch* [1903] 1 K.B. 444) in order to surmount that difficulty.
29 See Smith, *Short Commentary on the Law of Scotland*, p. 175.

alarming the sovereign in circumstances which could otherwise only have given rise to a charge of high treason.[30]

Such offences as treason and treason felony have both an internal and external aspect, and in the case of somewhat similar offences this aspect of internal order becomes accentuated. It has recently become clear that the Official Secrets Act 1911 can have an inhibiting effect upon some political demonstrations, and is not limited to offences of espionage or sabotage in the generally accepted use of those terms.[31] In a more strict sense of the maintenance of public order in the community there is, in Scotland, the offence of mobbing and rioting, which is constituted by the act of several persons acting in concert to achieve an illegal purpose, or to achieve a lawful purpose by the illegal means of using threats of violence. There must be some element of common purpose, which may, however, arise after a meeting has come about accidentally even if with lawful purposes, e.g., if carried away by oratory a crowd starts to act in a tumultuous manner.[32] In England there are a series of offences, unlawful assembly, rout and riot, which are of increasing gravity, dealing with the same problem. In effect each of these offences corresponds to a stage in the seriousness of any mass meeting.[33] On top of the common law crimes there is, in Scotland, the crime under the Riot Act 1714 (now repealed in England by the Criminal Law Act 1967). That Act contains a proclamation which may be read where twelve or more persons are assembled riotously and tumultuously to the disturbance of the peace. The proclamation calls upon those present to disperse, and the Act creates a more serious offence if they do not do so within the hour. It must be emphasised that the Act supplements, but does not displace, the common law.

There is, under the general law, a communal responsibility in respect of riots which appears in two forms. There is an obligation on every citizen to aid in the maintenance of public order,[34] an obligation which appears in an accentuated form in the obligation of magistrates to maintain order, and of the armed forces to aid the civil power. The circumstances in which force may be used require nice judgment, since if the use of force is deemed excessive or premature a criminal charge against both those who invoke the force and against those who exercise it may result. If it is not invoked timeously a criminal charge against those responsible for maintaining the public peace may likewise arise.[35]

---

[30] The Treachery Act 1940, passed to deal with the special conditions in the last war, ceased to have effect in 1946.
[31] *Chandler* v. *D.P.P.* [1964] A.C. 763.
[32] Compare *H.M. Advocate* v. *Wild* (1854) 1 Irv. 552, where the ultimate purpose might be considered lawful, but the means were not, with *H.M. Advocate* v. *Martin* (1886) 1 White 297, where the purpose itself was unlawful. See, too, Gordon, *Criminal Law.*
[33] For details of these offences, see, *e.g.,* Kenny, *Criminal Law.*
[34] Alison I, 534; *R.* v. *Brown* (1841) Car. & M. 314.
[35] *R.* v. *Pinney* (1832) 5 C. & P. 254, which appears to be equally applicable in Scotland. As to the duties of the armed forces, see Dicey, *Law of the Constitution,* App., Pt. V.

Fortunately, in recent times, the occasions for exercising such judgment have been rare. This communal responsibility is also manifest in the obligation of the community to pay for damage caused by a riot. This liability is now based on the Riot Act, the obligations being extended by the Seditious Meetings Act 1817, and in Scotland the procedure is now regulated by the Riotous Assemblies Act 1822. In England the equivalent regulation is to be found in the Riot (Damages) Act 1886,[36] and it is largely in this context that the question of riot has had any real significance in recent times.

Breach of the peace. Such offences look to conditions of considerable disturbance. More significant in ordinary times is the question of breach of the peace. The right to hold meetings is certainly not an absolute one, but it is wrong to consider that a meeting can be held only by tolerance. A predisposition in favour of meetings as part of the more general freedom of speech is evident in *Burgh of Dunblane, Petitioners*[37]; moreover, at common law magistrates cannot prohibit meetings in advance,[38] unless there is a fear of a breach of the peace. The question, however, resolves itself into one of time and place. Streets are for passage, and public parks and open spaces are for the general use of the public, and where holding a meeting conflicts with such primary purposes it is those purposes which may prevail.[39] There does not appear to be in this respect any difference in principle between static meetings and processions, though because of differences in their natures the application of the same principle may differ, since the former is the more likely to cause obstruction.

Public meetings. Greater difficulty arises from the fact that a public meeting or a procession may lead to a breach of the peace, either because the meeting itself becomes unruly, or because opponents of those holding the meeting are likely to attack the meeting. As to the first case, it seems clear that, if a meeting is of such character (held where it is) that it is likely to cause a breach of the peace (by reason, for example, of being insulting to the local inhabitants), those holding the meeting commit an offence.[40] In such cases the breach of the peace is foreseeable,

---

[36] *Capaldi* v. *Mags. of Greenock*, 1941 S.C. 310; *Coia* v. *Robertson*, 1942 S.C. 111; *Pompa's Trs.* v. *Mags. of Edinburgh*, 1942 S.C. 119; *Munday* v. *Receiver for Metropolitan Police* [1949] 1 All E.R. 337. The confused state of Scots law was criticised in *Coia*. By s. 235 of the Edinburgh Corporation Order Confirmation Act 1958, the payment of such sums is apparently made discretionary.
[37] 1947 S.L.T.(Sh.Ct.) 27; *Hutton* v. *Main* (1891) 19 R.(J.) 5 at 7. In *Aldred* v. *Langmuir*, 1932 J.C. 22 the possibility of land being dedicated to this purpose was contemplated. See, too, *Burden* v. *Rigler* [1911] 1 K.B. 337 and *Aldred* v. *Miller*, 1924 J.C. 117; and compare *Paterson* v. *Mags. of St. Andrews* (1881) 8 R.(H.L.) 117.
[38] *M'Ara* v. *Mags. of Edinburgh*, 1913 S.C. 1059.
[39] *M'Ara's* case, *supra*; *Aldred* v. *Miller*, 1924 J.C. 117; and *Aldred* v. *Langmuir*, 1932 J.C. 22.
[40] *Marr* v. *M'Arthur* (1878) 5 R.(J.) 38 at 43; *M'Ara* v. *Mags. of Edinburgh*, 1913 S.C. at p. 1074; *Wise* v. *Dunning* [1902] 1 K.B. 167, where a person having the intention of committing acts of such a type was bound over. It must be noted that that procedure for binding over does not now exist in Scotland.

and may be said to be directly provoked by those who hold the meeting. More difficulty arises when the meeting or procession is lawful, and when the fact of holding it is not of itself offensive to the inhabitants of a particular area, but when rivals are known to be likely to band together, and to offer violent opposition. That is to say, it is the conduct of others (not being those organising the meeting or procession) which is the prime cause of the breach of the peace. It is that situation which faced the court in *Beatty* v. *Gillbanks*,[41] where it was held that those who were innocent in their intent could not be bound over to keep the peace since " there was nothing in their conduct when they assembled which was either tumultuous or against the peace." The evidence showed, said Field J., that disturbances were caused by those antagonistic to the promoters of the procession. In Scotland when the same rivals, the Salvation Army and the Skeleton Army, came into collision it was held in *Deakin* v. *Milne* [42] that the Salvation Army had been properly convicted of breaking the public peace, in circumstances closely resembling those in *Beatty* v. *Gillbanks*. The cases may, however, be distinguished on the ground the procession of the Salvation Army itself in the latter case amounted to a disturbance of the peace, irrespective of the acts of others. The basis of the decision is not clear, and it may be (particularly if the views expressed in the opinion of Lord Craighill be accepted) that the possibility of conflict resulting from the acts of others would alone suffice to found a charge against the promoters of such a procession.[43]

These disputes about the interpretation of *Deakin* v. *Milne* may now have become purely academic. This consequence follows partly from the adoption of by-laws, such as that upheld in *Aldred* v. *Langmuir*,[44] and by sections in local Acts such as sections 184 and 186 and Part XXVII of the Edinburgh Corporation Confirmation Order 1967, giving to the magistrates the power to regulate or to prohibit processions. In part that consequence follows from the newer habit of charging different offences. In *Duncan* v. *Jones*,[45] the accused was charged with obstructing a police officer in the execution of his duty under the Prevention of

---

[41] (1882) 9 Q.B.D. 308; see, too, *Beatty* v. *Glenister* (1884) 51 L.T. 304; and see Goodhart, " Public Meetings and Processions " (1937) 6 C.L.J. 161; Wade, " Police Powers and Public Meetings " (1937) 6 C.L.J. 175; Glanville Williams, " Preventive Justice and the Rule of Law " (1953) 16 M.L.R. 407.

[42] (1882) 10 R.(J.) 22. That part of the decision which rests upon the effect of the proclamation by the magistrates must now be rejected in view of *M'Ara's* case, *supra*. See also *Whitchurch* v. *Millar* (1895) 23 R.(J.) 1; and *Jordan* v. *Burgoyne* [1963] 2 Q.B. 744; where, however, the offence was a statutory one, see *post*.

[43] This view would accord with *R.* v. *Justices of Londonderry* (1891) 28 L.R.Ir. 440, which was in *Wise* v. *Dunning* preferred to *Beatty* v. *Gillbanks*. In general principle *Beatty* v. *Gillbanks* appears preferable, and on the first reading suggested above *Deakin* v. *Milne* is not inconsistent with that. Earlier in *Marr* v. *M'Arthur* (1878) 5 R.(J.) 38 there was insistence upon an intent to provoke a breach of the peace.

[44] 1932 J.C. 22.

[45] [1936] 1 K.B. 218; and see the criticism of that case in 6 C.L.J. at p. 177 *et seq.* A more serious attack on the logical foundations of *Duncan* v. *Jones*, and a warning against the dangers of its extension, is to be found in Daintith, " Disobeying a Policeman—A Fresh Look at *Duncan* v. *Jones*," in [1966] *Public Law* 248.

Crimes Acts 1871 and 1885 (which are United Kingdom statutes). Fearing a breach of the peace (though the accused had at the time committed none) a police officer required the accused to hold the meeting elsewhere. On her refusing to do so she was taken into custody, and charged with the offence in question. Such a charge circumvents the difficulties of *Beatty* v. *Gillbanks*, and is built upon the foundation of the obligation of the police to maintain order, and was in effect foreseen by Lord Dunedin in *M'Ara's* case.[46] It raises the issue, however, of who is to judge the likelihood of a breach of the peace. It is said that the apprehension by the police of a breach of the peace must be reasonable, but it has also been said that " I think that a police officer charged with the duty of preserving the Queen's peace must be left to take such steps as, on the evidence before him, he thinks proper." [47] Such assertions, if too much weight were given to them, might effectively make the police judges of whether or not meetings should take place. It must, therefore, be remembered that there has, at any rate in Scotland, been an insistence upon the discretion to be used in interfering with public meetings.[48]

Further powers of regulating processions are given by the Public Order Act 1936. That Act prohibits (s. 1) the wearing of a uniform which indicates association with a political organisation at any public meeting, or in a public place. It prohibits (s. 2) the organisation of quasi-military formations, either to usurp the functions of the normal forces of law and order, or for displaying force in connection with the promotion of any political purpose, and (s. 4) prohibits the carrying of offensive weapons at any public meeting. Further by section 3, the chief officers of police (or in burghs in Scotland, the magistrates) are given power to impose conditions upon processions in the interest of the preservation of the peace. Further (s. 3 (2)) the chief constable may apply to the magistrates of any burgh [49] for an order prohibiting for a period not exceeding three months all or any class of public processions within the area, and the magistrates may (with the consent of the Secretary of State) make such an order. In London it is the Commissioner of Police of the City or of the Metropolitan Police who, with like consents, may make such an order.

In one particular respect the law has now been strengthened. The Race Relations Act 1965 prohibits anyone in control of a place of "public resort" which includes hotels, theatres and places of public resort maintained by a local authority to practise discrimination on the grounds of colour, race or ethnic or national origins. It is also an

---

46 1913 S.C. at p. 1074.

47 *Piddington* v. *Bates* [1960] 3 All E.R. 660 at 663, *per* Lord Parker C.J.

48 *Aldred* v. *Miller*, 1924 J.C. 117.

49 Borough or urban district in England; and see generally Ivamy, "The Right of Public Meeting" (1949) *Current Legal Problems* 183; and see Public Order Act 1963.

offence to limit the transfer of a tenancy on these grounds. Further, under section 6 it is an offence to stir up hatred against any group distinguished on these grounds, either by written matter or by any words used in a public place or public meeting. The Act also strengthens section 5 of the Public Order Act 1936 by adding to the offence of using threatening or abusive words in a public place or meeting so that a breach of the peace is likely the offence of similarly distributing or displaying any writing or sign likely to have those effects.[50] Here it has been held in *Jordan* v. *Burgoyne*[51] that a speaker must take his audience as he finds it, so if the audience is one of hooligans and words are spoken insulting hooligans, so that a breach of the peace is likely, an offence is committed.

The meetings hitherto spoken about are largely those occurring in public places, though the provisions of the 1936 Act relating to uniforms, etc., apply also to public meetings held in private places. That Act also strengthened the Public Meetings Act 1908, making it an offence to disrupt the conduct of a public meeting. The Act of 1936 enables a constable, at the request of the chairman of the meeting, to demand the name and address of those suspected of an offence under the Act of 1908. Thus there is preserved an element of responsibility and control on the part of those holding such a meeting, while at the same time extending the scope of the forces of public order.

Even apart from that statute it must be noted that a breach of the peace may occur in a private place.[52] More important, however, is the question of the right of the police to attend such meetings. It has been held in England that the police have the right to enter when there are grounds for believing that a breach of the peace may be committed, or seditious speeches made.[53] It must, however, be noted that in the particular case the meeting was advertised as open to the public, and that it was as members of the public that the police entered. The authority of this case—*Thomas* v. *Sawkins*—is doubtful. No general right of the police to enter private premises is admitted,[54] and the principle of the case appears to be inconsistent with the theory of the Public Order Act 1936. There is of course a right to enter in hot pursuit, and where it appears that offences are being committed which will otherwise go undetected the police may enter under the general law. They may also enter as members of the public, where an indiscriminate

---

50 A private individual has no right to seek to enforce the Act by means of an injunction: *Thorne* v. *B.B.C.* [1967] 2 All E.R. 1225, and prosecutions are under the control of the Attorney-General in England. See, for the general application, *R.* v. *Britton* [1967] 1 All E.R. 486.

51 [1963] 2 Q.B. 744.

52 *Young* v. *Heatly*, 1959 J.C. 66; *Dougall* v. *Dykes* (1861) 4 Irv. 101; *Hendry* v. *Ferguson* (1883) 10 R.(J.) 63; but see 1959 S.L.T.(News) 229.

53 *Thomas* v. *Sawkins* [1935] 2 K.B. 249; but see 6 C.L.J. 22.

54 *Davis* v. *Lisle* [1936] 2 K.B. 434 denies it in England. It is denied universally in the United Kingdom by the general insistence upon search warrants.

invitation has been given to the public. It is to be doubted how far
Thomas v. *Sawkins* should be relied on beyond these circumstances.

FREEDOM OF PROPERTY

As has already been mentioned an assumption of the freedom of property
appears in many branches of the law, though the courts will insist upon
reasonableness in measures taken to defend property and in orders
which will be made by courts in that defence.[55] Perhaps the most
common reflection of this recognition is in relation to the right of search.
Cases of the taking of property against the payment of compensation are
regulated by the ordinary law, and normally present no constitutional
issues.[56] The inviolability of a man's house is maintained by both the
criminal and the civil law, and again no constitutional issues arise.
Conflict with the interests of the state does, however, arise in relation
to the right of search. In basic principle there is no real difference
between the law of Scotland and England. The principle of the right
of property means in this context that (except with consent or in extraordinary circumstances) a warrant is required for entry into a man's
property, and further that the invasion of property must be confined
within necessary limits, which means in this context that the warrant
shall be sufficiently specific. These principles were firmly established in
England in *Wilkes* v. *Wood*[57] and *Entick* v. *Carrington*.[58] In the former
a warrant which was general as to the persons to be arrested and the
papers to be seized was held invalid. In the latter Lord Camden C.J.
emphasised that the legality of the warrant must be demonstrated, and
strongly rejected a justification of state necessity which had been put
forward: " With respect to the argument of state necessity, or a
distinction that has been aimed at between state offences and others,
the common law does not understand that kind of reasoning." He also
rejected the argument based on utility that general searches were a means
of detecting offenders by discovering evidence. Similar principles were
affirmed in Scotland in *Bell* v. *Black and Morrison*,[59] where a like
" fishing " warrant for the seizure of papers, not as evidence, but in
the hopes of finding traces of guilt, was as strongly condemned. Equally
there is an insistence on specification or other like precautions in relation

---

[55] *Clark* v. *Syme*, 1957 J.C. 1; *Hay's Trs.* v. *Young* (1877) 4 R. 398; and *Winans* v.
Macrae (1885) 12 R. 1051.
[56] Cases such as *Att.-Gen.* v. *De Keyser's Royal Hotel* [1920] A.C. 508 or *The Burmah
Oil Case*, 1964 S.C.(H.L.) 117 are exceptional. The absence of a specific constitutional protection of property undoubtedly excludes the possible considerable amount
of litigation on the issue of what is " taking " as against " regulation." This argument or distinction underlies *Hartnell* v. *Minister of Housing and Local Government*
[1965] A.C. 1134.
[57] (1763) 9 St.Tr. 1153.
[58] (1765) 19 St.Tr. 1029; *R.* v. *Rees* (1963) 107 S.J. 536.
[59] (1867) 5 Irv. 57; see, too, the later proceedings in (1865) 3 M. 1026, where views are
expressed even more strongly. See earlier *Mackenzie* v. *Marchmont* (1704) II Fount.
246.

to the warrant.[60] More recently these cases were discussed in *Stewart* v. *Roach*.[61] It appears from that case that apprehension or a charge is not a necessary preliminary to the grant of a warrant, provided that there is serious suspicion, and provided that the warrant is sufficiently specific.

It is evident that there is here a question of balance, and so in exceptional cases search without warrant is permissible. Thus, where after an arrest (which was without warrant) a search was made it was held justified, even though without warrant, on grounds of urgency.[62] The issue remains a live one because of this conflict of ends, and because a right of search may itself be abused, stretching farther than is authorised by the warrant. It is at this point that a difference between the laws of England and Scotland becomes apparent. In England it has been held that a wrongful search may be excused *ex post facto* by the discovery of evidence of a crime and that such evidence, albeit wrongfully obtained, is freely admissible.[63] In Scotland a different rule prevails. Such evidence is not necessarily excluded, but account is taken of all the circumstances of the case including the seriousness of the charge.[64] In these cases Lord Cooper brought out clearly in his opinions the interests which have to be balanced one against the other, and as a result the courts assume their proper (though arduous) role of maintaining that balance, a role which is abandoned in *Elias* v. *Pasmore*.[65] The issue also appears in new forms. The practice of intercepting telephone conversations when authorised by a warrant was accepted and approved of in 1957 by a committee of Privy Councillors.[66] It is, however, to be doubted whether such warrants, if challenged, could stand up to the earlier rules against general warrants.

---

[60] *Nelson* v. *Black and Morrison* (1866) 4 M. 328, where a balance is struck between the sanctity of property and the interest of the community in the suppression of crime by the insistence upon proper safeguards against oppression.

[61] 1950 S.C. 318, before a court of seven judges. *M'Lauchlan* v. *Renton*, 1911 S.C.(J.) 12 was also there discussed and disapproved. See, too, on the civil side, Rights of Entry (Gas and Electricity Boards) Act 1954. Again the importance of local legislation should be noted; the Edinburgh Corporation Order Confirmation Act 1967, Part XXIX, gives wide powers of search, entry and arrest.

[62] *H.M. Advocate* v. *M'Guigan*, 1936 J.C. 16. Exceptions are also made under such statutes as the Official Secrets Act 1911, s. 9, or the Incitement to Disaffection Act 1934, s. 2, which are akin in cause to the special powers of arrest in the Public Order Act 1936, s. 7.

[63] *Elias* v. *Pasmore* [1934] 2 K.B. 164; and see Wade, " Police Search " (1934) 50 L.Q.R. 354.

[64] See *Pringle* v. *Bremner & Stirling* (1867) 5 M.(H.L.) 55; and particularly the restatement of principles in *Lawrie* v. *Muir*, 1950 J.C. 19; *M'Govern* v. *H.M. Advocate*, 1950 J.C. 33, and their application in *H.M. Advocate* v. *Turnbull*, 1951 J.C. 96, which has similarities with *Elias* v. *Pasmore* and *H.M. Advocate* v. *M'Kay*, 1961 J.C. 47. For a good comparative study on " The Admissibility of Evidence Procured through Illegal Searches and Seizures " see Cowen and Carter, *Essays on the Law of Evidence*.

[65] Which is supported by *Kuruma* v. *The Queen* [1955] A.C. 197.

[66] See Cmnd. 283. A shift of emphasis is noticeable. Lord Camden and Lord Cooper were concerned with the protection of those who might well be guilty. The report comments that under its procedure there is no likelihood of the ordinary *law-abiding* citizen being affected (§ 143) (italics supplied).

The protection of the accused. It is clear that in the cases just discussed there is a large element of " due process of law." That is to say that convictions should be obtained by means which are fair to the accused. This element may produce inconvenience to the police, but it is essential to the liberty of individuals, and to the maintenance of the rule of law in any real sense. That concept spreads out into many rules evolved for the protection of the accused. While an arrested person may be searched, further tests upon him without his consent are excluded.[67] Much more rigid are the rules which protect the accused from questioning once he has been taken into custody or once suspicion has settled upon him, since then the dangers are all the greater.[68] In effect any questioning is limited to an elucidation of what has already been said, and all the circumstances are considered from the aspect of fairness to the accused. A somewhat similar position in England exists under the Judges' Rules,[69] but the Scottish rules operate more stringently to protect the accused. In England a breach of the rules does not necessarily exclude statements made by the accused, but in Scotland the exclusion of statements improperly made is more rigorous than is the exclusion of real evidence.

There remains, though, in Scotland, an element of judicial discretion, notably as to the point of time from which the rules are to apply. This discretionary element, and the somewhat similar discretion in relation to real evidence, is important. While it is true that an action can be raised for illegal searches, this may prove to be an inadequate deterrent, particularly having regard to the present difficulties in raising actions against the police. A more effective deterrent as far as the police are concerned is the fact that a conviction obtained by the use of such faulty evidence may not be upheld. Were rules to be laid down in general terms they would have to take account of extreme cases, and might well be inappropriate in others.[70] Thus the discretionary element ensures that the police will, in their proper anxiety to secure a conviction, stop well short of the borderline. A firm rule might mean that in all cases they would go to that border, even when such conduct was not fully justifiable.

---

67 *M'Govern* v. *H.M. Advocate*, 1950 J.C. 33; and see *Reid* v. *Nixon*, 1948 J.C. 68 (and see now Road Traffic Act 1962, s. 2, and the Road Safety Act 1967, s. 2). As to consents, see *M'Kie* v. *H.M. Advocate*, 1958 J.C. 24; and on the civil side *Whitehall* v. *Whitehall*, 1958 S.C. 252; *W.* v. *W.* (*No.* 4) [1963] 2 All E.R. 841.

68 *Chalmers* v. *H.M. Advocate*, 1954 J.C. 66; *Wade* v. *Robertson*, 1948 J.C. 117; *H.M. Advocate* v. *Aitken*, 1926 J.C. 83; *Manuel* v. *H.M. Advocate*, 1958 J.C. 41.

69 As to which, and as to their force, see Archbold, *Criminal Pleading and Evidence*, § 1118, and the Appendix to Marshall, *Police and Government*, which gives the 1964 revision.

70 See the refusal to lay down absolute rules in *Reid* v. *Nixon*, *supra*, note 67. The aspect of fairness to the accused has many other aspects; see, *e.g.*, *H.M. Advocate* v. *Olsson*, 1941 J.C. 63. See generally Coutts, *The Protection of the Accused*, and La Fave and Remington, " Controlling the Police " (1965) 63 Michigan L.R. 987.

FREEDOM OF THE PERSON

The rules already discussed have an obvious bearing upon the freedom of the person, but that topic must be more generally treated. It falls to be considered from the aspect of the criminal law, and from that of the civil law.

Arrest. On the criminal side, there is first the insistence, in normal circumstances, on a warrant to arrest, which must be issued by a magistrate. This insistence on a warrant here, as in the case of search, provides a safeguard attributable to the distribution of powers. Liberty in these respects is considered to be too precious to be watched over by one person or body alone. Thus those concerned with the investigation of crime have to go outside that particular machinery and justify their requirements. The warrant must be specific, and not general, but if the name of the person to be arrested is unknown a description will suffice. The necessities of life require some modification; so, both in England and Scotland, arrest without warrant is justifiable in certain circumstances. In Scotland a constable may arrest without warrant if he sees a crime being committed and there are reasonable grounds for considering that otherwise the criminal will abscond, or where, subject to like conditions, he is credibly informed that a crime has been committed by a particular individual. Again all the circumstances must be taken into account, *e.g.,* if the arrested person has no known abode, or the nature of the possible punishment makes absconding likely.[71] So, too, at common law, the police have (as has been seen) the right to arrest to prevent a breach of the peace. In addition to these common law powers statutory powers are also conferred.[72] These powers may be exercised upon suspicion, and it must be noted that the police are protected in that exercise by the fact that no action will lie for wrongous arrest against them unless malice or want of probable cause can be shown.[73]

The police have the right to call for the aid of ordinary citizens. A private citizen himself has also a separate right to arrest with a view to handing over the arrested person to the police as soon as possible. This right is, however, much more hedged about, and is not so extensive as that of the police, since it is a right which is perhaps more open to abuse in the hands of a private citizen. So, arrest upon suspicion is

[71] See particularly *Peggie* v. *Clark* (1868) 7 M. 89; *Leask* v. *Burt* (1893) 21 R. 32; *Melvin* v. *Wilson* (1847) 9 D. 1129, where carrying a peacock in the early hours of the morning was held to be sufficiently suspicious to justify arrest. *Cf. Harvey* v. *Sturgeon,* 1912 S.C. 974 (a respectable business man carrying an alarm clock at 5.30 p.m.); and see Hume, *Criminal Law,* II, p. 75; Alison, *Criminal Law,* II, p. 117.

[72] See, *e.g.,* the Public Order Act 1936, s. 7; Road Traffic Act 1960, s. 6 (4); but such powers are narrowly construed.

[73] *Robertson* v. *Keith,* 1936 S.C. 29; *Beaton* v. *Ivory* (1887) 14 R. 1057; *M'Gilvray* v. *Main* (1901) 3 F. 397. For the sequel to *Beaton* v. *Ivory,* see Vol. 17, *Accounts and Papers* (1888), No. 446, as to the reimbursement of the costs of Sheriff Ivory.

not justified,[74] and any delay in handing over to the police will give rise to liability.[75] In principle the position in England is similar, but it seems that with the exception of breach of the peace arrest without warrant by the police was only justifiable in cases of felony.[76] Similarly citizens may arrest, but not upon suspicion, and delay in handing over to the police will likewise create liability.[77] To a large extent the old law is reproduced and clarified by the Criminal Law Act 1967, s. 2. That Act abolished felonies as a distinct category of crimes and thus the position of arrest without warrant had to be clarified. A sharp distinction is made in section 2 (3) as compared with section 2 (4), the first giving powers to any person where an arrestable offence *has* been committed, the second giving power to a constable to arrest where he reasonably suspects that such an offence has been committed.

Because of its dangers arrest without warrant is confined within narrow limits and when the power is exercised, the position must be regularised, as by bringing the arrested person before a magistrate without delay. Moreover, he who arrests must at the time explain the reasons to the arrested person, unless they are sufficiently evident from the whole circumstances, and the explanation given must be a true one.[78]

Bail. Assuming detention, the person detained has the right to apply for release on bail. There are two stages: first, there is an application for release on bail before commitment for trial. Since this is the stage of investigation there is a weighting in favour of the views of the prosecutor.[79] In the second place there is bail after commitment for trial. The issue is in Scotland regulated by the Bail (Scotland) Act 1888, and the position has been summarised by saying that the applicant has a right to have his application heard and that bail should be granted unless there is good reason to the contrary.[80] At this stage the accused (as well as the prosecution) may appeal from a decision as to bail. In England the principles on which bail is granted or refused are somewhat similar, the governing consideration being that the accused shall appear

---

74 Hume, *Criminal Law*, II, p. 76.
75 *Mackenzie* v. *Young* (1902) 10 S.L.T. 231.
76 Archbold, *Criminal Pleading*, § 2809; 2 Co.Inst. 52; *Dumbell* v. *Roberts* [1944] 1 All E.R. 326; and on police powers, see Glanville Williams, " Demanding Name and Address " (1950) 66 L.Q.R. 465.
77 *Walters* v. *W. H. Smith and Son Ltd.* [1914] 1 K.B. 595; *John Lewis & Co.* v. *Tims* [1952] A.C. 676.
78 *Christie* v. *Leachinsky* [1947] A.C. 573, the principles of which appear to be applicable in both jurisdictions. There Lord Simon emphasises the general background and (at p. 587) gives a detailed exposition.
79 The Bail (Scotland) Act 1888 gives a right to the prosecutor to appeal against a decision to grant bail, though it seems that an appeal by the accused to the power of the High Court akin to the *nobile officium* is competent: *Milne* v. *M'Nicol*, 1944 J.C. 151; and see in England *R.* v. *Guest* [1961] 3 All E.R. 1118. By the Criminal Justice (Scotland) Act 1963, s. 37, courts are given power to review their decisions in respect of bail.
80 *Mackintosh* v. *M'Glinchy*, 1921 J.C. 75; and see *H.M. Advocate* v. *Quinn & Macdonald*, 1921 J.C. 61; previous convictions may put the onus on the accused to show why bail should be allowed: *Young* v. *H.M. Advocate*, 1946 J.C. 5; and Renton and Brown, *Criminal Procedure*, p. 44 *et seq.*

for trial, but it is possible that their application is somewhat less liberal than in Scotland.[81]

Release. In Scotland the main rules for securing a speedy trial and the release of those held on criminal charges spring from the Act Anent Wrongous Imprisonment 1701, an Act for which the later years of the Stuarts had shown the need.[82] The position is now regulated by the Criminal Procedure (Scotland) Act 1887, s. 43. If a person has been committed for trial, and has not within sixty days been served with an indictment he may serve notice on the Lord Advocate that, if an indictment is not served within fourteen days, the prosecutor will be called on to show cause in the High Court why he should not be released. If no indictment is served and the court is not satisfied as to the reason for delay, the court orders release after three further days unless an indictment is served meanwhile. Release in such circumstances does not prevent a prosecutor raising a fresh indictment and obtaining a warrant for a fresh committal. The Act, however, provides, in that event, against the possibility of further delays.

More importantly, section 43 also provides that if the accused has been imprisoned for eighty days, then, unless he is brought to trial and the trial concluded within 110 days from his committal until liberated in due course of law he shall be released and be free of the crimes charged. The period may only be prolonged where it can be shown that delay was caused by the illness of the accused or of a witness or by some other circumstance for which the prosecutor is not responsible.[83] It will be noted that the Act secures the early service of an indictment and an early trial, it does not of itself deal with the period between arrest and committal for trial but that period can be controlled by the High Court of Justiciary in exercise of its special powers.[84] Regulations to secure a speedy trial, though somewhat different in detail, are to be found in England in the Habeas Corpus Act 1679 and the Assizes Relief Act 1884.[85] The Habeas Corpus Acts go further, however.[86] The Act of 1679 applicable to imprisonment on criminal matters enabled a writ of habeas corpus to issue, requiring the production of the prisoner, so that it covered cases of detention without legal warrant, and the period

---

[81] See Archbold, *Criminal Pleading*, § 201 *et seq.*; and see generally the essay in Smith, *Studies Critical and Comparative.*

[82] Sir George Mackenzie in his *Vindication*, commenting on his part in detentions without trial, says: "these things may be accounted severe, but not illegal." Imprisonment without cause and delays in trial was one of the grievances in the Claim of Right. Nevertheless, some power to secure release had existed; see the case of Janet Richmond (1661); and other remedies were available: Hume, *Criminal Law*, II, p. 96.

[83] See generally Renton and Brown, *op. cit.*; as to the running of time where detention for other reasons supervenes, see *Wallace* v. *H.M. Advocate*, 1959 J.C. 71.

[84] And by civil courts in actions for wrongous imprisonment.

[85] Though they may be sometimes difficult to work in modern conditions: *R.* v. *Campbell* [1959] 1 W.L.R. 646.

[86] See Jenks, "The Story of Habeas Corpus" (1902) 18 L.Q.R. 64; Holdsworth, *H.E.L.*, Vol. IX; (1949) 65 L.Q.R. 30; and (1950) 66 L.Q.R. 79.

before committal for trial.[87]   The Act of 1679 was extended, by that
of 1816, to detention other than on a criminal charge, and thus gave a
much wider significance to the writ.   By the Act of 1862 the application
of these Acts was confined to colonies or foreign dominions of the Crown
where no court existed capable of issuing it.[88]   Procedure in relation
to applications for the writ has been reformed by the Administration of
Justice Act 1960, which, by section 14, provides that in a criminal
matter it may only be refused by a Divisional Court of the Queen's
Bench Division, and that no second criminal or civil application shall
be made on the same grounds.[89]   That Act further by section 15 makes
possible an appeal in criminal or civil matters.

Civil cases.   There is one possible advantage in the habeas corpus
procedure.   In principle, though modern practice varies, it requires the
production of the person detained, and in certain circumstances that
could be a considerable merit.   It has also, in its modern form, the
advantage that it is a universal remedy, in that it may be used no matter
what the form or cause of detention.   It may thus be used for a wide
range of civil purposes, including such matters as the custody and
guardianship of infants,[90] or to challenge the validity of orders of
extradition or deportation.[91]   It has in many cases been supplemented
or effectively superseded under particular pieces of legislation which
have provided particular remedies,[92] but even in such cases it remains a
powerful residual weapon.

The fact that on the criminal side the broad purposes of habeas corpus
are achieved under the Criminal Procedure Act means that in Scotland
something else has to be found for the protection of personal liberty
in the civil sense.[93]   It is clear that the law had long recognised the
gravity of wrongous imprisonment,[94] even though there was not any
consistency in that recognition.   At times relief might be got by petition
to the Privy Council, and, after the abolition of the Privy Council, by
petition to the Lords of Justiciary.[95]   In cases of civil arrest, a petition
for suspension and liberation was appropriate to secure release.   It

---

[87] It cannot be granted where a person is serving a sentence imposed by a competent
court: *Ex p. Hinds* [1961] 1 W.L.R. 325; *Re Wring* [1960] 1 W.L.R. 138; *R.* v.
Board of Control, ex p. Rutty [1956] 2 Q.B. 109.

[88] In *Re Mwenya* [1960] 1 Q.B. 241 these terms were held to embrace a protectorate.

[89] See also *Re Kray* [1965] 1 All E.R. 710 as to the power of the Lord Chancellor.

[90] *Barnardo* v. *McHugh* [1891] A.C. 388; and see Bromley, *Family Law*, Chap. XIV.

[91] *R.* v. *Governor of Brixton Prison, ex p. Schtraks* [1963] 1 Q.B. 55; *R.* v. *S. of S.
for Home Affairs, ex p. Soblen* [1962] 3 W.L.R. 1145; *R.* v. *Governor of Brixton
Prison, ex p. Soblen* [1963] 2 Q.B. 243.   In the first *Soblen* case detention of an
alien was challenged by habeas corpus proceedings.   In the second the same procedure was used to challenge a subsequent deportation order.

[92] *e.g.*, under the Mental Health Act 1959.

[93] It is true that in *Paterson* v. *Wright* (1736) Mor. 17069 the penalties under the Act
of 1701 were applied equally to a private citizen who had wrongfully detained
another, but see Fount. II, 267.

[94] Balfour's *Prackticks*—Of privie imprisonment of the King's lieges (*Tit.* Criminal
Causes).

[95] See the case of Mackenzie of Assynt in Hume, *Criminal Law*, II, Chap. III.

seems that today that procedure is appropriate where detention follows upon the judgment of an inferior court. Where detention has some other basis, *e.g.*, an order under the Mental Health Act,[96] and there is some document which is capable of being attacked, an action for reduction would appear to be appropriate. In other cases, such as those dealing with the detention of children, it appears that the procedure by petition is both competent and effective.[97] The *nobile officium* of the Court of Session, and the equivalent power of the High Court of Justiciary (which is not excluded by a statute covering a portion of the ground[98]), appear to afford sufficient residual powers to guarantee protection against any unauthorised detention.

These differences in the procedure for securing release may have consequences upon the grounds upon which release may be obtained. The procedure by petition is clearly capable of bringing more of law and fact upon the record, and it remains to be determined, for example, whether an answer that an individual was detained for contempt of the House of Commons (which can be a good answer in habeas corpus proceedings) would be a sufficient answer in Scotland, assuming that the aid of the courts is invoked before the Serjeant at Arms has carried the alleged contemnor out of the jurisdiction.[99]

Apart from these remedies to secure release, it must be remembered that in both jurisdictions infractions of the liberty of the individual are zealously watched by the civil law. "In cases of patrimonial damage," it has been said, "excesses of error and bona fides have sometimes been admitted, but not in cases of false imprisonment. The liberty of the subject is so secured that it cannot be violated with impunity even by mistake."[1] Despite the changes in society, that at least appears to be one of the principles to which the courts must adhere, though adherence may impose heavy burdens upon them.

RELIGIOUS TOLERANCE

It was, perhaps, inevitable that a revolutionary movement such as the Reformation should itself have had some authoritarian results, and that those who had achieved it should deny to others that religious freedom for which they themselves had fought. The Act for Securing the Protestant Religion (and the significant place which that had in the Union Compact) is but one mark of the depth of feeling which had been

---

[96] Or see earlier as to letters of impressment *Smith* v. *Jeffrey*, Jan. 24, 1817, F.C. or *Napier* v. *Browning*, Jan. 19, 1781, F.C. (whether the mates of smuggling ships enjoyed the same immunities as those of more normal trading ships).

[97] *Leys* v. *Leys* (1886) 13 R. 1223.

[98] *Keith* v. *H.M. Advocate* (1875) 3 Coup. 113.

[99] Preliminary questions about the United Kingdom character of that officer are also involved.

[1] *Laing* v. *Watson and Mollison* (1791) 3 Pat.App. 219; see, too, *Kuechenmeister* v. *Home Office* [1958] 1 Q.B. 496.

engendered, and which, coupled with other factors, delayed the legislative recognition of religious toleration which had, in fact, arrived considerably earlier.

In the political world religious disabilities were steadily removed. The effective repeal of the Test and Corporation Acts in 1828, the Catholic Emancipation Act 1829, the Jews Relief Act 1858, the Oaths Act 1888, had the combined effect of removing religious barriers from political life. The movement towards religious toleration spread into other branches of life. In the Scottish universities tests had not been applied to students, and those applied to professors were progressively abolished from the Universities (Scotland) Act 1853.[2] Elsewhere the establishment of such institutions as University College London helped to widen the doors to university education, and those doors were legally opened in Oxford and Cambridge by the University Tests Act 1871. In schools, a like process of liberalising was operative, so that, both in England and in Scotland, the public system of education is freed from any religious discrimination.[3] In relation to marriage laws (particularly as to the places of celebration of marriages) a like process has continued. In effect, therefore, the establishment of religious toleration is virtually complete, subject to limitations imposed by the requirements of public order,[4] and to the reservation to the state of the right of determining who is a minister, or what is a religion where issues of public order arise.[5] It is arguable whether in this instance the achievement of this freedom has not been, in part at least, achieved because of the absence of any specific guarantee. The presence of such a guarantee may have the effect of affording the necessary handhold for a minority to force its views on a majority,[6] and thus of frustrating arrangements such as those existing under the administrative schemes for the individual local education authorities in Scotland whereby members of the various churches are co-opted to the Education Committee. It may also be that the fact of the establishment of the Church of Scotland and of the Church of England may paradoxically have contributed something to this evolution.

2 Though this Act was prompted not so much by a general spirit of religious toleration as by the particular circumstances of the Disruption. In fact the test had earlier been often disregarded or evaded in relation to lay chairs.

3 The provisions of the Education (Scotland) Act 1946 may be said to be somewhat more liberal than those of the Education Act 1944, but in practice there is no real distinction.

4 R. v. Senior [1899] 1 Q.B. 283; and Glanville Williams, Criminal Law, The General Part, 2nd ed., § 241. While the Race Relations Act 1965, ss. 1 and 6, do not affect this question, s. 7, amending s. 5 of the Public Order Act 1936 as to the display of signs, etc., could extend the protection of religious groups.

5 Walsh v. Lord Advocate, 1956 S.C.(H.L.) 126.

6 Compare Engel v. Vitale, 370 U.S. 421, 8 L. ed. 2d 601 (1962) and Sutherland, The Law and the One Man amongst the Many.

FREEDOM OF ASSOCIATION AND ECONOMIC LIBERTY

Just as movements of thought and changes in society were reflected in the growth of religious toleration, so also, eventually, were the economic changes of the nineteenth century reflected in the recognition of a freedom of association, the right of masters or men to band together for the furtherance of their interests. These issues have long been treated as raising questions of individual liberty and of public policy. The Combination Act 1801 can be said to look to the liberty of the individual master and, indeed, may be said to have guarded that liberty too well. The watch that the law has always kept upon exclusive privileges marks the abiding elements of public policy. The passing years and economic movements made it clear that the concept of liberty embedded in the Act of 1801 was an inadequate one, and ultimately, by the Trade Union Act 1871, trade unions (whether of employers or workmen) were accepted as lawful, despite the fact that their purposes might be in restraint of trade. Thereafter the ability of trade unions to act was increased, in particular by the Trade Disputes Act 1906, allowing peaceful picketing, providing that inducing another to break a contract is not actionable if done in pursuance of a trade dispute, and conferring upon unions and their officials an immunity from tortious liability.[7]

At the back of this legislation lay a series of what may be regarded as unfortunate decisions in the courts, each of which had to be rectified by legislation.[8] The legislation itself is piecemeal and exists against a general background of relevant law which is confused and difficult to understand.[9] In many respects the effect has been to recognise the existence of trade unions, but to exclude their activities from the purview of law.[10] Thus there remain problems still to be determined. The limits of the right to strike (which is recognised) are uncertain. The Trade Disputes and Trade Unions Act 1927 had declared illegal strikes which had any object beyond furthering a trade dispute within the trade or industry and were designed or calculated to coerce the government. This Act was repealed by the Trade Disputes and Trade Unions Act 1946, and uncertainties exist about the lawfulness of, for example, a general strike. It seems that in practice the only general limits set to the right to strike are those imposed by the law of sedition, though the actual conduct

---

[7] Further protection is given, e.g., by Conspiracy and Protection of Property Act 1875, s. 3. See, generally, Citrine, *Trade Union Law*; Samuels, *The Law of Trade Unions*.

[8] *R.* v. *Duffield* (1851) 5 Cox C.C. 384; *Taff Vale Ry.* v. *Amalgamated Society of Railway Servants* [1901] A.C. 426 (as to tortious liability); *Amalgamated Society of Railway Servants* v. *Osborne* [1910] A.C. 87 (reversed by the Trade Union Act 1913, permitting the use of union funds for certain political purposes).

[9] e.g., as to conspiracy consider *Crofter Hand Woven Harris Tweed Co.* v. *Veitch* [1942] A.C. 435. The clarity of the law has not been aided by *Rookes* v. *Barnard* [1964] A.C. 1129 (in which the threat to strike in breach of contract was held to be capable of amounting to the tort of intimidation) and by the Trade Disputes Act 1965, passed to reverse that decision. See also *Square Grip Reinforcement Co. Ltd.* v. *Macdonald*, 1968 S.L.T. 65. The whole matter is now before a Royal Commission.

[10] Trade Union Act 1871, s. 4.

of a strike may be affected by the rules governing public order. Under the Conspiracy and Protection of Property Act 1875, breaches of contract which affect the supply of gas, water or electricity may be criminal offences (though assuming due notice is given the Act in no way prevents a strike). Similarly acts done in furtherance of a dispute could be offences under regulations made after a declaration of an emergency under the Emergency Powers Act 1920 (as amended by the Emergency Powers Act 1964, which enables a proclamation to be made when there is a threat of the dislocation of national life). The Act of 1920, however, recognises implicitly the right to strike. Section 2 (1) provides that no regulation made under that Act shall make it an offence for any person to take part in a strike, or peacefully to persuade any other person to take part in a strike, and also provides that no regulation shall impose any form of a compulsory military service or industrial conscription. In effect, therefore, it is only the manner in which a strike is conducted which can conflict with regulations, and not the strike itself. Thus no official balance between the interests of trade unions and those of the state has as yet been struck, and it seems improbable that any much greater precision of the law is to be expected. The invocation of the Emergency Powers Act 1920 on any occasion may itself show changes in outlook.

It may be noted that as respects combinations of employers, the law has of late become more direct in protecting the public interest, through the mechanism in particular of the Restrictive Practices Court and less forcefully through the Monopolies Commission. Under the Restrictive Trade Practices Act 1956, agreements restricting prices, conditions of supply, quantities to be produced, persons to whom goods are to be supplied or the processes of manufacture to be applied to goods are (with certain exceptions) to be registered. Under section 21 the restrictions are to be deemed contrary to the public interest unless the Restrictive Practices Court is satisfied that one (or more) of the conditions set out in that section is fulfilled. These conditions are such as could justify the restriction on grounds of the public interest, but the restriction must not exceed what is reasonable for that purpose.[11] Similarly under the Monopolies and Restrictive Practices (Inquiry and Control) Act 1948 (as amended), the Monopolies Commission must (particularly under section 14) have regard to the public interest in reaching any conclusion on a reference to it. The scope of the latter Act was extended by the Monopolies and Mergers Act 1965, which brought the supply of services of any description within the jurisdiction of the Commission, extended the powers of the Board of Trade and gave to the Commission powers of control over mergers which are significant, either because of the capital involved or because of the dominant position of the enterprises involved.

11 See Wilberforce and Campbell, *Restrictive Trade Practices and Monopolies.*

Thus, questions of liberty in the economic field may be coming increasingly within the area of law, and again questions of balance between public and private interest are clearly posed, though they are as yet obscurely answered. Much of the town and country planning regulation and its extensions in the fields of the location of industry, under the Local Employment Act 1960 or the Control of Office and Industrial Development Act 1965, illustrate the same development. The problems are, however, more difficult to solve than those of the traditional and more fundamental issues of individual liberty, and no consistent theory of law is yet apparent; partly, or largely, for the reasons discussed at the end of the last chapter. Nevertheless, the existence of these problems should be observed, they emphasise that problems of liberty falling within the traditional heads have not been finally solved, and that those traditional heads are not themselves exhaustive. Indeed, these developments in the field of economic activity produce problems which are not all related to the conflicts of communal interests (in the sense of state interests) and individual interests, they also produce problems of the conflict of the interests of the individual as against those of a private group, and of those problems the law must take notice. On the one side there are questions of the legitimacy of the use by trade associations of devices such as stop-lists, fines, etc., to enforce their regulations.[12] Some attempt has been made to meet some of these problems by section 24 of the Act of 1956, which outlaws certain forms of sanction, but again all that is clear is that the law has not yet reached a full development. Similar problems arise on the other side, when expulsion or exclusion from a trade union may have serious effects upon the ability of an individual to earn his livelihood, and attention has turned to these also. The courts have recently shown a greater readiness to intervene than was once the case.[13] There is, however, a reluctance so to do. This reluctance springs partly from unhappy judicial intervention in the past, partly from the circumstance that, by reason of history, so much of labour law is outside the bounds of ordinary law and hence a feeling has grown up that it should be so,[14] and partly because this is inherently an area in which law operates with difficulty. A like reluctance may be observed in the regulation of similar problems which arise in connection with bodies controlling professional organisations.[15] There is then a residual judicial control, but its scope has not been firmly settled.

[12] *Thorne* v. *Motor Trades Association* [1937] A.C. 797.
[13] *Lee* v. *Showmen's Guild* [1952] 2 Q.B. 329; *Barnard* v. *National Dock Labour Board* [1953] 2 Q.B. 18; *Bonsor* v. *Musicians' Union* [1956] A.C. 104; and see generally Rideout, *Right to Membership of a Trade Union*; *Hiles* v. *Amalgamated Society of Woodworkers* [1967] 3 All E.R. 70 and *Nagle* v. *Feilden* [1966] 2 Q.B. 633.
[14] To that feeling a long history, reaching back to the Tolpuddle Martyrs and the trial of Muir, contributes. Consider, *e.g.*, the views expressed in cases such as *Faramus* v. *Film Artistes' Association* [1963] 2 W.L.R. 504.
[15] Lloyd, " The Disciplinary Powers of Professional Bodies " (1950) 13 M.L.R. 281.

Conclusion. Such uncertainties in the law are perhaps inevitable. In all questions relating to the liberties of the individual there can be observed a balancing or conflict of interests, particularly between the interests of the individual and the interests of the group which is the state. It was that problem of balance which prompted Lincoln's question " Must a state be too strong for the liberty of its subjects, or too weak for its own protection? " That question remains an important one. Yet, put in that form it conceals an important fact. The state itself exists simply for the fulfilment of the individual. The conflict is not between the interests of two rivals, the state and the individual, it is between the personal or localised interests of the individual and his communal or generalised interests. It is then clear that the balance that will be struck at any one time will be dictated by a judgment of the respective values of those two groups of interests, a judgment which must vary according to the circumstances in which it is made. Thus the balance will change. The purpose in striking the balance does not. The purpose is the achievement of the dignity of man.

The mechanism for achieving that balance is the law. The legal device which is used both to embody and to achieve the communal interests within a society is, at one level, that body which we call the state. Divorced from this connection with its members, for whom it exists, " the state " is either a meaningless or a dangerous concept. It is meaningful and acceptable only as a mechanism for attaining the liberty of man, his freedom of thought, speech, action and self-expression. This aim, in our society at least, must endure. It is as means to attaining that end that all constitutional rules and institutions must be judged. For themselves alone constitutional institutions have no value, they have value only as means to an end. Constitutional rules have in themselves no sanctity; they too are the means to an end, and must be judged not by their history alone but by their efficiency as such means (an efficiency which may either be aided or diminished by that history). Their study should then not be an arid one, and should the author have made it so, the fault is his. If then, at the end of a survey of some of those rules and institutions (a survey which may, perhaps, have obscured their purpose), the author is allowed to declare what he believes that ultimate purpose to be, let him roundly declare that, in his view, it is simply the achievement, so far as is humanly possible, of the freedom of man.

APPENDIX

EXTRACT FROM THE EUROPEAN CONVENTION ON HUMAN RIGHTS

Article 1

The High Contracting Parties shall secure to everyone within their jurisdiction the rights and freedoms defined in Section 1 of this Convention.

SECTION I

Article 2

(1) Everyone's right to life shall be protected by law. No one shall be deprived of his life intentionally save in the execution of a sentence of a court following his conviction of a crime for which this penalty is provided by law.

(2) Deprivation of life shall not be regarded as inflicted in contravention of this Article when it results from the use of force which is no more than absolutely necessary:

(a) in defence of any person from unlawful violence;

(b) in order to effect a lawful arrest or to prevent the escape of a person lawfully detained;

(c) in action lawfully taken for the purpose of quelling a riot or insurrection.

Article 3

No one shall be subjected to torture or to inhuman or degrading treatment or punishment.

Article 4

(1) No one shall be held in slavery or servitude.

(2) No one shall be required to perform forced or compulsory labour.

(3) For the purpose of this Article the term " forced or compulsory labour " shall not include:

(a) any work required to be done in the ordinary course of detention imposed according to the provisions of Article 5 of this Convention or during conditional release from such detention;

(b) any service of a military character or, in case of conscientious objectors in countries where they are recognised, service exacted instead of compulsory military service;

(c) any service exacted in case of an emergency or calamity threatening the life or well-being of the community;

(d) any work or service which forms part of normal civic obligations.

Article 5

(1) Everyone has the right to liberty and security of person.

No one shall be deprived of his liberty save in the following cases and in accordance with a procedure prescribed by law:

(a) the lawful detention of a person after conviction by a competent court;

(b) the lawful arrest or detention of a person for non-compliance with

347

the lawful order of a court or in order to secure the fulfilment of any obligation prescribed by law;

(c) the lawful arrest or detention of a person effected for the purpose of bringing him before the competent legal authority on reasonable suspicion of having committed an offence or when it is reasonably considered necessary to prevent his committing an offence or fleeing after having done so;

(d) the detention of a minor by lawful order for the purpose of educational supervision or his lawful detention for the purpose of bringing him before the competent legal authority;

(e) the lawful detention of persons for the prevention of the spreading of infectious diseases, of persons of unsound mind, alcoholics or drug addicts or vagrants;

(f) the lawful arrest or detention of a person to prevent his effecting an unauthorised entry into the country or of a person against whom action is being taken with a view to deportation or extradition.

(2) Everyone who is arrested shall be informed promptly, in a language which he understands, of the reasons for his arrest and of any charge against him.

(3) Everyone arrested or detained in accordance with the provisions of paragraph (1) (c) of this Article shall be brought promptly before a judge or other officer authorised by law to exercise judicial power and shall be entitled to trial within a reasonable time or to release pending trial. Release may be conditioned by guarantees to appear for trial.

(4) Everyone who is deprived of his liberty by arrest or detention shall be entitled to take proceedings by which the lawfulness of his detention shall be decided speedily by a court and his release ordered if the detention is not lawful.

(5) Everyone who has been the victim of arrest or detention in contravention of the provisions of this Article shall have an enforceable right to compensation.

Article 6

(1) In the determination of his civil rights and obligations or of any criminal charge against him, everyone is entitled to a fair and public hearing within a reasonable time by an independent and impartial tribunal established by law. Judgment shall be pronounced publicly but the press and public may be excluded from all or part of the trial in the interest of morals, public order or national security in a democratic society, where the interests of juveniles or the protection of the private life of the parties so require, or to the extent strictly necessary in the opinion of the court in special circumstances where publicity would prejudice the interests of justice.

(2) Everyone charged with a criminal offence shall be presumed innocent until proved guilty according to law.

(3) Everyone charged with a criminal offence has the following minimum rights:

(a) to be informed promptly, in a language which he understands and in detail, of the nature and cause of the accusation against him;

(b) to have adequate time and facilities for the preparation of his defence;

(c) to defend himself in person or through legal assistance of his own choosing or, if he has not sufficient means to pay for legal assistance, to be given it free when the interests of justice so require;

(d) to examine or have examined witnesses against him and to obtain the attendance and examination of witnesses on his behalf under the same conditions as witnesses against him;

(e) to have the free assistance of an interpreter if he cannot understand or speak the language used in court.

Article 7

(1) No one shall be held guilty of any criminal offence on account of any act or omission which did not constitute a criminal offence under national or international law at the time when it was committed. Nor shall a heavier penalty be imposed than the one that was applicable at the time the criminal offence was committed.

(2) This Article shall not prejudice the trial and punishment of any person for any act or omission which at the time when it was committed was criminal according to the general principles of law recognised by civilised nations.

Article 8

(1) Everyone has the right to respect for his private and family life, his home and his correspondence.

(2) There shall be no interference by a public authority with the exercise of this right except such as is in accordance with the law and is necessary in a democratic society in the interests of national security, public safety or the economic well-being of the country, for the prevention of disorder or crime, for the protection of health or morals, or for the protection of the rights and freedoms of others.

Article 9

(1) Everyone has the right to freedom of thought, conscience and religion; this right includes freedom to change his religion or belief and freedom, either alone or in community with others and in public or private, to manifest his religion or belief, in worship, teaching, practice and observance.

(2) Freedom to manifest one's religion or beliefs shall be subject only to such limitations as are prescribed by law and are necessary in a democratic society in the interests of public safety, for the protection of public order, health or morals, or for the protection of the rights and freedoms of others.

Article 10

(1) Everyone has the right to freedom of expression. This right shall include freedom to hold opinions and to receive and impart information and ideas without interference by public authority and regardless of frontiers. This Article shall not prevent States from requiring the licensing of broadcasting, television or cinema enterprises.

(2) The exercise of these freedoms, since it carries with it duties and responsibilities, may be subject to such formalities, conditions, restrictions or penalties as are prescribed by law and are necessary in a democratic society, in the interests of national security, territorial integrity or public safety, for the prevention of disorder or crime, for the protection of health or morals, for the protection of the reputation or rights of others, for preventing the disclosure of information received in confidence, or for maintaining the authority and impartiality of the judiciary.

Article 11

(1) Everyone has the right to freedom of peaceful assembly and to freedom of association with others, including the right to form and to join trade unions for the protection of his interests.

(2) No restrictions shall be placed on the exercise of these rights other than such as are prescribed by law and are necessary in a democratic society in the interests of national security or public safety, for the prevention of disorder or crime, for the protection of health or morals or for the protection of the rights and freedoms of others. This Article shall not prevent the imposition of lawful restrictions on the exercise of these rights by members of the armed forces, of the police or of the administration of the State.

Article 12

Men and women of marriageable age have the right to marry and to found a family, according to the national laws governing the exercise of this right.

Article 13

Everyone whose rights and freedoms as set forth in this Convention are violated shall have an effective remedy before a national authority notwithstanding that the violation has been committed by persons acting in an official capacity.

Article 14

The enjoyment of the rights and freedoms set forth in this Convention shall be secured without discrimination on any ground such as sex, race, colour, language, religion, political or other opinion, national or social origin, association with a national minority, property, birth or other status.

Article 15

(1) In time of war or other public emergency threatening the life of the nation any High Contracting Party may take measures derogating from its obligations under this Convention to the extent strictly required by the exigencies of the situation, provided that such measures are not inconsistent with its other obligations under international law.

(2) No derogation from Article 2, except in respect of deaths resulting from lawful acts of war, or from Articles 3, 4 (para. (1)) and 7 shall be made under this provision.

(3) Any High Contracting Party availing itself of this right of derogation shall keep the Secretary-General of the Council of Europe fully informed of the measures which it has taken and the reasons therefor. It shall also inform the Secretary-General of the Council of Europe when such measures have ceased to operate and the provisions of the Convention are again being fully executed.

Article 16

Nothing in Articles 10, 11 and 14 shall be regarded as preventing the High Contracting Parties from imposing restrictions on the political activity of aliens.

Article 17

Nothing in this Convention may be interpreted as implying for any State, group or person any right to engage in any activity or perform any act aimed at the destruction of any of the rights and freedoms set forth herein or at their limitation to a greater extent than is provided for in the Convention.

Article 18

The restrictions permitted under this Convention to the said rights and freedoms shall not be applied for any purpose other than those for which they have been prescribed.

INDEX